Second Edition

T0332054

Advanced Management Accounting

Maurice L. Hirsch, Jr.

Southern Illinois University at Edwardsville

SOUTH-WESTERN
CENGAGE Learning

Australia • Brazil • Japan • Korea • Mexico • Singapore • Spain • United Kingdom • United States

For product information and technology assistance,
contact **emea.info@cengage.com**.

For permission to use material from this text or product,
and for permission queries,
email **clsuk.permissions@cengage.com**.

British Library Cataloguing-in-Publication Data
A catalogue record for this book is available from the
British Library.

ISBN: 978-1-86152-676-2

Cengage Learning EMEA
Cheriton House, North Way, Andover, Hampshire, SP10 5BE,
United Kingdom

Cengage Learning products are represented in Canada by
Nelson Education Ltd.

For your lifelong learning solutions, visit
www.cengage.co.uk

Purchase your next print book, e-book or e-chapter at
www.CengageBrain.com

Printed by Lightning Source, UK

Preface

Managers throughout an organization are faced with rapid changes in the external and internal environments that the organization faces. Therefore, those managers concerned with relevant information for internal decision making must be provided information that is not only timely but also allows them to be flexible in the light of changing conditions. The preface of the first edition said, in part:

> Management accounting seems to be at a crossroads. While there are many computer-integrated manufacturing facilities in use or being built, there are also a great number of efficient labor-oriented manufacturing plants. Since both environments exist simultaneously, the treatment of several subjects needs to be broader. . . .
>
> Another crossroads of sorts is the reaffirmation of the need for independent management accounting information. Managers should be wary of using financial accounting information to make management decisions. . . .

These crossroads still exist. If anything, the environment is even more dynamic today than it was just a few years ago. In addition, the movement toward strategic management has accelerated. Finally, the heart of the matter is still the same—information for decision making and the role of the management accountant in the accumulation, analysis, and use of that information. Thus, the themes of this book are *managers must have relevant information within a framework of strategic management* and *managers must consider a dynamic environment*.

This book can fit in various places in the curriculum. With 150-hour programs, this book is appropriate for a third course in management accounting at the senior or graduate level. In addition, it can be successfully used as a major text in the junior-level second course that follows a sophomore management accounting course when a strong management accounting track is pursued. Finally, the book fits well into an MBA program for those with a management accounting background. In all applications, students are expected to have a background in cost-volume-profit analysis, tactical decision making, capital budgeting techniques, and the rudiments of product costing for financial accounting. Several quantitative techniques are covered. Students should have some background in simple linear regression and a basic knowledge of statistics and probability. Sufficient review material is available if such a background exists.

CHANGES IN THE SECOND EDITION

There have been significant changes throughout this edition. However, the basic perspective and level of presentation is the same as the first edition. As with the first edition, Chapter 1 deals with information, the major theme of this book. This chapter sets the stage by examining the behavioral effects of information. In addition, Appendix 1A—Guidelines for Case and Memorandum Preparation is expanded. Chapters 2 and 3 are completely new and represent an expansion of the first edition's Chapter 2—an exploration of the issues facing management accountants. Chapter 2 starts with a history of management accounting to lay a foundation of where it is today and where it is going in the future. This is followed by a framework for accounting information and a discussion of activity-based costs and management. Chapter 3 moves the reader into strategic management with a discussion of value chains and management philosophies/techniques such as the Theory of Constraints, just-in-time, and life-cycle costing. The themes and information introduced in these first three chapters are integrated throughout the book. Within these chapters and as the book progresses, readers are asked to think about the various methods and philosophies that are being advanced in order to see how they can work together and where they differ.

Chapter 4 deals with simple and multiple linear regression and combines two chapters from the first edition. Chapter 5, on the learning effect, and Chapter 6, on decisions with constrained resources, have been revised to tie in with changes made elsewhere in the text. Chapter 7, on extensions of the cost-volume-profit model, includes some models resulting from studies in Germany. Chapter 8, on the cost and benefit of information, is revised to fit in with other revisions, as are Chapters 9 and 10, which deal with variances and variance investigation, respectively.

Chapter 11, on allocation issues, has been rewritten and reorganized, includes new material, and ties service department pricing to transfer pricing, which is covered in Chapter 15. Chapter 12, Strategic Management, is rewritten from scratch. It comes back to reinforce the material in Chapters 2 and 3 while moving ahead to form the basis for Chapters 13–15. Chapter 13, on capital asset acquisition, is reorganized and rewritten from the perspective of strategic management. It also includes more discussion of qualitative measures as well as issues like what will happen to a firm if an investment is *not* made.

Chapter 14, on performance evaluation, has been extensively rewritten to include not only financial quantitative measures but also nonfinancial quantitative and qualitative measures as well as the results of field studies in the United States, Japan, and other countries. Chapter 15 deals with transfer pricing and has been updated and reorganized in this edition. Finally, in addition to Appendix A, which contains relevant tables, Appendix B lists a variety of books and articles so that inquiring readers can begin to explore particular interests more deeply.

Instructors should find this book flexible and open. They can combine several chapters together, as well as customize the order of coverage. Even though quantitative techniques are found in many chapters, those wishing to stress this area less can go from Chapters 1–3 right to Chapter 7 or beyond. Some combinations of chapters are as follows:

Introductory block	Chapters 1, 2, and 3
Regression	Chapters 4 and 5
Linear programming	Chapter 6
Uncertainty/risk	Chapters 7, 8, and parts of 10 and 13
Variances	Chapters 9 and 10
Strategic management	Chapters 11, 12, 13, 14, and 15

Hopefully, this book will inspire the reader to ask questions about all aspects of management accounting. The traditional assumptions are changing. There is now a challenge to determine whether management accountants can creatively meet current information needs. This book should help in that process.

My thanks to all those who contributed to the first edition. I appreciate the support of Southern Illinois University at Edwardsville and the comments and suggestions I get from my students and colleagues there. Special thanks to Michael Costigan and Linda Lovata. I am in debt to Mary Draper of South-Western Publishing Company for her insight and commitment to make this the best book possible. My thanks go to the following reviewers who read drafts of this edition and significantly contributed to its final form.

Jacob G. Birnberg
University of Pittsburgh

Harold B. Cook
Central Michigan University

Paul A. Dierks
Wake Forest University—Graduate School of Management

Susan F. Haka
Michigan State University

Cynthia D. Heagy
University of Houston—Clear Lake

Paul R. Koogler
Southwest Texas State University

Linda L. Nelms
University of North Carolina at Asheville

Mary S. Rolfes
Mankato State University

Maurice L. Hirsch, Jr.

Contents

Part 1

Information and Management Accounting

Chapter 1

Information and Human Behavior

Silence is never so impenetrable as when the whisper of steel on paper strives to pierce it. I sit in a labyrinth of solitude jabbing at its bulwarks with the point of a pen—jabbing, jabbing, jabbing.[1]

Times and technology might have changed since Beryl Markham wrote the above, but the basic issues are the same: how can we effectively communicate information? Accountants are concerned with collecting and interpreting data; rearranging, abstracting, and combining data in order to get relevant information; considering the information and coming to conclusions and/or decisions; and communicating the process, the information, and the outcomes to others. In any specific situation, accountants must define their task, the composition and needs of the intended audience, and the most effective and efficient way to communicate with that audience. Choices include:

---

[1] Beryl Markham, *West with the Night* (Berkeley, Calif.: North Point Press, 1983), p. 145.

1. Relevant information, given the task and the audience
2. Audience characteristics that might affect how they perceive and/or use information
3. Form, order, and format to present information

These topics form not only the basis of this chapter but also the foundation of all the following material. If accountants are to maintain their position as providers of relevant information for management decision making, they must continue to build skills in oral and written communication. In addition, operating managers increasingly want accountants to expand their role and be part of the decision-making process rather than just providers of information. Increased expectations add to the choices that accountants make for information elicitation and presentation.

INFORMATION AND DATA

There is a difference between information and data. Data are things that we observe. Records show statistics such as direct labor hours worked over a year in a printing company, pounds of feed used in a month in a horse boarding and training stable, or charges to patients at a hospital over the last five years. By themselves these data are merely facts. Information, on the other hand, is relevant news. Given a decision to make, we look at the available raw data, choose relevant information, and then organize it and analyze it. If the result is something that can affect managers' decisions, then we have created information.

Types of Information

Information has to have value to the decision maker. Managers can create many different types of information. In doing so, they need to make explicit choices about information content, format, order, aggregation, level of sophistication, and so on.

Information can be included in an annual report, in the daily stock listings in *The Wall Street Journal*, in a written memorandum that is a verbal analysis of data, and in the body language and tone of a manager speaking to his or her superior. Thus, information takes on many forms, and it provides the central theme of this book. This chapter deals with some basic concerns about the behavioral dimensions of information. Chapters 2 and 3 deal with changes in information needs brought about by changes in the internal and external environment businesses face. Chapters 4 through 7 are concerned with information useful in quantitative models. Chapter 8 considers information's cost versus its benefit. Chapters 9 and 10 explore the use of information in operational control. Chapters 11 through 15 involve information issues dealing with allocation, strategic planning, capital budgeting decisions, performance evaluation, and transfer pricing.

While it may seem obvious, almost every subject that we deal with as managers concerns the interface between creators and users of information. Many of these interactions involve not just the exchange of information but also an emotional involvement by the participants. Examples include budget setting and the resulting evaluation process, transfer pricing decisions between decentralized segments of a firm, and variance reports. Thus, information is more than just news. Information can also have a behavioral dimension.

As accountants we must be concerned that the information decision makers use will result in the best decisions possible at the time. What data did the manager see before participating in standard setting or budgeting? How many of these data became relevant information to the manager? How did the manager *use* the information?

Our choices will be based on the perceived usefulness of information about a particular subject and the cost of obtaining that information. How managers present information will also depend on the audience they are addressing— the decision makers who need the information. In addition to choosing how to communicate, managers must possess the oral and written communication skills necessary to transmit information and conclusions to others.

Information and the Accountant

Accountants recognize that one of their principal functions is to provide information to facilitate decision making for planning and control. Statement 1C from the Institute of Management Accountants states:

> Management accountants have a responsibility to: communicate information fairly and objectively; disclose fully all relevant information that could reasonably be expected to influence an intended user's understanding of the reports, comments, and recommendations presented.[2]

This is an ethical statement about objectivity. For many years it was implicitly assumed that accounting information is "objective, unbiased, neutral."[3] In recent years that view has been challenged. For example, Caplan argued that

> The objectivity of the management accounting process is largely a myth. Accountants have wide areas of discretion in the selection, processing, and reporting of data.[4]

---

[2] Statement 1C, June 1, 1983, *Objectives: Standards of Ethical Conduct for Management Accountants* (New York: National Association of Accountants), p. 1.

[3] Accounting Principles Board, *Basic Concepts and Accounting Principles Underlying Financial Statements of Business Enterprises* (New York: American Institute of Certified Public Accountants, 1970), pp. 10, 37.

[4] Edwin Caplan, *Management Accounting and Behavioral Science* (Reading, Mass.: Addison-Wesley Publishing Company, Inc., 1971), p. 31. Also see A. Thomas, "Useful Arbitrary Allocations," *The Accounting Review* 46:3 (July 1971), pp. 472–479.

Some people assume that an accountant's role is to provide unbiased information for decision making. The assumption is that there is a single set of facts waiting to be reported and that the accountant's job is to *find* them. This view has been challenged; accountants now argue that the selection of data for reporting to decision makers is not a neutral, unbiased activity. The facts are too numerous and may be too costly to collect. Thus the accountant must consciously and subconsciously make choices. In some cases the accountant might even want to influence the decision, and this wish is reflected in the information he or she chooses to present.

Information and the Individual

The accountant chooses what data to collect, how to analyze these data, and how to present information to decision makers. Besides factors such as cost or availability, the information provider's personal psychological makeup is a part of this choice process. Each of us possesses a set of biases, techniques, and structures that affects our perceptual choices both in the presentation and in the use of information. Our choices are made in light of who we are as individuals. Thus, it is appropriate for us to look at some dimensions of information perception, use, and selection.

HUMAN INFORMATION PROCESSING

Human information processing is a field of study taking us beyond the premise that all you need in order to make good decisions are the facts. Many studies in this area have shown that different people use information differently. Some people seem able to understand and *use* much more complex information than others. Some need a greater quantity of information for decisions. Some people are more comfortable with numerical information than others. Equations might be useful for some decision makers, while anything mathematical might turn others off. A person's experience and personality can affect his or her use and perception of information. For example, what one person may classify as subjective, another might classify as objective. We are also learning more about how form, order, and level of aggregation of information can affect decision-making behavior. Accountants are amassing hard evidence in this field that can be used and expanded.

With easy access to word processors and easy-to-use quantitative programs, it is possible for an attitude to develop that more is better. People even thought that the computer would replace human judgment because, with all the data that can be generated, much routine decision making would become trivial. However, we know now that people do not respond well to too much data. They reach a saturation point that is called channel or information overload. It is like trying to fill a soda bottle from a 55-gallon drum: only so much of the liquid gets in while the rest is wasted.[5] Some information is ignored, some is selected due to the comfort or bias of the decision maker, and some is just discounted.

Cognitive Complexity

Cognitive complexity is one of the subjects studied in human information processing. Before this area is explained, consider a case example.

Illustration: Troy Printing Company   Troy Printing Company has a computer-based job-order costing system. Troy prints various trade magazines, catalogs, and specialty work such as posters and promotional material. Some jobs are quite regular in format and scheduling, while others come in at the last minute and are very diverse in specifications. Rich Cassady, president, and Alice Perez, the company's chief accountant, want to report job cost information for the use of lead workers on various pieces of equipment, departmental forepersons, the scheduling and production staff, the company's estimating staff, and for themselves. While issues of cognitive complexity are not really handled independently of other information processing problems, we can look at how Cassady and Perez need to make choices in this area.

Considerable data are available regarding the costs of a job. There are actual cost and standard cost data. Data are available from the various departments (camera work, printing, binding, shipping) in the production sequence. There are fixed costs and variable costs. Some jobs create overtime because they are received late, while others are run on overtime at the convenience of Troy's management.

As Cassady and Perez have remarked, various people need to have some of this information to make relevant decisions. We can assume for the sake of this illustration that Cassady is more able to deal with complex data and can better use complex information than the shipping department foreman. Cassady might be very comfortable with an organized computer output showing various dimensions of actual costing compared to standards used to estimate a job, a breakdown by department of fixed and variable costs, as well as a dimension of controllability, just to name a few examples. As president, he has an ongoing interest in bidding new jobs and seeing how profitable each current job has been. His decisions include not only short-range planning and control but also issues of supplier contracts, union negotiations, new printing or binding equipment, new market segments, and so on. The decisions are complex, and the job cost data with all their complexity are but one part of Cassady's full set of information. He needs to be flexible in his use of information from various sources both within and

---

[5] There are direct applications of this concept in L. Revsine, "Data Expansion and Conceptual Structure," *The Accounting Review* 45:4 (October 1970), pp. 704–711; and H. Miller, "Environmental Complexity and Financial Reports," *The Accounting Review* 47:1 (January 1972), pp. 31–37.

without the company and to organize all this information in such a way that he can best use it for the decisions at hand.

The shipping department supervisor has a different need for information. His decisions regard crews, supply costs, scheduling, and efficiency. Not only is he less comfortable with complex data, but also he needs less information in order to do his job. While he needs to be flexible in his use of information, his approach can be much more ordered and regular than Cassady's or Perez's. While Cassady concerns himself with complex external issues such as the economy or market research, the department supervisor may have only specific worker problems to deal with (sickness, a new baby) as external concerns. The internal issues confronting the supervisor also are limited to the scope of his department. Thus, this supervisor needs a simpler set of information for simpler decisions than does top corporate management. Do not infer, however, that people lower in the hierarchy are lower in cognitive complexity. In fact, one might find a chief executive who cannot deal with complex information and a departmental supervisor who can.

Even within top management there are differences in how information is used and how much is needed. Perez and Cassady might have different abilities to handle complex information. For example, Perez may be able to handle more complexity and ambiguity than Cassady, but her job entails using fewer dimensions of information than Cassady's.

Several factors are evident in Troy Printing's information needs. They include the need to provide relevant information to people at different levels of management. These people have different needs for information: the information must be relevant to each person's area of decision making. Some people seem better able to deal with abstract information, while others need more details. The study of human information processing (HIP) offers us ways to explore these factors.

One of the main bodies of HIP research is concerned with cognitive complexity. Several authors propose two dimensions in the use of information for decision making. Driver and Mock[6] call these dimensions the *amount of information* used and the *degree of focus*. A person who uses a minimal amount of information and focuses on one, clear-cut solution to a problem is at one end of the continuum; at the other end is a person who uses all relevant information that she or he can get (obviously weighed by benefit versus cost) and develops multiple analyses and solutions. Keep in mind that we are dealing with two dimensions and not just one. A person might

---

[6] See M. Driver and J. Mock, "Human Information Processing, Decision Style Theory, and Accounting Information Systems," *The Accounting Review* 50:3 (July 1975), pp. 490–508, for a good review of the literature and references in this area. Also see H. M. Schroder, M. J. Driver, and S. Struefert, *Human Information Processing* (New York: Holt, Rinehart & Winston, Inc., 1967), Chapters 1–3; and P. L. Hunsaker, "Incongruity Adaptation Capability and Risk Preference in Turbulent Decision-Making Environments," *Organizational Behavior and Human Performance* 2 (1975), pp. 173–185.

be quite able and willing to use a great deal of information but not be able to move beyond a simple focus on a singular solution.

Amount of Information   Assume that Troy Printing's management is considering new product lines. If Cassady is able to use much information successfully and can focus on multiple solutions, he might review all the operating specifications of current equipment along with production schedules and cost reports to determine the time available and the type of job Troy would be able to handle. In addition, he would call in various equipment manufacturers, sound out competitors and customers, and seek other information relevant to what compatible types of work were available and who was currently printing these jobs. Just with this set of concerns, Cassady could accumulate quite a bit of information to review.

However, if Cassady wanted to use only a minimal amount of information, he might concentrate on a few simple items. He would not expand this data set but rather would be satisfied with just enough information to yield some answers. There is no right or wrong for this or any other dimension of human information processing. There are successful managers on both ends of the spectrum (and unsuccessful ones as well).

Degree of Focus   The other dimension of using information is the focus of Cassady's analysis: To what end is the information going to be used? A simple focus would be to find one product that would use existing slack time in a reasonably profitable way. The focus at the other extreme would be to find several products or sets of products to use existing capacity as well as options entailing new equipment and perhaps buildings.

Now put these dimensions together. If Cassady is both a minimal information user and has a singular focus, he may come up with a short-range plan based limited data to fill existing capacity. It may very well be nonoptimal in either the short or long term. If he has a multiple focus, he may use a limited amount of information to propose several of the alternatives. However, he will have very little hard information on each of the alternatives.

If Cassady can use a maximum amount of information but has a single-solution focus, he may choose the alternative with the highest expected utility. His analysis will be thorough but directed toward a singular problem. The most complex style is being able to use a maximum amount of information while also looking at multiple objectives and solutions. This will yield a more complete analysis and a full set of options together with an assessment of the strengths and weaknesses of each. However, successful decision makers can and do come from each style combination; complexity can be good or bad—it depends on the situation at hand.

Decision Styles   Driver and Mock[7] use the term *decision style* to describe the combinations of these two dimensions. The four styles they propose are as follows:

---

[7] Driver and Mock, "Human Information Processing."

Style	Information	Focus
1. Decisive	Minimal	One solution
2. Flexible	Minimal	Multiple solutions
3. Hierarchic	Maximum	One solution
4. Integrative	Maximum	Multiple solutions

While research has shown most people are dominant in just one style, mixed styles are possible. People who have hierarchic and integrative styles use a maximum of information and are cognitively complex. Thus, a person who successfully uses a great deal of information can, by definition, deal with complexity.

As you think through the four proposed decision styles, you can think about how you and your friends use information. In your decision to attend a particular university and to pursue a certain major or degree program, what was the kind and amount of information you gathered? Did you focus on a single solution such as courses in accounting or on multiple solutions balancing general education and accounting, how your decision might affect an entry-level job, and how it ought to affect your life years after graduation? As you think through different decision-making scenarios, you will begin to see where you seem comfortable on the amount of information and degree of focus dimensions. In addition, you will see that these two dimensions themselves are affected by the decision at hand.

Conceptual Levels

To this point in the discussion we have seen that people can use different amounts of information and that they can focus on a unique solution or on multiple solutions in decision making. As accountants, we are interested not just in general taxonomy but in knowing more about how information is used. How we choose to present information is intertwined with how our audience can best use it. Miller and Gordon[8] look at a part of cognitive complexity called **conceptual level**. For example, let us compare the conceptual level of the decisive style and that of the integrative style. The decisive style (using minimal information directed toward a singular solution) implies that the decision maker will "satisfice" (i.e., choose a solution that meets very basic criteria) rather than optimize and will have intolerance for much information. Such a person will look at summary figures such as total variances or earnings per share or just the return on investments of a project and may make reasonable decisions, but based on little information. A decision maker with an integrative style (using maximum information directed toward multiple solutions) can look into figures in a report,

---

[8] D. Miller and L. Gordon, "Conceptual Levels and the Design of Accounting Information Systems," *Decision Sciences* 6 (1975), pp. 259–269. This article contains a good bibliography on the subject.

analyze the assumptions, integrate external factors, and consider various per-spectives in the process of arriving at a set of solutions. Thus, the decisive style involves a low conceptual level and the integrative style a high one. It is important to note that no style is *better* than another. Good decision makers (and bad ones, too) come from each decision style.

Environmental Complexity   Even if each of us has a dominant decision style, there is some range of complexity (conceptual level) over which we vary. While our ability to use information is in part learned behavior, it is affected by what is happening now in our environment. This factor is called **environmental complexity.** Consider a well-organized report that is full of recognizable relevant information, and compare it with an unorganized, poorly labeled report containing the same raw information. In the first instance we would be better able to *use* the information (or some of it), no matter what our decision style. In the second instance our ability to use the information would be impaired by an environmental factor: poor organization and communication of the material. This subject area is addressed later in this chapter and in Appendix 1A.

The dimensions of conceptual level and environmental complexity are illustrated in Figures 1-1 and 1-2. Figure 1-1 shows that each individual has an optimal level of abstractness. If a person is presented with a piece of information and no more, he or she is not motivated to use much more than a simple decision style. At the other end of the spectrum, if an individual

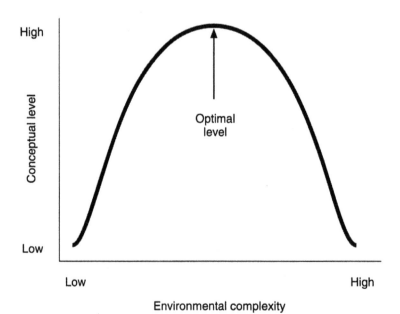

Figure 1-1   A Person's Optimal Level of Abstractness

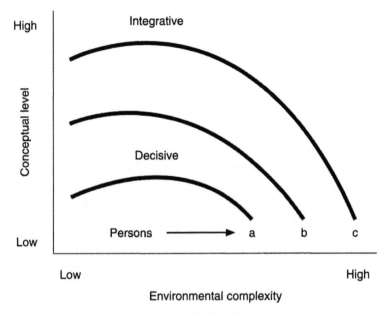

Figure 1-2   Persons Differing in Ability to Use Abstract Information

is swamped with too much information, he or she will retreat to a simple style to be able to deal with this overload. Thus, the idea that accountants and others (engineers, market researchers, personnel experts) should simply give managers all the facts can lead to the managers' throwing up their hands and using very simple decision rules. Somewhere in the middle lies an optimal range of complexity and conceptual level for decision making.

Figure 1-2 compares people who have different abilities to use complex information. The lowest curve (curve *a*) might be someone with a decisive style, the highest (curve *c*) a person with a hierarchic or integrative style.

Cognitive Complexity and Management Accountants

This discussion has direct application to accounting information. For example, both Revsine and Miller[9] have looked at trends to expand data in corporate annual reports. Each author concludes that too much information can reduce a person's ability to deal with abstract ideas. This has implications for internal reports as well. The objective is to find the appropriate amount of information for the decision at hand and to present that information in a way that is useful to the decision maker.

Information that accountants prepare for other managers can be of various levels of diversity and structure. For example, the advent of the computer

---

[9] Revsine, "Data Expansion and Conceptual Structure"; and Miller, "Environmental Complexity and Financial Reports."

and of canned programs for certain analyses (such as regression and correlation analysis) has resulted in managers' receiving nearly every piece of data that can be generated. The format may be designed by a statistician with no regard for relevance to the problem at hand. Given this bewildering array of data, it is no wonder that the manager might look at some summary piece of information and ignore the rest.[10]

Cognitive Limits

All the maximization models that we use (such as linear programming and expected value) are based on the assumption that the decision maker is an economic person. An *economic person* is characterized as an expected utility maximizer. He or she is rational—a perfect information processor. However, few people fit this idealized framework.[11] Most of us are *administrative persons*[12] who cannot cope with every bit of information and therefore tend to look at key result areas. For example, in considering a product's value to the company, the administrative person might look only at separable margin or market share.

Administrative people seem to want to "satisfice" rather than maximize. Thus, when a reasonable solution is found, they accept it, and there is no drive to find an optimal solution. As part of this process, they tend to limit the research process for information; they want to look at familiar situations and perpetuate existing decisions. This orientation has been called *bounded rationality*.[13]

Accountants as preparers and users of information are faced with a conflict. They and their audience are limited by levels of cognitive complexity and by the basic decision style they use. In addition, all the quantitative models we use that are supposed to promote optimal behavior are in opposition, in some ways, to a person's natural tendency to "satisfice." No wonder that the adopting of sophisticated techniques has lagged behind the development of the techniques themselves.

PERSONALITY DIMENSIONS AND INFORMATION USE

The material presented earlier on cognitive complexity shows that different people can fall on different complexity curves, and that material also introduces

---

[10] Managers tell various horror stories about, for example, some 50 pages of PERT diagrams they receive from subcontractors. If there is information contained in the 50 pages, it is ignored, since the data set is just too complex.

[11] For a full discussion of various sources for this material, see S. Kerr, R. J. Klimoski, J. Tollier, and M. A. Von Glinow, "Human Information Processing," in J. Leslie Livingstone, *Managerial Accounting: the Behavioral Foundations* (Columbus, Ohio: Grid, Inc., 1975), pp. 169–192.

[12] The pioneering ideas were set forth by Herbert A. Simon, *Administrative Behavior: A Study of Decision Making Processes in Administrative Organization*, 2nd ed. (New York: The Free Press, 1975).

[13] Simon, *Administrative Behavior*.

us to the topic of how personality traits affect information use. Each of us brings into a job situation the total of who we are and what we have learned. Our personal history includes how we deal with our feelings, what our self-image is, and what our need structure is at the time, to name just a few dimensions.[14] We are the product of our own choices as conditioned by what we have learned from our parents, teachers, and supervisors over the years. We possess various communication skills that we have learned and developed. All these factors and more are part of our personality and style and have an effect on how we use information. As accountants, we should know what variables affect the use of information so that we understand better what choices we have to make when selecting and presenting information.

Psychological Type

The idea of psychological type was developed by Jung. Isabel Briggs Myers refined Jung's original ideas and developed four dimensions of psychological type as well as a scale to measure these dimensions: the Myers-Briggs Type Indicator or MBTI.[15] The dimensions of type are

EI: Extroversion–Introversion
SN: Sensing–Intuition
TF: Thinking–Feeling
JP: Judgment–Perception

Let us look at a couple of these dimensions to see how they might affect information creation, perception, and use. The EI dimension for Extroversion–Introversion involves how we deal with the outside world. If a group of people who are more introverted were given a problem to solve and they all met together, it would be common for them to read quietly all the information they were given and to formulate their thoughts internally before sharing them with others. A more extroverted group, in contrast, may start discussing the situation immediately and may review information and formulate thoughts orally as the meeting progresses. Many meetings in business involve some participants who are introverted and some who are more extroverted. The oral flow of information might be affected by the group's composition.

---

[14] For references regarding feelings and self-image, see such books as M. James and D. Joungeward, *Born to Win* (Reading, Mass.: Addison-Wesley Publishing Company, Inc. 1971); T. Harris, *I'm OK, You're OK* (New York: Harper & Row, Publishers, 1967); C. Rogers, *On Becoming a Person* (Boston: Houghton Mifflin Company, 1961). Refer also to A. Maslow's hierarchy of needs as described in his book, *Toward a Psychology of Being*, 2nd ed. (New York: Van Nostrand-Reinhold Company, 1968).

[15] I. Briggs Myers, "Myers-Briggs Type Indicator" (Palo Alto, Calif.: Consulting Psychologists Press, Inc., 1977). Two good references in this area are I. Briggs Myers, *Gifts Differing* (Palo Alto, Calif.: Consulting Psychologists Press, Inc., 1980) and G. Lawrence, *People Types & Tiger Stripes* (Gainesville, Fla.: Center for Applications of Psychological Type, Inc., 1982).

The Sensing–Intuition (SN) dimension deals with how we process information. People who are more sensing like to deal with things in a linear fashion, going step by step. They may be able to get from the first step to the last but may not have a good idea of the whole picture. At the intuitive end of the SN dimension is the person who sees the first few steps and then may be able to jump to a conclusion or to see the whole thing. However, that same person may not be able to accomplish all the steps to get to the solution of the problem. We can see the difference between more sensing and more intuitive people if we look at how people deal with different subjects within this book. The review material on production variances in Chapter 9 is more procedural and may be easier for the more sensing person to understand. The material is this chapter involves more abstract ideas and may be easier for the more intuitive person to comprehend.

These dimensions are presented as descriptions of an individual's preferred behavior. They are neither good nor bad. People can choose to modify their behavior. In addition, these dimensions are a continuum. Most people fall somewhere on one side or the other, but are not, for example, totally sensing with zero intuition. However, we can see the different choices we could make about how to create or use information on the basis of these dimensions. As an example, you might want to give someone directions to a new restaurant. Ask yourself how you would give these directions to a person who is more sensing as compared to a person who is more intuitive.

This is a new area for research. For a while, most studies were descriptive but recent studies have used psychological type as a predictor of action. For example, Stumpf and Dunbar used a laboratory experiment and found that there are different decision-making biases displayed by people with different combinations of the SN and TF dimensions.[16] However, not all studies produce significant results.

There are direct implications of knowing the psychological type of an intended audience given a particular task even if we cannot predict behavior consistently. For example, assume an audience is, in general, more sensing than intuitive: that is, they are more comfortable with information given in a direct, linear fashion. If your task is to write a memorandum giving them information useful for a particular decision, knowing their affinity for sensing will help you present the information in a way that is more effective. The task might change. If you are a group leader (instructor) who is trying to both utilize your audience's preference for sensing and expand their ability/comfort with intuition, you might make different choices in how you present things.

---

[16] Stephen A. Stumpf and Roger L. M. Dunbar, "The Effects of Personality Type on Choices Made in Strategic Decision Situations," *Decision Sciences*, Vol. 22 (1991), pp. 1047–1072.

Locus of Control

A group of authors looking at human information processing proposes that locus of control can affect how an individual uses information.[17] Locus of control is a concept originated by Rotter to describe how a person perceives the question of who controls his or her destiny.[18] If a person thinks that he or she is in control, that person has an internal framework (locus of control). If, on the other hand, a person feels that he or she is at the mercy of the environment and that he or she has little personal control, then that person's locus is external. Tests have been developed to measure relative positions on this continuum, and added dimensions of internality and externality rather than just an overall scale have been posited.[19] Some researchers have demonstrated that people with an internal locus of control make different decisions and seem to use information differently from those more externally oriented.[20] For example, in certain situations, it is possible that people who are more externally oriented may believe that all information is totally objective and that they can do little to affect outcomes. Internally oriented decision makers may feel they can change the odds of success and make decisions based on their being more in control of the situation than the externally oriented person would. The above is basically theoretical since it has not been tested empirically.

n-Achievement

Another dimension that has received attention is n-achievement, a measure of the achievement motivation of an individual.[21] High achievers tend to set reasonable goals that may have some moderate degree of risk but seem normally attainable. A person with a high motivation to achieve usually is a problem solver, a person who is willing to assume responsibility. The idea of accepting a moderate degree of risk (not wanting a situation either too easy or too risky) is borne out in many studies in psychology.[22] As with locus of control, n-achievement is measurable.

---

[17] Kerr and others, "Human Information Processing"; and J. Dermer, "Human Information Processing and Problem Solving: Implications for Accounting Research" in Livingstone, *Managerial Accounting: The Behavioral Foundations*, pp. 169–208.

[18] See J. B. Rotter, "Generalized Expectancies for Internal Versus External Control of Reinforcement," *Psychological Monographs* 80:609 (1966), pp. 1–28.

[19] For example, B. Collins, "Four Components of the Rotter Internal–External Scale: Belief in a Difficult World, a Just World, a Predictable World, and a Politically Responsive World," *Journal of Personality and Social Psychology* 29:3 (1974), pp. 381–391.

[20] Maurice L. Hirsch, "Disaggregated Probabilistic Accounting Information: The Effect of Sequential Events on Expected Value Maximization Decisions," *Journal of Accounting Research* 16:2 (Autumn 1978), pp. 254–269.

[21] D. C. McClelland, J. D. Atkinson, R. A. Clark, and E. L. Lowell, *The Achievement Motive* (New York: Appleton-Century-Crofts, Inc., 1953).

[22] See, for example, Ward Edwards, "Behavioral Decision Theory," *Annual Review of Psychology* 12 (1961), pp. 473–498.

Research suggests that the need for achievement and the elements of locus control (or attribution) are related.[23] Persons who attribute successes to themselves (internal locus of control) tend also to experience pride in accomplishment. Because positive esteem-enhancing feelings mediate from self-attribution of success, these persons tend eagerly to approach future task challenges. So long as this association pattern is repeated whenever progress or accomplishment is perceived by an individual, he or she sets in motion the conditions to develop a higher-than-average need for achievement.[24] After all, the achievement motive has long been characterized as the capacity for taking pride in accomplishment.[25] However, persons who attribute success to luck, powerful other people, or easy tasks do not experience pride in accomplishment (since they do not see themselves as the cause of the success) and thus are ambivalent about future task challenges. Persons who are strong external attributers thus do not form the mental-emotional association necessary for developing achievement motivation.

Personality Dimensions and Accounting Information

We have begun to identify dimensions of the psychological and behavioral makeup of a person, including the person's self-image, psychological type, position on the internal–external locus of control dimension, and a measure of achievement motivation. We do not mean this discussion to provide an exhaustive list of such variables, only an introduction to the subject so that we can see that information might be used by different people in different ways.

Certainly we can hope that if we know the personality characteristics of our audience, we can fashion our information in such a way as to promote its most effective use. However, this may not be possible for many reasons. Some authors state that there is some dependency between the decision at hand and the personality characteristics of the decision maker. For example, a person who is high in n-achievement might react differently in one capital budgeting decision than in another one.[26] Stumpf and Dunbar state that it is important to see the extent that a bias is systematic.

---

[23] Bernard Wiener, *Achievement Motivation and Attribution Theory* (Morristown, N.J.: General Learning Press, 1974).

[24] Curtis W. Cook and Ruth E. Cook, "Achievement Motivation Can Be Managed: A Coaching Strategy of Attribution Change," Southern Illinois University at Edwardsville, School of Business, working paper.

[25] J. W. Atkinson, *An Introduction to Motivation* (New York: Van Nostrand-Reinhold Company, 1964), p. 241.

[26] W. McGhee, M. D. Shields, and J. G. Birnberg, "The Effects of Personality on a Subject's Information Processing," *The Accounting Review* 53:3 (July 1978), pp. 681–697. A good summary of prior research and some of the dimensions we identify in this chapter is found in Michael D. Shields, "The Effects of Accounting Information on Managerial Decision Making," in Ferris and Livingstone *Management Planning and Control: The Behavioral Foundations*, rev. ed. (Beaver Creek, Ohio: Century VII Publishing Co., 1987), pp. 219–245.

While people are not likely to exhibit the same bias all of the time, they may exhibit a particular bias a modest percentage of the time—and they may exhibit many different biases.[27]

Others argue that the very nature of accounting involves ambiguity and vagueness.[28] We are told to investigate *large* or *significant* variances; we often have ambiguous states of nature, criteria for decisions, and constraints; yet we often propose decision models that presume simple yes/no responses. For example, we build objective functions and constraints as input into a linear programming model. The outcome is definitive: make this much of that product and that much of another product. The constraints we pose for the model are quite precise, while those that really impinge on our final decisions might be much more ambiguous. Thus, if we were to work on how to present the outcome of a linear programming model to managers, not only would we have to deal with personality dimensions and form, order, and format issues but also with the possible ambiguity of the inputs and constraints. These might interact so that decision makers with similar personality characteristics would make different decisions given the same information, or a single decision maker would make different decisions in similar settings. Thus, while we have begun to identify the kinds of issues and dimensions that can affect behavior, we have not yet developed clear, useful models incorporating these variables. We may never be able to do so. It is, however, important to begin to raise these questions so that we are aware of these dimensions and how they can influence information use. In addition, by becoming aware of how each of us might be different from one another in some dimensions but alike in others, we can be open to how successful information processing and decision making can take on many forms.

FORM, ORDER, AND FORMAT OF INFORMATION

The preceding discussion of human information processing and personality attributes provides us with an awareness of some of the dimensions that affect information presenters and receivers. These concerns can serve as a basis for our thinking about information presentation and elicitation. We can see, for example, that too much or too little information can limit its use in a particular decision-making setting. This leads to a discussion of the form, order, and format of information.

---

[27] Stumpf and Dunbar, "The Effects of Personality Type," pp. 1063–1064.
[28] Awni Zebda, "The Problem of Ambiguity and Vagueness in Accounting," *Behavioral Research in Accounting*, Vol. 3 (1991), pp. 117–145.

How to Present Information

We can present information in many ways:

1. Orally or in written form
2. Live or recorded (e.g., video, voice mail)
3. Hard copy (plain paper, fax) or electronic copy (electronic mail)
4. Text, graphs, or spreadsheets
5. Handouts or overhead slides

These choices are a sample of the many that exist. Each can be expanded to include choices that arise, say, after you decide to present information to someone in written (hard copy) text form using a word processing program, a particular font, and a laser printer.

When choosing how to present information, the key question continues to be: *Given a task and a particular audience, how can I present information most effectively and efficiently?* If the task is to present medical research findings to an audience comprising other medical researchers, the presenter might choose to hand out in advance detailed text and tables outlining the research and then to present summary information orally and with the use of slides. On the other hand, if a consulting group is going to present the results of their analysis and conclusions regarding a particular business problem, they might choose to create a brief handout containing outline points they are going to cover in their oral presentation. The detailed output from their study would then be left with the client after the oral report. These are explicit choices, with many dimensions, that information presenters must make.

Order of Information

Given the task and the audience, what is the best order of information? It's akin to the old question, "I have some good news and some bad news. Which do you want to hear first?" Some things have a logical order. Restaurant menus usually list appetizers, main courses, side dishes, and desserts in that order.[29] This seems reasonable given the pattern of the order of the meal. The order of some things is fairly well set by rules; for example, an income statement following generally accepted accounting principles (GAAP) will start with revenues and end with income. However, in cases not bounded by GAAP or other external requirements, the accountant must make choices about information order.

For example, assume that plant management has analyzed several investment opportunities for new capital equipment. Upper management has asked that plant managers present the results of their findings and that they

---

[29] Even this is specific to certain cultures. In Hong Kong, for example, soups are listed after entrees since that is when soups are served.

discuss all projects investigated, whether or not they are to be recommended. The plant managers may present the findings in many different ways:

1. Listing the projects alphabetically
2. Listing in the order of investment capital needed
3. Listing in the order of net present value
4. Listing by degree of risk
5. Listing recommended projects before rejected ones
6. Listing based on other than financial criteria (e.g., needed due to regulations followed by those recommended to maintain/gain market share, increase quality, and so on)

There is some evidence that the order of information can affect how that information is used.[30] In the example above, order can affect the perceived ranking of various alternatives. What message is implied by ranking projects by relative risk versus their effect on quality or market share? Should projects be listed using more than one order? How should they first be presented and how should they be listed in a summary of those recommended?

Order can affect the perceived relevance of information. If minor points are covered first, the reader might assume that the body of the report is irrelevant. For this reason, many writers tend to summarize major points at the beginning of a report and then develop these issues in the main text. See Appendix 1A for further discussion of this point.

While we do not know if or how our choice of order can affect decisions in many cases, we often have a good, although quite subjective, idea of how order affects the receiver. If a manager is going to present both critical and complementary information regarding the performance of a subordinate, she might present the more negative material first, work through the feelings that might be generated by such information, and then finish with positive feedback. Although this might be fairly subconscious, the manager is making a choice regarding order.

Level of Aggregation

Aggregation refers to how detailed or summarized a set of information is. For example, earnings per share is a highly aggregated figure, while a list of all the accounts receivable would be disaggregated information. Though issues involving cognitive complexity are concerned with what various types of information to present, choices about aggregation have to do with the level of summarization of whatever type is chosen.

Aggregation can have an effect on information on both the input and the output sides. A manager must choose what data to use to define the benefits and costs of an alternative course of action. Aggregating too much

---

[30] See Lowell Bourne, *Order Effects in Accounting Variance Reports: A Laboratory Experiment* (unpublished Ph.D. dissertation, Washington University, St. Louis, 1976).

can distort information or at least reduce the amount of information in a set of data.

A discussion of variances (see Chapter 9) involves the differences between looking at an overall material variance (aggregated) or at material price, mix, and use variances (disaggregated), all divisions of the overall material variance. Another example of aggregation is the use of a weighted-average contribution margin. The individual contribution margins in dollars and in percent are lost by this aggregation.

Aggregation certainly is an issue at the output end. In fact, certain management principles implicitly assume increasing levels of aggregation. The idea of management by exception is built on giving fewer and fewer details in reports as they go to higher and higher levels of management.

A new field involving information for the executive is emerging from the wealth of computer hardware and software available to most executives in the modern office. What information is useful to the executive? How should it be presented? New computer technology allows a very flexible approach to what the executive sees. Summary reports can come up on the screen and, if the manager so desires, backup material can be called up to analyze or support the aggregated first report.

Managers need to make explicit choices on the aggregation issue. Various studies show that level of aggregation or disaggregation can have an effect on perception and decision-making behavior. Malcom discusses this choice in the context of sales variances.[31] He shows that if a firm has four similar products, there are eighteen different ways to present sales data. Aggregating one way or another may tend to hide certain trends and may lead managers to improper conclusions. He concludes that sales variances should be aggregated only if the products are homogeneous in most respects.

Quite a few studies, including work by Barefield, by Ronen, by Hirsch, and by Lewis and Bell, have explored the issue of aggregation and accounting information.[32] Barefield looked at whether decision makers made better choices when given condensed (aggregated) information regarding operating variances or when they were given more (disaggregated) information. In this experiment, Barefield found that the subjects did better with more information.

However, Ronen, Hirsch, and Lewis and Bell show that simple disaggregated information can lead people to make nonoptimal choices. As defined

---

[31] R. E. Malcom, "The Effect of Product Aggregation in Determining Sales Variances," *The Accounting Review* 52:1 (January 1978), pp. 162–169.

[32] R. Barefield, "The Effect of Aggregation on Decision Making Success: A Laboratory Study," *Journal of Accounting Research* 10:2 (Autumn 1972), pp. 229–242; J. Ronen, "Some Effects of Sequential Aggregation in Accounting on Decision-Making," *Journal of Accounting Research* 9:2 (Autumn 1971), pp. 307–332; Maurice L. Hirsch, "Disaggregated Probabilistic Accounting Information," *Journal of Accounting Research* (Spring 1978), pp. 254–269; B. Lewis and J. Bell, "Decisions Involving Sequential Events: Replications and Extensions," *Journal of Accounting Research* 23:1 (Spring 1985), pp. 228–239.

earlier, economic man is an expected-value maximizer.[33] In a simple decision setting with all other factors being equal, most decision makers will choose that alternative with the highest expected value. However, these studies show that people will choose an alternative with a lower expected value when given certain disaggregated information.

Therefore, there is a conflict on level of aggregation just as there is in the cognitive-complexity area. How aggregated should data be? How aggregated should reports be? Highly aggregated information tends to hide or even cut out certain items that might be of great value in a particular analysis. Too much disaggregation may lead to suboptimal decisions from a different perspective.[34] Like the other concepts considered in this chapter, level of aggregation interacts with many other variables.

Designing Computer Screens

A practical and current example of these concerns can be found in the design of what you see on a computer terminal's screen. When you sit at a microcomputer or at a terminal for a large, mainframe computer, you interact with the program and system by responding to the various screens and menus generated by the program. Here is a good example of how issues of form, order, and format all come together on a small screen.

A user will need to enter into a conversation with the system using the CRT screen and the keyboard. Even here some basic rules apply. Conversations should be complete in themselves, should use readily available data, should have a definite beginning and end, should be cancelable at any time, and should provide the ability to review and correct entries before the conversation is ended. The type of conversation would be quite different for a part-time user who goes to the library and wants to find certain source material on the library's computer as compared with an airline ticket agent who spends full time at a terminal and who has received specialized training.

Guidelines are important for designing screen layout. First you must select what goes on the screen. Criteria according to Arthur Andersen & Co., for example, include relevance to the user, proper level of detail, completeness, a logical way to get to other screens when one is not enough, related subfunctions on the same screen when there is room, and a screen that takes into account the terminal being used and the operating system's response ability.[35]

Screens can be zoned. "Window" technologies employ zoned screens with several programs displayed at once. Even with one program, the designer

---

[33] Assume that expected value and expected utility are identical. While this may not always be the case, it holds sufficiently so that this is not a restrictive assumption.

[34] Another interesting discussion of aggregation is in J. Ronen, "Nonaggregation Versus Disaggregation of Variances," *The Accounting Review* 49:1 (January 1974), pp. 50–60.

[35] This is based on material in Arthur Andersen & Co. "Consulting Division Technical Information Release 4 (10/1/80), Conversation and Screen Design Guidelines" (Chicago, Ill.: Arthur Andersen & Co.).

must decide where the headings will be, and where the general applications of the program will go and where to display messages from the program. Choices are also made on what to put in the most desirable position of the screen (defined in most programs as the upper left); what to highlight, reverse video, underline, and so on. All these issues need to be addressed explicitly when creating screens for users. The point of this section is that we have to make similar choices for any type of information we create, whether it is oral, written by hand, or generated by computer.

Stochastic versus Deterministic Information

Many chapters in this book discuss assessment of risks, measurement of uncertainty, and sensitivity analysis. However, most of the information we see is deterministic. An annual report shows a single figure for net income, and each account balance is reported as a single figure in the balance sheet. Cost-volume-profit models and discounted cash flow models generally use single values. We use specific data for an objective function and constraints in linear programming. In all these cases a full set of information includes some assessment of risk. Accounts receivable or inventory could be expressed using a 95 percent confidence interval. Discounted cash flow models and linear programming can reflect uncertainty through simulation and sensitivity analysis. However, there is a problem regarding the use of such information. As one report states:

> Certainly a more complete decision model may be specified using probabilities, but do users deal with probabilities in a consistent, "rational" way, as every good "economic man" should? The information specialist should know the answers to such questions. . . .[36]

This is a crucial question to all aspects of behavior and information. It is quite easy to say that mathematical models are better than heuristic ones or that specifically dealing with uncertainty is more complete than just making point estimates. However, we have very little evidence on how people use this information. For example, much of our thinking about how people use stochastic information comes from studies involving gambling odds and decisions from the psychology literature.[37] Any extrapolation of these studies into accounting is tenuous at best.

---

[36] "Report of Committee on Managerial Decision Models," American Accounting Association, *The Accounting Review* (Supplement 1969), pp. 42–76.

[37] Ward Edwards did a whole series of such studies in the 1950s and 1960s. For example, see "Probability Preferences in Gambling," *American Journal of Psychology*, no. 66 (1953), pp. 349–364; and "The Prediction of Decisions Among Bets," *Journal of Experimental Psychology* 50:3 (1955), pp. 201–214.

THE EFFECTS OF POWER ON INFORMATION

According to Pfeffer, most definitions of power are based on the notion that one person can make another person do something, even when that other person resists.[38] At the beginning of this chapter, we discussed objectivity. When power comes to play, information can be selected and presented in ways that enhance the power of the individuals or groups who control information. Pfeffer goes on to describe political strategies and tactics for manipulating information to one's own advantage. For example, if someone favors a particular course of action, that person may select certain criteria for evaluating the performance that favor his or her position. People may use information "to justify a decision, as contrasted with making the decision."[39] Outside experts may be hired as a way to influence the decision process. The information presented by experts is accepted as valid because it comes from a knowledgeable source. These experts may be engaged because a particular participant in the situation knows they will give certain recommendations that favor that participant's position. It is interesting that Pfeffer states that consultants are used most frequently in the area of designing a new information system, the conduit for all information for the entire company.[40] Persons in power can really influence the type and quality of information that managers will see. Those people who control the information flow can have a major impact on decisions that are based on available information.

Thus, in our effort to deal with choices regarding information, we also must take into account the likelihood that some individuals or groups will be attempting to control the nature, amount, and format of the information in ways that enhance their own power. Just as it is unlikely that information is unbiased and neutral, it is also unlikely that there will be no power or political considerations.

INFORMATION ELICITATION

The discussion to this point has focused on information presentation. The same issues apply when eliciting information from others. For example, in both eliciting and presenting information we must be aware of the sensitivity of information, its order, and its level of aggregation.

---

[38] J. Pfeffer, *Power in Organizations* (Marshfield, Mass.: Pitman Publishing, Inc., Jeffery Pfeffer, 1981), p. 2.

[39] Pfeffer, *Power in Organizations*, p. 140.

[40] Pfeffer, *Power in Organizations*, p. 145.

Objective versus Subjective Information

At one extreme, objective information is a set of facts. We can ask, for example, the dimensions of a particular piece of equipment. At the other end of the spectrum might be personal opinions about whether a salesperson believes a particular customer will accept a price change. Eliciting information regarding probabilities is a good example of this continuum. In some cases we are certain about information; in other situations we have some evidence about the range of values a variable might assume. Finally, there are times that we have no way to assess such a range and any estimate would be quite arbitrary. We can call these three levels *certainty, risk,* and *uncertainty.* In many cases we are eliciting information where either risk or uncertainty exists. In most cases involving risk, we are dealing with subjective assessments of that risk, since there are few examples of objective probabilities.

Types of Information

Managers want to find information in many different areas. As accountants, we might want to know the process a manager uses to evaluate new products, decide among competing suppliers for a new piece of equipment, or propose the best way to close a sale. Accountants want information to evaluate how they can be most effective in helping managers make good decisions. If, say, we are interested in providing financial and nonfinancial, quantitative as well as nonquantitative, information to managers to help them assess the performance of department heads under their supervision, we want to make sure that we understood the current process and information used. Members of the accounting staff would interview supervisory managers or seek information through written questionnaires. The accounting staff would want to know what information is sensitive to the supervisor. A supervisor might feel defensive about certain types of information and want to know if and how what the accountant is writing down in the interview could be used against him. The order of questioning in an interview might lead to going off on certain useful or not-so-useful tangents. Questioners will also have to decide what background information to provide to respondents in advance. How much is appropriate? How much should they say about the purpose of the interview and its outcomes? Although they want to be informative and get the best possible responses, they do not want to influence the responses.

The above example is meant to provide an illustration of the types of questions that the information solicitor might have. These concerns seem quite similar to those of the information presenter. They revolve around the most efficient and effective way to garner information given a task and audience. In addition, we might explore the aspects of eliciting a particular type of information: probabilities.

Eliciting Probabilities

Earlier discussion in this chapter has shown that while theoretically we can say that models are more useful if they explicitly recognize risk, we are less sure how people use information containing probabilities. The elicitation of probabilities is thus another area of concern.

There are three dimensions to the problem of eliciting probabilities.[41] First, does the manager elicit information from himself, or do others (such as the accounting department) elicit information either orally or in writing?

Second how is probability information considered and presented? One way is to get direct assessments regarding probabilities, odds, means and variances, and so on. Another way is to get some specific dollar figures. For example, a manager could say it is equally likely to have the following three sales ranges: $100,000 to $300,000, $300,001 to $700,000, and $700,001 to $900,000.

Third, should probabilities be elicited directly or indirectly? A direct estimation is illustrated by the manager's statement above. An indirect method is to infer probabilities *given* that decisions have been made. This involves going backward from the decision to the probabilities. For example, the accountant could ask a manager to state his estimate of profits if 100,000 units of product A were produced at a variable cost of $75 with a selling price of $125 per unit. This estimate could be compared to estimates based on other production levels, variable costs, selling price, and so on. The accountant could then derive a probability distribution based on these various values.

ORAL AND WRITTEN COMMUNICATION OF INFORMATION

In this section we explore the need for good oral and written communication skills; complete our discussion of task and audience while adding a new dimension, role; and discuss feedback in the communication process.

Need for Good Communication Skills

In the past few years, accounting professionals have been sending a clear message to university accounting departments—we need accounting personnel who not only know their field but also know how to communicate effectively through both writing and speaking. Thirty percent of the accounting firms surveyed by *The Wall Street Journal* (1986, July 15) reported dissatisfaction with the communication skills of entry-level accountants. Another study[42] cited poor

---

[41] For a good summary and complete references see G. R. Chesley, "Elicitation of Subjective Probabilities: A Review," *The Accounting Review* 50:2 (April 1975), pp. 325–337.

[42] National Association of Accountants *Management Accounting Campus Report*. Montvale, N.J.: National Association of Accountants, May 1989.

writing skills as a major reason for job terminations among entry-level accountants. Others report that practicing CMAs place great importance on communication skills (speaking, writing, and listening) and were dissatisfied with the training they had received in formal courses involved with communication.[43] Another study looked at controllers of United States corporations who are CMAs.[44] Respondents rated, among other things, the importance of different skills and characteristics for entry-level management accountants, reporting that the following were either very important or extremely important: thinking skills (95 percent), problem-solving skills (97 percent), listening skills (91 percent), writing skills (92 percent), and speaking skills (73 percent). They also said entry-level management accountants were either very weak or extremely weak in: writing skills (55 percent) and verbal skills (49 percent). The authors conclude:

> Writing, listening, verbal, and overall management skills were identified as either important skills . . . or as current weaknesses. . . . The need for these skills indicates that more practice in public speaking, writing, and group discussion is warranted in all phases of the accounting curriculum.

They go on to suggest:

> . . . the CMA's conclusions that students' technical accounting knowledge might be sacrificed for greater concentration on problem solving and thinking skills suggest that faculty might need to rethink course designs and activities.[45]

The need for better communication and analytical thinking skills is also called for in the report of the American Accounting Association Committee on the Future Structure, Content, and Scope of Accounting Education (the Bedford Committee).[46] In response to such findings, practitioners, university accounting departments, and students have begun to take a serious look at the communication skills needed to enter the business world. In addition, we are realizing that courses in accounting skills need to be combined with training in analytical thinking and both oral and written communication skills. Without the integration of skills training, those entering the work force are seriously shortchanged, with possible detrimental consequences to their careers and hopes of advancement.

Accounting involves communicating information to others. Although it is important to deal with how personality types, power, form, order, and format

---

[43] David E. Stout, Donald E. Wygal, and Katharine T. Hoff, "Writing Across the Disciplines: Applications to the Accounting Classroom," *The Bulletin of the Association for Business Communication* (Denton, Tex.: University of North Texas), 53.4, (1990), pp. 10–16.

[44] Adel M. Novin, Michael A. Pearson, and Stephen V. Senge, "Improving the Curriculum for Aspiring Management Accountants: The Practitioner's Point of View," *Journal of Accounting Education*, Vol 8 (1990), pp. 207–224.

[45] Novin, Pearson, and Senge, p. 220.

[46] American Accounting Association (AAA) Committee on the Future Structure, Content, and Scope of Accounting Education, "Future Accounting Education: Preparing for the Expanding Profession," *Issues in Accounting Education* 1 (1990), pp. 168–195.

affect how information is received, at the core is this need to acquire and use excellent analytical thinking and communication skills. Many think that knowing "good English" is somehow divorced from either analytical thinking or being able to communicate. However, what we think and how we communicate are completely intertwined. Thinking can be quite abstract at times, but if we want to tell someone else about an idea or a conclusion, we are usually going to organize our thinking in words and, through various oral and written avenues, communicate those words to our audience.

Logical Thinking

The key to communication comes before organization, form, and format. Managers must logically analyze a situation. If managers think logically and act on the basis of that logic, the communicating techniques that are explored, the techniques that are used, and the conclusions reached become easier. Communication is then a logical extension of the analytical process. The ability to use logical analysis is the key to overall management accounting.

Role, Audience, and Task

The basic question posed so far is *given the task and the audience, how can we most effectively and efficiently communicate?* We have discussed some of the aspects of both task and audience but need to expand our discussion and add another dimension: role.

Role involves the information provider's function. For example, is she operating alone or as a member of a team? Is she acting as an advisor or a decision maker? In any task, the role the information provider is to play must be explicit; audience and role are a matched set. The *audience* is the constituency being addressed: a peer, supervisor, subordinate, customer, supplier, or member of the board of directors, for example. As with role, audience must be clearly defined. Consulting with a client often requires different skills than communicating with peers within the same department. Talking to production managers might involve different skills than dealing with salespeople. Communicating with a large, diverse audience involves different choices than an informal meeting with a supervisor.

Finally, there is the *task*, the specific assignment. Defining task involves not only the expected content but also the organization, form, format, and personnel required to accomplish it. A task of, say, gathering and organizing information for another's use is different from using that information and coming to an operating decision based on it.

Role, audience, and task are interrelated. It is important to have a clear definition of each before starting a project; if a person is unclear about any of these three aspects, there is the possibility that the results will be unsuccessful. It is possible that the person assigning the role, audience, and task is unclear about what he wants; or he may know what he wants but communicates his wishes in an ambiguous way. If so, it is your responsibility to ask questions in order to find out what is required for success. There is the old "hairy beast" story, which involves a ruler who asks his hunters to go into the forest and bring him back a beast. However, each time a different animal is presented to him, he roars his disapproval at the hunter for bringing in the wrong beast and sends him back into the forest. The audience is clear (the ruler), but it is not so apparent what the role and task are for the hunters; they can only achieve the ruler's unstated goals by chance.

The specific definitions of role, audience, and task can evolve as the work goes forward. What started out as a simple information gathering task might turn out to be more complex than anticipated. What was assumed to be certain now looks as if it is more uncertain and the decision maker must make several explicit assumptions. You might have been told that you were going to present your analysis and conclusions to a single member of management, but as the work progresses you might decide that more people should be the audience.

Feedback

Feedback is the reaction and information we give others that allows them to learn and improve. Information providers can present feedback to audiences and vice versa. Effective feedback is a vital element in integrated skills training. Some issues in feedback design and implementation are (1) considering the form and format of feedback, (2) using peers to give each other feedback, (3) asking questions rather than giving answers, (4) reviewing drafts of reports, and (5) learning how to evaluate others' work.

Form and Format Issues   Feedback can be formal or informal, in writing or oral, from a single person or from a group. Feedback can come from the attention, or lack of it, given by the audience. It can come from the questions that are asked at the end of a presentation.

Feedback Among Peers   The more general discussion about information elicitation and presentation applies to feedback as well. People often do not want to hear even well-meaning criticism; however, often feedback from peers, if given in a noncompetitive way, is seen as less threatening. In fact, if several colleagues make similar recommendations regarding a draft of a report, this can be confirming evidence to the preparer.

Asking Questions versus Giving Answers   It is natural that people want to know what the "right" answer is as well as a natural tendency for some to want to tell others what they *think* is the right answer. However, in many cases it is more important to ask questions rather than to give answers. Questions can address lack of clarity about an issue: "What do you mean here?" If a person offers no argument or evidence to back up his or her assertion, ask "Why?" or "What is the evidence to support your assertions?" Questions should not include a hidden agenda where you have an opinion and want the other to guess what it is. For example, if a report jumps between subjects and does not have adequate transitions, it would be better to state this than to ask "Do you need a transition here?" Even with suggestions about a need for transitions between ideas or a point that is dropped prematurely, criticism can be couched in questions such as "I am having problems with a lack of transition between ideas; what could you put here so that the reader can better follow your shift in subjects?" and "This seems incomplete to me; what can you put here to help me understand it better?"

Dealing with Drafts   The text you are now reading started out as a draft using a word processing program. The draft was sent to possible adopters and was given to students for class use. Each provided feedback that could be used to improve the final product. Exposing drafts for feedback allows someone else who is not as close to the work as the author to evaluate it from a neutral position and to offer aid, an extremely important part of any oral or written communication.

Evaluating the Work of Others   In an accounting class you get a grade based on a set of expectations. Instructors are in the position of evaluating the performance of students, and they usually have developed an explicit set of outcomes and ways to evaluate. Managers are often in the same position. They must evaluate the worth of a report or the progress of an employee toward promotion. Much as it is important to have an explicit role, audience, and task, it is just as critical to know the evaluation criteria you will use to judge success—and to communicate those criteria to the people you will evaluate. It is also important to know the evaluation that will be applied to you. Feedback can also be provided by the presenter to the audience—it is a two-way street. Effective appraisal of our work allows us to improve and communicate better.

SUMMARY

This chapter raises questions about how we process information, how personality dimensions can affect information use, the effect of power on information and offers a discussion about form, order, and format issues and what is entailed in coupling good analytical thinking and communication skills. In some sense the material raises more questions than it answers. We do not address the cost of information, but that is important (and is covered later in the text). The point is to nurture a concern about information elicitation and presentation. If we are aware that these issues exist, we can make conscious choices about how we will address them. Entire courses and books are devoted to many of the subjects discussed. We have crammed a good bit of new material into a few pages.

The material is integral with the other areas that follow. Keep the subjects introduced in this chapter active in your thinking as you deal with all the subjects that follow. At times this material is explicitly referred to while at other times it is implicit in the discussion. As with some other topics we discuss, the objective of this chapter is mostly to raise questions rather than to give answers. It is up to you to ask these questions and to come up with your own conclusions as you proceed through the balance of the book.

❖ *APPENDIX 1A*

GUIDELINES FOR CASE AND MEMORANDUM PREPARATION[47]

INTRODUCTION

Cases and expanded problems are a way to include more real-world issues and problems in a course. They can be very broad and include general, strategic issues, or they can be more focused and deal with a specific problem at hand. When we discuss these cases or expanded problems, we can develop and integrate the ideas that are introduced in the text and/or other readings. Such an oral analysis in class, when coupled with a written presentation, helps develop analytical thinking skills and oral and written communication skills as well. The objective of this appendix and assignments that result from it is to use case analysis and memorandum preparation as surrogates for real-world tasks, roles, and audiences.

These guidelines deal with two types of written assignments: a shorter memorandum to management and a longer case analysis (our substitute for a more formal report). These two differ in format and may differ in perspective.

Cases   Cases deal with from one to several issues, usually contain several pages of information, and require you to present an in-depth analysis of several pages. You may be asked to respond to a case as a neutral third

---

[47] For a more complete discussion of written and oral communication issues, see Maurice L. Hirsch, Jr., Robert Anderson, and Susan L. Gabriel, *Accounting and Communication*, (Cincinnati: South-Western Publishing Company), 1994.

party (i.e., a student) writing to another neutral third party (i.e., your instructor), or you may be asked to assume the role of a consultant or a member of management writing to a particular audience in the company (e.g., the president, the plant manager, and so on). Assignments will specify your role and your audience. Depending on the case at hand, the task might need further definition.

Memoranda   Shorter assignments provide an opportunity to develop skills in communicating with management in mostly single-issue settings. The background material is usually shorter than case material. Memoranda will be from the perspective of either a consultant or a member of management writing to a particular audience in the company (as explained above). Assignments will specify role, audience, and task.

Various instructors (like other supervisors) have specific requirements for case analysis and presentation or memorandum formats; this is a general guideline. If an instructor wants to deviate from this guideline, he or she will tell you so specifically.

BASIC REQUIREMENTS

Microcomputers and Word Processing   You are expected to be familiar with the use of microcomputers and with at least one word processing package. Microcomputers give you the ability to draft, redraft, and edit your material. You are required to use microcomputers for all cases and memoranda.

Writing Skills   What you present and how you present it are intertwined. This is how you are evaluated in the work place. You are expected to possess basic skills in English. This means that you must write and think clearly; present your information in an organized format; keep your audience's needs firmly in mind; use correct grammar, spelling, sentence and paragraph structure, reference citation, and so on. You might purchase the most recent edition of a style book such as the *Harbrace College Handbook* with MLA documentation style. If your campus has a writing laboratory, you may want to use it.

Background Knowledge   You are expected to possess basic knowledge about American business in general. You should read *The Wall Street Journal*, a major business magazine, and a national news magazine on a regular basis. If appropriate, use the library to gain background information about a particular company and/or industry.

Definition of Purpose   Make certain that you understand what your purpose is for each writing task. Clarify your role and clarify your audience.

If you are uncertain of the purpose behind your writing a case or memo, ask your instructor for clarification.

Audience Analysis   No writing assignment can be successfully completed without spending some time defining and analyzing your audience. Ask yourself the following questions: Who will be reading this? What is my relationship with the reader(s)? What do my readers already know about the subject? Do my readers have strong feelings about this subject? By answering these questions, you will have an audience profile that will help shape both what you say and how you say it.

Analysis versus Restatement   Many students confuse analysis with restatement. Restatement is a summary of the facts in a situation. An analysis involves critical thinking and requires that you go beyond the facts and answer the following questions: So what? What is the ramification of this information? How does this information affect the present or future situation? What kind of an impact does this information have on my audience? All memoranda and cases require analysis; mere restatement is insufficient.

Names and Abbreviations   Names of individuals and companies should first be stated in full. Do not substitute "Co." for "Company," "Incorporated" for "Inc.," or any change at all in the given name of a company. Define your abbreviations. For example, you could state, "In 1989, the situation at Federal Paper, Inc. (Federal) involved . . ." From that point on, you could refer to the company as just Federal. Once you have defined an abbreviation, use it consistently. The first time names are used they should be stated in full. If you want to abbreviate an individual's name, use the last name (e.g., Smith for Robin Smith) or use Ms. Smith. Your perspective will dictate how formal or informal you should be with names.

Supporting Schedules   All supporting schedules, exhibits, graphs, and tables must be properly labeled and referred to in your analysis. Supporting materials that contain numbers can be called an exhibit or table, but graphical material should be referred to as a figure. Exhibits and/or figures should be numbered in the order they are referred to in the paper. When you refer to a specific exhibit, refer to it as "Exhibit 1" rather than "exhibit 1." All exhibits, tables, or figures must have a heading that is descriptive of their content as well as an exhibit, table, or figure number identifying order of presentation.

You are encouraged to generate material that would be useful for exhibits and/or figures by using programs such as Lotus 1-2-3, graphics packages, a regression package, or a linear programming package. However, be selective in what you want to include. Take your audience, role, and task into consideration; carefully format your exhibits, make sure they are properly titled, and provide appropriate references to sources. Finally, make sure all abbreviations are defined.

Use of Jargon   Make sure you get specific instructions from your instructor regarding the use of jargon (topic- or industry-specific terminology) and the inclusion of background information. You should be able to present your analyses without jargon, buzzwords, or clichés if asked to do so.

Environmental Constraints   Each set of problems has some constraints imposed by the internal and external environment of the situation. You should clearly state what these constraints are. They may limit how you present your analysis, what problems you are supposed to address, and what information is available, to name a few constraints.

CASES

A case is a glimpse of a real-world situation where you are limited in what you know by the brief information contained on a few pages. Sometimes the case issues are clear, and sometimes they are not. However, you can see what problems are emerging and can see the kinds of decisions needed to solve these problems. A lack of complete information is not an excuse for avoiding dealing with the case issues.

Reading the Case

First read and reread the case, to get an overall understanding of the situation and supporting facts. When you reread the case, take notes about key facts, assumptions, and issues. Outline what analytical techniques are appropriate to help you gain additional needed information (e.g., net present value analysis, simple or multiple linear regression, and linear programming). Look at existing quantitative information to see if it is accurate, consistent, and well presented. Look at the case questions (if any), and formulate an idea about how to approach your analysis.

Avoid rushing to a conclusion as you read a case. If you do, you might overlook important information or you may distort information to fit some preconceived idea. Second, be sure you fully understand the case before you try to work on any appropriate numerical analysis. Third, be careful to differentiate between facts, estimates, and assumptions or suppositions.

As you read, ask yourself a broad range of questions. What are the problems and opportunities here? What information is given that will aid you in solving these problems? What information is lacking that you might need? What is going on here anyway? Why are these problems still unsolved?

What is happening between the people in this company? When you use an appropriate analytical technique, what do you hope to learn? How sensitive is your analysis to changes? How probable are these changes? What assumptions and/or estimates do you have to make?

You should be very careful not to confuse the basic problem with its symptoms. For example, a decline in sales is probably a symptom of a problem and not the problem per se. Make sure you understand what background information is required. Depending on the case, you might have to discuss factors inside the organization (management team, marketing issues, finances, and so on) and outside the organization (industry makeup, foreign competition, economic conditions, governmental regulations, and so on). The more a problem is related to strategic planning issues, the more it will be important to identify the strengths and weaknesses of a firm in relation to its internal and external environment.

In analyzing and planning how to respond to a case, do not be limited by the specific questions asked in the case. Do not feel bound to address specific questions in a lock-step manner. Remember that a case should be used as a springboard for any relevant issues that can usefully be brought into the analysis. Also remember that you will be writing this response after having done all the supporting analysis. Thus, there should be a feeling of integration about your presentation. For example, if there are four sequential parts to a case, your answers to part 1 should not be presented as if you had not read and solved parts 2, 3, and 4.

Since a case extends the text in many instances, do not expect that you can always find specific text references or techniques for your analysis or solution. You might have to integrate several ideas and/or techniques from several sources.

General Form and Format Guidelines

Perspective of Writer and Reader   Make your perspective clear and consistent. Are you writing a formal paper with all references in the third person? Is your approach from the perspective of a member of management or as a consultant to management? Who is your audience? Is it your instructor reading the report as a neutral third person, or is your instructor playing the role of a specific member of the management of a company involved in the case?

If you are writing a formal paper (sometimes referred to as a classic case presentation), take the detached role of a person who is observing the information and problem(s) and who is analyzing and commenting about appropriate issues. Your audience is another person who is detached from the situation at hand. Instructions should be clear about how much information your audience requires (how much is known background information and how much you should explain and/or summarize).

If you are writing from the perspective of an outside consultant hired by the company or a member of the management of a company, you are working with management to deal with appropriate issues in the case. The case instructions or specific instructions from your instructor will let you know what perspective to take and who your audience is. Knowing your audience should help you define how much background information or explanation is appropriate.

Headings   Headings help to form transitions between sections and help the reader know where you are going. In addition, they provide a good framework for your analysis and help you write a more organized paper. You are expected to use appropriate headings.

General Writing Guideline

The following is a general writing guideline for a case presentation that will have to be amended depending on your assigned perspective (neutral, consultant, member of management) and specific instructions from your instructor.

Executive Summary   Some instructors will want a paper to start with an executive summary where, in about one page, you summarize your recommendation(s), basic findings (problems and pertinent information), and necessary explanations. This section should be brief and to the point. A statement of the problem and identification of alternate courses of action can follow this summary.

Beginning/Introduction   The introduction to your analysis should include a statement of the problem(s) you have identified. You should state how you have approached the analysis and solution to the case problems and what you have identified as alternate courses of action. If quantitative techniques are called for, you should justify their use. List the decisions you need to make and whether they are dependent and/or sequential. If you have made assumptions and/or estimates, state them clearly and justify them. If there is necessary information that you deem relevant, call attention to that fact. Finally, include a brief summary of the conclusions you have reached (including actions recommended). Make sure you demonstrate that there is specific evidence in the case to support your position. In addition, some instructors want you to summarize relevant background information as a part of your presentation while others want you to assume that the reader is fully familiar with the case material.

This section sets the tone for all that follows. Make sure that you build a sufficient foundation regarding the problems or issues, the facts, your approaches, and so on. Make sure it is clear to the reader what you are doing and why you are doing it.

Middle/Analysis   This is the heart of the paper, where you present your analysis and how you went about forming conclusions. What criteria are you using to select a final course of action? What are the results of your analysis? Make sure to support your analysis. Do not make assertions without evidence or argument to support them. Here is where you need to spend the greatest amount of time and space. Your conclusions and recommendations should be clear and logically follow your analysis. Finally, there must be a way to measure the consequences of your recommendations. Therefore, this section should include the following:

1. Identification of viable courses of action that are open to the organization or the individual in the case/problem. Not all such courses of action may be explicitly delineated in the case.
2. Explanation of the criteria that will be used to select the final course of action. If criteria are mentioned in the case, you should evaluate them and justify their use. If no criteria are presented, you should develop realistic and applicable criteria through your analysis of case information and through your examination of secondary sources.
3. Selection of a course of action and identification, in a step-by-step fashion, of how this course of action will be implemented. If it is appropriate, assign specific and detailed duties and responsibilities to specific individuals. Establish a time table. Be as complete as possible with your plan.
4. Discussion of means to measure the consequences of your recommendation(s). Establish standards by which the success or failure of your proposed course of action should be judged. If realistic in terms of the case, you should establish a system of rewards (positive and negative) for named individuals or officials based upon the standards and objectives you set.

You should build a logical presentation in this section. You will probably have to integrate several ideas and issues. Organization and the use of headings is quite important, as everything should flow in a logical order. It should be clear to the reader how you have come to your conclusions and why you have chosen a particular choice.

End/Conclusion   Your ending section should summarize the solutions to the problems you defined in the introduction. If there are remaining problems that are unanswered, state them and what you would do to resolve them. Give your recommendations. This final section should bring everything together so there is a natural end to the paper. There should be no surprises nor new material in this section; everything should flow logically from the previous sections and must be fully supported by discussion and facts presented prior to the conclusion.

MEMOS TO MANAGEMENT

Some assignments require that you write a memorandum to management about a specific problem at hand. In most instances, such memoranda will be shorter and more focused than case analyses and presentations. The general guidelines above regarding names, headings, supporting schedules, jargon, and environmental constraints apply to memoranda just as much as to cases. Although a memorandum is shorter than a case presentation, the general organizational writing guidelines apply. Other things to consider when preparing a memo include the following:

1. Use a proper memo format that includes a heading, to whom the memo is addressed, who wrote the memo, the date, and the subject. Make sure to align names (see below). Also see that your name appears on the memo so you can receive proper credit! As an example of a memorandum format, see Figure 1A-1.
2. Be direct and to the point. Do not use fancy words and avoid jargon as much as possible. Define your audience and make sure you provide information in a way that such a person or persons can understand what you are saying. If you were the person you are addressing, how would you want information presented to you?
3. Make your purpose clear. Executives are busy: if you do not grab their attention and hold it, they tend to scan your report with little interest or just throw it away. Make it clear what response you would like from the reader.
4. Use the opening of a memo to establish a link between what you have been asked to do and your report (memo). At the end of the memo, tie things together and end so that the reader feels good about your work and knows you are available to answer additional questions. Set the stage for future work/assignments.

MEMORANDUM

To: John Jones, Sales Manager
From: Mary Smith, XYZ Consulting Company
Date: August 13, 1992
Subject: Analysis of Current Planning Issues

John, this memo is in response to your request for us to analyze your current performance evaluation procedures. We believe you will be pleased with the results of our work. First of all, we see the following issues to resolve: . . .

Figure 1A-1 Illustration of Memorandum Format

If you are an outside consultant writing to your client, you might not want to use the memo format suggested above and illustrated in Figure 1A-1. Rather, you would attach a cover letter to the client and the body of your analysis would be in an attached report. This is really a subtle difference between internal memoranda and external reports.

PROBLEMS AND CASES

1-1.   Creating a Company—an In-Class Exercise

You will be part of a small group that will be formed the first day of class. Your group will be assigned *one* of the following situations. In each case, your role is a group of people just starting a company. When you meet together in class, assume that role in your discussion. When you are required to give an oral report, assume that your management group is meeting with other entrepreneurs who are going through the same process and that you are sharing what you have learned and decided with them. In that role, you are also expected to ask questions as appropriate of other groups.

Manufacturing Company

You and your associates are just starting a manufacturing company that will supply components to various automobile companies (the "big three" as well as U.S. plants of foreign firms). You will operate out of a single factory in rural Illinois near a major interstate highway. You are meeting today to discuss the outline of the information you will need in order to be effective decision makers and managers. During your exchange of ideas, consider the external environment of the firm, including regulatory concerns; the internal organizational structure and facilities environment; and information you will need for planning, operating, controlling, and making both short-term and long-term decisions.

At the end of the meeting, you are expected to give an oral report regarding the conclusions you reached. Make sure to be explicit about any assumptions you made regarding your company or its environment.

Service Company

You and your associates are just starting a company that will provide information services to callers and to those hooked up to the system by modems on their computers. You will be specializing in retail goods and will have information regarding prices and availability of items not only from national mail-order companies but also from locally owned stores throughout Missouri and Illinois. The company will be located in an office in rural Illinois near St. Louis, Missouri. You are meeting today to discuss the outline of the information you will need in order to be effective decision makers and managers. During your exchange of ideas, consider the external environment of the firm, including regulatory concerns; the internal organizational structure and facilities environment; and information you will need for planning, operating, controlling, and making both short-term and long-term decisions.

At the end of the meeting, you are expected to give an oral report regarding the conclusions you reached. Make sure to be explicit about any assumptions you made regarding your company or its environment.

Retail Company

You and your associates are just starting a retail plant and flower nursery in St. Charles, Missouri, a suburb across the Missouri River from St. Louis. You are meeting today to discuss the outline of the information you will need in order to be effective decision makers and managers. During your exchange of ideas, consider the external environment of the firm, including regulatory concerns; the internal organizational structure and facilities environment; and information you will need for planning, operating, controlling, and making both short-term and long-term decisions.

At the end of the meeting, you are expected to give an oral report regarding the conclusions you reached. Make sure to be explicit about any assumptions you made regarding your company or its environment.

1-2. Behavior and Information

Edwin Caplan has observed the following:

> The efficiency and effectiveness of human behavior and decision making within organizations is constrained by: (1) the inability to concentrate on more than a few things at a time; (2) limited awareness of the environment; (3) limited knowledge of alternative courses of action and the consequences of such alternatives; (4) limited reasoning ability; and (5) incomplete and inconsistent preference systems. As a result of these limits on human rationality, individual and organization behavior is usually directed toward attempts to find satisfactory—rather than optimal—solutions.[48]

Required:

Comment on the preceding quotation, referring to the chapter material and bringing in specific examples to illustrate your discussion. Be sure to do the following:

1. Explain the five constraints Caplan proposed.
2. Explain how these constraints are important to managerial and cost accounting.

1-3. Human Resource Accounting (CMA Adapted)

During the 1970s several authors wrote about human resource accounting (HRA).[49] The idea was not only to recognize the investment in land and equipment that a manager is held responsible for, but also to evaluate that manager on how he or she develops human resources. In a company that uses residual income or return on investment and ignores human assets, it is possible that managers will choose to maximize short-term profits by eliminating training seminars and conferences, company-financed college programs, and the like. This may achieve a better return on investment (ROI) in the current period, but it may have negative effects on future profits. With this as a brief introduction to HRA, consider the following situation.

The consumer products division of the Liberty Manufacturing Company experienced reduced sales in the first quarter of 19X8 and has forecasted that the decline in sales will continue through the remainder of the year. The profit budgeted in the

---

[48] E. Caplan, *Management Accounting and Behavioral Science*, pp. 31–33.

[49] See R. Likert, *The Human Organization* (New York: McGraw-Hill Book Company, 1967); and E. Flamholtz, *Human Resource Accounting* (Belmont, Calif.: Dickinson Publishing Co., Inc., 1974).

original 19X8 profit plan was about 40 percent less than that of the prior year. Fortunately, Liberty's other divisions budgeted improved profits in 19X8 over 19X7.

The top management of Liberty believes in a decentralized organization, and division managers have considerable latitude in managing the operations of their divisions. Division managers receive bonuses of a specified percentage of division profits in addition to their annual salaries.

At the end of the first quarter of 19X8, John Spassen, the manager of the consumer products division, felt that drastic action was needed to reduce costs and improve the performance of his division. As one step to reduce costs he dismissed twenty highly trained, skilled employees. Only five of them are expected to be available for reemployment when business returns to normal in 19X9.

The top management, upon reviewing the steps taken by Spassen, was concerned about the consequences of releasing the twenty skilled employees. Company officials had recently attended seminars on human resource accounting and wondered whether Spassen would have taken that particular action had a cost-based human resource accounting system been in operation.

Required:
1. Evaluating human assets or resources is a difficult question. Some authors propose a cost-based system founded on measurable costs, while others advocate a more general approach such as a present value of future worth to the company. Using this situation as an example, what is accounted for in a cost-based HRA system?
2. How could the company use information from a cost-based HRA system in deciding whether to dismiss the twenty skilled employees?
3. What other information would be useful in evaluating this decision?

1-4. The Issue of Control

One of the theories discussed in this chapter, that of cognitive complexity, involves the idea of confusion. Obviously, knowledge should be designed to reduce confusion. Some authors have stated that we humans are very intolerant when faced with confusion. In fact, we may even accept someone who is a dictator as long as we will be given order (and confusion will disappear). Recent history has lent some support to this proposition.

Required:
Using the resources of this chapter (and additional resources if so requested by your instructor), discuss the issues of control and confusion reduction. What is the management accountant's role in these matters?

1-5. Human Information Processing

The Shop 'n Save Corporation is run by Robert Lennon. The company operates a chain of retail quick-shop stores that are open 24 hours a day. All the stores are located in a major eastern metropolitan area. The company started ten years ago with one store and over the years has expanded to fifteen stores. Mr. Lennon is the majority shareholder in the company, and the other shares are owned by two other persons. Mr. Lennon is a C.P.A. and a lawyer. He is quite bright in simple mathematics and algebra but has had no formal training in subjects such as calculus. He has a good memory and can recall details of various events affecting the company and financial data about the company. The management team in the central office is fairly small; besides the president, Mr. Lennon, there is an accountant-bookkeeper and an administrative vice president. John Carlton, the vice president, has had little formal education. Although he completed high school, he did not complete college. However, he is both bright and industrious.

Mr. Lennon likes to be in control of most situations. He tends to centralize decision making. In addition, he tends to keep information in his head rather than having a management information system. Even the financial accounting data must sometimes be explained to the other shareholders, since various adjustments between stores and differences between cash and accrual accounting have caused some confusion in the interpretation of financial statements. Several of these discrepancies grew with the business. While the accounting system was adequate for a single store, it needs improvement for the multiple-store current status.

The nature of this business is high-volume, low-profit. While the company has grown, it has encountered severe cash flow difficulties from time to time. All the investors have had to put in investment capital or lend money to the corporation over its life. Up until now, the minority investors have been fairly inactive in an ongoing review of the business. They have accepted information given to them by Mr. Lennon at face value and have accepted his analysis of current situations. However, with increasing interest rates and increasing investment in the company, the outside investors want to improve the information network at the company so that they might better determine how the company is doing.

Required:
Assume that you have been hired as a consultant to the outside investors. Describe and critique the current situation and the problems that you see. Your description and analysis should include the concepts outlined in this chapter as well as appropriate concepts from other chapters. What recommendations would you make to the outside investors and to management, and how would you implement these recommendations?

1-6. Assessing Risks

The managers of Rose, Inc., are contemplating several new projects. Rubin Stein, company treasurer, is aiding the various managers in these analyses. Mr. Stein and his staff are responsible for presenting net present value data and other pertinent information to Charles Largo, company president, who will make the final decision on which project or projects to accept.

Rose is a decentralized company. The projects under consideration are from five different divisions. Divisional managers have done some preliminary gathering of data to analyze the projects, but they are looking to the accounting staff to help them get together all the information needed. The operating divisions are classified by central management as expense centers. In addition to these operating divisions, there is a sales division. Operating divisional managers and the sales manager have met to discuss the viability of the various projects. These meetings have been preliminary, and more are needed.

The equipment division is contemplating entering the manufacture of car-wash equipment. The sales division would set up regional wholesalers of the equipment. This type of equipment is modular and would have both an original-equipment and replacement-equipment market.

The electronics division is considering a new cordless telephone. The technology for making such a telephone is quite new, and research and development costs would be entailed if the company were to embark on the project. The units could be marketed both to the government and to wholesalers and retailers.

The chemical division is considering a line of car-wash chemicals, which would be manufactured even if the equipment division did not produce car-wash equipment. The technology for these chemicals is fairly straightforward. Marketing would be handled by the sales force of Rose.

The other two projects under consideration are similar in nature to the three described above.

Required:
1. How should members of the accounting staff work with the various managers in this case?
2. What information is necessary in order to make an adequate analysis for the president?
3. How would the staff aid in eliciting this information and in assessing risks for each of the three projects outlined above?

1-7. Time and Information: A Conflict?

In an article in *Harvard Business Review,* a trio of authors[50] traced the corporate strategy planning process through four distinct phases. They reported in part:

> Most companies trace the origins of a formal planning system (Phase I) to the annual budgeting process where everything is reduced to a financial problem. Procedures develop to forecast revenue, costs, and capital needs and to identify limits for expense budgets on an annual basis. Information systems report on functional performance as compared with budgetary targets. . . .
>
> A principal weakness of Phase II and III strategic planning processes is their inescapable entanglement in the formal corporate calendar. Strategic planning easily degenerates into a mind-numbing bureaucratic exercise, punctuated by ritualistic formal planning meetings that neither inform top management nor help business managers to get their jobs done. . . .

Required:
1. This quotation seems to outline a possible conflict between the information-generating process and an annual timetable. Does such a conflict exist? How does it curtail the flow of useful information?
2. What are the processes by which this conflict is resolved and information becomes more useful for strategic planning purposes?

1-8. Defining Communication (CMA)

The management accountant, as an information processor, must effectively utilize both personal communication skills and the organization's formal communication system. Inherent to both interpersonal and formal organizational communication are

---

[50] Frederick W. Gluck, Stephen P. Kaufman, and A. Steven Walleck, "Strategic Management for Competitive Advantage," *Harvard Business Review,* 58:4 (July–August 1980), pp. 154–161.

barriers which limit the effectiveness of communications and which must be recognized and appropriately managed.

Required:
1. Define and explain what is meant by the terms "effective interpersonal communication," and "effective formal organizational communication."
2. Use practical examples to briefly describe at least three barriers to effective interpersonal communication that management accountants may create in the course of their work.
3. Use practical examples to briefly describe at least three barriers to effective formal organizational communication that management accountants may encounter.

1-9. Reviewing an Accounting Information System (CMA Adapted)

The B & B Company manufactures and sells chemicals for agricultural and industrial use. The company has grown significantly over the last ten years but has made few changes in its information gathering and reporting system. Some of the managers have expressed concern that the system is essentially the same as it was when the firm was only half its present size. Others believe that much of the information from the system is not relevant and that more appropriate and timely information should be available.

Dora Hepple, Chief Accountant, has observed that the actual monthly cost data for most production processes are compared with the actual costs of the same processes for the previous year. Any variance not explained by price changes requires an explanation by the individual in charge of the cost center. She believes that this information is inadequate for good cost control.

George Vector, one of the production supervisors, contends that the system is adequate because it allows for explanation of discrepancies. The current year's costs seldom vary from the previous year's costs (as adjusted for price changes). This indicates that costs are under control.

Vern Hopp, General Manager of the Fine Chemical Division, is upset with the current system. He has to request the same information each month regarding recurring operations. This is a problem that he believes should be addressed.

Walter Metts, President, has appointed a committee to review the system. The charge to this "System Review Task Force" is to determine if the information needs of the internal management of the firm are being met by the existing system. Specific modifications in the existing system or implementation of a new system will be considered only if management's needs are not being met. William Afton, assistant to the president, has been put in charge of the task force.

Shortly after the committee was appointed, Afton overheard one of the cost accountants say, "I've been doing it this way for fifteen years, and now Afton and his committee will try to eliminate my job." Another person replied, "That's the way it looks. John and Brownie in general accounting also think that their positions are going to be eliminated or at least changed significantly." Over the next few days, Afton overheard a middle management person talking about the task force, saying, "That's all this company thinks about—maximizing its profits—not the employees." He also overheard a production manager in the Mixing Department say that he believed the system was in need of revision because the most meaningful information he received came from Brad Cummings, a salesperson. He stated, "After they have the monthly sales meeting, Brad stops by the office and indicates what the sales plans and targets are for the next few months. This sure helps me in planning my mixing schedules."

Afton is aware that two problems of paramount importance to be addressed by his "System Review Task Force" are (1) to determine management's information needs for cost control and decision-making purposes and (2) to meet the behavioral needs of the company and its employees.

Required:

1. Discuss the behavioral implications of having an accounting information system that does not appear to meet the needs of management.
2. Identify and explain the specific problems B & B Company appears to have with regard to the perception of B & B's employees concerning
   a. The accounting information system
   b. The firm
3. Assume that the initial review of the System Review Task Force indicates that a new accounting information system should be designed and implemented.
   a. Identify specific behavioral factors that B & B's management should address in the design and implementation of a new system.
   b. For each behavioral factor identified, discuss how B & B's management can address the behavioral factor.

1-10. Budgets and Communication (CMA Adapted)

An effective budget converts the objectives and goals of management into data. The budget often serves as a blueprint that represents management's plan for operating the business.

The budget frequently is the basis for control. Management performance can be evaluated by comparing actual results with the budget.

Thus, creating the budget is essential for the successful operation of an organization. Finding the resources to implement the budget (i.e., the process of getting from a starting point to the ultimate goal) requires the extensive use of human resources. The manner in which the people involved perceive their roles in the budget operation is important to the successful use of the budget as an effective management tool for planning, communicating, and controlling.

Required:

Communication plays an important part in the budget operation whether an imposed or participatory budgetary approach is used.

1. Describe the differences between the communication flows in these two budgetary approaches.
2. Discuss the behavioral implications on the communication process for each of these budgetary approaches.

1-11. External Users of Information (CMA)

Company annual reports have become large documents. They now include such sections as letters to the stockholders, descriptions of the business, operating highlights, financial review, management discussion and analysis, segment reporting, and inflation data as well as the basic financial statements. The expansion has been due, in part, to a general increase in degree of sophistication and complexity in accounting standards and disclosure requirements for financial reporting. The expansion also is reflective of the change in the composition and level of sophistication of its users. Current users include not only stockholders but financial and securities analysts, potential investors, lending institutions, stockbrokers, customers, employees, and, whether the reporting company likes it or not, competitors. Thus, a report that was designed as a device for communicating basic financial information has increased its scope either to meet the needs of an expanding audience or meet the need to expand the audience.

Conflicting views on the value of annual reports range from failing to provide adequate data to meet the intent of the report, to providing an unfathomable information overload.

Required:
1. The task of the preparer of an annual report is the communication of information from the corporation to targeted users.
   a. Identify and discuss the basic factors of communication that must be considered in the presentation of this information.
   b. Discuss the communication problems a corporation faces in preparing the annual reports that result from the diversity of the users being addressed.
2. Evaluate the effectiveness of current annual reports as communication devices for each of the following users:
   a. Current and potential stockholders
   b. Financial analysts
   c. Employees
3. Discuss the effect on the communication of information to all users as a consequence of knowing that competitors will read and analyze the annual report.

1-12. Tailoring Information for the User (CMA)

Communication is an inherent process in organizations. Consequently, management must make the communication process work for the benefit of its organization. Managers should examine the dynamics of their organization's process of communication in order to be sure that the information sent will be valuable to the intended receivers. A common format for sending information is regularly distributed reports displaying quantitative and financial data.

A portion of Arguay Company's Comprehensive Inventory Control Report is presented on page 46. The report was designed by the company's data processing department at the suggestion of the plant manager. The report is sent regularly to the production manager, purchasing manager, and cost accounting manager.

Required:
1. Explain the following concepts and indicate how they may be blocks to effective communication:
   a. Credibility of the sender
   b. Knowledge of the receiver
   c. Content appropriateness
   d. Overload

Arguay Company
Comprehensive Inventory Control Report
Week Ended August 8, 19X1

Part Number	Quantity			Standard Cost Per Unit	Total Actual Costs	Variance
	Inventory on Hand	Used	Purchased			
. . .						
53 Series						
. . .	. . .	. . .	. . .	. . .	. . .	. . .
5397	175	8,433	8,556	$1.0325	$9,033	$ (199)
5398	215	9,717	9,810	.0786	765	6
. . .	. . .	. . .	. . .	. . .	. . .	. . .
Total 53 Series	12,387	647,305	649,077	.6438	423,068	(5,192)
54 Series						
. . .	. . .	. . .	. . .	. . .	. . .	. . .
5401	1,191	15,448	16,352	.3597	5,723	159
5402	1,723	37,236	35,897	.5500	19,815	(72)
. . .	. . .	. . .	. . .	. . .	. . .	. . .
Total 54 Series	42,786	1,437,233	1,435,865	.7490	1,074,173	1,290
. . .	. . .	. . .	. . .			
Total Inventory	708,113	10,797,828	10,872,560	1.4350	15,657,100	(54,976)

Note: The series of dots (i.e., . . .) represent other data omitted from the report to simplify presentation.

2. On the basis of the segment of Arguay Company's Comprehensive Inventory Control Report presented, explain which of the concepts in Requirement 1, if any, would be a block to effective communication with the
   a. Purchasing manager
   b. Production manager
   c. Cost accounting manager

1-13. Communication (CMA)

Communication is necessary to support the basic social needs of the employee—acceptance, recognition, and security. Communication is the primary means for an organization to transmit information necessary to ensure the satisfactory achievement of corporate goals and objectives. Within any business entity, formal communication consists of basically three types: downward, horizontal, and upward.

Required:
1. Describe the three types of formal communication (downward, horizontal, upward) and for each give an example of how the communication process supports the accomplishment of corporate goals and objectives.
2. Identify and discuss a potential problem that occurs for each type of formal communication and indicate the action that could be taken by (1) the employee and (2) the corporate management to resolve the problem you present.

1-14. Form and Format (CMA)

George Watkins, Vice President of ISOT Manufacturing Company, made a request for an operational audit of the corporate human resource management system. Two months ago, the audit was assigned to Bill Barnett, a senior internal auditor. ISOT introduced the human resource management system eight years ago, and it has been modified and enhanced periodically to provide managers more effectively with needed information abut the company's 15,000 employees. Josh Simmons, Director of Human Resource Planning and Management, designed the original system and has managed it to date.

Bill Barnett has collected all the data for his report. He has found some significant differences from standard procedures for the identification and assessment of potential manager replacements and also some significant differences from standard data recording procedures. The internal audit department's practice is to write the audit report in such a way as to encourage Simmons to accept it and act on its recommendations. However, during the summary of findings in the final interview with Simmons, Barnett perceived Simmons as defensive and likely to resist acting on audit report recommendations.

As Barnett prepares to write the report to accomplish the internal audit department's objectives, there are a number of factors in report preparation that he should consider. The format, for example, can affect the reader's attitude toward the report.

Required:
1. Identify and describe four factors other than format that Barnett should recognize as he decides how to write this report.
2. Explain how each of the four factors identified in Requirement 1 is important in achieving the internal audit department's objective of having Simmons accept the report and act on its recommendations.

1-15. Upward Communication (CMA)

Communication is the exchange of information and the transmission of meaning. An organization cannot perform effectively without adequate communications. Emphasis on organizational communication has intensified since World War II, and this heightened concern has been widely reported in the business literature. This literature has challenged the rhetoric of manipulation and the one-way stream of communication flowing from the top to the bottom of an organization. As a result, organizations are placing increasing value on upward communications and are establishing special mechanisms to encourage use of this communication channel.

Required:
1. Identify the benefits for both superiors and subordinates that can be expected from improved upward communication.
2. Describe the barriers or deterrents to upward communication that may exist in organizations.
3. Describe the organizational atmosphere that should exist for effective upward communication.
4. Identify specific actions that could be taken by an organization to encourage upward communication.

1-16. Power (CMA)

Power is the potential ability to affect the behavior of others and is generally related to the control of valued or scarce resources. Power can be based on either organizational status or personal attributes and can be divided into five types: legitimate power, reward power, coercive power, referent power, and expert power.

Influence exists when a person consciously or unconsciously exercises power to affect the behavior or attitudes of others. The distribution of power in organizations is rarely what it appears to be on organizational charts or in job descriptions because certain organizational departments and/or certain individuals are generally more influential than others.

Required:
1. Describe each of the five types of power identified above.
2. Some organizational departments have more power than others. Describe at least three factors that may make an organizational department more influential than others.
3. Individuals who seek and acquire influence have certain attributes. Describe at least three of these attributes.

1-17. Senders and Receivers (CMA)

Tabor Industries is an established manufacturer of refrigeration equipment for supermarkets. While gross sales have been steadily increasing, net profits have not kept pace. It is generally believed that production is not as efficient as possible and that better cost controls need to be instituted.

To help address these problems, Warren Renson, Vice President and Production Manager, decided to involve the work force in making suggestions. He sent the following memo to all production line and staff employees.

Date: December 1, 19X9
To: Production Line and Staff Employees
From: Warren Renson

Let's improve production together. We need your input. I know we can make production more efficient. A suggestion box system is hereby implemented. We will pay an appropriate percentage of the savings to the employee who makes any suggestion that is implemented. Send your suggestions to my office. I look forward to hearing from you.

The suggestion box system has been in operation for a full year now, and Renson is annoyed and disappointed with the results. Only three worthwhile suggestions have been received, and only one of these has had any measurable impact on production efficiency. Many other suggestions were submitted, but they were all for the benefit of the employees.

Required:
1. Communications can be misunderstood at various levels.
   a. Describe at least four personal characteristics, attributable to both senders and receivers, that can cause communication problems.

b. Describe at least three organizational characteristics that may be barriers to effective communication.

2. Explain why the suggestion box systen. failed at Tabor Industries.

3. Recommend at least four ways in which Tabor Industries might improve its communication with employees in order to increase production efficiency.

1-18. The Repertory Theatre of St. Louis[51]

In February 1987, Mark Bernstein, the recently hired managing director of The Repertory Theatre of St. Louis (The Rep) met with Peter Bunce, a local corporate leader who was the president and chairman of the Board of Directors of The Rep. In this conversation, Bunce stated:

> As a result of all the changes we've had in the professional leadership at the theatre over the last several years, the Board seems to be left with a funny mixture of information. There is too much financial information and it's confusing and not well organized.
>
> The board has a different role to play than a board of, say, a manufacturing company. The information we receive must be relevant to our role. As you know, all our Board members do this as volunteers and need clear, concise information that they can grasp at a glance.
>
> With the correct professional leadership in place, we need to revise the form and substance of the financial information we present to the Board. In addition, we should explore what qualitative information seems relevant. Revising information for the board should be one of your first priorities; we would like to see a new system in place by June so we can use it as we begin our new fiscal year and new season of plays.

The Rep, located in Webster Groves, MO, a suburb of St. Louis, celebrated its 20th birthday in Fall 1986. Over its 20-year history, the theatre has been administered by a succession of five artistic directors, the current artistic director having taken over in Fall 1986. In addition, a new managing director, a position with equal rank to the artistic director but with different duties, took office in February 1987. The new managing director, Mark Bernstein, was charged with the task, among others, of organizing and presenting financial and managerial information to the Board of Directors and its committees.

Background of The Repertory Theatre of St. Louis

The theatre was founded to bring a professional repertory company to the St. Louis area and as an enhancement of the Webster College's (now Webster University) Theater Conservatory program. From the beginning, it was a professional theatre, as opposed to a community theatre, or one where students and instructors from the college put on their performances. Thus, the theatre was originally a division of the college, but separate from its academic theatre program.

After a few successful years, audience attendance dropped and finances suffered. In fact, because of the great losses the college endured, the theatre "went dark" (closed down) for a year. At this point, since the theatre was such a financial burden

---

[51] Hirsch, Maurice L., Jr., and Mark Bernstein, "The Repertory Theatre of St. Louis Case," *Journal of Accounting Education*, Vol. 8 (Elmsford, N.Y.: Pergamon Press, 1990), pp. 153–182.

to the college and the president thought the theatre could only prosper· if it were independent from the college, an independent, not-for-profit corporation was formed, the Loretto-Hilton Repertory Theatre, Inc., and an independent Board of Directors was recruited from various community and business leaders interested in theatre and the arts. This organization continues to this day and is now known as The Repertory Theatre of St. Louis or The Rep.

Repertory or Regional Theatres The regional or repertory theatre movement in the United States usually involves theatres that present new works, classics, modern American plays, and other works which would not usually be presented in the area by, say, national touring companies or other commercial, for-profit theatres. Regional theatres are fully professional with actors belonging to Actors Equity and various support groups belonging to appropriate craft and professional unions.

In the main, companies such as The Rep are founded by an artistic director who has a vision for a theatre in a community and who has gathered the resources and lay support to bring this vision to a reality. This was not the case in St. Louis. Webster College founded the theatre and hired an artistic director. He remained with the theatre until the theatre became a separate corporation.

Regional theatres present plays either in one time block (i.e., the same play is on stage for several weeks) or in what is called rolling or rotating repertory (i.e., a series of plays are presented in rotation during a several-week period). The Rep has consistently chosen the former route and it presents six plays on what is called the "mainstage," a space seating 733 people, and another three plays to a smaller audience in the "studio" space which seats up to 125.

As part of the separation of The Rep from Webster University, the university provides free rent to The Rep for the use of the Loretto Hilton Center, where the two stages and craft shops are housed, as well as office space in two nearby buildings. The mainstage space contains a thrust theatre with the audience surrounding the stage. The studio space is an open room which can be changed for each play.

Professional Management Most regional theatres are run by either an artistic director or a combination of an artistic and a managing director. The artistic director has complete authority over the program that the theatre offers. He or she must provide artistic leadership for the organization within the budget that is available. If there is a managing director, that person is in charge of the business affairs of the organization. The current organization of The Rep consists of both an artistic director and a managing director.

After The Rep became a separate not-for-profit corporation, a new director was hired. That person held the title of producing director (since his job really entailed elements of being both an artistic and a managing director) and was at The Rep from 1972 to 1980, eight seasons. His successor was artistic director for three seasons, 1980–1983. Because of some financial problems during those years, the then head of production, Steven Woolf, was promoted to the job of managing director, a job that was established at that time and that held equal rank with the artistic director in the management of the organization.

Differences in artistic vision led to the artistic director leaving in 1983 and, while a nationwide search was conducted for a new artistic director, for two years Mr. Woolf assumed the title of acting artistic director, as well as performing the duties of managing director. A new artistic director was hired during the second year of this period, 1984, but his duties did not begin until the next season.

Beginning with the 1985–1986 season, the new artistic director embarked on an ambitious plan to increase the artistic base of the theatre. He hoped to bring several new designers, directors, and actors to St. Louis and needed a larger budget to fulfill his plans. The board responded by meeting his challenge with additional contributed capital and projected the increases that would be needed in subscription and single ticket sales in order for the plan to work. The season, however, did not meet audience approval and fell short of revenue projections. Therefore, the theatre was left with an accumulated deficit of about $300,000 after the 1985–86 season. At this point, Mr. Woolf became artistic director and a search was started for a new managing director. That search culminated in the hiring of Mark Bernstein who took office in February 1987, during the first season in which Steve Woolf was artistic director. The theatre staff and the board sensed that a new age of stability seemed to be at hand with this management team.

Lay Leadership As a not-for-profit corporation, The Rep is governed by a Board of Directors consisting of up to 48 members from the Greater St. Louis area. The board meets several times a year. At its regular meetings the board hears oral reports from the artistic director regarding the current season and future plans, written and oral reports from the managing director regarding financial and marketing matters, and written and oral reports from the director of development on the status of current fund raising efforts. In addition, board committees report on their work on long-range planning, by-laws, fund raising, benefits/parties, etc., as appropriate.

There is a balance of power between the board and the professional leadership in the theatre. The board's main functions are to set general policies, to map the long-range directions for the theatre, to help fund the resources needed to mount the program it has accepted from the artistic director, and to oversee the finances of the theatre. Within the approved budget, the professional managers are given fairly free rein to choose a season and to expend funds in order to bring that season about. Thus, for example, the artistic director chooses the entire artistic season and, along with the managing director, is charged with presenting that season within the revenue and expense parameters that the board has approved. Table 1 is a list of plays presented in both theatre spaces over the past several years.

Certain board committees meet on a regular basis. The Executive Committee, the Finance committee, and the Development Steering Committee meet monthly. These committees get into more detail in their discussions than the board at large. Business items and reports are first presented to the Executive Committee before they come before the board.

Financial Background

Revenues The theatre gets its funds from earned income (revenue from sales of subscriptions and single tickets, as well as some other items such as parking, refreshments, program advertising, etc.), from funding agencies, and from contributions. Funding agencies include regional, state, and federal money, as well as private and community foundations interested in the arts such as the Arts and Education Council of St. Louis.

Table 1
The Repertory Theatre of St. Louis List of Mainstage and Studio Plays

	Mainstage	Studio
1983–84	The Glass Menagerie The Dining Room Tintypes Sleuth Medea The Importance of Being Earnest	True West The Unseen Hand and Killer's Head Tongues and Savage Love
1984–85	A Raisin in the Sun 'Master Harold' and the Boys The 1940's Radio Hour Dial "M" for Murder The Price The Comedy of Errors	Waiting for Godot Still Life Annulla, An Autobiography
1985–86	Twelfth Night Under Statements Little Shop of Horrors The Mighty Gents Golden Boy A Streetcar Named Desire	The Marriage of Bette and Boo Tom and Viv Miss Julie Botiford

1986–87	All My Sons
	The Rainmaker
	The Foreigner
	Ma Rainey's Black Bottom*
	The Flying Karamazov
	  Brothers in the Juggle and
	  Hyde Show
	The Phantom of the Opera
		Billy Bishop Goes to War
		Lucky Lindy
		Beyond Here Are Monsters

* Because of casting and directoral problems, *Sizwe Banzi Is Dead* was substituted for *Ma Rainey's Black Bottom*.

Private contributions come from corporations and individuals. There is an Endowment Fund and ongoing programs for annual giving to the theatre.[1] Public funding has varied over the years as a function of the quality and vision of the work presented as well as the funds that were available. Federal funding of the arts has been curtailed in the 1980s. Table 2 shows the major sources of revenue for The Rep for fiscal years ending 1983 to 1987.

Expenses Expenses include the general overhead of running the theatre (management personnel, marketing, fund raising, accounting, utilities, etc.) and the production and artistic expense of putting on the six mainstage and three studio productions. Table 3 shows the major expense categories for the 1983 to 1987 period.

TABLE 2
The Repertory Theatre of St. Louis' Sources of Revenue

	Budget FY87	FY86	FY85	FY84	FY83
Ticket Sales	$ 978,250	$ 906,172	$1,035,162	$ 949,057	$ 905,716
ITC*	87,500	85,927	81,002	48,465	57,655
Interest/Endowment	50,000	59,886	77,734	66,803	53,549
Other Earned Income	124,000	91,110	111,466	99,533	89,571
Public Funding	672,500	605,500	450,100	457,465	457,025
Private Contributions	460,000	399,522	364,989	270,861	269,604
Special		130,511**	95,000***		
In-Kind Contributions	197,872	197,876	186,864	173,416	144,076
Total Revenues	$2,570,122	$2,476,504	$2,402,317	$2,065,600	$1,977,196

Notes:

*ITC stands for the Imaginary Theatre Company, a touring program of The Rep designed to introduce theatre at the primary and secondary school level throughout Missouri.

**In FY86, a Challenge Drive was conducted amongst the Board of Directors to raise additional funds to support the new artistic director's expanded programming.

***In FY85, a piece of real estate was contributed to The Rep, valued at $95,000.

During these and previous years, subscriptions were as follows for the mainstage:

1986–87	9,175
1985–86	11,656
1984–85	12,557
1983–84	12,523
1982–83	14,142
1981–82	16,566
1980–81	16,192
1979–80	15,531

TABLE 3
The Repertory Theatre of St. Louis' Expenses

	Budget FY87	FY86	FY85	FY84	FY83
Administration	$ 935,951	$1,090,815	$1,088,358	$ 884,855	$ 823,792
Production	627,289	790,036	642,988	591,360	572,653
Artistic	722,157	825,942	387,085	298,297	343,232
ITC	85,000	81,785	71,051	52,480	56,668
In-Kind Facilities	197,872	197,876	186,864	173,416	144,076
Total Expenses	$2,568,269	$2,986,454	$2,376,346	$2,000,408	$1,940,421

Finance Committee   While the staff, particularly the managing director, is responsible for budgeting, the Board of Directors has a Finance Committee that is responsible for oversight of the budget and the managing of all investment and borrowing. The Endowment Fund is invested in high-grade bonds and other securities as well as certificates of deposit.

Working Capital   As was stated, beginning the 1986–1987 season, the theatre was currently in a deficit position. In previous years, when there was no deficit to contend with, it was usual to have cyclical cash needs which were financed through a working capital line of credit with a local bank. There was a heavy cash inflow during the spring when subscriptions were renewed and a heavy cash need as plays were produced over the season from September through the following Spring. However, with no cash reserves left, the theatre needed a much larger line of credit than usual. All the endowment of the theatre was pledged as collateral for this line of credit; thus, there was no financial flexibility left in the organization.

The debt seemed manageable in the short run, but the Board of Directors was uneasy about it. Because the theatre could sustain no losses of any magnitude, the deficit became an inhibition to more adventuresome programming and new programming initiatives (e.g., summer productions, a series of play readings, etc.).

Management Information   At the time of the conversation between Mark Bernstein and Peter Bunce, February 1987, the board received about the same set of information that theatre staff received. Most of these forms are shown in Tables 4 through 9. This same set of forms went to the Finance Committee, the Executive Committee of the Board, and to the board itself as shown.

The major financial accounting system was computerized but there was no link between the accrual accounting system and a budgeting model. Budgets were prepared on independent electronic spreadsheets along with many handwritten calculations and schedules.

The computerized accounting system generated a 35 page report on the general ledger each month. In discussing this report, Mr. Bernstein stated:

> The 35 page report is so finely detailed, it gives you the impression of tiny pieces rather than a complete picture. There is just too much there to assimilate at once. It's not organized in a useful fashion. I think it should be summarized into a more useful form before anyone can draw conclusions from it. The current management and board information is an attempt to do this. However, I think it can be done better.

There was some difference of opinion about the current reports. Since the timing of the receipt of revenue is often unrelated to when expenses are incurred, some questioned the validity of month-by-month reporting. In addition, while the board wanted a report showing revenue and cost for each play, staff did not think this report was useful. Mr. Bernstein stated:

> We choose a season that consists of big plays and/or works involving music as well as smaller plays with, say two or three actors and one set. It's a balance of programming and a balance of available artistic dollars. We do not expect each production to cost the same. However, ticket buyers, whether buying a six-play subscription or a ticket for a single show, pay a price that is the same regardless of the play they are seeing.

TABLE 4
Key Indicators as of January 31, 1987

	ACTUAL			PROJECTED		
	OCTOBER	NOVEMBER	DECEMBER	JANUARY	FEBRUARY	MARCH
SUBSCRIPTION SALES						
YTD TARGET	630000	630000	630000	630000	630000	630000
ACTUAL	650973	654163	654163	654162	654163	654163
VARIANCE	20973	24163	24163	24162	24163	24163
FUND RAISING						
YTD TARGET	165750	249950	288400	327450	349900	378925
ACTUAL	236197	246338	330802	351801	364900	388925
VARIANCE	70447	−3612	42402	24351	15000	10000
PUBLIC FUNDING						
YTD TARGET	278385	379985	496120	560655	578040	578040
ACTUAL	247500	395250	546422	562337	578040	578040
VARIANCE	−30885	15265	50302	1682	0	0
SINGLE TICKETS						
YTD TARGET	62000	70000	110000	144000	180000	220000
ACTUAL	56771	66886	131054	154579	195000	240000
VARIANCE	−5229	−3114	21054	10579	15000	20000
TOTAL REVENUE						
YTD TARGET	775452	1041142	1357027	1634945	1853514	2056072
ACTUAL	811193	1049611	1481823	1654719	1873514	2086072
VARIANCE	35741	8469	124796	19774	20000	30000
TOTAL EXPENSE						
YTD TARGET	946916	1162266	1367663	1623063	1906612	2165782
ACTUAL	983697	1191333	1404521	1658744	1996612	2285782
VARIANCE	36781	29067	36858	35681	90000	120000
BORROWING						
YTD TARGET	250000	250000	200000	450000	550000	550000
ACTUAL	250000	280000	130000	230000	425000	475000
VARIANCE	0	30000	−70000	−220000	−125000	−75000

In addition, there is the question of fixed costs. I am convinced that in the short term (a season) that our basic production staff is fixed regardless of the choice of plays for that season. For example, our costume shop consists of six people: a shop head, two drapers, two stitchers, and a crafts person. In order to produce anything more than a two-person play, we would need the full crew of six people. For large productions, we add people to the costume shop and to the scene shop.

Even if we were to, say, eliminate a mainstage production or to eliminate the studio season of three plays, I believe we could not reduce the staff requirements. At best, if we shortened the season, we could reduce the time we hire production people from 35 weeks to some lesser number.

Tied in with the revision of board information requested by Mr. Bunce, Mr. Bernstein decided to revamp the information system for internal decision making as well.

In addition, one of the things that seemed lacking was a strategic plan. While long-range planning had been the practice, the changes in artistic direction and the new management team led both staff and the board to realize that the theatre needed to carefully spell out its mission, goals and objectives, and strategies. To this end, a retreat was held in May 1987, attended by a professional facilitator in these matters, the Executive Committee of the Board, and all the key staff members of The Rep. Table 10 is a summary of a superordinate goal statement and some more immediate goals and objectives. Mr. Bernstein thought that information going to the board should include measures to see if the long-range plan was being achieved.

TABLE 5
Revenue/Expense Report—*The Foreigner* as of January 31, 1987

	ACTUAL	BUDGET	DIFFERENCE
REVENUE			
SUBSCRIPTION	108387	105000	3387
SINGLE TICKET	69675	50000	19675
GROUP	4601	3300	1301
STUDENT MAT	1992	6500	−4508
TOTAL	184655	164800	19855
EXPENSE			
SETS	35450	33940	1510
PROPS	7697	7750	−53
LIGHTS	12614	11855	759
SOUND	5588	5570	18
COSTUMES	16880	17215	−335
ARTISTIC	85330	70026	15304
TOTAL	163559	146356	17203
NET	21096	18444	2652

TABLE 6
Monthly Dept Expense/Revenue as of January 31, 1987

| EXPENSE | JANUARY | | YEAR TO DATE | | |
DEPARTMENT	ACTUAL	BUDGET	ACTUAL	BUDGET	VARIANCE
ADMINISTRATIVE	28131	29337	215696	218982	−3286
PR/MARKETING (1)	26265	24506	200144	146205	53939
SUBSCRIPTIONS	0	0	165720	120136	45584
DEVELOPMENT	5947	8880	59274	73551	−14277
BOX OFFICE	8713	8403	70221	73694	−3473
FRONT OF HOUSE	1797	1628	9073	8695	378
INCOME PROJECTS	3970	3693	21511	22674	−1163
OTHER TECH (2)	9712	7658	60942	55005	5937
SETS (3)	59334	26444	198483	179285	19198
PROPS	6904	9009	41557	44922	−3365
ELECTRICS (4)	11671	10575	51870	57241	−5371
SOUND	4306	7734	24992	36954	−11962
COSTUME	17736	18181	84127	106427	−22300
ARTISTIC (5)	56848	77674	412285	431234	−18949
ITC (6)	12889	21678	42849	48058	−5209
TOTAL	254223	255400	1658744	1623063	35681
REVENUE					
SUBSCRIPTION (7)	84000	105000	409135	399000	10135
SINGLE TICKET (8)	20413	34000	154579	144000	10579
GROUP TICKET (8)	6343	9800	33512	39200	−5688
STUDIO (9)	5653	8533	16497	21283	−4786
OTHER (10)	15284	6500	108908	114357	−5449
GRANTS (11)	15915	64585	562337	560655	1682
FUNDRAISING (12)	20999	39050	351801	327450	24351
ITC (13)	4289	10500	17950	29000	−11050
TOTAL	172896	277968	1654719	1634945	19774

NOTES ON MONTHLY DEPT. EXPENSE/REVENUE REPORT

1. This reflects the continuing problem with marketing and with program advertising revenues.
2. Timing of lump billing from Webster University on the Director of Operations for the Loretto Hilton Center salary—still expect other tech to be over $5,000 for year.
3. Start of *The Phantom of the Opera* set costs. As was reported earlier, these costs are expected to be over budget.
4. Last of student run crew cost for *The Foreigner*.
5. Large underage due to small cast size of *Sizwe Banzi Is Dead* instead of larger *Ma Rainey's Black Bottom*—the underage will be used by *The Phantom of the Opera* music and other costs.
6. Underage due to timing of spring tour start-up costs—note related underage in ITC revenue also.
7. Timing in recognition of subscription income—clears out last month's overage.
8. *Sizwe Banzi Is Dead* has not done as well as had been hoped.
9. *Lucky Lindy* single ticket receipts have yet to be deposited and will probably be somewhat under budget.
10. Overage due to timing in receipt of program ad income.
11. Timing in recognition of Regional Arts Commission grant—reverses last month's overage.
12. Expected underage after last month's overage.
13. Timing in receipt of touring fees.

TABLE 7
Income Statement for the Month Ended as of January 31, 1987

	BUDGET	ACTUAL	VARIANCE
REVENUE			
SUBSCRIPTIONS	$105,000	$ 84,000	($ 21,000)
SINGLE TICKETS	34,000	20,413	(13,587)
GROUP SALES	9,800	6,343	(3,457)
STUDIO THEATRE SALES	8,533	5,653	(2,880)
OTHER EARNED REVENUE	6,500	15,284	8,784
PUBLIC FUNDING	64,535	15,915	(48,620)
FUNDRAISING	39,050	20,999	(18,051)
IMAGINARY THEATRE CO.	10,500	4,289	(6,211)
WEBSTER UNIV. IN-KIND	0	0	0
TOTAL REVENUE	$277,918	$172,896	($105,022)
EXPENSE			
ADMINISTRATIVE EXPENSE	$ 29,337	$ 28,131	1,206
MARKETING & PUBLIC REL	24,506	26,265	(1,759)
SUBSCRIPTIONS	0	0	0
DEVELOPMENT	8,880	5,947	2,933
BOX OFFICE	8,403	8,713	(310)
FRONT OF HOUSE	1,628	1,797	(169)
INCOME PROJECTS	3,693	3,970	(277)
SUBTOTAL SUPPORT EXP	$ 76,447	$ 74,823	1,624
OTHER TECHNICAL EXPENSE	$ 7,658	$ 9,712	(2,054)
SETS EXPENSE	26,444	59,334	(32,890)
PROPS EXPENSE	9,009	6,904	2,105
ELECTRICS EXPENSE	10,575	11,671	(1,096)
SOUND EXPENSE	7,734	4,306	3,428
COSTUME EXPENSE	18,181	17,736	445
ARTISTIC EXPENSE	77,674	56,848	20,826
IMAGINARY THEATRE CO.	21,678	12,889	8,789
WEBSTER UNIV. IN-KIND	0	0	0
SUBTOTAL TECH & ARTISTIC	$178,953	$179,400	(447)
TOTAL EXPENSE	$255,400	$254,223	1,177
NET INCOME/(LOSS)	$ 22,518	($81,327)	($103,845)

TABLE 8
Income Statement as of January 31, 1987

	ACTUAL YEAR-TO-DATE			PROJECTED REMAINDER OF YEAR			COMBINED TOTAL FOR FULL YEAR		
	BUDGET	ACTUAL	VARIANCE	BUDGET	ACTUAL	VARIANCE	BUDGET	ACTUAL	VARIANCE
REVENUE									
SUBSCRIPTIONS	399000	409135	10135	231000	245865	14865	630000	655000	25000
SINGLE TICKETS	144000	154579	10579	106000	132921	26921	250000	287500	37500
GROUP SALES	39200	33512	-5688	20800	26488	5688	60000	60000	0
STUDIO THEATRE SALES	21283	16497	-4786	16967	16753	-214	38250	33250	-5000
OTHER EARNED INCOME	114357	108908	-5449	59643	65092	5449	174000	174000	0
PUBLIC FUNDING	560655	562337	1682	111845	112663	818	672500	675000	2500
FUNDRAISING	327450	351801	24351	132550	108199	-24351	460000	460000	0
IMAGINARY THEATRE CO.	29000	17950	-11050	58500	72550	14050	87500	90500	3000
WEBSTER UNIV. IN-KIND	0	0	0	197872	197872	0	197872	197872	0
TOTAL REVENUE	1634945	1654719	19774	935177	978403	43226	2570122	2633122	63000
EXPENSE									
ADMINISTRATIVE EXPENSE	218982	215696	3286	114507	105263	9244	333489	320959	12530
MARKETING & PUBLIC REL	146205	200144	-53939	73720	84781	-11061	219925	284925	-65000
SUBSCRIPTIONS	120136	165720	-45584	0	0	0	120136	165720	-45584
DEVELOPMENT	73551	59274	14277	33862	48139	-14277	107413	107413	0
BOX OFFICE	73694	70221	3473	33849	37322	-3473	107543	107543	0
FRONT OF HOUSE	8695	9073	-378	4685	4307	378	13380	13380	0
INCOME PROJECTS	22674	21511	1163	11391	12554	-1163	34065	34065	0
SUBTOTAL SUPPORT EXP	663937	741639	-77702	272014	292366	-20352	935951	1034005	-98054
OTHER TECHNICAL EXPENSE	55005	60942	-5937	22551	24384	-1833	77556	85326	-7770
SETS EXPENSE	179285	198483	-19198	44871	94758	-49887	224156	293241	-69085
PROPS EXPENSE	44922	41557	3365	12214	19079	-6865	57136	60636	-3500
ELECTRICS EXPENSE	57241	51870	5371	24134	29405	-5271	81375	81275	100
SOUND EXPENSE	36954	24992	11962	14509	20732	-6223	51463	45724	5739
COSTUME EXPENSE	106427	84127	22300	29176	38526	-9350	135603	122653	12950
ARTISTIC EXPENSE	431234	412285	18949	290923	354872	-63949	722157	767157	-45000
IMAGINARY THEATRE CO.	48058	42849	5209	36942	45151	-8209	85000	88000	-3000
WEBSTER UNIV. IN-KIND	0	0	0	197872	197872	0	197872	197872	0
SUBTOTAL TECH & ARTISTIC	959126	917105	42021	673192	824779	-151587	1632318	1741884	-109566
TOTAL EXPENSE	1623063	1658744	-35681	945206	1117145	-171939	2568269	2775889	-207620
NET INCOME/(LOSS)	11882	-4025	-15907	-10029	-138742	-128713	1853	-142767	-144620

TABLE 9
Projected Cash Flow 1986–1987 as of January 31, 1987

	ACTUAL							PROJECTED					COMBINED TOTAL
	JUNE	JULY	AUGUST	SEPT	OCT	NOV	DEC	JAN	FEB	MAR	APRIL	MAY	
INFLOWS													
TICKETS	23597	11771	25761	90680	45096	26321	72187	26959	49700	209000	341000	155000	1077072
OTHER EARNED	6299	5408	1140	12630	16347	34268	7018	16062	10500	10500	10643	5000	135815
SPECIAL							72827				72827		
PUBLIC FUNDING	35083	6000		132083	98750	98750	184506	14450	17385		22230	22230	631467
FUNDRAISING	26800	12610	11491	37401	84112	27069	105884	50161	22450	29025	31375	55075	493453
OTHER	1965	10351				2080	6910	4288	10000	15500	28000	5000	84094
TOTAL INFLOWS	93744	46140	38392	272794	244305	188488	449332	111920	110035	264025	433248	242305	2494726
OUTFLOWS													
ADMINISTRATIVE	54922	64941	59853	104569	106354	86812	69972	86719	87790	104780	113538	88318	1028568
PRODUCTION	12376	16410	51101	73490	72811	60040	64523	98737	95314	95137	36147	4685	680771
ARTISTIC	17783	28881	39293	81341	65624	53969	71947	50340	139965	120975	58049	12894	741061
OTHER	3180	5197	1362	2036	2037	3909	11448	12874	11898	13943	8503	1641	78028
TOTAL OUTFLOWS	88261	115429	151609	261436	246826	204730	217890	248670	334967	334835	216237	107538	2528428
EXCESS DEFICIT	5483	−69289	−113217	11358	−2521	−16242	231442	−136750	−224932	−70810	217011	134767	−33700
CASH BEG BALANCE −97902	−92419	−161708	−274925	−263567	−266088	−282330	−50888	−187638	−412570	−483380	−266369	−131602	−33700
ANTICIPATED BORROWING	100000	150000	300000	250000	250000	280000	130000	230000	425000	475000	275000	125000	

TABLE 10
Results of Weekend Retreat on Strategic Planning—Superordinate Goal and Other Goals and Objectives—May 1987

Ultimately, the special magic and joy of live performance helps to keep the flame of humanity alive in our civilization. No mere goal statement can hope to capture this essence. However, those of us who accept the charge of guiding this Theatre need some basis for determining whether we are meeting that charge. In this spirit, we aspire to:

1. Become the pre-eminent theatre in this metropolitan region.
2. Be regarded as an indispensable institution in this metropolitan region.
3. Function in such a way that the public will come to expect an uncompromising standard of quality in every facet of our operation.
4. Attract outstanding professionals in the field to join our work.
5. Achieve financial strength and stability through:
   a. Building a net subscription base of 14,000 by 1989–1990 and 16,000 by the end of 1991–1992.
   b. Retaining on average not less than 70% of subscriptions with a goal of 75%.
   c. Operating at least at break-even over the period.
   d. Eliminating the current deficit.
   e. Securing dependable sources of revenue of not less than 150 percent of the current annual base.

Required

It is now December 1987, and Mr. Bernstein has asked you to help him design an information system and reporting formats for the board that would be relevant and timely.[2] Both the staff and board are anxious that information include not only appropriate quantitative facts, but also qualitative information. You have been hired by Mr. Bernstein as his assistant and you are to write a report to him outlining your suggestions. The existing reports shown as exhibits to the case should be used as a starting point in your discussion. What are the strengths and weaknesses of these reports individually and as an information package? What changes do you recommend and why? Your report should be specific, showing examples of various forms, reports, and/or graphs that you propose.

Endnotes

1. Endowment funds are invested, used as collateral for working-capital loans, and income from these funds becomes part of the current operating budget. Annual giving funds are used as part of the current operating budget.

2. Mr. Bunce wanted a new system in place by June. However, for the purposes of this case, December is a better starting point since it is in the middle of the season and both budgeted and actual information are available to use in suggested reports.

Chapter 2

Issues Confronting Management Accounting—Part I

writing from the publishers.

Today, the entire financial community has awakened both to the fact that cost accounting is no longer applicable, and that something must be done. Unfortunately, they are not going back to the fundamentals, the financial statements logic, and seeking there answers for these important business questions. Instead, the financial community is totally immersed in an attempt to save the obsolete solution.

"Cost drivers" and "activity-based costs" are the names of these fruitless efforts.[1]

The TOC (Theory of Constraints) approach is a short-run, powerful optimization procedure. It emphasizes increasing the throughput of the organization and determining what prevents throughput from being higher. . . . In attempting to increase throughput, TOC advocates see little benefit from detailed analysis of operating expenses.

---

[1] Eliyahu M. Goldratt, *Sifting Information Out of the Data Ocean: The Haystack Syndrome* (New Haven, Conn.: North River Press, 1990), pp. 39–40.

Consequently, Goldratt and Fox do not attempt to analyze or allocate operating expenses. In effect, operating expenses are treated as a big blob. So if some traditional methods of overhead allocation have been accused of treating overhead as a big blob, the TOC approach defines operating expenses as an even bigger blob because it includes direct labor in addition to overhead. The TOC approach is not concerned with tracing operating expense to products or doing anything about it. . . .

. . . [TOC] is useful for short-term cost forecasting and optimization, [but] we believe it is misleading for most other decisions on products, such as product mix, pricing, and make-versus-buy.[2]

To meet the challenges of the globally competitive and world-class manufacturing environment, American management must identify the information necessary for effective business decisions. Although there was a well-established paradigm for such information, managers are amending or discarding that model and incorporating concepts known as just-in-time, continuous improvement, activity-based costing, Theory of Constraints, value added, value chain, life-cycle costing, and so on. As is illustrated by the two quotations above, there are those who see some of these models as the core of a new approach and define other ideas as being either in conflict or not as central.[3] Opinions differ, however, about which concept to place at the center and which at the periphery. Thus, while there are many new ideas to consider and old ones to reevaluate, there is no consensus on how to proceed.

This chapter and the next introduce these emerging areas of discussion. We will show the basics of each of these models as well as pointing out what their advocates and critics say about them. While we do draw some conclusions, the basic objective of these chapters is to provide enough background (and

[2] Robert S. Kaplan in "Contribution Margin Analysis: No Longer Relevant/Strategic Cost Management: The New Paradigm," Michael A. Robinson, ed., *Journal of Management Accounting Research*, Vol. 2 (Sarasota, Fla.: American Accounting Association, Fall 1990), pp. 3, 5.

[3] Here and in other chapters, you will find opening quotations that present actual or apparent conflicting points of view. As you develop your own perspective about each subject area, you can reexamine these authors' statements and decide what you agree or disagree with.

reference material) that the reader can make his or her own analysis and conclusions about the usefulness of these ideas in various settings. Proponents present many of the emerging topics and philosophies as quite different from one another, but although there are aspects that are different, sometimes similarities are overlooked. Some apparent differences might be actual harmony. Based on learning about different perspectives, our own experiences, and the overall long-term strategies of the organization where we work, it is up to us to decide what fits together and is effective.

MANAGEMENT ACCOUNTING: RESPONDING TO THE ENVIRONMENT

In order to fully understand today's managerial practices, it is useful to review how managerial accounting has responded to its environment in the past. Management accounting was created by managers as a response to their information needs. Much in the same way that current managers and authors have suggested ways to deal with the environment of the 1990s, past managers responded to their own changing situation. Much of this is documented by Johnson and Kaplan, who trace cost management and cost accounting from the 1800s until today.[4] Many of the basics of what we now call management and cost accounting were derived long ago. For example, the ideas of associating labor and overhead costs with the conversion of raw materials into finished products and using costs as a way to control a business seem to come from mechanized textile mills of the early 1800s. The objective was to see how labor and overhead could be controlled to make profits. Up to that time, the piecework, manual nature of textile manufacturing meant that manufacturing took place at home and there was an external market for what people were willing to pay. With mechanization, labor was now a direct input within the factory rather than contracted for externally, so there was the possibility of increasing profits by controlling labor and overhead.

In the late 1800s, large manufacturers such as Carnegie Steel Company moved toward what could be called job order costing. Andrew Carnegie used cost sheets to monitor all the costs associated with the tons of rails that were produced. He seemed interested in knowing incremental costs so that he could price in a way to fill existing manufacturing capacity. However, as with the textile mills, cost information was being used in a single-product company. The change from the past was the investment needed to

---

[4] H. Thomas Johnson and Robert S. Kaplan, *Relevance Lost: The Rise and Fall of Management Accounting* (Boston: Harvard Business School Press, 1987). This section is but a brief summary of the points raised by Johnson and Kaplan. The richness of the history can only be gained by reading the book itself.

produce steel products and the concept of covering incremental costs to fully utilize existing production equipment. At this stage, managers distinguished between differential costs and those associated with long-term assets (sunk costs).

Management accounting also developed in retailing where, for example, Marshall Field's traced revenues and costs (cost of merchandise and separable departmental operating costs) to departments and dealt with these departments as responsibility centers. Johnson and Kaplan attribute the interest in management accounting as a way that managers could look at internal operations.[5] Heretofore, the market had set costs when many operations were subcontracted (for example, piecework for textile operations), but now, as these processes moved inside a business, managers could no longer look to the market to set costs. They needed information to allow them to manage in this new environment. However, little attention was placed on information for long-term planning or capital asset acquisition.

One of the biggest changes that occurred at the end of the 1800s and beginning of the 1900s was the emergence of vertically integrated companies that produced several different products. However, most of these companies retained a fairly centralized management philosophy and adopted many of the methods and measures used by the single-product companies that preceded them. These new companies did develop budgets for planning and control of their diverse operations and devised the concept of return on investment to gain a level playing field when comparing the results from different types of divisions.

Johnson and Kaplan point out that before the 1920s, managers looked at underlying transactions. At DuPont Powder Company, for example, managers looked at materials consumed as well as the costs of other inputs. The actual consumption of resources could be compared to standards, and operations in one department of a plant could be compared to those of the same area in another plant. The focus was on the control of inputs for a more efficient operation. Johnson and Kaplan call this focus *cost management*.[6] With the growth of complex companies and the need for intracompany and intercompany comparison, managers began losing the link to inputs (transactions, activities) and looking more to return on investment and the bottom line. Thus, the fully allocated costs generated for financial accounting became the surrogates for plant operations. Johnson and Kaplan call this the change from cost management to *cost accounting*; this is not just a change in terms but in philosophy. It's interesting to see that current writings use the term *management* (for example, activity-based management, strategic management), a return to this earlier emphasis.

In addition, from the 1800s onward, even with mechanization of industry, the focus was on people. Labor was a significant component of the total cost of manufacturing. Much of cost accounting has been based on the notion

---

[5] Johnson and Kaplan, *Relevance Lost*, Chapter 2.
[6] Johnson and Kaplan, *Relevance Lost*, Chapters 4 and 5.

that (1) labor is a short-term variable cost, (2) labor is a significant portion of total manufacturing costs, and (3) overhead is related to labor consumption. In some industries today, not only is the nature of labor changing, but also the percent of labor to total cost is dropping. In some cases, labor is becoming more of a fixed cost rather than variable as has been the model for decades. For example, a manufacturer of plastic products in the Midwest has a basic labor force that comes in daily. Even though they are paid by the hour, unless they are laid off for some period of time, they work 40 hours each week. If there is insufficient manufacturing work, then these employees work on maintenance. At a manufacturer of original parts for the automobile industry, this same situation holds. There, when production slows down, in addition to maintenance, employees might be found in the office doing secretarial work.

There are places, however, where labor is still variable in the short term and is a significant part of total costs. In the printing industry, for example, where paper might be supplied by the customer, labor and supervision can make up 75 percent of total manufacturing costs. In addition, labor is scheduled only when there is work to be done. People might be laid off on a daily basis depending on the work load. Thus, there is not a clear characterization that we can generalize about the significance of labor nor about its variability.[7] However, there seems to be general agreement that the existing cost accounting paradigm will evolve to take into account the emerging environment of most businesses.

The External Environment

In recent years the news has been filled with the woes of American business and how companies in other countries are outproducing and outmarketing American products. In fact, we are seeing the demise of certain industries. For example, there have been no television manufacturers in the United States since 1992, when Zenith, the last assembler/manufacturer, moved its operations to Mexico. Quality has come to the forefront. The meaning of the phrase "made in Japan" has changed dramatically over the years following World War II. Although it used to portray something that was low in quality, it now denotes the highest quality standards.

The very nature of competition has changed. We are now in a world trading arena, and the nature of that arena is changing in both Europe and Asia. The year 1992 marked the beginning of a new relationship among the members of the Common Market. There are no trade barriers between any of the countries in that relationship, and efforts progress to have a common

---

[7] There is some argument about this point. Some authors report studies showing that labor is no longer a material part of total costs. Although this is certainly true in many industries, it is less true in others, as the example shows.

currency as well. The breakup of the Eastern bloc has affected not only the European map but also that of Asia. Finally, in 1997 the British crown colony of Hong Kong will become part of the People's Republic of China.

In addition, we are faced with different countries doing business in ways that are not like those of the United States. For example, the subsidy arrangements for various countries differ so that an industry that virtually stands on its own in one country might be heavily subsidized and/or controlled in another. All of this leads to changing needs for information by managers.

Early competition from foreign companies concentrated on products with long production runs and high volume. The first automobiles that Japanese companies brought into America were low cost, low frill, and no option. As we discuss below, many existing cost systems in U.S. companies showed that long-run items were less profitable per unit than short-run ones. With a single, plantwide overhead rate, for example, any specific costs relating to short-run or customized products were absorbed as part of the costs for all (especially long-run) products. U.S. automobile makers continued a variety of lines and options, virtually building a car to a customer's specifications. Their cost systems were faulty and told managers that this was efficient even with set-up costs and changeover times: in essence, these managers lost control over incremental costs. The next step was for foreign manufacturers to reduce set-up or changeover time so that they could produce a wide variety of products and options and still maintain the competitive edge with American companies in both cost and quality. The Japanese firms in particular recognized incremental costs associated with short runs and strived to eliminate as many of such costs as possible. American managers, by contrast, did not know the problem existed.

The Internal Environment

In response to changes in the marketplace, U.S. companies have been investing in new manufacturing technology and revising some of the ways they manage their businesses. Robotics have been introduced in many companies as has computer-integrated manufacturing (CIM). At a minimal level, robots are doing tasks better and/or cheaper than humans in some industries. Other industries are aiming for a completely automated manufacturing operation where people act as service/maintenance personnel rather than as direct labor.

Other firms have reorganized their operations into *manufacturing cells*. Here, instead of like equipment being lined up side by side, a variety of equipment needed for a single product (or product group) is arranged in a minifactory concept. In one Illinois firm that makes brake parts for the replacement market, a manufacturing cell was set up for the entire operation from working on precast components through the boxing of the final part for shipment to dealers. Instead of workers doing a single operation (tending a similar machine) as they might do in a traditional operation, those involved in cell manufacturing do all the jobs in the cell and help each other as bottlenecks appear.

Cost management is given increased emphasis in organizations that had heretofore partially ignored it. In the health care industry, for example, as the total cost of care has risen, it has become increasingly important to see what incremental costs are associated with a particular service or treatment. This is necessary both from the perspective of what insurance carriers are willing to pay in reimbursement and in establishing a needs assessment for the purchase of multimillion-dollar equipment.

Other responses to the current reality have been continuous improvement (kaizan), just-in-time inventory and management philosophy, activity-based costing, and the Theory of Constraints. We explore these and other theories and practices and look at how changes in theory and practice should change management accounting practice. The first topic is activity-based costing, a model to return to the basic idea of cost management.

ACTIVITY-BASED COSTING

Activity-based costing (ABC) directs managers' attention to the activities that cause an organization to have a certain set of financial, human, and physical resources in place. In addition, ABC stresses a more accurate assignment of costs. In this section, we discuss some costing issues and in the next we focus on the resources themselves.

Product Costs for Managerial Decision Making

For managers to decide how much to charge for a product or service or how to meet competition from other U.S. or foreign companies, they must have reasonable estimates of the resources committed and consumed for each product or service offered. When there was little or no competition for specific products, it was sufficient to have a cost system that was less accurate for a particular product or product group. However, recent history shows that foreign competitors gained a foothold in the U.S. market by targeting specific products. Thus, with specific competition comes the need for specific costs. With some costs it is easy; if, say, $20 worth of materials or purchased parts is used in manufacturing a product, there is no question that this cost should be included in the cost of the product and that it is accurate. However, if we look at a cost such as rent on the factory building or the plant manager's salary, it is impossible to determine how much of such costs were incurred to produce each product. On one end of the spectrum there are *separable* or *traceable costs*; these costs are discrete to the product and, if the product is not made, these costs will disappear.[8] At the other end of this continuum are *common costs*, resources and costs that are in place regardless of the particular products or services offered and that relate to producing, selling, or administering more than one product or service.

Direct Variable Manufacturing Costs   Traceable costs are also called *direct costs*. In the traditional model that has been used in management and cost accounting for decades, accountants and operating managers have classified materials and labor as both variable and direct. A firm making automobile engines, for example, needs an engine block for each engine produced. Thus, the cost of parts such as the engine block is both variable (total costs change when production changes) and direct (used for that product on a one-to-one basis).[9] Labor might or might not be variable and/or direct. If labor is truly variable, that is, laborers are hired only when there is work and paid an hourly rate or piece rate for their efforts, and if there is a one-to-one relationship between labor effort and production, then labor is both variable and traceable to that production (unit).

For example, in the printing of this book, each section of the book (group of pages) was produced on a printing press operated by a crew of people. During the printing of each section, the focus of activity by these people was entirely on that section. Thus, the costs are traceable to each unit of production. Let us compare this to a process that generates multiple products, say, an oil refinery. Workers who feed crude oil into the refining process are not dealing with just one product; the refining process yields dozens of products from the basic raw material. Thus, while the costs of the laborers are direct to the entire process, they cannot be traced on a one-to-one basis to each product produced. The costs are traceable; rather than to a unit of production, they are attributable to the joint process that yields the multiple products.

Common Manufacturing Costs   At the other end of the spectrum from direct costs are common costs. Examples of common manufacturing costs include factory rent, insurance on the plant, costs to heat and light the factory, the plant manager's salary, and so on. As long as the company has the plant, such costs exist regardless of the particular products made or the quantity of each product in a given period.[10] For managerial decision making,

---

[8] As we will discuss, some costs will disappear immediately. These costs include materials and other direct variable costs. Others may disappear over time, such as moving a full-time engineering position to halftime or not filling jobs when they become open.

[9] A single component like an engine block can be used in more than one model of an automobile. However, its consumption (cost) will still be on a one-to-one basis for whatever car it is used. A one-to-one relationship means that the movement of a single independent variable has a completely predictable effect on resources used. A further discussion of one-to-one, many-to-one, and one-to-many relationships is found in Chapter 11, which deals with allocation issues.

[10] Although it is possible to argue with this statement, the general idea is correct. There are base costs that are common on a broad scale.

common costs present a problem. Clearly such resources and their costs will not go away if a particular product or product line is dropped; however, in pricing, for example, common costs have to be considered or the company runs the risk of losing money.

Other Direct Manufacturing Costs Some manufacturing costs are traceable to a product but are not variable. If labor is virtually a fixed cost but, like the press crew printing a section of a book, can be traced in an unambiguous way to a particular product, that cost is direct. Other examples include the cost to set up a production line to make a particular product, engineering time used in planning and supervising the manufacturing of a product or product line, shipping department costs associated with a product, and inventory management costs linked to certain components or products.

It should be relatively straightforward to trace such direct costs to the products that use the resources. If a machine's crew uses eight hours to produce a batch of a product, then that fraction of their cost (eight hours out of, say, forty hours) is direct and traceable to those products. If the average labor cost for such a crew was $30 per hour and if 1,000 units were produced over an eight-hour span, total labor costs that are direct to that production are $240 (8 hours at $30 per hour) and the labor cost per unit is $0.24 ($240 divided by 1,000 units produced). If this batch of pro-ducts caused production to cease while machinery was adjusted for that particular run, then there is a direct set-up cost that can be attributed to that product. There might be inspection of products as they are made; such costs are also direct.

Other costs are direct to the product but might be associated with the product as a whole rather than with a particular production run. For example, suppose a company produces frames for automobiles and uses robotic machinery to weld pieces of the frame together. Engineers and programmers determined how the welding robots were to work and programmed the computers that run them. These are basically one-time costs. There are other costs to maintain the efficiency and effectiveness of the production line robots. Although these costs are direct to the product over the long term, the portion to assign to each production run or unit of product is more difficult to determine as compared to the labor example above. Companies may decide to estimate the life of a product (how long it is expected to be a viable product in its present form) and the quantity to be produced over the product's life, and then assign a portion of these costs based on these estimates. If a product is expected to have an economic life of three years and sell a total of 3,000,000 units in that period of time, total direct product costs relating to engineering and programming would be divided by 3,000,000 and applied on a unit basis over the three-year period.

Nonmanufacturing Direct Costs Besides the costs to make a product, there might be costs traceable to a product or product line but incurred in other areas of a company. For example, if part of the sales department is associated with one product line, those costs are direct to that line. Sales commissions are a good example of direct nonmanufacturing costs; others might include salaries of people who provide customer service for a product line.[11] If the part of the accounting function that includes accounts receivable has one person who deals with the receivables from a product line, again we have direct costs for that line. When managers are trying to determine what resources are consumed by a particular product line or model of a product, these costs are just as important to trace as manufacturing costs.

Resources are put into place and used for specific reasons. While some resources are common to all production or general management functions, it is important for managers to know as accurately as possible what resources are directly attributable to a particular division, to a plant, to a product line, and to a product in order to make effective decisions. Thus, wherever possible, managers should trace costs to their sources: the activities that generate the need for the resources. This is the core of ABC and activity-based management.

Accuracy versus Precision

This is a good time to discuss *accuracy* versus *precision*. Too often we focus on finding an answer that is carried to four decimal places (it *looks* precise) and ignore how accurate the data are that were used to make up the estimate. When managers try to determine why resources exist in a company, they should concentrate on accuracy and not worry too much about precision. If a programmer is writing instructions for robotic equipment and is performing other functions within the data processing department as well, it is not important to be too fine in measuring *exactly* how much of her time is spent in one function or the other. It is useful, however, to find out that about 25 percent of her time is spent in programming for robotic manufacturing, about 25 percent in dealing with general ledger programming, and about 50 percent in working on general systems design for the company. Not much is gained to say that 24.6 percent or 26.2 percent of the programmer's time is spent with the robotic equipment. Some authors claim that accuracy is being right to the first digit (for example, is it in the 20 percent range or the 30 percent range?).[12] Precision might make a manager think the answer "looks" better, but often precision to four places yields no different analysis than a more gross figure; it might encourage the manager to assume that the information is more exact than it really is.

---

[11] Some customer service cost may be direct to a particular group of customers. While the discussion focuses on products and product lines, there are other ways to classify and assign direct costs.

[12] For example, see Robert Kaplan, "Accounting Critic Robert Kaplan," *INC.* (April 1988), p. 64.

Tracing versus Allocation

When managers assign costs based on a cause-and-effect relationship, this is *tracing* or *attributing* costs. For example, if we were to do a study and find that one of the engineers employed by a company spent virtually all of her time dealing with a certain product group, we would have sufficient evidence that this cost can be traced to that group: if the product group were discontinued, that engineer could be fired or the resources associated with her time reassigned to other needs (and other ways to trace her cost). On the other hand, *allocation* is the assignment of costs where there is little or no cause and effect. If we decide to assign the cost of a plant manager to all products based on machine hours, this is an allocation; there is no relationship between the level of machine use and the resource. In the balance of this book, we will use the terms *tracing* and *allocating* only in the sense of these definitions. This is important because other authors use allocation in a more general sense to mean any assignment of cost regardless of causality.

TRACING ACTIVITIES

As stated at the outset, the object of ABC is to trace activities in order to focus attention on why resources were consumed (and, therefore, to control the activity and thereby the resource) and to use accurately traced costs as inputs for various managerial decisions. All costs are traceable to some level. The discussion above illustrated costs that are traceable to a unit of production (material, labor), to batches (set-up and inspection costs), and to joint processes (labor during a refining operation). Even common costs (for example, plantwide expenses such as a plant manager's salary or property taxes) are traceable—but to the plant itself.

Hierarchy of Activities

Cooper studied 50 cost systems in 31 companies and proposes a hierarchy of how resources are consumed by looking at the following activities:

1. *Unit-level* activities, which are performed each time a unit is produced
2. *Batch-level* activities, which are performed each time a batch of goods is produced
3. *Product-level* activities, which are performed as needed to support the production of each different type of product
4. *Facility-level* activities, which simply sustain a facility's general manufacturing process[13]

---

[13] Robin Cooper, "Cost Classification in Unit-Based and Activity-Based Manufacturing Cost Systems," *Journal of Cost Management.* (New York: Warren, Gorham, & Lamont, Fall 1990), p. 6.

Cooper proposes that costs from the first three levels should be assigned to products using appropriate drivers while costs associated with the fourth level should either be treated as a period expense or assigned to products through an arbitrary allocation process. This hierarchy allows managers to assign costs as appropriate to the decision at hand. It recognizes that all costs are traceable to some level, but that it is not necessarily useful to assign all costs to units of product.[14]

Focus on Resources

Activity-based costing and management is supposed to focus managers' attention on the control of resources through the control of the activities that cause these resources to be in place. For example, if a plant has an engineering department with ten engineers, managers should look at that set of resources and ask why it is there. If we are to assume that the plant needs at least one engineer (we can call this a core or basic fixed cost), then what are the activities that require the other nine? Using Cooper's different activity levels, engineering time and resources can be attributed to batch, product, and facility activities. We can subdivide some of Cooper's categories if needed. If, say, an engineer were assigned to an entire product group, customer class, or geographical area, we could further refine the hierarchy. However, the basic idea remains: trace resources to the activities that cause them. This is the first stage of a two-stage process.

Two-Stage Assignment Process

While costs such as materials and variable, traceable labor can be assigned directly to units of product, overhead costs are assigned using a two-stage process. This basic process is the same in both traditional and ABC systems; the difference is how these assignments are made and whether they are made (i.e., whether facility-level costs are allocated).

The first stage is to assign costs to a cost center. This means looking at resources and dividing them up into groups based on the activities that cause the resources to be there, as discussed above. The second stage is to assign costs, as appropriate, to products based on a causal driver. The second stage is where traditional and ABC systems differ, because the traditional system has relied almost solely on volume-related measures such as direct labor (hours or cost) as the single driver used to assign costs to products, while an ABC system looks at the hierarchy and causal activities as the basis for cost assignment and uses both volume- and nonvolume-related drivers.

---

[14] Others argue that such allocations do serve useful purposes. See Jerold L. Zimmerman, "The Costs and Benefits of Cost Allocations," *The Accounting Review* (July 1979), pp. 504–521.

Product versus Period Costs

Traditional cost accounting systems differentiate between product and period costs using the basic financial accounting definitions. Thus, the only costs assigned to products are those that financial accounting defines as product or inventoriable costs. While a portion of the salary of a manufacturing department's supervisor is allocated to products, none of the costs associated with the salesperson whose sole assignment is that product are assigned to the product. Under the traditional model, any cost classified as a period cost is expensed in the period and little effort is taken to associate that cost with any of the levels in Cooper's hierarchy. However, under activity-based costing, the focus is on resources and the activities that cause them. Thus, there is no longer a division between product and period costs as defined by financial accounting. Instead, managers should look at causality.

We are not advocating the change of information needed for financial accounting and the basic ways that product and period costs are differentiated. However, managers should establish different ways to aggregate information given their decision-making needs. Before illustrating the differences between traditional and ABC cost systems, let us establish a basic framework for cost systems.

SYSTEMS FOR MANAGERIAL DECISION MAKING

What Johnson and Kaplan call the movement from cost management to cost accounting was caused by a focus on financial accounting numbers rather than underlying economic reality. With the ascendancy of return on investment and the development of what both practitioners and academics have called cost accounting, all manufacturing costs were assigned to units of product. Managers wanted to know inventory valuation because they were concerned about cost of goods sold and income. However, as both managers and authors have pointed out for decades, there is a need for differential information given the decision at hand. Thus, while managers (and supporting cost accounting information) seem to have focused on financial accounting information, one of the side effects of the activity-based costing and other current movements is to refocus managers' attention on relevant information for decision making.

It is important for managers to differentiate between cost of products for managerial decisions and product costs for financial and tax accounting. If we can accurately trace costs to products (all costs, not just manufacturing costs) and if we can develop ways to deal with common costs, it is possible that financial accounting will change as a result of this discussion.

Three different systems are useful for accumulating managerial information for decision making. The following model has three ongoing systems as well as room for ad hoc information.

Ongoing Systems

1. *Cost of products for managerial decision making.* This system provides traceable cost information showing how each product or product line uses resources (causes a company to have resources). The focus is on traceability and no differentiation is made between product costs and period costs, between manufacturing and nonmanufacturing costs and resources. Thus, as appropriate, costs can include research and development, design, data processing, marketing, distribution, and customer service as well as manufacturing.

2. *Product costs for financial accounting.* This system follows prescribed procedures for financial accounting. Product costs include only manufacturing costs. While the same sense of direct/traceable costs is maintained in this system as is in the first system, more problems are inherent in this system with the necessity of dividing common costs (for example, fixed manufacturing overhead) among products and units of product, as we discuss below.

3. *Operational control.* There is a need for information beyond just unit-cost or product information, per se. Within a manufacturing operation, managers want to know if they are operating efficiently and effectively. How much material is being used? What are the measures of throughput in the manufacturing process? Are budgets being met? These are examples of operational control information.

Ad Hoc Needs

Special Studies: While operations are an ongoing process, from time to time managers perform special studies. As an example, managers investigate whether existing equipment should be replaced, decide whether to introduce a new product or discontinue an old one, and determine what price to charge for goods given a temporary condition of excess capacity. The ongoing systems should provide useful information for these special studies. Some additional information might have to be gathered as well. Although such studies are by their very nature different in some respect each time they are conducted, it is not necessary for most companies to have a whole series of systems in place to address these needs. Managers might not start each analysis from scratch; they might have a basic spreadsheet model they use in similar situations. The point is that there is no ongoing system maintained for such special studies or that the normal system does not routinely generate information for special studies.

Comparison of Traditional and Activity-Based Systems

The following illustration uses data shown in Exhibit 2-1; the illustration continues in Exhibits 2-2 and 2-3.[15] Samantha, Inc. has a single plant with

---

[15] The contents of these exhibits were generated using Lotus 1-2-3 and are included in SAMANTHA.WK1, which is available from your instructor. By changing some of the basic data, you can see the effects on costs and income for each product.

Exhibit 2-1
Samantha, Inc.—Basic Data

	Product 1	Product 2	Product 3	Total
Suggested prices/unit	$ 50.00	$ 60.00	$ 70.00	
Units produced and sold	5,000	30,000	100,000	
Direct materials/unit	$ 15.00	$ 20.00	$ 25.00	
Direct labor information:				
Labor hours per unit	0.1	0.2	1	
Rate per hour $12.00				
Labor hours used	500	6,000	100,000	106,500
Labor hours available (budgeted)				106,500
Machine use information:				
Machine hours per unit	0.3	0.3	1	
Machine hours used	1,500	9,000	100,000	110,500
Machine hours available (budgeted)				110,500
Batch information:				
Units per batch	100	150	1,000	
Machine hours per set-up	2	1	1	
Variable overhead at budgeted activity				$ 607,750
Fixed manufacturing overhead (traced):				
Cost centers				
Supervision	$18,000	$ 18,000	$ 25,000	$ 61,000
Depreciation	10,000	30,000	30,000	70,000
Engineering	20,000	25,000	90,000	135,000
Maintenance	10,000	20,000	30,000	60,000
Material handling	5,000	13,000	52,000	70,000
Set-ups (below)	18,750	37,500	18,750	75,000
Total traceable costs	$81,750	$143,500	$245,750	$ 471,000
Facility-level costs				1,329,000
Total fixed manufacturing				$1,800,000
Set-up costs (batch-related):				
Annual costs				$75,000
Number of set-ups	50	200	100	
Total machine hours	100	200	100	400
Total set-up cost assigned	$18,750	$ 37,500	$ 18,750	$ 75,000
Sales and administrative costs:				
Unit- and product-level cost	$10,000	$ 46,000	$ 95,000	$ 151,000
Facility-level costs				400,000
Total				$ 551,000

Exhibit 2-2
Samantha, Inc.—Comparative Income Statements

A. Traditional Costing System: All overhead allocated using direct labor hours.

Unit cost	per hour	Product 1	Product 2	Product 3
Materials		$ 15.00	$ 20.00	$ 25.00
Labor	$12.00	1.20	2.40	12.00
Variable overhead (DLH)	5.71	0.57	1.14	5.71
Fixed overhead	16.90	1.69	3.38	16.90
Total		$ 18.46	$ 26.92	$ 59.61

Pro Forma Income Statement
Traditional Cost System—Absorption Costing

	Product 1	Product 2	Product 3	Total
Revenue	$250,000	$1,800,000	$7,000,000	$9,050,000
Costs of goods sold	92,305	807,660	5,961,000	6,860,965
Gross profit	$157,695	$ 992,340	$1,039,000	$2,189,035
Selling and administrative expenses				551,000
Income before taxes				$1,638,035

B. Activity-Based Costing System: Only unit- and product-level costs assigned to products. Facility-related costs not allocated.

Unit cost	per hour	Product 1	Product 2	Product 3
Materials		$ 15.00	$ 20.00	$ 25.00
Labor	$12.00	1.20	2.40	12.00
Variable overhead (MH)	5.50	1.65	1.65	5.50
Fixed overhead (traced)		16.35	4.78	2.46
Total		$ 34.20	$ 28.83	$ 44.96

Pro Forma Income Statement
ABC System—No Allocation of Facility-Level Costs

	Product 1	Product 2	Product 3	Total
Revenue	$250,000	$1,800,000	$7,000,000	$9,050,000
Direct manufacturing costs	171,000	865,000	4,495,750	5,531,750
Direct manufacturing margin	$ 79,000	$ 935,000	$2,504,250	$3,518,250
Direct sales and administrative costs	10,000	46,000	95,000	151,000
Direct margin	$ 69,000	$ 889,000	$2,409,250	$3,367,250
Facility-level costs				
Manufacturing				1,329,000
Sales and administrative				400,000
Income before taxes				$1,638,250

three products. Although there are limits when using simplified examples such as this one, the major points are generalizable to a more complex setting.

1. The traditional cost accounting model employs a volume-based driver such as direct labor hours (or dollars) or machine hours for the assignment of all manufacturing overhead costs while the activity-based costing (ABC) model assigns unit-, batch-, and product-level costs to products, leaving facility-level manufacturing overhead unallocated.[16]

2. The traditional cost accounting model ends up with a cost of goods sold based on absorption costing and includes only product costs as defined in financial accounting. This framework is most appropriate for financial accounting statements. Even if results are recast in a contribution margin format, the major distinction is between variable costs (both product and period costs that relate to a volume-based driver) and fixed costs. The ABC model focuses on managerial decision making, generating product costs that cross the boundary between manufacturing and nonmanufacturing activities, and keys in on tracing of costs.

3. Even with the ABC model, there are basic issues to address.
   a. Even if a cost is attributable, it might be sunk and, therefore, not relevant for certain decisions.
   b. Some costs are treated as attributable, but, in reality, they are not avoidable.
   c. Certain costs, such as set-ups or inspection, are attributable to a cost center but might not really be traceable to products. In this case, some volume-related allocation does take place.
   d. Managers still use fully allocated costs for many decisions. While many advocate that this practice cease, we must also address how ABC would handle absorption costing.

Exhibit 2-1 includes the basic information for the illustration. Samantha has three products that vary in total production. We assume that production equals sales and that Samantha is working at capacity in order to avoid a difference in income caused by any form of absorption costing.[17] Note that information is given regarding direct labor hours, machine hours, and batch- and product-level costs for each product. In addition, facility-level (common) costs are shown.

The first part of Exhibit 2-2 is a traditional, direct-labor-based, absorption costing, financial accounting income statement. Unit costs include materials, labor, and variable and fixed overhead. All overhead is assigned using direct labor hours. Cost of goods sold for each product is its unit costs times units sold. All sales and administrative costs are shown in a lump sum as

---

[16] Some managers allocate facility-level costs, an issue we address in point 3.

[17] For a review of how absorption costing affects income, see a basic management or cost accounting text.

period expenses. The only profitability information that we have from this type of statement is either unit or total gross margin (or gross profit). However, gross margin includes an allocation of facility-level costs as well as a single driver (labor hours) for the assignment of other overhead costs.

Exhibit 2-2 also includes an activity-based costing income statement. Assume that a study of cost centers and activities yields the information shown about unit and batch costs in Exhibit 2-1. Also assume that this study reveals that variable overhead is related to machine hours rather than direct labor hours. In the ABC example, unit costs include materials, labor, variable overhead (using machine hours as the driver), and only attributable fixed overhead. We could also have included nonmanufacturing unit, batch, and product costs, but we chose to highlight these as a separate line item. Thus, there is a *direct manufacturing margin* which is the difference between revenue and traceable manufacturing costs, and a *direct margin* where traceable nonmanufacturing costs have been deducted from the direct manufacturing margin. The major difference in product costs is caused by the tracing of $471,000 of fixed costs to specific products. The results of the ABC model in Exhibit 2-2 show that if, say, Product 1 were to be dropped from the product line, the result would be a lost margin of $69,000. Over a reasonable period of time, about $181,000 in costs would be avoided and $250,000 in revenues lost per year if such a decision were made. We will discuss this assumption later. Finally, facility-related costs are not allocated to products in this exhibit, but instead, they are treated as period costs. Note that the total income from both methods is the same (any difference is due to rounding).

The two parts of Exhibit 2-2 illustrate the differences in traditional versus activity-based costing. In addition, the exhibit highlights product costs for financial accounting as compared to cost of products for managerial decision making. However, as stated above, there are potential problems with activity-based costing.

Some Issues to Resolve in Activity-Based Costing

Activity-based costing focuses managers' attention on resources and the activities that cause these resources. By controlling the activities, managers can reduce costs. There is an assumption, therefore, that if an activity is reduced, over some reasonable period of time, costs will also reduce somewhat proportionally. Let us look at two examples of costs that might not change as activity goes down even if these costs are traceable to an appropriate activity level.

Traceable Sunk Costs   Sunk costs are, by definition, not relevant to decisions since such costs are unaffected whatever alternative is chosen for a current decision. In ABC, managers might trace the use of certain equipment to a product. The cost of this dedicated equipment is usually reflected in its depreciation, an allocation of a sunk cost. In the Samantha example, there is a total of $70,000 per year in traceable depreciation, but this cost might not reflect the opportunity cost of using these resources. The depreciation probably does not relate to either the net realizable value of these assets or the replacement cost. The real economic event that would take place if a product that had dedicated machinery were to be discontinued would be the use of that machinery for another product or the net sales value of the disposal of the machinery and the present value of the lost depreciation tax effect foregone. Therefore, if separable depreciation is a material amount, its inclusion in an ABC product cost is suspect since its annual amount is the result of an allocation and the asset's cost is sunk. In addition, including these costs might lead to managers making the wrong product mix choice.

Traceable Costs That Are Not Avoidable   Earlier in this chapter we looked at a company with ten engineers in its engineering department. Under activity-based costing, it is common for managers to undertake a study of engineering time to see what activities cause these resources. Say that one engineer with an annual salary of $40,000 spends about 50 percent of her time on one product group, 25 percent on another group, and the remaining 25 percent on general (facility) problems. Under ABC, 50 percent of that person's salary and departmental support costs would be assigned to the first product group, 25 percent to the second, and 25 percent would go to facility-level costs.

If the first product were dropped, there is the implicit assumption that about $20,000 (0.50 × $40,000) would be saved. In fact, most companies would not move this engineer to half time; her free time would be reassigned. Perhaps if there were several moves at the same time to drop products, the company could save a whole engineering position. However, if this is so, then the real cost is at the facility level and not the product level as posited in the ABC tracing of that engineer's costs. Thus, *depending on the decision at hand*, managers would want to disaggregate ABC information to show which costs are sunk (such as depreciation) and which are traceable but not avoidable (like 50 percent of an engineer's cost).

Quasi-Allocations   In some batch-related costs, such as set-ups and inspections, managers might be able to make first-stage cost assignment based on causality but have less success in the second stage. In the Samantha example, Exhibit 2-1 shows that first-stage cost assignment to the set-up function is $75,000. It is possible that these costs include a core set of costs, which would not go away unless the plant were closed, and some other costs that are avoidable if, say, Product 1 or 2 were to be dropped. It is also possible that all $75,000 are long-term fixed costs and are not avoidable as long as the set-up function remains. Let us look at this last assumption first and then return to the earlier one.

Under ABC it is normal to assign set-up costs to product (the second stage) using some driver such as machine hours or labor hours. Managers would want to see what relevant activity is associated with set-ups. In the Samantha example, the $75,000 is assigned using machine hours. If the $75,000 in set-up costs are long-term fixed costs, then the assignment using machine hours is really an allocation. Even if Product 1 were to be dropped, there would be no savings in set-up costs. If we relax this assumption a bit and allow for some of the costs to be both separable and avoidable if a product were dropped, the problem still remains for those costs common to the set-up function. Again, managers should be careful when such costs are used in an ABC system and should be aware of the difference between traceable and avoidable.

Activity-Based, Absorption Costing

While we do not advocate allocating facility-level costs to products, much research shows that managers want to use absorption costing as a basis for transfer pricing (as the basis for a surrogate for market prices) and segment and managerial performance evaluation (as part of return on investment and residual income), for example. Since advocates of ABC point to the increased accuracy of activity-based costs, managers must be made aware of when and how common costs are allocated.[18] By nature, certain allocation methods might be deemed more reasonable than others, but none make a cost more accurate.

Exhibit 2-3 illustrates three different ways to allocate the facility-level costs ($1,329,000): first using direct labor hours, the old standby; second using machine hours, the appropriate driver for variable overhead in the illustration and the basis for set-up cost assignment; and finally, in proportion to the amount of traceable overhead shown in Exhibit 2-1. As you can see, these different allocation methods yield quite different results at the product gross margin level. In moving from the traditional model shown in the first part of Exhibit 2-2 through the three different ways to apply common fixed overhead in Exhibit 2-3, Product 3 looks more and more profitable while Product 1 moves in the other direction. However, as stated above, *none of these methods yields a more accurate cost than another.*

Even where managers do not allocate facility-level costs, this same problem can persist at another level. The engineering department with ten engineers might have nine who can be traced to various activity levels while there is a tenth engineer who is the supervisor. In many ABC systems, common costs for this engineering department are assigned on the same basis as the other nine engineers' time/costs are assigned. Thus, relative traceable costs are the basis for common cost allocation. Although the consequences are smaller

---

[18] Certain authors propose there are conditions that must be met in order for activity-based costs to be relevant. For example, see Eric Noreen, "Conditions Under Which Activity-Based Cost Systems Provide Relevant Costs," *Journal of Management Accounting Research*, Vol. 3, (Sarasota, Fla.: American Accounting Association, Fall 1991), pp. 159–168.

Exhibit 2-3
Samantha, Inc.—Pro Forma Income Statements
Activity-Based Costing—Absorption Costing

A. Allocate Facility-Level Costs Using Direct Labor Hours

	Product 1	Product 2	Product 3	Total
Revenue	$ 250,000	$1,800,000	$7,000,000	$9,050,000
Cost of goods sold	177,239	939,873	5,743,637	6,860,750
Gross profit	$ 72,761	$ 860,127	$1,256,363	$2,189,250
Selling and administrative expenses				551,000
Income before taxes				$1,638,250

Where facility-level manufacturing costs are allocated using:

Direct labor hours	$12.48 per hour		
Per unit	$ 1.25	$ 2.50	$ 12.48

B. Allocate Facility-Level Costs Using Machine Hours

	Product 1	Product 2	Product 3	Total
Revenue	$ 250,000	$1,800,000	$7,000,000	$9,050,000
Cost of goods sold	189,041	973,244	5,698,465	6,860,750
Gross profit	$ 60,959	$ 826,756	$1,301,535	$2,189,250
Selling and administrative expenses				551,000
Income before taxes				$1,638,250

Where facility-level manufacturing costs are allocated using:

Machine hours at	$12.03 per hour		
Per unit	$ 3.61	$ 3.61	$ 12.03

C. Allocate Facility-Level Costs Using Relative Traceable Overhead

	Product 1	Product 2	Product 3	Total
Revenue	$ 250,000	$1,800,000	$7,000,000	$9,050,000
Cost of goods sold	401,670	1,269,908	5,189,172	6,860,750
Gross profit	($151,670)	$ 530,092	$1,810,828	$2,189,250
Selling and administrative expenses				551,000
Income before taxes				$1,638,250

Where facility-level manufacturing costs are allocated using:

Relative traceable overhead				
Total traceable costs	$ 81,750	$ 143,500	$ 245,750	$ 471,000
Percent of total	17.36%	30.47%	52.18%	100.00%
Allocation of facility cost	$ 230,670	$ 404,908	$ 693,422	$1,329,000
Per unit	$ 46.13	$ 13.50	$ 6.93	

than allocating all facility-level costs based on relative traceable costs, the results are similar and should be avoided where possible.

The above discussion is not a criticism of activity-based costing. In fact, as we have illustrated earlier in the chapter and summarize below, ABC is a distinct improvement over traditional costing systems because it focuses managers' attention on controlling resources and knowing what activities or transactions cause resource use. Rather this is a warning that many of the same problems that exist with traditional systems continue with ABC. Managers should not be lulled into accepting a new model without recognizing its limitations and being careful to make explicit choices in its use.

How ABC Improves on Traditional Cost Systems

By recognizing that resources are the results of activities or transactions, ABC focuses managers' attention on those resources so that they can be controlled. By tracing costs to the unit, batch, product, or facility level, managers can more accurately assign costs and make better decisions regarding pricing and product mix, for example. Inherent in this discussion is not only the inaccuracy of a traditional system in many cases but also some biases introduced with a single, direct-labor-based cost driver.

In the Samantha example, the three products vary in production levels from 5,000 to 100,000 units. A comparison of the traditional costing system shown in Exhibit 2-2 to an ABC system shows that the cost of Product 1 (the lowest-volume product) is much higher under ABC while that of Product 3 (the highest-volume product) is much lower. This is common when comparing the results of these two systems. Under a traditional costing system, products with high labor content (which would include those with long production runs) get a disproportionately high allocation of overhead costs. Costs associated with products and batches are treated as if they are unit related under the traditional system. Thus, high-volume, high-labor-content products are overcosted while low-volume products are undercosted. Activity-based costing removes this inaccuracy by tracing costs appropriately. Even with the problems identified above, ABC systems remove the basic bias that is part of a traditional costing system, assigning too much cost to high-volume products.

SUMMARY

To this point, we have been looking at changes in how we accumulate costs given an emerging competitive environment. In this chapter we examined how managers seek information to reflect their needs given the internal and external environment of the firm. This historical perspective provides a framework for understanding systems for managerial decision making and analyzing how traditional and activity-based costing systems work. This chapter concentrates on differentiating product costs for financial accounting and managerial decision making. Chapters that follow deal more specifically with operational control and information for special studies.

In addition to the changes in the competitive arena, changes that are causing managers to rethink basic management philosophies are taking place within the internal environment of many firms. This ties in with the above examination of cost tracing and a concentration on controlling resources, but it is also much broader. In the next chapter we look at the Theory of Constraints, just-in-time, total quality control, and other aspects of a more general change in management thinking that ties what is included in this chapter to the overall strategic planning process of a firm.

PROBLEMS AND CASES

2-1. Productivity (CMA)

An examination of the productivity rates of industrialized countries shows a pattern of productivity growth during the two immediate post-World War II decades (1950–1970). This period of growth has been followed by a constant slowing of the growth rate that has continued into the 1980s. A general belief exists that the slowing of the growth rate has reached a crisis level.

Productivity growth rates of Japan and the United States are often compared. For instance, Japan experienced an average productivity growth rate of 7.2 percent from 1950 to 1965. This rate dropped to 3.1 percent in the late 1970s. The United States' absolute productivity was much higher than Japan's from 1950 to 1965. However, the United States' leadership position in absolute productivity is now threatened due to a much slower rate of increase. An implication of the slowing of the productivity growth rate is that the United States and other countries having similar productivity patterns may experience a reduction in their standards of living.

As a function of the concern over productivity levels and in an attempt to maintain a competitive position in the world market, industry and unions in the United States seem to be moving away from rigid work rules that were bargained during periods of greater growth and are adopting more flexible job structures. Examples of such work rule changes drawn from recent concessions on the part of unions include decreasing the size of work crews, increasing the breadth of job descriptions, decreasing paid break times and lunch periods, decreasing use of seniority as a single factor in promotions, and increasing various types of job design techniques such as job rotation.

Required:
1. Define the term *productivity* and explain why productivity is important.
2. Discuss the basic relationship and interaction between the level of the standard of living and the level of productivity and how this relationship and interaction affect the motivation of workers.
3. Discuss the likely effect on the worker attitudes in firms where there have been work rule concessions.

2-2. Traditional Cost System (CMA)

Many companies now recognize that their cost systems are inadequate for today's powerful global competition. Managers in companies selling multiple products are making important product decisions based on distorted cost information, as most cost systems designed in the past focused on inventory valuation. In order to elevate the level of management information, current literature suggests that companies should have as many as three cost systems for (1) inventory valuation, (2) operational control, and (3) activity-based costing which is also known as individual product cost measurement.

Required:
1. Discuss why the traditional cost system, developed to value inventory, distorts product cost information.
2. Identify the purpose and characteristics of each of the following cost systems.
   a. Inventory valuation.
   b. Operational control.
   c. Activity-based costing.
3. a. Describe the benefits that management can expect from activity-based costing.
   b. List the steps that a company, using a traditional cost system, would take to implement activity-based costing.

2-3. Defining Factory Overhead (CMA)

Moss Manufacturing has just completed a major change in its quality control (QC) process. Previously, products had been reviewed by QC inspectors at the end of each major process, and the company's ten QC inspectors were charged as direct labor to the operation or job. In an effort to improve efficiency and quality, a computerized video QC system was purchased for $250,000. The system consists of a mini-computer, 15 video cameras, other peripheral hardware, and software.

The new system uses cameras stationed by QC engineers at key points in the production process. Each time an operation changes or there is a new operation, the cameras are moved, and a new master picture is loaded into the computer by a QC engineer. The camera takes pictures of the units in process, and the computer compares them to the picture of a "good" unit. Any differences are sent to a QC engineer, who removes the bad units and discusses the flaws with the production supervisors. The new system has replaced the ten QC inspectors with two QC engineers.

The operating costs of the new QC system, including the salaries of the QC engineers, have been included as factory overhead in calculating the company's plant-wide factory overhead rate which is based on direct labor dollars.

The company's president is confused. His vice-president of production has told him how efficient the new system is, yet there is a large increase in the factory overhead rate. The computation of the rate before and after automation is shown below.

	Before	**After**
Budgeted overhead	$1,900,000	$2,100,000
Budgeted direct labor	1,000,000	700,000
Budgeted overhead rate	190%	300%

"Three hundred percent," lamented the president. "How can we compete with such a high factory overhead rate?"

Required:
1. a.   Define "factory overhead," and cite three examples of typical costs that would be included in factory overhead.
    b.   Explain why companies develop factory overhead rates.
2.   Explain why the increase in the overhead rate should not have a negative financial impact on Moss Manufacturing.
3.   Explain, in the greatest detail possible, how Moss Manufacturing could change its overhead accounting system to eliminate confusion over product costs.
4.   Discuss how an activity-based costing system might benefit Moss Manufacturing.

2-4. Product Profitability (CMA)

Olat Corporation produces three gauges. These gauges measure density, permeability, and thickness and are known as D-gauges, P-gauges, and T-gauges respectively. For many years the company has been profitable and has operated at capacity. However, in the last two years prices on all gauges were reduced and selling expenses increased to meet competition and keep the plant operating at full capacity. Third quarter results, as shown below, are representative of recent experiences.

OLAT CORPORATION
Income Statement
Third Quarter 19X3
($000 omitted)

	D-Gauge	P-Gauge	T-Gauge	Total
Sales	$900	$1,600	$ 900	$3,400
Costs of goods sold	770	1,048	950	2,768
Gross profit	$130	$ 552	$ (50)	$ 632
Selling and administrative expenses	185	370	135	690
Income before income taxes	$(55)	$ 182	$(185)	$ (58)

Mel Carlo, president, is very concerned about the results of the pricing, selling, and production policies. After reviewing the third quarter results he announced that he would ask his management staff to consider a course of action that includes the following three suggestions.

- Discontinue the T-gauge line immediately. T-gauges would not be returned to the line of products unless the problems with the gauge can be identified and resolved.
- Increase quarterly sales promotion by $100,000 on the P-gauge product line in order to increase sales volume 15 percent.
- Cut production on the D-gauge line by 50 percent, a quantity sufficient to meet the demand of customers who purchase P-gauges. In addition, the traceable advertising and promotion for this line would be cut to $20,000 each quarter.

George Sperry, controller, suggests that a more careful study of the financial relationships be made to determine the possible effect on the company's operating results as a consequence of the president's proposed course of action. The president agreed and JoAnn Brower, assistant controller, was given the assignment to prepare an analysis. In order to prepare the analysis, she gathered the following information.

- All three of the gauges are manufactured with common equipment and facilities.
- The quarterly general selling and administrative expense of $170,000 is allocated to the three gauge lines in proportion to their dollar sales volume.
- Special selling expenses (primarily advertising, promotion, and shipping) are incurred for each gauge as follows.

	Quarterly Advertising and Promotion	Shipping Expense
D-gauge	$100,000	$ 4 per unit
P-gauge	210,000	10 per unit
T-gauge	40,000	10 per unit

- The unit manufacturing costs for the three products are as follows.

	D-Gauge	P-Gauge	T-Gauge
Raw material	$17	$ 31	$ 50
Direct labor	20	40	60
Variable manufacturing overhead	30	45	60
Fixed manufacturing overhead	10	15	20
	$77	$131	$190

- The unit sales prices for the three products are as follows.

D-gauge	$ 90
P-gauge	$200
T-gauge	$180

- The company is manufacturing at capacity and is selling all the gauges it produces.

Required:
1. JoAnn Brower has suggested that the Olat Corporation's product-line income statement as presented for the third quarter of 19X3 is not suitable for analyzing proposals and making decisions such as the ones suggested by Mel Carlo.
   a. Explain why the product-line income statement as presented is not suitable for analysis and decision making.
   b. Describe an alternative income statement format that would be more suitable for analysis and decision making, and explain why it is better.

2. Use the operating data presented for Olat Corporation and assume that President Mel Carlo's proposed course of action had been implemented at the beginning of the third quarter of 19X3. Then evaluate the president's proposed course of action by specifically responding to the following points.

    a. Are each of the three suggestions cost effective? Your discussion should be supported by a differential analysis that shows the net impact on income before taxes for each of the three suggestions.

    b. Was the president correct in eliminating the T-gauge line? Explain your answer.

    c. Was the president correct in promoting the P-gauge line rather than the D-gauge line? Explain your answer.

    d. Does the proposed course of action make effective use of Olat's capacity? Explain your answer.

3. Are there any nonquantitative factors that Olat Corporation should consider before it considers dropping the T-gauge line? Explain your answer.

2-5. Numerically and Manually Controlled Machines

Don Fogarty, manager of the Data Processing Department of Rutman Industries, had just been summoned to the office of the president of the company, David Werner. Werner was concerned that the costs in data processing had risen dramatically over the last year (mainly due to hiring new programmers) and that current performance reports showed the department to be behind with a large backlog of unfinished work.

Rutman Industries made custom parts for various automobile manufacturing companies. Most parts went through one to three operating departments. In each department, production managers had the option of scheduling the parts on numerically operated machines or on manually operated machines. The numerically operated machines needed specific programming by the Data Processing Department. During the last year there had been a significant trend by the production managers to schedule most of their work on the numerically operated machines, thereby creating an increasing load for the data processing programmers.

In his conversation with Fogarty, Werner pointed out that while the performance reports for the various production departments looked good (set-up time was down), the rising cost of programmers was ruining the overall profit picture for Rutman Industries. Fogarty was directed to solve the problem by increasing productivity and limiting hiring.

On his way back to his office, Fogarty got into a discussion with Kay Wilson, the chief cost accountant. Wilson told Fogarty that the information that Werner was getting was indicative of what was going on. As she explained it, production departments were charged for actual machine set-up time as well as operating labor and overhead and material use. Factory overhead included the Data Processing Department in that a predetermined rate was charged to each department per labor hour within that department. This was done on a standard basis for the year in advance. Costs of new hires in Fogarty's department were borne by the department since it was considered unfair to charge an operating department for personnel changes or efficiencies (inefficiencies) brought about during the year. However, Wilson was also concerned about the trend away from the manually operated machines. She stated that some parts would be made more efficiently on the manual machines and she could not understand why these machines were being underutilized. She also had received purchase requests for more numerical machines even though the manual machines were relatively new and were about as cost effective as the numerically controlled machines for most basic moderate-length production runs.

Required:
As Fogarty's assistant you have been assigned the task of recommending a course of action. What is the problem at Rutman? How can it be solved?

2-6. Overhead Rates (CMA)

MumsDay Corporation manufactures a complete line of fiberglass attaché cases and suitcases. MumsDay has three manufacturing departments—molding, component, and assembly—and two service departments—power and maintenance.

The sides of the cases are manufactured in the Molding Department. The frames, hinges, locks, and so on are manufactured in the Component Department. The cases are completed in the Assembly Department. Varying amounts of materials, time, and effort are required for each of the various cases. The Power Department and Maintenance Department provide services to the three manufacturing departments.

MumsDay has always used a plantwide overhead rate. Direct labor hours are used to assign the overhead to its product. The predetermined rate is calculated by dividing the company's total estimated overhead by the total estimated direct labor hours to be worked in the three manufacturing departments.

Whit Portlock, Manager of Cost Accounting, has recommended that MumsDay use departmental overhead rates. The planned operating costs and expected levels of activity for the coming year have been developed by Portlock and are presented by department in the schedules (000 omitted) that follow.

	Manufacturing Departments		
	Molding	**Component**	**Assembly**
Departmental activity measures			
Direct labor hours	500	2,000	1,500
Machine hours	875	125	
Departmental costs			
Raw materials	$12,400	$30,000	$ 1,250
Direct labor	3,500	20,000	12,000
Variable overhead	3,500	10,000	16,500
Fixed overhead	17,500	6,200	6,100
Total departmental costs	$36,900	$66,200	$35,850
Use of service departments			
Maintenance			
Estimated usage in labor hours for coming year	90	25	10
Power (in kilowatt hours)			
Estimated usage for coming year	360	320	120
Maximum allotted capacity	500	350	150

	Service Departments	
	Power	**Maintenance**
Departmental activity measures		
Maximum capacity	1,000 KWH	Adjustable
Estimated usage in coming year	800KWH	125 hours
Departmental costs		
Materials and supplies	$ 5,000	$1,500
Variable labor	1,400	2,250
Fixed overhead	12,000	250
Total service department costs	$18,400	$4,000

Required:
1. Calculate the plantwide overhead rate for MumsDay Corporation for the coming year using the same method as used in the past.
2. Whit Portlock has been asked to develop departmental overhead rates for comparison with the plantwide rate. The following steps are to be followed in developing the departmental rates.
   a. The Maintenance Department costs should be allocated to the three manufacturing departments using the direct method.
   b. The Power Department costs should be allocated to the three manufacturing departments using the dual method, i.e., the fixed costs allocated according to long-term capacity and the variable costs according to planned usage.
   c. Calculate departmental overhead rates for the three manufacturing departments using a machine hour base for the Molding Department and a direct labor hour base for the Component and Assembly Departments.
3. Should MumsDay Corporation use a plantwide rate or departmental rates to assign overhead to its products? Explain your answer.

2-7. Productivity Improvement (CMA)

Improved productivity is considered an important way to reduce or control expenditures during periods of inflation. Productivity improvement can be obtained in a variety of ways including additional capital investment and more effective employee performance. The three cases presented below focus on attempts to increase employee productivity without added capital investment.

Case 1   The Customer Complaints Department is in charge of receiving, investigating, and responding to customer claims of poor service. The volume of paperwork is very large and is growing because each complaint requires the processing of several forms and letters. A large staff is required for handling this processing. There is a wide span of control, with fifteen to twenty staff members reporting to each supervisor. The number of complaints processed per worker has shown a noticeable decline in recent months.

The department manager recommends that supervisors require increased performance. They should do this by setting performance objectives, making their presence more obvious, monitoring breaks and lunch hours, and seeing to it that talking among staff members is strictly curtailed. The supervisors should also make the staff aware that failure to achieve performance objectives will result in a negative evaluation of their performance.

Case 2 A department of an insurance company in charge of processing medical-related claims has had its budget reduced even though the number of claims has been increasing. This reduction comes after very small annual appropriation increases in prior years. Given the recent rate of inflation, the actual resources available to do the work have decreased.

Top management recently has specified that certain claims be processed within forty-eight hours of receipt, a requirement that leads to special handling of such claims. Consequently, the budget reduction causes the processing of other claims to be delayed even further. The department manager complains that the budget cuts and the priority treatments of certain claims will reduce the department's over-all productivity.

This manager recommends that top management allow all managers to partici-pate more actively in the budget development and budget adjustment during the budget year. Further, once the general objectives for a department are established, the department manager should be allowed to set the priorities for the work to be accomplished.

Case 3 Investigative auditors within a welfare agency are responsible for detect-ing cases of welfare fraud. Because of the latest recession, the number of welfare fraud cases was expected to be significantly higher than in recent history. However, the number of cases discovered has not increased significantly. This may be due to the fact that investigators are becoming discouraged because of the lack of follow-up action taken on their findings. Cases are backed up in legal processing. Even when the individuals are found guilty, the penalties are often very light. The investigators wonder if all their time and effort to uncover the fraudulent claims are justified.

The manager of the Investigative Audit Department has recommended an annual performance incentive program for the investigators which is related only to the number of cases of fraud detected. The annual performance evaluation report would be filed in each investigator's personnel record and each investigator's annual salary adjustment would be based primarily upon the number of fraud cases detected. Currently, evaluations relate to the number of cases closed with a conviction.

Required:
For each of the three cases presented, discuss whether or not the proposal of the department manager will improve productivity within the department. Explain, in detail, the reasons for your conclusion in each case.

2-8. Information Costs (CMA)

The Independent Underwriters Insurance Co. (IUI) established a Systems Depart-ment two years ago to implement and operate its own data processing systems. IUI believed that its own system would be more cost effective than the service bureau it had been using.

IUI's three departments—Claims, Records, and Finance—have different require-ments with respect to hardware and other capacity-related resources and operating resources. The system was designed to recognize these differing needs. In addition, the system was designed to meet IUI's long-term capacity needs. The excess capacity designed into the system would be sold to outside users until needed by IUI. The estimated resource requirements used to design and implement the system are shown in the following schedule:

	Hardware and Other Capacity-Related Resources	Operating Resources
Records	30%	60%
Claims	50	20
Finance	15	15
Expansion (outside use)	5	5
Total	100%	100%

IUI currently sells the equivalent of its expansion capacity to a few outside clients.

At the time the system became operational, management decided to redistribute total expenses of the Systems Department to the user departments based upon actual computer time used. The actual costs for the first quarter of the current fiscal year were distributed to the user departments as follows:

Department	Percentage Utilization	Amount
Records	60%	$330,000
Claims	20	110,000
Finance	15	82,500
Outside	5	27,500
Total	100%	$550,000

The three user departments have complained about the cost distribution method since the Systems Department was established. The Records Department's monthly costs have been as much as three times the costs experienced with the service bureau. The Finance Department is concerned about the costs distributed to the outside user category because these allocated costs form the basis for the fees billed to the outside clients.

James Dale, IUI's Controller, decided to review the distribution method by which the Systems Department's costs have been allocated for the past two years. The additional information he gathered for his review is reported in the three tables that are on the following page.

Dale has concluded that the method of cost distribution should be changed to reflect more directly the actual benefits received by the departments. He believes that the hardware and capacity related costs should be allocated to the user departments in proportion to the planned, long-term needs. Any difference between actual and budgeted hardware costs would not be allocated to the departments but remain with the Systems Department.

The remaining costs for software development and operations would be charged to the user departments based upon actual hours used. A predetermined hourly rate based upon the annual budget data would be used. The hourly rates that would be used for the current fiscal year are shown on page 94.

TABLE 1
Systems Department Costs and Activity Levels

| | Annual Budget | | First Quarter | | | |
| | | | Budget | | Actual | |
	Hours	Dollars	Hours	Dollars	Hours	Dollars
Hardware and other capacity-related costs	—	$ 600,000	—	$150,000	—	$155,000
Software development	18,750	562,500	4,725	141,750	4,250	130,000
Operations—						
Computer-related	3,750	750,000	945	189,000	920	187,000
Input/output-related	30,000	300,000	7,560	75,600	7,900	78,000
		$2,212,500		$556,350		$550,000

TABLE 2
Historical Utilization by Users

| | Hardware and Other Capacity Needs | Software Development | | Operations | | | |
| | | | | Computer | | Input/Output | |
		Range	Average	Range	Average	Range	Average
Records	30%	0–30%	12%	55–65%	60%	10–30%	20%
Claims	50	15–60	35	10–25	20	60–80	70
Finance	15	25–75	45	10–25	15	3–10	6
Outside	5	0–25	8	3–8	5	3–10	4
	100%		100%		100%		100%

TABLE 3
**Utilization of Systems Department's
Services in Hours—First Quarter**

| | Software Development | Operations | |
		Computer-Related	Input/Output
Records	425	552	1,580
Claims	1,700	184	5,530
Finance	1,700	138	395
Outside	425	46	395
Total	4,250	920	7,900

Function	Hourly Rate
Software development	$ 30
Operations	
Computer related	$200
Input/output related	$ 10

Dale plans to use first quarter activity and cost data to illustrate his recommendations. The recommendations will be presented to the Systems Department and the user departments for their comments and reactions. He then expects to present his recommendations to the management for approval.

Required:
1. Calculate the amount of data processing costs that would be included in the Claims Department's first quarter budget according to the method James Dale has recommended.
2. Prepare a schedule to show how the actual first quarter costs of the Systems Department would be charged to the users if James Dale's recommended method were adopted.
3. Explain whether James Dale's recommended system for charging costs to the user departments will:
   a. Improve cost control in the Systems Department.
   b. Improve planning and cost control in the user departments.
   c. Be a more equitable basis for charging costs to user departments.

2-9. The Electronics Assembly Plant[19]

Background   The Electronics Assembly Plant has been a part of the parent corporation for about ten years. It was acquired as part of a much larger acquisition that involved the retention of the top management of the acquired company. These managers had been promised that corporate headquarters would adopt a "hands-off" policy toward the Electronics Assembly Plant. The parent corporation has existed for about fifty years and is a highly decentralized, fully diversified holding company consisting of two service groups and four manufacturing groups. Each of these six groups has a highly developed management staff experienced in their own industries. The Electronics Assembly Plant is an oddity in that it is the only manufacturing unit in one of the service groups.

While the assembly plant has an experienced manufacturing staff, it is headed by a manager with no prior manufacturing experience. The purchasing-manager position has been vacant for an extended period and staff turnover has been high throughout the plant. The computer system has been enhanced and a new manufacturing software package has been implemented to help in planning the acquisition and use of manufacturing resources (an MRP system). This new system is not yielding the expected benefits and in many cases the system output is being ignored by shop-floor personnel.

In line with its philosophy of decentralization, and its hands-off policy, the parent corporation has provided little direction to the management of the assembly plant. The question of management control has become critical over the past three years. The assembly plant has been able to sell everything it can produce, yet its operating and

---

[19] This case used by permission of the Institute of Management Accountants. IMA or IMA adapted.

financial results are far less positive than would be expected during a national economic recovery.

Management Response   Because the parent corporation has four manufacturing groups, its internal audit staff has developed audit techniques designed to measure manufacturing effectiveness and to identify opportunities to improve effectiveness. When the reports coming from the assembly plant began to show a deteriorating condition in terms of days' receivables, inventory turnover, inventory shrinkage, cash flow, ROI, and cost of sales, the corporate audit staff recommended a thorough review to identify opportunities to strengthen the operations.

The assembly plant and its parent service-group management were not anxious to subject the plant to an examination by a corporate staff group. In spite of numerous requests to arrange the review, and after selected contact between senior managers at both units, the management control review was delayed until inventory turnover was less than 1.0, over $2 million (30 percent of total) of receivables were delinquent more than 120 days, and the inventory shrinkage approached 10 percent of cost of goods sold.

The review of the assembly plant was completed late last year by a two-person team of internal manufacturing consultants with combined manufacturing experience of more than fifteen years. The results of their review are summarized in the report provided in the exhibit that follows. The report was sent to the plant manager for use in developing an action plan to correct significant weaknesses in control.

Required:
After reviewing the exhibit, put yourself in the position of the corporate controller in considering the following questions:

1. What should the plant controller do to assist manufacturing management in responding to the conditions in the plant?
2. How should the actions for improvement be prioritized, and how much consideration should be given to the question of "too much change too quick"?

Exhibit 1
Report of the Internal Management Consulting
Team for the Electronics Assembly Plant
Principal Observations

Master Scheduling
Marketing, the master scheduler, and production personnel have not coordinated their efforts to develop and execute a valid master schedule and a detailed production plan.

-   The master schedule has fluctuated significantly on a month-to-month basis (see Attachment 1). Planning, as it applies to the production, inventory, and purchasing functions, cannot occur if the production targets are continually changing.
-   A formal system has not been devised to assign mutually agreeable priorities between marketing and manufacturing to ensure timely completion or provide the necessary replanning mechanism for work orders.
-   Failure to establish and meet weekly production goals results in a month-end crunch, overtime, and inefficiencies in the operation.
-   The master schedule does not involve capacity requirements planning (how many people and/or machines are required to meet the production schedule)

Exhibit 1 (continued)

to determine if the plan can be executed. No mechanism exists to identify the causes of missed production targets or to devise corrective actions.

Inventory Accuracy

The minimum inventory accuracy level necessary to support material requirements planning is 95 percent.

* Review of cycle-counting results, performed by cycle counters for the week ending September 14, yields the following results:

  Of 89 "A" items counted, 23 (25.8 percent) agreed in quantity to the perpetual inventory records.
* Access to the storeroom is not limited to authorized personnel.
* Documents used to update inventory transactions within the plant and between outside storage locations are not numerically controlled (there is no accountability for numerical sequence and disposition).
* Production and inventory planners do not utilize MRP action notices because of the lack of integrity of the data input.
* A continuing comprehensive cycle-counting program would support MRP and the inventory planning function.

Purchasing

Review of the purchasing department revealed the following:

* Vendor history information is not utilized or analyzed in relation to purchasing decisions.
* Competitive bidding and multiple sourcing is limited due to time constraints and lack of emphasis.
* Maintenance of open and closed purchase orders is not performed by purchasing personnel.
* Follow-up of late deliveries, inaccurate quantities, and poor quality could be improved. In addition, no effort is made to slow down purchases that are no longer needed as early as we originally planned.
* Purchase orders are not entered into the EDP system on a timely basis. During our review there were 59 pallets of material being held by the receiving department due to a lack of purchase orders and/or data entry on the system.

Shop Floor Control

* Work orders are randomly released to the shop. Consequently, no plan is developed to take advantage of scheduling similar products in succession.
* Failure to keep work-order lots together, along with the routings and blueprints, results in difficulties related to job completion and work-order reporting.
* Production planners release work orders to the stockroom for picking. This permits a backlog to build up in a staging area instead of controlling the work orders and work-in-process inventories via the shop floor control function. During our review there were 246 orders staged that were short at least one part. This is usually due to parts intended for one order being used on another order. The effect is a loss of visibility of this inventory, excessive work-in-process inventory, and an increased risk of obsolescence because of a failure to integrate engineering and design changes.

Exhibit 1 (continued)

- Blueprints at the wrong revision level are available to shop floor personnel when building products.

Quality Control

Troubleshooting is a bottleneck operation. It was observed that:

- Technicians are involved in performing testing, repair, and troubleshooting. Lower paid personnel can, and do, perform testing and repair after the technician has identified the problem. Neither time nor historical statistics are used for planning the troubleshooting function nor are any allowances built into the routings or scheduling assumptions.

Attachment 1

A master schedule in an MRP environment should not fluctuate more than 5 to 10 percent (maximum) in total between months. The following is an analysis of scheduling changes for the top 10 products (31 percent of sales dollars) during a recent three-month period.

Product		July	August	September
1. SMT-1	1st revision	121% decrease	7.4% decrease	7.4% decrease
2. DI-3	1st revision	21% decrease	11% decrease	11% decrease
	2nd revision		18% increase	25% increase
3. SMT-2	1st revision	53% decrease	37% decrease	37% decrease
	2nd revision		78% increase	78% increase
4. ZU-355	1st revision	50% increase	no change	no change
	2nd revision		25% increase	25% increase
5. DI-X3	1st revision	6% increase	14% increase	14% increase
	2nd revision		65% increase	75% increase
6. 3185-3	1st revision	25% increase	no change	no change
	2nd revision		61% increase	61% increase
7. CMP-1	1st revision	33% increae	no change	50% increase
	2nd revision		33% increase	no change
8. SMT-1L	1st revision	8% increase	18% increase	no change
	2nd revision		28% increase	no change
9. DI4A	1st revision	14% increase	no change	no change
	2nd revision		222% increase	no change
10. CP35	1st revision	no change	no change	no change

2-10. The Portables Group[20]

Background

Tektronix, Inc., headquartered in Portland, Oregon, is a world leader in the production of electronic test and measurement instruments. The company's principal product

---

[20] This case used by permission of the Institute of Management Accountants. IMA or IMA adapted.

since its founding in 1946 has been the oscilloscope (scope), an instrument that measures and graphically displays electronic signals. The two divisions of the Portables Group produce and market high- and medium-performance portable scopes.

Tektronix experienced almost uninterrupted growth through the 1970s based on a successful strategy of providing technical excellence in the scope market and continually improving its products in terms of both functionality and performance for the dollar. In the early 1980s, however, the lower-priced end of the division's medium-performance line of scopes was challenged by an aggressive low-price strategy of several Japanese competitors. Moving in from the low-price, low-performance market segment in which Tektronix had decided not to compete, these companies set prices 25 percent below the U.S. firm's prevailing prices. Rather than moving up the scale to more highly differentiated products, the group management decided to block the move.

The first step was to reduce the prices of higher-performance, higher-cost scopes to the prices of the competitors' scopes of lower performance. This short-term strategy resulted in reported losses for those instruments. The second step was to put in place a new management team whose objective was to turn the business around. These managers concluded that, contrary to conventional wisdom, the Portables Group divisions could compete successfully with foreign competition on a cost basis. To do so, the divisions would have to reduce costs and increase customer value by increasing operational efficiency.

Production Process Changes

The production process in the Portables Group divisions consisted of many functional islands, including etched circuit board (ECB) insertion, ECB assembly, ECB testing, ECB repair, final assembly, test, thermal cycle, test/QC, cabinet fitting, finishing, boxing for shipment, and shipment. The new management team consolidated these functionally-oriented activities into integrated production lines in open work spaces that allow visual control of the entire production area. Parts inventory areas were also placed parallel to production lines so that at each work station operators would be able to pull their own parts. This in essence created an early warning system that nearly eliminated line stoppages due to stockouts.

Additional steps that were taken in the early to mid 1980s to solve managerial and technical problems include implementation of just-in-time (JIT) delivery and scheduling techniques and total quality control (TQC), movement of manufacturing support departments into the production area, and implementation of people involvement (PI) techniques to move responsibility for problem solving down to the operating level of the divisions. The results of these changes were impressive: substantial reductions in cycle time, direct labor hours per unit, and inventory, and increases in output dollars per person per day and operating income. The cost accounting group had dutifully measured these improvements, but had not effectively supported the strategic direction of the divisions.

Cost Accounting System

Direct Material and Direct Labor   Figure 1 shows the breakdown of the total manufacturing cost of the newest portable scopes produced with the latest technologies. In most cases, material and labor are easily traced to specific products for costing purposes. Prior to the mid 1980s, however, the divisions' attempts to control direct labor had been a resource drain that actually *decreased* productivity.

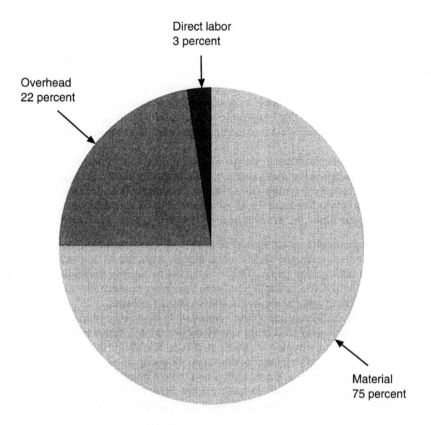

Direct labor
3 percent

Overhead
22 percent

Material
75 percent

Figure 1 Manufacturing Costs

There were approximately twenty-five production cost centers in the Portable Instruments Plant. Very detailed labor efficiency reports were prepared monthly for each cost center and each major step in the production process. In addition, an efficiency rating for each individual employee was computed daily. Employees reported the quantity of units produced and the time required to produce them, often overestimating the quantity produced to show improved efficiency against continually updated standards. The poor quality of the collected data resulted in semi-annual inventory write-downs when physical and book quantities were compared.

"The inadequacy of our efficiency reporting system became clear when we analyzed one of our new JIT production lines," commented Michael Wright, Financial Systems Application Manager. "On a JIT manufacturing line, once the excess inventory has been flushed out, it is essentially impossible for any person to work faster or slower than the line moves. However, if one person on the line is having a problem, it immediately becomes apparent because the product flow on the line stops. Corrective action is then taken, and the line is started up again.

"On that line, the system told us that the efficiency of each of the workers was decreasing. However, stepping back from the detail of the situation allowed us to look at the overall picture. We found that the costs incurred on the line were going down and its product output was going up. Obviously, it was becoming more, not less, efficient."

The quantity of direct labor data collected and processed also was a problem. Production employees often spent twenty minutes per day completing required reports when they could have been producing output. Additionally, the accounting staff was processing 35,000 labor transactions per month to account for what amounted to 3 percent of total manufacturing cost. "Transactions cost money," observed John Jonez, Group Cost Accounting Manager, "and lots of transactions cost lots of money."

In response to these problems, the group accounting staff greatly simplified its procedures. It abandoned the measurement of labor performance for each operation, and greatly reduced the number of variances reported. The number of monthly labor transactions fell to less than 70, allowing the staff to spend more time on overhead allocation and other pressing issues.

Overhead The product costing system allocated all manufacturing overhead costs to products based on standard direct labor hours. A separate rate was computed for each manufacturing cost center. This system led to rapidly increasing rates; the direct labor content of the group's products had been continually decreasing for years, while overhead costs were increasing in absolute terms.

"Because the costing system correlated overhead to labor, our engineers concluded that the way to reduce overhead costs was to reduce labor," commented Jonez. "The focus of cost reduction programs therefore had been the elimination of direct labor. However, most of this effort was misdirected, because there was no correlation between overhead cost incurrence and direct labor hours worked. Our system penalized products with proportionately higher direct labor, but it wasn't those products that caused overhead costs. We proved that. We attacked direct labor and it went down, but at the same time overhead went up.

"We therefore knew that we needed a new way to allocate overhead. More fundamentally, we needed a way for the cost accounting system to support the manufacturing strategy of our group. The objective was clear—to provide management with accounting information that would be useful in identifying cost reduction opportunities in its operating decisions as well as provide a basis for effective reporting of accomplishments."

Approach to Method Change

Initial Steps The first step taken by Wright and Jonez in developing a new overhead allocation method was to establish a set of desirable characteristics for the method. They decided that it must accurately assign costs to products, thus providing better support for management decisions than the old method. It must support the JIT manufacturing strategy of the Portables Group. It also must be intuitively logical and easily understandable by management. And finally, it must provide information that is accessible by decision makers.

The next step was to interview the engineering and manufacturing managers who were the primary users of product cost information. These users were asked, "What is it that makes your job more difficult? What is it that makes certain products more difficult to manufacture? What causes the production line to slow down? What is it that causes overhead?" The answers to these questions were remarkably consistent—there were too many unique part numbers in the system. This finding revealed a major flaw in the ability of the direct labor-based costing method to communicate information critical for cost-related decisions. Manufacturing managers realized there were substantial cost reduction opportunities through the standardization of component parts, but there was no direct method to communicate this idea to design and cost-reduction engineers who made part selection decisions.

Although difficult to quantify, some costs are associated with just carrying a part number in the database. Each part number must be originally set up in the system, built into the structure of a bill of materials, and maintained until it is no longer used. Moreover, each part must be planned, scheduled, negotiated with vendors, purchased, received, stored, moved, and paid for. Having two parts similar enough that one could be used for both applications requires unnecessary duplication of these activities, and therefore unnecessary costs.

Standardizing parts results in several indirect benefits. Fewer unique part numbers usually means fewer vendors and greater quality of delivered parts. It also means smoother JIT production, fewer shutdowns of manufacturing lines, and greater field reliability. These observations led to a preliminary consensus on the need to develop a product costing method that would quantify and communicate the value of parts standardization.

Cost Analysis "To confirm our assessment," stated Jonez, "we segmented the total manufacturing overhead cost pool. The costs of all cost centers comprising the pool were categorized as either material-related or conversion-related based upon rules developed in conjunction with operating managers. [See Exhibit 1.]

"Material-related costs pertain to procurement, scheduling, receiving, in-coming inspection, stockroom personnel, cost-reduction engineering, and information systems. Conversion-related costs are associated with direct labor, manufacturing supervision, and process-related engineering. Application of the rules results in an approximately 55/45 split between material overhead (MOH) and conversion overhead (COH). This finding further confirmed the inadequacy of the existing method, which applied all overhead based on direct labor."

The accounting analysts decided to focus their initial efforts on the MOH pool. To improve their understanding of the composition of the pool and thus assist them

---

Exhibit 1
Rules for Overhead Segmentation by Cost Center Classification

(1) *Production.* The overhead costs of any cost center containing direct labor employees are assigned 100 percent to the COH pool.

(2) *Group/Division/Product Group Staff.* The total costs of any manufacturing staff cost center are assigned 50 percent to the COH pool and 50 percent to the MOH pool.

(3) *Group/Division/Product Group Support.* The total costs of any manufacturing support cost center (e.g., Material Management or Information Systems) are assigned 100 percent to the MOH pool.

(4) *Manufacturing Cost-Reduction Engineering.* The total costs of any cost-reduction engineering cost center are assigned 100 percent to the MOH pool.

(5) *Manufacturing Process-Related Engineering.* The total costs of any process-related engineering cost center are assigned 100 percent to the COH pool.

in developing a method for its allocation, Wright and Jonez consulted operating managers and further segmented it into:

1. Costs due to the value of parts,
2. Costs due to the absolute number of parts used,
3. Costs due to the maintenance and handling of each different part number and
4. Costs due to each use of a different part number.

The managers believed that the majority of MOH costs were of type (3). The costs due to the value of parts (1) and the frequency of the use of parts (2 and 4) categories were considered quite small by comparison.

The analysts therefore concluded that the material-related costs of the Portables Group would decrease if a smaller number of different part numbers were used in its products. This cost reduction would result from two factors. First, greater volume discounts would be realized by purchasing larger volumes of fewer unique parts. Second, material overhead costs would be lower. "It was the latter point that we wanted our new allocation method to focus on," commented Wright.

"Our goal," continued Jonez, "was to increase customer value by reducing overhead costs. Our strategy was parts standardization. We needed a tactic to operationalize the strategy."

Required:

1. Using assumed numbers, develop a cost allocation method for material overhead (MOH) to quantify and communicate the strategy of parts standardization.
2. Explain how use of your method would support the strategy.
3. Is any method which applies the entire MOH cost pool on the basis of one cost driver sufficiently accurate for product decisions in the highly competitive portable scope markets? Explain.
4. Are MOH product costing rates developed for management reporting appropriate for inventory valuation for external reporting? Why or why not?

2-11. J.J. West Life Insurance Company[21]

Background

Insurance provides a means of dealing with risk. Some risks can be avoided, while other risks can be anticipated and planned for. Still other risks, which can be financially devastating, cannot be avoided or planned for with certainty. Insurance is a means of dealing with the financial consequences of these other risks.

An underlying principle of insurance is that a group can collectively sustain losses that would be too great for any one member of the group to absorb. Each individual in the group pays a premium for coverage regardless of whether or not they have a loss. This principle makes it possible for insurance to pay thousands of dollars in benefits to an individual in return for hundreds of dollars in premium. The ability to do this consistently over the long-term is dependent upon the skills and judgment of the group's insurance company.

---

[21] The statistics in this case are based on the mid-1980s. This case used by permission of the Institute of Management Accountants IMA or IMA adapted.

Early Approaches   A simple approach to insurance that was attempted up through the late 1800's was the assessment society. A group of people, often a fraternal organization, would agree to provide death benefits for its members by assessing each surviving member a share of the cost of the benefit payment when a member died. Each member paid the same assessment amount, regardless of age, health or any other distinguishing risk characteristics. As the group aged, assessments became more frequent, making the recruitment of new and, especially younger members more difficult. As the group dwindled in size, each member's assessments began to increase. Eventually, the money ran out and the assessment society failed.

The failure of the assessment society represents an example of *adverse selection*. That is, the tendency of the members of a group with poorer than average health, in relation to the entire group, to apply for and continue to receive coverage in a greater proportion than the rest of the group. This can occur when the classification of the risk to be insured is either non-existent or insufficient. Risk classification is a means of reviewing relevant information about an applicant in determining what level of risk of loss they represent.

Early efforts to consider risk classifications were subjective in nature. In the 1600's, applicants for insurance would appear before the underwriter to answer questions about health, lifestyle and the purpose of the insurance. Using this information, the underwriter would determine whether the applicant should be issued insurance and how much, and what would be the appropriate premium rate. Since the classification was not particularly scientific, the early policies issued were quite limited.

The underwriter seeks to answer the same questions today, but with far more useful information. In the 1700's, a mathematical basis for an age-based *mortality* table was developed through the study of the records of a town in what is now Poland. The table determined the probability of death occurring at each year of age for the group studied. Eventually, *morbidity* tables were established, which showed the rate of sickness and injury occurring among given groups of people categorized by age. These tables allowed life and health insurers to take a person's age into account in determining the appropriate cost (premium) for insurance. For the first time insurers had the ability to incorporate fairness into the issuance of their products. That is to say, people with similar risks were to be treated similarly.

Modern Insurance   From these early efforts came modern life and health insurance. These coverages are of two distinct types; Group and Individual.

Group insurance can be traced to the early assessment societies. However, there are some notable differences. The modern group is made up of people of varied risks who pay premiums at the same rate. Some of these people may be otherwise uninsurable due to medical problems or hazardous occupations. However, they are afforded reasonable rates because their poorer risks are offset by other members of the plan who represent less risk than the average for the group. The group is insurable provided it is large enough and has a steady influx of new members that reflect the population the group is based upon (avoiding the *adverse selection* problem noted above). These plans are funded (paid for) in a variety of ways. Plans of adequate size (i.e., 100 or more lives) are experience rated. That is, the insurance company calculates the premium rate based partially on the prior loss experience of the plan and the insurance company pays the losses out of the premium. If losses are less than expected, there is an underwriting gain. If losses exceed expectations there is an underwriting loss. In either case the premium would be adjusted in the future. Another approach taken by still larger groups is to self-fund a plan. Under this arrangement the plan sponsor (employer) does not pay a premium. They pay a fee to the insurance company to administer their plan and directly bear the cost of all claims up to an established maximum, at which point a "cap policy" pays any additional claims. These approaches are only used to fund health plans. Group life plans and smaller health plans are "pooled" with other plans to more effectively spread the risk.

Modern insurance has certain underwriting guidelines enabling this system to work. The group must be brought together for a reason other than to obtain insurance. If not, it will be populated predominantly by people who already need the benefits for existing problems and not insurance. The typical modern group is a company offering life, health and disability insurance to its employees.

There must be *adequate participation* by the group (a specific percentage of the employee population must join the plan), or else there is little likelihood the insured's level of risk will match that of the employee population upon which the premium is based. The law of large numbers will not operate properly if the group gets too small. The smaller the group, the less the chances are that the group's experience will reflect the predicted results. In addition, insufficient participation may indicate that there is an alternative insurance plan which is siphoning off a specific segment of the group, thus negating the risk classification of the group as a whole. If only older or sicker participants are left in the plan, the premium charged will be insufficient to pay the claims, resulting in higher premiums isolating the high risk individuals further. This would defeat the purpose of group insurance.

Additionally, once the plan is established, employees should not be able to elect coverage only when they know they are about to incur claims (i.e., at the onset of an illness or injury). To prevent this from occurring all *late entrants*, those seeking insurance after an initial eligibility period, are required to establish that they are insurable. This is accomplished through questions on the insurance application regarding the health of the applicant for the purpose of determining if they have a serious illness such as cancer, heart disease, hypertension, diabetes, or acquired immunodeficiency syndrome (AIDS). If a catastrophic claim is a certainty it is not in the best interest of the insurance company or the other members of the group to provide insurance to the applicant as this will affect their future premium rate.

Pre-existing condition clauses are found in most health plans to curtail expenses the insurer and, ultimately, the employer must pay for conditions that the insured was treated for during a defined period of time prior to the effective date of insurance. Approaches to this include, but are not limited to, incident maximums (a limit on how much the insurer will pay for the illness in question), being ineligible for a defined period for the specific condition, or requiring a *treatment-free* period prior to eligibility for the specific condition (i.e., not receiving treatment for the condition for a defined period not to exceed a defined maximum period).

Individual insurance is a type of coverage for which the concept of fairness becomes especially important. Fairness depends on grouping together people with similar characteristics such as age, sex and health and calculating a premium based on the group's level of risk. Those with the same risks should pay the same premiums for individual life, health or disability insurance. For individual insurance each policy is underwritten separately. For each application the underwriter determines whether or not to issue the policy, how much insurance should be provided, and which premium rate classification the applicant should receive.

Risk Classification   Risk classification is based on information from the application, health statements, or physical examinations regarding the applicant's age, sex, health, geographic location, occupation, hobbies and habits. All of these characteristics have a "reasonably" predictable effect on a person's future health care costs and longevity. It is important to note that the purpose of this fact gathering is not to diagnose an illness, but to classify the risk. Individuals are matched to risk classifications which have been previously established and have had rates determined for them. The risk classifications have been set for any segment of the population for which the average mortality and morbidity can be predicted with accuracy.

This is accomplished through the use of loss statistics for the industry. These statistics are compiled by organizations such as the American Council of Life Insurers (ACLI) and the Health Insurance Association of America (HIAA).

Additionally, individual insurance companies accumulate their own statistical data which reflects their own experience. Advances in information processing have allowed the industry to continually refine these classifications having the effect of grouping insureds with others who more closely reflect the same level of risk as themselves.

The effect that information gathered on the application has on the level of risk varies. A terminal illness has a virtual certainty of causing death in the near future. A person in this situation is uninsurable. The risk of death from a risky habit (e.g., smoking or hang-gliding), when considered along with other factors, is not a certainty, but results in an increased probability of death versus someone without the same habits and would result in a higher premium rate. Once insured, a change in a person's health will not affect their coverage if the coverage is properly maintained. If material information is withheld or misstated by the applicant, the insurance company can contest the contract for a defined "contestability period," usually two years, after its issuance.

Once the insurer has all the necessary information about the applicant's risk the insurance decision can be made. An applicant may be rated standard and charged normal rates. He or she, because of higher risk, may be rated substandard and charged higher premiums, perhaps also including some limitations on the terms of the coverage. Or, because the risk is too high, an applicant may be declined for insurance. In practice only about two percent of individual life insurance applications are not accepted and about five percent are rated substandard. These risk ratings may be different between companies dependent upon their underwriting practices.

Being rated as uninsurable by one company does not necessarily mean insurance cannot be obtained from another company. Also, risk ratings change as technological advances result in new methods to treat previously terminal illnesses.

It is important that the risk classification process be efficient. The additional cost of refinements to the risk classification process should not exceed the reduction in expected claims from the less refined risk classification. Conversely, any arbitrary setting of limits on the medical information insurers can use will cause low-risk policyholders to subsidize high-risk policyholders resulting in higher costs. The theoretical goal of pricing a given risk classification is to develop a premium rate which is financially sound for the insurance company and its other policyholders, fair to the insured and permits economic incentives for wide-spread competition and availability of coverage. Laws, regulation and public opinion constrain risk classification systems within broad guidelines of social acceptability which must be balanced against the potential economic side effects of adverse selection or market dislocation (resulting in coverage which is either prohibitively expensive or unavailable). The underwriting process should not be unfairly discriminatory, nor should it conflict with basic individual human or civil rights. However, it should enable fair and accurate risk classification on a prospective basis.

The regulated environment in which the insurance industry operates is controlled predominantly by the individual states at this time. All products (policies) must be approved by each state in which they will be sold. The company and its agents must be licensed in a state before they can solicit sales. Through this mechanism the states control what products will be offered and how they will be sold and administered. Typically, states require that insurers make their full portfolio of products available to their residents. This prevents insurers from selectively not writing business that state regulations make unprofitable.

Group and individual insurance differ in that group insurance seeks to establish a risk classification for an entire group while individual insurance underwriting attempts to assess the risk classification for each individual applicant. In the group all individuals pay the same blended premium rate, whereas with individual insurance each insured should pay a rate similar to those presenting a similar risk. While some underwriting and administrative processes differ to take advantage of the economies of scale by large groups, the basic underlying concepts are the same. Insurance is based on the sharing of risks and the laws of probability to predict mortality and morbidity. The cost of participating in it is determined based on the probability of the risk coming to fruition. Once it is known with reasonable certainty that an event is about to occur, the laws of probability no longer apply; the risk is 100 percent. Put simply, insurance only works if you purchase it before you need it. Conversely, once insurance is purchased and properly maintained, it cannot be taken away.

In addition to trying to accurately classify and price risks, the insurance industry also actively tries to lessen the cost of losses incurred. One example of this is the sponsoring of medical cost containment approaches such as medical care management. Health benefits are generally paid according to a plan of benefits established to cover a broad range of situations. This process will not necessarily always provide for the most efficient use of healthcare dollars while minimizing the cost to the insured. Medical care management allows for more flexibility to be brought into the process by providing appropriate care in a cost effective manner. This is one of many efforts currently being undertaken by the insurance industry to limit the current rapid escalation in health care costs.

J.J. West

The J.J. West Life Insurance Company is a provider of life, accident and health, and disability insurance products. It markets these products to individuals and groups in all 50 states and the District of Columbia. J.J. West ranks among the top 10 percent of all companies in the industry as measured by premiums. The company does not engage in any other business. J.J. West is envied by its competitors for its large book of group business from Fortune 500 clients as well as for its strong marketing organization. While the group market has historically been the company's strongest market segment J.J. West has recently shown significant strength in individual lines.

J.J. West has competitive underwriting guidelines in all markets. The underwriters, which are located in the Branch Offices, are supposed to use all tools legally available to them in making their decisions. All applications for individual life insurance coverage above $250,000 require a medical examination. All applications for individual medical and disability coverages must be accompanied by a satisfactory medical history. As is the industry standard, applications submitted with a medical exam or medical history that generate a mortality rate of 150 percent (a mortality rate 50 percent higher than a person with no abnormal risk), or more, will classify an individual as not acceptable by West's standards and will be rejected. The company does not offer substandard rates.

Medical applications are also required for all individuals insured under group policies that cover 15 or fewer people. Management believes that it is too costly to require physicals for individuals in groups of more than 15. Management also feels that this policy provides West with a competitive advantage. Most of its competitors require medical applications for groups of 20 or fewer individuals. Large group coverages also have a physical medical application requirement for those individuals who do not apply for coverage immediately upon employment or at the inception of the group policy. Groups of 15 or more individuals make up 70 percent of West's group business.

Management feels confident with its underwriting guidelines. Although there has been some recent increase in loss experience for individual lines coverages, the company has historically outperformed its peers.

Management considers the contract provisions contained in the company's policies as standard for the industry. Accident and health policies have a three month treatment-free period for pre-existing conditions, and the range of benefits that are offered by the company meet or exceed any that are offered by West's competitors. Management does not feel that these provisions add or detract from West's competitive position; however, they do feel that the responsiveness of West's Claim Department and its overall service does provide a competitive advantage.

The company has 200 Branch Offices located throughout its marketing area, including offices in the 50 largest metropolitan areas as ranked by the census bureau. Each of the offices perform sales, claims and premium accounting functions. Branch Offices are evaluated and bonuses awarded on meeting or exceeding prduction quotas and on how well they control marketing and underwriting costs. Claim costs are considered to be uncontrollable and are not factored into the Branch evaluation.

Marketing considerations require that detailed results of all office activity be reported to the Senior Vice President, Field Operations, every Thursday. Office activity is manually captured and accumulated in personal computers until transmitted to the Home Office on leased telephone lines. Once transmitted to the Home Office, information from all offices is accumulated and various production, claims and financial reports are prepared for field management. Field management considers this system to be responsive to their needs. It is flexible and can be easily enhanced.

The company has recently installed a new automated claims system. This system is capable of handling all three lines of business and allows claims examiners to record a significant amount of data on its data base, including payment, claim, and claimant information. Of great importance to the Claims Department is the new system's ability to speed up the payment process. It is felt that this ability will further enhance the company's competitive position.

Another of the innovations that claims management is proud of is the fact that for the first time claim examiners can classify losses by medical condition. For example, if death, medical treatment, or disability is the result of pneumonia, the examiner has a specific diagnostic code for pneumonia. The prior system only had the ability to record general medical conditions such as respiratory disease. Examiners have been instructed to be as specific as possible when entering the cause of loss so that a more detailed history of causes of loss can be maintained. General medical conditions will not be accepted by the system. The system is capable of summarizing information contained in its data base and generating different levels of management reports using any of the data fields.

The company's cost accounting system accumulates all costs by functional department. Each department then allocates these costs to individual product lines. In most cases departments allocate costs to product lines using formulas developed over many years. Management has become disenchanted with this process. Of prime concern is the inability of product line management to verify the accuracy of costs allocated to their products. They are especially skeptical of the allocations received from the Branch Offices.

Senior Management has become increasingly aware of the AIDS epidemic. They have read about the spread of the disease in the national press and view AIDS as a potential threat to West. Exhibit 1 summarizes facts about the disease and the financial threat to the insurance industry posed by the disease. In recent months, they have seen many companies change their underwriting policies. Several companies have also pulled out of selected markets.

The actuaries have also been concerned about the small number of reported AIDS cases. They have not been able to identify enough AIDS related claim data with which to either project the AIDS exposure to West or to price products to reflect the increased exposure. Of particular concern to the actuaries is the fact that West's claims do not reflect the reported experience of its peer competitors or of the Centers for Disease Control.

As CFO, Senior Management has come to you to see if you can answer the following questions:

Required:
1. Given the achievable objectives of a cost accounting system for an insurance company:
   a. Is the system currently in place adequate to accurately measure the company's AIDS related costs?
   b. Describe enhancements (if any) that should be made to the company's cost accounting system.
2. What steps can J.J. West take to limit its exposure to AIDS? Would you recommend the same actions for both group and individual lines of business?
3. If a state enacts legislation prohibiting insurance companies from using the results of blood tests and AIDS questions on insurance applications, what would you recommend if faced with the question of whether to continue to offer life, medical, and disability coverage in that state?
4. Given the fact that your claims data base does not have sufficient data for the actuaries to project the company's exposure, what, if any, data can you identify that would allow you to make an estimate of exposure? You do not need to limit your analysis to company data.

Exhibit 1
AIDS Background

The AIDS Virus

Acquired Immunodeficiency Syndrome (AIDS) is an infectious disease caused by the Human T-cell Lymphotropic Virus Type III (HTLV-III). It is believed to be a new disease in human beings. Its major effect is the complete loss, by the body's immune system, of the ability to fight certain kinds of infection. Bodily fluids, blood and semen seem to be the primary method of disease transmission at this time. Persons at high risk of acquiring the virus are men who are homosexually or bisexually active, intravenous drug abusers, persons receiving infected blood products intravenously, and children born of infected mothers. At intermediate risk are persons, especially women, who engage in heterosexual sex with members of high-risk groups.

As with most other viruses there exists a clinical spectrum of disease associated with the HTLV-III infection. At one end of this spectrum rests the totally asymptomatic individual with a positive antibody test who may or may not develop the disease and who may or may not be infectious to others. At the other end of the spectrum lies the unfortunate person with full-blown AIDS and an expected short-term mortality of 100 percent. In between are those infected by the virus who have developed associated syndromes such as AIDS Related Complex (ARC), or the lymphodenopathy syndrome. The Center for Disease Control (CDC) estimates that for every patient with AIDS there are eight patients with ARC; the CDC is forced to make estimates because ARC is not a reportable disease.

As can be seen from the following tables, most AIDS cases come from certain large cities and states where the homosexual population is predominately located and is concentrated in the age groups under 50 years of age. In New York City, AIDS is now the leading cause of death for males in the 30 to 39 year age group.

AIDS State Distribution As of March 3, 1986		AIDS Cases Per Million Population As of March 3, 1986	
State	**Percentage of AIDS Cases**	**SMSA of Residence**	**Cases Per Million Population**
New York	33%	New York, NY	605.7
California	23	San Francisco, CA	590.7
Florida	7	Miami, FL	333.4
New Jersey	6	Newark, NJ	232.5
Texas	5	Los Angeles, CA	198.1
Other	26	All Other	38.9
Total	100%		

Source: Centers for Disease Control Weekly Surveillance Report, March 3, 1986.

It should be noted that the distribution of AIDS cases may be even more concentrated than the figures above represent. There is evidence that suggests that some AIDS victims facing impending death go back to their hometowns in their final months. This would have the effect of "spreading" the geographic statistics.

Exhibit 1 (continued)

The CDC reports that approximately half of the reported AIDS cases are in the 30–39 age category. Since females account for only 6 percent of reported AIDS cases, the age breakdown is not sex distinct and is summarized in the following table.

AIDS Age Group
As of March 3, 1986

Age	Percentage of AIDS Cases
0–12	1%
13–19	0
20–29	21
30–39	47
40–49	21
49+	10
Total	100%

Source: Centers for Disease Control Weekly Surveillance Report, March 3, 1986.

Since AIDS cases first began to be reported in June 1981, the number of new cases has grown substantially. Whereas in 1981, there were 201 cases reported, in 1985 there were 8,406 cases. The 1986 number is expected to exceed the total reported for all previous years. During the fourth quarter of 1986 an average of 58 AIDS cases were being reported daily to the CDC. This translates to 21,170 cases on an annual basis. This figure does not take into account the 20 percent under reporting estimated by the CDC. Factoring in the 20 percent, the rate of newly reported cases may be approaching 25,500 on an annual basis.

Even more alarming to the experts is the number of Americans believed to be already infected with the virus. Because the virus has a long incubation period (believed to be three to five years), we can only estimate future damage. The CDC estimated 500,000 to 1,000,000 infected Americans. Other estimates are as high as 2,000,000. However, these are soft figures extrapolated from a very small data base. Estimates of the number of those infected who will come down with AIDS also varies. The CDC has estimated 5 to 19 percent, although this number is in the process of being revised upward. An epidemiologist at Johns Hopkins has suggested 30 to 50 percent. And Dr. Anthony Fauci, Director of the National Institute of Allergy and Infectious Diseases and an authority on AIDS, believes 40 percent of those infected will eventually develop AIDS and die from it. He estimates a million Americans are presently infected and that the number will jump to two or three million in the next five to ten years.

While we really do not know how many people are infected with the AIDS virus, it is believed that a reasonable estimate would be in the neighborhood of one million. Assuming that at least one third of these will develop the disease and die from it, we are talking about 300,000 deaths in the next few years. And if Dr. Fauci is correct this number could reach a million within five to ten years. So far there is no effective treatment for AIDS.

Exhibit 1 (continued)

Blood Tests

A very important aspect of the AIDS problem for the insurance industry is the issue of blood tests, their reliability and their legality. In March 1985, the FDA approved the Enzyme Linked Immunosorbent Assay (ELISA) test for detecting antibodies to the AIDS virus. This test will not diagnose AIDS (there is no test which can clearly identify individuals in the earliest stages of AIDS), but will detect the presence of the AIDS antibody in human semen or plasma. If the antibody is present in a sample from a person in a high-risk group, he or she probably was exposed to the virus and was infected long enough to develop antibodies to it. However, if this test is done randomly from the general population, it can produce false positives.

The Public Health Service advises that a positive test from a random selection of the general population should be repeated. If the repeated test is positive, the reliability is improved, but still is not as reliable as the test when done in the select high-risk group. Thus, the use of another test is recommended to confirm the positive ELISA results. Generally, the Western Blot test is used for this purpose. This too, is an antibody test but one that is rather time-consuming and expensive. If the two ELISA's plus the Western Blot are positive, there is a 99.9 percent chance you have a true positive for whom the mortality ratio is 2,500 percent (25 times that of a healthy person) in the first few years.

There is another test used in conjunction with AIDS and that is the T-cell Test. This test determines the status of the immune system and, as such, is not an antibody test. The AIDS virus destroys T helper cells thereby depressing the immune system. The normal ratio is 2:1. A ratio of 1:1 is highly suggestive and less than 1:1 is positive. A positive means the pathological or disease process is active. However, the test will not tell the cause of the immunosuppression: congenital, medications, or a virus. Thus it must be used in combination with other information to determine whether an individual has been infected with the AIDS virus.

The Legislative Issue

Insurance companies do business subject to a variety of risk-classification legislation. These laws prohibit unfair discrimination between individuals of the same class and of equal expectation of life (life insurance), or of essentially the same hazard (accident or health insurance). They also prohibit unfair discrimination based on age, sex, sexual preference (in a few states), and marital status. This legislation may impact, and possibly restrict or limit, the potential procedures established by insurance companies to deal with the AIDS problem.

Arguments against AIDS testing are that they violate an individual's civil rights, that insurance companies cannot assure that results would be kept confidential, and that the tests are not 100 percent reliable. The industry contends that insurance companies have always used the results of medical examinations to evaluate insurability and have never had a problem keeping the results of medical tests confidential.

In their efforts to influence state legislatures to prohibit insurance companies from testing for AIDS exposure or from using positive tests to deny insurance to applicants, gay rights groups and others have raised the issue of the false positive factor in the antibody tests. And, to some extent, these groups have been successful. In California, the results of antibody tests may not be used in determining insurability. In Wisconsin, the legislature initially prohibited conditioning of insurance coverage

Exhibit 1 (continued)

or determining rates on the existence or results of antibody tests, but then amended the law to remove these restrictions if the tests are approved by the state epidemiologist and insurance commissioner.

While California and Wisconsin have passed laws on the testing issue, other states are considering prohibitive legislation. The New York Legislature has a proposal before it that would prevent companies from requiring a blood test for AIDS, because they say such tests are medically inconclusive and that a majority of people who do test positive in an AIDS test do not develop the disease.

The District of Columbia has enacted the most stringent legislation to date. Insurers are prevented from testing high-risk applicants until 1991. After the five-year period, insurers not only must obtain permission from the superintendent of insurance to test applicants and to adjust premiums for those who test positive, but also must only use tests approved by the public health commissioner. Even if applicants test positive for AIDS or have impaired immune systems, insurers will be obligated to provide coverage for them on the same basis as for all other applicants.

Impact on the Insurance Industry
If, as most authorities believe, at least one million people have already been infected with the AIDS virus, the worst is yet to come. The 18,000 AIDS cases to date will pale when compared to a possible 300,000 or more cases in the next few years.

Any estimate of the impact of AIDS on the insurance industry must be recognized as being highly speculative at this time. As AIDS is a relatively new disease there is very little data with which to work. Additionally, many insurance companies do not have the mechanisms in place to capture AIDS related data.

The Health Insurance Association of America (HIAA) has just concluded its survey of AIDS claim experience as reported by two-thirds of its member companies. The total payout to date on reported claims approximates $100 million. The period covered for these expenses is non-specific. It represents a mix of claims first reported in 1985 and early 1986. Not included in the survey are ARC claims. The number of claims reported were rather small; however, based on this survey, the following claim cost information was developed:

Claim Type	Number of Claims	Average Claim Cost	Total Claim Cost
Medical	514	$38,000	$19,532,000
Life	906	$32,000	$28,992,000
Disability	235	$29,000	$ 6,815,000

One reason for the small number of reported cases is the difficulty companies had in identifying and capturing their AIDS claim experience. Additionally, the CDC estimates a 20 percent under reporting of AIDS cases. Thus it is likely that the total claims payout significantly exceeds $100 million.

Of interest in the survey is the $38,000 figure reported for medical care. This represents in-hospital and out-of-hospital expenses and is significantly lower than the $147,000 CDC estimate of average medical expenses for AIDS patients. The large discrepancy might be accounted for by the introduction of medical case man-

Exhibit 1 (continued)

agement for these claims. Some insurance companies have reported that case management has reduced claim costs from $140,000 to $40,000. Another contributing factor to the discrepancy may be the muddled clinical picture of what AIDS is and how you extract it from a claims data base. Thus, it is likely that the $38,000 figure represents under reporting as companies may not have captured all claim experience or anticipated future experience. The correct figure more likely is somewhere between $40,000 and $100,000.

Assuming HIAA's figures are a reasonable estimate of what is happening, the average claimant cost (the total of life, medical and disability) is at least $100,000. Multiplying this figure by 300,000, the industry is looking at, at least, a $30 billion dollar payout in the next several years and an even greater payout if the number of cases is in excess of 300,000 which is possible, especially if AIDS spreads to the general population. It should also be remembered that these projected costs do not include ARC claims.

The study also found that AIDS claims were heavily concentrated during the period in the first and second years after issue of a life insurance policy. Twenty-two percent of AIDS death claims by amount were in each of the first two policy years. This pattern suggests that persons bought life insurance who knew or suspected that they were infected by the AIDS virus. The inherent danger of this situation to life insurance companies, and the lack of fairness to other policyholders who must support the resulting claims costs, is obvious.

While the death benefit for all incurred claims due to AIDS averaged $33,471, 97 of 1,024 reported claims were for $100,000 or more, 28 were for $200,000 to $300,000, 3 for $500,000 to $600,000 and 3 claims were for $1 million. These figures underline the potentially disastrous financial impact of a handful of large claims from persons who apply for life insurance with the knowledge that they have been infected by the AIDS virus.

It is also likely that the total claim amounts are understated due to the lack of specific identification and coding of some death claims that were, in fact, caused by the AIDS virus.

Chapter 3

Issues Confronting Management Accounting—Part II

. . . the field of cost management is both broad and rather loosely defined. The best approach to a definition I can find appears in the book *Cost Management for Today's Advanced Manufacturing*. Its effort to define cost management confirms the fuzzy nature of the term:

> To some, it means cost accounting and the determination of product cost. To others, it means the measurement of nonfinancial, operational factors of production. Still others say it is management accounting and therefore totally separate from external reporting requirements.[1]

The confusion about what constitutes cost management is understandable because it is a new field that combines elements from three older fields:

- Management accounting;
- Production; and
- Strategic planning.[2]

---

[1] C. Berliner and J. A. Brimson, eds., *Cost Management for Today's Advanced Manufacturing* (Boston: Harvard Business School Press, 1988), p. 41.

[2] This is part of the introduction by Robin Cooper to *Emerging Practices in Cost Management*, Barry Brinker, ed. (Boston: Warren, Gorham, & Lamont, 1990), p. xiii. This volume is a good compendium of various aspects of cost management.

The terms *strategic cost management* and *cost management* are prevalent in the literature. As shown above, they are umbrella terms that incorporate a broader spectrum of interest than what we had thought of as traditional management or cost accounting. In Chapter 2, we looked at one part of cost management: costs related to products as organized for use in financial accounting and in managerial decision making. Inherent in the discussion of activity-based costing (ABC) and other subjects in Chapter 2 is the notion that accounting information is to serve decision makers as they pursue the strategic goals of an organization. In this chapter, we look at some of the broader issues confronting managers and management accountants as we adjust to an ever more dynamic manufacturing and competitive environment. Here we examine more general management philosophies, such as the Theory of Constraints (TOC), just-in-time (JIT), and total quality control (TQC), as well as other aspects of cost management, such as life-cycle costing and value chains. We will tie these ideas to those in the previous chapter as well as discuss how they are related to other topics that follow. As with the discussion of ABC, the objective here is to examine these ideas and to ask questions about them.

VALUE CHAINS

As a framework to help organize what follows, we first present the idea of value chains. Shank and Govindarajan define a *value chain* for any firm as "the linked set of value creating activities all the way from basic raw material sources through to the ultimate end-use product delivered into the final consumers' hands."[3] An example would be the value chain that brings this book into your hands. It starts with land and forest management for the raw resources needed to make paper, petroleum exploration and drilling coupled with other chemical processes to make ink, and the raw resources needed for glues and other materials. This stream goes through the manufacture of the basic materials that make up this book and intersects with the chain linking the author's creativity through press-ready copy. Finally, there is the printing and binding of the book as well as the production of any support materials (for example, solutions manual, computer software). Although in some cases the entire chain might be accomplished by a single company, in most cases companies choose what part of the chain to pursue. For this book, there are paper and ink companies, a publishing company, an author, a printer, a binder, various companies associated with the

---

[3] John K. Shank and Vijay Govindarajan, "Strategic Cost Management: The Value Chain Perspective," *Journal of Management Accounting Research*, Vol 4, Fall 1992 (Sarasota, Fla.: American Accounting Association), pp. 179–197.

transportation of the book and related materials, and, finally, the store from which it was originally purchased.

Companies make choices about where they are in the value chain. These are strategic planning issues since such decisions set the tone for the resources needed given the mission of the firm. Such decisions are usually based on maximizing a company's strengths. In addition, once managers have chosen a particular position in the value chain (and evaluated that position vis-à-vis their competitors), there are other decisions about how to interact with what is happening upstream (anything before it gets to the company) or downstream (anything that comes after in the chain). Some of these decisions are not in the control of a company.

Being strong in a particular area is not enough to guarantee success. Firms must have strengths that improve their capability to compete in the market place. Although there are many different types of strategic moves that can put a company in a good position relative to its rivals, all successful competitive strategies boil down to two basic approaches.

1. Firms can compete on the basis of offering the best price for a good product. In order to turn a profit using this strategy (which is called *cost leadership*), firms must have lower costs than their competitors.
2. Firms can offer a unique product that customers are willing to pay more for. This type of strategy is called *differentiation*.

For a company to gain a cost advantage over its competitors or to create a unique product, managers should *not* look at the firm as a whole to lower costs or to differentiate.[4] Instead, Porter suggests managers look at all the activities a firm performs to produce, sell, and service a product—and do a similar analysis of the activities of competitors. This is organized under Porter's value chain, which incorporates both the primary and support activities a firm performs. After creating a value chain for the firm (this corresponds to choosing what part of the value chain makes sense for the company, as discussed above), managers should assign costs to each activity. By looking at the company's costs and activities and comparing these with information about competitors, managers can design a strategy to reduce costs below those of competitors.

Deciding what part of the value chain to pursue, and then using Porter's idea of preparing a value chain, is time consuming. However, it ties in well with activity-based management and certainly is an important task for accountants to engage in.

To illustrate a set of choices regarding value chains, Shank and Govindarajan use the example of a printing press manufacturer who decides, given the demand of various printers, to make a press that will take paper with a width of three meters. Upstream paper manufacturers are affected since they will have to make paper that will fit these new presses. This new

---

[4] See Michael Porter, *Competitive Advantage* (New York: Free Press, 1985).

width might affect overall waste or the purchase or renovation of paper-making equipment. On the other hand, upstream decisions might affect those later in the chain. If the availability of wood for paper pulp is curtailed or expanded or if there are government regulations that require more recycled paper, price might be affected. As a result, publishers might alter the size of their products.

Value chain analysis is not limited to what part of the chain a company addresses and the relationships it makes in other parts of the chain. In addition, companies might divide their own portion of the chain into a value chain within the firm; each segment of the company would have some part of the chain. This allows a strategic management focus for segment managers, promotes the discussion and elimination of unnecessary overlap, and establishes outcome measures for segment and managerial performance evaluation.

Value chain issues and ABC/ABM seem to work together. Once a particular part of the chain is chosen and links established both upstream and down, then resources are put into place and traced with appropriate drivers. The value chain provides the basic strategic planning link while ABC and ABM involve the day-to-day administration of the strategies to accomplish overall goals and objectives. Chapter 12 discusses strategic planning in more detail.

Many companies talk about *value added* (the cost to convert raw materials into finished products). As discussed in Chapter 2, a midwestern printing company looks at revenue less the cost of paper as VAM (value-added manufacturing). Value added seems to focus attention only on what happens within a company rather than identifying and working with what happens before and after a product passes through that company's portion of the value chain. At a midwestern printing company specializing in newsstand publications, managers work with paper and ink companies to make sure raw materials purchased are completely compatible with the company's printing and binding equipment and can fulfill customer needs. In addition, management works with different parts of the distribution channel to lower costs and increase efficiency of delivery. If managers are evaluated solely on what happens within a single department, they might lose sight of the value chain interrelationships and overall long-term profitability would suffer.

Shank and Govindarajan point to calculational difficulties within a firm, including establishing a value for intermediate products, identifying linkages across activities, and computing an estimate of supplier and customer margins. They suggest starting with every point in the chain where an external market exists. This helps define segments of the chain and estimates of margins along the chain.

These authors propose several stages to strategic management using the value chain perspective.

1. Identify value chain stages. This includes any parts of the chain that can have an effect on the company.

2. Identify strategic options. This might mean looking at strategies for different parts of the chain within a company.
3. Assign costs and revenues to value chain stages. Trace differential costs and revenues to each stage. This might also mean estimating margins for suppliers and customers, as discussed above.
4. Estimate market-based transfer prices. If there are intermediate products, what "price" will be charged to the buying segment in the chain. (This concept is further developed in Chapter 15.)
5. Estimate investment in assets for each part of the chain.

Here is a piece in the puzzle to fit in with the concepts we review in Chapters 2 and 3. ABC/ABM, JIT, TOC, life-cycle costing, and value chains are all based on achieving long-term strategic goals.

THEORY OF CONSTRAINTS

The Theory of Constraints is proposed as a management philosophy to attain strategic goals within the portion of the value chain that a company defines for itself. Traditionally, managers have looked to measures such as net income to see if a firm is making a return. This income can be compared to a relevant set of assets employed by the firm to get return on investment (ROI) or return on net assets. Within the income statement, gross profit is supposed to show margin from the sale of products. Raw materials, in-process inventory, and finished goods inventory are treated as assets, something of future value unless they are too large. These traditional measures of return are redefined by proponents of the Theory of Constraints.

In the Theory of Constraints (TOC), managers' attention is directed to increasing *throughput* (revenue from sales less material costs for goods sold), having appropriate levels of *inventories* (all the money that the system has invested in purchasing things it intends to sell), and minimizing *operational expenses* (all the money the system spends in order to turn inventory into throughput)[5] by actively managing internal and external constraints. You can see how this differs from the traditional financial and managerial accounting models. Rather than gross margin (revenue minus fully absorbed costs of goods sold) or contribution margin (revenue minus variable costs), throughput is revenue minus only material costs. Fox defines a *constraint* as "anything that prevents the system from achieving higher performance versus its goal . . . to make money today and in the future."[6] TOC helps managers identify internal and external constraints, decide how to make the

---

[5] These definitions come from Goldratt, Eliyahu M. and Jeff Cox, *The Goal*, 2nd rev. ed. (Eli Goldratt, 1992), pp. 60–62. Please read this book for a complete background of TOC and to gain a basic understanding of Goldratt's philosophy.
[6] See Robert E. Fox, "The Constraint Theory," *Cases from Management Accounting Practice*, Vol. 8, James T. Mackey, ed. (Montvale, N.J.: Institute of Management Accountants, 1992), pp. 1–16.

best use of the constraints, subordinate other things to the exploitation of the constraints, and reduce the constraints' limitations on the system's performance.

Constraints

Let us first look at an internal constraint such as a bottleneck operation in the production process. A *bottleneck* occurs when a resource is limited so that the needs to use that resource exceed its capacity. The basic idea in TOC is to make sure that the products given first priority through the bottleneck are components and products that can be sold rather than ones that will end up sitting in process or waiting in the warehouse for some possible future need. Manufacturing constraints are identified by looking at where capacity for throughput (making products for sale, not for inventory) is less than demand. Once we identify the various constraints in the system, the next step is to see the throughput per unit of constrained resource (in dollars per hour or per person—whatever the proper measure is for that resource) for each product (or component) that passes through that constraint. This transition in thinking is similar to how we move from cost-volume-product analysis with no constraints to one with constraints.

When there are no constraints, a manager wants to maximize contribution margin by making products with the highest individual contribution margins per unit. If each product uses constrained resources equally, the same decision rule holds. However, when products use resources unequally and some resources are constrained, then we want to maximize contribution margin *per the scarce resource*. The next step is to either use some modeling program such as linear programming (as discussed in Chapter 6) or a more dynamic process such as TOC.

Fox[7] presents the following example. A company has two products called *P* and *Q*. The manufacturing process is shown in Figure 3-1. Note that all four manufacturing departments (A through D) are used to make both products. Times for each process as well as other operating data are shown in Figure 3-1.

Assume that the market will accept up to 100 P's and up to 50 Q's per week at the prices shown in Figure 3-1. Thus, if demand is met, the profit of the company will be as follows:

	P	Q	Total
Market demand potential	100 units	50 units	
Price	$ 90	$ 100	
Raw material costs	45	40	
Contribution	$ 45	$ 60	
Total contribution	$4,500	$3,000	$7,500
Operating expenses (without material)			6,000
Profit per week			$1,500

[7] Fox, "The Constraint Theory." While this example is rudimentary, it illustrates some of the basic ideas of TOC. More complex examples use computer simulation to show how TOC can be used in a dynamic environment.

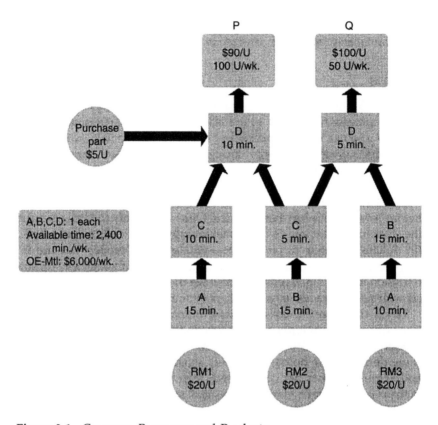

Figure 3-1 Company Resources and Products

However, there is not enough capacity to make both 100 P's and 50 Q's per week given the information in Figure 3-1. Exhibit 3-1 shows that resource B would have to produce at 125 percent of capacity in order to meet this demand. Thus, resource B is the constraint (bottleneck operation) that managers should look at first.[8]

The next step is to decide how to make the best use of the constraint. Writers such as Goldratt and Fox call this exploiting the constraint.[9] Exhibit 3-2 shows that while product Q has the higher contribution margin per unit (the better product with no constraints), product P has a higher margin per constrained resource (minutes) in resource B. This leads to the third step, subordinating everything to the fact that (1) resource B is constrained and (2) product P has the better margin in the constrained resource. Thus, managers would want to make all that the market demands per week of product P and use any remaining capacity to produce Q. The results of this decision are shown in Exhibit 3-3.

---

[8] Fox, "The Constraint Theory," Figure 4, p. 6.
[9] Fox, "The Constraint Theory."

Exhibit 3-1
Capacity Loads of Production Resources to Meet Market Demand[10]

Resource	Load/Week	Available Time/Week	Percent of Available
A	$15 \times 100 = 1,500$ $10 \times 50 = \underline{500}$ 2,000	2,400	2,000/2,400 = 83%
B	$15 \times 100 = 1,500$ $15 \times 50 = \underline{750}$ $15 \times 50 = \underline{750}$ 3,000	2,400	3,000/2,400 = 125%
C	$10 \times 100 = 1,000$ $5 \times 100 = \underline{500}$ $5 \times 50 = \underline{250}$ 1,750	2,400	1,750/2,400 = 73%
D	$10 \times 100 = 1,000$ $5 \times 50 = \underline{250}$ 1,250	2,400	1,250/2,400 = 52%

Exhibit 3-2
Margin Per Constrained Resource Minute

Product	P	Q
Price	$90	$100
Raw material costs	45	40
Contribution per unit	$45	$ 60
Time on constraint B (minutes)	15	30
Contribution per constraint minute	$ 3	$ 2

Summary of TOC Focusing Steps

Thus, to summarize, the objective of TOC is to increase throughput while managing inventories and decreasing operating expenses. The basic steps to achieve this end are to

1. Identify the constraints.
2. Decide how to make the best use of the constraints.
3. Subordinate all other decisions to the decision in step 2.
4. Reduce the constraints' limitations on the system's performance.
5. Go back to step 1.

---

[10] Fox, "The Constraint Theory," Figure 5, p. 7.

Exhibit 3-3
Projected Profit Maximizing Constrained Resource B

Product	P	Q	
Potential demand	100	50	
Resource B—produce maximum P	15 × 100 = 1,500 minutes		
Balance left of resource B	2,400 – 1,500 = 900 minutes		
Use balance to produce Q	900/30 = 30 units		
Produce given constraint	100	30	
Contribution per unit	$ 45	$ 60	
Total contribution	$4,500	$1,800	$6,300
Operating expenses (less materials)			6,000
Weekly profit			$ 300

We have illustrated steps 1–3 above. Step 4 could be accomplished by increasing capacity through additional resources for the constraint or changing the way the constraint is used.

Our illustration is for an internal physical constraint (as opposed to an external constraint, such as market demand or material availability, or an internal policy constraint). If the constraint were to be in the marketplace, the same type of analysis would hold; the measures and remedies would be modified to take the new constraint into account. Once one constraint is dealt with, others become binding and the process goes on indefinitely (step 5).

TOC, Continuous Improvement, and Dynamic Environment

Authors and managers who discuss TOC applications warn that this is not a one-time process. Recently, a manager of a manufacturing company that makes replacement parts for agricultural equipment told of his company's use of TOC. The initial results were excellent; profitability went up and orders were met on time. However, after this initial success, the managers became complacent and thought their work was done. They did not realize once their original constraints were handled other constraints would appear. They focused efforts on those original constraints, which were no longer a problem, and did not address new ones. Thus, one important component of TOC is continuous improvement and the realization that the process never stops: new constraints keep emerging.

A second part of the story is the dynamic nature of TOC in actual operations. Constraints are not as static as the illustration above might imply. During the normal course of production, there are shifts in sales demand, customer needs, capacity (breakdowns, downtime for preventative maintenance), need for trained employees for specific functions, transportation options, and other internal and external variables. TOC envisions a dynamic management process that can adapt almost instantaneously to changes in the environment. Training modules for TOC employ simulations where several variables can and do change, thus directing a manager's attention to a new constraint and training the manager to use the five-step process to deal with it. TOC and modeling techniques such as linear programming share an emphasis on constraints, but TOC emphasizes the dynamic nature of binding constraints. As we will see in Chapter 6, linear programming usually deals with more static sets of constraints.

The concept of value chains and the decisions that seem to result from it are linked with TOC. In TOC managers are directed to look at constraints. It's not set-up time in general on which to focus but, rather, set-up time on a constrained resource. A manager puts much more effort in increasing production output from a constrained resource than on one that has significant excess capacity. In the same regard, looking at the value chain within a company allows managers to identify opportunities to help the company's overall competitive position and long-term profitability. Funds might be cut from one area and added to another if the result is appropriate to the long-term strategy and the portion of the chain the company has chosen to address.

Accounting Information and TOC

TOC is unconcerned with tracing costs. The quotation from Goldratt at the beginning of Chapter 2 illustrates his concern with traditional cost accounting. Goldratt has classified everything into throughput (T), inventories (I), and operating expenses (OE). He proposes that there is a problem in product costs (used for financial accounting) and the terminology that accompanies such cost measurements.[11] After criticizing the allocation process used in product costs for financial accounting, he reorganizes the notion of net profit (NP) as follows:

$$NP = \Sigma_p(T - OE)_p$$

This equation takes financial accounting net income and recasts it using TOC terms. Income becomes the sum of the separate incomes from each of the products that are made and sold. With a gross margin (part of income) per product, Goldratt says this equation implies that a company can think individually about profits on a product-by-product basis. He poses that profit is something that applies only to the company. He wants us to eliminate from our vocabulary terms such as *product margin* and *product cost*. Even *contribution margin* is a suspect term: contribution margin calculations contain labor and variable overhead, and TOC advocates argue that such costs

---

[11] This discussion comes mainly from Eliyahu M. Goldratt, *Sifting Information Out of the Data Ocean: The Haystack Syndrome* (New Haven, Conn.: North River Press, 1990), Chapter 8.

are plantwide and are fixed in the short run. Instead, Goldratt wants managers to concentrate on throughput (which only includes the material costs associated with a product) and on operating expenses as a whole.

In Chapter 2 we discussed issues of allocation versus attribution as well as tracing costs under ABC and including only attributable costs at the facility level. In addition, we proposed an organizing framework that considers costs based on the way they are utilized (valuing inventories for financial accounting, making decisions about products, controlling the enterprise, and looking at special studies).

For many operating managers, planning and performance measures are tied to the basic product costs their companies generate for financial reporting. We can see from previous discussion that product costs using the traditional cost accounting model are suspect. Thus, performance measures based on these costs might motivate managers to make poor decisions. Goldratt's request that we do away with our cost terms and concentrate our attention on throughput, inventories, and operating expenses seems in concert with the basic thrust of ABC and ABM: seeing how resources came into place and controlling the activities that caused them. (However, ABC does not focus on constrained resources.) The questions that Goldratt asks can be answered under the framework of ABC while not neglecting the basics of TOC. He defines information as "an answer to the question asked."[12] The organizing ideas proposed in Chapter 2 seem to fulfill this definition.

JUST-IN-TIME

Just-in-time (JIT) is a management approach that not only deals with reducing inventory costs, something akin to a focus of TOC, but also presents a way to think about the manufacturing process in general. JIT is coupled in many cases with Kanban and with other approaches from Japanese management philosophies. Foster and Horngren state that JIT "is a philosophy that focuses on performing activities as they are needed by other internal segments of an organization."[13]

JIT inventory and production is not a new concept. Its basis is having inventory available only when it is needed. For example, for a local bottler of soft drinks empty bottles take up space, have little value by themselves, and are costly to store. It has been the norm for years to have the bottle suppliers deliver bottles as they are needed on the production line, so in that respect, part of the philosophy of JIT has been around a long time. The

---

[12] Goldratt, *Sifting Information*, p. 85.

[13] George Foster and Charles T. Horngren, "Cost Accounting and Cost Management in a JIT Environment," *Emerging Practices in Cost Management*, Barry J. Brinker, ed. (Boston: Warren, Gorham, & Lamont, 1990), pp. 199–209.

recent emphasis on JIT involves more than delivery of goods to a purchaser so that they are used immediately instead of stockpiled; the philosophy now involves all aspects of purchasing and manufacturing.

Let us take a company with a single product that goes through five departments before it gets to the shipping department. As goods in the shipping department reach a specific level (reorder point), finished goods are produced by Department 5. As components in Department 5 fall below a certain level, Department 4 works to replenish them. This same set of signals goes all the way back to the purchasing function. This is called a *pull* system; nothing is done until needed by the next department. The opposite is a *push* system where production is scheduled to fill capacity, which often results in large in-process and finished goods inventories. Often bottlenecks appear as several orders try to make it through a binding constraint. With a pull system, the date of delivery is used as a starting point and everything is coordinated and scheduled back through the production process to make sure that date is achieved. In addition, push systems are often linked with performance measures valuing working at or near capacity. Managers are often motivated to make components that are easy and efficient to manufacture to fill capacity effectively even when there might not be a need for these components for many months in the future. Current work might be sacrificed in order to accomplish a long production run of such components.

Part of this concept is to reduce in-process inventories as much as possible and to reduce all support department costs. Such costs are *non-value added* since they are not part of actually converting raw materials into final products. Proponents of JIT argue that the reason many companies keep large buffers of work in process is to even out scheduling and to adjust for parts that are rejected during inspection. Thus, if a company attacks its scheduling problems and has higher quality, it can substantially reduce or eliminate work-in-process inventories.

Work flow and scheduling have at least two dimensions. First, many companies organize their productive facilities by machine type (functional). This means that in-process goods must travel from department to department, as the process to complete them requires machines of different kinds. Although in some firms this makes sense, in others such a layout causes high inventories. It takes time to store goods, remove them from storage, and transport them around the plant. Second, the focus on cost centers and individual worker performance and responsibility can contribute to uneven and inflexible scheduling. The top part of Figure 3-2 shows a traditional shop floor. Pockets of inventory develop and staging areas are needed because of all the work to move in-process inventory around the plant.

The manufacturing cell helps managers eliminate work in process. A cell is a minifactory within the plant, consisting of all the machinery and people needed to manufacture a specific group of components. Rather than a component going back and forth to different machine areas, all the machinery

Conventional

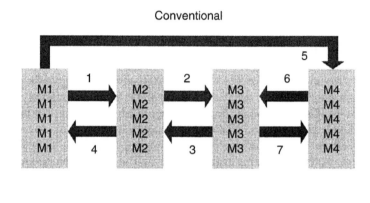

Cell

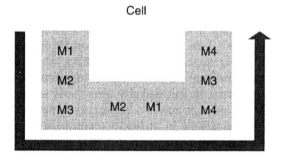

Figure 3-2   Conventional and Cell Manufacturing

for one or more types of component is brought to one place. As part of the change to manufacturing cells, workers typically are part of a cell production team. No longer is one person responsible for one type of machine while another is responsible for another type; now, all the workers within a manufacturing cell cross-train and work on all positions within the cell. Thus, idle time is reduced and work in process is virtually eliminated. In one midwestern plant making parts for the replacement automotive market, the change to cells freed up almost one-third of the plant and allowed the parent company to move a production line to that plant from another of their facilities. The bottom portion of Figure 3-2 represents a cell environment.

Kanban

A technique for managing JIT is Kanban; there must be some regular signal that tells managers when to produce and how much to produce. Briefly, a *Kanban* is a tag that is attached to the containers or racks on which components are kept. Let us again use the example of a company with a single product that must pass through five producing departments. Assume that we are dealing with Department 3. As soon as parts in a container supplying Department 3 are being used, a worker takes the Kanban (tag) and places it in a box with other Kanban for that component. As with other techniques for a reorder point, managers preset a number of Kanban as a signal that replenishment is needed. Empty containers and the same number of Kanban are taken to the prior department, Department 2. An equal number of full containers are withdrawn from Department 2. Each of these new containers has a production Kanban attached to it. The worker who is withdrawing these containers takes the production Kanban and the Kanban she has brought with her (withdrawal Kanban) and places them into a box within Department 2. These are accumulated in Department 2 until a predetermined level is reached signaling production of the component. Components produced by Department 2 are kept in Department 2 until Department 3 withdraws them as described above. This same process flows from the shipping area back to the purchasing function.

Push versus Pull Inventories

JIT and Kanban *pull* inventory through production. In the strictest sense, the only department that knows a production schedule is the shipping department. All other departments produce based on inventory being pulled from the end of the production line; they manufacture only to meet a need. This is contrasted to a push system where goods are manufactured for inventory, the production schedule is known throughout the plant, and manufacturing is geared toward a daily output figure in every department.

Advocates of the pull system claim to have better line balancing; there is less buffer inventory and better utilization of capacity, which causes multiple savings. Not only are there savings in raw material, work in process, and finished goods inventories (and their attendant use of space and support costs), but also a more balanced line means that less overall capacity is needed, which means a lower investment in capital and human resources. Part and parcel of this process is worker flexibility. In order for JIT to work properly, workers have to be able to move from one area to another (even outside their cells) to go where they are needed.

JIT and Cost Management

Foster and Horngren propose four fundamental aspects of JIT:

1. Managers would eliminate all resources and activities that do not add value to a product.
2. Quality is paramount and rework is virtually eliminated.
3. Managers strive for continuous improvement in efficiency.
4. The visibility of value-added activities versus non-value-added ones increases so that it is clear when JIT objectives are being met.

They go on to say that JIT helps in getting more accurate cost information since managers focus on resources and tracing (i.e., JIT is compatible with

ABC).[14] This allows the same kind of management attention to resources that is proposed both by ABC and TOC ideas.

However, as with ABC, Goldratt has criticisms of JIT. On the one hand, he lauds the fact that JIT and TQM (total quality management) make managers look at inventories as a burden rather than an asset. On the other hand, he accuses JIT practitioners of acting as if all resources are independent: it is just as good to reduce lead time in one operation as it is in any other; reducing set-up times, per se, is good. Goldratt argues there are interdependent resources and variables. With a resource that is not a constraint (and might never be one), there is no advantage to reducing set-up time or increasing throughput: there is no opportunity cost[15] associated with these actions. He calls his approach a change from looking at the *cost world* to the *throughput world*.[16]

While some authors might propose that looking at the new alphabet soup of ABC, TOC, and JIT, for example, means mutually exclusive alternatives, others argue that we are really looking at different dimensions and approaches to the same problem: how to be profitable in the long run given an ever changing internal and external environment. Thus, operating managers should understand the basics of all of these ideas and adopt the particular hybrid that suits their company's particular needs. More than ever before, it is important for management accountants to be innovative and flexible in their approaches to measuring costs and success.

LIFE-CYCLE COSTING

Another way to organize thinking within a value chain is to look at life-cycle costing. All products go through a life cycle starting with the research and development stage that precedes actual introduction to the marketplace, the embryonic stage where the product begins to gain a toehold in the market, the growth stage as it expands to meet its potential, the mature stage where it is no longer new or unique but holds its place, and the final stage, aging, where managers decide when it is best to cease production and to use resources for other things. Life cycles can be quite short or lengthy. Compare, for example, LED watches with basic steelmaking in the United States. LED watches were the rage for about a year until LCD watches replaced them; they went from introduction to withdrawal in that time period. In contrast, the basic process for making steel has not changed for decades. The industry has slowly moved from mature to aging, but only recently has there been a threat from foreign competition that might lead to ending production.

---

[14] Foster and Horngren, "Cost Accounting," p. 199.
[15] Note, however, that if workers are cross-trained, there is an opportunity cost.
[16] Goldratt, *Sifting Information*, Chapter 10.

As we shall see in Chapter 14 on segment performance evaluation, the life cycle of the technology and products made at a division or segment of a company have an effect on how that segment should be evaluated. Our focus here, however, is on costs associated with product life cycles and how to treat them for both cost of products for managerial decision making and operational control.[17]

Before a product is ready for market, the company typically has invested in research and development of the product itself, manufacturing techniques to be used to make its components, and programming for numerically controlled machines used in its manufacture. In addition, besides the costs to make a product, there are traceable nonmanufacturing costs. The company has incurred market research costs, current marketing costs, costs of developing channels of distribution, and after-sales service costs. All the costs associated with the product must somehow be amortized over the life of the product for long-run profitability.

The main problem in associating costs (even traceable ones) with a product is determining if the costs are sunk and, therefore, not relevant for product decisions. Consider research and development or market research costs. Managers find that a significant portion of these kinds of costs do not result in a salable product. Decisions to proceed or to cease development are regularly made on all sorts of products. Our basic instinct is to make sure that such decisions are based on incremental revenues and costs and that sunk costs are ignored. How, then, can we argue that sunk costs should be part of product life-cycle costs and should be recovered over a product's existence? Unfortunately, as we pointed out in Chapter 2, we have this same problem in ABC when we look at other sunk costs such as depreciation associated with machinery traceable to a particular product or product group. It is this separability of costs by products that Goldratt criticizes.

We can start to solve this problem by looking at how we analyze decisions to purchase a significant asset, a subject that will be dealt with in Chapter 13. In a capital budgeting analysis, managers look at all the costs associated with a project from its inception to its end. This is really life-cycle costing with a present value weighing such costs against potential benefits. From a financial point of view, if a proposal has a negative net present value at the appropriate discount rate, it should be rejected at least from the quantitative financial perspective. Even if there are no new assets to be put into place for a new product, the same kind of analysis would also be appropriate. Is a proposed product at its proposed price coupled with preproduction, production, and distribution/service costs going to be profitable?

Japanese companies have been adept at what is called *product churning*: the same basic product (say, a video camera) is repackaged with a few nonconsequential changes. The object is to make customers perceive this as a completely new and advanced product; this scheme seems to have worked.

---

[17] We will not deal with how such costs are treated for financial accounting purposes.

These firms are quite effective in very short product life cycles. This places pressure on competitors who might become confused about where to jump into the market. What features should they include? Will they accurately guess the next new version of their competitors' product or be perceived by customers as being behind the time?

Product churning results in very short life cycles. While there are some positive aspects of this practice, it is interesting to see reports in the press that profitability is suffering at some of these companies. These press reports state that managers are going to begin relying more on American analytical techniques such as discounted cash flow analysis. In essence, then, these companies will be looking at life-cycle costing. The basic idea of life-cycle costing is in harmony with ABC: we are focusing managers' attention on resources and the activities that cause those resources to be in place. In addition, life-cycle costing and value chains are quite similar in their emphasis.

FIELD RESEARCH

Many of the ideas in Chapters 2 and 3 come from observations in the field. What are practicing managers doing to adjust to the changing environment? There is a renewed interest today in what is called field research to find out what companies are doing, what works, and what does not seem to be working. Most new ideas in management come from practicing managers, and academics can aid in the process by observing, recording, and working with managers as change evolves. We can help synthesize what we are seeing in the field so that others can learn without going through the pain of experience. Much of what is written about ABC is based on extensive field research. Shank and Govindarajan base their ideas in part on what they observed in the field. Goldratt wrote about TOC after seeing companies struggle with constrained resources and trying to help them.

Chapters 2 and 3 highlight some of the results of current field research. Other studies are found in later chapters. You are encouraged to read the original work of these authors and to explore the idea of field research as a way to gain an understanding of both problems and solutions. By looking at what is happening and the various proposals to address current problems, you can integrate these ideas and choose those parts that seem appropriate in a given situation.

SUMMARY

Chapters 2 and 3 cover some emerging ideas in cost management. We have covered such subjects as activity-based costing, Theory of Constraints, and just-in-time. In this chapter, we present the concepts of value chains and strategic management as a framework for these and other techniques or management philosophies. As part of establishing the goals and objectives of a company, managers choose where a segment or the entire company fits in the value chain.

The Theory of Constraints is a way that managers can focus on any binding constraint and opportunity costs associated with that constraint. By subordinating all other decisions to that constraint and then working to modify or eliminate the constraint, they can adapt to a dynamic environment and achieve the long-run strategies of the company. Just-in-time is another method to achieve strategic goals. JIT focuses attention on inventory management and the opportunity cost associated with significant in-process inventories. Such a philosophy fits in well with shifts to cell manufacturing. Finally, life-cycle costing allows managers to look at resources needed depending on the stage in a product or product group's life cycle. All three of these ideas allow managers to concentrate on strategic management.

PROBLEMS AND CASES

3-1. Job Order and Process Costing

After a discussion of job order costing and the objective of recording the cost of material, labor, and overhead by job, John Y. Lee states the following about job order costing with the new manufacturing technology:

> In a flexible manufacturing environment . . . , workers (and even materials) are frequently transferred between job orders to insure a smooth flow of process. This will certainly upset the accounting department's attempt to trace the costs of three elements to different job orders.[18]

Required:
1. How will job order costing be affected by production cells and computer-integrated manufacturing? Expand on the comments by Lee and explore other areas as well.
2. How will process costing be affected? Will JIT affect process costing differently from job order costing?

3-2. Just-In-Time Inventory

The management of Prima Manufacturing is considering switching to just-in-time inventory. Besides the changes in plant layout and materials flow during the production process, information has been gathered on raw material costs as follows:

	Current	Just-in-Time
Average investment in materials	$6,900,000	$1,380,000
Annual freight charges	$ 470,000	$1,615,000
Ordering costs	$ 37,000	$ 96,000

---

[18] John Y. Lee, *Managerial Accounting Changes for the 1990s*, McKay Business Systems (1987), p. 50.

Just-in-time inventory would mean a much more frequent delivery schedule than is currently in place. Managers estimate that inventory carrying costs are 22 percent of inventory value.

Required:
1. What is just-in-time inventory? Explain how this concept goes beyond shorter delivery schedules for raw materials.
2. Should Prima Manufacturing adopt a just-in-time policy?
3. Recommend and demonstrate some sensitivity analysis on the figures you used to solve part 2.

3-3. Just-in-Time (CMA)

The management at Megafilters Inc. has been discussing the possible implementation of a just-in-time (JIT) production system at its Illinois plant, where oil filters and air filters for heavy construction equipment and large, off-the-road vehicles are manufactured. The Metal Stamping Department at the Illinois plant has already instituted a JIT system for controlling raw materials inventory, but the remainder of the plant is still discussing how to proceed with the implementation of this concept. Some of the other department managers have grown increasingly cautious about the JIT process after hearing about the problems that have arisen in the Metal Stamping Department.

Robert Goertz, manager of the Illinois plant, is a strong proponent of the JIT production system, and recently made the following statement at a meeting of all departmental managers. "Just-in-time is often referred to as a management philosophy of doing business rather than a technique for improving efficiency on the plant floor. We will all have to make many changes in the way we think about our employees, our suppliers, and our customers if we are going to be successful in using just-in-time procedures. Rather than dwelling on some of the negative things you have heard from the Metal Stamping Department, I want each of you to prepare a list of things we can do to make a smooth transition to the just-in-time philosophy of management for the rest of the plant."

Required:
1. The just-in-time (JIT) management philosophy emphasizes objectives for the general improvement of a production system. Describe several important objectives of this philosophy.
2. Discuss several actions that Megafilters Inc. can take to ease the transition to a just-in-time (JIT) production system at the Illinois plant.
3. In order for the just-in-time (JIT) production system to be successful, Megafilters Inc. must establish appropriate relationships with its vendors, employees, and customers. Describe each of these three relationships.

3-4. Implementing Just-in-Time (CMA)

Over the past several years, many companies have made the decision to implement a just-in-time (JIT) production system. There have been varying degrees of success with JIT as the implementation process is dependent on many factors such as management commitment to the process and employee acceptance of the process. In addition, a company must be willing to change the way it thinks about its employees, suppliers, and customers if it is going to be successful in using JIT procedures.

Required:
1. In general, describe several actions that a company can take to facilitate an organizational change.
2. To ensure the success of a just-in-time (JIT) production system, describe the relationship a company must establish with its
   a. suppliers.
   b. customers, and
   c. employees.
3. The success of a JIT production system requires changes in management skills and behavior.
   a. Describe at least two changes in management skills and management behavior that will be required to ensure a successful transition to a JIT production system.
   b. Identify several steps a company can take to achieve the changes described in Requirement 3.a above.

3-5. Changing Cost Information (CMA)

Dartmoor Inc.'s main business is the publication of books and magazines. Alan Shane is the production manager of the Bridgton Plant which manufactures the paper used in all of Dartmoor's publications. The Bridgton Plant has no sales staff and limited contact with outside customers as most of its sales are to other divisions of Dartmoor. As a consequence, the Bridgton Plant is treated as a cost center for reporting and evaluation purposes rather than as a revenue or profit center.

Shane perceives the accounting reports that he receives to be the result of an historical number generating process that provides little information that is useful in performing his job. Consequently, the entire accounting process is perceived as a negative motivational device that does not reflect how hard or effectively he works as a production manager. In discussions with Susan Brady, controller of the Bridgton Plant, Shane said, "I think the cost reports are misleading. I know I've had better production over a number of operating periods, but the cost reports still say I have excessive costs. Look, I'm not an accountant; I'm a production manager. I know how to get a good quality product out. Over a number of years, I've even cut the raw materials used to do it. The cost reports don't show any of this; they're always negative, no matter what I do. There's no way you can win with accounting or the people at headquarters who use these reports."

Brady gave Shane little consolation when she stated that the accounting system and the cost reports generated by headquarters are just part of the corporate game and almost impossible for an individual to change. "Although these reports are used to evaluate your division and the means headquarters uses to determine whether you have done the job they want, you shouldn't worry too much. You haven't been fired yet! Besides, these cost reports have been used by Dartmoor for the last 15 years."

From discussions with the operations people at other Dartmoor divisions, Shane knew that the turnover of production managers at the company was high, even though relatively few were fired. Typical comments of production managers who have left Dartmoor follow.

"Corporate headquarters never really listened. All they consider are those monthly cost reports. They don't want them changed, and they don't want any supplementary information."

"The accountants may be quick with numbers but they don't know anything about production. I wound up completely ignoring the cost reports. No matter what they say about not firing people, negative reports mean negative evaluations. I'm better off working for another company."

A copy of the most recent cost report prepared for the Bridgton Plan is shown below.

	Bridgton Plant Cost Report Month of November 19X1 (in thousands)		
	Master Budget	Actual Cost	Excess Cost
Raw material	$ 400	$ 437	$37
Direct labor	560	540	(20)
Overhead	100	134	34
Total	$1,060	$1,111	$51

Required:
1. Discuss Alan Shane's perception of
    a. Susan Brady, controller;
    b. corporate headquarters;
    c. the cost report; and
    d. himself as a production manager.

Include in your discussion how Shane's perceptions affect his behavior and performance as a production manager and employee of Dartmoor Inc.

2. Identify and explain at least three changes that could be made in the cost information presented to the production managers that would make the information more meaningful and less threatening to them.

3-6. Bottleneck Operation (CMA)

Bakker Industries sells three products (Products 611, 613, and 615) which it manufactures in a factory consisting of four departments (Departments 1 through 4). Both labor and machine time are applied to the products in each of the four departments. The machine processing and labor skills required in each department is such that neither machines nor labor can be switched from one department to another.

Bakker's management is planning its production schedule for the next several months. There are labor shortages in the community. Some of the machines will be out of service for extensive overhauling. Available machine and labor time by department for each of the next six months is listed below.

Monthly Capacity Availability	Department			
	1	2	3	4
Normal machine capacity in machine hours	3,500	3,500	3,000	3,500
Capacity of machines being repaired in machine hours	(500)	(400)	(300)	(200)
Available machine capacity in machine hours	3,000	3,100	2.700	3,300
Labor capacity in direct labor hours	4,000	4,500	3,500	3,000
Available labor in direct labor hours	3,700	4,500	2,750	2,600

Labor and Machine Specifications per Unit of Product					
Product	Labor and Machine time				
611	Direct labor hours	2	3	3	1
	Machine hours	2	1	2	2
613	Direct labor hours	1	2	—	2
	Machine hours	1	1	—	2
615	Direct labor hours	2	2	1	1
	Machine hours	2	2	1	1

The Sales Department's forecast of product demand over the next six months is presented below.

Product	Monthly Sales Volume
611	500 units
613	400
615	1,000

Bakker's inventory levels will not be increased or decreased during the next six months. The unit price and cost data valid for the next six months are presented on the next page.

Required:
1. Determine if the monthly sales demand for the three products can be met by Bakker Industries' factory. Use the monthly requirement by department for machine hours and direct labor hours for the production of Products 611, 613, and 615 in your calculations.
2. What monthly production schedule should Bakker Industries select in order to maximize its dollar profits? Support the schedule with appropriate calculations, and present a schedule of the contribution to profit that would be generated by the production schedule selected.

	Product		
	611	613	615
Unit Costs:			
Direct material	$ 7	$ 13	$ 17
Direct labor			
Department 1	12	6	12
Department 2	21	14	14
Department 3	24	—	16
Department 4	9	18	9
Variable overhead	27	20	25
Fixed overhead	15	10	32
Variable selling	3	2	4
Unit selling price	$196	$123	$167

3-7. Stanadyne Diesel Systems (A)[19]

The problem facing most manufacturers is that their facilities are not structured to meet the demands of a global marketplace, and there are many roadblocks that make the transition to an automated factory difficult. One of the most important, but least understood of these roadblocks is current cost management systems. These systems do not provide companies with the financial information necessary to manage the transition to a factory of the future.

James Brimson, 1986

Background

Stanadyne Diesel Systems manufactures and markets complex precision metal products and components of foreign and domestic industrial consumer goods. Its major products include diesel pumps, nozzles, fuel heaters, mechanical tappets, and related products used in the production of industrial and automotive diesel engines.

Stanadyne has experienced roller-coaster demand for its products in the 1980s. During the gasoline crisis, automobile manufacturers and consumers alike turned to diesel-powered automobiles to combat the high cost of gasoline. In conjunction with a major automobile manufacturer, the company embarked on a program of rapid expansion of production capacity to meet projected demand. Production peaked in 1984. The Plant Manager, Gene Brady, put it this way:

At the peak of production, we just couldn't hire people fast enough. Every day the plant foreman would run up to personnel to see if any qualified people had come in to interview. We were taking just about anybody, just to make sure we could keep up with the orders. And, we were managing by the seat of our pants. The growth was just too fast—everything was out of control.

---

[19] This case used by permission of the Institute of Management Accountants. IMA or IMA adapted.

This situation was not long-lived, though. Americans never truly came to love the diesel engine, especially the one containing Stanadyne parts. Due to quality problems with other components of the engine, the number and frequency of breakdowns put the product into an early grave. For the automobile manufacturer, a loss was incurred. For Stanadyne, it meant not only a substantial, and perhaps fatal, loss of business, but also a downturn exacerbated by extreme overcapacity. The company had invested a substantial amount in expanded capacity for which there was then no need.

A Unique Culture

Stanadyne is the direct descendent of a traditional metal-working job shop. In its early years it made various types of screws and bolts, using machinery quite advanced for its time. When talking about the company, managers refer to the impact the "job shop" mentality continues to have on the daily operations of the business.

Stanadyne has a strong, ingrown culture. This culture has its roots in its founders—individuals who worked as machinists prior to making the leap into owning their own business. Before its takeover by a conglomerate in 1987, the firm was able to boast a history of consistent promotion through the ranks. In fact, every president prior to 1987 started in the plant as a day worker. It is not a company characterized by ties and jackets, but rather by dirty hands and hard work.

The focus on promotion from within makes Stanadyne a unique company. Managers, from top to bottom, are "lifers." Most have never worked for another company. These individuals really know the company and its capabilities, and are willing to go the extra mile to ensure that high quality products are produced and shipped on time. Because of the long-standing tenure of the managers, most decision-making is done through meetings and informal networks, rather than through mandates from the top. It is a fully participating management in which everyone has a say in the process. This is reflected in the fact that every management employee with any tie to daily production attends an 8:00 a.m. meeting during which problems are aired and resolved in open forum.

The down side of Stanadyne's culture is the very informality that keeps its employees involved. Very few operating procedures are written down. Individuals make the organization run; if one person is out, the entire system slows down. Additionally, when problems occur people rather than new practices or approaches are looked to for solutions. In this loose organizational structure, individuals who take action to solve problems often do not pass along the information to others who could enact long-term solutions.

Just-in-Time Technology: A White Knight

Given the high costs that were embedded in the facility itself, Stanadyne had to find a way to produce a low marginal cost injector of high quality if lost sales were to be recouped. Facing stiff competition for its diesel injectors abroad, and no domestic market for automotive injectors, the company sought a new approach to gain a competitive edge.

In desperate straits, management, began to listen to individuals in the firm who believed that Just-in-Time (JIT) manufacturing was the approach that Stanadyne needed. Two managers played a key role in bringing the JIT approach to the company: Bill Holbrook, then the V.P. of Materials, and Jeff Anderson, who directly managed the materials planning group. Working together, Holbrook and Anderson crafted a plan for implementing the approach. They convinced their fellow managers of the benefits of JIT and related quality control techniques, and the group pursued implementation with a vengeance.

In the implementation phase, approximately 60 percent of the plant was reorganized into JIT cells, 20 percent into "Islands of Automation" (e.g., numerically controlled machines), and the remainder along functional lines. The cells themselves range from highly sophisticated robotic lines employing Kanban, electronic sensing devices and various forms of on-line quality control to others created simply by bringing old machines together. After cells were created, management relied on production personnel to reorganize their processes to achieve further efficiency gains in the production of components and subassemblies.

Due to the implementation of JIT techniques and additional efforts to standardize its products, Stanadyne has trimmed inventories from a high of $37 million in 1984 to $15 million in 1988. This has translated into a reduction of 19,000 square feet of inventory on the plant floor. Improved quality also has been achieved, with scrap down an average of 25 percent per year since 1984 to a 1988 level of $500,000, while the number of quality control inspectors has dropped substantially, down to 15 from a high of 60. Management believes that fully 80 percent of the benefits of implementing JIT methods have resulted from moving machines together, eliminating move and queue elements of process time.

Management Accounting in a JIT Setting

A key aspect of the JIT approach is the recognition of interdependence in the manufacturing process—that is, that the entire process is linked, and is constrained by the slowest machine or work center. This is common sense, but the traditional manufacturing literature stresses reducing the impact of interdependence by putting inventory buffers between machines. By contrast, the JIT approach considers inventory to be an area of waste to be eliminated.

For the management accounting system, several changes are suggested by the move to JIT. First, enhanced visibility and product-flow throughput lead to more emphasis on operational control measures. This is reflected in the use of various measures to monitor total processing time versus the time elapsed from raw materials release to finished goods. It is also reflected in control systems that match the level of controllability. The supervisor on the plant floor can control only direct costs; upper management is responsible for indirect items. Everyone's goal is to remove waste and to gain better control of the plant's processes.

Additional changes occurring in practice include the simplification of inventory tracking (e.g., backflushing), the use of rolling averages of actual costs to monitor continuous improvement performance goals, and more widespread use of two-stage allocation processes that assign indirect costs to products based on consumption of resources instead of the use of overhead rates to spread the costs. Overall, the result is more focused and effective management accounting information systems that match the needs of the various decision-makers within the firms.

What has been the impact of JIT implementation on the management accounting system at Stanadyne? The company has made major changes in its basic plant control system. Two of the primary modifications are: (1) replacement of traditional standards-based control reports with "Business Reports," and (2) utilization of "checkbooks" for managing the plant floor. Both of these changes reflect the Controller's desire to match reporting formats with controllability criteria by focusing the attention of those who can affect change on the areas under their control. Additionally, the Controller continues to pursue the replacement of standard costs with actuals for operational control and performance evaluation, and to push this control to the lowest feasible level in the organization.

Business Reports Stanadyne has replaced its traditional full absorption cost-based reports with a contribution margin reporting format. A typical report generated by the new system is presented in Exhibit 1, whereas a traditional standards-based report, which is still generated by Stanadyne to meet corporate requirements, is shown in Exhibit 2. Maintenance of this dual system is viewed by Mike Boyer, the Controller, as follows:

> If we can't integrate with the financial accounting system we'll set up two information systems, because we have to know what it truly costs us to run the business.

The key characteristic of the revised management accounting system used by the plant is the *non*allocation of indirect costs to products. Hence, the income statement used internally to evaluate the plant's performance matches direct costs against associated revenues, and then presents indirect costs as separate, lump sum line items. This contribution margin approach focuses management's attention on items it controls while simplifying and refining the reporting process in the plant.

Exhibit 1
Business Report (000 $)

	Total	Pump	Nozzle	Filter	Other
Net Sales -OEM	2,000	1,000	500	200	300
—SERVICE	2,000	1,500	300	100	100
Total Net Sales	4,000	2,500	800	300	400
Direct Costs					
Material —OEM	800	400	150	100	150
—Service	700	500	100	50	50
—Variance	10	10	(10)	5	5
Total Material	1,510	910	240	155	205
Factory —OEM	725	400	200	75	50
—Service	525	300	100	75	50
—Variance	30	10	10	5	5
Total Factory	1,280	710	310	155	105
Direct Profit	1,210	880	250	(10)	90
Direct Profit %	30.3%	35.2%	31.3%	–3.3%	22.5%
Factory Overhead	300				
Selling & Admin.	100				
Engineering	100				
Tappet	50				
LIFO Setup	10				
Europe P/L	(2)				
Miscellaneous	252				
Income Before Taxes	400				
Return on Sales	10.0%				

Exhibit 2
Income Statement

Income Statement by Products	Dollar Amounts in Thousands			
	Total	O.E.	Service	Parts
Sales –Outside	7,500	2,500	2,500	2,500
–Subsidiary	0	0	0	0
–Intra/Inter/Subsidiary	0	0	0	0
–Returns/Allowances/Cash Disc.	0	0	0	0
Net Sales	7,500	2,500	2,500	2,500
Standard Cost of Sales				
Material Costs	750	250	250	250
Factory Costs	750	250	250	250
Non-Factory Costs	75	25	25	25
Total STD Variable Costs	1,575	525	525	525
Managed Factory	750	250	250	250
Managed Non-Factory	750	250	250	250
Committed	75	25	25	25
Total STD MGD/COMM	1,575	525	525	525
Income Per Estimate Card	4,350	1,450	1,450	1,450
Variances:				
Difference Replacement & Book Depr.	75	25	25	25
Lifo/Inv. Adj. Inflation	(75)	(25)	(25)	(25)
Inv. Discount/Selling				
Adj/Mps/Etc.	(75)	(25)	(25)	(25)
Total	(75)	(25)	(25)	(25)
Volume: Managed –Factory	75	25	25	25
–Non-Factory	(75)	(25)	(25)	(25)
Committed	75	25	25	25
Total Volume Variance	75	25	25	25
Estimate Card Variances	(75)	(25)	(25)	(25)
Spending: Variable –Material	75	25	25	25
–Factory	(75)	(25)	(25)	(25)
–Non-Factory	75	25	25	25
Managed –Factory	(75)	(25)	(25)	(25)
–Non-Factory	75	25	25	25
Committed	(75)	(25)	(25)	(25)
Total Spending Variance	0	0	0	0
Operating Income Contribution	4,275	1,425	1,425	1,425
Reserve and Inventory Adjustment				
Royalties Received	0	0	0	0
Capital Employed Income or Expense	75	25	25	25
Main Office Exp. ($584,000)				
Operating Income	4,350	1,450	1,450	1,450

The Controller's objective is to focus the accounting system on planning and control. Managers budget overhead items, and then use direct costs to control operations. The standards used to set flexible budget targets are based on ever-tightening rolling averages of actual costs. Boyer summarizes the management philosophy related to business reports in the following way:

> Why poison our outlook with full costs? We focus on controllable factors at the reporting level for managers. Putting overhead in broad buckets facilitates forecasting. Volume-based accounting measures are still used in forecasting and planning. . . . We look for a pure control approach. Namely, for each level of reporting we focus on control and traceability. . . . What we'd like to do is look at the business. We know the variable costs, and know the profit percentages we can make on these items, therefore we know how much we can afford in overhead. Our reporting system focuses on identifying those items we can change. At the top level there's little that can be done to direct costs (although on the plant floor these can be cut), but we do need to keep an eye on overhead items.

Checkbooks and Process Control   The philosophy noted above carries onto the production floor through the use of what management refers to as "checkbooks." These reports are maintained at the lowest level possible within the plant. An example checkbook is shown in Exhibit 3.

Exhibit 3
Cell Control Checkbook

Department 350
Prepared by ─────────

Vendor Name	Req. No.	Date Ordered	Part Number	Furnace Number	Qty. OD	Total Cost
Gas/Salts/Oils	Blank	10/01/86		All	0	$18,910.00
Baskets/Liners	Blank	10/01/86		All	0	3,795.50
Advanced ATM	78711	10/13/86	Carbon	Probes	3	2,345.00
Industronics	78714	10/13/86	Alnor	Cards	12	268.00
Kulas	78715	10/13/86	Type K	29"	8	145.50
Kulas	78715	10/13/86	Type K	Wire	1	132.00
Kulas	78715	10/13/86	Type K	18 × 36	4	368.75
Penn/Stokes	78716	10/13/86	V Lube	Vacuums	1	520.50
W. H. Barton	78718	10/13/86	Cooling	Chamber	1	1,680.00
W. W. Graingers	78719	10/13/86	Locks	Crib	6	38.00
Pittsburg	78720	10/13/86	Department	Paint	12	301.00
Sherwin/Will	78721	10/13/86	Department	Paint	4	289.50
Sherwin/Will	78721	10/13/86	Plastic	Buckets	6	102.00
W. W. Graingers	78723	10/24/86	Float	Assembly	2	28.00
					60	(28,923.75)
Opening Balance						30,052.68
Ending Balance						$ 1,128.93

The objective behind the development of checkbooks was to communicate to production supervisors their cost constraints. Each report is based on production in a particular department, with finished goods generating revenue-based deposits to the supervisor's "account." These credits are offset by deductions for direct materials, direct labor, set-ups, and other direct costs incurred in producing the products. The supervisor is given great latitude in managing his or her department, subject to the constraint that all scheduled production must be completed on time.

Supervisors are allowed to "save" for future expenses. Additionally, should a department exceed its budget for a certain level of output, the supervisor must immediately request additional funds from the plant manager. This forces a discussion of problems long before traditional cost accounting reports would be available, and enhances the communication process in the plant.

Checkbooks are balanced on a weekly basis, and status reports are generated for each department. This allows the supervisor to verify his or her charges, and to make any changes deemed necessary to current operations to prevent cost overruns. The checkbook approach supports Stanadyne's drive to change its accounting and management philosophy from that of a job shop to a process-oriented JIT facility.

Required:
1. What are the strengths and weaknesses of the new control reports developed by Stanadyne?
2. What changes could be made to improve the process control system?
3. Are these reports compatible with JIT manufacturing? Could they be used in a traditional manufacturing setting?

3-8. Stanadyne Diesel Systems (B)[20]

We've been running off direct costs for several years now. When we were faced with crisis, it was the best way to go. But now, as volumes pick up, I'm concerned about not knowing what it really costs, on a full cost basis, to make our products. How can I make sure we are covering our costs?

Mike Boyer, Controller
Stanadyne Diesel Systems

Background
Stanadyne Diesel Systems has undertaken a revolutionary change to its internal reporting system in response to competitive pressures and the demands of supporting a Just-in-Time manufacturing environment. The system, described in case (A), is focused on control. Indirect costs are not allocated to products, but are reported based on lines of responsibility. This informal system has recently been sanctioned by corporate management.

Reminiscent of the direct cost versus full cost controversies of the 1960s, Mike Boyer, Stanadyne's Controller, is wrestling with the tradeoffs made earlier in changing to direct costing. The approach he is taking, rather than moving away from the control-oriented system described earlier, is focused on developing different cost systems for different purposes.

---

[20] This case used by permission of the Institute of Management Accountants. IMA or IMA adapted.

The mentality of the accounting group at Stanadyne is that they provide a service that extends beyond basic report writing, detailed transaction analysis, and issuance of monthly scorecards. An active group, they consider the key questions guiding their efforts to be: Do you know what you are doing? Why? What are you measuring? Developing a good plan and thinking about the information needed both to manage ongoing operations and to support strategic decision-making are key priorities in this group.

The Controller's Problem

Although the Controller's proactive role in the organization is one of the factors contributing to the turnaround at Stanadyne, several issues have recently been raised within the accounting group. The Chief Cost Accountant summarized his view as follows:

> I'm not particularly in favor of decoupling the management accounting system from the financial. I think we would benefit most from an integrated approach, one which factors in both managerial and financial reporting requirements.

One system or two? This is one area of controversy in the firm as the tensions between financial and managerial reporting requirements are brought to the surface.

Stanadyne has been maintaining, separate from the management reporting system, an elaborate system of cost pools to support full cost inventory valuation. In full cost reports, indirect costs—which are not assigned to production in the management reports—are allocated to the various products. Operating decisions are made using direct costs, but Boyer continues to use full costs in answering Marketing's requests for pricing information. Marketing, then, receives both direct cost information in the management reports, and full cost numbers.

The problem facing the Controller arises from this dual system. Overhead tracking, which has been decoupled from the management reporting system, is performed in a corner—the realm of the cost accountant. The control and pricing support functions of overhead reporting are separated under this arrangement. More serious, though, is the increasing tendency by Marketing to use the control reports in making pricing decisions rather than the full cost numbers provided by accounting. Pricing below full cost is thus becoming a routine practice rather than a conscious decision made on the basis of detailed profitability analysis.

Activity Accounting

The full cost versus direct cost argument brings Stanadyne full circle in this controversial area. Many accountants believe that full cost profit margins are the appropriate measure of product line profitability in today's manufacturing environment, due to increasingly large pools of indirect costs. This is essentially the realization being voiced by Boyer. However, he does not consider a return to traditional methods of cost allocation to be a viable option:

> The detail on our fully absorbed cost statements is a problem. I would like to be able to track indirect costs to products, and I want those costs to be accurate. In fact, if we can't make good decisions from the product line statement, then why prepare it? But tracking overhead costs—well, we just don't have a good idea of what causes them.

This is a familiar concern among practicing accountants. The movement to identify and use cost drivers in the tracking and assignment of overhead costs arose partly from the recognition that full costs are more important than ever. Activity accounting has tremendous appeal in this setting—at least at the conceptual level. But how can a company with limited resources find the expertise, time, and money to design and implement such a system? Despite these questions, the Controller has decided to begin a study of activity accounting at Stanadyne.

The basic framework being used in the study is shown in Figure 1. Each individual in the overhead group is being asked to list the basic activities that he or she performs, to state what inputs are required and what outputs result from each activity, and finally, to estimate activity time and frequency of occurrence. Combined with payroll data, the beginning of a database can be constructed, as suggested by Figure 2.

The objective is to provide a flexible database of activities that can be accessed on multiple dimensions to support operating decisions, pricing, and ad hoc reporting requirements. The question of what is cost can be approached differently depending on the use to be made of the information. One such use is to identify those activities which add value to the company's products and those which do not.

Potential Problems

The move toward white collar accountability at Stanadyne and other companies underscores the appropriateness of the JIT philosophy—the continuous elimination of waste in the process of value added manufacturing—for factory support activities as well as production activities. However, activity accounting for overhead workers requires some form of time/cost reporting on an ongoing basis. These workers typically have not been held directly accountable for their use of time.

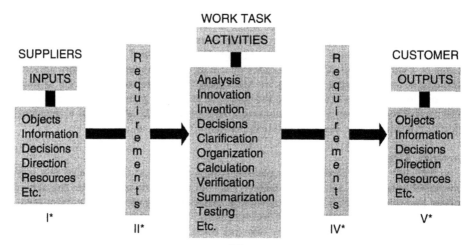

Figure 1 Framework for Activity Accounting Study

* Summary of the Model: All work may be thought of as occurring within a system. The system involves the "Supplier" providing inputs (I) based upon sets of requirements (II) to the "Work Task" (III) and its activities. The activities of the work task add value to the work and make it conform to other requirements (IV) before providing it as an output (V) to the "Customer."

Stanadyne personnel are predictably concerned about the outcome of the activity accounting project, as reflected in this comment by Boyer:

> Our people are nervous—and stressed. We're looking to add to this tension, and it may be the straw that breaks the camel's back. They will think it's another way to cut out more people, and they won't want to cooperate. Sure we need the information, but I just don't know if we can get it without damaging the fragile relationships we have with our people.

This is an interesting challenge. Several forms of dysfunctional behavior have been detected in public accounting, where time-based reporting has been used for years.

A chargeback system is both an accounting process to monitor resource usage and a mechanism for attaching the costs of these resources to the activities and/or products they support. McKinnon and Kallman (1987) suggest that a complete chargeback system should:

1. Record usage at a level that identifies all resources consumed.
2. Identify the individual performing the work as well as the process, product, or department receiving benefit.
3. Summarize usage based on classifications that impart the greatest amount of information (i.e., match the information use). The focus is on not only dollars expended but also the type of resource consumed and the level of service provided.
4. Report the summarized usage at regular intervals to identify significant trends and characteristics.

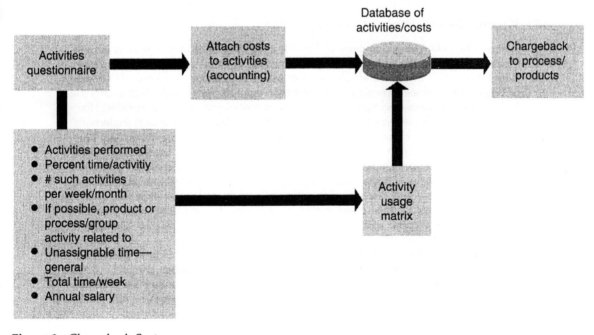

Figure 2   Chargeback System

These include overstating the time spent on tasks, shifting time from one task to another, and reporting as completed tasks that were never undertaken.

The critical issue may be how the information is used. If its use is restricted to product cost measurement and inventory valuation, people will have little incentive to misreport. But if the data are used for control and performance evaluation purposes, some falsification of reports may be expected. Finally, if the data are used to "weed out" individuals doing non-value added work, the accountant may be considered by some employees to be acting as their judge and potential executioner.

The concept of activity accounting is intuitively appealing, suggesting overhead costs can be analyzed and traced based on the activities that cause them. Implementing the concept, however, is far from simple. It requires a change in mindset among indirect labor groups, and a defined level of accountability not found in many existing systems. If used improperly, it could serve to divide, rather than to support and integrate, the people in an organization. As a new approach to cost analysis, activity accounting needs to be closely examined for both its benefits and its potential dangers.

Required:
1. Is direct costing information appropriate for operating decisions? For pricing decisions?
2. What problems are firms likely to encounter as they attempt to structure and implement activity accounting systems? What is your opinion of the approach being used by Stanadyne?
3. Should the management accounting system consist of one integrated database, or should separate cost systems be developed for different purposes?
4. Should accountants assume the role of reporting value added and non-value added activities? Why or why not?

3-9. Wharton Manufacturing Company (A)[21]

Wharton Manufacturing Company of Texas is a job-shop fabricator of steel structures. Customers include the utility industry and various lighting applications companies. Wharton is one of five manufacturing entities within the Construction Products Division of Wharton Industries Incorporated. With similar manufacturing capabilities, each site has a general manager who maintains independent control and fiscal responsibility. However, the home office is responsible for all marketing, quotations, and design engineering.

These central functions communicate closely with each manufacturing site. They frequently consult about available capacity and lead time with branch operations. About 50% of product shipments are custom orders with the remainder produced from existing designs. All sites use a costing system incorporating standard material, labor, and variable and fixed burden rates. Allocation of burden expenses to discrete part numbers is done using direct labor hours. The company uses formulas combining sales volume with contribution margin percentages to pay sales agents and marketing personnel.

The Texas plant has two broad types of product: large poles and small poles. Each is further subdivided into four product groups. While most product demand follows the activity of the construction industry, certain products are somewhat seasonal. The three basic competitive issues are price (lowest cost), product presence (high quality

---

[21] This problem used by permission of the Institute of Management Accountants.

and up-to-date features), and responsiveness (reduced lead times and due date performance). All three are important for most products offered, although some customers tend to favor one or two over the other. For example, short lead time, in some cases, may be less important than low price and high quality.

Theory of Constraints Implementation

Starting in late 1986, the Texas plant began researching the application of the Theory of Constraints (TOC). After much discussion, the plant identified its constraint operations. Management then decided to exploit and subordinate the other resources to the constraint. Time buffers of in-process inventory were set up in front of the constraint operations and shipping as protection from disruptions. Figure 1 is a schematic layout of the plant showing the constraints and time buffers. Unfortunately, facing a very dismal future at the start of 1987, the Texas plant temporarily laid off 40% of its personnel. However, after a couple of months, when TOC was up and running, staffing returned to normal.

With the introduction of TOC, Drum-Buffer-Rope scheduling replaced the manufacturing resource planning (MRP) system. Under MRP, the objective of the company was to keep all resources in the plant as busy as possible. This policy was followed even if it meant making repetitive items to forecasted, in excess of current, demand. However, often after installation of TOC, finished goods inventories were cut and all items (including repetitive ones) were made only to customer order. The plant's management changed its focus from efficiency for all operations to concentrating on improving productivity for the constraint operations. Performance measures for the support resources changed from traditional efficiency measures to evaluation of how well they fed the buffers. There is only one drawback: to buffer against long lead times and because of unreliable vendors, increases in raw material inventories were necessary.

Theory of Constraints Results

Overall results for the first year of using TOC were impressive. Improvements occurred in the areas of price, product presence, and responsiveness. Shipments increased while fixed costs remained relatively constant. Thus, actual unit costs were lower. Quality, measured by the ability to meet the customer's needs, improved. Finally, improvements in the plant's responsiveness to the marketplace occurred. Due date performance (on-time shipments) improved from a low of 70 percent the previous year to the mid 90 percent range. Lead times fell by nearly 50 percent. Management found it no longer needed finished inventories. Most important, earnings for the year were up 154 percent and return on equity increased by 132 percent.

Stagnation and Challenges

Implementation of the TOC methods spread to the other manufacturing sites the following year. Drum-Buffer-Rope scheduling replaced the MRP scheduling system and an intensive reeducation program occurred for key people throughout the Division.

However, a negative result was that competition also intensified from rival domestic and foreign companies. So the company fought to keep market share by lowering prices, shortening lead times, and improving due-date performance.

Unfortunately, in spite of increasing shipment volume, profits for the Texas plant were only slightly better than the previous year. The outlook for future profits was clouded by a combination of market price erosion and inflationary operating expenses.

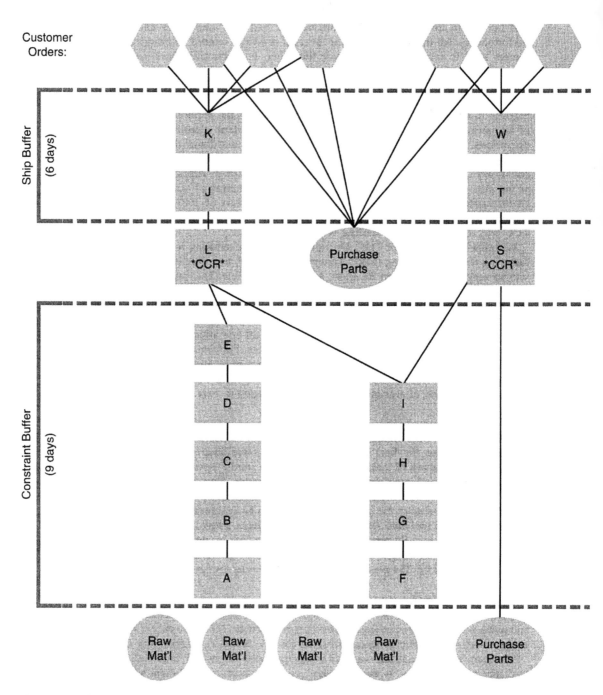

Figure 1   Wharton Plant Layout

Required:
1. In 1987 the company decided to cut finished goods. What do you think was the basis for this decision?
2. During the first year of operations under TOC, how did the company avoid a reduction in reported income from reducing finished goods inventories?[22]
3. Should the Division expand its application of TOC beyond the shop floor?
4. Should the Division use activity-based costing for reevaluation of its product lines? Give a thorough explanation of your reasoning.
5. What pricing strategies can the central marketing and quotations group use to improve future profitability?
6. Once marketing refocuses its efforts to bring in business that least penalizes the constraint, isn't it conceivable that the constraint will change?
7. During the off season, the constraint on the system actually was in the market. Should constraint theory pricing policy be changed during the off season?

Appendix to Figure 1:   Establishing regions in each buffer supports the process of ongoing improvement; management simply monitors each region. Jobs that do not appear as scheduled are holes requiring investigation. Region size varies from company to company; for example, region one consists of jobs due in the next 24 hours; region two may be those due in the next 72 or 48 hours; and so on. Another company may use a different size region.

These regions form an important early warning system. Buffer management actively tracks not only region one holes, but also those holes occurring in region two. Of course, region one holes will get the most attention. They require expediting to prevent the loss of throughput. Region two analysis is also important in that it gives the users valuable information about "potential troublemakers." However, resources that routinely cause holes in region one are areas receiving maximum attention from management. It is the cause of these holes that should have their protective capacity increased to prevent future problems. Protective capacity increases don't necessarily require additional capital or staffing. Simple methods such as focusing on preventive maintenance efforts or productivity improvements may avoid additional capacity costs. Thus the buffering allows a temporary, low-cost, solution until the problems can be eliminated.

3-10. Wharton Manufacturing Company (B)[23]

Implemented the previous year, the Drum-Buffer-Rope system had a positive impact on the plant's productivity. Unit costs fell as volumes increased while fixed costs remained relatively constant. However to continue to improve, the plant managers needed to resolve certain issues. There were suspicions that inappropriate accounting assumptions directed marketing to seek a less profitable product mix. The problem was that current cost accounting systems reconciled the operating results to the planned income statement figures. Thus, the cost accounting data

---

[22] This is the usual income effect when using full costing for inventory reporting. When inventory levels rise, more fixed overhead charges are deferred to future periods. As inventory levels fall these prior period fixed costs become expenses for the current period. If inventories do not change, and spending levels remain the same, the fixed overhead costs incurred will equal the changes expensed as Cost of Goods Sold.

[23] This problem used with permission of the Institute of Management Accountants.

followed the same assumptions as traditional accounting systems. They did not recognize short-term opportunity costs. Similarly, traditional manufacturing management systems ignored short-term constraints. However, this all changed under the Theory of Constraints (TOC). In order to determine the company's next move, management developed a TOC product line throughput analysis.

TOC focuses on short-term constraints. The aim is to increase the contribution per constraint hour. To manage under TOC, accounting classifications must change to record costs as throughput, operating expenses, or investments. Fortunately, the existing cost system provided most of the information needed. According to TOC, throughput is the net sales less raw materials costs, outsourcing costs, and other minimal variable costs like electricity. However, the accuracy of the current accounting system was an issue.

The company found its standard raw material data was too aggregated to separate out the costs as defined by TOC. The accounting problem was to identify the variable costs that were assigned to throughput and those that were assigned to operating expenses. TOC defined some of the existing variable overhead costs as fixed and some as variable. TOC, for example, defines such supply items as weld wire, gases, and electricity as variable but other items like indirect labor as fixed. Thus after an analysis using TOC definitions some of the costs previously classified as variable under traditional accounting were now treated as operating expenses. The total costs remained the same but now throughput costs were less than variable costs.

Nonetheless, care had to be taken as an overriding priority to not change external financial reporting. Thus, the internal cost system had to produce data for both TOC and accrual accounting assumptions. When completed, these changes did allow a more accurate calculation of product line throughput. Throughput was now the net sales less standard material costs plus the revised standard variable burden. Meanwhile, the company still retained the ability to perform traditional gross profit calculations (see Exhibit 1).

Product-line routing files disclosed the use of constraint resources for each customer order. Using this data, management did an historic analysis on previous shipments to calculate the throughput and constraint time for each product. Changes in periodic internal reports allowed the calculation of this new information for each customer order. The company could now calculate the throughput per constraint hour. This compared with the calculation of traditional gross margin, or the gross profit percentage for each product line.

Management's analysis confirmed the company's suspicion that some products were not as lucrative as shown by the traditional cost system. Equally important, it also showed that one of its products, 4T, was far more rewarding than previously thought.

When centralized engineering, marketing, and quotations personnel received this sales data they developed a plan to capitalize on the potential of the 4T product line. A value of $500 per hour was chosen as the breakeven constraint hour margin. The new policy was to price the product at what the market would bear, but never less than $500 per hour.

The new constraint pricing method for an order was far simpler than the traditional method. However, despite this or perhaps because of it, the quotation personnel routinely checked their calculations with the Texas plant to get final pricing approval. This was not due to a lack of knowledge, however, but rather from a certain nervousness. Consequently, quotes were cross-checked using both traditional and constraint theory methods. Often accrual accounting gross margins that fell

Exhibit 1
Traditional Gross Margin Analysis
Profit Analysis Comparison
Product 4T, Order #739-88

Gross Order Revenue	$208,950	
Less Deductions from Sales:		
Freight Expense to Customer	$ 5,800	
Commissions to Agent	$ 10,095	$ 15,895
Net Sale		$193,055
Cost of Goods Sold:		
Raw material @ Standard	$133,918	
Direct Labor	$ 16,235	
Variable Burden	$ 20,897	
Total Cost of Goods Sold @ Standard		$171,050
Gross Margin $		$ 22,005
Gross Margin %		11.4%

(Order not acceptable, less than traditional minimum threshold of 20%)

Constraint Theory Profit Analysis

Gross Order Revenue	$208,950	
Less Deductions from Sales:		
Freight Expense to Customer	($ 5,800)	
Commissions to Agent	($ 10,095)	
Net Sale		$193,055
Throughput Calculation:		
Raw Material @ Standard	$133,918	
Variable Throughput Spending (See case)	$ 6,238	
Total Material and TOC Variable Expense		$140,246
Net Throughput $		$ 52,809
Total constraint resource time required for order:		102.9 hours
Constraint theory return (throughput/constraint time):		$ 513/hr.

(Order is acceptable, greater than the minimum threshold of $500/hour.)

below the previously held 20 percent return criteria showed yields of more than the $500 per hour.

Exhibit 1 details an actual order for product 4T. It is typical of the type of bids starting 1988. Because of long lead times, the effect of the TOC bids did not really start to flow from the Texas plant until early 1989.

Figure 1 graphically depicted earnings before tax and net sales volume for the periods 1986 through 1990. The first year (1986) showed results before the installation of Drum-Buffer-Rope. With the implementation of TOC there was a dramatic

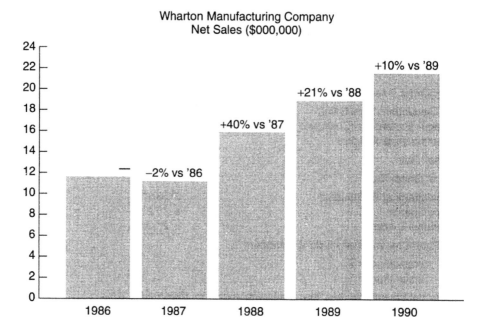

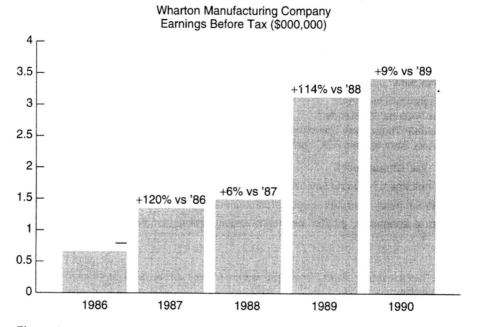

Figure 1

improvement the following year. In 1988 there was a large increase in sales, yet only a modest increase in earnings. The last two years showed the effect of the constraint theory influence on product mix. Although sales showed good increases, the earnings for these fiscal periods again doubled over 1988's results.

Required:
1. What changes were made to the traditional accounting measures with the introduction of TOC?
2. Given the current complaints about accounting systems creating a short-term decision mentality, how does TOC support long-term strategic goals?
3. How did the decisions made using TOC influence the financial statements?
4. What considerations must be included in the design of the TOC incentive system? How do these systems articulate appropriately with the financial statements?
5. Given the concerns of a more competitive world, will TOC support learning and innovation?

Part 2

Tactical Forecasting and Decision Making

Chapter 4

Estimating Cost Behavior: Linear Regression

I'm a scientist and I know what constitutes proof. But the reason I call myself by my childhood name is to remind myself that a scientist must also be absolutely like a child. If he sees a thing, he must say that he sees it, whether it was what he thought he was going to see or not. See first, think later, then test. But always see first. Otherwise you will only see what you were expecting. Most scientists forget that. . . .[1]

Managers need information to see what is going on in the external and internal environments of their organizations. In many cases, managers can use quantitative models to produce information that will be useful in their decision-making process. This chapter is the first of a series dealing with various quantitative models and techniques. In this chapter we explore simple

---

[1] Douglas Adams, *So Long, and Thanks for all the Fish* (New York: Harmony Books, 1985), p. 165.

and multiple linear regression. In Chapter 5, we look at curvilinear models —specifically the learning effect. Chapter 6 deals with linear programming as a technique that can help managers deal with limited resources. Finally, Chapter 7 covers extensions of the cost-volume-profit model.

Our interest in these models is from the perspective of practicing managers: we want to know what models are appropriate in different decision settings and how to use the models. We are interested in how to accumulate appropriate data as input for models and how to interpret the outputs we receive from computer programs. Although the derivation of these models is important, the discussion in this book does not deal with this aspect. Instead, we will concentrate on the practical use of models in everyday decision settings.

LINEARITY: THE BASIC ASSUMPTION

This chapter deals with how to estimate cost and other behavior using linear regression. By definition, then, we are assuming a linear function. The most basic linear model managers use is the

$$profit = (price - variable\ cost)quantity - fixed\ cost$$

model we find in cost-volume-profit (CVP). In the simple, deterministic CVP model, managers know which costs are fixed and which are variable. In addition, quantity or volume (usually defined as units) is the independent variable that can affect total variable cost and, therefore, total cost. There is some debate about the use of the CVP model as the cost structure of some manufacturing firms is changing (see Chapter 7). However, the basic idea of looking at which costs remain constant with changes in volume and which costs change as volume increases or decreases lies at the heart of estimating the cost of products, budgeting, analysis of a potential capital asset acquisition, and other information gathered by managers. This same CVP model forms the basis of our discussion of linear regression and correlation analysis.

Assumptions of the Deterministic CVP Model

If we are going to use a model, it is always important to know its limits and assumptions. While some models are quite robust even if some basic assumptions are violated, others might be so sensitive to assumptions that if the assumptions are violated, the model might not provide useful information. We start with the assumptions of the deterministic CVP model. Although a condition of certainty might be suspect, it is a good place to start. A clear deterministic model can then be used as the basis for a more complex stochastic model.[2]

The assumptions of deterministic CVP analysis are

1. The basic linear profit (and cost) equation is an accurate representation of how profits (costs) behave.
2. The basic model holds within a relevant range defined by both quantity and time.
3. Unit revenues and variable costs remain constant within the relevant range (that is, there are no quantity discounts or demand-related changes in prices or costs).
4. Fixed costs remain the same within the relevant range (that is, there are no stepped fixed costs).
5. Volume is the only variable that affects changes in total revenues and total variable costs.[3]

Thus, profits and costs are linear within the relevant range and are affected by changes in volume. Managers are assumed to be able to define unambiguously which costs are fixed and which are variable. All parameters of the CVP model are known with absolute (or relative) certainty.

A basic discussion of CVP analysis also includes the notion that the CVP model with its relevant range concept is a simplified (but useful) abstraction of the linear portion of the economists' model of total revenue and total cost curves. Figure 4-1 shows this idea graphically.

While we know that costs and revenues behave as depicted in Figure 4-1, we can use the CVP model to make estimates of revenues, costs, and profits within the linear (or near-linear) relevant range of this graph.

Problems with CVP Analysis

The CVP model is a robust one; even when some of its assumptions are violated, it still may yield useful information for planning and decision making. However, there are some problems with this model. Assume for the sake of an illustration that managers have determined the following for a single product department:

Price per unit	$10.00
Variable costs per unit	$ 6.00
Departmental fixed costs	$24,000/month

One of the basic assumptions is that we know that the $10 price will not change during this period. Managers should ask if prices are really certain. Will there be a range around the $10 figure and, if so, what kind of range? We also assume that the $6 variable cost per unit is firm. Again managers

---

[2] CVP under conditions of uncertainty is covered in Chapter 7.
[3] There are other assumptions, including the assumption that production equals sales, but they are not relevant to this discussion.

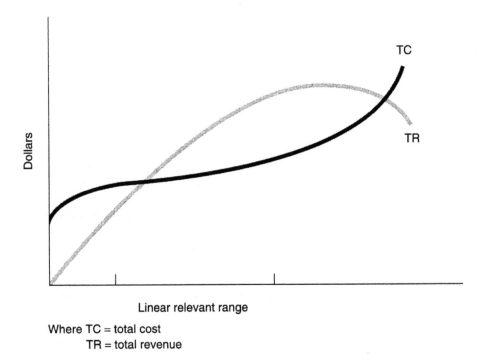

Where TC = total cost
TR = total revenue

Figure 4-1 CVP and Economists' Profit Model

can ask if this is so. For example, would materials costs go down if contracts for larger quantities were made due to higher anticipated volume? A more basic problem is that this simple example may implicitly assume that the managers of this department have unambiguously defined traceable fixed and variable costs (and their appropriate drivers) in contrast to other costs that are common. It also means that managers possess sufficient knowledge to distinguish fixed costs from variable ones. This may be difficult to do.

As an illustration based on a real situation, a power company operating coal-fired generating facilities classified the cost of coal and the cost of cleaning the steam boilers as variable and all other costs as fixed. When asked why this is so, the manager replied "because we think that's the way it is." The company had no objective evidence for this judgment, only the thoughts of the managers. While management might be entirely correct in this case, they might also be incorrect. It would be valuable to develop objective criteria and evidence regarding which costs are variable and which are fixed.[4]

---

[4] Henry R. Schwartzbach, "The Impact of Automation on Accounting for Indirect Costs," *Management Accounting* (December 1985), p. 47 reports that only 13 percent of firms responding to his questionnaire use a statistical basis for establishing the basis for overhead allocation. He comments that because "most companies do not validate their choice (of allocation bases) statistically, it is not surprising that they do not change bases as operations change."

Another problem is that the CVP model uses changes in volume as the only factor affecting changes in total cost. Certainly we can expand our notion of volume to include more than just units produced and sold. However, although volume-related measures (units, direct labor hours, machine hours, and pounds of material, for example) are important drivers, other factors such as batches, number of products, and time or season might affect costs. Thus, we cannot assume that volume-related measures are the only ones to investigate and use.

In some sense, basic CVP analysis assumes that fixed costs are either common or separable in a very basic way (e.g., to a department). As we have seen with our discussion of ABC, costs (fixed or variable) can be the results of activities at the unit, batch, product, process, or facility level.

In addition to looking at appropriate drivers, the basic nature of the mix of fixed and variable costs is changing in some firms. As firms adopt numerically controlled machines and robotics, they might become much more capital intensive. In addition, in many firms not only is labor a smaller part of total costs, but also direct labor is becoming a *de facto* fixed cost at least in the short term. Thus, it becomes even more important to look at our basic assumptions and to see what the emerging reality holds.

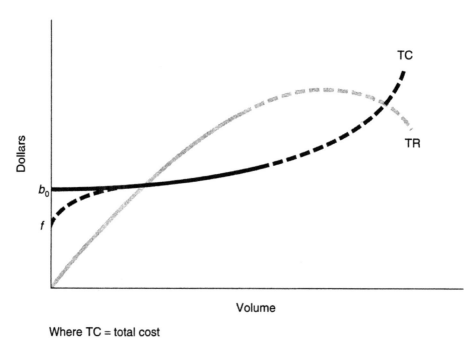

Where TC = total cost
TR = total revenue

Figure 4-2   Building Linear Estimates

After looking at changes brought about by new technology and/or competitive pressures, managers are still left with some basic questions about costs. They want to be able to get objective evidence regarding

1. which costs are variable and which are fixed,
2. what factor(s) affect each variable cost, and
3. the size of the variation around estimated costs.

As a result, managers use techniques such as linear regression to yield answers to these questions.

Under CVP analysis assuming certainty, managers more or less calculate total costs rather than estimate them. When we relax the binding (and somewhat unrealistic) condition of certainty, managers now want to predict costs (the dependent variable) given different levels of the independent variable. This prediction is based on two other estimates: the linear intercept and the variable cost per unit of the independent variable.

In this discussion we change the notion of *fixed cost* to one of a *linear intercept*. Refer to Figure 4-2, which is an expanded version of Figure 4-1 showing the linear portion of the total cost curve graphed so it intersects the y axis. While point b_0 shows the linear intercept, point f depicts fixed costs at zero volume. Thus one change from the CVP model to a cost estimating model is how we define the fixed portion of total costs. The most basic change, however, is how managers estimate both the fixed and variable elements of cost.

SIMPLE LINEAR REGRESSION

The total cost portion of the CVP model is

$$\text{Total Cost} = \text{Fixed Cost} + (\text{Variable Cost} \times \text{Quantity})$$

This can be translated into a more generic form

$$y = b_0 + b_1 x$$

where y = total cost (dependent variable)
b_0 = linear intercept
b_1 = variable cost per unit of the independent variable
x = units of the independent variable (e.g., direct labor hours, machine hours, volume, pounds of material)

The Linear Regression Model

In this section we will review the simple linear regression model. The basic idea of simple linear regression [or *ordinary least squares (OLS)*] is to find the statistically best estimate of $y = b_0 + b_1 x$. We move from the CVP notion that y is easily determined, because we know what b_0 and b_1 are, to having to estimate y (we now call the dependent variable y' or y *prime*) by finding the statistically best estimates of both b_0 and b_1. In the OLS method, this best estimate is the line that minimizes the sum of the squared differences between actual and predicted costs. In formula form this is

$$\text{Min } \Sigma(y - y')^2$$

where y = actual costs
$\quad\quad\quad y'$ = estimated costs

We can illustrate simple linear regression and correlation analysis using the data in Exhibit 4-1, which are plotted in a scatter diagram in Figure 4-3. The results of a computer program using this set of data are in Exhibit 4-2. Thus, based on the OLS model, the estimate of overhead costs is

$$y' = \$759.46 + \$7.51x$$

This is graphed in Figure 4-4 (page 164). Note how about half the observations fall above the line and about half below it.

Plotting the Data

As Figure 4-2 shows, we are trying to look at the linear portion of a total cost line. Plotting the data is a good way to begin this process to see if a

Exhibit 4-1
Lucas Manufacturing
Cost Data

Observation	Machine Hours	Overhead Cost
1	500 hours	$ 4,606
2	350	3,618
3	590	5,325
4	585	5,556
5	425	3,809
6	400	3,832
7	450	3,988
8	576	5,329
9	565	4,777
10	334	3,326
11	490	4,176
12	385	3,733
13	530	4,396
14	567	4,957
15	472	4,169
		$65,597

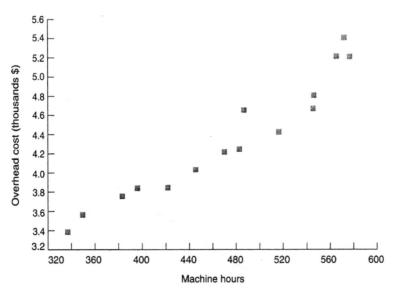

Figure 4-3 Lucas Manufacturing: Plot of Overhead Costs and Machine Hours

Exhibit 4-2
Lucas Manufacturing
Regression and Correlation Analysis

UNWEIGHTED LEAST SQUARES LINEAR REGRESSION OF OHCOST

PREDICTOR VARIABLES	COEFFICIENT	STD ERROR	STUDENT'S T	P
CONSTANT	759.46	325.03	2.34	0.0361
HOURS	7.5087	6.6513E-01	11.29	0.0000

R SQUARED	0.9074	RESID. MEAN SQUARE (MSE)	4.766E+04
ADJUSTED R SQUARED	0.9003	STANDARD DEVIATION	218.3

SOURCE	DF	SS	MS	F	P
REGRESSION	1	6.0744E+06	6.0744E+06	127.44	0.0000
RESIDUAL	13	6.1964E+05	4.7665E+04		
TOTAL	14	6.6941E+06			

DURBIN-WATSON STATISTIC 2.3188

P VALUES, USING DURBIN-WATSON'S BETA APPROXIMATION:
  P (POSITIVE CORR) = 0.7461, P (NEGATIVE CORR) = 0.2539

EXPECTED VALUE OF DURBIN-WATSON STATISTIC 1.9789
EXACT VARIANCE OF DURBIN-WATSON STATISTIC 2.4359E-01

Note: Scientific notation is used in this exhibit. For example, the residual mean squared is 4.766E+04. This means that you should move the decimal point to the right four places to get (rounded) 47,660. Looking at the exact variance of the Durbin-Watson statistic, this would be 0.24359, since it is 2.4359E-01.

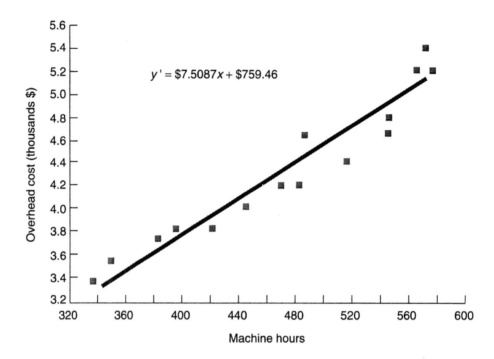

Figure 4-4   Lucas Manufacturing: Simple Linear Regression

linear model is appropriate. Figure 4-3 shows a somewhat linear pattern, which is accentuated by overlaying the calculated regression line on the data points, as shown in Figure 4-4. Note, however, that there is a pattern to the data. The first four points fall above the regression line, seven of the next eight fall below, and the final three above. Thus, the data show a slight curve and we know going into our analysis that if these data are representative, we are using a linear approximation for estimating. Plotting also allows a visual search for outlier observations, as is discussed below.

We started with the notion that managers could define fixed and variable costs (the CVP model). We extended this to the simple linear regression model and correlation analysis where managers can see if there is evidence of a relationship between a dependent variable (overhead costs in this example) and an independent variable (such as machine hours). While the OLS method gives us the best estimates of both the linear intercept and the variable cost coefficient, we must look at other measures to see if these estimates are usable. Our focus is on the expected variability around our estimates. If, for example, we could say that our estimates of both b_o and b_1 were so good that we expect no variation around them, then (assuming basic assumptions of the model are not violated) we have excellent parameters to forecast overhead costs. On the other hand, if we find tremendous variability around our estimates, then we may not be able to use them to predict cost behavior. We look at the standard error of the slope (s_{b_1}), the standard error of the intercept, the coefficient of determination (r^2), and the standard error of the forecast (S_f) as ways to gain objective evidence whether our estimates are statistically significant.

Objective Measures

When deciding whether to use the output from a linear regression model as the basis for forecasting future cost behavior, a manager should first be satisfied that there are no problems with the data and that the assumptions of linear regression have not been violated. We cover these points later. Next, the manager can apply some objective measures to see if the estimates generated in the linear regression output are statistically significant. Finally, once these first two sets of conditions are satisfied, the manager can subjectively assess the model and decide whether and how to use it. This section deals with the objective measures.

Standard Error of the Slope   A good place to start is to see if the estimate of the variable coefficient (the slope) is statistically significant. This is accomplished by calculating the standard error of the slope and then, using it to determine a 95 percent confidence interval around b_1, seeing if we can reject the null hypothesis that B_1, the true, unknown variable cost coefficient, equals zero. If we can reject the null hypothesis (that there is no relationship between the independent and dependent variable), we can then accept the alternate hypothesis that $B_1 \neq 0$. If so, then we will also accept b_1 as the best estimate of variable costs.

Using the output from Exhibit 4-2, we see that the standard error of the slope is 0.665. (We review all the formulas for determining measures such as s_{b_1} in the appendix to this chapter.) There are n-2 or 13 degrees of freedom with the 15 observations in this example. Using the t-table in Appendix A, the t-value for a 95 percent confidence interval ($t_{.025}$) is 2.16. This means that a 95 percent confidence interval around the estimate of the slope is

$$b_1 \pm t_{.025}s_{b_1}$$

7.51 + or − (2.16 × 0.665)
7.51 + or − 1.44 or a range of 6.07 to 8.95

This range does not intersect with zero. Therefore we can reject the null hypothesis and accept the alternate hypothesis. If this range were, say, −1.2 to 12.4, then we could not reject the null hypothesis since we would not be sure if the slope was positive, negative, or flat.

t-**Test**   Another way of assessing the significance of the slope is to use a *t*-test. We can rearrange $b_1 \pm t_{.025}s_{b_1}$ to find out what value of t will yield zero at one end of the range of b_1.

We want the *t*-value where $b_1 = t\, s_{b_1}$. This is found at

$$t = \frac{b_1}{s_{b_1}}$$

In our example,

$$t = \frac{7.51}{0.665} = 11.3$$

Thus, b_1 would have to fall over 11 standard deviations before its value would hit zero. The probability of this is almost zero. Both the computed *t*-value and the probability of b_1 being zero are shown in the computer output in Exhibit 4-2. In our case, the critical *t*-value is 2.16. If the *t*-test yielded a value less than 2.16, say, 1.5, then we could not reject the null hypothesis that $B_1 = 0$.

If we cannot objectively reject the null hypothesis that $B_1 = 0$, we cannot use the estimates generated by the regression model. If we cannot objectively say that there is a statistical relationship between, say, overhead costs and machine hours, we cannot say that overhead costs will change as machine hours rise or fall. In fact, our best estimate of costs might be the simple arithmetic average y.

The Standard Error of the Linear Intercept   We can apply the same analysis to looking at the linear intercept (b_0) as we did with the slope. However, the consequence of the linear intercept not being statistically significant is different than it is when we look at the slope. In the case of Lucas Manufacturing, Exhibit 4-2 shows that the computed *t*-value is 2.34, which is greater than the critical value of 2.16. Thus, we can reject the null hypothesis that $B_0 = 0$ and use b_0 as our best estimate of the intercept.

In the case of the *slope*, if there is no statistical significance we would not use the regression output at all in its present form, because we would not have evidence that there was a relationship between costs and hours in the example. Therefore, first we should be satisfied that we do have such a relationship for the slope. Then, if we cannot reject the null hypothesis regarding the *intercept*, we are not sure if the intercept is zero, negative, or positive. Thus, there is a relationship between the dependent and independent variable, but we are unsure about the intercept. In this case managers have two options. First, since the intercept is probably close to zero if the intercept is not significant, they can ignore their uncertainty about its value and use the regression output as generated. However, a better approach is to specify in the regression program that the intercept is zero and to recalculate the slope given $b_0 = 0$.[5]

Coefficient of Determination   The coefficient of determination or r^2 (sometimes called the *goodness of fit* of the model given the data) is the measure used to see how good an overall estimate has been generated by the regression equation. As developed in the appendix to this chapter, r^2 involves a ratio of

$$r^2 = 1 - \frac{\text{unexplained variance}}{\text{total variance}}$$

The unexplained variance is due to difference between the actual observations (y) and estimated costs (y') at each level of the independent variable. This term, $(y - y')$, is called the *error term* or a *residual*. It is what is left over as the difference between the data and the regression model. The unexplained variance is the sum of the squared residuals $\Sigma(y - y')^2$. Therefore, if the residuals are very small, then r^2 will be near 1. If the residuals are quite large, then r^2 approaches zero. In the case of the Lucas Manufacturing example, r^2 is about 0.90.

There are two different explanations of r^2. First, in this case about 90 percent of the movement in overhead costs is related to movement in machine hours. The other 10 percent is due to either random fluctuations or to other independent variables that we have not identified. The second explanation is that using the regression estimates is a 90 percent better predictor of costs than using the simple arithmetic mean of costs.

The coefficient of determination does not imply that there is a cause-and-effect relationship between the dependent and independent variables. It means only that a statistical relationship exists. In fact, the r^2 of 0.90 in Exhibit 4-2 would be the same if the independent and dependent variables were reversed (that is, if we were trying to predict machine hours given overhead costs).

In the computer printout in Exhibit 4-2, we have an objective measure of the goodness of fit. In simple linear regression, the t-test for the slope is

---

[5] Virtually all regression programs allow the user to specify whether to calculate the intercept or to set the intercept to zero. Once you have run the program and seen that the null hypothesis regarding the intercept cannot be rejected, then rerun it with the intercept set to zero. However, this limits your ability to use other parts of the regression package (e.g., Durbin-Watson statistic).

also the test for the significance of r^2. As we discuss below, with multiple regression, we look at the F-test for an overall objective evaluation of the regression equation. However, in simple linear regression there will never be a conflict between the t- and F-tests. Thus, we can rely on the t-test to help us not only with the slope but also with the goodness of fit of the regression equation.

Standard Error of the Forecast

We have established that y' is our best statistical estimate for total costs if the data requirements, assumptions, and objective measures are met. However, y' is only a point estimate of, say, overhead costs at a specified level of machine hours (x). The standard error of the forecast (S_f) allows managers to build a confidence interval around that estimate. The basis for the standard error of the forecast is the *standard error of the estimate, S_e*. As with the coefficient of determination, the basic part of the standard error of the estimate is the sum of the squared residuals.[6] The regression program used to generate Exhibit 4-2 identifies the standard error of the estimate as STANDARD DEVIATION with a value of about $218. Therefore, in order to calculate a 95 percent confidence interval around y' using the standard error of the estimate, we would use the critical value of $t(t_{.025} = 2.16$ with 13 degrees of freedom) and the standard error. Thus, for, say, 390 machine hours our estimate of overhead costs would be

$$y' = \$759 + (\$7.51)(390) = \$3,688$$

and a 95 percent confidence interval would be

$$y' \pm t_{.025} \, S_e = \$3,688 \pm (2.16)(\$218) = \$3,217 \text{ to } \$4,159$$

The Effect of the Independent Variable   If used as illustrated above, the entire regression line and a 95 percent confidence interval around it would look like Figure 4-5. However, to be more accurate, the manager's assessment of a useful range around the estimated cost, y', should take into account the effect of the independent variable, x, on the variance. The closer x is to its mean, x, $(x = 481$ in the example from information in Exhibit 4-3), the more the standard error of the estimate is a good measure of cost variability. As a manager wants estimates further and further away from the mean, we are getting to the edges of the relevant range and expect more variability. This is shown graphically in Figure 4-6.

The effect of x on the variability of estimated cost can be incorporated by using the standard error of the forecast (S_f).

---

[6]The formula for the standard error of the estimate is shown in the appendix to this chapter.

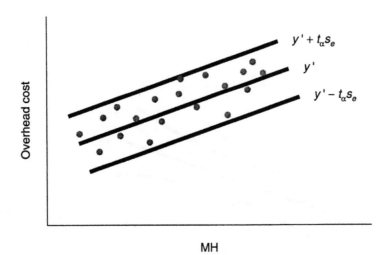

Figure 4-5 Confidence Interval Using S_e

Exhibit 4-3
Lucas Manufacturing
Standard Error of the Forecast

MH in Order X_f	$(X_f - X)^2$	S_f	$(S_f - S_e)$
334	21,687	245	27
350	17,231	241	23
385	9,267	234	16
400	6,604	232	14
425	3,166	228	10
450	978	226	8
472	86	225	7
490	76	225	7
500	351	225	7
530	2,375	227	9
565	7,011	232	14
567	7,350	232	14
576	8,974	234	16
585	10,761	235	17
590	11,823	236	18
Sum	107,740		

S_f at mean machine hours:

481	0	225	7

where   Mean = 481.2667
        S_e = 218

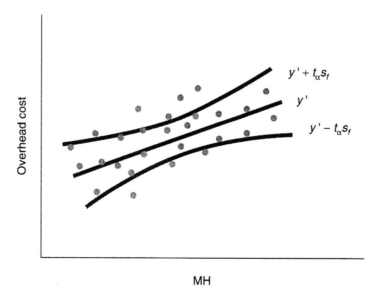

Figure 4-6 Confidence Interval Recognizing the Effect of the Independent Variable

(1)
$$S_f = S_e \sqrt{1 + \frac{1}{n} + \frac{(x_f - \bar{x})^2}{\Sigma(x_f - \bar{x})^2}}$$

x_f is the value of x used for estimating y' (like 390 hours). S_f for 390 hours is \$233 (S_f for 400 hours is \$232, as shown in Exhibit 4-3). This figure is not substantially different from the \$218 standard error of the estimate. Even at 590 direct labor hours, S_f rises only to \$236 (see Exhibit 4-3).

Therefore, while statistically it is more accurate to use the standard error of the forecast (S_f), as a practical matter it may be reasonable to use the standard error of the estimate (S_e) as was shown above for calculating a range around estimated costs.

Size of the Standard Error

It is difficult to establish criteria for what level of S_f (or S_e) is considered acceptable. This is a subjective judgment affected by the use of the regression results. The first steps in deciding to use regression results are to make sure that the objective tests are met and that there are no problems with data or violation of assumptions. Once this is established, then managers will decide if an r^2 is high enough or S_f low enough; the fact that a regression is statistically significant does not mean it is useful. If a 95 percent confidence interval yields a range that a manager judges as too broad, she might not be willing to use coefficients from the regression as part of her estimating model. She is then faced with the problem of what other model might be better (objectively and subjectively).

ASSUMPTIONS OF LINEAR REGRESSION

Included in the discussion about the various statistical measures of a regression equation's usefulness as well as the discussion about data needs are several assumptions that are important. If these assumptions are not met, there can be problems in using regression results.

Models Have Assumptions

Most models have assumptions that are a specified part of the model. In earlier discussion, the assumptions of the cost-volume-profit model were outlined. In some cases, if various assumptions are not met, the model may still be useful but in some reduced way. In other cases, a violation of an assumption may invalidate the model. Finally, techniques do exist for trying to adjust the data or the model when some assumptions are not met. An example of this is what to do if the intercept is not significant. An alternate OLS model was proposed to solve this problem.

Knowing the assumptions of a model allows managers to use the model better. They know inherent strengths and weaknesses and can adjust how they use the results from a model accordingly.

Assumptions of Linear Regression Analysis

Major assumptions include the following:

1. Representative observations
2. Constant variance (homoscedasticity)
3. Error terms (residuals) normally distributed
4. Observations independent of one another
5. Data are linear[7]

We will discuss the idea of *representative observations* in the section on data requirements. It is important to recognize that even one observation that is not representative can have a serious effect on the regression equation. If, say, in the Lucas Manufacturing example the first observation had been aberrant and was recorded as $5,500 instead of $4,606 for 500 machine hours.

---

[7] Some nonlinear data can be converted to a linear relationship, as illustrated in Chapter 5 on the learning effect.

The result of this, as you can confirm by changing the data in Exhibit 4-1 and running a new regression, is to raise the slope from $7.51 to $7.66 per machine hour and to reduce r^2 from 0.90 to 0.80. This is the effect of only one outlier. Many computer programs identify outliers so that managers can examine the data in order to see if it is recorded properly and is representative. The possibility of outliers is another reason why many managers plot data as a first screen of usefulness.

Managers should not eliminate outlier observations without good cause. Proper screening is appropriate, as is looking at how data are recorded. Observations should be adjusted or removed only if there is good cause.

Another aspect of representative data is whether the relationship depicted by using the data makes *economic sense*. Is there a reason to believe that costs are affected by the chosen independent variable? Is that variable an imperfect reflection of a more basic variable? Even if we get a significant set of figures from a regression and correlation analysis, are the results *sensible?* As an illustration, in a study estimating costs at an electric utility based on changes in kilowatt hours (kwh), there were significant regression results relating mowing and grounds maintenance costs to kwh. This does not make sense. Will the grass grow more quickly if more power is generated? Perhaps the real independent variable was outside temperature. Generation goes up as it is warmer and air conditioning is used. The variable of interest then would be weather and not kwh.

Constant Variance   In order to make statistical inferences using the regression equation and the standard error of the estimate, the standard error itself must be constant. Thus, in the Lucas Manufacturing example where the standard error of the estimate (S_e) is $218, it would be difficult to, say, create a 95 percent confidence interval at 300, at 400, and at 500 direct labor hours if a manager knew that the variance (or its square root, the standard error) was changing. Constant and nonconstant variances (homoscedasticity and heteroscedasticity) are illustrated in Figure 4-7. There are many data sets where heteroscedasticity as shown in Figure 4-7(b) is prevalent. It is reasonable to expect some larger variance at higher levels of an independent variable (because, for example, of the increased difficulty of control at higher levels of activity). (This, by the way, is a logical explanation for using S_f instead of S_e).

Independence of Error Terms   A key assumption is that the error terms (or residuals), $(y - y')$, are independent and are normally distributed. If a pattern of error terms exists, one of the basic tenets of OLS regression is broken. Tied in with the error terms being independent is the assumption that observations themselves should be independent.

Independence of Observations   There are several things that cause dependence between observations. Inflation over time is one main cause.

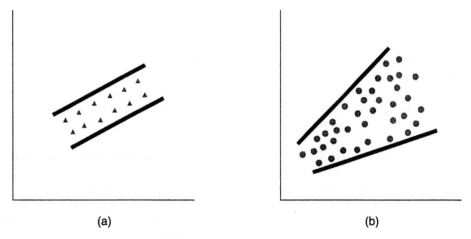

Figure 4-7   Constant and Nonconstant Variances

Thus, if one knows costs in 1993, 1994 costs will be affected just by the passage of time due to annual inflation. In other cases, costs of one period bec ome tied to costs of a previous period. For example, if a plant geared up a second shift and hired and trained skilled personnel, management might be loath to fire these people immediately upon a turndown in volume. Several months may pass before these skilled people would be laid off. Thus there is dependence between observations.

Serial Correlation

Serial correlation (or *autocorrelation*) occurs when there is dependence between observations (or error terms). The best test for autocorrelation is the Durbin-Watson (DW) statistic. Many regression and correlation packages calculate not only the DW statistic, but also give a measure of the serial correlation that exists. Exhibit 4-2 on page 163 shows a DW statistic of 2.32. A rough rule of thumb is that the DW statistic should be near 2.0. If it is too far below 2.0, there is positive serial correlation; if it is too far above 2.0, there is negative serial correlation.

In the Lucas Manufacturing example, Exhibit 4-2 shows that the expected value of the DW statistic is about 2.0 (1.98) and that the probability of negative correlation (since the DW is above the expected value) is about 0.25, not significant.[8]

---

[8] There are two points about the use of the DW statistic. First, the output shown in Exhibit 4-2 shows only the probability of negative or positive correlation and not the correlation itself. Second, if the correlation were shown (it is -0.18 in this case), we are dealing with a simple r rather than r^2. Thus, a correlation of, say, 0.70 can be translated into a relationship of about 0.49 (0.70^2).

Time-Series versus Cross-Sectional Data   There are two usual types of data. *Time-series* data are observations across time (months, years). A typical time-series data set would be, as in Lucas Manufacturing, fifteen months of data for one department's overhead and machine hours. Cross-sectional data are several observations at one period of time. For example, costs for 15 different retail outlets for a single day (or month, or year) would be cross-sectional data. While serial correlation can be detected in both types of data, it is much more usual (and logical) to see it in time-series data.

Ways to Eliminate Serial Correlation   If serial correlation exists, managers will want to see if the data can be adjusted to remove it. For example, if there is a specific price index that managers can use to deflate the data, it can be used to help remove serial correlation. Another way is to use the absolute values of the *first difference* of the data instead of the data themselves.[9] If there had been serial correlation using the data in Exhibit 4-1, then, for the first observation, instead of using 500 hours and $4,606, we would use (350 – 500) 150 hours and ($3,618 – $4,606) $988 with first differences. This reduces the observations from 15 to 14. The result is a regression based on

$$(y_t - y_{t-1}) = b_0 + b_1 (x_t - x_{t-1})$$

It is important not just to apply some technique such as deflating the data or using first differences. Managers should seek out the causes of the serial correlation and try to eliminate them from the data. This is a more accurate way to adjust the data.

A way to detect autocorrelation even without a DW statistic is to plot the residuals and look for a pattern. Figure 4-8 shows the plot of the residuals from the data in Exhibit 4-1. As you can see, there is no apparent pattern, a visual affirmation that the residuals are random and normally distributed. We will see illustrations of a pattern in the residuals in our discussion of the learning effect in Chapter 5.

Problems with Autocorrelation   When autocorrelation exists, the estimates of the intercept and the slope are unaffected. However, if there is positive autocorrelation, the standard error of the slope is understated and the slope might seem significant when it really is not. Thus, we might reject the null hypothesis that $B_1 = 0$ when we should have accepted it. Conversely, if there is negative serial correlation, the standard error of the slope is overstated and we might not reject the null hypothesis when we should have. In the first case, we run the risk of accepting that there is a relationship

---

[9] There are other methods for dealing with serial correlation; this discussion is just an introduction to the topic.

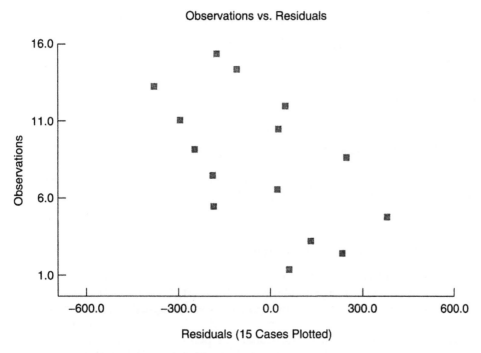

Figure 4-8 Lucas Manufacturing Plot of Residuals

between the dependent and independent variables when there is not one. In the second case, we run the risk of rejecting the regression equation when there really is an association between the dependent and independent variables.

MULTIPLE LINEAR REGRESSION

In many cases a dependent variable is associated with more than one independent variable. At times, managers might know of several independent variables that they believe could help explain, say, shipping costs. Therefore, they would test various combinations of these variables to see which combination results in the best model overall. In other cases, after running a simple linear regression and finding that r^2 is low, managers might reanalyze the situation and see if they can identify other independent variables that might improve the goodness of fit. This section deals with *multiple linear regression and correlation analysis* as a logical extension of the simple linear OLS model. In addition, we look at additional assumptions and tests when we have more than one independent variable. Finally, we look at step-fixed costs.

Measures Used to Evaluate the Multiple Regression Model

The model and measures developed above are expanded to take into account more than one independent variable:

estimate of costs: $y' = b_0 + b_1 x_1 + b_2 x_2 + \cdots + b_n x_n$
goodness of fit: adjusted r^2
variation around regression
   estimate: S_f (or S_e)
variation of estimate parameters: $s_{b_0}, s_{b_1}, s_{b_2}, \cdots, s_{b_n}$

All the measures used for simple regression are calculated in an extended form for multiple regression. The biggest change comes with the coefficient of determination.

Adjusted Coefficient of Determination

The availability and ease of computer programs for regression and correlation analysis might encourage managers to try a large assortment of independent variables, whether they make economic or logical sense or not. Adding independent variables can explain more and more of the movement of the dependent variable; each additional independent variable makes the resulting model more complex, however. The *adjusted coefficient of determination* discourages incorporating variables that will make little marginal change in the unexplained variance, because it incorporates the number of independent variables so the adjusted r^2 is lowered, all things being equal, as the number of independent variables increase.

As shown in the appendix to this chapter, the formula for the unadjusted coefficient of determination incorporates only the numerators of the unexplained and total variances since the denominators [$(n - 1)$ for a sample] cancel out. The adjusted coefficient of determination is

$$\text{adjusted } r^2 = 1 - \frac{\dfrac{\Sigma(y - y')^2}{n - j - 1}}{\dfrac{\Sigma(y - \bar{y})^2}{n - 1}} = 1 - \left(\frac{n - 1}{n - j - 1}\right)(1 - r^2)$$

where the unexplained variance includes j, the number of independent variables, in its denominator. Even with one independent variable, the coefficient of determination is changed. Exhibit 4-2 shows the results from a simple linear regression and shows that the adjusted r^2 is a bit lower than the unadjusted version.[10]

---

[10] Not all computer programs provide an unadjusted r^2 and not all provide an adjusted r^2. Look at the output and read the documentation for a program to be sure which measure you are getting.

As the number of independent variables rises, the unexplained variance portion of the equation rises and the adjusted coefficient of determination falls. However, this can be offset by increasing the sample size (number of observations, n).

F-Test for Multiple Coefficient of Determination

Most computer regression and correlation programs list an F-statistic. This measure is used to test the null hypothesis that the adjusted multiple coefficient of determination (sometimes called ρ) is zero. The F-statistic is a ratio with a numerator of

Regression sum of squares/$k - 1$ or   SSR/$k - 1$,

which is really the explained variance (the difference between estimated costs and the mean). The denominator is the unexplained variance

Error sum of squares/$n - k$ or   SSE/$n - k$

where k is the number of variables (both dependent and independent) and n is the number of observations.

F-ratios are similar to computed t-statistics in simple linear regression. If the computed F-ratio is greater than the critical F-ratio with $(k - 1)$ and $(n - k)$ degrees of freedom, then the null hypothesis that $\rho = 0$ can be *rejected* and the regression results are significant. Many computer programs not only show the computed F-statistic but also the probability associated with the null hypothesis.[11]

COLLINEARITY

One of the basic assumptions of multiple regression is that the independent variables are not correlated with each other. The high correlation of independent variables is called *multicollinearity* or just *collinearity*. Some cases of collinearity are fairly obvious. For example, if a machine requires a crew of three workers to operate it, for every machine hour there will be three direct labor hours. This is perfect correlation between these independent variables and an illustration of collinearity. If a manager were to use *both* machine hours and direct labor hours as independent variables to estimate cost, then the results could be quite confusing.

---

[11] This is just an introduction to the F-statistic. Tables are not given because they are complex and because computer output usually shows the probability for us; thus, a comparison has already been made with the critical value and we need not do this manually.

Basic Illustration

Exhibit 4-4 shows data for separable conversion costs (labor and overhead) for one of the products of the Spartan Company. In addition, data are shown for units produced, machine hours, direct labor hours, and season of the year. We will use all these figures as the discussion progresses.

Although a manager could choose to run about every combination of variables to get the best relationship with costs, it is easy to see by looking at the data that labor hours are virtually fixed and that season, by itself, probably would not be a good predictor of costs. Therefore, the two most promising simple regression models are

Exhibit 4-4
Spartan Company
Conversion Costs

Observation	Conversion Costs	Units	Machine Hours	Direct Labor Hours	Season
1	$311,100	1,500	3,150	2,000	0
2	204,500	1,200	2,300	2,200	0
3	286,400	1,400	3,050	2,200	0
4	270,500	1,260	2,700	2,200	0
5	251,100	900	2,020	2,200	1
6	213,500	1,000	1,900	2,000	1
7	288,700	1,300	2,430	2,000	1
8	366,200	1,700	3,750	2,000	1
9	219,900	1,150	2,010	2,000	1
10	346,700	1,600	3,100	2,000	1
11	303,000	1,500	3,350	2,000	0
12	261,400	1,350	2,540	2,000	0
13	264,944	1,400	2,600	2,000	0
14	303,554	1,450	3,000	2,000	0
15	245,734	1,200	2,560	2,100	0
16	254,235	1,100	2,400	2,100	0
17	232,722	1,000	1,800	2,100	1
18	296,589	1,300	2,450	2,000	1
19	319,777	1,450	2,800	2,000	1
20	335,367	1,575	3,100	2,000	1
21	337,223	1,625	3,400	2,000	1
22	345,389	1,550	3,150	2,000	1
23	207,678	1,200	2,300	2,000	0
24	250,289	1,300	2,450	2,000	0

where: Season = 1 is summer
Season = 0 is not summer

1. Conversion costs as a function of units
2. Conversion costs as a function of machine hours

The results of these two models are shown in Exhibit 4-5 (page 180).

The results show two models that are quite close. Although the measures for machine hours are slightly higher than those for units, with the exception that the intercept for units is not significant, the two models are both useful. A choice between them would have to be made on subjective, rather than objective, measures. If managers decide to use units as the independent variable, then they will probably rerun the model forcing the intercept to zero.

Multiple Regression

Various combinations of the four independent variables can be run to identify the best multiple regression relationship and to ascertain if this relationship is better than either of the simple regression models shown in Exhibit 4-5. First we will look at combinations of units, machine hours, and direct labor hours, and later we will incorporate season as we look at dummy variables. Exhibit 4-6 shows the results from the following relationships:

1. Conversion costs as a function of machine hours and units
2. Conversion costs as a function of machine hours, units, and direct labor hours

In the first model in Exhibit 4-6 (page 181), conversion costs as a function of machine hours and units, the overall regression is significant (F-statistic of 36.50 with p-value of 0.0000) but neither of the t-values for units or machine hours are significant. Given an adjusted r^2 of 0.76, this does not seem logical. It is also not logical given the unadjusted r^2 for each of these variables in Exhibit 4-5 (0.75 for both units and machine hours individually).

In the second model, not only do we see the same problems as in the first (significant F-statistic but units showing a t-value that is not significant) but also direct labor hours is shown with a *negative* coefficient. This implies that the more labor hours used, the lower the cost.

These problems are caused by collinearity, a high correlation between independent variables. Exhibit 4-7 shows a simple correlation matrix of all the variables. Note that the correlation between units and machine hours is over 0.90; these two variables are highly collinear.

How to Detect Collinearity   If multiple regression results yield coefficients with opposite signs from those that are logical to expect or where there are coefficients that are not significant in a regression with a high adjusted r^2 and a significant F-value, there is a good possibility that collinearity exists. In addition, the use of a correlation matrix can show collinearity directly before a regression is run.

Exhibit 4-5
Spartan Company
Simple Regression and Correlation Analysis

1. Conversion cost as a function of units produced (UNITS):

```
UNWEIGHTED  LEAST  SQUARES  LINEAR  REGRESSION  OF  COSTS

PREDICTOR
VARIABLES     COEFFICIENT   STD  ERROR    STUDENT'S  T      P
---------     -----------   ---------     -----------    ------
CONSTANT      2.3094E+04    3.2179E+04        0.72       0.4805
UNITS         192.51        23.836            8.08       0.0000

R  SQUARED              0.7478    RESID.  MEAN  SQUARE  (MSE) 5.954E+08
ADJUSTED  R  SQUARED   0.7363    STANDARD  DEVIATION          2.440E+04

SOURCE          DF       SS            MS           F         P
---------       --    ----------    ----------    -----     ------
REGRESSION       1    3.8839E+10    3.8839E+10    65.23     0.0000
RESIDUAL        22    1.3099E+10    5.9541E+08
TOTAL           23    5.1938E+10

DURBIN-WATSON  STATISTIC  1.7083
P  VALUES,  USING  DURBIN-WATSON'S  BETA  APPROXIMATION:
  P  (POSITIVE  CORR)  =  0.2115,  P  (NEGATIVE  CORR)  =  0.7885

EXPECTED  VALUE  OF  DURBIN-WATSON  STATISTIC        2.0288
EXACT  VARIANCE  OF  DURBIN-WATSON  STATISTIC        1.5309E-01
```

2. Conversion costs as a function of machine hours (MACHHRS):

```
UNWEIGHTED  LEAST  SQUARES  LINEAR  REGRESSION  OF  COSTS

PREDICTOR
VARIABLES     COEFFICIENT   STD  ERROR    STUDENT'S  T      P
---------     -----------   ---------     -----------    ------
CONSTANT      6.3440E+04    2.6807E+04        2.37       0.0272
MACHHRS       80.764        9.8343            8.21       0.0000

R  SQUARED              0.7540    RESID.  MEAN  SQUARE  (MSE) 5.807E+08
ADJUSTED  R  SQUARED   0.7429    STANDARD  DEVIATION          2.410E+04

SOURCE          DF       SS            MS           F         P
---------       --    ----------    ----------    -----     ------
REGRESSION       1    3.9164E+10    3.9164E+10    67.45     0.0000
RESIDUAL        22    1.2775E+10    5.8068E+08
TOTAL           23    5.1939E+10

DURBIN-WATSON  STATISTIC   1.6539
P  VALUES,  USING  DURBIN-WATSON'S  BETA  APPROXIMATION:
  P  (POSITIVE  CORR)  =  0.1896,  P  (NEGATIVE  CORR)  =  0.8104

EXPECTED  VALUE  OF  DURBIN-WATSON  STATISTIC        2.0067
EXACT  VARIANCE  OF  DURBIN-WATSON  STATISTIC        1.5425E-01
```

Exhibit 4-6
Spartan Company
Multiple Regression and Correlation Analysis

1. Conversion costs as a function of units (UNITS) and machine hours (MACHHRS):

UNWEIGHTED LEAST SQUARES LINEAR REGRESSION OF COSTS

PREDICTOR VARIABLES	COEFFICIENT	STD ERROR	STUDENT'S T	P
CONSTANT	3.6458E+04	3.2043E+04	1.14	0.2680
UNITS	93.664	64.291	1.46	0.1599
MACHHRS	44.212	26.860	1.65	0.1146

R SQUARED   0.7766   RESID. MEAN SQUARE (MSE) 5.525E+08
ADJUSTED R SQUARED 0.7553   STANDARD DEVIATION   2.351E+04

SOURCE	DF	SS	MS	F	P
REGRESSION	2	4.0336E+10	2.0168E+10	36.50	0.0000
RESIDUAL	21	1.1602E+10	5.5249E+08		
TOTAL	23	5.1938E+10			

DURBIN-WATSON STATISTIC 1.6215
P VALUES, USING DURBIN-WATSON'S BETA APPROXIMATION:
  P (POSITIVE CORR) = 0.2204, P (NEGATIVE CORR) = 0.7796

EXPECTED VALUE OF DURBIN-WATSON STATISTIC   2.0336
EXACT VARIANCE OF DURBIN-WATSON STATISTIC   2.6399E-01

2. Conversion costs as a function of units, machine hours, and direct labor hours (LABHRS):

UNWEIGHTED LEAST SQUARES LINEAR REGRESSION OF COSTS

PREDICTOR VARIABLES	COEFFICIENT	STD ERROR	STUDENT'S T	P
CONSTANT	3.0283E+05	1.6380E+05	1.85	0.0793
UNITS	48.959	67.423	0.73	0.4762
MACHHRS	59.125	27.338	2.16	0.0428
LABHRS	-121.08	73.128	-1.66	0.1134

R SQUARED   0.8035   RESID. MEAN SQUARE (MSE) 5.102E+08
ADJUSTED R SQUARED 0.7741   STANDARD DEVIATION   2.259E+04

SOURCE	DF	SS	MS	F	P
REGRESSION	3	4.1735E+10	1.3912E+10	27.27	0.0000
RESIDUAL	20	1.0204E+10	5.1018E+08		
TOTAL	23	5.1939E+10			

DURBIN-WATSON STATISTIC 1.6552
P VALUES, USING DURBIN-WATSON'S BETA APPROXIMATION:
  P (POSITIVE CORR) = 0.2371, P (NEGATIVE CORR) = 0.7629

EXPECTED VALUE OF DURBIN-WATSON STATISTIC   2.0694
EXACT VARIANCE OF DURBIN-WATSON STATISTIC   3.0601E-01

Exhibit 4-7
Spartan Company
Correlation Matrix

SIMPLE CORRELATIONS

	COSTS	LABHRS	MACHHRS	UNITS	SEASON
COSTS	1.0000				
LABHRS	-0.3387	1.0000			
MACHHRS	0.8684	-0.1504	1.0000		
UNITS	0.8648	-0.2818	0.9341	1.0000	
SEASON	0.2206	-0.4656	-0.1044	0.0045	1.0000

Results of Collinearity   What happens with a regression equation where the independent variables are collinear? Can management use these results or must they be rejected? The answer to this last question is both yes and no.

The coefficients of a regression equation are supposed to yield the marginal cost of increasing that independent variable by one while holding everything else constant. The equation using both machine hours and units is:

$$\text{estimated conversion costs} = \$36{,}458 + \$93.66 \text{ units} + \$44.21 \text{ machine hours}$$

For the moment let us ignore the low *t*-values for the two independent variables. If a manager wanted to know the additional cost of adding one more unit *while holding machine hours constant*, ideally he or she would say that it is about $94. However, this is not valid since units do not change independently from machine hours; if units go up, machine hours go up as well. With collinearity, the manager cannot use individual coefficients to estimate marginal costs.

However, if a manager is interested only in estimating total conversion costs and does not care about the marginal costs *per se* making up that total cost, then a regression including collinear independent variables can be used. Obviously, all the variables must be significant for an equation to be used—with or without collinearity.

STEP-FIXED COSTS

In many circumstances, firms see step-fixed costs within the relevant range of observations. For example, the addition of a second shift might not change variable costs but may require additional supervisors. In a situation where labor is virtually fixed, as in our basic illustration, when volume reaches a certain level, additional labor might be needed. Other examples include changes in utility bills caused by the season of the year. Many summer-peaking electric utilities charge quite a bit more for power consumed in the summer versus that used in the other seasons of the year.

Dummy Variables

In order to deal with a step-cost condition, managers can use dummy variables. A dummy variable takes on a value of 1 or 0 denoting a "yes" or "no" condition regarding the step function. Thus, in the Spartan Company example we might say season will take on the value of 1 if it is summer and 0 in all other seasons.

Because machine hours and units are the best simple regression models (and because we cannot use them together due to collinearity), Exhibit 4-8 (page 184) shows the results of multiple regression models using these variables coupled with season.

As with the two simple regression models, we are again faced with choosing between the two models in Exhibit 4-8 based mostly on subjective measures. Both show significant t-values for the independent variables and a significant F-statistic. Neither has a significant intercept. While the adjusted r^2 of the machine hours and season model is better than the units and season model, the Durbin-Watson statistic for the latter model is better than the former. However, in either case, we can see the result of the dummy variable, season.

How to Use Dummy Variables

We can now compare the two simple regression models with the multiple regression models using a dummy variable for season.

Conversion costs as a function of season and/or units:
 estimated costs = $23,094 + $192.51 units
 estimated costs = $12,422 + $192.29 units + $20,237 season

Conversion costs as a function of season and/or machine hours:
 estimated costs = $63,440 + $80.76 machine hours
 estimated costs = $39,331 + $83.82 machine hours + $29,386 season

Since we specified that the dummy variable is 1 in summer and 0 in other seasons, we have really defined a step-fixed cost; therefore, the dummy variable becomes an adjustment to the intercept in summer. In the case of the machine hours model, the intercept will be $32,659 in summer and $12,422 otherwise; in the other model, the intercept will be $68,717 in summer and $39,331 otherwise. Given the overall measures associated with these

Exhibit 4-8
Spartan Company
Multiple Regression and Correlation—Dummy Variable

1. Conversion costs as a function of machine hours and season

UNWEIGHTED LEAST SQUARES LINEAR REGRESSION OF COSTS

PREDICTOR VARIABLES	COEFFICIENT	STD ERROR	STUDENT'S T	P
CONSTANT	3.9331E+04	2.2242E+04	1.77	0.0915
MACHHRS	83.821	7.8503	10.68	0.0000
SEASON	2.9386E+04	7880.4	3.73	0.0012

R SQUARED   0.8520   RESID. MEAN SQUARE (MSE) 3.660E+08
ADJUSTED R SQUARED 0.8379   STANDARD DEVIATION   1.913E+04

SOURCE	DF	SS	MS	F	P
REGRESSION	2	4.4253E+10	2.2126E+10	60.46	0.0000
RESIDUAL	21	7.6856E+09	3.6598E+08		
TOTAL	23	5.1939E+10			

DURBIN-WATSON STATISTIC 2.3887

EXPECTED VALUE OF DURBIN-WATSON STATISTIC   2.0718
EXACT VARIANCE OF DURBIN-WATSON STATISTIC   32.829

2. Conversion costs as a function of units and season

UNWEIGHTED LEAST SQUARES LINEAR REGRESSION OF COSTS

PREDICTOR VARIABLES	COEFFICIENT	STD ERROR	STUDENT'S T	P
CONSTANT	1.2422E+04	3.0106E+04	0.41.	0.6841
UNITS	192.29	22.008	8.74	0.0000
SEASON	2.0237E+04	9229.8	2.19	0.0397

R SQUARED   0.7948   RESID. MEAN SQUARE (MSE) 5.076E+08
ADJUSTED R SQUARED 0.7752   STANDARD DEVIATION   2.253E+04

SOURCE	DF	SS	MS	F	P
REGRESSION	2	4.1280E+10	2.0640E+10	40.66	0.0000
RESIDUAL	21	1.0659E+10	5.0758E+08		
TOTAL	23	5.1939E+10			

DURBIN-WATSON STATISTIC 2.0714

EXPECTED VALUE OF DURBIN-WATSON STATISTIC   2.0933
EXACT VARIANCE OF DURBIN-WATSON STATISTIC   26.511

two multiple regression models, it seems that managers would have a more useful model using both season and either machine hours or units as compared to using either machine hours or units alone.

DATA REQUIREMENTS

Any statistical method is only as good as the data entered in the model. A simple example will illustrate this point. Several years ago a consulting firm conducted a study to see if there were a relationship between various cost elements at the electric-generation facilities of an Eastern public electric utility and kilowatt hour production. In one such regression run the monthly data for maintenance costs included two negative figures of over -$50,000. Because it is unusual (if not impossible) to have a negative maintenance expense, the researchers asked the utility's managers to justify these figures. The response was that during the previous several months the amount of supplies and parts expensed had exceeded the actual supplies and parts used. Thus, the negative entries reflected a reversing entry moving parts *back into* inventory. Obviously, there was no way to adjust the data to find the correct expenses each month and any regression equation would have been meaningless from a practical concern unless the data were cleaned up.

Accurate Cost Records

Perhaps one of the biggest problems is making sure records accurately reflect proper recording of costs. In the case of the electric utility, in order to have accurate records for a future analysis managers would have to record actual maintenance costs on a monthly basis. They must make sure any materials that were issued but not used were returned to inventory that month. In other cases it is not so much a matter of changing the way costs are recorded but of looking through the data to see if errors have taken place.

Leads and Lags

Cost data can lead or lag changes in the independent variable. It is common that electric, gas, telecommunications, and water bills, for example, lag from 30 to 60 days behind their use. Thus, in estimating utility cost as a function of production, managers must be careful to match the correct costs with production.

Maintenance costs can precede or follow heavy use of machinery. In seasonal or cyclical businesses, maintenance will be performed at times when production requirements are low. For example, a heavy equipment construction contractor in the Chicago area would probably do major maintenance functions in the winter months while the equipment was otherwise idle. Any estimate of costs relating to activity should take this timing into account.

Representative Data

The costs used in a regression analysis should be representative of costs at volumes within the relevant range. Outlier observations (i.e., a cost that is very high or very low given the level of the independent variable) change the estimates of b_0 and b_1 in the regression equation. Thus, when a plot of the data, an inspection of the data, or a warning in the printout from a computer regression program shows that there is an outlier, managers should investigate these figures to see if errors exist in cost recording and/ or if the costs are representative of normal operations.

In addition, the time period and range of observations should be neither too short (narrow) nor too long (broad); however, there should be enough observations available to make a reasonable estimate. For example, monthly data for three months is clearly an inadequate length of time. On the other extreme, however, monthly data for ten years might not be useful. Not only will costs change over time as a function of the economy and inflation, but technological changes can make older data obsolete.

Allocations

Many costs include allocations. For example, it is possible that, say, some general office expense was allocated to overhead before the regression for Lucas Manufacturing shown in Exhibit 4-2 was run. If $1,400 in monthly fixed cost had been allocated, then the intercept would be $1,400 too high if we were to consider only separable overhead costs. On the other hand, if costs had been allocated to overhead based on $1.50 per machine hour, then the slope would be overstated by $1.50 per hour. To look at only separable costs, we would have to adjust the original data in Exhibit 4-1. If $1,400 per month had been allocated, then overhead costs should be reduced by $1,400 each. If the allocation had been at $1.50 per machine hour, then the overhead costs would have to be reduced by $1.50 times machine hours for each observation.

As a review problem, rerun the data in Exhibit 4-1 first by subtracting $1,400 from each value of overhead. This will also allow you to use the option of forcing the intercept to zero since, after adjusting the data, the t-test for the intercept is 1.97 with our critical value of 2.16. Next, go back to the original set of data in Exhibit 4-1 but this time remove $1.50 times machine hours from each of the values for overhead. The results of these two regressions are shown in Exhibits 4-9 and 4-10.

Exhibit 4-9
Lucas Manufacturing
Regression and Correlation Analysis:
Overhead Costs Adjusted to Remove $1,400 in Allocated Fixed Costs

A. Basic estimates

UNWEIGHTED LEAST SQUARES LINEAR REGRESSION OF OHCOSTA

PREDICTOR VARIABLES	COEFFICIENT	STD ERROR	STUDENT'S T	P
CONSTANT	-640.54	325.03	-1.97	0.0704
HOURS	7.5087	6.6513E-01	11.29	0.0000

R SQUARED	0.9074	RESID. MEAN SQUARE (MSE)	4.766E+04
ADJUSTED R SQUARED	0.9003	STANDARD DEVIATION	218.3

SOURCE	DF	SS	MS	F	P
REGRESSION	1	6.0744E+06	6.0744E+06	127.44	0.0000
RESIDUAL	13	6.1964E+05	4.7665E+04		
TOTAL	14	6.6941E+06			

DURBIN-WATSON STATISTIC 2.3188

P VALUES, USING DURBIN-WATSON'S BETA APPROXIMATION:
   P (POSITIVE CORR) = 0.7461, P (NEGATIVE CORR) = 0.2539

EXPECTED VALUE OF DURBIN-WATSON STATISTIC 1.9789
EXACT VARIANCE OF DURBIN-WATSON STATISTIC 2.4359E-01

B. Forcing linear intercept to zero

UNWEIGHTED LEAST SQUARES LINEAR REGRESSION OF OHCOSTA

NOTE: MODEL FORCED THROUGH ORIGIN

PREDICTOR VARIABLES	COEFFICIENT	STD ERROR	STUDENT'S T	P
HOURS	6.2178	1.2668E-01	49.08	0.0000

R SQUARED	0.9942	RESID. MEAN SQUARE (MSE)	5.748E+04
ADJUSTED R SQUARED	0.9938	STANDARD DEVIATION	239.8

SOURCE	DF	SS	MS	F	P
REGRESSION	1	1.3848E+08	1.3848E+08	2409.12	0.0000
RESIDUAL	14	8.0475E+05	5.7482E+04		
TOTAL	14	1.3929E+08			

Exhibit 4-10
Lucas Manufacturing
Regression and Correlation Analysis:
Overhead Costs Adjusted to Remove $1.50 per Machine Hour

UNWEIGHTED LEAST SQUARES LINEAR REGRESSION OF OHCOSTB

PREDICTOR VARIABLES	COEFFICIENT	STD ERROR	STUDENT'S T	P
CONSTANT	759.46	325.03	2.34	0.0361
HOURS	6.0087	6.6513E-01	9.03	0.0000

R SQUARED	0.8626	RESID. MEAN SQUARE (MSE)	4.766E+04
ADJUSTED R SQUARED	0.8520	STANDARD DEVIATION	218.3

SOURCE	DF	SS	MS	F	P
REGRESSION	1	3.8899E+06	3.8899E+06	81.61	0.0000
RESIDUAL	13	6.1964E+05	4.7665E+04		
TOTAL	14	4.5095E+06			

DURBIN-WATSON STATISTIC 2.3188

P VALUES, USING DURBIN-WATSON'S BETA APPROXIMATION:
   P (POSITIVE CORR) = 0.7461, P (NEGATIVE CORR) = 0.2539

EXPECTED VALUE OF DURBIN-WATSON STATISTIC 1.9789
EXACT VARIANCE OF DURBIN-WATSON STATISTIC 2.4359E-01

In the case of Exhibit 4-9, all the measures of the usefulness of the regression remain the same with the exception of the calculated t-value for the intercept. As stated above, we cannot reject the null hypothesis that B_0 = 0. Thus, we have rerun the regression forcing the intercept to zero (through the origin). Note what this does to the computed t-value for the slope and for r^2: both increase considerably.

Another side effect of this illustration is the negative intercept shown at the top of Exhibit 4-9. It is a good example of why managers cannot interpret the intercept as a reflection of fixed costs at zero volume. Although the intercept is not significant in this example, there are other cases where a negative intercept would be. Remember that the data are from a relevant range. While it is not intuitively appealing, the slope from that range may be such that the regression line, if extended to the axis, would show a negative intercept. Managers should question negative intercepts but should not necessarily reject them just because they are negative.

Exhibit 4-10 shows the results if costs were allocated on a variable basis at $1.50 per machine hour. As stated above, the slope goes down by $1.50. This seems appropriate because you removed $1.50 per hour from the data before you ran the regression. In addition to a reduction in the slope, r^2 goes from 0.90 to 0.86 and the computed t-value for the slope goes from 11.29 to 9.03. Both of these changes are related and logical. If $1.50 per machine hour of allocated costs were included in the original data, then, at least for *that* portion of overhead costs, there is a perfect correlation between costs and machine hours: allocated costs were *added* to separable costs at $1.50 times machine hours. By removing these allocated costs from the data set, we have also reduced the degree of association between these costs and machine hours. This affects the coefficient of determination. In addition, while the slope is reduced by $1.50 (from $7.51 to $6.01), the standard error of the slope stays the same since each residual $(y - y')$ is unchanged. Thus, the computed t-value of b_1/s_{b_1} goes down since the numerator is lower while the denominator is the same. To test the assertion that the residuals are unchanged, pick a value of machine hours (say, 500) and calculate y' and then the residual $(y - y')$, first using the original data in Exhibit 4-1 and then the adjusted data when you removed $1.50 per hour. You will find that at 500 hours the residual is $93 in both cases.

CROSS-SECTIONAL DATA

The major illustrations to this point have used time-series data. The following example shows a cross section of data at one period of time. Crane, Inc. has 17 regional warehouses for mail-order computer supplies. Chris Crane, president, is trying to estimate shipping costs for the items the company sells. She has identified the following as possible relevant variables:

weight (in pounds)
size (length + width + height in inches)
fragile (percent of shipments)
warehouse location

While she is not certain that these variables will all be significant, she believes them all to be relevant, logically associated with shipping costs, and not collinear. The data that the Accounting Department has accumulated appear in Exhibit 4-11 (page 190). Results reflect that Ms. Crane's assumptions are valid. Exhibit 4-12 (page 191) shows the regression results and a correlation matrix for all the variables. From goodness of fit to lack of serial correlation to lack of collinearity, this is a good estimate of shipping costs.

This illustration provides a model that managers can use to look at marginal costs. Thus, for example, total costs will go up by over $43 per pound with size, fragility, and location held constant. The same marginal cost statements could be made for each of the independent variables.

Cross-sectional data differ from time-series data in that the former involve several observations at one period of time while the latter consist of several observations over time. While serial correlation is more usually associated

Exhibit 4-11
Crane, Inc.
Shipping Data

Warehouse	Weight	Size	Fragile %	Location	Cost
1	43	350	20	1	$30,366
2	35	450	37	1	31,502
3	46	560	10	0	28,390
4	45	360	25	0	29,174
5	60	330	10	1	29,237
6	40	420	12	0	27,879
7	54	435	34	1	32,216
8	40	410	14	0	28,332
9	48	480	22	0	29,496
10	42	510	9	0	28,246
11	44	380	35	1	31,081
12	52	520	23	0	30,992
13	42	420	25	1	30,923
14	48	450	10	1	29,196
15	45	400	15	0	28,124
16	50	360	20	1	29,576
17	38	500	32	0	31,347

Where: Location = 1 is city; location = 0 is rural

with time-series analysis, it can also occur using cross-sectional data. Remedies are discussed earlier in this chapter.

STEPWISE LINEAR REGRESSION

Some computer packages allow a user to hunt for the best regression models. This process is stepwise linear regression. For example, say that a manager wanted to examine the Crane example. One choice for the manager would be to run every possible combination of variables and then to choose the best model or models available. Even for a relatively uncomplicated problem like this one with four independent variables, the following fifteen models could be run.

Four-Variable Models
weight, size, fragile, location

Three-Variable Models
weight, size, fragile
weight, size, location
weight, fragile, location
size, fragile, location

Two-Variable Models
weight, size
weight, fragile
weight, location
size, fragile
size, location
fragile, location

One-Variable Models
weight
size
fragile
location

Exhibit 4-12
Crane, Inc.
Regression and Correlation Analysis

1. Correlation matrix

SIMPLE CORRELATIONS

	COST	FRAG_PCT	LOCATION	SIZE	WAREHOUSE	WEIGHT
COST	1.0000					
FRAG_PCT	0.8704	1.0000				
LOCATION	0.5270	0.3172	1.0000			
SIZE	0.0150	-0.0575	-0.5091	1.0000		
WAREHOUSE	0.0597	0.0286	-0.0722	0.1331	1.0000	
WEIGHT	0.0336	-0.2357	0.2483	-0.2109	0.0398	1.0000

CASES INCLUDED 17   MISSING CASES 0

2. Cost as a function of fragile percent (FRAG_PCT), location, size, and weight

UNWEIGHTED LEAST SQUARES LINEAR REGRESSION OF COST

PREDICTOR VARIABLES	COEFFICIENT	STD ERROR	STUDENT'S T	P
CONSTANT	2.2311E+04	1409.6	15.83	0.0000
FRAG_PCT	117.45	13.618	8.62	0.0000
LOCATION	976.64	287.04	3.40	0.0052
SIZE	6.0166	2.0449	2.94	0.0123
WEIGHT	43.257	20.380	2.12	0.0553

R SQUARED	0.9153	RESID. MEAN SQUARE (MSE)	2.119E+05
ADJUSTED R SQUARED	0.8871	STANDARD DEVIATION	460.3

SOURCE	DF	SS	MS	F	P
REGRESSION	4	2.7485E+07	6.8713E+06	32.43	0.0000
RESIDUAL	12	2.5424E+06	2.1187E+05		
TOTAL	16	3.0028E+07			

CASES INCLUDED 17   MISSING CASES 0

DURBIN-WATSON STATISTIC 1.8998

EXPECTED VALUE OF DURBIN-WATSON STATISTIC 1.8374
EXACT VARIANCE OF DURBIN-WATSON STATISTIC 4.7482

After running all these models, a manager would apply the rules we have discussed (goodness of fit, t-tests, F-tests, checking for serial correlation and/or collinearity, and so on). Imagine, though, that instead of four possible useful independent variables, a manager had twenty or one hundred independent variables. Think of the number of regression models that would have to be checked! Stepwise linear regression helps in such large problems. This form of the regression model automatically compares all models and prints out those that are the best for each variable level. Thus, for the Crane example, since there is only one four-variable model, it would be reported. The best of the four three-variable models, the best of the six two-variable models, and the best of the four one-variable models would also be shown. (Manuals for such programs should be consulted to find out how the word "best" is defined.)

There is a danger in using the stepwise regression technique. A manager may be tempted to create a huge data set with little reason for many of the variables to be included. He or she may think that a naïve "hunting trip" may yield useful results. This violates a prime assumption of linear regression, the economic/logical sense of a proposed relationship. Thus, managers need to be as careful in creating good data sets with the simplest and with the most complex of models.

REGRESSION AND NEW MANAGEMENT ACCOUNTING TRENDS

Activity-based costing and management (ABC/ABM) are based on knowing what activities or transactions cause the acquisition and/or use of resources. Theory of Constraints advocates want managers to look at throughput per scarce resource as part of dealing with a dynamic environment of changing constraints. Regression and correlation analysis can provide needed input for ABC/ABM and TOC. These and other costing and management systems need a manager to have as accurate information as possible. Regression and correlation analysis allows managers to establish objective measures of relationships: more accuracy.

SUMMARY

Simple and multiple linear regression are everyday tools managers can use to aid in estimating cost and other behavior. The basic assumptions and data requirements for both simple and multiple regression are the same and are based, in some ways, on the assumptions of the basic cost-volume-profit model. As with all models, managers should not only be knowledgeable about underlying assumptions but also know which assumptions are so important that their violation means that the resulting estimates cannot be used. Managers should look at data, possible variables to use, and output with an eye not only for objective measures but also for logic and reasonableness. Models have the potential of helping managers make estimates and decisions; they do not replace managerial judgment.

The discussion to this point has covered the linear model. While this model is the easiest to use, managers do find situations where costs are nonlinear. The next chapter covers this topic.

❖ *APPENDIX 4A*

SIMPLE LINEAR REGRESSION AND CORRELATION FORMULAS

The basic formulas relating to simple linear regression start with the normal equations

$$\Sigma y = nb_0 + b_1\Sigma x$$
$$\Sigma xy = b_0\Sigma x + b_1\Sigma x^2 \tag{A1}$$

which are based on minimizing the sum of the squared deviations. This term, $\Sigma(y - y')^2$, forms the basis for many of the other parts of simple linear regression.

Coefficient of determination   If a manager had a set of data like that in Exhibit 4-1 but thought that machine hours (as well as any other independent variable) had little or no effect on costs, a reasonable way to estimate overhead costs would be to sum the 15 observations and get an arithmetic average cost by dividing by 15, or $65,597, from Exhibit 4-1, divided by 15 equals $4,373. This would be the estimate of costs at any level of machine hours if there were not a relationship between costs and hours. If managers wanted to look at some variability around this sample mean, they would use the variance of

$$\sigma^2 = \frac{\Sigma(y - \bar{y}_i)^2}{n - 1} \tag{A2}$$

where: y_i = the individual cost data points
        n = the number of observations

In estimating costs using the OLS regression method, managers create another average cost, y'. For example, the estimate of overhead costs at 390 machine hours using the output from the Lucas Manufacturing example in Exhibit 4-2 is $y' = \$759 + (\$7.51)(390) = \$3,688$, rounded.[12] Thus, *on average*, costs are expected to be about \$3,688 at 390 machine hours. Managers do expect some variability around this estimate. If we consider y' an average, then its variance would be

$$\sigma^2_{y'} = \frac{\Sigma(y - y')^2}{n - 1} \tag{A3}$$

Formula (A2) yields a variance relating actual costs to the arithmetic mean. Formula (A3) is a variance based on the relationship of actual to predicted costs where the mean is y'. These two formulas show two pieces of a variance:

actual cost − average cost   = the total variance
actual cost − estimated cost = the unexplained variance

Note that the numerator of the unexplained variance is the sum of the squared residuals which, as we have stated, are caused by random fluctuations or variables that we have not identified. Thus, this variance is unexplained by the regression results. Using these two terms, the coefficient of determination is

$$r^2 = 1 - \frac{\Sigma(y - y')^2}{\Sigma(y - \bar{y})^2} \tag{A4}$$

where the denominators of the two variances cancel out.

Standard Error of the Estimate   The standard error of the estimate is

$$S_e = \sqrt{\frac{\Sigma(y - y')^2}{n - 2}} \tag{A5}$$

As shown on page 169, the standard error of the estimate is the primary part of the standard error of the forecast in formula (1).

Standard Error of the Slope   The standard error of the estimate also plays a significant part in the standard error of the slope.

---

[12] We round both the intercept and the slope since nothing is gained in accuracy by carrying these estimates out to several places.

$$S_{b_1} = \frac{S_e}{\sqrt{\Sigma x^2 - n\bar{x}^2}} \qquad \text{(A6)}$$

Standard Error of the Intercept   The standard error of the slope is the core of the standard error of the intercept.

$$S_{b_0} = S_{b_1} \sqrt{\frac{\Sigma x_j^2}{n}} \qquad \text{(A7)}$$

PROBLEMS AND CASES

4-1. Data Requirements

Fences, Inc., wants to estimate overhead so they can build standard costs for their products. The accounting staff has assembled data for the past 48 months. It looks as if machine hours should be the best predictor of overhead costs. However, besides machine hours (and cost), data on labor hours are also available. In looking into the data provided by the staff you find that in the first year there was a major machine breakdown that shut the plant down for a month. In addition, countywide reassessment of property taxes occurred both in the first and in the third year. Inflation had been a significant factor four years ago but the rate had tapered off from 8 percent to a current 3 percent. Labor all belonged to a union and received an increase at the beginning of year three. Due to a new nuclear plant, utility rates had almost doubled about a year ago.

Required:
As a consultant to management, what would you recommend? What data seem useful? How can Fences, Inc., estimate factory overhead?

4-2. Effects of Inflation (CMA)

Effects of inflation, if not adequately incorporated in planning and not properly accounted for in the evaluation of performance, can result in misleading information and, consequently, inappropriate decisions by company management.

In an effort to properly recognize inflation for planning and control purposes, a major corporation established a program for the education of its management called "Effectively Managing with Inflation." The program identified measurements or situations that required the effect of inflation to be specifically incorporated into the analysis. Four of the items covered in the program are as follows:

- Service business versus manufacturing business.
- Segment expansion/contraction.
- Operating margins.
- Return on investment.

Required:

For each of the four items listed above:

1. Indicate how company management may be led to incorrect decisions when inflation factors are not properly identified and incorporated into the analysis.
2. Suggest adjustments which could be incorporated into the analysis to properly recognize and account for the effects of inflation.

4-3. Interpretation of Regression Results

You have been hired as a consultant by a mail order company that deals in sophisticated electronic products for industry. The managers of the company are looking at shipping costs at each of their eighteen regional warehouses. Shipments and total costs at these facilities for one month are as follows:

Warehouse	Shipments	Cost
1	34	$47,756
2	71	98,249
3	32	45,181
4	37	47,927
5	73	98,139
6	30	66,559
7	27	58,292
8	61	79,068
9	42	66,438
10	67	85,665
11	25	62,579
12	28	59,464
13	32	47,249
14	65	93,705
15	37	66,535
16	21	52,274
17	33	49,229
18	45	58,073

Results of a computer program relating costs to shipments are as follows:

	RIGHT-HAND VARIABLE	ESTIMATED COEFFICIENT	STANDARD ERROR	T_STATISTIC	PROB.
1	Shipment	919.865849876	(124.52666) T = 7.38690		0.000
2	Constant	26849.108560794	(5653.74810) T = 4.74890		0.000

```
SAMPLE SIZE                      =            18        (DF = 16)
     SUM OF SQUARED RESIDUALS    =    1244300356.191228
              VARIANCE (MSE)     =      77768772.261951
  STANDARD ERROR (ROOT MSE) =    8818.660457
                   R-SQUARED     =           0.773263
```

```
      ADJUSTED  R-SQUARED   =            0.759092
      F-STATISTIC ( 1, 16)  =           54.566275  (ρ=0.0000)
     SUM  OF  RESIDUALS     =           -0.000000
DURBIN-WATSON  STATISTIC    =            1.685734
```

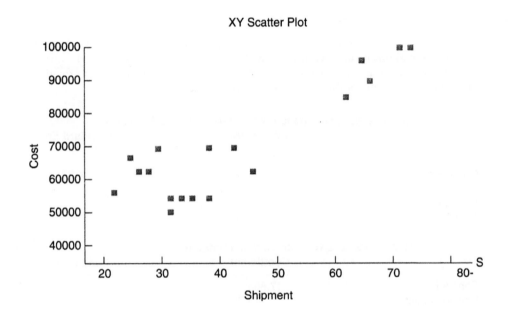

XY Scatter Plot

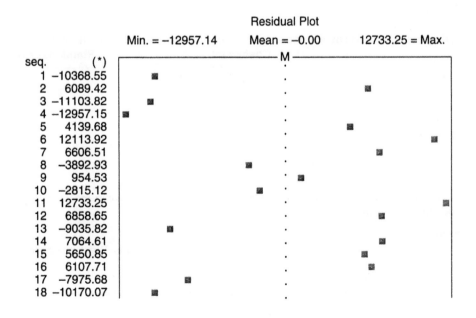

Residual Plot

Min. = −12957.14	Mean = −0.00	12733.25 = Max.

seq.	(*)
1	−10368.55
2	6089.42
3	−11103.82
4	−12957.15
5	4139.68
6	12113.92
7	6606.51
8	−3892.93
9	954.53
10	−2815.12
11	12733.25
12	6858.65
13	−9035.82
14	7064.61
15	5650.85
16	6107.71
17	−7975.68
18	−10170.07

Required:

Write a report to management in which you discuss the validity of the data used and your interpretation of the regression results as presented. If appropriate, provide other evidence that may help management to predict shipping costs based on number of shipments.

4-4. Interpretation of Results

Metal Pole Company has run a series of regressions as a step toward a flexible budget for manufacturing overhead. On the basis of machine hours and units of output, the following results were obtained. While the data have not been provided, there were no serious outliers, nor were there any gaps in the data.

Regression 1: Overhead cost as related to machine hours

	Coefficient	Standard Error
Constant	−32,657	
Machine hours	16.57	4.32

$r^2 = .77$
$S_e = 3,456$

Regression 2: Overhead cost as related to units of output

	Coefficient	Standard Error
Constant	17,865	
Units of output	13.76	3.87

$r^2 = .61$
$S_e = 3,973$

Regression 3: Overhead cost as related to machine hours and units of output

	Coefficient	Standard Error
Constant	−15,373	
Machine hours	7.37	3.31
Units of output	10.44	3.81

$R^2 = .79$
$S_e = 1,623$

In addition, a correlation matrix showed a .86 relationship between machine hours and units of output.

Required:
1. Determine the computed t-values for all three regression runs. What is the meaning of a computed t-value?
2. Explain the meaning of r^2 in regressions 1 and 2 as well as R^2 in regression 3.
3. Explain the meaning of a negative intercept in regression runs 1 and 3.

4. Using the results of regression 3, what is the estimate of overhead costs if there are 3,000 machine hours and 2,000 units of output? How much will that estimate change if units go up by 100 but machine hours remain the same?

5. Evaluate each set of regression results. Point out the strengths and weaknesses of each regression. Write a note to management choosing and justifying one of these results.

4-5. Interpret and Explain Results (CMA)

The Lockit Company manufactures door knobs for residential homes and apartments. Lockit is considering the use of simple and multiple linear regression analysis to forecast annual sales because previous forecasts have been inaccurate. The sales forecast will be used to initiate the budgeting process and to identify better the underlying process that generates sales.

Larry Husky, the controller of Lockit, has considered many possible independent variables and equations to predict sales and has narrowed his choices to four equations. Husky used annual observations from twenty prior years to estimate each of the four equations.

Following is a definition of the variables used in the four equations and a statistical summary of these equations:

S_t = Forecasted sales (in dollars) for Lockit in time period t
S_{t-1} = Actual sales (in dollars) for Lockit in time period $t - 1$
G_t = Forecasted United States gross national product in time period t
G_{t-1} = Actual United States gross national product in time period $t - 1$
N_{t-1} = Lockit's net income in time period $t - 1$

Statistical Summary of Four Equations

| | | | Coefficients | | | | |
| | | | Dependent Variable (Intercept) | Independent Variable (Rate) | Standard Error of the Estimate | Coefficient of Correlation | t-Value |
Equation	Dependent Variable	Independent Variable(s)					
1	S_t	S_{t-1}	+$ 500,000	+$ 1.10	$500,000	+.97	5.50
2	S_t	G_t	+$1,000,000	+$ .00001	$510,000	+.95	10.00
3	S_t	G_{t-1}	+$ 900,000	+$.000012	$520,000	+.90	5.00
4	S_t		+$ 600,000		$490,000	+.98	
		N_{t-1}		+$ 10.00			4.00
		G_t		+$.000002			1.50
		G_{t-1}		+$.000003			3.00

Required:

1. Write Equations 2 and 4 in the form $y = a + bx$.
2. If actual sales are $1,500,000 in 19X1, what would be the forecasted sales for Lockit in 19X2?
3. Explain the meaning and significance of the coefficient of correlation.

4. Why might Larry Husky prefer Equation 3 to Equation 2?
5. Explain the advantages and disadvantages of using Equation 4 to forecast annual sales.

4-6. Explain Results (CMA Adapted)

John Wood, a financial analyst for a major automobile corporation, has been monitoring the funds used in advertising campaigns and the funds used for automobile factory rebates. Financial data have been accumulated for the last twenty-four months along with customer sales, i.e., automobiles sold. Wood contends that there may be a relationship between the level of automobile sales and funds expended on advertising and/or factory rebates. If such a relationship can be determined, the company may be able to estimate sales demand based upon various levels of funding commitments for one or both types of expenditures.

Regression equations and supporting statistical values were developed for the various relationships between variables and are presented below. The meanings of the notations used in the equations are as follows:

$$A = \text{Advertising funds in } \$100,000$$
$$R = \text{Funds for factory rebates in } \$1,000,000$$
$$D = \text{Customer sales demand (automobiles sold) in } 10,000 \text{ units}$$

	Equation 1	Equation 2	Equation 3	Equation 4
Equation	$D = 2.455 + .188A$	$D = 2.491 + .44R$	$R = 6.052 + .005A$	$D = -.184 + .186A + .437R$
Coefficient of correlation	.643	.560	.014	.838
Coefficient of determination	.414	.314	.0002	.703
Standard error of the estimate	1.325	1.434	2.202	.922
Reliability of the coefficient of correlation at 5 percent and:				
• 22 degrees of freedom	.404	.404	.404	
• 21 degrees of freedom				.498

Required:
1. If the corporation is projecting advertising expenditures amounting to $1,500,000 and factory rebate expenditures amounting to $12,000,000 for the next time period, calculate expected customer demand in units using:
   a. Equation 1.
   b. Equation 4.
2. Assume that Equation 4 is employed to estimate a total customer demand of 104,160 automobiles for a time period. Using a 95 percent confidence level, determine the range of automobile sales that could occur during the time period.
3. Select the regression equation which would be most advantageous to predict customer sales demand and explain why it is the best.

4. Explain the significance of Equation 3 and its value for the regression analysis evaluation.
5. Each of the regression equations includes a constant.
    a. Discuss the meaning of the constant term included in regression Equation 2.
    b. What is the significance of the value being negative in regression Equation 4? Explain your answer.

4-7. Simple Linear Regression and Outlier Observations

Tracy Valve Company manufacturers valves used mainly in plumbing and air conditioning. As part of a current emphasis to try to better associate costs with what seems to drive them, Ann Durham, the chief management accountant, has asked you to look at the following cost and machine hour figures. Twenty grinding machines are part of this sample.

Machine	Department Costs	Machine Hours
1	$67,425	2,503
2	82,308	3,215
3	71,452	2,763
4	76,957	2,888
5	81,118	3,173
6	87,778	3,304
7	70,396	2,623
8	81,538	3,053
9	66,719	2,598
10	75,837	2,833
11	83,764	3,255
12	83,579	3,142
13	75,558	2,937
14	67,857	2,645
15	80,468	3,003
16	79,709	3,113
17	77,091	2,870
18	67,030	2,607
19	73,606	2,865
20	68,588	2,535

Required:
1. With a computer program, analyze the above data using simple linear regression and correlation analysis. Your computer work should include appropriate graphs of the data and of the residuals. Write a note to Ms. Durham stating what your conclusions are about these data and the relationship between machine hours and cost.
2. After you have run your primary analysis but before she had received your memo, Durham sees that there was an error in the first observation. New data show a cost of $77,000 instead of $67,425. Rerun all your computer analyses and tell Durham the effect of this one new data point.

4-8. Time Series—Inflation

The managers of Spartan Manufacturing, a small third-world company in an unstable area, are trying to develop an overhead application measure for the upcoming year. Costs and machine hours, the variable that management thinks is most associated with the overhead costs, are shown below for the past year.

Period	Hours	Cost
1	125	$ 5,915
2	183	6,432
3	245	8,162
4	95	6,297
5	163	7,260
6	226	8,334
7	217	9,242
8	155	7,921
9	203	9,186
10	233	10,697
11	177	9,961
12	189	9,802

Required:
1. Using a computer program, analyze the above data and assess the relationship between cost and hours. Graph the data and the residuals as part of your analysis.
2. Over lunch with the Minister of Finance you find out that the ongoing inflation rate in this country is about 4 percent a month. Adjust the data and run a new regression and correlation analysis.

4-9. Allocated Costs

The president of Oxymoron Corporation has asked you to look at the following overhead and machine hour figures for the forming department and give her an estimate of how to apply overhead to units of product.

Machine Hours	Overhead Cost
2,234	$ 69,142
3,451	116,191
4,523	121,550
2,188	68,097
3,264	111,503
3,895	127,940
4,752	140,343
2,955	85,576
3,952	128,733
4,285	123,798
3,737	120,355
3,523	111,996
2,586	77,155
4,383	134,282
4,237	135,856

Required:

1. Using the above data and simple linear regression, estimate the rate per machine hour that should be applied for overhead in this department. Evaluate the results obtained from a regression computer program.

2. The president informs you that she has been advised that $10,000 per observation of allocated fixed costs were inadvertently included in the above figures.

    a. Without running a new regression, what is the effect of this information on the estimate of the intercept, the cost per machine hour, r^2, S_e, and S_b?

    b. Now run a new regression and correlation analysis and verify that your analysis is correct. What is your evaluation of this new regression without allocated costs included?

3. The president now informs you that she was wrong in part 2. Instead of a flat $10,000 per observation, allocated costs were $10 per machine hour and were included in the original figures. Repeat the requirements for 2a and 2b with this new information.

4-10. Change in Cost Function

Data appear below for overhead costs in the milling department of Tenney Manufacturing, a defense contractor. Tenney's management is trying to assign overhead costs as part of their cost-plus contract arrangement with the Department of Defense.

Month	Hours	Cost
Jan, 19X7	4,211	$110,037
Feb	4,781	119,638
Mar	3,901	103,770
Apr	4,360	110,572
May	3,571	97,110
June	3,915	106,027
July	4,444	114,388
Aug	4,185	107,538
Sept	4,128	108,709
Oct	3,981	106,841
Nov	3,611	98,519
Dec	3,444	105,327
Jan, 19X8	3,313	102,026
Feb	3,415	102,807
Mar	3,009	96,554
Apr	3,161	98,782
May	3,237	100,534
June	3,367	102,172
July	3,115	97,099
Aug	2,876	93,588

Required:

Assist management in determining a way to apply overhead based on hours. First run a regression, a plot of the data, and a plot of the residuals using all the data. As a result of analyzing these results, make recommendations to management and run new regressions and plots as appropriate.

4-11. Stickiness of Costs

Manx Manufacturing, a major subcontractor in the automobile industry, is trying to establish a flexible budget for overhead. Data for the past 15 months appear below. Management believes that overhead costs are best related to machine hours.

Month	Machine Hours	Overhead Cost
Jan, 19X3	9,345	$376,267
Feb	8,123	331,367
Mar	8,954	356,016
Apr	9,124	360,586
May	8,877	359,531
June	8,651	345,599
July	9,144	368,729
Aug	5,465	223,046
Sept	5,723	235,005
Oct	5,377	225,702
Nov	4,567	196,559
Dec	5,195	184,401
Jan, 19X4	4,545	156,695
Feb	4,737	163,914
Mar	5,009	177,932

Production was curtailed in August 19X3. Management thought that this was only temporary and did not make some necessary cost adjustments based on lower production for a few months. Finally these cost adjustments were made.

Required:
1. Analyze the above data for 15 months using regression and correlation analysis. Plot the data and the residuals as part of your analysis. Write a memo to the management of Manx explaining your conclusions.
2. If there are other regression analyses that you want to run as a result of your conclusions in part 1, do so and explain the results that you obtain.

4-12. Time Series versus Moving Average (CMA)

The Glenall Company is a maker of numerous small industrial items. In some cases the items are sold individually, but most are sold in combinations. The market for these products is extremely competitive. Recently, the company has been losing sales because of stock shortages. The product demand, production, and inventory history by month for the 19X3–19X4 fiscal year are reproduced below.

Month	Sales Demand	Production	Ending Inventory
July	9,400	10,000	5,600
August	10,200	10,000	5,400
September	10,200	10,000	5,200

Month	Sales Demand	Production	Ending Inventory
October	15,300	12,000	1,900
November	15,600	12,000	0
December	15,800	16,000	200
January	18,300	16,000	0
February	19,300	18,500	0
March	19,600	19,500	0
April	15,900	19,500	3,600
May	16,200	16,000	3,400
June	17,200	16,000	2,200

All production schedules for each product are planned by an ad hoc committee composed of both production and sales personnel. On the fifth of every month, production is determined for the coming month. Demand is determined by actual sales and unfilled orders received since the fifth of the prior month. There are no back orders. Thus, sales that cannot be filled within sixty days of receipt are lost. Once production runs are determined, they cannot be easily changed without substantial set-up, sequencing, and raw material carrying costs.

The production manager blames faulty demand forecasts for the current crisis while the sales manager blames the production manager for not keeping enough safety stock on hand to satisfy customer demand. Company officials are not satisfied with the current forecasting method and have decided that a more sophisticated basis should be employed. Two models that have been proposed are a three-month moving average and a time-series regression.

Amy Chew of Glenall's Planning Department was assigned to develop both models and was told that both models are to be based on historical data. She developed the moving average model to forecast demand for the coming month based upon the actual sales demand for the prior three months as shown below.

$$D_t = \frac{\sum_{i=1}^{3} D_{t-1}}{3}$$

where: D_t = forecasted sales demand for coming month
D_{t-1} = actual sales demand for prior month i

The model based on the time-series analysis was developed through the use of the least squares method. The demand was regressed on a trend with four seasonal components, i.e., each quarter of the year was considered a seasonal component. The fourth quarter seasonal factor was actually incorporated into the intercept term. The resulting model is reproduced below.

$$D_T = 11,100 + 488\ T + S_i$$

where: D_T = forecasted sales demand for month T
T = the month in the time series (e.g., July 1 X3 = 1)
S = quarterly seasonal factor
i = applicable quarter; i = 1, 2, or 3

S_1 = seasonal factor for first quarter (July, August, September); value = –2,110

S_2 = seasonal factor for second quarter (October, November, December); value = +2,060

S_3 = seasonal factor for third quarter (January, February, March); value = +4,100

r^2 = .99

F-statistic = 467

The seasonal factor to be used in the model depends upon the month for which the sales demand is being forecasted; for example, the forecast for January means the third quarter seasonal factor would be applicable.

Required:
1. Forecast Glenall Company's sales demand for July 19X4 using:
   a. the moving average model.
   b. the model based on the time-series analysis.
2. Compare and contrast, in general terms, the model based on the time-series analysis with the moving average model with respect to:
   a. complexity.
   b. applicability to Glenall Company.
3. If past sales trends continue for Glenall Company in the future, which of the two models will yield the more accurate forecast for future sales demand? Explain your answer.

4-13. Cost Prediction and Allocation[13]

You are a staff member of the controller's department of the REG Company. The company produces and sells five products (rear axles, front axles, transmissions, chassis, and motors; referred to henceforth as products A, B, C, D, and E). For budgeting purposes it is necessary to estimate the factory overhead costs for January and February of 19X3. Also, it is necessary to determine the overhead application rate(s) for 19X3. You have been given this assignment. The memo requesting you to do this included the following information:

1. Overhead costs recorded in 19X1 and 19X2:

	19X1	19X2
January	$348,077	$951,013
February	506,297	509,049
March	454,759	614,348
April	435,517	534,805
May	517,108	579,023
June	600,914	618,611
July	484,831	662,031
August	433,080	519,370
September	473,406	569,046
October	556,618	544,753
November	491,223	490,512
December	546,336	545,186

---

[13] This case was written by Ronald V. Hartley, "Cost Prediction and Allocation," *Issues in Accounting Education* 2:1 (American Accounting Association, Spring 1987), pp. 141–151.

2. Effective September 19X1, several of the stamping machines were replaced.
3. There are other data in the system (your instructor is the "system" for this pur-
    pose) that might be helpful to you in completing the assignment. Requests for this
    information must be submitted in *writing*.

Required:
Prepare a report to the controller that communicates your recommendation concerning:

1. Overhead costs to be budgeted for January and February, 19X3.
2. Overhead application rate(s) to be used in 19X3 under full absorption costing.

4-14. Sources of Data[14]

Automobile manufacturers try to predict sales in order to help with their annual
planning as well as gain a more long-term view of capital requirements. You have
been hired as a consultant to Elliott Manufacturing, a supplier of bumpers to the
industry. You have the data attached in Exhibit 1 consisting of annual figures for
retail sales of passenger cars, disposable personal income in 1987 dollars, the index
of consumer sentiment, the total civilian unemployment rate, and interest rates as
represented by the six-month commercial paper rate.

Sales are in thousands of cars, income in billions of 1987 dollars, sentiment in an
index with 100 as the base, unemployment in percent, and interest in percent. Retail
passenger car sales, disposable personal income, the unemployment rate, and the
commercial paper rate can be found in *Survey of Current Business*.[15] This same source
can be used to find annual figures for the Index of Consumer Sentiment.

The data in Exhibit 1 go through 1991. Fill in data for these same five variables
for 1992 through the present.

Required:
You are part of a team that has been hired as consultants to Elliott Manufacturing.
You are responsible for making an oral report to management coupled with a full
written analysis in which you deal with all parts of this and the following problem.
Present your analysis and findings in a coherent and organized manner. Make sure
that tables, figures, and graphs (whether for the written report or as handouts for
the oral report) are clear, well organized, and have adequate labels and titles. The
items that follow here and at the end of the next problem are meant as a guide to
your analysis rather than an outline for the final reports.

1. Fill in the table to the present. Cite the source, issue, and page for all additional
    data.
2. Using a computer regression program, do the following:
    a. Plot each of the variables over time
    b. Graph income versus sales
    c. Run a regression of sales against income; also run a regression of sales
        against sentiment

---

[14] Problems 4-14 and 4-15 were written by Donald Elliott.
[15] *Survey of Current Business* is a monthly publication of the Bureau of Economic Analysis of
the United States Department of Commerce. The blue pages in the middle of each monthly
issue contain annual and monthly data on many useful economic series, such as measures of
income, production, inventories, prices, trade, employment, and finance. The yellow pages contain data previously published in *Business Conditions Digest*, consisting of monthly data for
indicators of economic and business activity.

Exhibit 1

Year	Sales	Income	Sentiment	Unempl	Interest
1966	9,035	1,734.3	93.80	3.80	5.55
1967	8,347	1,811.4	94.10	3.80	5.10
1968	9,655	1,886.8	93.10	3.60	5.90
1969	9,582	1,947.4	88.20	3.50	7.83
1970	8,403	2,025.3	76.50	4.90	7.72
1971	10,227	2,099.9	81.10	5.90	5.11
1972	10,872	2,186.2	90.40	5.60	4.69
1973	11,350	2,334.1	76.10	4.90	8.15
1974	8,775	2,317.0	64.00	5.60	9.84
1975	8,539	2,355.4	70.50	8.50	6.32
1976	9,994	2,440.9	85.40	7.70	5.35
1977	11,046	2,512.6	86.80	7.10	5.60
1978	11,164	2,638.4	79.40	6.10	7.99
1979	10,559	2,710.1	66.00	5.80	10.91
1980	8,979	2,733.6	64.40	7.10	12.29
1981	8,535	2,795.8	70.70	7.60	14.76
1982	7,980	2,820.4	68.00	9.70	11.89
1983	9,179	2,893.6	87.50	9.60	8.89
1984	10,394	3,080.1	97.50	7.50	10.16
1985	11,039	3,162.1	93.17	7.20	8.01
1986	11,450	3,261.9	94.80	7.00	6.39
1987	10,278	3,289.6	90.60	6.20	6.85
1988	10,639	3,404.3	93.73	5.50	7.68
1989	9,903	3,471.2	92.80	5.30	8.80
1990	9,499	3,538.3	81.60	5.50	7.95
1991	8,388	3,509.0	77.60	6.70	5.85

    d. Run a regression of sales using the four variables as the independent variables; store the residuals

    e. Forecast sales for the next two years using the regression in d.· (*Hint*: you must first forecast all the exogenous variables before you can use the regression to forecast sales.)

3. Look at the plot for sales. Would you expect a forecast of sales from a simple linear trendline to be very accurate?

4. Look at a plot of income. Would you expect a forecast of income from a simple linear trendline to perform well?

5. Would linear trendlines be useful in forecasting sentiment, the unemployment rate, and/or the interest rate?

6. Look at the regression results in part 2.

    a. For the simple regression of sales and income, what is your assessment of the results?

    b. For the multiple regression of sales and the other four variables, how do these results compare with the simple regression model? Comment especially on r^2, the *t*-statistic, and the Durbin-Watson statistic. Do all of the coefficients have proper signs? Explain.

7. Look at the years following 1973 in your tables and graphs. Was there any obvious break in behavior after this period? What do the residuals show? What caused this to occur? How could this be accommodated in the multiple regression model? Would knowledge of the years in which strikes had occurred also be helpful in understanding the residuals? How?

8. How did tax reform affect 1986 auto sales? How did the Gulf War affect auto sales in the early 1990s? Will your regression as specified here take these factors into account? Explain briefly.

9. How did you forecast income, sentiment, unemployment rate, and interest rate? Do your forecasts for automobile sales show growth or decline? How are these forecasts related to the forecasts for income, sentiment, unemployment rate, and interest rate?

10. Do you think that your forecast is realistic? Explain briefly.

4-15. Model Building

This is a continuation of the previous problem. In that problem, the model needs improvement or may even be misspecified and, therefore, not forecast very accurately. Consider the theoretical specification of the model used in this regression. The dependent variable was automobile sales and the independent variables were income, an interest rate, the unemployment rate, and consumer sentiment. The functional form was linear. No lagged variables were used.

Required:
As in the last problem, in your role as consultants, the following are meant as a guide to your analysis rather than as an outline for this part of your oral and written reports to management.

1. Outline your own theoretical model of automobile sales. What variables have you considered for your model? Justify your choices.

2. What signs should the coefficients of these variables have according to theory? Why?

3. Consider measures of the theoretical variables listed in part 1. Go to the library and find annual data for the sample period for at least one of these variables that did not appear in the original specification in the previous problem. Define this new variable. Explain how you have measured it, cite your data source(s), and list the values of this variable for the sample period.

4. Revise your data set by inserting your additional variable(s) and any updated information you can find on the existing variables.

5. Look at the dependent variable. Can you come up with a better definition of that variable (with a resulting set of data) that will yield a better specification of the model (i.e., higher r^2)? (*Hint*: minivans and utility vehicles are considered to be light trucks.)

6. Consider the functional form of the regression specification. Must the model be linear? What alternate functional forms might you try? How must you transform your data to estimate these alternative functional forms? Create transformed variables for your data.

7. Estimate and evaluate your models. Which model has the best diagnostic statistics? How does the performance of these new models compare with the model in problem 4-14?

8. Forecast automobile sales (using your revised definition of the dependent variable and the revised data) for the next two years' using your best model. Explain and justify your predicted values for the exogenous variables. How do these forecasts of future automobile sales compare with your forecasts from the previous problem?

4-16. Cost Estimating in the U.S. Brewing Industry[16]

Hobie Leland, Jr., had just completed his MBA and accepted a job with the Pabst Brewing Company in Milwaukee, Wisconsin. His initial assignment was to estimate the cost-volume relationship of Pabst vis-à-vis several of its competitors in the United States brewing industry. He first made an analysis of the internal records of Pabst and discovered that since 1962 Pabst had been a single-line-of-business company. Prior to 1962, it also had owned a soft-drink company (Hoffman Beverage Company), and the accounting records did not separately report the costs associated with the brewing and soft-drink operations. Hobie decided to base his analysis on the 1962–1980 period and collected the data shown in Table 1 at the end of this case. In 1962 Pabst operated brewing plants in four locations—Milwaukee, Wisconsin (dating back to 1844), Peoria Heights, Illinois (1934), Newark, New Jersey (1946), and Los Angeles, California (1953). In 1971 a new plant in Pabst, Georgia, was brought into operation. On January 30, 1979, Pabst acquired a Portland, Oregon, brewery from the Blitz-Weinhard Company. In September 1979, the Los Angeles plant (with a capacity of 1.350 million barrels) was permanently closed. The total annual capacity of the five remaining breweries operating in 1980 was 18.9 million barrels.

This case is divided into decisions that Hobie had to make regrading an appropriate model for cost-volume relationships at Pabst and other issues when comparing Pabst to some of its competitors.

Required:
You have been hired as a consultant to the management of Pabst Brewing Company. Their accounting staff has provided you with the information contained in the case and the data in Tables 1, 2, and 3. In addition, you will be provided with a printout of some regression results obtained by the staff. This case takes some fancy footwork in that the data are all from 1962–1980, but you are writing this report in the 1990s. While you are responsible for knowing as much about the beer industry in general and Pabst in particular, it is impossible for you to update the data set to include information beyond that given in the case given changes in ownership, companies going out of business, and so on.

Your task is to prepare a written report for Pabst's senior management in which you:

1. Analyze the data in Table 1 and identify problems that might occur in using these data to estimate cost-volume relationships at Pabst.
2. Discuss how to deal with inflation. The Wholesale Price Index of Beer is provided as a way to deflate data. Discuss the problems with using this measure for this purpose and either provide evidence that this is the best measure to use or present the case for another deflator. Here and in other areas, it is important to know something about the industry or a particular brewer.

---

[16] This case was written by George Foster. Copyright 1981 by the Board of Trustees of the Leland Stanford Junior University.

3. Analyze the data in Table 2 and identify problems that might occur in using these data to estimate cost-volume relationships for Pabst's competitors.

4. Analyze the data in Table 3 and identify problems that might occur in using the cross-sectional data to estimate cost-volume relationships in the brewing industry.

5. You will be provided with regression results for the following models where C_t is cost of sales and V_t is barrels of beer sold over the 1962–1980 period:

   Pabst $C_t = b_0 + b_1 V_t$

   Deflated Pabst $C_t = b_0 + b_1 V_t$

   Deflated Pabst $(C_t - C_{t-1}) = b_0 + b_1(V_t - V_{t-1})$

   Deflated An-Busch $(C_t - C_{t-1}) = \mathbf{b_0} + b_1(V_t - V_{t-1})$

   Deflated Olympia $(C_t - C_{t-1}) = b_0 + b_1(V_t - V_{t-1})$

   Deflated Schlitz $(C_t - C_{t-1}) = b_0 + b_1(V_t - V_{t-1})$

   Industry $C_t = b_0 + b_1 V_t + b_2$ (number of employees)

   Adjusted industry $C_t = b_0 + b_1 V_t + b_2$ (number of employees)

   Industry $C_t = b_0 + b_1 V_t$

   Adjusted industry $C_t = b_0 + b_1 V_t$

   You will also be provided with various graphs of the data and the residuals from most of these regression models as well as the matrix of correlation coefficients for the data in Table 3. Without using technical terms or jargon, you are to analyze each of these models. Specifically, you are to:

   a. Discuss why the third model is better than the first or second models to predict Pabst's costs. Inform management about the problems with autocorrelation, what it means, and why you are trying to eliminate it.

   b. Discuss the multiple regression models. Which of the two is better? Why? What are the problems of multicollinearity, what does it mean, and why should you try to eliminate it?

   c. Using the best models from Table 1 and 2 data and the best model from Table 3 data, what inferences can you draw for Pabst's management regarding Pabst's costs versus those of their competitors? Do you get confirming or conflicting results from these two sets of models?

   While you can assume that Pabst's management is familiar with the data, be careful to be informative, to use good organization, to explain where appropriate, and to avoid going into your own internal frame of reference. You are required to seek additional information from other sources that will allow you to fully analyze this case. Information sources include, but are not limited to, the library and brewers. Use current information coupled with these past data to draw your conclusions.

TABLE 1
Pabst Brewing Company: 1962–1980

Year	Cost of Sales[a] ($000,000s)	Barrels Sold (000,000s)	Wholesale Price[b] Index of Beer
1962	166.943	5.844	.533
1963	184.981	6.672	.533
1964	206.666	7.444	.535
1965	229.200	8.219	.536
1966	252.122	9.047	.540
1967	285.380	10.123	.552
1968	313.070	10.910	.557
1969[c]	305.044	10.225	.570
1970	324.391	10.517	.596
1971	367.779	11.797	.611
1972	395.559	12.600	.612
1973	431.398	13.128	.623
1974	530.769	14.297	.719
1975	630.160	15.669	.759
1976	696.039	17.037	.769
1977	688.045	16.003	.794
1978	720.258	15.367	.848
1979[d]	765.303	15.115	.933
1980	832.018	15.091	1.000

[a] The level of detail in Pabst's Annual Report for the "Costs of Sales" item has increased since 1962. The 1980 Annual Report broke this item into three components:

Cost of Goods Sold	$607.526
Federal Excise Taxes	$133.539
Marketing, General and Administrative Expenses	$ 90.953
	$832.018

[b] The Wholesale Price Index of Beer is Index 0261-01 (Malt Beverages) in the Bureau of Labor's Wholesale Price Index. Prior to 1967, the Index was labeled 1441 (Malt Beverages). Index 0261-01 has 1967 as the base year (=100); the index is rescaled to make 1980 the base year (=1.000).

[c] On June 30, 1958, Pabst acquired the Blatz Brewing Company. On September 2, 1969, under a court-ordered divestiture, Pabst sold the Blatz brands to G. Heileman Brewing Company, Inc. In the 1968 fiscal year, sales of Blatz brands totaled 1.854 million barrels.

[d] On April 2, 1979, Pabst acquired the Blitz-Weinhard Company, a Portland based brewer. The results of operations of Blitz are included since the date of acquisition. The 1978 sales of Blitz were approximately $41.9 million.

TABLE 2
Other U.S. Brewing Companies: 1962–1980

Year	Anheuser Busch Cost of Sales ($000,000s)	Barrels Sold (000,000s)	Olympia Brewing Cost of Sales ($000,000s)	Barrels Sold (000,000s)	Jos. Schlitz Cost of Sales ($000,000s)	Barrels Sold (000,000s)	Wholesale Price Index of Beer
1962	392.752	9.035	59.617	1.742	236.650	6.869	.533
1963	416.025	9.397	60.336	1.776	269.476	7.833	.533
1964	452.979	10.370	72.715	2.168	284.894	8.258	.535
1965	504.351	11.841	82.849	2.461	295.250	8.607	.536
1966	569.967	13.575	90.941	2.678	326.238	9.467	.540
1967	662.433	15.535	97.464	2.867	356.145	10.382	.552
1968	759.554	18.393	106.711	3.075	398.089	11.904	.557
1969	780.340	18.712	118.942	3.375	479.278	13.709	.570
1970	915.527	22.202	120.088	3.379	527.530	15.129	.596
1971	1038.996	24.309	112.549	3.094	594.473	16.708	.611
1972	1128.319	26.522	122.354	3.330	686.034	18.906	.612
1973	1321.302	29.887	134.867	3.637	782.975	21.343	.623
1974	1673.241	34.097	178.426	4.301	922.335	22.661	.719
1975	1861.545	35.196	256.494	5.574[b]	1046.954	23.279	.759
1976	1624.704	29.051[a]	342.104	7.163[c]	1102.017	24.162	.769
1977	2046.453	36.640	342.341	6.831	1073.224	22.130	.794
1978	2479.349	41.610	359.100	6.662	1047.224	19.580	.848
1979	3016.654	46.210	354.638	6.029	1050.281	16.804	.933
1980	3509.500	50.200	388.542	6.091	997.658	14.954	1.000

[a] The 1976 Annual Report of Anheuser Busch noted that "the decline in beer sales volume was the result of a three-month work stoppage" (p. 4).

[b] On March 1, 1975, Olympia acquired the brewery operations of Theodore Hamm Company. The 1975 results reported by Olympia include the 1975 results of Hamm's from the date of acquisition. In 1974, Hamm's had sales of $105.314 million. Included in the acquisition was a brewing facility in St. Paul, Minnesota.

[c] Effective December 29, 1976, Olympia acquired the net assets of Lone Star Brewing Company. The 1976 results reported by Olympia include the results of Lone Star for the January 1, 1976, to December 31, 1976, period. In 1975 and 1976 the total net sales of Lone Star Brewing Company were $61.332 million and $53.068 million respectively. Included in the acquisition was a brewing facility in San Antonio, Texas. Also included in the acquisition was a truck-leasing operation. The net sales of the truck-leasing operation were $11.275 million in 1975 and $12.686 million in 1976.

TABLE 3
U.S. Brewing Industry: 1980

Firms	Fiscal Year	Cost of Total Sales ($000,000s)	Barrels Sold (000,000s)	Number of Total Employees[a]	Number of Brewing Plants	Ratio of Beer Sales($) to Total Sales($)[b]	Total Sales ($000,000s)[c]
Anheuser-Busch Companies	12/31	3509.500	50.200	18,040	10	.92	3822.400
Jos. Schlitz Brewing	12/31	997.658	14.954	6,100	6	>.90	1027.743
Adolph Coors Company	12/31	923.608	13.779	9,650	1	.87	1021.198
G. Heileman Brewing	12/31	771.293	13.270	5,600	10	.88	840.784
Olympia Brewing	12/31	388.542	6.091	2,164	3	.92	391.974
F & M Schaefer	12/31	204.898	3.572	1,342	1	1.00	209.075
Genesee Brewing	4/30	165.476	3.604	932	1	1.00	177.245
Falstaff Brewing	12/31	96.061	1.600	594	3	1.00	95.574
Pittsburgh Brewing	10/31	48.786	.993	416	1	1.00	49.804

[a] Three of the five companies having non-beer activities provide in their 1980 10K a breakdown of the number of employees in each activity:

 Coors : "The Company has approximately 9,650 employees. Of those, approximately 1,100 employees work full-time in construction and engineering and approximately 2,100 work for the Company's six subsidiaries which produce ceramic products" (p. 6).

 Heileman : "The Company has approximately 5,600 employees of which 3,650 are employed in brewing operations, 1,600 are employed in baking operations and 350 are employed in other areas" (p. 4).

 Olympia : "The number of persons employed on December 31, 1980 was 2,164 of whom 374 were engaged in the leasing business" (p. 6).

[b] The ratio of beer sales to total sales is computed with the numerator being before the deduction of excise taxes on beer.

[c] Total sales of Pabst in 1980 were $853.441. Table 3 excludes the second largest U.S. brewing company, Miller Brewing Company, which is a fully owned subsidiary of Philip Morris. Beer sales of Miller Brewing in 1980 were $2,542.300 million (34.300 million barrels). Table 3 also excludes privately held companies, e.g., Stroh Brewing Company and General Brewing Company.

Chapter 5

Curvilinear Relationships: The Learning Effect

We live in a forest and rarely see the fence that surrounds it. For us the forest in which we dwell is the entire universe; within it we carry on the affairs of our daily lives, unaware of what lies beyond the fence, unaware even that the fence is there. Within that forest, we walk on paths laid down for us. It is we who walk; that is our accomplishment, and no mean achievement at that. Our lives as lived convey one dominant image of our fundamental nature: intelligent, thoughtful, reflective, complex, we may be; but machines we clearly are.[1]

---

[1] Edward E. Sampson, *Ego at the Threshold: In Search of Man's Freedom* (New York: Dell, 1975), p. 20.

There is evidence that people learn to do certain tasks faster as they repeat them. Earlier discussion focused on a linear model of costs where marginal costs are presumed constant within the relevant range. However, we can incorporate the notion of learning where marginal cost (time) goes down as production rises. These models are curvilinear and the relationship depicted is called a *learning effect* or *learning curve*.[2]

THE LEARNING PROCESS

We can all think of examples of when we have learned. The first time you used a word processing program might have involved a lot of searching and making mistakes in commands. As you worked more and more with the same program, you gained confidence, remembered needed commands, and progressively worked faster. At some point, however, you reached the limit of your speed, given the program, the task, and your own ability. The same thing could be said about learning how to analyze and interpret the output from a regression and correlation analysis program. Each time you use such an output, you might be able to come to conclusions more quickly. Again, you will reach some plateau where learning will cease. The idea behind the material in this chapter is to look at models whereby we might describe learning in a way that will help us to estimate costs, set prices, budget, evaluate performance, and so on, for both manufacturing and support tasks. In addition, we explore how changes in manufacturing technology have affected the use of learning curve models.

Businesses have used the learning effect for over 50 years. There are several models that describe learning, but managers seem to choose two main representations. The first is the marginal time model, which states that the marginal time to produce a unit (or batch) goes down by some percent. The second, the cumulative average model, professes that as cumulative production doubles, the cumulative average time to produce a unit (or batch) goes down by some percent. For example, early studies of the aircraft industry showed a 20 percent decline as production doubled.[3] However, it is common practice to express learning models in terms of the value *to* which cumulative average time declines. Thus, a decline of 20 percent would be called an 80 percent learning curve. Such a curve could be graphed as shown in Figure 5-1, where cumulative average time decreases as total production increases.

---

[2] Not all learning effects are curves over their entire range because there is usually a point where learning ceases.

[3] An early example is T. P. Wright, "Factors Affecting the Cost of Airplanes," *Journal of Aeronautical Science* (February 1936), pp. 122–128.

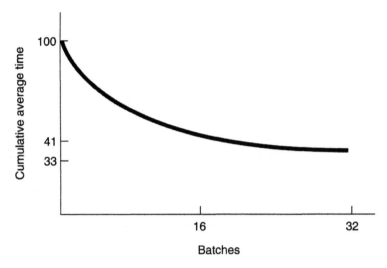

Figure 5-1   The Learning Effect

LEARNING CURVE MODELS

In the *marginal learning curve model*, the focus is on marginal time for a particular level of production, say, 11 units. Using this model we would calculate marginal time for the eleventh unit. Total time would be the estimate of the marginal times for all 11 units added together. In contrast, in the *cumulative average model*, calculations show the cumulative average time for all 11 units. Total time for 11 units would be the estimate of cumulative average time for 11 units times 11. Both the marginal and cumulative average time models use the same basic formula; however, the definitions of the terms of the formula change between the two models. In addition, these are two separate and distinct models each describing learning differently. Later we compare the two to illustrate this difference.

Marginal Model

The marginal model states that *marginal* time (cost)[4] goes down by a set percent each time production doubles. An example is found in Exhibit 5-1. Assume that a production process has an 80 percent learning effect. Under the marginal model, the time for the second unit (a doubling point) would be 8 hours if the first unit took 10 hours. At the next doubling point, 4 units, the time for the *fourth* unit would be 80 percent of that for the second unit,

---

[4] Learning affects time. In cases where labor is a variable cost, it would also affect cost directly. In cases where labor is essentially a fixed cost, productivity (capacity) is affected with learning. Thus, time really is the core factor under consideration.

Exhibit 5-1
Marginal Learning Curve Model

Units of Production	Marginal Time	Cumulative Time
1	10 hours	10 hours
2	8	18
4	6.4	
8	5.12	
16	4.096	

Exhibit 5-2
Marginal Learning Curve Model
Formulas

Marginal time: $y = ax^b$

where: y = marginal time for the xth unit
a = time for the first unit
x = number of units (e.g., first, second, etc.)
b = the learning exponent

the learning exponent:

$$b = \frac{\ln \text{ learning curve}}{\ln 2}$$

Note: The discussion will use the term ln for natural logs. You can use log base 10 (log), and the results will be the same even if the intermediate figures are different.

or 6.4 hours (0.80 × 8). This same process is carried out at all the doubling points of production.

Cumulative time for units produced to date is not easily determined without formulas. It is easy to see that cumulative time for two units equals 18 hours in the example since we have the marginal time for both the first and second units. However, we do not have the marginal time for the third unit and, therefore, cannot directly give the cumulative time for four units. This problem increases as we double to 8 units and higher.

Without formulas, we seem limited to calculating marginal time at doubling points. We cannot, for example, figure the marginal time for the seventh unit or the cumulative time for 7 units. Thus we need basic formulas for a general approach to the learning problem. These are shown in Exhibit 5-2. Thus, with the marginal time formula, we can calculate the marginal times for the first 4 units of production as shown below. First, assume that there is an 80 percent learning curve. The learning exponent, then, is[5]

$$b = \ln 0.80/\ln 2 = -0.3219$$

and marginal (and cumulative times) are as follows for the first four units:

Unit	Marginal Time	Cumulative Time
1	$y = (10)(1^{-0.3219}) = 10$	10
2	$y = (10)(2^{-0.3219}) = 8$	18
3	$y = (10)(3^{-0.3219}) = 7.021$	25.021
4	$y = (10)(4^{-0.3219}) = 6.4$	31.421

Note that the cumulative times were calculated by adding the marginal times.

Cumulative Average Model

In the cumulative average time model, the *cumulative average time* for, say, two units (using an 80 percent learning effect) is 80 percent of the time for the first unit. An example like the figures in Exhibit 5-1 is presented in Exhibit 5-3. Cumulative average time is calculated in the same way that marginal time was calculated in the earlier model; the definitions have changed. Total cumulative time is easy to calculate since we can multiply the cumulative average time by the number of units produced to yield, for example, $4 \times 6.4 = 25.6$ hours for four units.

Exhibit 5-3
Cumulative Average Learning Curve Model

Units of Production	Cumulative Average Time	Cumulative Time
1	10 hours	10 hours
2	8	16
4	6.4	25.6
8	5.12	40.96
16	4.096	65.536

---

[5] Note that since the log of a number less than 1 is negative, the learning exponent will always be negative. Some authors show this by modeling as follows: $y = ax^{-b}$. However, the models are the same. In addition, we will round the learning exponent to four places. When working on a calculator or on a computer, such rounding will not take place.

Exhibit 5-4
Cumulative Average Learning Curve Model
Formulas

Cumulative average time: $y = ax^b$

where: y = cumulative average time for x units
a = time for the first unit (batch)
x = cumulative units (batches) produced
b = the learning exponent

the learning exponent:

$$b = \frac{\ln \text{ learning curve}}{\ln 2}$$

Total cumulative time
Total cumulative time is (cumulative average time) × (cumulative production). In formula form this is:
$xy = (x)(ax^b) = ax^{b+1}$

As with the earlier model, managers cannot be limited to doubling points. Thus, the basic formulas shown in Exhibit 5-4 reflect the cumulative average model. Note that the basic formula *seems* the same. However, since the definition of y is now cumulative average time and not marginal time, the two formulas are quite different. In addition, there is a formula for total cumulative time in Exhibit 5-4.

There is no easy formula in this cumulative average model for marginal time.[6] Marginal time can be calculated by subtracting cumulative time for, say, 4 units from cumulative time for 3 units to get the marginal time for the fourth unit. Thus, we would have the following for the first 4 units.

Unit	Cumulative Average Time	Cumulative Time	Marginal Time
1	$y = (10)(1^{-0.3219}) = 10$	10	10
2	$y = (10)(2^{-0.3219}) = 8$	16	6
3	$y = (10)(3^{-0.3219}) = 7.021$	21.063	5.063
4	$y = (10)(4^{-0.3219}) = 6.4$	25.6	4.537

Exhibit 5-5 shows a comparison of the two models. In the top part of the exhibit, both models are shown with an 80 percent learning curve. The cumulative average time model shows lower times than the marginal model at a given learning percent. In the bottom half of the exhibit, the marginal model is shown at a 72 percent learning effect while the cumulative average time model remains at 80 percent. The idea is to see if there is any direct comparison between the two models. You can see that incremental times

---

[6] Some authors use the formula *marginal time* = $a(b +1)x^b$. However, this formula does not always yield results equivalent to the other formulas, especially at low values of x.

Exhibit 5-5
Cumulative Average and Marginal Time Models Compared

A. Comparison using same learning percent

Learning percent	80%		80%
First unit	10		10
Learning exponent	−0.3219		−0.3219

	Cumulative Average Time				Marginal Time		
Units	Cumulative Average Time	Total Time	Incremental Time		Incremental Time	Total Time	Cumulative Average Time
1	10.00	10.00	10.00		10.00	10.00	10.00
2	8.00	16.00	6.00		8.00	18.00	9.00
3	7.02	21.06	5.06		7.02	25.02	8.34
4	6.40	25.60	4.54		6.40	31.42	7.86
5	5.96	29.78	4.18		5.96	37.38	7.48
6	5.62	33.70	3.92		5.62	42.99	7.17
7	5.34	37.41	3.71		5.34	48.34	6.91
8	5.12	40.96	3.55		5.12	53.46	6.68
9	4.93	44.37	3.41		4.93	58.39	6.49
10	4.77	47.65	3.29		4.77	63.15	6.32
11	4.62	50.83	3.18		4.62	67.77	6.16
12	4.49	53.92	3.09		4.49	72.27	6.02
13	4.38	56.93	3.01		4.38	76.65	5.90
14	4.28	59.86	2.93		4.28	80.92	5.78
15	4.18	62.73	2.87		4.18	85.11	5.67
16	4.10	65.54	2.81		4.10	89.20	5.58

B. Comparison using different learning percents

Learning percent	80%		72%
First unit	10		10
Learning exponent	−0.3219		−0.4739

	Cumulative Average Time				Marginal Time		
Units	Cumulative Average Time	Total Time	Incremental Time		Incremental Time	Total Time	Cumulative Average Time
1	10.00	10.00	10.00		10.00	10.00	10.00
2	8.00	16.00	6.00		7.20	17.20	8.60
3	7.02	21.06	5.06		5.94	23.14	7.71
4	6.40	25.60	4.54		5.18	28.33	7.08
5	5.96	29.78	4.18		4.66	32.99	6.60
6	5.62	33.70	3.92		4.28	37.27	6.21
7	5.34	37.41	3.71		3.98	41.24	5.89
8	5.12	40.96	3.55		3.73	44.98	5.62
9	4.93	44.37	3.41		3.53	48.51	5.39
10	4.77	47.65	3.29		3.36	51.86	5.19
11	4.62	50.83	3.18		3.21	55.07	5.01
12	4.49	53.92	3.09		3.08	58.15	4.85
13	4.38	56.93	3.01		2.97	61.12	4.70
14	4.28	59.86	2.93		2.86	63.98	4.57
15	4.18	62.73	2.87		2.77	66.75	4.45
16	4.10	65.54	2.81		2.69	69.44	4.34

for the models begin to converge as production rises. In addition, the order of the columns shows the basic order of calculation. With the cumulative average model, you move from cumulative average time to total time to marginal time, while in the marginal time model the order is reversed.

Neither model is better. Each reflects different ideas of learning. As discussed later, these are not the only two models that are proposed, but they seem to be the most used.[7] Much of the discussion that follows employs the cumulative average time model and the formulas in Exhibit 5-4. However, the ideas expressed could just as easily apply to the marginal time model.

ESTIMATING LEARNING CURVE PARAMETERS

In the examples shown in Exhibit 5-5, the time for the first unit and the learning effect are known. While it is possible that an analysis of past data and/or engineering studies will yield estimates of these two parameters, managers can use a linear transformation of the data coupled with the estimating techniques discussed in Chapter 4. Before discussing the use of ordinary least squares linear regression, we will show how to transform data to a linear form.

The basic formulas for the learning effect shown in Exhibit 5-4 are

$$\text{cumulative average time:} \quad y = ax^b$$
$$\text{total time:} \quad xy = ax^{b+1}$$

Linear transformations of these formulas can be obtained by using logarithms[8] as follows:

$$\ln y = \ln a + b \ln x$$

and

$$\ln xy = \ln a + (b + 1) \ln x$$

Thus, data for, say, cumulative production and total cumulative times can be transformed into logarithmic form and then the unknown parameters can be estimated. The general transformation will change the curvilinear pattern of data shown in Figure 5-1 on page 217 to a linear pattern shown in Figure 5-2.

---

[7] Examples include Diane D. Pattison and Charles J. Teplitz, "Are Learning Curves Still Relevant?" *Management Accounting* (February 1989), pp. 37–40, where both models are illustrated, as compared to James Geiger and Raymond L. Winn, III, "Leader/Follower Competition in the Department of Defense," *Journal of Cost Management for the Manufacturing Industry* (Spring 1987), pp. 13–24, where just the marginal time model is used.

[8] Again, we are staying with natural logarithms denoted ln, and the antilog will be found using the e^x function. In addition, it is possible to use curvilinear regression directly instead of performing a log transformation on the data for linear regression.

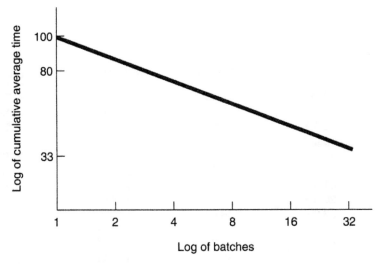

Figure 5-2 Linear Tranformation of Learning Effect

As an example of estimating learning curve parameters, we will use the data in Exhibit 5-6 for the American Royal Co. American Royal makes communication equipment both for the government and for private industry. Management knows from past experience that there is a learning effect in its production process. Currently, component #919 is being produced, and the data in Exhibit 5-6 reflect current experience.

These data are presented in a total time form. It is possible that cumulative average time was kept, but, even if not, it certainly can be calculated by dividing by total production. Thus a full set of data (including logarithms) for units, cumulative average time, and total time is shown in Exhibit 5-6.

Simple Linear Regression

Ordinary least squares regression (OLS) and correlation analysis can be applied to learning situations, using logarithmic data. Since we know that we are expecting a curvilinear function, there is little gained by looking at a linear regression using the raw data. Instead, we make the log transformations as shown in Exhibit 5-6 and use these in our regression and correlation analysis. The results are as follows:

Total Time

$$\text{LNTOTTIME} = 2.3137 + 0.7353 \text{ LNTOTPROD}, \ r^2 = 0.996,$$
$$t_{b_1} = 68.33, \ t_{b_0} = 61.22 \quad \text{and} \quad S_e = 0.0557$$

where: LNTOTTIME $= \ln xy$
      LNTOTPROD $= \ln x$

Exhibit 5-6
American Royal Co.
Assembly—Part #919

Case	TOTPROD	TOTTIME	LNTOTPROD	LNTOTTIME
1	2.000	16.40	0.6931	2.7973
2	3.000	22.80	1.0986	3.1268
3	5.000	34.00	1.6094	3.5525
4	8.000	45.28	2.0794	3.8129
5	12.000	65.52	2.4849	4.1824
6	15.000	76.65	2.7081	4.3392
7	21.000	86.31	3.0445	4.4579
8	26.000	111.54	3.2581	4.7144
9	33.000	148.83	3.4965	5.0028
10	38.000	131.10	3.6376	4.8760
11	45.000	168.75	3.8067	5.1284
12	53.000	180.20	3.9703	5.1941
13	64.000	206.08	4.1589	5.3283
14	72.000	226.80	4.2767	5.4241
15	78.000	245.28	4.3567	5.5024
16	85.000	267.26	4.4427	5.5882
17	90.000	282.71	4.4998	5.6444
18	95.000	298.11	4.5539	5.6975
19	102.000	319.81	4.6250	5.7677

Where: LNTOTPROD = ln (total production)
LNTOTTIME = ln (total time)
TOTPROD   = total production
TOTTIME   = total time

The Durbin-Watson statistic is 2.45 and, therefore, does not indicate a problem with serial correlation. However, as we will discuss below, there is a reason why the Durbin-Watson statistic is muted using these data. As you can confirm, a plot of the residuals shows no unusual pattern. (As a review problem, run a regression using the raw data and plot the residuals. You will find a distinctive pattern and a very low Durbin-Watson statistic.)

We can translate these results into cumulative average time by just deducting 1 from the estimate of the slope.[9] Thus, we would have

Cumulative Average Time
$\ln y = 2.3137 - 0.2647 \ln x$

---

[9] You can see that it is important to keep track of what each variable means. In the total time model, the slope is $(b + 1)$ while in the cumulative average time model it is just b. In addition, we must realize that the estimate of the intercept is the log of a. We use the total time, since it ties with total cost (y') used in Chapter 4.

As you can verify, the only difference in regression outputs is that the co-efficient of determination is higher for the first regression (total time) than the cumulative average time results. This is caused by the slope being larger in the total time model while the standard error of the estimate and the standard error of the slope remain constant. Thus, the unexplained variance is a bit smaller.

The results of the regression and correlation analysis yield a learning curve percent of

$$b = \text{In learning curve percent/In 2}$$
$$-0.2647 = \text{In learning curve percent/0.6931}$$
$$\text{In learning curve percent} = -0.1835$$

The antilogarithm of -0.1835 is about 83 percent. The antilogarithm of the intercept is about 10.[10] Thus, our estimate of the time for the first unit is 10 hours and there seems to be an 83 percent learning curve.

Batches and Units

Many times, data are collected on batches of production. Thus, instead of unit data, one might have a batch of 100 or 1,000 units. This poses no problem as long as a manager keeps the data straight. The intercept, a, becomes the time for the *first batch* instead of the first unit. The independent variable, x, becomes *batches* rather than units.

There is a good reason to deal with batches rather than with units. In large runs, the first few units may not be a good estimate of the production process, even without learning. There might be fluctuations in time that are not indicative of the process. Therefore, batch data may be a more accurate means of estimating, since such fluctuations would tend to even out in a batch.

CONDITIONS FOR LEARNING

Not all processes evidence a learning effect. Even if there is learning, it can take on several forms (two of which have already been discussed). Learning might go on for several batches or cease after only a few batches. No matter what the process, at some point learning will cease.

When Learning Occurs

Learning is correlated to the amount of labor in a process as well as preplanning. In general, the higher the proportion of labor in a production

---

[10] As in our discussion in earlier chapters, no accuracy is gained by carrying these figures to several decimals.

process, the more there is a chance for learning to occur. Assembly departments, even in high-technology industries, are especially subject to learning because of the hands-on nature of the work. Take a department where workers place computer chips into preprinted circuit boards and solder connections. Each type of board is a bit different and the tasks vary. Such an operation is a likely candidate for learning. However, highly automated procedures might be paced by the machine and not the worker. Although there could be an initial period of training to become familiar with the process in general, there would be little learning for any particular component manufactured. For example, in a plant that manufactures engine cradles for a particular model of automobile, the production line might consist of cell manufacturing with various operations linked by robots moving work in process. Final assembly is accomplished through a robotics welding line where workers are more attendants than hands-on assemblers. In such a situation, there is relatively little learning. Not only is the process controlled by machines, but also a single product is made over many years until the basic design of the automobile changes.

Preplanning tends to reduce the amount of learning on the job. Thus, if workers are trained in a nonproduction setting or there is a considerable amount of human engineering done to reduce a slow startup of production, there will be a higher learning curve percent (less learning). Preplanning should reduce the time for the first unit as well. Contrast this to a production process that starts up with little preplanning. Here the first units might take a longer time to make as workers "feel" their way through the process. However, there is a greater chance for learning as production increases.

It is important to make sure that learning is associated with improvements in worker performance when doing the same job using the same equipment. Any increases in productivity that are caused by better materials, new machinery or methods, or changes in the sequence of processing are not related to learning as modeled here. While it is important to achieve improvements in time (cost) from whatever source, managers must be sure to identify sources of savings so that budgets, standards, pricing, and so on reflect a cause-and-effect reality. As with any estimations, managers must make sure that data are clean. The data problems are no different from those discussed in the previous chapters.

Alternate Forms of Learning

The cumulative average model shows learning occurring at a steady rate. As long as learning is continuing, cumulative average time drops by the same percent. There are other forms of learning that can occur.

With an *asymptotic* learning curve, marginal time per unit decreases at a decreasing rate rather than at a constant rate. Other models rely more on a relevant range concept so that early production (or very high production) is excluded from estimates as being nonrepresentative of a mid-range of learning. Operations research courses cover a wide range of such models. In addition, many companies have developed their own learning models based on years of experience with their product lines and facilities.

Cessation of Learning

It would be rare for learning to go on forever. There comes a time when machine and/or human capacity has reached a practical maximum. At best, production achieves a *steady state* where marginal time remains constant. It is just as important to predict when this steady state will come about as it is to predict the parameters of the learning curve.

Data can be collected from past production to see when it is usual for learning to cease. In the case of new equipment, engineering studies may show theoretical limits to productivity. However, managers should not ignore constraints on production that are caused by behavioral factors. Peer pressure or union regulations may limit output. Changes in supervisory practices may affect motivation. Turnover or vacations may interrupt a learning curve (or even reverse it for a while).

If learning reaches a steady state, incremental (marginal) time becomes constant, and cumulative average time will continue to fall. For cumulative average time to stabilize, incremental time would have to increase; unlearning would have to occur. Look back at Exhibit 5-6 where there are 19 observations covering a total of 102 units produced to date. Our earlier regression estimates were based on the notion that learning continued in the same functional form over the entire range of production. However, a review of Exhibit 5-6 shows that marginal times stabilize somewhere between 70 and 80 units. We do not have the marginal times *per se* but can look at average times for units starting at that level.

$$(245.28 - 226.80)/(78 - 72) = 3.08$$
$$(267.26 - 245.28)/(85 - 78) = 3.14$$
$$(282.71 - 267.26)/(90 - 85) = 3.09$$
$$(298.11 - 282.71)/(95 - 90) = 3.08$$
$$(319.81 - 298.11)/(102 - 95) = 3.10$$

It looks as if learning has ceased. Thus, if we were going to estimate total time for, say, 90 units, we would underestimate if we continued to use the learning percent from a regression that incorporated all 19 observations. This is even more important as we estimate production beyond what has been made so far.

Review Problem

As a review problem, use only the first 15 observations from Exhibit 5-6 and run a new regression and correlation analysis. The results should be as follows:

Total Time

$$\ln xy = 2.335 + 0.7255; \ r^2 = 0.996$$

The t-values are still quite high for the intercept and the slope (over 50 each) and the Durbin-Watson statistic is 2.8349, quite a bit higher than previously computed using all 19 observations. Our new estimate of a learning percentage, as you can verify, is still about 83 percent. The real damage, then, of using the original regression would be in assuming that learning continued through all 102 units. Such misestimation is important at any level but can be quite severe if learning ceased, say, after about 20 units. At the level illustrated for American Royal, the curve had flattened out a bit and the cost of an estimating error is not as great. If we used an 83 percent learning curve, we would expect that 102 units should take 287 hours $[(10)(102^{0.7255}) = 286.58]$. This can be compared to the actual recorded time of 320 hours. Now that management has evidence that learning has ceased, they can use a marginal time of about 3.1 hours for all units over current levels.

Managers want to look at data for this type of a regression as closely as they do for any other type. We have now added a dimension because we are looking to see where learning ceases. Plots of the data and residuals might help such an analysis.

PRACTICAL USES OF LEARNING CURVES

The learning curve model is a practical aid to managerial planning in several areas, including pricing, standard setting and variance reporting, budgeting, and production planning. Use of the learning effect yields better information for decision making.

Pricing

Pricing plays an ever-increasing role in the success of a business. Foreign manufacturers have garnered the lion's share of many markets, especially in labor-intensive products. If learning exists, its recognition and inclusion in pricing formulas can help to achieve more business.

As an example, refer back to Exhibit 5-6 on page 224 for part #919 for American Royal Co. We now know that learning ceased at about 70 to 80 units. Say that we were earlier in the process, had made only 38 units, and estimated the 83 percent learning effect. Assume that costs are as shown in Exhibit 5-7 and that American Royal's management wanted an estimate on making an additional 20 units of the component.

Exhibit 5-7
American Royal Co.
Costs—order #919

Materials	$200.00 per unit
Labor and variable overhead	$ 25.00 per hour
Fixed overhead	$ 35.00 per hour based on practical capacity

If managers had ignored learning, they would have assumed that it would take about 10 hours per unit to make all units produced.[11] Each unit would cost $800 given this assumption, as shown below.

Materials	$200
Labor and variable overhead (10 × $25)	250
Fixed overhead (10 × $35)	350
Total	$800

This assumes using fully absorbed costs. We might want to look only at separable costs, which are about $450 per unit. More specifically, managers should focus on the $250 and variable overhead associated with labor, because these are the resources that would be affected by learning.

If learning is included in the estimates, managers would use the 83 percent learning curve as follows. Total time to make 38 units is 131.1 hours. Total time to make 58 units would be $xy = (10)(58^{0.7312}) = 194.7$ or an additional 63.6 hours (194.7 − 131.1) for 20 units. This is compared to 200 hours if an estimate of 10 hours per unit had been used or 69 hours if 3.45 hours, the average time for 38 units (131.1/38), had been used. At $25 per hour for labor and variable overhead, the estimation error is $3,410 [(200 − 63.6)$25] using variable costs or $8,184 [(200 − 63.6)($25 + $35)] if fully absorbed costs are used. If average time per unit for 38 units had been used (3.45 hours), the estimation error would be 5.4 hours (69 - 63.6) or $135, using variable labor and overhead, or $324 with full costs if the average cost for 38 units had been used.

Thus, in pricing (and in all other uses of learning curves), managers should be careful to use the learning percentage within its relevant range. The use of the learning curve can substantially reduce estimation errors where learning exists.

---

[11] There are other assumptions you could make. For example, perhaps managers would look at total time to date and get cumulative average time and use that as their base for the next 20 units. The estimating error would be different, but the point is the same as using 10 hours per unit.

Standards and Standard Cost Variances

The same points regarding pricing can be repeated under standard setting. Standards are only meaningful if they reflect what managers can expect from production. If departmental performance is to be judged at least partially by standard cost variances, then managers should incorporate learning into standard inputs, given outputs achieved. Assume that a company has determined that the standard costs for direct labor and variable overhead for a product are

Direct labor: $20 per hour
Variable overhead: $15 per hour

Engineering studies have shown that 8 hours are expected for the first batch (a batch is 25 units) and that they hope for an 85 percent learning curve. During the first month of production, the following standard costs are recorded:

Week	Production	Direct Labor	Variable Overhead
1	50 batches	$2,440	$1,830
2	40	1,240	930
3	60	1,600	1,200
4	50	1,200	900

Using the standard cost per hour data provided above, this translates to the following hour figures, as you should verify.

Week	Production	Cumulative Production	Incremental Hours	Total Hours
1	50 batches	50 batches	122	122
2	40	90	62	184
3	60	150	80	264
4	50	200	60	324

Using the learning curve that engineering has estimated as a standard, the following would be the standard input of hours given the outputs achieved (you should verify these figures):

Week	Production	Cumulative Production	Standard Incremental Hours	Standard Total Hours
1	50 batches	50 batches	159.85	159.85
2	40	90	90.84	250.69
3	60	150	119.96	370.65
4	50	200	91.31	461.96

Labor efficiency and variable overhead efficiency variances for the four weeks would be as follows, based on the data presented above.

Week 1
labor efficiency variance = (122 − 159.85) $20 = $757 F
variable overhead efficiency variance = (122 − 159.85)$15 = $568 F

Week 2
labor efficiency variance = (62 − 90.84) $20 = $577 F
variable overhead efficiency variance = (62 − 90.84)$15 = $433 F

Week 3
labor efficiency variance = (80 − 119.96)$20 = $799 F
variable overhead efficiency variance = (80 − 119.96)$15 = $599 F

Week 4
labor efficiency variance = (60 − 91.31)$20 = $626 F
variable overhead efficiency variance = (60 − 91.31)$15 = $470 F

There seems to be a clear trail of favorable variances. Were these variances the result of good management? abnormal conditions? a misestimate of the learning curve? This is a good time to do some sensitivity analysis on the learning curve. Assume that records show the first batch did take eight hours as estimated. What would be the learning curve percent that would reduce these variances to near zero? If such a new percent can be found (most or all of the variances near zero), then an investigation may have to take place to see whether such a change is permanent or was something abnormal for this period.

Perhaps the best way to solve for a new learning curve would be to use an electronic spreadsheet program where changes in either a or b would show changes in estimated time and a variance between actual and estimated time. In such a program, an 81 percent learning curve (while holding a constant) produces the following variances:

Week	Labor Efficiency	Variable Overhead Efficiency
1	$ 4.47 U	$ 3.36 U
2	8.95 U	6.71 U
3	34.60 U	25.95 U
4	40.19 U	30.14 U

Thus, it looks as if there is an 81 percent learning curve instead of the 85 percent curve originally estimated. Is this a change that should be incorporated into future production estimates? Questions like this tie into the discussion on variance investigation covered in Chapter 10.

When calculating standard cost variances, managers also have to make sure that learning has not ceased. If efficiency variances have been pretty much in line but then a string of unfavorable variances occurs, management has a good clue that learning might have ceased.

In the above example, fixed overhead was not addressed. Let us say that fixed overhead is based on practical capacity. Management must take into account the fact that the same hours of capacity can produce many more units of production if learning is present.

Budgeting and Production Planning

The entire budgeting cycle is affected if learning applies to the production process. The sales department will be able to deliver more units in a shorter time. Production and purchases budgets will have to be adjusted to take learning into account. Cash budgets will need to reflect learning both on the inflow and outflow sides.

SUMMARY

The learning curve or learning effect is a practical management tool reflecting decreases in cumulative average time as cumulative production increases. Managers can use simple linear regression to estimate the parameters of the learning curve. As with any estimate, managers must make sure that the data are relevant and representative and that they are within a relevant range. Two main models (the cumulative average time and marginal time models) are discussed.

Learning does not occur in all situations. Processes that have the greatest potential for learning involve a high ratio of labor and labor-paced manufacturing. In addition, the less preplanning done in such situations, the more learning will take place. There has been recent discussion regarding learning and a computer-integrated manufacturing (CIM) environment. Some argue that learning will continue to be important since there will still be assembly areas that are labor intensive. Others argue that there will be a reduced learning effect due to much more preproduction engineering and to a robotics-oriented manufacturing plant. Finally, even in cases where learning is evident, learning does not go on forever since there are physical and psychological limits to production.

Some examples are given to show how the learning effect is used in pricing, standard cost variances, and budgeting and production planning. Sensitivity analysis and problems with relevant range assumptions are discussed with these examples. The result is an easy-to-use decision aid for management.

PROBLEMS AND CASES

5-1. Estimating Learning Effect

Data for the assembly department of the Foxes Machine Company for a particular part is as follows:

Number of Batches	Total Time (Hours)
1	200
2	330
3	420
4	520
5	590

Required:
Using the above data, estimate the learning curve using linear regression. Plot the data both before and after transformation.

5-2. Variance Analysis

The Gummie Company makes electronic components for industrial and governmental clients. Most contracts run for several years. For example, a Defense contract may last five years. While the company knows there is learning, especially in the assembly department, they have not estimated specific learning for each job, but assume a 90 percent learning curve for all jobs for labor and variable overhead.

Each order is treated as a job. Management wants to monitor how actual performance compares to the budget for each job. For example, data on two jobs is as follows:

| | Job | |
	AB–10	OP–12
Total number of units to be delivered	12,000	6,000
Number completed to date	7,000	2,000
Labor and variable overhead costs to date	$162,180	$ 78,300
Cost for first 100 units (= budget)	$ 3,800	
Total budgeted cost for entire order		$192,000

The cost of the first one hundred units is not available for job OP-12 because of input error on the computer. In addition, no one seems to be able to find the sheet showing the total budgeted cost for job AB – 10.

Required:
Determine the costs that should be accumulated for each job at its current state of completion. What can you say about actual versus budgeted costs for these two jobs?

5-3. Bidding and Learning

Southstar Aircraft is currently bidding on a new medium-range transport for the European market. A French-German consortium is bidding against Southstar and the expected bid price is $24,000,000 per airplane.

Southstar has been through some recent refinancing and management has decided that they need to earn at least $3,200,000 on each aircraft of this variety. Estimates of relevant costs for this model are as follows:

Materials and purchased parts, per plane	$11,200,000
Labor and variable overhead, first plane	15,200,000
Estimated learning curve on conversion costs	85%

Required:
1. Determine whether or not Southstar can meet the $24,000,000 for 16 airplanes and still earn its required profit margin.
2. Determine the learning curve that will make Southstar just meet the target contribution margin at a price of $24,000,000 per plane.

5-4. Regression Analysis and Learning

The following data pertain to the lathe operation on part 10840.

Batches	Cumulative Average Cost
1	288
2	236
3	207
4	190
5	178
6	167
7	159
8	152
9	147
10	142
11	138
12	135
13	132
14	130
15	128
16	126

Required:
1. Plot the data and run a linear regression analysis using the raw data. What problems do you see given the data and the use of a linear regression model?
2. Appropriately transform the data. Plot the transformed data and run a linear regression analysis using the transformed data. What is the estimated learning curve percent?
3. Look at incremental costs. If appropriate, run a new estimate of learning based on a relevant range of batches. Evaluate this estimate as compared to that in part 2.

5-5. Standard Costs and Bidding (CMA)

The Kelly Company plans to manufacture a product called Electrocal which requires a substantial amount of direct labor on each unit. Based on the company's experience with other products which required similar amounts of direct labor, management believes that there is a learning factor in the production process used to manufacture Electrocal.

Each unit of Electrocal requires 50 square feet of raw material at a cost of $30 per square foot for a total material cost of $1,500. The standard direct labor rate is $25 per direct labor hour. Variable manufacturing overhead is assigned to products at a rate of $40 per direct labor hour. The company adds a markup of 30 percent on variable manufacturing cost in determining an initial bid price for all products.

Data on the production of the first two lots (16 units) of Electrocal is as follows:

- The first lot of eight units required a total of 3,200 direct labor hours.
- The second lot of eight units required a total of 2,240 direct labor hours.

Based on prior production experience, Kelly anticipates that there will be no significant improvement in production time after the first 32 units. Therefore, a standard for direct labor hours will be established based on the average hours per unit for units 17–32.

Required:
1. What is the basic premise of the learning curve?
2. Based on the data presented for the first 16 units, what learning rate appears to be applicable to the direct labor required to produce Electrocal? Support your answer with appropriate calculations.
3. Calculate the standard for direct labor hours which Kelly Company should establish for each unit of Electrocal.
4. After the first 32 units have been manufactured, Kelly Company was asked to submit a bid on an additional 96 units. What price should Kelly bid on this order of 96 units? Explain your answer.
5. Knowledge of the learning curve phenomenon can be a valuable management tool. Explain how management can apply the learning curve in the planning and controlling of business operations.

5-6. Learning Effect and Bidding (CMA)

Catonic Inc. recently developed a new product that includes a rather complex printed circuit board as a component (Catonic's part number PCB-31). Although Catonic has the ability to manufacture the PCB-31 internally, the circuit board is purchased from an independent supplier because the company's printed circuit line has been operating at capacity for some time.

The first contract for 50 units of the PCB-31 was awarded to Rex Engineering Company in September 19X2 on the basis of a competitive bid. Rex was significantly lower than other bidders. Additional orders for 50 units each were placed with Rex as shown in the purchase history schedule below. Rex has proved to be a reliable supplier of other component parts over a period of several years.

Date Ordered	Quantity	Unit Price	Total Price
September 15, 19X2	50	$374	$18,700
November 15, 19X2	50	374	18,700
January 1,19X3	50	374	18,700
February 1, 19X3	50	374	18,700

Mark Polmik, a buyer for Catonic, has determined that the next order for PCB-31 should be for 600 units. He has contacted Kathy Wentz, a Rex salesperson. Polmik indicated that the next PCB-31 order would be for 600 units and that he believed that Catonic should receive a lower unit price because of the increased quantity. Wentz provided a proposal of $355 per unit for the 600-unit contract a few days later.

Polmik has scheduled a meeting with Wentz for next week for the purpose of negotiating the 600-unit contract. He has asked Catonic's cost accounting department for assistance in evaluating the $355 unit price for the PCB-31 circuit board.

The price bid on the original contract for 50 units was estimated to be a "full cost" based price since, at that time, Catonic was not sure if there would be future contracts for the PCB-31 board. The cost of materials included in the PCB-31 is estimated to be $180 per unit. Cost accounting is fairly sure that Rex applies overhead at 100 percent of direct labor and employee benefit cost. Because Rex Engineering recently received a good deal of coverage by the local media when a strike was narrowly averted, the labor and fringe benefit costs at Rex are known to be approximately $20 per hour. The printed circuit line at Rex is very similar to the one at Catonic, and Rex's overhead is believed to be approximately 50 percent variable and 50 percent fixed. Similar work at Catonic evidences a 90 percent learning curve effect.

Using the foregoing data, the price of a fifty-unit order is estimated to be comprised of the following cost components:

Materials	$	180
Labor and employee benefits (4 labor hours × $20)		80
Overhead (100 percent of labor and employee benefits)		80
Full cost of PCB-31 component	$	340
Profit contribution (10 percent of full cost)		34
Unit price	$	374
Units purchased		50
Total contact price		$18,700

Required:
1. Prepare a schedule that may be used by Mark Polmik during his meeting with Kathy Wentz next week. This schedule should incorporate the learning curve effect that Rex would have experienced on the first 200 units produced and should be of use to Polmik in negotiating a contract with Rex Engineering.
2. The learning curve (also known as a progress function or an experience curve) was first formally recognized in the 1920s. Since that time the learning effect has been observed in a number of different industries. The general form of the learning curve may be expressed as $y = ax^b$.
   a. What are the implications of an 80 percent learning curve as opposed to a 90 percent learning curve?
   b. Identify factors that would tend to reduce the degree of learning that takes place in an industrial operation.

5-7. Learning Effect and Variances[12]

The engineering department of Jodi Trailers has estimated 100 direct labor hours for the assembly of the first trailer of a new horse trailer line. The standard labor

---

[12]This problem is based on an example by Woody M. Liao, "Consideration of Learning Effects in Efficiency Variance Analysis," *Cost and Management* (January-February 1982), pp. 30–32.

rate is $10 per hour. During the last month, ten trailers were assembled in 900 direct labor hours. Labor costs were a total of $9,900.

Required:
1. Calculate a labor rate and a labor efficiency variance for production to this point.
2. Assume that the company has experienced a 90 percent learning effect on previous new trailers. Recalculate the variances in part 1 including the effect of learning.
3. The efficiency variances in each of parts 1 and 2 are different. Under standard costing that ignores the effect of learning, what is the amount of direct labor that would be moved to Work in Process given the production of ten trailers? Use the information that you have generated in parts 1 and 2 to create and label appropriate variances that will fill the gap between actual labor costs of $9,900 and standard costs ignoring learning.
4. The managers of Jodi Trailers are concerned that variance analysis was delayed until after ten units were produced. They would have liked unit-by-unit feedback. Using the data below, calculate an efficiency variance due to learning and an efficiency variance due to factors other than learning for each unit.

Trailer	Actual Hours	Cumulative Hours
1	100	100
2	98	198
3	96	294
4	94	388
5	92	480
6	88	568
7	86	654
8	84	738
9	82	820
10	80	900

5. Evaluate the variance reporting system of parts 1 through 4.

5-8. Learning Effect and Variances—Additional Data

This problem builds on problem 5-7. Another five trailers were built in the next month and results showed the following based on labor rates of $11 per hour.

Trailer	Cumulative Labor Costs
11	$10,780
12	11,660
13	12,551
14	13,442
15	14,322

Required:
1. Using the same format as part 2 of problem 5-7, calculate the efficiency variance for the additional five units in total and by unit.
2. Using the same format as parts 3 and 4 of problem 5-7, calculate efficiency variances due to learning and due to factors other than learning.
3. Comment on the variances you have calculated.

5-9. Sourcing Decision (CMA)

The Henderson Equipment Company has produced a pilot run of 50 units of a recently developed cylinder used in its finished products. The cylinder has a one-year life, and the company expects to produce and sell 1,650 units annually. The pilot run required 14.25 direct labor hours for the 50 cylinders, averaging .285 direct labor hours per cylinder. The last cylinder in the pilot run required .194 direct labor hours. Henderson has experienced an 80 percent learning curve on the direct labor hours needed to produce new cylinders. Past experience indicates that learning tends to cease by the time 800 parts are produced.

Henderson's manufacturing costs for cylinders are presented below.

Direct labor	$12.00 per hour
Variable overhead	10.00 per direct labor hour
Fixed overhead	16.60 per direct labor hour
Material	4.05 per unit

When pricing products, Henderson factors in selling and administrative expenses at $12.70 per direct labor hour. All selling and administrative expenses except sales commissions (2 percent of sales) are independent of sales or production volume.

Henderson has received a quote of $7.50 per unit from the Lytel Machine Company for the additional 1,600 cylinders needed. Henderson frequently subcontracts this type of work and has always been satisfied with the quality of the units produced by Lytel.

Required:
1. If the cylinders are manufactured by Henderson Equipment Company, determine
   a. the average direct labor hours per unit for the first 800 cylinders (including the pilot run) produced. Round calculations to three decimal places.
   b. the total direct labor hours for the first 800 cylinders (including the pilot run) produced.
   c. the marginal direct labor hours for the 800th cylinder produced. Round calculations to three decimal places.
2. After completing the pilot run, Henderson Equipment Company must manufacture an additional 1,600 units to fulfill the annual requirement of 1,650 units. Without prejudice to your answer in Part 1, assume that

   • the first 800 cylinders produced (including the pilot run) required 100 direct labor hours, and
   • the 800th unit produced (including the pilot run) required .079 hours.

   Calculate the total manufacturing costs for Henderson to produce the additional 1,600 cylinders required.
3. In order to maximize profits, determine whether Henderson Equipment Company should manufacture the additional 1,600 cylinders or purchase the cylinders from Lytel Machine Company. Support your answer with appropriate calculations.

Chapter 6

Short-Term Planning with Constraints on Resources

Oh, give me land, lots of land under starry skies above.
Don't fence me in.[1]

In Chapter 3, the Theory of Constraints (TOC) was introduced as a way of managing constraints in a dynamic environment. Although there are many aspects to TOC, one basic premise is to maximize the amount of throughput (revenues less the cost of material to produce goods sold) while minimizing inventory and operating expenses. TOC is a broad-based concept that really involves how an organization is managed; it goes beyond tactical uses of constrained resources. In this chapter, we look at such short-term uses. Linear programming allows managers to make short-term mix decisions that

---

[1] Cole Porter, "Don't Fence Me In" (New York: Warner Bros.).

optimize profit. By its very nature, linear programming constraints tend to be more static than those addressed by TOC.

SHORT-TERM DECISION MAKING WITHOUT CONSTRAINED RESOURCES

In the TOC example in Chapter 3, we looked at two products that each used resources in a different way and that also had differing contribution margins. If there were no limits on any of the resources (internal or external) and if managers decided that they wanted to market only one of the two products, the one with the larger contribution margin per unit would be picked, all other things remaining equal. However, in some sense, the idea of no constrained resources is a fiction or, at least, does not happen often. There always seems to be a constraint of some kind. Even in the example above, there is the constraint of marketing only one product or the other.

THE EFFECT OF CONSTRAINED RESOURCES

Firms usually have limits on several important variables both within the firm and in the external environment. If a company is looking at alternate uses of excess capacity (floor space, machine capacity, and so on), the constraint is the amount of excess available. However, the point above is still valid: the first part of most analyses involves looking at per-unit margins (preferably contribution margin). As with the discussion of TOC, the next step is to define the relevant constraints. Internally this can mean strategic choices, personnel, equipment, space, materials, utility availability, and funds. In the external environment, limits include the economy, value chain limits, the market in general and specific markets, regulations, and politics. Given these constraints, managers can calculate the margin (or cost) per unit of scarce resource for all the alternatives under consideration. While TOC looks at a single constraint at a time (see the example in Chapter 3), managers are often faced with decisions where there are multiple short-term constraints and it is not intuitively obvious how to balance different products and different constraints.

For example, Mann Exploring is considering two products, a folding camp seat and a camp stove. The contribution margins of each are

    seat: $12.00/unit
    stove: $ 9.00/unit

There are no incremental fixed costs for either product. Clearly the seat has a better contribution margin per unit than the stove. If the market is wide open and Mann could sell virtually all it could produce, the seat would yield higher profits than the stove, *ignoring any constrained resources*. As stated, this is the first step in how most managers look at using resources.

First, let us begin with a single constraint: capacity (time). This allows us to build on the earlier TOC example. Mann's engineers state that the seat takes $\frac{1}{2}$ hour to produce, while the stove takes $\frac{1}{3}$ hour. While the seat has the higher contribution margin *per unit*, the stove has the higher contribution margin *per hour*, the scarce resource.

Contribution Margin

Seat: 2 per hour @ $12 = $24/hour
Stove: 3 per hour @ $ 9 = $27/hour

Thus, with a single constrained resource (time), making the stove would yield higher profits.

Even before we begin to discuss other quantitative constraints, a company might consider some strategic and subjective constraints. For example, a company might not opt to make only one of the products but, rather, might choose to make some of each. Managers might be concerned with having a broader product line. These kinds of constraints can be incorporated in the model, as we shall see later.

LINEAR PROGRAMMING MODEL

With a single constrained resource, once managers know the contribution margin per unit of that resource, they can choose which product(s) to make and know the economic consequences of their choices. For example, for every hour that managers devote to seat production, they will lose $3 when compared to using that same capacity to make stoves. However, as we add other constraints and more products, the mix choices are not easy to see and the economic consequences become more difficult to ascertain. Thus, managers use linear programming to aid them in decision making and allow them to see the consequences of different choices given the constraints. **Linear programming** is a mathematical optimization model that provides the best (most profitable) use of constrained resources. This is done by looking at the contribution margins of all products that can use these resources (*maximization* of total contribution margin) or by the costs of these products (*minimization* of costs). We illustrate both maximization and minimization problems; in some senses they are mirror images of each other.

Basic Maximization Problem

The general ideas presented in this section set the stage for most uses of linear programming. We start off with two products and a single constraint, and then we add one additional constraint. If you understand this two-variable, two-constraint example, little effort is needed to extend your understanding and use of this quantitative tool to more complex settings.

The Objective Function   A manager should set a specific objective. In the Mann Exploring example, the objective is to get the highest profits possible given any constrained resources. Since there are no incremental fixed costs associated with either product, profit is *maximized* by finding that combination of the two products that will yield the highest total contribution margin. This is stated in linear programming terms as a *maximization problem* where the *objective function* shows the linear combination of the products and their unit contribution margins. In this example, the objective function is

$$\text{Max } Z = \$12 \text{ seat} + \$9 \text{ stove}$$

where Z is total contribution margin, *seat* is the number of folding seats produced (and sold), and *stove* is the number of stoves produced (and sold). Although it may seem trivial to define these terms, it is extremely important that there is common agreement because the definition needs to remain constant throughout the entire problem.

Constraints   As was developed earlier, one possible set of limited resources is capacity. In this case, 1,000 hours are available. If it takes $\frac{1}{2}$ hour for each seat and $\frac{1}{3}$ hour for each camp stove, production in total will be a linear combination of seats and stoves so that not more than 1,000 hours are used. For capacity, this constraint is:

$$\tfrac{1}{2} \text{ seat} + \tfrac{1}{3} \text{ stove} \leq 1,000 \text{ hours}$$

This is shown graphically in Figure 6-1. If only seats are produced, Mann can make up to 2,000 units (1,000 hours/$\frac{1}{2}$ hour per unit). If only stoves are produced, the upper limit is 3,000 units (1,000 hours/$\frac{1}{3}$ hour per unit). What is the maximum contribution margin available to Mann with only one constraint? We can check the two end points.

$$2,000 \text{ seats} \ @ \ \$12 = \$24,000$$
$$3,000 \text{ stoves} \ @ \ \$ 9 = \$27,000$$

This is consistent with our previous conclusion: camp stoves have a higher contribution margin per hour of capacity. Note that we can also check any

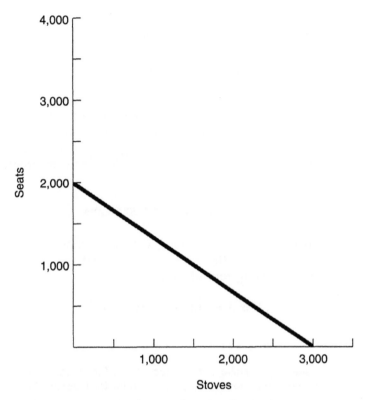

Figure 6-1 Mann Exploring: Capacity Constraint

linear combination falling on the constraint line. (We would ignore points falling under the constraint since Mann would not be fully utilizing all its resources at, say, 800 hours.) If Mann produced 1,000 seats, 500 hours would be used, leaving 500 hours to produce 1,500 stoves. Total contribution margin would be $25,500 (1,000 seats @ $12 plus 1,500 stoves @ $9). While this is better than producing only seats, it is not as good as producing only stoves. This same trend would be shown for any combination of the two products. Thus, with only one constraint, the objective (maximizing profits) is reached by producing 3,000 stoves and getting a total contribution margin of $27,000.

Additional Constraints   The first constraint above relates to time on one of the two machines that both of these products use during production. The second machine also has limited capacity, 1,200 hours. The folding seats take 0.3 hours on this machine while the camp stoves take 0.6 hours. Using the same analysis as before, we have the following as contribution margins per unit of the second scarce resource:

Contribution
Margin

Seat: $3\frac{1}{3}$ per hour @ $12 = \$40$/hour
Stove: $1\frac{2}{3}$ per hour @ $\$9 = \$15$/hour

It should be obvious that the folding seats will have the higher contribution margin per hour for this resource because not only do they use half the time as the stoves, but the contribution margin per unit is higher as well. If we incorporate this information into a constraint for linear programming, we have:

0.3 seat + 0.6 stove ≤ 1,200 hours

This new constraint is graphed along with the constraint for the first machine in Figure 6-2. With these two variables and the two constraints, the full linear programming formulation is:

Max Z = $12 seat + $9 stove

subject to

$\frac{1}{2}$ seat + $\frac{1}{3}$ stove ≤ 1,000 (constraint for Machine 1)
0.3 seat + 0.6 stove ≤ 1,200 (constraint for Machine 2)

To this we add some implied constraints (called *nonnegativity constraints*) that we cannot produce fewer than zero of either product.

seat ≤ 0,   stove ≤ 0

Although we should show these nonnegativity constraints to be complete when we write out the objective function and other constraints, they are really implicit and are included automatically in any computer program that yields the optimal linear programming solution.[2]

Graphic Solution

Figure 6-2 allows us to solve this constrained resource problem without any quantitative methodology. We can see which linear combination of the two products yields the highest total contribution margin. If there were more

---

[2] It is not necessary to use nonnegativity constraints as input into linear programming computer models or when solving them by hand. The basic algorithm, the simplex method, automatically incorporates them into the solution.

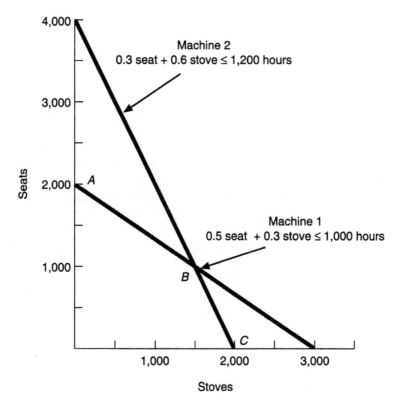

Figure 6-2   Mann Exploring: Two Constraints

than two products, we could not find the solution graphically unless we graphed in more than two dimensions. Since many real-world situations involve hundreds of products and hundreds of constraints, we will need a mathematical solution. However, from the graph of a two-product, two-constraint problem we can learn much that can be extended into a complex problem setting. In Figure 6-2, three points are identified. Point A is producing 2,000 seats with a contribution margin of $24,000 as was developed earlier. This would use all the Machine 1 capacity (2,000 × 0.5 = 1,000 hours) but would leave 600 hours of Machine 2 capacity unused (a *slack* resource), since 2,000 × 0.3 = 600 hours out of 1,200 hours available.

If point C is chosen, 2,000 stoves will be produced. Note at this juncture that we cannot choose 3,000 stoves as we did in the one-constraint problem since the new constraint (Machine 2) limits *feasible* solutions below the limits placed by Machine 1 hours. At 2,000 stoves total contribution margin is $18,000 ($9 × 2,000) and while all of Machine 2 capacity is used up (0.6 × 2,000 = 1,200 hours), there is slack capacity on Machine 1 of $333\frac{1}{3}$ hours (1,000 − ($\frac{1}{3}$ × 2,000). Point B is a linear combination of seats (1,000 units) and stoves (1,500 units). The total contribution margin is

1,000 seats @ $12 + 1,500 stoves @ $9 = $25,500

We can check other points on the constraint lines delineating the *feasible solution space* of the graph, but point B will prove to have the highest total contribution margin.

Figure 6-3 is an expansion of Figure 6-2 that includes the objective function (called an *isoprofit* line) at $25,500. This dashed line intersects with the feasible solution space only at the meeting of the two constraints. One thousand seats and 1,500 stoves use all of *both* constraints, as you should verify. The isoprofit line can be graphed in the same manner as constraints. First choose a level of total contribution margin (like $25,500) and find the intersection with the axes by assuming first that the company makes only seats ($25,500/$12 = 2,125 seats) and then that only stoves are made ($25,500/$9 = 2,833.33 stoves). As with constraints, the isoprofit line moves in a parallel fashion as the total margin changes upward or downward. In order to maximize total profit in a maximization problem, the isoprofit line must be moved as far to the right (higher) as possible while still staying in the feasible solution space.

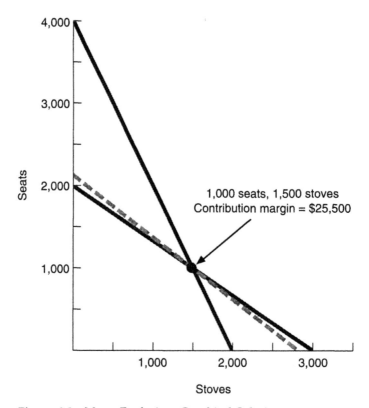

Figure 6-3 Mann Exploring: Graphical Solution

Linear Programming Tableaus

Tables (called *tableaus*) can be constructed to depict the linear programming model. There is little need today to use these tableaus to solve a linear program by hand using what is called the simplex method. Computers also use the simplex method to solve these problems. Even though many computer outputs are "user friendly," it is important to understand tableaus and to be able to read and interpret them in order to see the logic behind the computer solution.

The Initial Tableau   The solution starts at the origin. Assume that we make zero of both products. Thus, there will be *slack* amounting to 1,000 hours for Machine 1 and 1,200 for Machine 2. We will now define *slack variables* to account for any excess time. Thus, our constraints are now

0.5 seat + 0.3333 stove + Machine 1 slack = 1,000 hours
0.3 seat + 0.6 stove + Machine 2 slack = 1,200 hours

In matrix (tableau) form this is:

Seat	Stove	Machine 1	Machine 2	
0.5	0.3333	1	0	1,000
0.3	0.6	0	1	1,200

When Mann makes no products, slack for the two machines equals 1,000 and 1,200 hours, respectively. This is shown in this initial tableau.

How to Read a Tableau   We have shown just the core of a tableau: the constraints. Look for columns where there is a single 1 and the rest of the numbers in the column are 0. *Machine 1* is such a column. Since the 1 appears in the first row, that row is associated with Machine 1. There are 1,000 hours left over as we had stated. Row 2 is for Machine 2 and reflects 1,200 hours available. The fact that the seat and the stove columns are not 1,0 or 0,1 reflects the fact that neither of these products is in the solution at this point.

The Final Tableau   The final tableau is the result of a computer (or hand) solution using the simplex method. In this method, an algorithm checks various possible points (like points *A*, *B*, and/or *C* in Figure 6-2) and selects the point with the highest contribution margin. The partial tableau of the solution for this example is:

Seat	Stove	Machine 1	Machine 2	
1	0	3.0	− 1.6667	1,000
0	1	− 1.5	2.5	1,500

Exhibit 6-1
Mann Exploring
Linear Programming Solution

```
MAX       12 SEAT + 9 STOVE
SUBJECT TO
        2)      .5 SEAT + .3333333 STOVE <=      1000
        3)      .3 SEAT + .6 STOVE <=      1200
END

LP OPTIMUM FOUND AT STEP       2

           OBJECTIVE FUNCTION VALUE

    1)         25500.0000

    VARIABLE           VALUE        REDUCED COST

      SEAT         1000.000000           .000000
     STOVE         1500.000000           .000000

      ROW       SLACK OR SURPLUS      DUAL PRICES

      2)               .000000        22.500000
      3)               .000000         2.500001

NO. ITERATIONS =       2
```

Using the same rules as we did in reading the initial tableau, row 1 is associated with folding seats (make 1,000) and row 2 with stoves (make 1,500). The fact that the two constraint columns are neither 1,0 nor 0,1 means *all of both constraints have been used* as we proved above. We will identify and show the use of the figures in the two machine columns in the section on sensitivity analysis.

Computer Solutions

There are several good computer programs that allow much flexibility of use and ease of interpretation. Solutions used herein are generated by LINDO.[3] Exhibit 6-1 shows the basic output for the linear program formulation and solution.

---

[3] LINDO is written by Linus Schrage and is available for IBM-compatible equipment. See *Linear, Integer, and Quadratic Programming with LINDO and LINDO User's Manual*, 5th edition (Palo Alto, Calif.: The Scientific Press), 1991.

SENSITIVITY ANALYSIS

A basic weakness of deterministic models managers use, such as linear programming, is the specificity of the figures that make up the formulas modeling the objective function and the constraints. For example, the two contribution margins per unit may change. Prices may go up or down in the marketplace. Variable costs may not remain the same. Who is to say that exactly 1,000 hours of Machine 1 time is available or 1,200 hours for Machine 2? What would happen to the solution of the Mann Exploring example if contribution margins changed? What would happen if more (or less) machine capacity were available? These are the types of questions we can answer using sensitivity analysis.

Objective Function Ranges

Currently the contribution margins are $12 for seats and $9 for stoves. What would happen if, for example, the contribution margin for seats rose to $14? If we go back to Figure 6-2 and examine points *A*, *B*, and *C* with this new contribution margin, we get

$$
\begin{aligned}
\text{Point } A: \quad & 2{,}000 \ @ \ \$14 & = \$28{,}000 \\
\text{Point } B: \quad & 1{,}000 \ @ \ \$14 + 1{,}500 \ @ \ \$9 = & 27{,}500 \\
\text{Point } C: \quad & 2{,}000 \ @ \ \$9 = & 18{,}000
\end{aligned}
$$

Now Point *A* has the highest total contribution margin and the solution calls for all seats and no stoves. At a unit contribution margin of $14, the folding seat is the best use of *both* scarce resources. This is shown below.

Seat	Stove	
$2 \times \$14 = \$28$/hour	$3 \times \$9 = \$27$/hour	Machine 1
$3\frac{1}{3} \times \$14 = \$46.67$/hour	$1\frac{2}{3} \times \$9 = \$15$/hour	Machine 2

Note that the contribution margin for stoves was held constant at $9 per unit. This is consistent with the basic notion of sensitivity analysis: how does the result change if we change a single variable and hold everything else constant?

What would happen if the contribution margin on seats fell to, say, $3 per unit (even though such a drop seems highly unlikely)? At a certain point, the $9 per unit contribution margin for stoves would yield higher contribution margins *per hour* for the two constraints. At this point, the solution would call for only stoves and no seats.

While we can solve for these upper and lower limits (a range of values) for the two contribution margins, computer programs can do this for us.

Exhibit 6-2
Mann Exploring
Sensitivity Analysis

RANGES IN WHICH THE BASIS IS UNCHANGED:

OBJ COEFFICIENT RANGES

VARIABLE	CURRENT COEF	ALLOWABLE INCREASE	ALLOWABLE DECREASE
SEAT	12.000000	1.500001	7.500000
STOVE	9.000000	15.000000	1.000000

RIGHTHAND SIDE RANGES

ROW	CURRENT RHS	ALLOWABLE INCREASE	ALLOWABLE DECREASE
2	1000.000000	999.999800	333.333400
3	1200.000000	600.000200	599.999900

Note: The computer sometimes carries figures out to an extent that may be confusing. For example, the *allowable decrease* for Row 3 is really 600 and not 599.9999.

Exhibit 6-2 shows a LINDO sensitivity analysis showing the ranges for the objective function coefficients.

In Exhibit 6-2 the upper and lower bounds on seat contribution margin are set at $13.50 and $4.50. If the contribution margin for the seat stays within this range, the solution will call for 1,000 seats and 1,500 stoves *holding everything else constant*. We have shown the results of one price outside this range ($14 for compasses). Exhibits 6-3 and 6-4 show computer solutions for a contribution of $13.52 (only 2 cents above the range limit) and for $4.45 (5 cents below the limit). These exhibits reaffirm the conclusions reached above: when the contribution margin for compasses exceeds the range, the solution will call for only folding seats and zero stoves; when the contribution margin for seats falls below the range, the solution will call for only stoves and no seats. Note that in both cases in this two-variable, two-constraint problem, when only one product is produced, there is slack in one constraint.

As the discussion about tableaus showed, the basic tableau has as many rows as there are constraints in the problem. Since each row must be identified with a variable, there are only the choices of the following in a solution when there are two constraints:

two slack variables (as in the initial tableau)
one product and one slack variable
two products

Exhibit 6-3
Mann Exploring
High Contribution Margin—Seat
Linear Programming Solution

```
MAX       13.52 SEAT + 9 STOVE
SUBJECT TO
        2)      .5 SEAT + .3333333 STOVE <= 1000
        3)      .3 SEAT + .6 STOVE <= 1200
END

LP OPTIMUM FOUND AT STEP 1

            OBJECTIVE FUNCTION VALUE

   1)          27040.0000

VARIABLE              VALUE           REDUCED COST

   SEAT          2000.000000             .000000
   STOVE             .000000             .013333

     ROW               SLACK OR
                  SURPLUS DUAL PRICES

     2)              .000000          27.040000
     3)           600.000000            .000000

NO. ITERATIONS = 1
```

This discussion (as well as Exhibits 6-1, 6-3, and 6-4) has included examples of three of these combinations. Obviously, we can come to the same conclusions regarding stove contribution margin as were reached about seat contribution margin. As long as that contribution margin stays within the range of $8 to $24, the basic solution is unaffected. If it goes over $24, then only stoves would be made; if it falls below $8, only seats would be made. In this part of the analysis the seat contribution margin is held constant at $12. Thus, the ranges of contribution margins that would not affect the basic solution are

	Range	Current
Seat:	$4.50 to $13.50	$12.00
Stove:	$8.00 to $24.00	$ 9.00

Both products seem sensitive to changes in prices or variable costs. For seats, contribution margin needs to rise only $1.51 for that product to domi-

Exhibit 6-4
Mann Exploring
Low Contribution Margin—Seat
Linear Programming Solution

```
MAX      4.45 SEAT + 9 STOVE
SUBJECT TO
      2)        .5 SEAT + .3333333 STOVE <= 1000
      3)        .3 SEAT + .6 STOVE <= 1200
END

LP OPTIMUM FOUND AT STEP 2

            OBJECTIVE FUNCTION VALUE

   1)           18000.0000

VARIABLE            VALUE          REDUCED COST

    SEAT           .000000             .050000
   STOVE       2000.000000             .000000

     ROW    SLACK OR SURPLUS      DUAL PRICES

      2)         333.333400          .000000
      3)            .000000        15.000000

NO. ITERATIONS = 2
```

nate the solution. For stoves, contribution margin must fall by only $1.00 for stoves to be eliminated from the solution. There is a reasonable chance that a combination of changes in prices and variable costs for *both* products could lead to just enough of a shift between these products that only seats would be called for in linear programming solution. Figure 6-4 shows the shift in the isoprofit line as the contribution margin of seats exceeds $13.50. At $13.50, the isoprofit line would fall exactly on the Machine 1 constraint line. As is shown, at $13.52 (the figure used in Exhibit 6-3) the line just clears the constraint line and shows graphically that the optimal solution is to make 2,000 seats.

Ranges for Constraints

In the basic solution to this example, both Machine 1 and Machine 2 capacity are fully utilized. Two questions can be asked regarding constraints. If there were more capacity available in, say, Machine 1, how much would

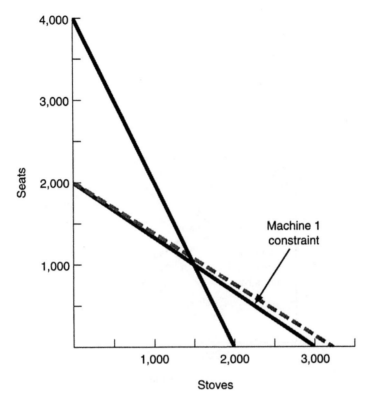

Figure 6-4   Mann Exploring: Change in Seat Contribution
Margin

Mann be willing to pay for it? Second, at what point would what we would
be willing to pay for additional Machine 1 capacity change? This section
addresses the second question while a following section addresses the first.
First, it is reasonable to assume there is some positive value to having at
least some additional capacity. Since the solution used up all of both constraints, additional resources *to a point* are welcome. If there were, say, 1,100
hours of Machine 1 capacity available, what would happen to this constraint? As Figure 6-5 illustrates, the constraint would move upward parallel
to the original constraint.

Two things are apparent on the graph. First, as the Machine 1 constraint
moves up, the intersection of the two constraints (the optimal solution) also
shifts so that fewer stoves and more seats are made. Second, this upward
shift cannot continue forever. At a certain point stove production will be
reduced to zero and can go no lower. Also, the Machine 1 constraint will
eventually fall *outside* the entire Machine 2 constraint. At that point Machine
1 is no longer a binding constraint and the sole relevant limited resource is

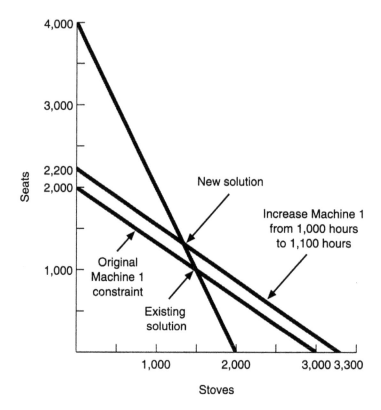

Figure 6-5 Mann Exploring: Change in Machine 1 Constraint

Machine 2 capacity. Exhibit 6-2 on page 250 shows the limits on the constraint. They are

Range	Current Constraint
Machine 1: $666\frac{1}{3}$ hours to 2,000 hours	1,000 hours
Machine 2: 600 hours to 1,800 hours	1,200 hours

At 2,000 hours, 4,000 seats would be produced (2,000/0.5 hr) and zero stoves would be made. Over 2,000 hours, Machine 1 is no longer a binding constraint to the problem. Conversely, the constraint line can move downward and to the left as resources are eliminated. If there are only $666\frac{2}{3}$ hours available on Machine 1, Mann would make 2,000 stoves ($666\frac{2}{3}$/0.3333) and no seats. As we established earlier, stoves have a higher contribution margin per hour on Machine 1 ($27 versus $24 per hour) while seats have a higher contribution margin per hour on Machine 2 ($40 versus $15 per hour). Thus, at $666\frac{2}{3}$ hours (or less) on Machine 1, that machine's capacity becomes the sole binding constraint. Since the contribution margin per hour for stoves is higher than seats on Machine 1, only stoves would be made. These same limits and discussion can be developed regarding the range for Machine 2.

If management could increase Machine 1 capacity to 2,100 hours, there would be 100 hours of excess capacity on hand. This would have a zero opportunity cost to the company since this time would be idle. What is the opportunity cost (additional contribution margin) that could be gained by having 1,100 hours available on Machine 1 (well below the 2,000-hour upper limit)? In the original computer printout there are figures called *dual prices* or *shadow prices* (see Exhibit 6-1 on page 248). These are

Row 2 $22.50
Row 3 $ 2.50

Rows 2 and 3 refer to the two constraints. (Row 1 is the objective function.) Repeating the basic final tableau presented on page 247, we have

	Seat	Stove	Machine 1	Machine 2	
Seat	1	0	3.0	−1.6667	1,000
Stove	0	1	−1.5	2.5	1,500

If Mann had one more hour of Machine 1 capacity available, the final tableau prescribes a shift of production: 3 more seats and 1.5 less stoves. The change in total contribution margin would be

$$(3)(\$12) + (-1.5)(\$9) = \$22.50$$

This shift in production is consistent with the graph presented in Figure 6-5. Thus, for each additional hour of Machine 1 capacity (up to an additional 1,000 hours), Mann could make an additional contribution margin of $22.50 per hour. The same analysis yields the following for Machine 2:

$$(-1.6667)(\$12) + (2.5)(\$9) = \$2.50 \text{ per hour}$$

From management's point of view, additional Machine 1 capacity is more desirable since so much more can be earned per additional hour of capacity.

Two-Variable, Two-Constraint Problems

In two-variable, two-constraint problems, we can clearly see the effect of changes outside the allowable ranges. In the case of the two products, if the contribution margin of one exceeds the range (holding the other product's margin constant), we know that we will make all of one product and none of the other. With two constraints, we can see that if one of the constraints rises to such an extent that it is no longer binding, there will be only one relevant constraint, the solution will call for making only one product, and there will be no opportunity cost (dual price) for additional capacity on the now nonbinding constraint. Thus, in two-variable, two-constraint problems, the results of going beyond the allowable range (holding everything else constant) on one variable or one constraint yield predictable results.

Within the allowable ranges we also have known effects. Holding the contribution margin of seats constant, if the contribution margin for stoves is anywhere between its upper and lower bounds as shown in Exhibit 6-2 ($8 to $24), the *mix* of the two products will not change. However, if the contribution margin per unit changes, then the total contribution margin (objective function value) changes.

In the case of constraints, as long as the amount of the constrained resource stays within its allowable range (holding everything else constant), the basic solution stays in place (e.g., make both seats and stoves in our example), but the *mix changes*. Thus, as illustrated, with an additional hour of Machine 1 capacity, the solution will call for 1,003 folding seats (the original 1,000 plus another 3 given the additional hour) and 1,498.5 stoves (1,500 less 1.5).[4]

This changes when we increase either the number of variables (products) or constraints. If we exceed the contribution margin range (or the range for a constraint) in a three-variable, four-constraint problem, we know that things will change but usually are not able to accurately predict what will happen. Thus, if a product's margin falls below its allowable range, we cannot say for certain that it will drop out of the solution; we only know that something will change. If a constraint goes above its allowable range, instead of the opportunity cost falling to zero, it might just change to a lower or higher amount. However, the basic points raised about sensitivity analysis are valid even if the results are not as easy to grasp in a larger problem.

Post-Solution Alterations

Sensitivity analysis allows managers to deal with the weakest part of the linear programming model: the exact equations required to set up the model. Even if a manager thinks that, say, costs will vary so that the contribution margin for stoves may be in a range of $8.80 to $9.20 per unit, some figure must be put in the objective function as the best estimate of that contribution

---

[4] Obviously, Mann would not make partial units. Thus, for all practical purposes we would talk about changes in two-hour increments for Machine 1, which would yield +6 seats and −3 stoves. Other alternatives involve rounding or using integer programming.

margin. The same holds true for the number of hours per unit and the total hours available on each machine. Using sensitivity analysis based on the original solution is one way to deal with these uncertainties.

Managers also have the option of altering any or all of the original data used in the problem formulation. Contribution margins can be varied outside the ranges shown in the solution as can righthand side variables (constraints). This may not seem too useful in the two-product, two-constraint case since managers have a clear idea what changes as figures exceed the range. However, in a four-product, twenty-constraint situation post-solution alterations may be the only way to grasp what changes imply for a revised solution.

In addition, managers may be dissatisfied with an original solution. If a solution calls for producing only one product and not the other, managers may think that this option is not reasonable given various long-term marketing considerations. Thus, they can add a constraint that forces a product to have a minimum quantity or to have a minimum percent of total production. Given the speed and ease of altering the equations and constraints, managers can make some changes and run new solutions. The new total contribution margin will be less than the original solution, and it will reflect the economic consequences of these changes. Managers can also estimate the cost of adding in a product where a solution calls for zero production by the use of the tableau and sensitivity analysis.

Review Problem

Assume that the seat contribution margin rose to $13.52 while the stove's stayed at $9. Exhibit 6-5 shows a full computer solution.

Required:
Using the information in this exhibit:

1. What is the optimal solution? What products will be made, and what is the total contribution margin expected?
2. Are both constraints fully utilized? If not, explain why not.
3. What is the opportunity cost for one additional hour of capacity for Machine 1? for Machine 2? Justify these figures from the tableau.
4. Why does *infinity* appear in the range analysis for both the objective function and the constraints?
5. Assume the president required that 100 stoves be made.
    a. What is the impact on the total contribution margin?
    b. How are Machine 1 and Machine 2 capacities affected?

(*Hint*: The tableau yields much of this information.)

Answers:
1. The optimal solution calls for 2,000 seats at $13.52 each or a total contribution margin of $27,040.

Exhibit 6-5
Mann Exploring
Review Problem

```
MAX       13.52 SEAT + 9 STOVE
SUBJECT TO
        2)    .5 SEAT + .3333333 STOVE <= 1000
        3)    .3 SEAT + .6 STOVE <= 1200
END

LP OPTIMUM FOUND AT STEP 2

           OBJECTIVE FUNCTION VALUE

    1)          . 27040.0000

VARIABLE            VALUE           REDUCED COST

     SEAT        2000.000000            .000000
     STOVE          .000000            .013333

     ROW      SLACK OR SURPLUS      DUAL PRICES

     2)            .000000          27.040000
     3)          600.000000            .000000

NO. ITERATIONS = 2

 RANGES IN WHICH THE BASIS IS UNCHANGED:

                    OBJ COEFFICIENT RANGES
   VARIABLE        CURRENT       ALLOWABLE      ALLOWABLE
                    COEF         INCREASE       DECREASE

     SEAT        13.520000       INFINITY        .020000
     STOVE        9.000000        .013333       INFINITY

                    RIGHTHAND SIDE RANGES
     ROW          CURRENT       ALLOWABLE      ALLOWABLE
                    RHS          INCREASE       DECREASE

      2         1000.000000     999.999900    1000.000000
      3         1200.000000      INFINITY      600.000000

THE TABLEAU
    ROW (BASIS)    COMPASS     STOVE    SLK  2    SLK  3
      1 ART          .000       .013    27.040     .000      27040.000
      2 SEAT        1.000       .667     2.000     .000       2000.000
      3 SLK  3       .000       .400     -.600    1.000        600.000
```

2. There are 600 hours unused on Machine 2 since

$$(2{,}000)(0.5) = 1{,}000 \text{ (Machine 1) out of 1,000 available}$$
$$(2{,}000)(0.3) = 600 \text{ (Machine 2) out of 1,200 available}$$

3. For Machine 1, the opportunity cost is $27.04 per hour up to an additional 1,000 hours. For each additional hour on this machine, 2 more seats will be made @ $13.52 each or $27.04 in total. Machine 2 excess capacity will be lowered by 0.6 for these two additional units. This information is contained in the final tableau. For Machine 2, the opportunity cost is zero since there is excess capacity. There is no benefit to Mann Exploring if additional hours were available.

4. In the case of an allowable increase for seats, seats are already the only product in the solution. Thus, increasing the contribution margin for the folding seat would not affect the solution. In the same way, since stoves are not included in the solution, no matter how much the contribution margin is decreased they still will not be in the solution. For the constraints, the infinite allowable increase for Machine 2 is related to the existing slack of 600 hours on that machine. Machine 2 is not a binding constraint for this problem as formulated. Adding infinite resources will not change that fact. Only by limiting Machine 2 to less than 600 hours (the amount currently used in the solution) will the solution be affected (less seats could be made).

5. The *reduced cost* in the exhibit for stoves reflects the opportunity cost per unit to add each stove to production. This is reflected in the final tableau as well. For each stove added to production the following happens:

$$
\begin{array}{llr}
\text{add 1 stove @ \$9.00} & = & \underline{\$9.0000} \\
\text{subtract } \tfrac{2}{3} \text{ seats @ \$13.52} & = - & 9.0133 \\
& & - \$0.0133
\end{array}
$$

Thus, the total contribution margin is affected by only $1.33 for 100 stoves, a small price to pay. Finally, if one stove is added to production (and two-thirds seats are deleted), Machine 2 capacity is affected by 0.4 hours as follows:

$$(-\tfrac{2}{3})(0.3) + (1)(0.6) = 0.4 \text{ additional hours used}$$

Summary

While a strength of linear programming is the necessity of coming up with fairly precise estimates for the objective function and the constraints, there is a balancing weakness in that these estimates may have a material amount of uncertainty surrounding them. The basic solution (and the final tableau from a simplex solution) gives managers guidance on how changes in prices, costs, production requirements, and constraint availability affect total contribution margin and production. Sensitivity analysis provides ranges for contribution margins. As long as contribution margins stay within these ranges, the production requirements do not change. Ranges for total constraint availability, along with the shadow prices (opportunity costs) for these constraints, indicate the value to a company of increasing (or the penalty of decreasing) available resources.

MINIMIZATION PROBLEMS

In many cases maximizing contribution margin is the same as minimizing costs. Production decisions often involve minimization rather than maximization problems for linear programming. A common minimization problem occurs when a single product has several components that are fairly interchangeable. For example, in producing animal feed or a certain grade of motor fuel, there may be substitutable material inputs where costs and characteristics are different. The objective, then, is to come up with a ton of feed or a gallon of fuel that is as cheap as possible but contains all the characteristics that make it usable and marketable. Thus, the objective function is to *minimize costs* rather than to maximize profits. As an example, assume the Waterway Oil Company seeks to produce a premium unleaded gasoline product that has the following characteristics:

1. Octane at least 95
2. Additives (anything other than refined crude oil) no greater than 40 percent

These characteristics have been developed in response to engineering and marketing concerns. (There are several other constraints that could be proposed but are not mentioned in order to deal with a simple example.) Obviously, an implicit condition (constraint) is that a gallon of fuel contains a total of one liquid gallon. Waterway's costs are

Raw gasoline	$0.30/gallon (*gas*)
Additive A	$0.695/gallon (*adda*)
Additive B	$0.74/gallon (*addb*)

Thus, the objective function is

$$\text{Min } Z = \$0.30 \text{ gas} + \$0.695 \text{ adda} + \$0.74 \text{ addb}$$

There are three constraints. The first deals with octane.

$$80 \text{ gas} + 125 \text{ adda} + 138 \text{ addb} \geq 95 \text{ octane}$$

In this constraint, gas and the two additives have different octane ratings. The combination of any grouping of the three must equal at least a 95 rating. The second constraint deals with the concern that additives make up no more than 40 percent of the total mix. This, for example, may be a governmental regulation.

$$\text{adda} + \text{addb} \leq .40$$

Exhibit 6-6
Minimization Example

```
MIN      .3 GAS + .695 ADDA + .74 ADDB
SUBJECT TO
        2)    80 GAS + 125 ADDA + 138 ADDB >= 95
        3)    ADDA + ADDB <= .4
        4)    GAS + ADDA + ADDB = 1
END

LP OPTIMUM FOUND AT STEP 2

          OBJECTIVE FUNCTION VALUE
  1)         .413793100

  VARIABLE            VALUE            REDUCED COST

       GAS          .741379                .000000
      ADDA          .000000                .053621
      ADDB          .258621                .000000

     ROW      SLACK OR SURPLUS         DUAL PRICES

      2)            .000000               -.007586
      3)            .141379                .000000
      4)            .000000                .306897

NO. ITERATIONS = 2

RANGES IN WHICH THE BASIS IS UNCHANGED:

                   OBJ COEFFICIENT RANGES
  VARIABLE      CURRENT         ALLOWABLE       ALLOWABLE
                COEF            INCREASE        DECREASE

       GAS       .300000         .239231       INFINITY
      ADDA       .695000       INFINITY          .053621
      ADDB       .740000         .069111         .440000

                   RIGHTHAND SIDE RANGES
     ROW        CURRENT         ALLOWABLE       ALLOWABLE
                RHS             INCREASE        DECREASE

      2        95.000000        8.200001       15.000000
      3          .400000      INFINITY           .141379
      4         1.000000         .187500         .102500
```

Exhibit 6-6 (continued)

THE TABLEAU

ROW	(BASIS)	GAS	ADDA	ADDB	SLK	2
1	ART	.000	.054	.000		.008
2	GAS	1.000	.224	.000		.017
3	SLK 3	.000	.224	.000		.017
4	ADDB	.000	.776	1.000		-.017

ROW	SLK	3	
1		.000	-.414
2		.000	.741
3		1.000	.141
4		.000	.259

Finally, we need a constraint that limits the combination of ingredients to one gallon. The following constraint reflects assumed relationships.

$$gas + adda + addb = 1$$

The solution should tell management the cost per gallon as well as the appropriate ingredients.

Exhibit 6-6 shows the computer solution, sensitivity analysis information, and final tableau for this problem. The solution calls for 0.741 gallons of gas (at $0.30 per gallon) plus 0.259 gallons of additive B (at $0.74 per pound) for a total price of $0.4138 per gallon. If additive A's cost were to drop more than $0.0536, it would enter the solution. Information on the constraints shows that the product is exactly 95 octane [$(80 \times 0.741379) + (138 \times 0.258621) = 95$], the additives are less than 40 percent of a gallon, and the one gallon constraint is satisfied.

The dual prices take on different meanings in a minimization problem. For example, if it were required to add one more octane point (from 95 to 96), the cost would go up by $0.0076. The final tableau shows you would *add* 0.017 gallons of additive B (at $0.74 per gallon) and use 0.017 *less* gallons of gas (at $0.30 per gallon) yielding an *increased cost* of $0.0076. (The computer program rounds the tableau numbers. Thus, this multiplication does not come out exact.) The dual price for the last constraint (a gallon must equal a gallon) is not too meaningful. Note that this constraint is not shown on the final tableau.

This example can also be used to illustrate what happens when the set of constraints chosen by mangers conflicts to the extent that no feasible solution is possible. Exhibit 6-7 shows the solution if gas had an octane rating of only 60 rather than 80. There is no way to satisfy the 95 overall

Exhibit 6-7
Infeasible Solution

```
MIN      .3 GAS +  .695 ADDA +  .74 ADDB
SUBJECT TO
        2) 60 GAS + 125 ADDA + 138 ADDB >= 95
        3) ADDA + ADDB <= .4
        4) GAS + ADDA + ADDB = 1
END


NO FEASIBLE SOLUTION AT STEP 0
SUM OF INFEASIBILTIIES = .487179E-01
VIOLATED ROWS HAVE NEGATIVE SLACK, OR (EQUALITY ROWS)
NONZERO SLACKS.
ROWS CONTRIBUTING TO INFEASIBILITY HAVE NONZERO DUAL
PRICE.

        OBJECTIVE FUNCTION VALUE

  1)         .497435900

  VARIABLE              VALUE         REDUCED COST

       GAS            .551282            .000000
      ADDA            .000000            .166667
      ADDB            .448718            .000000

      ROW      SLACK OR SURPLUS        DUAL PRICES

       2)            .000000           -.012821
       3)           -.048718           1.000000
       4)            .000000            .769231

NO. ITERATIONS = 0
```

octane ratings without violating the constraint limiting additives to no more than 40 percent of a gallon. You should verify this conclusion.

COMPLEX MAXIMIZATION PROBLEMS

While two-variable, two-constraint problems are easy to analyze, most real-world problems involve several variables and several constraints. It is not uncommon to have over 20 variables and 100 constraints for complex problems dealing with refineries, chemical production, and agricultural applications. Much in the same way that we can learn quite a bit about linear programming from looking at two-variable, two-constraint problems, we can also see the basics of complex problems by looking at just a few variables and constraints. Clearly what we learn in, say, a three-variable, four-constraint problem is applicable to one with 25 variables and 120 constraints.

Exhibit 6-8 shows the formulation, solution, sensitivity analysis, and final tableau for such a problem. The company produces three models of a product (Model A, Model B, and Model C). Constraints exist for four departments that these products use (all constraints are in hours). The result calls for all three products to be produced with a total contribution margin of about $30,000. There is slack capacity of about 7,800 hours in Department 1.

The final tableau in Exhibit 6-8 allows us to review how to read and use this important part of the linear programming output. The columns with zeros and a single 1 identify the four elements in the final solution: MODELA, MODELB, MODELC, and SLK 2 (which is Department 1). The rows with 1 in them identify which row relates to each of the four elements. We can again see that the number of variables in the solution equals the number of constraints. If, say, managers were looking at the possibility of adding 1,000 hours to Department 2, we can use the final tableau to see the change in both mix and contribution margin that would result.[5] First, we can see that the allowable increase for this department (SLK 3) is over 25,000 hours. Looking at the column labeled SLK 3, the following adjustments would occur with 1,000 more hours.

Model B production would rise about 170 units	+$1.25 × 169 = $211.25
Model A production would rise about 270 units	+$1.80 × 271 = 487.80
Model C production would fall about 340 units	−$2.00 × 339 = (678.00)
	$ 21.05

The final tableau shows that the contribution margin would change by about $22 (0.022 × 1,000), which is rounded from the $0.022034 shown as a dual price. The above approximation is reasonable since units are rounded to the nearest 10 and rounding in the final tableau would not yield exactly $22. We can conclude that adding 1,000 hours in Department 2 really adds very little to the company's profits. In order to make this analysis complete, slack capacity in Department 1 (SLK 2) would go down by about 220 hours (0.22 × 1,000). This can all be verified by rerunning the linear programming formulation shown in Exhibit 6-8 with the righthand side of row 3 changed from 47,000 to 48,000 hours.

---

[5] With the ease of using LINDO and other such computer programs, practicing managers might not use the final tableau to adjust mix and objective function value. Rather, they would probably alter the RHS variable for row 3 and rerun the problem. This approach is fine once a manager understands the basics of how such changes are made rather than relying on a "black box" to solve problems. It is in this spirit that we look at changes through the final tableau. They can always be verified by rerunning the linear program.

Exhibit 6-8
Complex Linear Programming Example—Original Formulation

A. Problem Formulation

```
MAX   1.8 MODELA + 1.25 MODELB + 2 MODELC
SUBJECT TO
       2)   2 MODELA + 3.5 MODELB + 4 MODELC <= 60000
       3)   4 MODELA + 3.5 MODELB + 2 MODELC <= 47000
       4)   5 MODELA + MODELB + 4.5 MODELC <= 70000
       5)   2.5 MODELA + 3 MODELB + 3.5 MODELC <= 50000
  END
```

B. Solution

```
        OBJECTIVE FUNCTION VALUE

        1)     29984.7500
```

VARIABLE	VALUE	REDUCED COST
MODELA	5966.102000	.000000
MODELB	1728.814000	.000000
MODELC	8542.373000	.000000

ROW	SLACK OR SURPLUS	DUAL PRICES
2)	7847.458000	.000000
3)	.000000	.022034
4)	.000000	.176271
5)	.000000	.332203

C. Sensitivity Analysis

```
RANGES IN WHICH THE BASIS IS UNCHANGED:
```

OBJ COEFFICIENT RANGES

VARIABLE	CURRENT COEF	ALLOWABLE INCREASE	ALLOWABLE DECREASE
MODELA	1.800000	.890909	.081250
MODELB	1.250000	.722222	.130000
MODELC	2.000000	.065000	.907407

RIGHTHAND SIDE RANGES

ROW	CURRENT RHS	ALLOWABLE INCREASE	ALLOWABLE DECREASE
2	60000.000000	INFINITY	7847.458000
3	47000.000000	25200.000000	10200.000000
4	70000.000000	7083.333000	35200.000000
5	50000.000000	5309.633000	7968.750000

Exhibit 6-8 (continued)

D. Final Tableau

```
THE TABLEAU
     ROW  (BASIS)   MODELA    MODELB    MODELC   SLK   2   SLK    3
       1  ART        .000      .000      .000       .000       .022
       2  SLK    2   .000      .000      .000      1.000       .220
       3  MODELB     .000     1.000      .000       .000       .169
       4  MODELA    1.000      .000      .000       .000       .271
       5  MODELC     .000      .000     1.000       .000      -.339

     ROW    SLK    4   SLK     5
       1      .176       .332  29984.750
       2      .163     -1.478   7847.458
       3     -.244       .217   1728.814
       4      .169      -.373   5966.102
       5      .088       .366   8542.373
```

Contribution Margin Sensitivity Analysis

Sensitivity analysis shows that the product contribution margins are quite sensitive to change. If the margin of Model A falls about $0.08 or Model B's goes down over $0.13 or Model C's rises about $0.07 per unit (looking at just one model at a time and holding the margins of the others constant), the basic solution will change. For example, what if managers misestimate either market price or variable costs for Model C and find out, after the fact, that the margin in the model for Model C should have been $2.10. What is the cost of that prediction error? Exhibit 6-9 shows the solution that managers would have seen if Model C's contribution margin had been estimated at $2.10 per unit.

The new solution calls for making only Models A and C. The objective function value is now $30,960 as compared to $29,985 in the original formulation. Thus, if the margin for Model C was really $2.10 when it was modeled as $2.00 per unit and if the product mix in Exhibit 6-8 were followed, the estimating error would be

Original mix with revised margin for Model C $29,985 + $0.10 × 5,966 ≈ $30,582
New total margin if new mix produced   30,960
    Estimating error   -$ 372

Changes in Resources Available

Exhibit 6-8 shows the allowable ranges for the three constrained departments. What will happen if one of the ranges is violated? As with changes

Exhibit 6-9
Change in Model C Contribution Margin

```
MAX      1.8 MODELA + 1.25 MODELB + 2.1 MODELC
SUBJECT TO
      2)   2 MODELA + 3.5 MODELB + 4 MODELC <= 60000
      3)   4 MODELA + 3.5 MODELB + 2 MODELC <= 47000
      4)   5 MODELA + MODELB + 4.5 MODELC <= 70000
      5)   2.5 MODELA + 3 MODELB + 3.5 MODELC <= 50000
END

      OBJECTIVE FUNCTION VALUE

      1)       30960.0000

VARIABLE          VALUE           REDUCED COST
    MODELA      3200.000000          .000000
    MODELB         .000000          .070000
    MODELC     12000.000000          .000000

      ROW     SLACK OR SURPLUS     DUAL PRICES
      2)       5600.000000          .000000
      3)      10200.000000          .000000
      4)         .000000           .168000
      5)         .000000           .384000

RANGES IN WHICH THE BASIS IS UNCHANGED:

                       OBJ COEFFICIENT RANGES
VARIABLE          CURRENT         ALLOWABLE        ALLOWABLE
                   COEF           INCREASE         DECREASE
    MODELA       1.800000          .043750          .300000
    MODELB       1.250000          .070000         INFINITY
    MODELC       2.100000          .420000          .035000

                       RIGHTHAND SIDE RANGES
      ROW        CURRENT         ALLOWABLE        ALLOWABLE
                  RHS            INCREASE         DECREASE
      2      60000.000000        INFINITY       5600.000000
      3      47000.000000        INFINITY      10200.000000
      4      70000.000000       7083.333000     5714.286000
      5      50000.000000       3181.818000     7968.750000
```

in contribution margin values, the result is not obvious with this many products and constraints. Exhibit 6-10 shows the results of reducing Department 4 resources from 50,000 hours to 40,000. Only Model A and Model C are made and there is slack in two departments.

Exhibit 6-10
Change in Resource Available

```
MAX      1.8 MODELA + 1.25 MODELB + 2 MODELC
SUBJECT TO
        2)   2 MODELA + 3.5 MODELB + 4 MODELC <= 60000
        3)   4 MODELA + 3.5 MODELB + 2 MODELC <= 47000
        4)   5 MODELA + MODELB + 4.5 MODELC <= 70000
        5)   2.5 MODELA + 3 MODELB + 3.5 MODELC <= 40000
END

LP OPTIMUM FOUND AT STEP 1

        OBJECTIVE FUNCTION VALUE

        1)      26344.4400

VARIABLE            VALUE          REDUCED COST
   MODELA        9388.889000          .000000
   MODELB           .000000          .722222
   MODELC        4722.222000          .000000

      ROW     SLACK OR SURPLUS      DUAL PRICES
      2)        22333.330000          .000000
      3)            .000000          .144444
      4)         1805.556000          .000000
      5)            .000000          .488889

NO. ITERATIONS= 1

RANGES IN WHICH THE BASIS IS UNCHANGED:

                      OBJ COEFFICIENT RANGES
VARIABLE           CURRENT          ALLOWABLE          ALLOWABLE
                    COEF            INCREASE           DECREASE
   MODELA         1.800000         2.200000            .371429
   MODELB         1.250000          .722222           INFINITY
   MODELC         2.000000          .520000           1.100000

                      RIGHTHAND SIDE RANGES
      ROW          CURRENT          ALLOWABLE          ALLOWABLE
                    RHS             INCREASE           DECREASE
       2        60000.000000        INFINITY        22333.330000
       3        47000.000000      2600.000000       24142.860000
       4        70000.000000        INFINITY        1805.556000
       5        40000.000000      2031.250000       10625.000000
```

Review Problem

Using the formulation in Exhibit 6-8, conduct sensitivity analysis as follows. In each case, rerun the linear program after the change and write down what happens to each product, the objective function value, and constraints (slack, shadow prices).

1. Look at the contribution margins (CM) for all three products.
   a. Change MODELA's CM so that it exceeds the allowable increase.
   b. Restore MODELA's CM to its original value and change MODELB's CM so that it exceeds the allowable increase.
   c. Restore MODELB's CM to its original value and change MODELC's CM so it exceeds the allowable increase.
   d. Restore MODELC's CM to its original value and repeat parts 1a through 1c by changing CMs so they fall below the allowable decrease.
2. Look at the righthand side ranges (amount of constraint available).
   a. Restore all three products' CMs to their original values. Change the righthand side value (RHS) for Department 1 so that it exceeds its allowable range.
   b. Restore Department 1's RHS to its original value and change the RHS for Department 2 so that it exceeds its allowable range.
   c. Restore Department 2's RHS to its original value and change the RHS for Department 3 so that it exceeds its allowable range.
   d. Restore Department 3's RHS to its original value and change the RHS for Department 4 so that it exceeds its allowable range.
   e. Restore Department 1's RHS to its original value and repeat parts 2a through 2d by going below the allowable range for each RHS.

As you should verify, the following should occur, with the changes asked for being looked at just one at a time:

Product	CM Exceeds Range	Slack Dept.
MODELA	MODELA goes up; MODELB drops out; MODELC goes down	Depts. 1, 4
MODELB	MODELA drops out; MODELB goes up; MODELC goes down	Depts. 1, 3
MODELC	MODELA goes down; MODELB drops out; MODELC goes up	Depts. 1, 2

Product	CM Falls Below Range	Slack Dept.
MODELA	MODELA goes down; MODELB drops out; MODELC goes up	Depts. 1, 2
MDOELB	MODELA goes down; MODELB drops out; MODELC goes up	Depts. 1, 2
MODELC	MODELA goes up; MODELB drops out; MODELC goes down	Depts. 1, 4

You should also see that the results in the first and last changes above (MODELA's CM exceeds range and MODELC's CM falls below range) yield exactly the same values for the variables and slack. Only the shadow prices are different. Likewise, the results for the analysis of MODELC's CM increasing, MODELA's CM decreasing, and MODELB's CM decreasing yield the same values for the variables and the amount of slack. Only the change in MODELB's CM exceeding the allowable range is not coupled with another change. You can see that in five out of six changes, however, MODELB drops out of the solution.

RHS Exceeds Range

Constraint	Products	Slack Depts.
Dept. 1	Since the allowable increase is infinity, there would be no change.	
Dept. 2	MODELA goes up; MODELB goes up; MODELC drops out	Depts. 1, 2
Dept. 3	MODELA goes up; MODELB drops out; MODELC goes up	Depts. 1, 3
Dept. 4	MODELA goes down; MODELB goes up; MODELC goes up	Dept. 4

RHS Falls Below Range

Constraint	Products	Slack Depts.
Dept. 1	MODELA goes up; MODELB and MODELC go down	Dept. 4
Dept. 2	MODELA goes down; MODELB drops out; MODELC goes up	Dept. 4
Dept. 3	MODELA drops out; MODELB goes up; MODELC goes down	Depts. 1, 4
Dept. 4	MODELA goes up; MODELB drops out; MODELC goes down	Depts. 1, 3

It is not easy (or intuitive in many cases) to predict what is going to change in cases with three or more variables. You can use a computer program to test the limits in ranges to find out the results. This is important to managers because some changes (e.g., dropping a product or increasing a product beyond a certain level) may not be easily adjusted for in current plans. This may give rise to additional constraints reflecting marketing concerns.

LINEAR PROGRAMMING AND THEORY OF CONSTRAINTS

Linear programming is a short-term model that is useful when managers have discretion over a mix of inputs and/or outputs given a fairly set group of constraints. At a petroleum refinery, for example, given the availability of different crude oils and additives as well as the needs of the marketplace, linear programming is a good method to best utilize inputs to produce the petroleum products. However, the constraints in linear programming are fairly static. Managers look to sensitivity analysis to see what constraints might be useful to address given the objective of maximizing margin or minimizing cost.

In TOC, the objective is maximizing long-term profits by direct managing of constraints. Besides the change from a short-term to a long-term perspective, TOC deals with a single constraint at a time and a dynamic environment where the constraint addressed and the throughput per constrained resource changes. This means that using linear programming and TOC might not lead to the same actions or the same long-term results.

In some senses, linear programming is limited by its formal constraints and short-term horizon. It need not be limited to just manufacturing and can include constraints in marketing, distribution, input availability, and so on. However, it does not include fluctuations or randomness in set-up times, processing times, arrival of orders, inspections, or breakdowns, which, taken in combination, are not accommodated by linear programming or its sensitivity analysis. Such fluctuations can cause the very bottlenecks TOC advocates say managers should attend to. Therefore, linear programming is presented as a short-term model that can be used only when it is appropriate either by itself or as part of other management models such as TOC.

USE OF LINEAR PROGRAMMING WITH OTHER MODELS

Different problems require different techniques for solution. There are times when two or more techniques could be linked together to aid a decision maker.

Linear Regression and Linear Programming

The objective function of a linear program involves costs. Managers can use forecasting/estimating tools like linear regression to predict costs. These costs can then become a part of the objective function of a linear program. In addition, regression measures can be useful in sensitivity analysis. For example, assume regression and correlation analysis were used to help determine the contribution margins in the Mann Exploring example earlier in this chapter. Contribution margins were estimated to be $12 for the seat and $9 for the camp stove. Sensitivity analysis revealed a range for these contribution margins as follows:

	Range	**Current CM**
Seat:	$4.50 to $13.50	$12
Stove:	$8.00 to $24.00	$ 9

If, say, a regression for labor costs on the stove had a standard error of the slope of $1, then a 95 percent confidence interval would say that the contribution margin could be in a range of $7 to $11 [$9 ± (2)($1)]. The lower end of this range is outside the allowable range on the linear programming solution. If costs rise more than 1 standard error (about 16 percent probability of occurrence), a new solution would call for no stoves to be produced. The combination of the regression and correlation analysis with sensitivity analysis in linear programming can allow an assessment of the likelihood that objective function or righthand side ranges will be exceeded.

Capital Budgeting and Linear Programming

When acquiring new equipment, management should determine the most effective way to use it. Thus, if a new machine is capable of producing several products, a linear program can be solved to indicate the optimal use of the resource. The resulting production can be built into the discounted cash flow estimate to see if the asset is worth acquiring.

SUMMARY

Linear programming is a decision aid when an organization is faced with competing uses of limited resources. The basic linear programming formulation requires good estimates of costs, prices, constraint use, and constraint limits. The same data problems discussed in Chapter 4 would pertain to all the quantitative models managers employ, such as linear programming. Computer solutions allow managers to quickly test limits on contribution margins and constraints via sensitivity analysis. Minimization and maximization problems are both illustrated. Linear programming, like most models, can be used in conjunction with other decision aids and forecasting tools.

PROBLEMS AND CASES

6-1. Effects of Learning

Audacity, Ltd., has just started manufacturing a new product line. Plant managers are working with the marketing personnel in order to determine the best possible combination of products to manufacture during the first month of these new items. Sara Arriba, plant engineer, has suggested that a linear programming solution be the basis for the production quantity discussion. The contribution margins for the two products in the original line are as follows:

Basic model: $120
Deluxe model: 195

Both products are made using three machines. The proposed prices and costs are shown below.

	Basic	**Deluxe**
Price	$615	$740
Variable costs:		
Materials, purchased parts	80	170
Labor (at $10/hour)	165	125
Overhead (at $20/machine hour)	250	250

Besides labor on the three machines, assembly labor is needed for the basic model after basic manufacturing. For the deluxe model, certain parts are purchased that are preassembled, with the balance being assembled during the machine operation. Machine capacities are as follows:

Machine 101   10,000 hours
Machine 105   8,000 hours
Machine 117   6,000 hours

Use per unit for the various products is:

	101	**105**	**117**
Basic Model	4 hours	7 hours	1.5 hours
Deluxe model	6 hours	4 hours	2.5 hours

Required:
1. Using the above information, formulate and solve a linear programming approach to the production decision. What is the proposed optimal combination of basic and deluxe models?
2. Management thinks that assembly will be subject to the learning effect. What rate of learning will change the optimal product mix called for in part 1?

6-2. Graphing and Interpretation of Results (CMA Adapted)

Home Cooking Company offers monthly service plans providing prepared meals that are delivered to the customers' homes and that need only to be heated in a microwave or conventional oven. The target market for these meal plans includes double-income families with no children and retired couples in the upper-income brackets.

Home Cooking offers two monthly plans: *Premier Cuisine* and *Haute Cuisine*. The Premier Cuisine plan provides frozen meals that are delivered twice each month; this plan generates a profit of $120 for each monthly plan sold. The Haute Cuisine plan provides freshly prepared meals delivered on a daily basis and generates a profit of $90 for each monthly plan sold. Home Cooking's reputation provides the company with a market that will purchase all the meals that can be prepared.

All meals go through food preparation and cooking steps in the company's kitchens. After these steps, the Premier Cuisine meals are flash frozen. The time requirements per monthly meal plan and hours available per month are presented below.

	Preparation	Cooking	Freezing
Hours required			
Premier Cuisine	2	2	1
Haute Cuisine	1	3	0
Total hours available	60	120	45

For planning purposes, Home Cooking uses linear programming to determine the most profitable number of Premier Cuisine and Haute Cuisine monthly meal plans to produce.

Required:
1. Using the notations P = Premier Cuisine and H = Haute Cuisine, state the objective function and the constraints that Home Cooking should use to maximize profits generated by the monthly meal plans.
2. Graph the constraints on Home Cooking's meal preparation process on graph paper or on a computer. Be sure to clearly label your graph.
3. Looking at all the corner points and points where constraints cross in the graph, what is the optimal mix of products that Home Cooking should produce and what is the value of the objective function at this optimal mix?
4. On the next page is part of a solution to this problem using LINDO. View each of the following as independent questions (i.e., go back to your original formulation before making each change requested).
   a. How would the optimal mix change if the price for Haute Cuisine were to be raised by $50 per plan sold? How would the value of the objective function be affected by the same change?
   b. How would the optimal mix change if the constraint for preparation were to be eliminated? (*Hint:* you might want to look at your graph to respond to this question.)
   c. How would the optimal mix change if the hours available for cooking were to be reduced by 30? How would this same change affect the objective function value?
5. What are the strengths and weaknesses of using linear programming to determine the mix of meal plans to offer?

```
        OBJECTIVE FUNCTION VALUE

1)          ????.00000

VARIABLE          VALUE              REDUCED COST
 PREMIER        ??.000000              ??.??????
 HAUTE          ??.000000              ??.??????

    ROW     SLACK OR SURPLUS        DUAL PRICES
     2)           .000000           45.000000
     3)           .000000           15.000000
     4)         30.000000             .000000

RANGES IN WHICH THE BASIS IS UNCHANGED:

                  OBJ COEFFICIENT RANGES
VARIABLE        CURRENT         ALLOWABLE        ALLOWABLE
                COEF            INCREASE         DECREASE
 PREMIER       ???.??????       60.000000        60.000000
 HAUTE         ???.??????       90.000000        30.000000

                  RIGHTHAND SIDE RANGES
    ROW         CURRENT         ALLOWABLE        ALLOWABLE
                RHS             INCREASE         DECREASE
     2         ???.000000       40.000000        20.000000
     3         ???.000000       60.000000        60.000000
     4         ???.000000       INFINITY         30.000000

THE TABLEAU
    ROW     (BASIS)      PREMIER      HAUTE    SLK    2    SLK    3
     1 ART               .000        .000     45.000       15.000
     2  PREMIER         1.000        .000       .750        -.250
     3    HAUTE          .000       1.000      -.500         .500
     4 SLK    4          .000        .000      -.750         .250

I   ROW    SLK    4
     1        .000   4500.000
     2        .000     15.000
     3        .000     30.000
     4       1.000     30.000
```

6-3. Product Mix Given Marketing Constraints[6]

Blackbird Oil Co. is planning for tomorrow's refinery production. Three different types of crude oil are available; some are only available in limited quantities. Crude oils (crudes) range from $35.00 per barrel to $42.00 per barrel as shown in Table 1, which follows. Note that a barrel is 42 gallons.

These crudes have different amounts of an impurity in them (see Table 1). Amounts of impurity are regulated by law. The impurity is expensive to remove. It costs $3.00 to remove (and discard) each gallon of impurity. Federal environmental standards limit the amounts of impurity to those shown in Table 2.

The crudes have intrinsically different compositions, which we will approximate as an "Intrinsic Octane" value (see Table 1). The octane rating is an average of the intrinsic octane ratings of the various crudes blended to produce the product. In addition, an additive is available for $20.00 per gallon. The octane rating is increased

TABLE 1

Grade of Crude Oil	Impurity Content	Cost per Barrel	Maximum Quantity (Millions Barrels)	Instrinsic Octane
A	1.0%	$42.00	.20	93
B	1.5%	39.00	Unlimited	89
C	2.7%	35.70	.08	83

TABLE 2

Product	Minimum Quantity (Million Gallons)	Price per Gallon	Maximum Impurity	Minimum Octane
Regular	8	$1.28	0.7%	89
Hi-Test	3	1.44	1.2%	95

by one point for each gallon of additive added to 1,000 gallons of fuel. Company standards require a minimum octane rating.

Two end products are of interests, Regular and Hi-Test. The company is committed to producing certain minimum quantities of each product, but they can sell all they can produce at the price shown.

Total refining capacity is .50 million barrels per day.

Required:
How much of each product should be produced, and how much of each crude should be purchased?

6-4. Determining a Labor Force

You are going to plan for operations for the Saw Mill during the next six months. Table 1, which follows, shows a forecast of sales for the six months. This forecast is

[6] Problems 6-3 through 6-7 were written by Robert Barringer.

changed into a man-hour forecast by using the estimate: for each man-hour of direct labor in the rough mill, they sell about $40 worth of finished goods.

The current labor force is 40. You may hire or fire as many as you wish at the beginning of the month. At the end of the sixth month, you must hire or fire sufficient workers to bring the final labor force back to 40. It costs $180 to hire and train a new worker; and $100 to fire a worker. The labor force during any month works a normal eight-hour day for each of the working days shown in Table 1.

TABLE 1

Sales Forecast ($1000)	Man-Hour Forecast (Man-Hours)	Working Days
200	5,000	21
330	8,250	22
220	5,500	21
270	6,750	21
360	9,000	19
300	7,500	21
1,680	42,000	125

Each month, the total labor force, working eight hours every working day, results in a total production measured in man-hours. Starting inventory plus production minus sales (all measured in man-hours) yields the ending inventory. It costs $0.80 to carry one man-hour in inventory for one month.

Current inventory is low; you may assume starting inventory to be 500 man-hours.

Required:
Assuming the forecast is fixed and known exactly, plan the following:

1. How many persons to hire or fire at the beginning of the each month.
2. Inventory at the end of the month based on production, sales, and starting inventory.

6-5. Advertising Plan for New Adult Soft Drink

An advertising manager for a new adult soft drink wishes to minimize costs of an advertising campaign to introduce his product. The manager expects to have an advertising budget of $155,000 and has asked you to ascertain how much total exposure can be obtained with these dollars.

Medium	Full Campaign	Audience
Television	$130,000	500,000
Newspaper	50,000	340,000
Billboard	12,500	75,000
TV Guide	25,000	170,000

The table above shows the cost for what the company's advertising agency calls a "full campaign," and the resulting total audience. In each medium, a fractional campaign is possible. Thus $20,000 spent on newspaper advertising would be a "40%

campaign," and would be expected to achieve an audience of 40 percent of 340,000, or 136,000.

It is possible to spend more money in any medium than the amount specified as a "full campaign," but each dollar above this amount reaches only half the audience specified above [e.g., $60,000 spent in newspaper advertising would reach 374,000 people (340,000 + $10,000 × 3.4) where $340,000/50,000 = 6.8/$ and 0.50 × 6.8 = 3.4].

For each medium, the manager has been given a tabulation of audience make-up by sex (F = female; M = male) and age, as follows:

	Age 20–30	Age 30–40	Age 40+
Television			
F	.07	.34	.06
M	.08	.37	.08
Newspaper			
F	.19	.09	.12
M	.39	.11	.10
Billboard			
F	.26	.19	.11
M	.20	.11	.13
TV Guide			
F	.10	.13	.27
M	.12	.11	.27

The manager's target is to reach a minimum of 90,000 females and 130,000 males in the 20–30 year range; 140,000 females and 126,000 males in the 30–40 year range; and 60,000 females and 50,000 males over 40.

Assuming the manager can reach and exceed this goal, different levels of importance are placed on reaching different segments of the population.

	Age 20–30	Age 30–40	Age 40+
F	1.00	.45	.20
M	.90	.45	.50

We shall call a female 20–30 an "effective target" (ET). Each male 20–30 that is reached is .90 ET, while each female 40+ is only .20 ET, and so on.

Required:
1. What is the minimum budget that will allow the advertising manager to reach the stated target population?
2. For this minimum budget, how many ET's are reached?
3. How many more ET's can be reached by spending a total of $155,000?

6-6. Cost of Supplies

Toledo is organizing an eight-day international fair. Among the various buildings for the fair, a restaurant has been built to serve meals to visitors. This eating establishment is divided into two parts—a cafeteria, which uses paper napkins, and a more formal restaurant, which uses tablecloths and linen napkins. Among other problems, the manager of the restaurant (the caterer) must minimize the expenses encountered in supplying clean napkins to customers for the complete period of the fair. The manager, eager to make decisions in a reliable way, asked the organizers of the fair to furnish a list of the estimated number of patrons at the formal restaurant, per day, during the eight days of the international show. The manager received the following list of figures:

First day	= 1,200	Fifth day	=	800
Second day	= 1,900	Sixth day	=	1,500
Third day	=	700	Seventh day	=	1,800
Fourth day	=	500	Eighth day	=	700

The caterer made a deal with a laundry on these terms: there will be a daily delivery and pickup of clean and soiled napkins in such a way that the laundry provides clean linens early in the morning and takes the used ones in the evening. The transportation cost is included in the washing service, which is 4 cents each for regular service, and 6.5 cents each for fast (or express) service. The normal service takes two days (one full working day), while express service can be performed overnight. In other words, a napkin that is used on the second day would be available for use again on the fourth day with regular service. Each new napkin costs 9.8 cents.

Required:
Prepare a plan in order to know:

1. How many napkins the manager must buy to assure a reliable flow.
2. How many napkins must be cleaned through normal service and how many must be cleaned through fast service, in order to minimize total expenses. The manager decided to send out all soiled napkins on the day of their use in order to avoid storing them, and to compute the optimal plan for the complete period by accepting, without modification, the figures received from the organizers.

6-7. Capital Purchase of Trucks

The Hammer Down Trucking Co. is planning to expand their fleet. They want to know how many trucks to purchase. Three types are shown in Table 1, which follows. Every other day the entire fleet will leave Chicago bound for St. Louis and the next day will return to Chicago. They will thus complete three round trips per six-day week. They have obtained authorization from the bank to borrow up to $453,000. This will limit the total number of trucks they can purchase.

Three kinds of cargo are available for them to carry. These are summarized in Table 2. The company managers have estimated the maximum of each type of cargo available to them at each pickup point. They have made commitments to carry a certain amount of some types, which sets a minimum amount in those cases.

<table>
<tr><th colspan="4">TABLE 1</th></tr>
<tr><th></th><th colspan="3">Operating Plus Amortization</th></tr>
<tr><th>Truck Type</th><th>Cost</th><th>Cost per Day</th><th>Tons</th></tr>
<tr><td>Regular tank</td><td>$12,000</td><td>$ 70</td><td>40</td></tr>
<tr><td>Copper</td><td>$24,000</td><td>$ 90</td><td>30</td></tr>
<tr><td>Glass</td><td>$33,000</td><td>$150</td><td>20</td></tr>
</table>

TABLE 2

Cargo Each Trip

Type of Cargo	Rev. per Ton Trip	Route	Minimum Required	Maximum Available
Regular	$ 3.00	Chi.—St. L.	0	220
		St. L.—Chi.	0	220
Corrosive	$21.00	Chi.—St. L.	20	180
		St. L.—Chi.	0	0
Other chemicals	$ 9.00	Chi.—St. L	20	200
		St. L.—Chi.	130	130

Regular cargo brings in $3.00 per trip per ton. This cargo may be carried in regular trucks or trucks with copper fittings. One chemical may be carried only in trucks with glass lining and glass fittings because of its corrosive properties. This cargo brings in $21.00 per trip per ton. Other chemicals may be carried in either copper or glass tanks but bring only $9.00 per ton per trip.

Required:
Determine how many of each of the three types of trucks Hammer Down Trucking should acquire.

6-8. Analyzing Results

Keith Products produces two models of its product: A and B. Both models must pass through at least two to three processing facilities: stamping, lathing, and assembly. The objective function and constraints for a linear programming solution to scheduling manufacturing are as follows:

```
MAX     $80  A  +  $100  B
SUBJECT  TO
         2)    3 A  +  3 B  <=   100  hours
         3)    4 A  +  8 B  <=   170  hours
         4)             B   <=    50  hours
```

The final tableau for the optimal solution is:

ROW	(BASIS)		A	B	SLK 2	SLK 3	SLK 4	
1	ART		.000	.000	20.000	5.000	.000	2850.000
2		B	.000	1.000	−.333	.250	.000	9.167
3		A	1.000	.000	.667	−.250	.000	24.167
4	SLK	4	.000	.000	.333	−.250	1.000	40.833

Required:
The idea of this problem is to see how computer programs get the limits they create. Since much sensitivity analysis information comes from the final tableau, use the tableau to answer the following questions:

1. How much will management be willing to pay for an additional 30 hours of stamping time?

2. If management bought an additional 25 hours of stamping time at a premium of $16 per hour over normal costs, what would be the new optimal solution (product mix, profit)? How much slack in assembly would be used up?
3. What is the meaning of the dual or shadow price? In what sense is it a price at all?
4. At what contribution margin will A drop out of the solution and only B will be made? What would the contribution margin of A have to be to make only A and no B? Show your work.

6-9. Sensitivity Analysis—Opportunity Cost

The Bistro Company has decided to produce the following amounts of each of their three products based on the results of a linear program as shown below:

Product A   0
Product B   260
Product C   320

The resulting contribution margin would be $22,040. The constraints pertain to three production machines that can be used to manufacture any combination of the three products. While the machines have a stated 2,000 hour availability each, there is some leeway of a few hours above that total. The linear program results that led to the manufacturing decision are as follows:

```
MAX      31 A + 22 B + 51 C
SUBJECT TO
         2)   2 A + 4 B + 3 C <= 2000
         3)   3 A + 1.5 B + 5 C <= 2000
         4)   5 A + 3 B + 2 C <= 2000

             OBJECTIVE FUNCTION VALUE
     1)          22129.0300

     VARIABLE           VALUE          REDUCED COST

         A            .000000            .032259
         B         258.064500            .000000
         C         322.580700            .000000

        ROW     SLACK OR SURPLUS      DUAL PRICES

         2)            .000000           2.161290
         3)            .000000           8.903226
         4)         580.645100            .000000
```

RANGES IN WHICH THE BASIS IS UNCHANGED:

VARIABLE	CURRENT COEF	OBJ COEFFICIENT RANGES ALLOWABLE INCREASE	ALLOWABLE DECREASE
A	31.000000	0.032259	INFINITY
B	22.000000	46.000000	.500014
C	51.000000	22.333330	.055557

```
                    RIGHTHAND SIDE RANGES
    ROW      CURRENT        ALLOWABLE        ALLOWABLE
             RHS            INCREASE         DECREASE

     2     2000.000000     750.000000       800.000000
     3     2000.000000    1333.333000      1250.000000
     4     2000.000000      INFINITY        580.645100
```

THE TABLEAU

ROW	(BASIS)		A	B	C	SLK 2	SLK 3
1	ART		.032	.000	.000	2.161	8.903
2	B		.065	1.000	.000	.323	-.194
3	C		.581	.000	1.000	-.097	.258
4 SLK	4		3.645	.000	.000	-.774	.065

ROW	SLK	4	
1		.000	22129.030
2		.000	258.065
3		.000	322.581
4		1.000	580.645

Required:

1. How sensitive is this solution to changes in the contribution margins of the three products? Be specific about changes in prices and costs for each product.
2. The Marketing Department has complained that there are customers who have been promised Product A and that they need at least 50 made. What would be the effect on total contribution margin, on production quantities for Products B and C, and on machine hour utilization if 50 Product A's were made?
3. During March, management committed resources to produce the product mix called for as shown above. However, after production had been started (and there was no way to alter production quantities for that month), there was a material price increase for one of the materials in Product C that amounted to $0.50 per unit. Formulate and run a new linear program based on this change in the contribution margin. What is the opportunity cost to management for making their original production decision?

6-10. Integer Programming

A chemical company wants to maximize profits on a product that sells for $0.30 per gallon. Suppose that increased temperature increases output according to the graph on the next page:

Required:

Assuming that production costs are directly proportional to temperature at $7.50 per degree of centigrade, how many gallons of the product should be produced? Formulate and solve an integer programming solution to this problem.

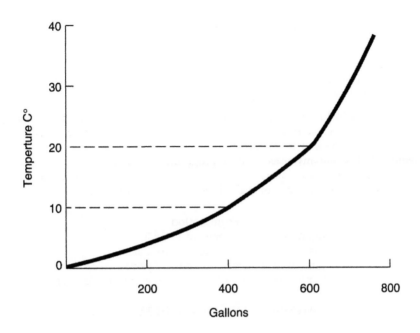

6-11. Comprehensive Case (CMA)

Jenlock Mill Company produces two grades of interior plywood from fir and pine lumber. The fir and pine lumber can be sold as saw lumber or used in the plywood.

To produce the plywood, thin layers of wood are peeled from the logs in panels, the panels are glued together to form plywood sheets, and then dried. The peeler can peel enough panels from logs to produce 300,000 sheets of plywood in a month. The dryer has a capacity of 1,200,000 minutes for the month. The amount of lumber used and the drying time required for each sheet of plywood by grade is shown below.

	Grade A Plywood Sheets	Grade B Plywood Sheets
Fir (in board feet)	18	15
Pine (in board feet)	12	15
Drying time (in minutes)	4	6

The only restriction on the production of fir and pine lumber is the capacity of the mill saws to cut the logs into boards. These saws have a capacity of 500,000 board feet per month regardless of species.

Jenlock has the following quantities of lumber available for July production.

Fir   2,700,000 board feet
Pine   3,000,000 board feet

The contribution margins for each type of output are as follows.

Fir lumber	$ .20 per board foot
Pine lumber	$ .10 per board foot
Grade A plywood	$2.25 per sheet
Grade B plywood	$1.80 per sheet

The demand in July for plywood is expected to be a maximum of 80,000 sheets for Grade A and a maximum of 100,000 sheets for Grade B. There are no demand restrictions on pine and fir lumber.

Jenlock Mill Company uses a linear programming model to determine the production quantities of each product. The correct formulation of the linear programming model and a summary of the solution of the model follow.

Formulation

F = board feet of fir lumber to be sold
P = board feet of pine lumber to be sold
A = number of sheets of Grade A plywood to be sold
B = number of sheets of Grade B plywood to be sold

$$\text{Maximize:} \quad .20F + .10P + 2.25A + 1.80B$$

Subject to:

Amount of fir available	F	$+ 18A + 15B$	$\leq 2{,}700{,}000$
Amount of pine available	$P +$	$12A + 15B$	$\leq 3{,}000{,}000$
Peeler capacity		$A + B$	$\leq 300{,}000$
Dryer capacity		$4A + 6B$	$\leq 1{,}200{,}000$
Saw capacity	$F + P$		$\leq 500{,}000$
Maximum demand:			
Grade A plywood		A	$\leq 80{,}000$
Grade B plywood		B	$\leq 100{,}000$

Summary of Solution

Summary of the Primal Problem

Solution Variables	Solution Values
Pine lumber to be sold	500,000 board feet
Grade A plywood to be sold	80,000 sheets
Grade B plywood to be sold	84,000 sheets
Slack items:	
Pine available	280,000 board feet
Peeler capacity	136,000 sheets
Dryer capacity	376,000 minutes
Demand for Grade B plywood	16,000 sheets

Nonsolution Variables	Oportunity Costs
Fir lumber to be sold	$.02
Constraining items:	
Fir available	$.12
Saw capacity	$.10
Demand for Grade A plywood	$.09

Ranges of the Restraining Values of the Constraints
(000 omitted)

Constraints	Initial Constraint Value	Lower Limit	Upper Limit
Amount of fir available	2,700	1,440	2,940
Amount of pine available	3,000	2,720	Infinity
Peeler capacity	300	164	Infinity
Dryer capacity	1,200	824	Infinity
Saw capacity	500		780
Demand for plywood			
Grade A	80	67	150
Grade B	100	84	Infinity

Ranges of Objective Function Coefficients

Objective Coefficient	Initial Value	Lower Bound	Upper Bound
Fir Lumber	$ .20	Negative infinity	$ .22
Pine lumber	$ .10	$ .08	Positive infinity
Grade A plywood	$2.25	$2.16	Positive infinity
Grade B plywood	$1.80	$1.50	$1.875

Required:

Refer to the *Summary of Solution* to answer each of the following requirements. The requirements are independent of each other.

1. How much fir, pine, Grade A plywood, and Grade B plywood should Jenlock Mill Company produce and what is the total contribution margin of this mix?
2. Will Jenlock Mill Company use all of its resources to their capacities during July if it follows the solution derived from the linear programming model? Explain your answer.
3. Two items regarding *fir* lumber appear under nonsolution variables: fir lumber to be sold with an opportunity cost of $.02 and fir available as a constraining item with an opportunity cost of $.12. Explain what these two items mean.

4. Assuming there is no change in price, should Jenlock Mill Company attempt to acquire any more fir for use during July, and if so, how much should be acquired? Explain your answer.

5. Jenlock Mill Company has been approached by one of its competitors asking Jenlock to sell it some drying time. How much, if any, drying time should Jenlock sell to its competitor? Explain your answer.

6. Jenlock Mill Company can acquire the use of additional mill saw capacity at the rate of $1,800 for an eight-hour day. The additional saw capacity can process 20,000 board feet of lumber in an eight-hour day. Should Jenlock acquire the use of extra saw capacity, and if so, how much time should it acquire? Explain your answer.

7. What is the range within which the contribution of the Grade B plywood can fluctuate before the optimal solution changes?

6-12. Linear Programming and Capital Budgeting

Background Kraus Printing Company is a commercial job printer. It is an old established firm, one of the largest of its kind in the South. It prints a wide variety of magazines and books on a contract basis. The company is owned and operated by Karen and Fred Kraus, who acquired control ten years ago following the retirement of their father. The younger members of the Kraus family are very ambitious and industrious. Under their leadership and in response to expanding sales volume, new, enlarged, and modern facilities have been built. However, this new plant is now operating at about capacity.

This phenomenal growth of the business must be attributed in part to a current trend for national publishers to print and distribute on a regional basis. For example, Kraus has recently contracted to print the southeastern edition of a leading national news daily. Also, they have just been contacted by a magazine publisher with a contract offer. This publisher, Leech Graphics, Inc., publishes an assorted line of entertainment publications including magazines on music, television, soap operas, and the rich and famous. The magazines are largely unoriginal and stereotyped but follow formats which Leech Graphics knows will sell. The publications sell for $6.00 a copy. They are of uniform length; therefore, the printing time, raw materials, and other inputs required to print each magazine are constants. Although no individual magazine is a "best seller," overall demand for these magazines is great. In fact, Leech Graphics has been unable to meet the demand. As a result and after careful market research, Leech has decided to increase output. Its present printers, however, are unable to supply significantly greater quantities. Thus, upon the recommendation of another publisher, Leech has approached Kraus Printing about a printing contract.

Leech offered Kraus a six-year contract under which Kraus would print a maximum of 100,000 copies a week of various magazines for the price of $1.69 each. This seemed to be a very attractive offer to Karen and Fred Kraus, so they immediately consulted their plant manager and finance officer for information relevant to deciding whether to accept the contract.

Plant Manager's Report The plant manager reported that new presses definitely would be needed. The present ones were not suited for this type of job and, in any case, were now being operated at virtual capacity. In addition, the manager noted that plant space was again becoming a problem for the firm and that only 1,488 square feet were not now in use. Karen and Fred Kraus asked the plant manager to contact the appropriate manufacturers for information on available machines.

On the following day, the plant manager informed them that contacts with manufacturers had revealed three different possibilities. Machine X had a cost of $150,000; each machine required 48 square feet of floor space and two workers, and would produce 480 copies each day. Machine Y cost $180,000, each requiring 55 square feet of floor space and three operators, and capable of producing 600 copies each day. Machine Z had a cost of $220,000; each one required 66 square feet of space and four workers, and would produce 760 copies each day. All three sets of production figures were based on the assumption of an eight-hour day and were derived from specifications quoted by the various manufacturers.

Additional information was provided by the plant manager. Given the current employment situation in the plant's locale, the manager estimated that no more than 72 new workers could be obtained at the present pay scale of $6 per hour. This restriction resulted in part from the level of skill required to handle the job. Materials cost was estimated at $.69 per copy. This included an allowance for waste, based upon past experience. Assuming the machines were operated eight hours per day, the plant manager estimated that the average daily cost for the special maintenance required by the new machines was $28, $32, and $36 per machine for machines X, Y, and Z, respectively.

Finally, the plant manager knew that accepting the contract from Leech Graphics would affect the incurrence of manufacturing overhead (over and above the cost of special maintenance requirements). The manager sent Karen and Fred Kraus a copy of the flexible budget for manufacturing overhead in the current year and attached this note: "At the present time, we charge each direct labor hour with manufacturing overhead of $2.10." A summary of the flexible budget, including the derivation of the $2.10 and a brief description of the costs included in the budget are presented in Exhibit 1, which follows on the next page.

Finance Officer's Report   The finance officer, after studying the firm's current financial position and the forecast of cash needs in the near future, reported that up to $5,000,000 of capital could be made available for investing in this venture. The firm's after-tax cost of capital was estimated to be 14 percent.

Regarding the tax implications of investments in new machinery, the firm's policy is to use the ACRS method to determine tax depreciation on any new long-lived resources. The finance officer's tentative opinion was that a five-year tax life would have to be used to determine tax depreciation on any of these three machines. It was felt that a proper time horizon for deciding whether to acquire any machinery was six years, since this was the duration of the contract proposed by Leech Graphics. The finance officer felt that estimating salvage values for special purpose printing equipment was very unreliable and was inclined to ignore this factor altogether in investment decisions. This officer estimated the marginal tax rate over the next six years to be 40 percent.

Required:
Frame these requirements within a case analysis format.

1. Within the constraints indicated, use linear programming (LP) to determine the optimal number and combination of each type of machine which Kraus Printing

Exhibit 1
Flexible Manufacturing Overhead Budget
For the Year 19XX
(rounded to nearest thousand $)

Cost	Volume (DLH)		
	80% Capacity	90% Capacity	100% Capacity
Indirect labor	$ 204,000	$ 230,000	$ 256,000
Supplies	178,000	200,000	222,000
Power	98,000	110,000	122,000
General and administrative	664,000	700,000	736,000
Plant management	250,000	250,000	250,000
Plant occupancy	400,000	400,000	400,000
	$1,794,000	$1,890,000	$1,986,000
Direct labor hours	800,000	900,000	1,000,000
Overhead per direct labor hour	$ 2.2425	$ 2.10	$ 1.986

Description of Costs

1. *Indirect labor:* cost of support for laborers operating printing machinery, including raw materials delivery, machinery set-up, clean-up, routine repairs, transportation of output to storeroom.

2. *Supplies:* cost of lubricants, clean-up materials, packing, and other miscellaneous materials used in production operations.

3. *Power:* cost of power to operate machinery. Basic utility costs for plant are included in plant occupancy costs.

4. *General and administrative:* An assignment of the firm's various general and administrative costs is made anually to the production area (as well as to the marketing area). The assignment formula for production for the current year is $380,000 + $0.3555 (DLH).

5. *Plant management:* the cost of salary for the plant's management and supervisory personnel.

6. *Plant occupancy:* various costs relating to provision of the basic plant capacity, including property taxes, building depreciation, machinery depreciation, heat, light, caretaking.

Co. should consider purchasing in order to accommodate the Leech Graphics contract. Your case analysis should justify the use of LP.

2. Analyze whether the acquisition of machinery, as indicated by the results in Requirement 1, would constitute a profitable use of the firm's investment capital. Assume 254 working days per year (this includes 6 holidays).

3. Offer guidelines for whether plant space now allotted for other printing jobs should be diverted to the Leech contract.

4. Offer guidelines for whether additional labor supply should be sought. (Note that the supply might be secured by a variety of means, e.g., a special training

program to expand the number of persons in the locale with the requisite skill, operating the plant six days a week, overtime.)

5. Should Kraus Printing consider subcontracting part of the Leech contract to some other printer? Explain.
6. The manufacturer of Machine Y is a very important supplier for Kraus Printing, and there is some feeling that the firm might be obliged to purchase some machinery from it if any is purchased. What are the implications of this possibility?
7. The production manager confides, "Of the three machines, Machine X is very revolutionary in its technology. For this reason, I cannot be as confident about the labor and raw materials estimates on it as I am about Machines Y and Z. Perhaps it would be worth the additional cost to investigate the reliability of these estimates further." Comment.

Hints:
1. For purposes only of standardizing the discussion of this problem, it is suggested that in the objective function you state the profit contributions for each machine in per-day terms. State any output constraint in the same terms. Assume a regular five-day work week.
2. It is urged that you work and discuss this problem in groups. For most students, there should be a synergistic effect from working the problem in a group instead of individually.
3. Because of the dearth of information about operations beyond the current year, your analysis in Requirement 2 will have to be rough. It is suggested you assume that costs, etc., throughout the six-year time horizon will be the same as you estimate in Requirement 1. Do your investment analysis on this basis, then qualitatively do a sensitivity analysis of the results. Assume the most current tax laws are in effect.

6-13. Comprehensive Case[7]

In November 19X4, the Bayview Manufacturing Company was in the process of preparing its budget for 19X5. As the first step, the company prepared a pro forma income statement for 19X4 based on the first ten months' operations and revised plans for the last two months. This income statement, in condensed form was as follows:

Sales revenue		$3,000,000
Materials	$1,182,000	
Labor	310,000	
Factory overhead	775,000	
Selling and administrative	450,000	2,717,000
Net income before taxes		$ 283,000

These results were better than expected and operations were close to capacity. However, Bayview's management was not convinced that demand would remain at present levels and hence had not planned any increase in plant capacity. Its equipment

---

[7] This problem is used with the permission of the American Accounting Association. Original problem by Professor Carl Nelson.

was specialized and made to its order; over a year's lead time was necessary on all plant additions.

Bayview produces three products; sales have been broken down by product, as follows:

100,000 of Product A at $20	$2,000,000
40,000 of Product B at $10	400,000
20,000 of Product C at $30	600,000
	$3,000,000

Management has ordered a profit analysis for each product and has available the following information:

	A	B	C
Material	$ 7.00	$ 3.75	$ 16.60
Labor	2.00	1.00	3.50
Factory overhead	5.00	2.50	8.75
Selling and administrative costs	3.00	1.50	4.50
Total costs	17.00	8.75	33.35
Selling price	20.00	10.00	30.00
Profit	$ 3.00	$ 1.25	$ (3.35)

Factory overhead has been applied on the basis of direct labor costs at a rate of 250 percent; and management asserts that approximately 20 percent of the overhead is variable and does vary with labor costs. Selling and administrative costs have been allocated on the basis of sales at the rate of 15 percent; approximately one half of this is variable and does vary with sales in dollars. All of the labor expense is considered to be variable.

As the first step in the planning process, the sales department has been asked to make estimates of what it could sell; these estimates, which have been reviewed by the firm's consulting economist and by top management, are as follows:

A 130,000 units
B 50,000 units
C 50,000 units

Production of these quantities was immediately recognized as being impossible. Estimated cost data for the three products, each of which requires activity of both departments, were based on the following production rates:

	Product		
	A	B	C
Department 1 (Molding)	2 per hour	4 per hour	3 per hour
Department 2 (Finishing)	4 per hour	8 per hour	4/3 per hour

Practical capacity in Department 1 is 67,000 hours and in Department 2, 63,000 hours; and the industrial engineering department has concluded that this capacity cannot be increased without the purchase of additional equipment. Thus, while last year Department 1 operated at 99 percent of its capacity and Department 2 at 71 percent of capacity, anticipated sales would require operating both departments 1 and 2 at more than 100 percent capacity.

Three solutions to the limited production problem have been rejected: (1) subcontracting the production out to other firms is considered to be unprofitable because of problems of maintaining quality; (2) operating a second shift is impossible because of a shortage of labor; and (3) operating overtime would create problems because a large number of employees are "moonlighting" and would therefore refuse to work more than the normal 40-hour week. Price increases have been rejected; although they would result in higher profits this year, the long-run competitive position of the firm would be weakened, resulting in lower profits in the future.

The treasurer then suggested that the Product C has been carried at a loss too long and that now was the time to eliminate it from the product line. If all facilities are used to produce A and B, profits would increase.

The sales manager objected to this solution because of the need to carry a full line and also maintained that there is a group of loyal customers whose needs must be met. The manager provided a list of these customers and their estimated purchases (in units), which total as follows:

A	80,000
B	32,000
C	12,000

It was impossible to verify these contentions, but they appeared to be reasonable and served to narrow the bounds of the problem, so the president concurred.

The treasurer reluctantly acquiesced, but maintained that the remaining capacity should be used to produce A and B. Because A yielded 2.4 times as much profit as B, the treasurer suggested that the production of A (in excess of the 80,000 minimum set by the sales manager) be 2.4 times that of B (in excess of the 32,000 minimum set by the sales manager).

The production manager made some quick calculations and said the budgeted production and sales would be about: ·

A	104,828
B	42,344
C	12,000

The treasurer then made a calculation of profits as follows:

A	104,828 at $3.00	$314,484
B	42,344 at $1.25	52,930
C	12,000 at ($3.35)	(40,200)
		$327,214

As this would represent an increase of almost 15 percent over the current year, there was a general feeling of self-satisfaction. Before final approval was given, however, the president said the new assistant would check over the figures. Somewhat piqued, the treasurer agreed, and at that point the group adjourned. The next day the preceding information was submitted to you as your first assignment on your new job as the president's assistant.

Required:
Prepare an analysis showing the president what should be done. Your analysis and presentation should include appropriate statistics, tables, and/or graphs presented in good order. Remember you are presenting an analysis to someone who has a minimal knowledge of computer modeling techniques and statistics.

Avoid jargon. Incorporate appropriate sensitivity analysis. Exhibits 1 and 2 contain information that you are able to obtain from the accounting system, which may help you to estimate an overhead cost breakdown into fixed and variable components different from that given in the case.

Exhibit 1
Direct Labor and Overhead Costs

Year	Direct Labor Cost (in Thousands)			Overhead Cost (in Thousands)		
	Dept. 1	Dept. 2	Total	Dept. 1	Dept. 2	Total
19X4	$140	$170	$310	$341	$434	$775
19X3	135	150	285	340	412	752
19X2	140	160	300	342	428	770
19X1	130	150	280	339	422	761
19X0	130	155	285	338	425	763
19W9	125	140	265	337	414	751
19W8	120	150	270	335	420	755
19W7	115	140	255	334	413	747
19W6	120	140	260	336	414	750
19W5	115	135	250	335	410	745

Exhibit 2
Sales and Selling and Administrative Expense
(in Thousands)

Year	Sales				Selling and Administrative Costs
	Product A	Product B	Product C	Total	
19X4	$2,000	$400	$600	$3,000	$450
19X3	1,940	430	610	2,980	445
19X2	1,950	380	630	2,960	445
19X1	1,860	460	620	2,940	438
19X0	1,820	390	640	2,850	433
19W9	1,860	440	580	2,880	437
19W8	1,880	420	570	2,870	438
19W7	1,850	380	580	2,810	434
19W6	1,810	390	580	2,780	430
19W5	1,770	290	610	2,670	425

Chapter 7

Extensions of Cost-Volume-Profit Analysis

Break-even analyses are an important technique for the planning, management and control of business processes. In *planning* they facilitate an overview of the individual effects of alternative courses of action on a firm's goals. . . . Break-even analyses are of importance in the day-to-day *management* of a business process when immediate decisions are to be based on simple criteria . . . . In the *control* of the business process the importance of break-even analysis lies in the fact that it uncovers the strengths and weaknesses of products, product groups or procedures, or of measures in general.[1]

I now believe at the broadest possible level that my support for the contribution margin concept was misplaced and short-sighted. In my view, looking back over those 25 years, what is really more simple-minded is to tout the advantages of contribution margin for real companies facing real business problems. In fact, it almost seems to be axiomatic, and let me call it Shank's Axiom. "If the problem is small

---

[1] Marcell Schweitzer, Ernst Trossmann, and Gerald H. Lawson, *Break-Even Analyses: Basic Model, Variants, Extensions* (New York: Wiley, 1992), p. 279.

enough so that contribution margin analysis is relevant then it can't have a very big impact on a company. And if the possible impact in a decision setting is major, if it can really affect a company in a major way, then it's silly to consider most of the factors to be fixed."[2]

There is a conflict in thinking about whether breakeven analysis continues to be a useful tool as the internal and external environments of business change. In this chapter we review this subject and conclude that such analysis remains relevant. In focusing attention on questions about the model and its extensions, we can better highlight its strengths and weaknesses. The basic cost-volume-profit (CVP) model is introduced in Chapter 4 along with assumptions of the deterministic, single-product model. In this chapter, we look at CVP sensitivity analysis, the model under conditions of uncertainty, links of CVP to linear programming and the Theory of Constraints (TOC), and how to deal with perishable products in a CVP analysis. Chapter 13, which covers capital asset acquisition decisions, deals with long-term cash flow breakeven analysis incorporating the time value of money.

IS CVP ANALYSIS STILL RELEVANT?

As companies adopt new technologies, fixed costs rise and variable costs drop as a percent of total costs. Even costs heretofore classified as variable (e.g., hourly labor) are becoming more fixed in that, in the short term, laborers are often hired for 37.5 or 40 hours a week with little chance of being laid off.[3] In these companies, labor is almost considered a part of overhead rather than "direct labor" as it has been thought of in the past. Thus,

---

[2] John K. Shank as part of a panel discussion reported in Michael A. Robinson, ed., "Contribution Margin Analysis: No Longer Relevant/Strategic Cost Management: The New Paradigm," *Journal of Management Accounting Research* Vol. II (Fall 1990). Sarasota, Fla.: American Accounting Association, p. 17.

[3] In 1984, there were reports of such contracts. See, for example, *The Economist*, July 7, 1984, U.S. edition, p. 5. However, evidence of this is even earlier: Hormell tried guaranteed annual wages in the late 1950s.

in some companies variable costs are reduced to the cost of material with virtually the rest of the costs of manufacturing fixed.[4]

In addition, many companies are adopting variants of an activity-based costing (ABC) system where the emphasis moves from looking at cost behavior (variable or fixed) and, instead, focuses on why resources are in place and to what level or activity these resources can be traced. Managers might be less interested in contribution margin and more interested in a margin that includes all costs traceable to that product, product group, or customer. Robert Kaplan argues that the dichotomy of all costs being variable and fixed leads managers to believe that fixed costs are just there as a result of being in business and that managers need not worry about why they are there or about controlling them. With such a scenario, managers would emphasize contribution margin.[5]

In the possible conflict between ABC and TOC in an earlier chapter, we saw that elements of the dissension might be interpreted as champions of different causes promoting their own at the expense of the other's model. In the question about the usefulness of CVP analysis, we have no specific models to deal with, only whether a venerable model has outlived its usefulness. One position is that the need to use CVP analysis is reduced or eliminated since (1) there is only a small percentage of variable to total costs and (2) managers' attention should be directed to why resources are in place rather than cost behavior per se. The second position is that there is nothing in the model that seems limited by rising contribution margin percentages (as variable costs drop) or in looking at separable costs and combining notions of CVP analysis with ABC (or even TOC). Why should it be a given that a certain set of fixed costs is in place and that managers would not be interested in them if they used CVP analysis?[6]

An emphasis on ABC/ABM and even a division between short-term and long-term variable costs does not mean we should drop CVP analysis. It still provides us with a basic decision-making tool that, in many ways, is the underpinning of newer philosophies. In addition, as is demonstrated throughout this chapter, it is a practical, understandable model that is becoming more robust with the use of electronic spreadsheets and all that means for extensions to the model and for sensitivity analysis. Its basic strength is that it allows managers to investigate a wide range of scenarios and examine a wide variety of dimensions as they analyze business problems.

In addition, there is evidence that CVP continues to be used as an ongoing management tool. Schweitzer, et al. produced a book reflecting German

---

[4] As with earlier discussion, there is the notion of long-term variable costs and fixed costs. The former consist of costs that could be eliminated if the activities causing them were to cease while the latter are costs that will be in place as long as that kind of resource (machine or human) is needed at the company.

[5] Robinson, "Contribution Margin Analysis: No Longer Relevant," pp. 2–3.

[6] Both Charles T. Horngren and Germain B. Boer support CVP analysis and these views in the panel discussion reported in Robinson, "Contribution Margin Analysis," pp. 21–28.

CVP practices.[7] Their book includes case evidence of the use of CVP analysis and its extensions. Interest seems sufficient in the basic model and its extensions that this book has been published in English, Japanese, and Chinese. Kim and Song report about practices among Japanese, Korean, and U.S. firms. Their research shows that "contribution margin is an important financial measure for 83% of Japanese corporations. . . ." This measure is used by 59 percent of U.S. firms and 40 percent of Korean firms responding.[8] While Shank's opening quote purports that there are no success stories using CVP analysis or any complex problems where it applies, Schweitzer et al. and Kim and Song seem to provide refuting evidence.

The CVP model has always had its limitations, as do most simple models. Its simplicity is both its strength and its weakness. The simple, single-product, deterministic model was never more than a broad way to assess profitability. All the extensions of the model have their own sets of assumptions and limitations. Basic CVP analysis coupled with sensitivity analysis is still intuitively appealing to students and managers alike since it forms the basis for an intuitive understanding of cost structure and what affects profits. Thus, the model is no less useful today than it ever was. As things change, we must be ever more aware of the restrictions of any model we use. However, that does not mean that a model should be discarded just because change is taking place. Nor does it mean that our thinking about this model cannot be adapted given an increased awareness about costs and resource management.

In the sections that follow, the CVP model is presented in the light of today's thinking. No model is useful in all situations. Thus, it is up to you as a manager to determine when you believe it's appropriate to use in a real-world environment.

COST-VOLUME-PROFIT SENSITIVITY ANALYSIS

The basic single-product, deterministic CVP model is represented as follows:

after-tax profit = [(price − variable cost)quantity − fixed cost](1 − tax rate)

or

$$\Pi = [(P - V)Q - F](1 - T)$$

---

[7] Schweitzer et al. *Break-Even Analyses: Basic Model, Variants, Extensions.*

[8] Il-Woon Kim and Ja Song, "U.S., Korea, & Japan: Accounting Practices in Three Countries," *Management Accounting* (August 1990). Montvale, N.J.: National Association of Accountants, pp. 26–30.

where: Π = after-tax profit
 P = price per unit
 V = variable cost per unit
 Q = quantity produced and sold
 F = fixed costs of the period
 T = tax rate

While managers might give a point estimate for each variable in this profit model, they are aware that these variables are not certain. This means that they can use single- or multiple-variable sensitivity analysis or can try to incorporate a stochastic model and get various confidence intervals. This section deals with sensitivity analysis, with the incorporation of risk later in the chapter.

In basic sensitivity analysis, managers do not assess probabilities to associate with any of the variables. Instead, they may vary one element at a time to see its effect on income. For example, assume the managers of Rosehips Company, a manufacturer of a single vitamin supplement, are using CVP analysis to help with planning for the upcoming year. Basic information and a projected income statement are shown in Exhibit 7-1 (see next page) along with cost-volume-profit breakeven analysis.

Current net income is $26,400 based on 80,000 units, a price of $7.00, variable costs of $4.20 (including a 10 percent sales commission or $3.50 per unit without sales commissions), fixed costs of $180,000, and a tax rate of 40 percent. This exhibit was set up with an electronic spreadsheet. Basic information is placed in a Data Section at the top of the spreadsheet, along with a pro forma income statement. This is followed by a series of breakeven analyses. Exhibit 7-2 shows the same analysis but with the formulas shown for the spreadsheet. Electronic spreadsheets allow great flexibility for sensitivity analysis. In this case, the managers not only calculated the standard breakeven quantity and breakeven sales dollars but also looked at the breakeven level for the price, variable cost, and fixed cost elements of the model, assuming all other variables are held constant.

Thus, these managers have established breakeven limits for the major variables. This is a good first step in moving from a deterministic to a stochastic model. A comparison of current and limit values shows the following:

	Current Value	Limit Value	Percent Change
Quantity	80,000	64,286	−19.64%
Price	$7.00	$6.39	− 8.71%
Variable cost[a]	$3.50	$4.05	+15.71%
Fixed cost	$180,000	$224,000	+24.44%

[a]The variable cost does not include commissions of 10 percent of sales.

Exhibit 7-1
Rosehips Company
Cost-Volume-Profit Analysis
Basic Analysis

```
Data Section:

        Quantity                      80,000 units

        Price                          $7.00
        Variable costs
          Material                      2.00
          Labor                         1.00
          Overhead                      0.50
          Commissions        10.00%     0.70 (percent of sales)
                                     ---------
        Total variable costs           $4.20

        Contribution margin            $2.80

        Period fixed costs
          Manufacturing              $100,000
          Sales                        50,000
          Administrative               30,000
                                     ---------
        Total period fixed costs     $180,000

        Tax rate                        40%

Pro Forma Income Statement

        Revenue (80,000 units   *    7.00 price)   $560,000
        Cost of Goods Sold
          Materials                 $160,000
          Direct labor                80,000
          Variable overhead           40,000
          Fixed costs                100,000
                                   ---------
                                                    380,000
                                                   ---------
        Gross profit                                180,000

        Other expenses
          Sales - variable          $56,000
          Sales - fixed              50,000
          Administrative - fixed     30,000
                                   --------
                                                    136,000
                                                   ---------
        Income before taxes                          44,000
        Taxes at 40%                                  17,600
                                                   ---------
        Net income                                  $26,400
```

Cost-Volume-Profit Analysis*

Breakeven quantity	64,286 units
Contribution margin percent	40.00%
Breakeven sales	$450,000
Breakeven price holding Q, F, and V constant	$6.39
Breakeven variable cost holding P, F, and Q constant (holding commissions constant)	$4.05
Breakeven fixed costs holding P, V, and Q constant	$224,000

*See Exhibit 7-2 for the formulas for each of these parts of the CVP analysis.

Exhibit 7-2
Rosehips Company
Cost-Volume-Profit Analysis
Spreadsheet Formulas

	A	B	C	D	E	F	G	H
1								
2								
3								
4								
5								
6	Data Section:							
7								
8		Quantity			80,000 units			
9								
10		Price			$7.00			
11		Variable costs						
12		Material			2.00			
13		Labor			1.00			
14		Overhead			0.50			
15		Commissions	10.00%		0.70	(percent of sales)		
16					----------			
17		Total variable costs			@SUM(E12 .. E15)			
18								
19		Contribution margin			$2.80			
20								
21		Period fixed costs						
22		Manufacturing			$100,000			
23		Sales			50,000			
24		Administrative			30,000			
25					----------			
26		Total period fixed costs			@SUM(E22 .. E24)			

Exhibit 7-2 (continued)

```
27        A        B        C        D        E        F        G        H
28                 Tax  rate                          40%
29
30  Pro Forma Income Statement
31
32               Revenue (+E8 units    *    +E10      price) +C32*E32
33               Cost of goods sold
34                  Materials                  +$E$8*E12
35                  Direct labor               +$E$8*E13
36                  Variable overhead          +$E$8*E14
37                  Fixed costs                +E26
38                                             ---------
39                                                             @SUM(E34 .. E37)
40                                                             ---------
41               Gross profit                                  +G32-G39
42
43               Other expenses
44                  Sales - variable           +E8*E15
45                  Sales - fixed              +E23
46                  Administrative - fixed     +E24
47                                             ---------
48                                                             @SUM(E44 .. E46)
49                                                             ---------
50               Income before taxes                           +G41-G48
51
52               Taxes at        40%                           +C52*G50
53                                                             ---------
54               Net income                                    +G50-G52
55
56
57
58
59
60
61
62  Cost-Volume-Profit Analysis
63
64     Breakeven quantity                      +E26/E19 units
65     Contribution margin percent             +E19/E10
66     Breakeven sales                         +E26/F65
67
68     Breakeven price holding
69        Q, F, and V constant      (((((E17-E15)*E8)+E26)))/(E8*(1-D15))
70
71     Breakeven variable cost holding
72        P, F, and Q constant          (((E8*E10*(1-D15))-E26)/E8)
73        (holding commissions constant)
```

Exhibit 7-2 (continued)

	A	B	C	D	E	F	G	H
74								
75	Breakeven fixed costs holding							
76	P, V, and Q constant				+E8*E19			

This preliminary analysis appears to show that profits are fairly sensitive to a small change in selling price (8.71 percent change or $0.61).[9] However, it may be that other variables should cause more concern with managers because there is a higher likelihood that they are subject to change or that there is an interrelationship among variables.

Managers can also vary more than one variable at a time to see the effect on profits. Exhibit 7-3 shows two variations of the Rosehips example. The Data Section from Exhibit 7-1 has been modified to show two additional sets of estimates, and the lower portion of the exhibit reflects an abbreviated contribution margin income statement to highlight changes in key segments of the model: contribution margin, fixed costs, and income. In the first revision, managers are looking at changes related to higher-quality materials (up $0.20 per unit) coupled with higher selling price (up $1.00). Even with quantity sold down by 10,000 units, the result is a substantial increase in profits. The second set of revised values reflects a slight drop in volume and selling price coupled with a small increase in material and labor, as well as in variable and fixed manufacturing overhead. The result of these changes drives income below breakeven.

Using multiple variables is similar to different budget levels in flexible budgeting. Managers can easily look at the possibilities that exist given their own decisions as well as changes in the external environment.

CVP ANALYSIS UNDER CONDITIONS OF UNCERTAINTY

While the basic model assumes deterministic values for the relevant variables, managers need some way to explicitly recognize that all of these inputs may be random variables. There have been many models dealing with CVP under conditions of uncertainty, starting with Jaedicke and Robichek.[10] Driscoll et al. divide the several articles that followed Jaedicke and Robichek along two dimensions: risk (which, in a single-product case,

---

[9] Normally, sensitivity analysis would show that the dollar change in sales price per unit and variable costs per unit are identical. In this case, however, the sales commission changes this relationship. With the commission, $(1 - 0.1)P = V$. Thus, $(0.90)(\$0.61) = \$0.55$.

[10] R. Jaedicke and A. Robichek, "Cost-Volume-Profit Analysis Under Conditions of Uncertainty," *The Accounting Review* (October 1964). Sarasota, Fla.: American Accounting Association, pp. 917–926.

Exhibit 7-3
Multiple-Variable Sensitivity Analysis

DATA SECTION:

	Original Value	Revised Value #1	Revised Value #2
Quantity	80,000	70,000	78,000
Price	$7.00	$8.00	$6.90
Variable costs			
Material	$2.00	$2.20	$2.10
Labor	1.00	1.00	1.20
Overhead	0.50	0.50	0.55
Commissions	0.70	0.80	0.69
Total variable cost	$4.20	$4.50	$4.54
Contribution margin	$2.80	$3.50	$2.36
Period fixed costs			
Manufacturing	$100,000	$100,000	$105,000
Sales	50,000	50,000	50,000
Administrative	30,000	30,000	30,000
Total period fixed	$180,000	$180,000	$185,000
Tax rate	40%	40%	40%

SOLUTION:

	Original Value	Revised Value #1	Revised Value #2
Contribution margin	$224,000	$245,000	$184,080
Fixed costs	180,000	180,000	185,000
Income before taxes	$ 44,000	$ 65,000	($ 920)
Taxes	17,600	26,000	(368)
Income	$ 26,400	$ 39,000	($ 552)

deals with the variance of a product's selling price or cost variables) and the assumptions and methods for dealing with uncertainty.[11]

Early writers looked at a single variable, sales, and considered other variables deterministic. For example, assume that quantity in the Rosehips example is normally distributed with an expected value of 80,000 units and a standard

---

[11] D. Driscoll, W. Lin, and P. Watkins, "Cost-Volume-Profit Analysis Under Uncertainty: A Synthesis and Framework for Evaluation," *Journal of Accounting Literature* (1984), p. 86.

deviation of 10,000 units. Thus, sales are $n(80,000, 10,000)$. Using a normal probability table (Table A1 in the Appendix), we can find the probability of breaking even. Breakeven quantity is 64,286 units (Exhibit 7-1). This quantity is 1.57 standard deviations $[(64,286 - 80,000)/10,000]$ below the mean. The probability of breaking even or less is about 6 percent, as you should verify.

This same analysis can be used to find the probability of achieving any level of profits. Say, for example, managers would like to know the probability of a net income after taxes of at least $50,000. The volume needed for this level of profits is about 94,048 units.

$$\frac{\$180,000 + \dfrac{\$50,000}{(1 - .40)}}{\$2.80} = 94,048$$

Then $(94,048 - 80,000)/10,000 = 1.4$ standard deviations above the mean. This implies that there is only an 8 percent chance of making at least $50,000 net income. This basic model deals with the assessment of sales risk and this risk is incorporated into CVP analysis. It is limited by the use of a single random variable (sales quantity) and the assumption of a normal distribution.

Problems with the Normal Random Variable Model

Two sets of problems arise with the assumption that the random variables are normally distributed. One set deals with how managers can assess the mean and standard deviation of the variables, and one set involves the assumption of a normal distribution.

Eliciting Probabilities   Let us assume at this point that the random variable under analysis is sales volume. Managers will want to have a fairly good idea of what the expected value (mean) and the standard deviation are for sales volume before they would be willing to use a model that relies on such measures. Many managers seem to have trouble with the concept of probability distributions. It would be unusual that one could go to the Sales Manager and ask for an estimate of the mean and standard deviation of sales, assuming that sales are normally distributed. A blank look might follow such a question. Thus, managers who are collecting information may have to elicit probabilistic estimates about sales volume in other ways.

Most discussions about probability start off with a discrete distribution. Later discussion then moves to a continuous distribution. One can use this same approach in eliciting probabilities from management.[12] Perhaps last year's sales level is a good place to start. A manager can be asked to guess whether sales will be at that level this year. Then the following questions can focus on the lowest volume of sales that could be expected and the

---

[12] There is a good discussion of eliciting probabilities in G. R. Chesley, "Elicitation of Subjective Probabilities: A Review," *The Accounting Review* (April 1975), pp. 325–337.

highest volume. From there, the missing information could be filled in and estimates of a mean and standard deviation could follow. Note that this means taking imperfect data about a distribution and smoothing it out to get some estimates to use in the normal probability model.

As you can see, even with this process there are several areas that can cause a less than useful result. While the normal probability distribution is continuous and unbounded, the probabilities and sales volumes with which they are associated in this estimating process are discrete and the distribution is bounded (lowest and highest sales volumes). Even so, this is a reasonable way to start. While there may be theoretical parameter estimation problems, it would be a rare manager that would take a resulting probability of, say, making $50,000 in net income as absolute fact to the last decimal place. More often than not, such a practical probability assessment (like an 8 percent probability of making net income of $50,000 or more in the Rosehips Company example) would be taken as a broad measure. Managers might interpret this as a "small chance of achieving our goals" rather than using the actual probability per se.

Problems with Normal Distribution Assumption   In the examples involving Rosehips Company, the only variable that was investigated was sales volume. This leaves three other general classes of variables (price, variable cost, and fixed costs). Under the general model proposed by Jaedicke and Robichek, all four variables would be normally distributed and independent. In addition, profit would then be normally distributed with a mean and standard deviation derived by standard formulas for combining normal variables. There seem to be at least two problems with the Jaedicke and Robichek model. First, there is no evidence to suggest that the variables in the model are independent. While we can assume away the fact that price and quantity are related in deterministic CVP analysis, this assumption cannot be treated so lightly in a stochastic analysis.[13] In addition, other authors have pointed out that, while one could assume that an additive combination of variables (like contribution margin per unit) is normally distributed, mathematical analyses show that the product of normally distributed variables is more often not normally distributed.[14] Total contribution margin is the product of sales volume and contribution margin per unit and, therefore, probably is not normally distributed.

Other authors have proposed models to compensate for the above criticisms. However, most are still based on a normal or lognormal approach and suffer from the same general problem of making a specific distributional

[13] The Driscoll, Lin, and Watkins article (see footnote 11) is a good analytical article on all the models covering CVP and uncertainty. They cover points like the one just addressed, for example.

[14] See J. Kottas and H. Lau, "A General Approach to Stochastic Management Planning Models: An Overview," *The Accounting Review* (April 1978). Sarasota, Fla.: American Accounting Association, pp. 389–401.

assumption that is open to question.[15] In addition, almost all these models allow the basic random variables to take negative values. Thus, depending on the mean and standard deviation for, say, sales volume, there could be a significant probability that volume was negative. This cannot happen any more than, say, variable cost can be positive. Thus, as hinted in the section on eliciting probabilities, some of the random variables under question may have real bounds and may not be symmetrical.

Other Ways to Deal with Uncertainty

There are two general classifications of the other ways that have been proposed to deal with uncertainty. One is to relax the distributional assumptions about the random variables and try to back into some descriptive statistics that will allow a manager to make assessments, for example, of the probability of breakeven. The other class of models uses simulation as a way to deal with multiple variables with different distributions.

For example, Chebychev's inequality, which is discussed by Buzby,[16] is an estimating technique that allows a distribution-free assessment of probabilities.[17] However, since it is such a broadbrush approach, resulting probabilities are so general as to be of little use to managers. This same criticism can be leveled at most if not all of the models that do not rely on a distribution assumption. Thus, the models that call for a normal or lognormal random variable are exact to use, but the underlying assumption of normality may be so suspect that the model cannot be used. Models that ignore an assumption about distribution, however, lack precision and may be useless to managers. There still remains the simulation model. Simulation allows performing a quite complex sensitivity analysis with all of the variables being changed.

A LINEAR PROGRAMMING APPROACH TO CVP ANALYSIS UNDER UNCERTAINTY

While the above discussion can be expanded to deal with a multiproduct company, the limitations of such analysis become more severe, especially when coupled with constrained resources that can be used for different products. Several authors have proposed linear programming as a way to deal with multiproduct breakeven analysis and joint resources.

---

[15] Schweitzer et al. summarize these models in *Break-Even Analyses*, pp. 228–236.

[16] S. Buzby, "Extending the Applicability of Probabilistic Management Planning and Control Models," *The Accounting Review* (January 1974). Sarasota, Fla.: American Accounting Association, pp. 42–49.

[17] Chebychev's inequality says that C percent of any set of numbers will fall within the range of $\bar{x} \pm h\sigma$, where

$$C = 1 - \frac{1}{h^2}$$

Linear Programming and the Deterministic CVP Model

Schweitzer et al. illustrate a use of linear programming as a way to deal with multiproduct breakeven given joint constrained resources.[18] Assume a firm has two products, x_1 and x_2. The authors use linear programming to see if breakeven can be achieved given scarce resources (defined below as variables x_3 to x_5). What seems unique is their objective function where they want to minimize the deviations above or below the linear representation of the contribution of two products, x_1 and x_2. In other words, a feasible solution would be a value either above or below breakeven using stated contribution margins for the two products and making production mix subject to the three constrained resources. They propose that with several constraints and fixed costs, it is often difficult to find a combination of products that exactly yields breakeven. Thus, their objective function finds that combination of products that deviates the least from breakeven.

The formulation of their example is in Exhibit 7-4. There are three constrained resources (rows 2, 3, and 4). Note that the slack variables have been set up to yield equality rather than using our normal ≥ or ≤ signs. Row 5 consists of the contribution margins of the two products (8.00x_1$ and 5.50x_2$) and the two slack variables, x_6 and x_7, which are the deviations above or below the contribution line that are to be minimized. Only one of these two variables (both of which form the objective function) can have a value in the final solution, since there can either be a deviation above or one below a target contribution margin (or breakeven), not both.

Exhibit 7-4 also shows the solution given a target contribution margin of $16,000. The solution calls for 1,645 x_1 and 516 x_2 along with excess capacity in the row 2 and row 3 constraints. Since both x_6 and x_7 are not in the solution (each of their values is zero), the target contribution margin can be achieved [(1,645.161 × $8.00) + (516.129 × $5.50) = $16,000].

Review Problem

Raise the target contribution margin from $16,000 to $25,000 (change the last constraint) and rerun the minimization problem from Exhibit 7-4. What is the output indicated? Your solution should show that the best you can do is to produce 1,454 x_1 and 1,154 x_2, or a total contribution margin of $17,977. The solution will also show that the variable defined as deviation below the target contribution margin, x_6, equals 7,023, the value of the deficiency below the target of $25,000.

Incorporating Uncertainty into the Linear Programming CVP Model

Miller and Morris propose a linear programming approach for choosing the best *ex ante* mix of products and providing some measures of risk associated

---

[18] Schweitzer et al., *Break-Even Analyses*, pp. 122–127.

Exhibit 7-4
Linear Programming and CVP Analysis

```
MIN      X6 + X7
SUBJECT TO
      2)    6 X1 + 27 X2 + X3 = 54000
      3)    6 X1 + 7 X2 + X4 = 16800
      4)    20 X1 + 6 X2 + X5 = 36000
      5)    X6 - X7 + 8 X1 + 5.5 X2 = 16000
END
             OBJECTIVE FUNCTION VALUE
   1)        .000000000
```

VARIABLE	VALUE	REDUCED COST
X6	.000000	1.000000
X7	.000000	1.000000
X1	1645.161000	.000000
X2	516.129000	.000000
X3	30193.550000	.000000
X4	3316.129000	.000000
X5	.000000	.000000

ROW	SLACK OR SURPLUS	DUAL PRICES
2)	.000000	.000000
3)	.000000	.000000
4)	.000000	.000000
5)	.000000	.000000

RANGES IN WHICH THE BASIS IS UNCHANGED:

OBJ COEFFICIENT RANGES

VARIABLE	CURRENT COEF	ALLOWABLE INCREASE	ALLOWABLE DECREASE
X6	1.000000	INFINITY	1.000000
X7	1.000000	INFINITY	1.000000
X1	.000000	.000000	10.333330
X2	.000000	3.100000	.000000
X3	.000000	.000000	.123016
X4	.000000	.000000	.596154
X5	.000000	INFINITY	.000000

RIGHTHAND SIDE RANGES

ROW	CURRENT RHS	ALLOWABLE INCREASE	ALLOWABLE DECREASE
2	54000.000000	INFINITY	30193.550000
3	16800.000000	INFINITY	3316.129000
4	36000.000000	4000.000000	8939.131000
5	16000.000000	1976.923000	1600.000000

with this choice.[19] Some of their assumptions may ease the problems regarding assuming a normal distribution discussed above. Exhibit 7-5 shows the basic assumptions of an example from this article and the following discussion is based on that example. In this illustration, four products can be manufactured. There are means and variances for revenue per unit and for costs of various resources and there are assumed uses of these constrained resources.

Using constraints shown in the exhibit, we can derive the objective function as follows (as you should verify):

	Product 1	Product 2	Product 3	Product 4
Revenue r_1	$33	$35	$25	$31
Resource 1 p_1	−4	−6	−2	−4
Resource 2 p_2	−25	−20	−15	−20
Resource 3 p_3	−3	−4	−5	−3
Contribution margin	$ 1	$ 5	$ 3	$ 4

For example, the contribution margin for product 1 is the revenue of $33 less:

Resource 1:	2 × $2 = $ 4
Resource 2:	5 × $5 = $25
Resource 3:	3 × $1 = $ 3

The result of a linear programming solution to this objective function and set of constraints is shown in Exhibit 7-6. The optimal solution calls for 100 of product 2 and 200 of product 4. No production is required for either product 1 or product 3. The optimal contribution margin is $1,300 (100 product 2 times $5 plus 200 product 4 times $4). Note that 700 units of resource 1 have been used (slack for that resource is 100 as shown under row 2 in the exhibit) while all of resources 2 and 3 have been used (slack equals zero for rows 3 and 4). Given this determination of quantities by the linear programming solution and the means and variances that were estimated for revenues and for resource costs, managers can determine the mean and standard deviation of total contribution margin.

First, total contribution margin will be:

$$C' = 100r_2 + 200r_4 - (700p_1 + 1,200p_2 + 1,000p_3)$$

as long as the bounds in the sensitivity analysis shown in Exhibit 7-6 are not exceeded.[20] Exhibit 7-7 on page 311 shows that the mean for total contribution

---

[19] R. Miller and M. Morris, "Multiproduct C-V-P Analysis and Uncertainty: A Linear Programming Approach," *Journal of Business, Finance, & Accounting* (Winter 1985), pp. 495–505.
[20] It is easier to look at total contribution margin in this way especially when calculating the variance for total contribution margin.

Exhibit 7-5
Linear Programming Example
Basic Data

	Product 1	Product 2	Product 3	Product 4
Revenue per unit (r_i)	r_1	r_2	r_3	r_4
Mean	$33	$35	$25	$31
Variance	1	2	1	2
Cost of resources (p_i)	p_1	p_2	p_3	
Mean	2	5	1	
Variance	1	2	0.25	

Assumptions:

1. The above variables are normally distributed and are independent of one another.
2. The constraints (use of resources) are assumed to be as follows:

$2x_1 + 3x_2 + x_3 + 2x_4 \leq 800$ (resource 1)
$5x_1 + 4x_2 + 3x_3 + 4x_4 \leq 1,200$ (resource 2)
$3x_1 + 4x_2 + 5x_3 + 3x_4 \leq 1,000$ (resource 3)

and all x_i are ≥ 0 and x_i represent products 1 through 4.

margin is $1,300 and the standard deviation is $1,929.[21] Remember that the model specified that all the variables were independent.

Thus, managers can compute the probability of a contribution margin ≥ 0 as

$(0 - 1,300)/1,929 = -0.674$ standard deviations below the mean

This is a probability of about 75 percent. The probability of making a contribution margin of at least $5,000 is

$(5,000 - 1,300)/1,929 = 1.918$ or about 3 percent

This model avoids the problem of multiplying two normal distributions together and getting a distribution that is not normal. In this model, quantity is determined *ex ante*. Revenues and resource costs are normally distributed and can be combined in a linear way so that the resulting distribution is normal. However, with an *ex ante* determination of all manufacturing quantities, there is nothing in the model to show change in profits given some assessment of the distribution of sales.

---

[21] The linear combination of variances is to add the variances together. Variance $(ax + by) =$ Variance $(ax - by) = a^2 \text{var}(x) + b^2 \text{var}(y)$ when all the variables are independent (i.e., the covariance is zero).

Exhibit 7-6
Linear Programming Results
Multiproduct CVP Analysis

```
MAX      PRODUCT1 + 5 PRODUCT2 + 3 PRODUCT3 + 4 PRODUCT4
SUBJECT TO
    2)   2 PRODUCT1 + 3 PRODUCT2 +   PRODUCT3 + 2 PRODUCT4 <=  800
    3)   5 PRODUCT1 + 4 PRODUCT2 + 3 PRODUCT3 + 4 PRODUCT4 <= 1200
    4)   3 PRODUCT1 + 4 PRODUCT2 + 5 PRODUCT3 + 3 PRODUCT4 <= 1000
END
LP OPTIMUM FOUND AT STEP 2
         OBJECTIVE FUNCTION VALUE
    1)        1300.00000


    VARIABLE         VALUE        REDUCED COST
    PRODUCT1         .000000        3.250000
    PRODUCT2      100.000000         .000000
    PRODUCT3         .000000        2.750000
    PRODUCT4      200.000000         .000000

        ROW    SLACK OR SURPLUS    DUAL PRICES
        2)        100.000000          .000000
        3)           .000000          .250000
        4)           .000000         1.000000
NO. ITERATIONS= 2

RANGES IN WHICH THE BASIS IS UNCHANGED:
                     OBJ COEFFICIENT RANGES
VARIABLE           CURRENT         ALLOWABLE       ALLOWABLE
                   COEF            INCREASE        DECREASE
PRODUCT1           1.000000        3.250000        INFINITY
PRODUCT2           5.000000         .333333        1.000000
PRODUCT3           3.000000        2.750000        INFINITY
PRODUCT4           4.000000        1.000000         .250000

                     RIGHTHAND SIDE RANGES
    ROW            CURRENT         ALLOWABLE       ALLOWABLE
                   RHS             INCREASE        DECREASE
    2            800.000000        INFINITY        100.000000
    3           1200.000000        133.333300      200.000000
    4           1000.000000        100.000000      100.000000
```

PERISHABLE PRODUCTS

There has been an implicit assumption in the discussion to this point that managers can adjust production to meet sales demand. Thus, if managers can estimate the mean and variance of sales quantity, they also have the

Exhibit 7-7
Standard Deviation—Contribution Margin

Product:	1	2	3	4
Quantity		100		200
Mean		$35		$31
Variance		$2		$2

Resource:	1	2	3
Quantity	700	1200	1000
Mean	$2.00	$5.00	$1.00
Variance	$1.00	$2.00	$0.25

Contribution Margin:
Mean:
$100r_2 + 200r_4 - (700P_1 + 1200P_2 + 1000P_3) = \$1,300$

Variance:

rev 2		rev 4		cost 1		cost 2		cost 3		variance
20000	+	80000	+	490000	+	2880000	+	250000	=	3720000

standard deviation = 1928.73

ability to wait until the actual sales level is known to commit manufacturing. If a product were not perishable, sales and production would not have to be equal since goods manufactured but not sold could be sold in the next period.

However, there are cases when products cannot be resold or stored for sale at a later date. In this case (often called the newsboy problem), managers must decide how many units to make. Unsold units will have a zero salvage value or some positive salvage value that is usually below the marginal costs of manufacturing.

Assume an optimal manufacturing quantity (much as was illustrated in the linear programming example) of x^*. Production must be set so that the expected value of selling an additional unit equals the expected value of the loss of making (or buying) the unit but not selling it. (This same kind of statement can be made for a retailer who buys perishable products.) Thus, in an expected-value sense, at this level of sales, the marginal revenue of selling one more unit should equal the marginal cost of producing it. This equality can be expressed as

$$cp = h(1 - p)$$

where:

p = probability of selling the unit
$(1 - p)$ = probability of not selling the unit

c = contribution margin per unit
h = loss sustained if unit is not sold, which is the variable cost per unit less salvage value, if any

From this, a manager can find the critical probability, p, as follows:

$$p = h/(c + h)$$

Consider the following example based on the Rosehips illustration. Assume that Rosehips's product is perishable and can be sold at $7 per unit, that the salvage value is $0.50, and that variable costs are $4.20 per unit. Thus,

$$p = (4.20 - 0.50)/(2.80 + 3.70) = 0.57$$

Thus, if there is at least a 57 percent chance of selling one more unit, it will be optimal to manufacture (buy) that unit.

This model can be used with a discrete distribution or a continuous one. With a continuous distribution, p is the probability that sales will be at least x^* while $(1 - p)$ is the probability of selling less than x^*. Refer to a normal probability table (Table A1 in the Appendix) to find the z value associated with a sales quantity with a probability of 0.57. This is associated with a z value of 0.18. There is a 57 percent chance of selling the optimal quantity or more. This means that besides the 50 percent from the mean up, there is another 7 percent below the mean. This 7 percent translates into the z value of 0.18. If we assume that sales quantity is $N(80,000, 10,000)$, then x^* is

$$80,000 - (0.18)(10,000) = 78,200 \text{ units}$$

The manufacturing of 78,200 units will realize a positive contribution margin (breakeven is 64,286 units as shown in Exhibit 7-1 on page 298).

As the salvage value rises, the resulting probability falls. Thus, at a salvage value of, say, $3,

$$p = 1.20/4 = 0.30$$

which translates into about 0.52 standard deviations above the mean and an optimal manufacturing quantity of 85,200 [80,000 + (0.52)(10,000)]. It is logical that managers would order (produce) more items if the expected value of a loss is going down.

SUMMARY

Cost-volume-profit analysis has traditionally been a basic, but robust, model for managers to use to help with short-term decisions regarding products as well as to be the basis for the flexible budget. Some argue that CVP analysis focuses managers' attention solely on price and variable cost and may promote ignoring fixed costs as a given. In addition, with the decrease of variable costs as a percentage of total costs in many companies, some think that CVP analysis has outlived its usefulness. However, there is substantial evidence that managers *use* this model and that there are pragmatic extensions to the basic model.

We are faced with the fundamental question we have with using any model: Under what circumstances is this model in its basic or extended forms useful? Managers are becoming increasingly aware that not all models, theories, cost systems, etc. are appropriate and/or cost efficient in all environments and situations. As with all models, CVP analysis has its limitations. For example, we want to deal with risk and find there are problematic distributional assumptions. However, using common sense, managers can combine sensitivity analysis, notions of risk, and mathematical programming *as appropriate* and have a useful model to aid in decision making.

PROBLEMS AND CASES

7-1. Perishable Products

Art Albert has a newsstand at the corner of Manhattan and Missouri streets. He must determine how many copies to order of the *Sunday Scoop*, the area's newspaper. Papers cost him $1.00, and he can sell them for $1.50. The *Scoop* does not allow him to return any unsold papers. This is small town, and Albert estimates the demand for papers to be as follows:

Demand	p(Demand)
50	0.05
51	0.13
52	0.19
53	0.21
54	0.24
55	0.12
56	0.06
	1.00

Required:
Determine the optimal number of papers to order.

7-2. Perishable Products

The *Sparta Plainsman* is a daily newspaper with a wide circulation throughout several small towns in Ohio. The paper has been plagued with returns of unsold copies, for which it gives full credit. The company charges its dealers $0.09 per copy, the same price it pays the dealers when it buys back unsold copies. Variable costs of printing are $0.03, and unsold copies can be converted to scrap paper, bringing in a net of $0.005 per copy.

Tom Swetnam, the publisher, has been trying to determine how many copies to print a day. Sales seem uniformly distributed between 5,000 and 7,000 copies a day.

Required:
How many copies should be produced each day?

7-3. CVP and Sensitivity Analysis

Required:
1. Build an electronic spreadsheet template similar to Exhibit 7-2. The sensitivity analysis shown in Exhibit 7-1 is all single variable. The limits and percent changes shown on page 297 are also for one variable at a time. Enter the data from Exhibit 7-1 into your template.
2. What is the effect of a 5 percent decrease in quantity coupled with a 5 percent increase in variable costs?
3. Resetting values to their original state, what is the effect of an increase of $15,000 in fixed costs coupled with a 3 percent drop in price?
4. Based on the changes in part 3, what would volume have to be to yield net income of $26,400?
5. Discuss the difference between this type of sensitivity analysis and the more traditional one-variable-at-a-time sensitivity analysis.

7-4. CVP Under Uncertainty

In the simple Jaedicke and Robichek model, only sales volume is considered a random variable. Consider the following example. The Werner Company has recently gone through a strategic planning session for all of its sales personnel. Based on past experience and on the goals and strategies set for the upcoming year, the following information is available about sales:

Mean sales for last five years:	100,000 units
Standard deviation of sales volume:	8,000 units
Last year's sales:	106,000 units
Goal for next year:	111,300 units (5% increase)

Other information regarding the company is as follows:

Price	$10.00 per unit
Variable costs	$ 4.80 per unit
Fixed costs	$450,000

Required:
1. What is the probability of at least breaking even?
2. What is the probability of achieving next year's sales goal?
3. What additional information do you want to be more confident about your probability assessments in the previous two parts?
4. How are your answers in parts 1 and 2 affected by a shift of the mean from 100,000 to 106,000?

5. Independent from your response to part 4, how are your answers to parts 1 and 2 affected by a reduction of the standard deviation to 4,000 units? by an increase in the standard deviation to 12,000 units?

7-5. Eliciting Probabilities

The Para Door Company has two operating divisions: wood doors and metal doors. The wood door manufacturing process is worker driven. Parts are lathed and finished out of pine and oak in various shapes and sizes. Very little automation is involved in this process. Skilled workers make up the majority of the labor force.

The metal door division is fully automated. Doors are completely formed, filled with insulation, and assembled on an automated stamping, forming, and assembly line that uses robots to transfer parts between machines.

You have been hired as a consultant to Para Door and have been asked to conduct a study to determine the mean and standard deviation of all inputs (material, labor, and overhead) for both divisions. The people you are going to work with are old hands at door manufacturing but few have had any training in statistics or quantitative models. They would be confused by the use of technical statistical jargon.

Required:
Write a report to management designing a plan to elicit probabilities to accomplish your task. The audience of this report is the management of the two operating divisions.

7-6. Linear Programming and Uncertainty

Review the linear programming solution to dealing with uncertainty. Sensitivity analysis in Exhibit 7-6 shows that the allowable increase in Product 2 margin is $0.333333.

Required:
1. Test the limit by increasing the contribution margin for Product 2 as a result of changing that product's Resource 3 use from 4 to 3.6. Run a new linear programming solution. What changes are there from the original solution?
2. When a value in the objective function is moving beyond its limit, it usually triggers a major change in the solution. Was there a major change? Why or why not?
3. Using the solution derived in part 1, recreate Exhibit 7-7.
4. What is the new probability of making at least $5,000?
5. Evaluate the linear programming model as a practical way to deal with uncertainty. What are its strengths and what are its weaknesses?

7-7. Uncertainty About Price and Variable Cost

Joey Tolbert, the production manager for Hill Street Enterprises, is uncertain about both the price and the variable costs for one of the company's main products. The market has been fairly stable lately and the Sales Department estimates that the mean price will be $25 with a standard deviation of $0.10.

The plant is using some new materials and, while fixed costs seem fairly set, there is some doubt about variable costs. Mean variable costs are estimated to be $15 with a standard deviation of $0.80. Both the distribution for price and for variable cost seem close enough to a normal distribution that this assumption can be used.

Required:

1. Mr. Tolbert has decided that he is willing to use these expected values and measures of variation in his decision process. With a unit contribution margin of $10 ($25 – $15), he is willing to produce additional units until the marginal increase in the variance of the contribution margin times .001 is greater than the marginal increase in total contribution margin. To the nearest hundred, find the production quantity indicated under this strategy.
2. If separable fixed costs per period are $70,200 and if management decides to produce the quantity you established in part 1, what is the probability that the firm will break even on this product?
3. What is the effect of a change in the standard deviation of price of $0.01 on the answers in parts 1 and 2? What is the effect of a change in the standard deviation of variable costs of $0.01 on parts 1 and 2?
4. Several criticisms have been made about CVP under conditions of uncertainty models that assume the variables are normally distributed. Do these criticisms apply here? Is this analysis useful to management?

7-8. Optimal Production Levels (CMA)

The PTO Division of the Galva Manufacturing Company produces power take-off units for the farm equipment business. The PTO Division, headquartered in Peoria, has a newly renovated, automated plant in Peoria and an older, less automated plant in Moline. Both plants produce the same power take-off units for farm tractors that are sold to most domestic and foreign tractor manufacturers.

The PTO Division expects to produce and sell 192,000 power take-off units during the coming year. The division production manager has the following data available regarding the unit costs, unit prices, and production capacities for the two plants.

	Peoria		Moline	
Selling price		$150.00		$150.00
Variable manufacturing cost	$72.00		$88.00	
Fixed manufacturing cost	30.00		15.00	
Commission (5%)	7.50		7.50	
G&A expense	25.50		21.00	
Total unit cost		135.00		131.50
Unit profit		$ 15.00		$ 18.50
Production rate per day	400 units		320 units	

*   All fixed costs are based on a normal year of 240 working days. When the number of working days exceeds 240, variable manufacturing costs increase by $3.00 per unit in Peoria and $8.00 per unit in Moline. Capacity for each plant is 300 working days.
*   Galva Manufacturing charges each of its plants a per unit fee for administrative services such as payroll, general accounting, and purchasing, as Galva considers these services to be a function of the work performed at the plants. For each of the plants at Peoria and Moline, the fee is $6.50 and represents the variable portion of G&A expense.

Wishing to maximize the higher unit profit at Moline, PTO's production manager has decided to manufacture 96,000 units at each plant. This production plan results in Moline operating at capacity and Peoria operating at its normal volume. Galva's corporate controller is not happy with this plan as he does not believe it represents optimal usage of PTO's plants.

Required:
1. Determine the annual breakeven units for each of PTO's plants.
2. Calculate the operating income that would result from the division production manager's plan to produce 96,000 units at each plant.
3. Determine the optimal production plan to produce the 192,000 units at PTO's plants in Peoria and Moline, and calculate the resulting operating income for the PTO Division. Be sure to support the plan with appropriate calculations.

7-9. Projecting Profits (CMA)

RayLok Incorporated has invented a secret process to freeze light intensity and manufactures a variety of products related to this process. Each product is independent of the others and is treated as a separate profit/loss division. Product (division) managers have a great deal of freedom to manage their divisions as they think best. Failure to produce target division income is dealt with severely; however, rewards for exceeding one's profit objective are, as one division manager described them, lavish.

The DimLok Division sells an add-on automotive accessory that automatically dims a vehicle's headlights by sensing a certain intensity of light coming from a specific direction. DimLok has had a new manager in each of the three previous years because the predecessor manager failed to reach RayLok's target profit. Don Barnes has just been promoted to manager and is studying ways to meet the current target profit for DimLok.

The two profit targets for DimLok for the coming year are $800,000 (20 percent return on the investment in the annual fixed costs of the division) plus an additional profit of $20 for each DimLok unit sold. Other constraints on division operations are presented below.

- Production cannot exceed sales since RayLok's corporate advertising program stresses completely new product models each year, even though the "newness" of the models may be only cosmetic.
- The DimLok selling price may not vary above the current selling price of $200 per unit but may vary as much as 10 percent below $200.
- A division manager may elect to expand fixed production or selling facilities; however, the target objective that is related to fixed costs is increased by 20 percent of the cost of such expansion. Furthermore, a manager may not expand fixed facilities by more than 30 percent of existing fixed cost levels without approval from the Board of Directors.

Barnes is now examining data gathered by his staff to determine if DimLok can achieve its target profits of $800,000 **and** $20 per unit. A summary of these reports show the following.

- Last year's sales were 30,000 units at $200 per unit.
- The present capacity of DimLok's manufacturing facility is 40,000 units per year, but capacity can be increased to 80,000 units per year by an increase in annual fixed costs of $1,000,000.

- Present variable costs amount to $80 per unit, but if commitments are made for more than 60,000 units, DimLok's vendors are willing to offer raw material discounts amounting to $20 per unit, beginning with unit number 60,001.
- Sales can be increased up to 100,000 units per year by committing large blocks of product to institutional buyers at a discounted unit price of $180. However, this discount would apply only to sales in excess of 40,000 units per year.

Barnes believes that these projections are reliable, and he is now trying to determine what DimLok must do to meet the profit objectives assigned by RayLok's Board of Directors.

Required:
1. Calculate the dollar value of DimLok's present annual fixed costs.
2. Determine the number of units that DimLok must sell in order to achieve both profit objectives. Be sure to consider all constraints in determining your answer.
3. Without prejudice to your answer in part 2, assume Don Barnes decides to sell 40,000 units at $200 per unit and 24,000 units at $180 per unit. Prepare a pro forma income statement for DimLok showing whether or not Don Barnes' decision will achieve DimLok's profit objectives.

Part 3

Information for Production and Control

Chapter 8

Information: Cost versus Benefit

With . . . information economics, the management accounting process is not viewed as an attempt to obtain good cost
allocations or good variance analyses. Rather, the problem
is viewed as choosing an optimal information system in an
uncertain environment where the accounting information
system provides signals that help the decision maker or
cost analyst. . . . An information system is selected because
the expected benefits from improved decision making
exceed the expected costs of developing, implementing, and
operating the cost information system.[1]

Information is a commodity. Measurement consumes
resources.[2]

[1] Robert S. Kaplan, "The Impact of Management Accounting Research on Policy and Practice,"
in J. W. Buckley (ed.), *1981 Proceedings of the Arthur Young Professors' Roundtable*, Reston, Va.:
The Council of Arthur Young Professors, pp. 61–62.
[2] Charles T. Horngren, "Management Accounting: Where Are We?" *Management Accounting and
Control*, Robert Beyer Center of Managerial Accounting and Control, University of Wisconsin,
Madison (1975).

This chapter deals with the difference between getting and using information for yourself and obtaining information for a superior and the cost-versus-benefit trade-off in acquiring information. The first subject distinguishes between information for an individual gathered by that individual and information in a principal-agent environment. The second area deals with *information economics* and Bayesian revision of probabilities. Here we look at a model to judge the value of information given its acquisition cost. We expand this area in Chapter 10 when dealing with variance investigation. The objective here is more to expose you to a way of thinking, a means of analysis, than to propose a mathematical model that can be used on a daily basis. We are trying to operationalize the notion of whether the cost of a piece of information (or an information system) is worth the benefit derived.

INFORMATION FOR THE PRINCIPAL OR THE AGENT

In a proprietorship, the owner makes decisions for herself. This is contrasted to most other organizations where decisions are made at various levels of management by people who are agents rather than principals. Thus, a *principal* is someone who has ultimate authority and an *agent* is anyone acting on behalf of a principal. In a publicly held company, the principals are the stockholders and the agents are the directors and officers. In a partnership, the principals are the partners and the agents are the employees. This concept of principals and agents is called *agency theory*.[3]

Information Acquired Directly by a Principal

At the heart of agency theory is the notion that individuals act in their own self-interest. Thus, if a person is seeking information as a principal, he will use the information in a way that will further his self-interest. Even if we incorporate notions of short-term versus long-term well-being (e.g., social and ethical issues that might not affect a single decision but might affect an ongoing entity), people act in their own interest.

Information Acquired by an Agent

In most settings, information is gathered by agents rather than principals. We explore how to evaluate such agent managers in Chapter 14. Evaluation usually includes the notion of *behavior congruence*, where upper managers (principals in some sense) try to motivate subordinates (agents) to act

---

[3] A good review of agency theory can be found in Stanley Baiman, "Agency Research in Managerial Accounting: A Survey," *Journal of Accounting Literature* (Spring 1982), pp. 154–213.

in the same way that the principal would have acted in the same situation if the upper manager knew everything both parties knew (i.e., no information asymmetry). Efforts to acquire information by agents on the behalf of principals and efforts to motivate subordinates are not costless. Therefore, the agency relationship increases the cost of an information system. In an information-acquisition setting, the agent collects information to make decisions that are in the agent's best interest and, at the same time, are supposed to be in the best interest of the principal. There is an interdependency between the relevant, cost-effective information for a decision and the fact that an agency exists.

A principal wants an agent to act in the best interest of the principal. Principals acquire information themselves to see how agents are performing since they want to monitor agents' activities and motivate them. In addition, principals want to make sure that agents' representations are true. Thus, from several perspectives, principals are faced with many cost-benefit trade-offs in acquiring information for themselves.

Applications of agency theory include mathematical representations of this interrelationship and how they can affect information acquisition, analysis, and use. However, the practical implementation of these models is suspect due to their complexity. Therefore, while it is important to recognize that there is this interdependent relationship (actually, a series of them within an organization), we will not try to model them or show how they affect the cost-versus-benefit question.

DECISION TREES

Given that a principal or agent wants to acquire information, we can now look at the costs versus benefits of such information. However, before examining the information economics model, we will establish some basic terms. We start with a decision tree, which is illustrated in Figure 8-1. In this figure, boxes represent decisions (or actions), while circles represent states of nature. A manager has control over a decision; it is the manager's to make. Examples include whether to introduce a new product or not, whether to introduce the product regionally in a test market or to go nationally, and how to price the product. The number of alternatives from which a manager can choose is dependent on the decision. However, in making these decisions managers are faced with parts of the environment over which they have no control. These are called *states of nature*.

For example, competition may have a bearing on the decision to introduce a new product. There is some probability that there will be like products in the market. However, the manager has no control over the competition. Likewise, if a manager of a food concession at an outdoor sporting event is

State of nature

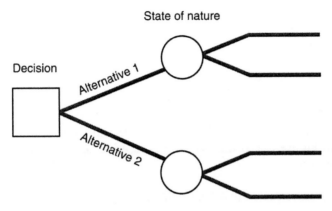

Figure 8-1   Decision Tree

deciding on how many vendors to hire that day, she has no control over the weather—a factor that could greatly affect sales outcome.

The decision tree in Figure 8-1 is a simple, one-decision example. Decision trees are solved (used) by calculating the expected value of each major branch and choosing the decision that has the higher (or highest) expected value. An illustration will help at this point.

The managers of Olathe Manufacturing are deciding whether to embark on a new advertising campaign (the decision, then, is *advertise* or *do not advertise*). There has been some discussion about the state of the market for their major products and, to simplify the discussion within the company, probabilities were assessed by the sales department regarding a *strong market* and a *weak market* (these are the states of nature), as shown below.[4]

Probabilities Regarding Market Strength

p(strong market)	0.60
p(weak market)	0.40
	1.00

Finally, the managers have estimated the profits they believe they could earn given each of these states of nature and whether the advertising program is adopted or not. These are called *outcomes* or *conditional values* and are as follows:

---

[4] Many decisions have more than two possible choices and many states of nature can have several conditions. In fact, states of nature do not have to be described by discrete probabilities and can use a continuous distribution such as the *normal distribution*. However, this discussion is not harmed by the simple two-alternatives and two-states-of-nature conditions illustrated.

Profits with Advertising Program
Strong market $80,000
Weak market   25,000

Profits Without Advertising Program
Strong market $60,000
Weak market   35,000

The decisions, the states of nature, and the outcomes are all illustrated together in Figure 8-2. If the decision is to advertise, the expected value of that decision is

$$\text{EV(advertise)} = (0.6 \times \$80,000) + (0.4 \times \$25,000) = \$58,000$$

and the decision to not advertise will yield the following expected value:

$$\text{EV(do not advertise)} = (0.6 \times \$60,000) + (0.4 \times \$35,000) = \$50,000$$

Thus, based on expected values, managers would choose to advertise since the expected value (EV) of that action is $8,000 higher than the EV (do not advertise). The two expected values are shown in Figure 8-2.

If management had information in advance that the market was going to be weak, however, they would reverse their choice since (1) the profits without advertising are $10,000 higher than with advertising when a weak market exists, and (2) the probabilities would now change so that p(strong market) = 0 and p(weak market) = 1.0. Since there is the possibility that additional information about the state of the market could change the

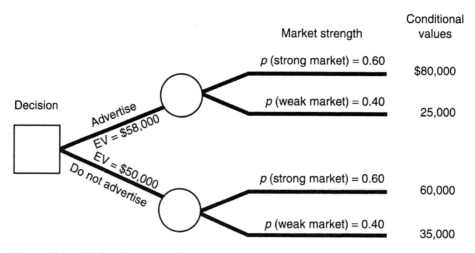

Figure 8-2 Olathe Manufacturing

decision indicated by a simple expected-value model, there is reason to evaluate the cost of such information in comparison to possible benefits. This leads into the discussion of information economics.

It is important to note at this point that if, say, the estimated profits with a weak market and no advertising were only $20,000 instead of $35,000, then there would be no reason to assess the value of additional information since the decision to advertise would be the wiser one given all states of nature. To generalize, then, *a piece of information can only be valuable if it can change the decision.* A manager would not want to pay for additional information when the decision would remain unchanged no matter what the information yielded.[5]

EXPECTED VALUE OF PERFECT INFORMATION

The decision tree example illustrates not only a visual framework for decisions, but also shows how the expected-value criterion is used. The *branch* of the tree (decision) that was chosen has the higher expected value ($58,000 versus $50,000). In theory, what would happen to the decision-making process if a manager had perfect information regarding whether the market was going to be strong or weak? As we have seen, if a manager knew the market was going to be strong, then the manager would choose to advertise and achieve a profit of $80,000, while if it were known that the market was weak, a choice would be made to not advertise, with a resulting profit of $35,000. Therefore, given these perfect choices, the highest expected value that could be derived would be as follows:

$$(0.6 \times \$80,000) + (0.4 \times \$35,000) = \$62,000$$

With no information in advance, the better expected value was $58,000. Now, with perfect information, the expected value has risen to $62,000. How much would a manager be willing to pay for perfect information? In this example it is a maximum of $4,000 ($62,000 – $58,000). If a manager in this case paid, say, $5,000 for perfect information, then profits would be reduced by that amount and would only total $57,000, less than the $58,000 in expected profits under a condition of no advance information.

Thus, the *expected value of perfect information* (EVPI) is the difference between the following:

expected value given perfect information – expected value with no information

---

[5] It is possible to argue that some managers like confirming information even if it does not change their decision. This argument is more behavioral than economic, however.

The EVPI can be used as a screen in deciding whether to go forward in an investigation of whether the benefit of a piece of information is greater than the cost. If the cost of information exceeds the EVPI, then that information is too expensive based on economic criteria.

INFORMATION ECONOMICS—
THE VALUE OF SAMPLE INFORMATION

It is rare that a manager can purchase perfect information. In most cases, perfect information is a concept and not a reality. However, managers can and do evaluate and purchase *sample information* and this provides a practical cost-benefit trade-off. For example, marketing surveys may provide information about the state of the market. Perhaps an analysis of leading indicators for various aspects of the economy and/or the specific industry would yield useful information to Olathe's managers. Consultants make their living providing valuable services to managers in such situations. The objective of the information economics framework, then, is to provide a structure for deciding whether to buy a certain set of sample (imperfect) information.

The first steps are outlined in our example above.

First, find the expected value of the various alternatives that are open to managers and choose that alternative with the highest (higher) expected value.

Second, find the EVPI by subtracting the results of step 1 from the expected value given perfect information.

Third, if the cost of information exceeds the EVPI, then the information should not be bought.

Fourth, if the information cost is less than the EVPI, then the following discussion leads to a cost-versus-benefit decision.

Bayesian Revision

Bayes' Theorem is used as the basis for the fourth step of the analysis. The basic notion of this model is for managers to take existing information (e.g., assessments of the market: strong or weak) and to combine this with new information (e.g., a market survey) in order to get a revised estimate of what is going on in the environment. If you can keep this basic notion in mind, then the model itself will make sense.

In this example, Olathe's managers are starting with their own assessment of the market. These are the *prior probabilities* before any new information is examined.

Probabilities of Each State of Nature

p(strong market)   0.60
p(weak market)   0.40

Let us assume some additional probabilities in this example. Assume that TRGI, a consulting company, is willing to conduct a market survey for Olathe. The objective is to see if the market is strong or weak. Naturally, Olathe's managers are interested in how successful TRGI has been in the past with similar surveys. In other words, how often have TRGI's results been correct? TRGI estimates that 85 percent of the time when a survey shows there is going to be a strong market, there actually is a strong market. However, 90 percent of the time when a survey shows that there is going to be a weak market, there is a weak market. It seems in this case that there is a higher accuracy in predicting a weak market given the reality of such a market. These assessments are called *conditional probabilities* since they are conditional on whether the market is actually strong or actually weak (the actual state of nature). In complete form (probabilities of being right and of being wrong), this information is as follows:

Conditional Probabilities Given a State of Nature

p(survey shows strong market I market is strong) = 0.85 (survey correctly predicts)
p(survey shows strong market I market is weak) = 0.10 (survey incorrectly predicts)
p(survey shows weak market I market is strong) = 0.15 (survey incorrectly predicts)
p(survey shows weak market I market is weak) = 0.90 (survey correctly predicts)

Thus managers have an existing assessment of the condition of the environment (prior probabilities) and can seek additional information that has conditional probabilities of being correct or incorrect, as illustrated above. When we combine these two using Bayes' Theorem, we can find the most interesting piece of information: the probability that the market is strong (or weak) *given* the results of the market survey. Assuming the consulting firm has been hired and a sample survey taken, managers will want probabilities to aid their choice (advertise or do not advertise), given the outcome of the survey. These are called *posterior probabilities* and are derived through the use of Bayes' Theorem.

At this point it is necessary to add notation to the discussion as shorthand for all the words in these conditional probabilities. A full set of notation for this example is contained in Exhibit 8-1. Obviously, if this were, say, a four-decision and six-states-of-nature problem, mathematical notation would become a necessity.

Thus, for our example, the managers of Olathe have the following information shown in notation form:

$$n_1 = \text{strong market} \quad \text{and} \quad n_2 = \text{weak market}$$

Exhibit 8-1
Probability Notation

Outcomes:
  States of nature n_i
  Probabilities of states of nature [and the sum of $p(n_i) = 1.0$] $p(n_i)$
The probabilities of the states of nature are also called *prior probabilities*.
Likelihoods or Conditional Probabilities:
  Samples s_i
  Probabilities of sample *given* state of nature $p(s_i | n_i)$
Posterior Probabilities:
  Probabilities of state of nature *given* sample results $p(n_i | s_i)$

Thus,

$$p(n_1) = 0.6$$
$$p(n_2) = 0.4$$

and

$$s_1 = \text{sample shows strong market}$$
$$s_2 = \text{sample shows weak market}$$
$$p(s_1 | n_1) = 0.85$$
$$p(s_1 | n_2) = 0.10$$
$$p(s_2 | n_1) = 0.15$$
$$p(s_2 | n_2) = 0.90$$

The Bayesian revision that yields the posterior probabilities is as follows:

$$p(n_i \mid s_i) = \frac{p(n_i) \; p(s_i | n_i)}{\Sigma \; p(n_i) \; p(s_i | n_i)}$$

Exhibit 8-2 shows the four posterior probabilities that can be calculated for this example. Obviously, the example could be expanded to include more than two states of nature and more than two results from sample information. However, an understanding of this simple example can easily be extended into a more complex one.

As can be seen by an examination of Exhibit 8-2, the sums of each of the two sets of posterior probabilities equal 1.0. This is logical and consistent.

Expected Value of Sample Information

To this point we have defined two actions that managers can take (advertise or do not advertise), two states of nature (strong market or weak market), prior probabilities about the states of nature, conditional probabilities

Exhibit 8-2
Posterior Probabilities
Olathe Manufacturing

$$p(n_1 | s_1) \;=\; \frac{p(n_1)\,p(s_1|n_1)}{p(n_1)\,p(s_1|n_1) + p(n_2)\,p(s_1|n_2)} \;=\; \frac{(0.60)(0.85)}{(0.60)(0.85) + (0.40)(0.10)}$$
$$=\; 0.927272$$

$$p(n_2 | s_1) \;=\; \frac{p(n_2)\,p(s_1|n_2)}{p(n_1)\,p(s_1|n_1) + p(n_2)\,p(s_1|n_2)} \;=\; \frac{(0.40)(0.10)}{(0.60)(0.85) + (0.40)(0.10)}$$
$$=\; 0.072727$$

$$p(n_1 | s_2) \;=\; \frac{p(n_1)\,p(s_2|n_1)}{p(n_1)\,p(s_2|n_1) + p(n_2)\,p(s_2|n_2)} \;=\; \frac{(0.60)(0.15)}{(0.60)(0.15) + (0.40)(0.90)}$$
$$=\; 0.20$$

$$p(n_2 | s_2) \;=\; \frac{p(n_2)\,p(s_2|n_2)}{p(n_1)\,p(s_2|n_1) + p(n_2)\,p(s_2|n_2)} \;=\; \frac{(0.40)(0.90)}{(0.60)(0.15) + (0.40)(0.90)}$$
$$=\; 0.80$$

regarding survey results given the actual state of nature, and posterior probabilities of the state of nature given the survey results. We now come back to the first question in this illustration: Should Olathe's managers hire TRGI to conduct a market survey? This is a cost-benefit trade-off. In order to answer this question, we will look at the maximum amount managers would be willing to pay TRGI for sample information (the survey) by first calculating the *expected value of sample information* (EVSI).

Given the posterior probabilities shown in Exhibit 8-2 and the conditional monetary values reflected in Figure 8-2, we look at expected values associated with the two actions (advertise or do not advertise) coupled with receiving either a strong or a weak market survey. The expected value of advertising or not advertising and receiving a market survey showing a strong market is

EV(advertising, strong market survey) = (0.9273 × $80,000) + (0.0727 × $25,000)
= $76,000

The expected value of no advertising and receiving a market survey showing a strong market is

EV(no advertising, strong market survey) = (0.9273 × $60,000) + (0.0727 × $35,000)
= $58,182

Therefore, the expected value of advertising coupled with a strong market is higher than the expected value of no advertising coupled with a strong market. It seems logical that, if the market is strong, advertising would have a positive effect on expected outcomes.

As a review of this material, calculate the expected values associated with the action of both advertising and not advertising with a weak market sample. You should see that the EV(advertise, weak market sample) = $36,000 while the EV(no advertising, weak market sample) = $40,000. Thus, if the survey shows a weak market, the better alternative is to not advertise.

Without additional information (the survey), we calculated that advertising would be the better action since EV(advertise) at $58,000 was greater than the EV(do not advertise) at $50,000. In order to find the EVSI, we should compare our optimal action given no additional information to an expected value that includes the effects of the sample information. We determined above that the better alternative is to advertise if there is a strong market ($76,000) and to not advertise if there is a weak market ($40,000). First we weight these values by the denominators in Exhibit 8-2. These are the $p(s_i)$ and are as follows:

$$p(\text{strong market sample}) = (0.60 \times 0.85) + (0.40 \times 0.10) = 0.55$$
$$p(\text{weak market sample}) = (0.60 \times 0.15) + (0.40 \times 0.90) = 0.45$$

These two add to 1.0 as we would expect. The resulting expected value, then, is

$$(0.55 \times \$76,000) + (0.45 \times \$40,000) = \$59,800$$

Since the expected value of the better action (advertise) with *no* information was $58,000, the expected value of sample information is

expected value of optimal actions given the information system less expected value of best decision given no information = $59,800 − $58,000 = $1,800

In other words, if the consulting company wanted to charge anything over $1,800, then its services would not warrant the expense.

This can be illustrated by adding in a cost for consulting. Say TRGI wants to charge $2,000 for its services. All the expected values would decrease by $2,000, which would yield a final expected value of $57,800 which is $200 less than the expected value when buying no additional information.

Managers can use the EVSI much in the same way as the EVPI as the screen for seeing if the economic benefits of an information system are greater than the costs. Microcomputer spreadsheets are very useful in doing sensitivity analysis with information economics. What would happen, say, if TRGI's estimates of the conditional probabilities were off? Exhibit 8-3 shows the results if $p(s_1 \mid n_1)$ is 0.75 instead of 0.85 and $p(s_2 \mid n_2)$ is 0.80 instead of 0.90. The EVSI drops from $1,800 to $200. This seems logical, since the surveys will yield information that is less accurate than originally illustrated.

Exhibit 8-3
Changes in Conditional Probabilities
Olathe Manufacturing

				Profits
p(n1)		0.6	a1|n1	$80,000
p(n2)		0.4	a1|n2	25,000
			a2|n1	60,000
			a2|n2	35,000

EV(a1)	$58,000		
EV(a2)	50,000		
Expected Value with Perfect Information			$62,000

EVPI $62,000   less $58,000 = $4,000

p(s1|n1)	0.75	p(s1)	0.53
p(s1|n2)	0.2		
p(s2|n1)	0.25	p(s2)	0.47
p(s2|n2)	0.8		
		Sum p(si)	1.00

Posterior probabilities

	A	B	A x B	divide by	p(si)	p(ni|si)
p(n1|s1)	0.6	0.75	0.45		0.53	0.849056
p(n2|s1)	0.4	0.2	0.08		0.53	0.150943
p(n1|s2)	0.6	0.25	0.15		0.47	0.319148
p(n2|s2)	0.4	0.8	0.32		0.47	0.680851

EV(a1,s1)	$71,698	best action is:
EV(a2,s1)	56,226	action 1
EV(a1,s2)	42,553	best action is:
EV(a2,s2)	42,979	action 2

Expected Value - Optimal Action - With Information
 ($71,698 x 0.53) + ($42,979 x 0.47) = $58,200

Expected Value of Sample Information

 $58,200   less $58,000   equals $200

Exhibit 8-4
Changes in Monetary Outcomes
Olathe Manufacturing

```
                                                                    Profits
p(n1)                                0.6          a1|n1           $80,000
p(n2)                                0.4          a1|n2            30,000
                                                  a2|n1            60,000
                                                  a2|n2            35,000


EV(a1)    $60,000
EV(a2)     50,000
Expected Value with Perfect Information                          $62,000

EVPI      $62,000       less      $60,000 =                 $2,000

p(s1|n1)       0.85          p(s1)        0.55
p(s1|n2)       0.1

p(s2|n1)       0.15          p(s2)        0.45
p(s2|n2)       0.9
                             Sum p(si)    1.00

Posterior probabilities
               A        B       A x B divide by       p(si) p(ni|si)
p(n1|s1)      0.6      0.85       0.51                 0.55 0.927272
p(n2|s1)      0.4      0.1        0.04                 0.55 0.072727

p(n1|s2)      0.6      0.15       0.09                 0.45      0.2
p(n2|s2)      0.4      0.9        0.36                 0.45      0.8

EV(a1,s1)                              $76,364 best action is:
EV(a2,s1)                               58,182              action 1

EV(a1,s2)                               40,000 best action is:
EV(a2,s2)                               40,000              action 2

Expected Value - Optimal Action - With Information
 ($76,364 x 0.55) + ($40,000 x 0.45) = $60,000

Expected Value of Sample Information

$60,000    less     $60,000    equals        $0
```

Exhibit 8-4 retains the original conditional probabilities but changes the monetary outcome for the action to advertise given a weak market from $25,000 to $30,000. In this case, the EVPI is reduced to $2,000 instead of $4,000 and the EVSI is now zero. Why is this so? The expected values for both actions coupled with a weak market survey are equal at $40,000. Thus, managers would be indifferent between the two possible actions. Therefore, no matter what the survey showed, managers would be as well off (or better off) by advertising; the survey information has no value since it cannot change the managers' decision. Both Exhibit 8-3 and 8-4 are presented virtually the way they would be using a microcomputer spreadsheet program. Since many intermediate figures are left out (formulas were used in spreadsheet cells), you should verify all the results from the original problem and the sensitivity analysis shown in Exhibits 8-3 and 8-4 by constructing a microcomputer spreadsheet template to solve this problem.[6]

Expected Opportunity Loss

The concept of *expected opportunity loss* (EOL) is analogous to EVPI. The EVPI of the Olathe Manufacturing example is $4,000. Thus, having perfect information increases our expected value by $4,000. This is the same as saying that an information system has the potential of saving us an expected loss (decrease in profits) of $4,000. Without information from the survey, managers would choose to advertise. With information from the survey indicating that the market was weak, managers would not advertise. Profits would then be $10,000 higher ($35,000 instead of $25,000), with a probability of 0.40 attached to the state of nature that the market is weak or an expected savings (avoided loss) of $4,000.

RISK AND REWARD—UTILITY FUNCTIONS

Up to this point in the discussion, *expected value* has been equated with *expected utility*. Thus, we have assumed risk neutrality for the decision maker. However, utility functions can be incorporated into the information economics model. Basically, instead of monetary outcomes, the outcomes are stated in a utility form. Assume that managers of Olathe are risk averse and have a utility function (U) that is $U(payoff) = \ln(payoff)$. Thus, the monetary payoffs will have to be converted to their natural logarithms. Otherwise, the process is identical to the one using monetary payoffs. The results are illustrated in Exhibit 8-5. When comparing this to Exhibits 8-3 and 8-4, note

---

[6] Create your spreadsheet in a generic manner so that any two-decision, two-states-of-nature problem could be solved using that template. You might figure out how to expand the template if, say, there were three states of nature instead of two.

Exhibit 8-5
Risk Averse Utility Function
Olathe Manufacturing

```
                                                          Utilities
p(n1)                       0.6              a1|n1        11.28978
p(n2)                       0.4              a1|n2        10.12663
                                             a2|n1        11.00209
                                             a2|n2        10.46310

EU(a1)     10.82452
EU(a2)     10.78650
Expected Utility with Perfect Information                 10.95911

EUPI       10.95911    less    10.82452 =         0.134588

p(s1|n1)       0.85         p(s1)       0.55
p(s1|n2)       0.1

p(s2|n1)       0.15         p(s2)       0.45
p(s2|n2)       0.9
                            Sum p(si)   1.00

Posterior probabilities
                   A       B     A x B divide by        p(si) p(ni|si)
p(n1|s1)          0.6    0.85    0.51                   0.55 0.927272
p(n2|s1)          0.4    0.1     0.04                   0.55 0.072727

p(n1|s2)          0.6    0.15    0.09                   0.45      0.2
p(n2|s2)          0.4    0.9     0.36                   0.45      0.8

EU(a1,s1)                           11.20518 best action is:
EU(a2,s1)                           10.96290           action 1

EU(a1,s2)                           10.35926 best action is:
EU(a2,s2)                           10.57090           action 2
```

Expected Utility - Optimal Action - With Information
(11.20518 x 0.55) + (10.57090 x 0.45) = 10.91976

Expected Utility of Sample Information

10.91976 less   10.82452 equals 0.095238

Monetary equivalents:
EVPI $1.10
EVSI $1.14

that the only changes are a shift from dollars to utility for outcomes and a conversion of EVPI and EVSI back into dollars at the end of the exhibit. Both EVPI and EVSI are virtually zero. The anomaly that EVSI (really EUSI) has a monetary value that is greater than EVPI (EUPI) is caused by the utility function's logarithmic makeup.[7]

Other utility functions can be substituted for this simple risk-averse model. The results using expected utilities can be different from those using expected monetary values. In this example, there is no expected utility for either perfect or sample information. In other examples, there may still be a positive EUPI but a zero EUSI or both positive EUSI and EUPI.

Use of Information Economics

Information economics includes several factors that might limit its usefulness. First of all, it is an expected-value model. In any individual case, actual outcomes will take on one of the conditional values (monetary or utility). In some cases, the expected value is not a conditional value. This is true in the Olathe example where, for example, profits with an advertising program are expected to be either $80,000 with a strong market or $25,000 with a weak market while the expected value of advertising is $58,000. Thus, the model is best used when applied to many problems. In the long run, using expected values works out.

Second, there are some questions about obtaining the prior and conditional probabilities needed for several states of nature and actions. This gets into the whole question of eliciting probabilities covered in Chapter 1. In addition, some of the outcomes might be continuous in nature rather than being discrete (e.g., levels of sales). However, managers might be able to use several discrete points as approximations for a continuous distribution.

Third, the idea of Bayesian revision and all these mathematical symbols might be perceived by some managers as too complex to deal with. With the aid of electronic spreadsheets, the computational burden of this model is quite small.

Finally, there is some evidence that managers really do not act as strict Bayesians in revising probabilities. Instead of the precise revisions moving from prior to posterior probabilities, as illustrated in this chapter, research shows that managers revise probabilities more conservatively.[8] Thus, not

---

[7] Expected utility (EU) may be a better term than expected value at this point. Also, see Chapter 5 on learning curves for a discussion about log functions.

[8] See Robert H. Ashton, *Studies in Accounting Research #17: Human Information Processing in Accounting,* Sarasota, Fla.: American Accounting Association (1982), Chapter 5, and P. Slovik and S. Lichenstein, "Comparison of Bayesian and Regression Approaches to the Study of Information Processing in Judgment," *Organizational Behavior and Human Performance* (November 1971), pp. 649–744.

only may the model seem complex to a manager, but even the manager that understands the mathematics of the model may not put full faith in the results since he may subjectively revise the posterior probabilities differently from Bayesian posterior probabilities.

Even with the lack of full acceptance of the model and the inherent problems of using a model deemed "too complex" by managers, information economics is a strong foundation for providing a useful way to evaluate whether benefit exceeds cost in an information buying choice.

SUMMARY

Information economics is a way to operationalize the concept of whether the benefit from information exceeds the cost of obtaining it. The discussion started with the concept of agency theory, that there is a set of interdependencies among people (principals and agents) that affects the choice of information (as well as alternatives chosen as viable). The following material assumes either that we are dealing with the principal or that there is no difference in what information would be needed and how it would be used given either a principal or agent. Decision trees were reviewed as a basic framework for notation and the expected-value model. From there, we investigate the expected value of perfect and of sample information and Bayesian revision of probabilities. Finally, we look at the possible limitation to the information economics model.

As stated in the beginning of the chapter, this discussion is really part of developing various analytical models for decision making. While we might want to derive all the probabilities and values and use the information economics model as in the Olathe illustration, we might also want to use it in a more abstract way. First, there is a real trade-off between cost and benefit for information. Second, even if we do not fully operationalize this model, we can use the notion of Bayesian revision (taking prior knowledge, incorporating new information, and revising our thinking) in basic analyses. Perhaps this is the most valuable part of this discussion.

PROBLEMS AND CASES

8-1. Decision Trees (CMA)

Various quantitative business methods are referred to as operations research or management science techniques. Many of these mathematical or statistical techniques can be applied by the management accountant to aid in business analysis and decision making. Decision tree analysis is one such technique that has proved useful to the management accountant.

Required:

1. Describe the environment and the circumstances for which decision tree analysis would be an appropriate decision model.
2. For decision tree analysis:
   a. explain what a decision tree is, including a description of its component elements.
   b. identify the mathematical or statistical concepts employed in the model.
   c. explain how the decision model works.
3. Two decision rules used in decision analysis are the maximax criterion and the minimax regret criterion. For each of these two decision rules:
   a. define the decision rule.
   b. explain the circumstances under which each rule would be employed.
4. The expected value of perfect information is often calculated in conjunction with decision tree analysis. Explain what is meant by the expected value of perfect information.

8-2. Value of Perfect Information

Flagston Publishing generally has a press run of 100,000 copies of *The Weekly*, a newsmagazine. The managers have been wondering whether this is optimal and have amassed the following information about demand, which they believe will hold true for the future:

Demand	p(Demand)
60,000	0.20
80,000	0.30
100,000	0.30
120,000	0.20

The magazine sells for $2, and the variable cost to print it is $0.60. Unsold magazines are destroyed.

Required:

Set up a payoff table to determine the optimal strategy and determine the expected value of perfect information.

8-3. Order Strategy

The Durham Flower Shoppe sells corsages. Orders must be placed once a week and, once the order has been placed, no more can be ordered that week. Corsages cost $1.50 and are resold at $4.00. Unsold corsages are discarded. Demand seems about normally distributed with a mean of 2,500 and a standard deviation of 600.

Required:

1. In order to maximize profits, what is the optimal number of corsages to order each week?
2. Without making any additional calculations, answer the following questions:
   a. What would be the effect on the optimal order quantity if the purchase price increased, with the selling price remaining constant?

    b. What would be the effect on the optimal order quantity if the standard deviation of demand were more than 600 corsages?

    3. How is this problem different from, say, that of the manager of a high-school reunion who was deciding on an order quantity of corsages (same costs, prices, demand) for the 25th Reunion this spring?

8-4. Maintenance Costs (CMA)

Sandstone Company uses a process that moves hot sand on a rubber conveyor belt. The useful life of a belt is stochastic, normally distributed with a mean of 15 weeks and a standard deviation of two-and-one-half weeks. Sandstone has always had Service Firm Inc. replace the belt on this system when it fails. The cost is $3,500 per replacement.

Service Firm has proposed a new arrangement intended to reduce the number of emergency repairs for replacing the belt when it fails. The offer is to replace a belt after a predetermined number of weeks of use, even if it is still usable, at a $500 discount. Of course, if the belt fails between the preventive replacement interval period, it would still be replaced immediately but at the regular charge, i.e., the discount would not be allowed.

Bill Thompson, Sandstone's Production Manager, has been asked to recommend a preventive replacement interval that would minimize average weekly belt cost. As a basis for his analysis, Thompson assembled the information presented below.

The first column of the table shows the preventive replacement intervals (in weeks) under consideration. The "Mean Life" column shows that a shorter preventive replacement interval also reduces the average service life of a belt.

The "Probability" column gives the probability for each preventive replacement interval that a belt will actually be replaced before it fails (and the $500 discount will be earned).

Preventive Replacement Interval	Mean Life	Probability
15	14.0	0.500
16	14.4	0.345
17	14.7	0.212
18	14.8	0.115
19	14.9	0.055

Required:

1. Explain what costs Sandstone Company will have to compare when deciding upon an appropriate preventive maintenance program.

2. Calculate Sandstone Company's average weekly belt cost under the current program of replacing the conveyor belt when it fails.

3. Determine the preventive replacement interval that would offer Sandstone Company the lowest total weekly belt cost.

4. If Service Firm Inc. were to increase the discount it offers for preventive maintenance, would this tend to reduce or increase the optimal interval? Explain your answer.

8-5. Decision Trees: Utility and Opportunity Costs (CMA)

George Eaton, a financial analyst with the Marketing Division of Ajax Industries, has been asked to evaluate the distribution alternatives for a new product. Eaton obtains the aid of two knowledgeable market analysts in the division to estimate the possible net present value of the cash flows from the alternatives and to assess the probabilities of each possibility.

The alternatives being considered are immediate national distribution or regional distribution with national distribution to follow if it is economically feasible. The possible cash flows and the probabilities associated with each alternative are presented as follows:

	Net Present Value of Cash Flows (in Millions of Dollars)	Probability of Cash Flow
Immediate National Distribution Only:		
High national results	$+10.0	0.30
Medium national results	+ 2.0	0.40
Low national results	− 3.0	0.30
		1.00
Regional Distribution Only:		
Excellent regional results	$+ 2.0	0.40
Moderate regional results	+ 0.5	0.40
Poor regional results	− 1.0	0.20
		1.00
National Distribution Following Regional Distribution:		
National Distribution as a Consequence of Excellent Regional Results:		
High national results	$+ 9.0	0.70
Medium national results	+ 2.0	0.20
Low national results	− 2.7	0.10
		1.00
National Distribution as a Consequence of Moderate Regional Results:		
High national results	$+ 8.0	0.30
Medium national results	+ 1.8	0.40
Low national results	− 3.0	0.30
		1.00
National Distribution as a Consequence of Poor Regional Results:		
High national results	$+ 7.0	0.10
Medium national results	+ 1.5	0.30
Low national results	− 4.0	0.60
		1.00

Required:

1. Formulate the decision tree framework for analyzing whether Ajax Industries should use national distribution or regional distribution with national distribution

to follow. Identify the probabilities and expected cash flows for each branch in the tree.

2. Using the maximum expected value criteria for decision-making purposes, indicate whether Ajax Industries should select national distribution or regional distribution with national distribution to follow. Support your decision with appropriate calculations.

3. Suppose Ajax Industries is conservative (risk averse) and wishes to minimize the expected value of taking any loss in making its decision. Determine whether Ajax Industries should select national distribution or regional distribution with national distribution to follow. Support your decision with appropriate calculations.

4. George Eaton and his associates are aware that determination of cash flows and probabilities involve subjectivity. Therefore, if any of these values are significantly in error, the reliability of the decision tree analysis could be in doubt. Describe a method by which the management can evaluate the possible consequences of errors in the estimates.

8-6. Expected Value of Sample Information[9]

Susan Baginski, the owner of some commercial property, has been offered two rental contracts from the same prospective lessee. Each contract is for a year and the lessee would be responsible for all occupancy costs including utilities, building insurance, and property taxes.

The first contract is for $30,000 per year plus $50 per unit of product sold by the lessee. The other contract is for $70 per unit sold with no base rent. This prospect seems to be the only one interested in the space available. Recent overbuilding in the area has cut demand drastically for at least a year. For the sake of this analysis, assume that the sale of units in this one year is independent of sales in any other year.

Required:

1. Construct a payoff table for the above options assuming that there are two states of nature: demand of 1,200 units or demand of 2,000 units. The probabilities associated with each level of demand are 40 percent and 60 percent respectively. What is the better choice based on expected value optimization?

2. What is the cost of prediction error? That is, what is the cost of, say, accepting the zero base rent and $70 per unit and then finding out that demand is only 1,200 units? What is the cost of accepting $30,000 base rent and $50 per unit and then demand turning out to be 2,000 units? Construct a table reflecting the cost of prediction errors.

3. Find the expected value of perfect information. Can you find it using the original payoff table and again using the table of prediction errors?

---

[9] This problem is based on Williamson, "Pressing Information Economies to Students," *The Accounting Review* (April 1982), pp. 416–419.

4. Find the expected value of sample information given the following facts. A consultant with a track record of being correct 80 percent of the time offers to do some sampling for you at a cost of $800. Sampling will result in one of two reports:

Pessimistic report—demand will be 1,200 units
Optimistic report—demand will be 2,000 units

Will it be worthwhile paying the consultant $800 for the information? (*Hint:* carefully consider what the conditional probabilities are for each report, given each state of nature.)

8-7. Expected Utility

Robin Fran, a manager of a plant making car bumpers, must decide whether to accept a special order on an experimental bumper. The cost of producing this bumper is unknown, but, for ease of estimating, she thinks a full production run will cost either $450,000 or $600,000 depending on set-up and running time. The customer has offered a fixed-price contract of $500,000. A payoff table reflecting the monetary values and Fran's estimates of the probability of each cost occurring are as follows:

	Cost	
	$600,000	**$450,000**
Accept order	−100,000	50,000
Reject order	0	0
Probability of cost$_i$	0.30	0.70

Ms. Fran bases her decisions on expected utility based on the following utility function:

$$U(x) = 1 - e^{-x/100,000} \quad \text{where: } x \text{ is monetary outcome}$$

Required:
1. Should she accept or reject the special order? Justify your answer. If there is a conflict between your numerical results and your decision, resolve that conflict.
2. Donna Kitchen, a consultant, has offered to analyze data from other manufacturers before Fran makes her decision. Kitchen charges $5,000 for her services. Based on past work with Ms. Kitchen, Fran estimates that if she spends the $5,000 with Kitchen and Kitchen comes up with data indicating that current production costs will be significantly less than anticipated, she then regards the $600,000 cost as occurring with a probability of 0.10 and the $450,000 production cost occurring with a probability of 0.90. Her full set of probability assessments is summarized below.

	Cost	
	$600,000	$450,000
Conditional probability of event		
given report indicating low current production cost		
(probability = 0.25)	0.10	0.90
given report indicating normal current production cost		
(probability = 0.50)	0.30	0.70
given report indicating high current production cost		
(probability = 0.25)	0.70	0.30

Should Ms. Fran purchase the information from Ms. Kitchen? (*Hint*: Make sure to label the probabilities that you have been given to see what you have and where you must go. The solution may be easier than you think.)

3. Ms. Kitchen has been using Rune stones to help in her predictions and she offers to guarantee her projections with certainty (perfect information) if Fran is willing to pay her $15,000. What is the expected utility of perfect information?

8-8. Comprehensive Case[10]

Background The Plastics Division of the United Chemical Co. manufactures and sells a line of raw materials used by plastic converters in the fabrication of components for durable goods manufacture. The Plastics Division has three manufacturing plants that employ a two-step process using 39 production lines. They manufacture 4,000 final products (grade/color combinations) for sale to 3,600 customers. Figure 1 describes the production facilities.

There are significant differences among the various production lines. Some grades of products can only be produced on certain lines. There are differences in equipment capacity which dictate the run size that is most efficient in each line (see Figure 2 for run size/cost relationships for the range of equipment sizes). These differences in the production lines require constant monitoring by production scheduling in order to match the mix and volume of sales orders with the production capabilities to achieve the most economic production results. The Plastics Division uses a standard cost system for evaluating the performance of the production facilities.

The financial reports being routinely prepared for use by division management currently include:

1. Income statement, balance sheet, and cash flow statement for the division as a whole.
2. Standard cost performance reports for manufacturing.

Upon special request, individual product-cost estimates are made. These estimates are usually used in pricing considerations.

---

[10] This problem is used by permission of the Institute of Management Accountants.

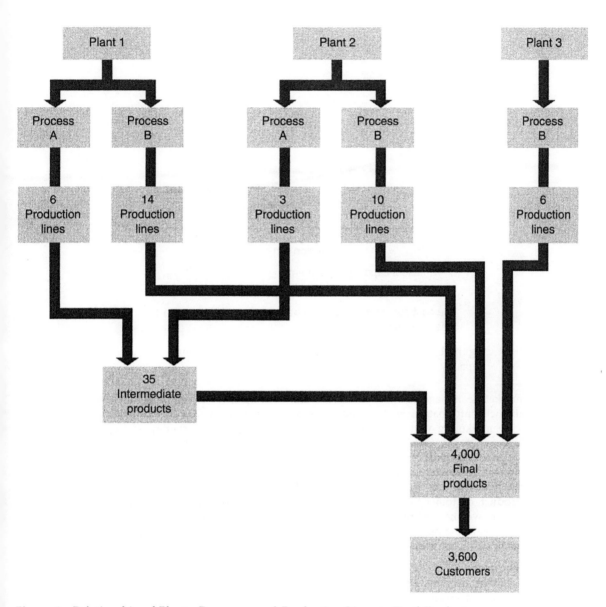

Figure 1   Relationship of Plants, Processes, and Production Lines to Final Products

The Current Environment   The division has grown rapidly in the past several years. Consequently, the business has become more complex because of the large number of customers, products, and production lines. The marketing department views the market (3,600 customers) as being made up of 5 major segments and 20 subsegments.

The controller, Bill Brown, has observed that the decisions being made by the manufacturing manager are quite different from the decisions required of the

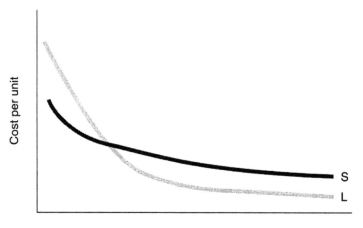

Production run size

S = Smallest capacity equipment
L = Largest capacity equipment

The cost curves for all other production lines fall between these two extremes.

Figure 2   Cost as a Function of Run Size and Equipment Capacity

marketing manager. Brown concluded that the different decisions require different financial information. He believed that through financial analysis his staff could provide marketing with data that could be used to guide marketing strategy and improve the profitability of the division. Brown observed that the lowest unit selling price of a product was about 30 percent of the division's highest priced product, and that the lowest unit cost was about 25 percent of the highest unit cost. He therefore reasoned that there must be a wide variation in profitability from product to product, customer to customer, and transaction to transaction. He concluded that a system was needed that would clearly define the profitability of each sale in order to provide the basis for marketing emphasis and pricing. But significant questions remained in his mind.

Required:
1. What are the critical information needs of (a) the marketing manager, (b) the manufacturing manager, and (c) the general manager?
2. How should a profitability analysis system use standard cost data?
3. How should a profitability analysis system be different from a manufacturing performance measurement system since they both use cost data?
4. What technique can be used in profitability analysis to digest and communicate the large amounts of data that constitute the individual transactions?

Chapter 9

Variances—An Expanded Treatment

Recently, a survey of controllers of manufacturing companies was conducted to determine the changes that have occurred in the past five years in the size of the smallest accounting unit covered by regularly available variance reports, the frequency with which these reports are issued, the number of variance accounts used, and the policy for investigating variances. The survey shows that companies now use smaller reporting units, issue reports more frequently, use more variance accounts, and have increasingly formalized exception procedures for both raw materials and direct labor. The survey suggests a trend toward disaggregated data. This indicates that the use of variance analysis is increasing.[1]

---

[1] Bruce R. Gaumnitz and Felix P. Kollaritsch, "Manufacturing Variances: Current Practice and Trends," *Journal of Cost Management* (New York: Warren, Gorham, & Lamont, Spring 1991), p. 64.

The financial data and management information generated by a cost accounting department is the result of a large data collection and internal control structure consisting of:

- Product and operation structures including engineering standards.
- Cost structures made up of material, labor, and overhead components.
- Inventory structures composed of multiple levels, categories, and locations.
- Transaction structures for recording of material movement and resource usage.
- Reporting structures for investigating variances, analyzing costs, and controlling inventory.

This infrastructure is often viewed as a constraining factor by line management in a manufacturing organization. A traditional interpretation of responsibility for internal controls can add layers of paperwork, cost, and inflexibility, which can in turn prevent an organization from responding rapidly to changing competitive and technological conditions.[2]

Traditional variance analysis is based on the use of standard costs and how actual results differ from standards. In a more generic sense, variances are measures that management can use to evaluate how results compare to some benchmark, to provide clues on areas that might be investigated, and possibly, to give managers a starting point for taking adaptive and corrective action. The two quotations that begin this chapter show us that on one hand the use of variances (based on a standard cost system) seems as strong as it ever was. In contrast, Walden, in the second quotation, points to some limitations in basic standard cost variances and his article suggests some improvements in how we accumulate, analyze, and present variance information. Others argue that the notion of standard costs (and, therefore, standard cost variances) is counterproductive since it focuses attention on a fixed

[2] Steven Walden, "Beyond the Variance: Cost Accounting Challenges for the 1990s," in Barry J. Brinker ed., *Emerging Practices in Cost Management* (New York: Warren, Gorham, & Lamont, 1990), pp. 181–182.

standard rather than continuous improvement. However, even with the various views on the efficacy of standards and on details of how information is to be gathered, analyzed, and communicated, the use of variances continues. As with other parts of management accounting, managers want to look at how the notion of variance analysis can be modified to fit their own circumstances and needs. For variance calculation, analysis, and reporting, that means going beyond the use of standard costs as the sole norm for comparison.

This chapter looks at both production and marketing variances. We start with a one-product company and then expand into multiple products for a more realistic environment. We go beyond the traditional standard cost variances to look at controllable versus uncontrollable variances and at what happens when standards change. A framework for choosing the level of aggregation of variances to calculate is suggested and, finally, we discuss how to choose to report variances to different levels of management.

VARIANCES: ESTABLISHING AN APPROPRIATE BASIS FOR COMPARISON

Traditional variance analysis (which is reviewed in the next section) is based on comparing actual results to those based on standard costs. Standards are developed based on engineering standards, past experience, statistical analysis, and management judgment. In most companies, standards are set at the beginning of the year and are used over the course of the year. Standards for variable costs involve both input costs (e.g., the cost per hundredweight of paper used in printing) and an input-output relationship (e.g., expected quantity of paper to be used for each 1,000 forms printed). As we review, standard cost variances can incorporate differences caused by, say, a permanent change in the market price of an input, a change in mix of inputs used, and other items related to either *changes of standards* or *uncontrollable changes*. However, the yardstick for comparison is still a fixed standard, even if it is amended to include changes or other factors.

At the other end of the spectrum is the notion of looking at continuous improvement. This idea is at the heart of much of current management thinking and practice. Standard costs are criticized as being fixed for a year. Anything better than standard is considered "favorable." Thus, if a manager could show the same favorable variance month after month, she would be rewarded under a standard cost system. However, a static favorable variance means that there is no continuous improvement going on; the manager has found a way to get an ongoing constant improvement but has moved no further.

In order to promote continuous improvement, managers might use some form of actual costs as a basis for comparison. Actual costs for the prior month might be modified for any unusual occurrences or costs and then used as the "standard" for the next month. A rolling average of actual costs over, say, three to six months is another basis.

Finally, not all bases for comparison need be in monetary form. Since companies are experiencing a rising percentage of fixed costs and with the advent of activity-based costing, managers can look at standards for transactions for various cost pools. These bases might either be standards or past experience.

The main point here is that each company should establish relevant bases for comparison. Current use of inputs and creation of outputs can be compared to these bases and managers can create meaningful variances to be used for the purposes outlined at the beginning of the chapter. With this in mind, the next section is a review of standard cost production variances. Even though the discussion is based on using standard costs, it does not take too much to amend the ideas to incorporate actual costs as an ever-evolving standard.

STANDARD COST PRODUCTION VARIANCES—A REVIEW

Standard cost variances usually assume that direct material, direct labor, and variable overhead costs are all variable production costs. Fixed production costs are confined to fixed manufacturing overhead for variance analysis. As we discussed earlier in the book, many companies are finding that labor is more of a fixed than a variable cost. However, this basic division of variable and fixed costs is still useful for many companies both here and abroad and provides a starting place for a review of standard cost production variances.

Standards

As discussed above, standard variable costs consist of the cost of the input factor times the standard quantity expected to achieve some output level. Thus, if labor is paid $15 per hour and it is expected to take two hours of labor to produce 100 units, the standard variable cost for direct labor would be $30 per 100 units or $0.30 per unit of output. These same kinds of standards for input costs and input use needed to achieve a level of output would be established for all variable costs.

Fixed cost standards are based on a period of time and not on units of production. By definition, fixed costs will not change as units change (within a relevant range of quantity and time). Therefore, managers can establish a standard (plan or budget) for fixed costs for a period like a year. At its most basic level, then, actual fixed costs for a period can be compared to the budget for that period.

For product costing for financial accounting, managers must assign a portion of fixed manufacturing costs to the cost of each unit produced. With standard absorption costing, budgeted fixed costs for a period are divided by some budgeted denominator activity (e.g., machine hours, number of set-ups), which eventually leads to a fixed-cost-per-unit figure. Since companies produce various types of products that may use differing amounts of a relevant input factor (such as machine hours), that input factor is often the denominator. Thus, if budgeted fixed costs are $500,000 per year and it is expected that 50,000 standard machine hours would be used in the year, the fixed overhead rate is $10 per standard machine hour. If a product used four standard machine hours per 100 units, this would translate to an allocation of fixed costs of $40 per 100 units or $0.40 per unit produced.

This example assumes a single basis for assigning overhead. Under activity-based costing (ABC) there can be multiple bases and overhead should be assigned by tracing costs as much as possible. However, even with ABC, there will be common costs that might be assigned (or will be assigned under full costing) using some single or multiple basis. Our discussion of variances could be made more complex by incorporating such multiple drivers, but the analysis would not be measurably improved. Therefore, a single activity is used.

Variable Cost Variances

Variable cost variances for one-input (or multiple inputs where the inputs are not interchangeable) examples can be divided into material, direct labor, and variable overhead variances. Within each one of these input variances, managers can calculate variances caused by differences in standard versus actual cost of the input factor and by differences in standard versus actual use of the input factor to achieve a given output. The first of these variances is called a *price, rate,* or *spending variance* for material, labor, and variable overhead, respectively. The second is called a *use* and/or *efficiency variance*.

There is a basic difference in the way these two variances are derived. The price, rate, or spending variance is based on the actual amount of input purchased (material) or used (labor). The price variance is the difference between the actual amount paid and the standard amount that should have been paid for that quantity. If a firm buys 35,000 gallons of a raw material for $73,000, a material price variance is the difference between $73,000 and how much should have been paid for those 35,000 gallons. If the standard cost per input (per gallon) is $2, then the total standard cost for 35,000 gallons is $70,000; there is therefore a $3,000 unfavorable material price variance. It is important to note that all variances calculated are evaluated (favorable or unfavorable) on how those variances affect profits.

Since the price, rate, or spending variance relates to inputs purchased, there is no need to know outputs achieved for these variances. In contrast, the use and efficiency variances ask the following question: Given the output produced, were the actual inputs more or less than the standard inputs for that level of production? For example, if standards called for $\frac{1}{2}$ gallon of raw material per unit of product and 3,000 units were produced, standard raw material use for that level of production would be 1,500 gallons. If more were used, then an unfavorable material use variance would occur; if less were used, then there would be a favorable variance.

Variance Formulas   It is important to derive the basic logic of variances before reviewing variable cost variance formulas. These formulas are just shorthand for the basic understanding developed above.

$$\text{price/rate/spending: } V_p = (\text{Actual Price} - \text{Standard Price})$$
$$\times \text{ Actual Quantity}$$
$$= (AP - SP)AQ$$
$$\text{use/efficiency: } V_e = (\text{Actual Quantity} - \text{Standard}$$
$$\text{Quantity}) \times \text{Standard Price}$$
$$= (AQ - SQ)SP$$

An Illustration   Exhibit 9-1 shows some standard cost data and actual production information for the Mundy Company.

Exhibit 9-1
Mundy Corporation
Standard Cost Information

	Per Unit
Standard Costs:	
Material—.3 lbs @ $10 per lb	$ 3.00
Direct labor—.2 hrs @ $12 per hr	2.40
Variable overhead—@ $15 per DLH	3.00
Fixed overhead—@ $50 per DLH[a]	10.00
	$18.40
Actual Costs and Use—April, 19X6:	
Material purchased:	$ 44,000 (4,000 lbs)
Material used:	2,900 lbs
Direct labor:	$ 23,000 (1,900 DLH)
Variable overhead:	$ 27,550
Fixed overhead:	$150,000
Production:	10,000 units

[a]Fixed overhead allocation is based on annual fixed overhead of $1,500,000 and 30,000 budgeted annual direct labor hours.

Variable standard cost variances, based on that information, are as follows:

Material

$$\text{Price:}^3 \ \$44,000 - (4,000 \text{ lbs} \times \$10) = \$4,000 \ U$$

or, to be consistent with the variance formulas:

$$\text{Price: } [(\$44,000/4,000) - \$10] \times 4,000 = \$4,000 \ U$$
$$\text{Use: } [2,900 \text{ lbs} - (10,000 \text{ units} \times .3 \text{ lbs})] \times \$10 = 1,000 \ F$$

Direct Labor

$$\text{Rate: } \$23,000 - (1,900 \text{ hrs @ } \$12) = 200 \ U$$

or,

$$[(\$23,000/1,900) - \$12] \times 1,900 = 200 \ U$$
$$\text{Efficiency: } [1,900 \text{ hrs} - (10,000 \text{ units} \times .2 \text{ hrs})] \times \$12 = 1,200 \ F$$

Variable Overhead

$$\text{Spending: } \$27,550 - (1,900 \text{ hrs} \times \$15) = 950 \ F$$

or,

$$[(\$27,550/1,900) - \$15] \times 1,900 = 950 \ F$$
$$\text{Efficiency: } [1,900 \text{ hrs} - (10,000 \text{ units} \times .2 \text{ hrs})] \times \$15 = 1,500 \ F$$

Since the variable overhead is applied based on direct labor hours, the variable overhead efficiency variance is really determined by labor efficiency. While managers can break out different labor and variable overhead efficiency variances, they are caused by the same thing: in this example, a savings of labor time.

Fixed Cost Variances

Fixed manufacturing overhead variances fall into two general categories: budget and application. The fixed overhead budget variance is the difference between the fixed overhead incurred in a period and the budgeted fixed overhead for that period. Units are irrelevant to this calculation. For April, Mundy's managers would want to know the difference between the $150,000 actually incurred and the budget for April (some portion of the annual budget of $1,500,000). If, say, the budget for April were $155,000, then the fixed overhead budget variance would be:

---

[3] In material price variances, it is usual that material purchased is used as the actual quantity. For material use variances, actual material used in production is appropriate as actual quantity.

$$\begin{aligned}
\text{Fixed Overhead Budget Variance} &= \text{Actual Fixed Overhead} - \text{Budgeted Fixed} \\
&\quad \text{Overhead} \\
&= \$150,000 - \$155,000 \\
&= \$5,000 \ F
\end{aligned}$$

The *fixed overhead application variance* (also called the *fixed overhead volume* or *denominator variance*) is the difference between the lump sum of fixed overhead budgeted for a period and fixed overhead applied to the units produced in that period. Mundy's fixed overhead application variance would be:

$$\$155,000 - (10,000 \text{ units} \times \$10 \text{ per unit}) = \$55,000 \ U$$

This means that production for that period is below the amount that would have been predicted based on budgeted fixed overhead. This is a good example of a place where financial accounting seems to have invaded a management accounting function. The application variance in this case is the difference between a predicted 15,500 units ($155,000 budget divided by $10 per unit fixed overhead) and the actual production of 10,000 units. This difference of 5,500 units is multiplied by the $10 per unit fixed overhead. In this and many cases, management might have a difficult time interpreting this variance. Perhaps it would be useful to find out what percentage of capacity is consumed by 10,000 units. Also, it might be good to ascertain the level of production that was budgeted for April. These pieces of information will help in the use of this variance. This is another illustration of the problem of trying to connect a fixed-cost-per-unit figure with lump sum fixed overhead. In most cases, the incurring of the $155,000 in fixed manufacturing cost has little to do with the level of production achieved in a particular month. Managers should investigate whether fixed overhead application variances are useful in any setting other than financial accounting, where there is a need to link actual costs to standard costs through the variance-calculation process.

CHANGE OF STANDARDS VARIANCES

As was stated at the outset, variances are only as good as the data recorded and the standards used for comparison. Much in the same way that confusion can take place with inadequate information regarding a variance (like the fixed overhead application variance above), there can be misleading variances when standards in use are not the most current. For this reason, most large computer-based product costing systems incorporate a *change of standards variance*. Say that Mundy's management finds out that material prices have changed on world markets and that instead of expecting to pay

$10 per pound, prices have now leveled off at $9 per pound. If variances were calculated based on the $10 figure, both the material price and material use variances would be incorrect.

Many managers do not want simply to change the material cost on their standard cost records. They may have approved annual budgets and want to be able to tie actual performance to those budgets. By incorporating change of standards variances along with other variances they can both create useful material variances, using the updated price for raw materials, and have a way to tie actual performance with their original budget standard. In this example, the change of standards variance would be valued at $1 per pound for all pounds bought and all pounds used.

This is a good place to begin to discuss the idea of disaggregation of variance information. In the example above, the two material variances[4] were

Price

$$\$44,000 - (4,000 \text{ lbs} \times \$10) = \$4,000 \ U$$

Use

$$[2,900 \text{ lbs} - (10,000 \text{ units} \times .3 \text{ lbs})] \times \$10 = \$1,000 \ F$$

Both of these are based on the old standard of $10 per pound. We can now relabel these variances as the total material price and the total material use variances. They can be disaggregated to include a change of standards variance as follows:

Price

$$\text{Current Price } \$44,000 - (4,000 \text{ lbs} \times \$9) = \$8,000 \ U$$
$$\text{Change of Standards } 4,000 \text{ lbs} \times (\$10 - \$9) = 4,000 \ F$$

Use

$$\text{Current Use } [2,900 \text{ lbs} - (10,000 \text{ units} \times .3 \text{ lbs})] \times \$9 = 900 \ F$$
$$\text{Change of Standards } [2,900 \text{ lbs} - (10,000 \text{ units} \times .3 \text{ lbs})] \times \$1 = 100 \ F$$

While the sum of these variances equals the unadjusted variances derived before, the disaggregated variances give more useful information than the aggregated ones. In this illustration of materials, the change of standards variances for price and use are based on different quantities. Management can combine the two variances, but they would make more sense as separate variance items.

Many computer programs allow an even broader set of options for managers in variance calculation. Besides original standards and current standards, managers can specify estimating standards (which may differ

---

[4] Alternate ways to calculate variances are shown throughout this chapter. It is limiting just to use the formulas in a fixed manner. Each alternate calculation yields the same result: the algebra is just rearranged.

from standards used to evaluate manufacturing performance). Standards are a basis for pricing. Estimating standards are set up based on how the job was bid. It is possible that the machinery figured in for a job was not used due to scheduling or other problems. Thus, the production standard for a job may differ significantly from the estimating standard. As with change of standards variances, using either production standards or estimating standards must be based on the relevance of the resulting variances.

CONTROLLABLE AND UNCONTROLLABLE VARIANCES

One of the key aspects of variance analysis, reporting, and use is to distinguish between variances that a manager could have avoided and those that could not be avoided. In a sense, the change of standards variance is an uncontrollable variance. If the market changes or if technology changes so that standards need to be revised, the manager has little control over variances that result from such shifts.

Uncertain Costs

We can extend the discussion from Chapter 7 on uncertainty and various cost estimates to derive a measure of controllable and uncontrollable variances under conditions of uncertainty. Let us say that a manager has estimated the cost for materials for a product. If there is uncertainty, the manager may have assigned probabilities to various cost estimates and, as a result, calculated an expected value and a standard deviation for costs. Similar estimates can be made for all elements of cost that pertain to the production of a product. Using these expected values, the manager makes decisions about how much of a product to produce and what cost components to employ to manufacture the product. If a manager is faced with limited resources, the costs and resulting contribution margins for various products may comprise the objective function in a linear program to find an optimal mix of products.

If the manager estimates incorrectly, then there is a variance. If the nature of the cost distribution changed between the original estimate and the actual production, then we have the same sort of problem outlined above in a change of standards variance. The difference is that we are dealing with a distribution of values instead of a single, certain value.

As an illustration, assume that a firm has a normal distribution of material costs with a mean of $150 and a standard deviation of $6 for its single product. Managers have derived this estimate through a survey of market conditions and prices. At this point, assume all other costs are certain. While this is a simplification of reality, it does no harm to the example. If the costs really are $150, then the firm plans to produce 5,000 units with the following results (all revenues and costs are assumed):

	Per Unit
Revenue	$500
Material	150
Labor	50
Overhead	200

$100 per unit × 5,000 units = $500,000

If material prices fall within the range estimated by management, there is a 95 percent confidence interval that profits[5] will be $100 ± (1.96 × $6) or from $88.24 to $111.76 per unit. Assume, however, that the nature of the distribution changed so that a new assessment of material cost would yield a mean of $200 and a standard deviation of $10. What has occurred is an error in forecasting. A new 95 percent confidence interval would yield a mean profit of $50 and a range of profits from $30.40 to $69.60. If management had had this information in advance, they could have investigated other pricing strategies, other production quantities, and/or other inputs. This will be illustrated below. In this case, not only has the mean of profits dropped to $50 ($100 less additional material costs of $50) but also the range of profits has become wider with a larger standard deviation for material costs. We can call this change in costs (and, therefore, profits) a *forecasting variance*. If management had been able to react to this shift in costs, perhaps it would have made a series of decisions that would have yielded a profit with a mean greater then $50. If so, then there was an opportunity cost associated with the change in costs, and a variance associated with this opportunity cost would also be calculated.

The ideas of *change of standards* and *forecasting* variances can be somewhat combined by referring to *ex-post variance analysis* as proposed by Demski.[6] Much as the previous example involves a specification of an original and a revised probability distribution for some or all the factors affecting costs, the Demski model relies on a prespecified model. In Chapter 6, linear programming solutions were proposed to maximize profits by producing an optimal mix of products given contribution margins for the products and constraints on productive capacity. The Demski model is based on a linear programming formulation as a basis for production decisions. As we saw in Chapter 6, if, say, a cost related to one product changed, a new solution could

---

[5] It is deliberate that the words "overhead" and "profit" are used. This may lead to some ambiguity about whether fixed overhead is included so that "profit" is really contribution margin. There is some controversy about the need to include fixed overhead per unit in unit costs used for planning and control. It would be especially appropriate to do so in a machine-intensive environment where overhead is applied based on units of production and/or some other causal variables.

[6] See Joel Demski, "An Accounting System Structured on a Linear Programming Model," *The Accounting Review* (October 1967), pp. 701–712.

call for a different mix of products and use of resources if the contribution margin for that product went above or below the boundaries specified in sensitivity analysis.

As an illustration, Onza Corporation is evaluating how to use its productive capacity during the next month. Based on data from marketing, production, and accounting, a linear programming problem was set up and solved as shown in Exhibit 9-2. Of the three products that could be manufactured, the linear programming solution calls for 6,000 Product A and 16,000 Product C, yielding a total contribution margin of $820,000. Let us assume that the cost of materials for Product A goes up $3 after the decision has been made and the production started. As can be seen from the sensitivity analysis in Exhibit 9-2, if the contribution margin for Product A falls by more than $2.50, then a new optimal solution is called for. This solution is shown in Exhibit 9-3.

The new solution calls for (about) 4,667 Product A, 1,000 B, and 15,667 C for a total contribution margin of $802,667. Unfortunately, management of Onza has already committed their resources and efforts to the original solution. The unforeseen change in price came too late for them to make a change. Given the change in material costs, the best that management could have achieved would be $802,000 (the original optimal contribution margin less $18,000 for the additional $3 per unit in variable costs for Product A). The difference between the budgeted contribution margin of $820,000 and the revised *ex-post optimal budget* of $802,000 is $18,000. This unfavorable difference can be termed a *forecasting variance.* It was uncontrollable in that management was faced with an ex-post fact to deal with and could not alter its actions in time.[7] However, a comparison can also be made between the actual contribution margin achieved and the ex-post optimal budgeted contribution margin. Assume that Onza achieved an actual contribution margin of $795,000. The $7,000 unfavorable difference between actual and ex-post budget is called an *opportunity cost* variance. Since $802,000 is the best that management could have achieved given the change of costs, that is the relevant yardstick for measurement.

Note that management could not really use the solution in Exhibit 9-3 as a measure of comparison. At an appropriate point, they committed their production to 6,000 Product A and 16,000 C. Thus, while it would have been optimal to use the solution suggested in Exhibit 9-3, it was not possible. The $667 difference between $802,000 that could be achieved given the original production decision and $802,667 as suggested in Exhibit 9-3 is also an opportunity cost to the company but not formally set out in this variance analysis.

---

[7] This does not imply that managers should not be held responsible for being poor forecasters.

Exhibit 9-2
Onza Corporation
Original Budget—Optimal Solution

```
MAX      30  PRODA + 50 PRODB + 40 PRODC
SUBJECT TO
         2)   PRODA + 3 PRODB + 2 PRODC <=   39000
         3)   PRODA + 2 PRODB + 2 PRODC <=   38000
         4)  2 PRODA + 3PRODB +  PRODC   <=   28000
END

LP OPTIMUM FOUND AT STEP 2

         OBJECTIVE FUNCTION VALUE

1)            820000.000

VARIABLE           VALUE          REDUCED COST
   PRODA       6000.000000            .000000
   PRODB          .000000           3.333332
   PRODC      16000.000000            .000000

    ROW    SLACK OR SURPLUS      DUAL PRICES
     2)       1000.000000            .000000
     3)          .000000          16.666670
     4)          .000000           6.666667

NO. ITERATIONS = 2

RANGES IN WHICH THE BASIS IS UNCHANGED:

                        OBJ COEFFICIENT RANGES
VARIABLE          CURRENT          ALLOWABLE          ALLOWABLE
                  COEF             INCREASE           DECREASE
   PRODA      30.000000          50.000000          2.499999
   PRODB      50.000000           3.333332          INFINITY
   PRODC      40.000000          20.000000          9.999995

                        RIGHTHAND SIDE RANGES
    ROW           CURRENT          ALLOWABLE          ALLOWABLE
                  RHS              INCREASE           DECREASE
     2        39000.000000         INFINITY        1000.000000
     3        38000.000000       1000.000000       24000.000000
     4        28000.000000      48000.000000        9000.000000
```

Exhibit 9-3
Onza Corporation
Revised Solution—New Cost Data

```
MAX      27 PRODA + 50 PRODB + 40 PRODC
SUBJECT TO
       2)      PRODA + 3 PRODB + 2 PRODC <= 39000
       3)      PRODA + 2 PRODB + 2 PRODC <= 38000
       4)    2 PRODA + 3 PRODB +   PRODC <= 28000
END

LP OPTIMUM FOUND AT STEP 1

          OBJECTIVE FUNCTION VALUE

   1)          802666.600

VARIABLE          VALUE           REDUCED COST
   PRODA       4666.667000           .000000
   PRODB       1000.000000           .000000
   PRODC      15666.670000           .000000

     ROW    SLACK OR SURPLUS      DUAL PRICES
     2)          .000000            .666666
     3)          .000000          17.000000
     4)          .000000           4.666667

NO. ITERATIONS= 1

RANGES IN WHICH THE BASIS IS UNCHANGED:

                          OBJ COEFFICIENT RANGES
VARIABLE          CURRENT          ALLOWABLE          ALLOWABLE
                  COEF             INCREASE           DECREASE
   PRODA       27.000000            .500000           7.000001
   PRODB       50.000000          17.000000            .666666
   PRODC       40.000000           1.999998          17.000000

                          RIGHTHAND SIDE RANGES
     ROW        CURRENT          ALLOWABLE          ALLOWABLE
                RHS              INCREASE           DECREASE
     2      39000.000000        3500.000000        1000.000000
     3      38000.000000        1000.000000        4666.667000
     4      28000.000000       47000.000000        7000.000000
```

Thus, in summary, the following are the relationships formulating the forecasting and opportunity cost variances:

forecasting variance = (Budgeted contribution margin − Ex-post contribution margin)

opportunity cost variance = (Ex-post contribution margin − Actual contribution margin)

Managers must be careful to investigate the cause of all significant variances. Even though the forecasting variance is defined as uncontrollable and the opportunity cost as controllable, this is not always the case. The delineation outlined above assumes that the managers committed the firm's resources and, therefore, the forecasting variance was out of their control. However, many times a manager has the time to react given a change. This adjustment may go all the way or only partially toward a revised optimum called for by the new information. Therefore, while we can nominally assign a variance as under or not under the control of a manager, this labeling should be investigated.

Overhead Variances

In the CPA Examination, the AICPA has also applied the term *uncontrollable variance* to the fixed manufacturing overhead application variance. As we discussed, this variance is caused by how overhead is applied and does not really relate to how a manager controls costs. Exhibit 9-4 presents a schedule of overhead variances based on the information developed before on the Mundy Company that not only differentiates between controllable and

Exhibit 9-4
Disaggregation of Overhead Variances

	4-way	3-Way	2-Way	1-Way
Variable Overhead	Efficiency $1,500 *F*	Efficiency $1,500 *F*	Controllable $6,450 *F*	
	Spending $950 *F*			
		Spending $5,950 *F*		Total $48,550 *U*
	Budget $5,000 *F*			
Fixed Overhead				
	Application $55,000 *U*	Application $55,000 *U*	Application $55,000 *U*	

uncontrollable variances but also extends our discussion about disaggregating variances. In the four-way analysis of overhead variances, managers have the fully disaggregated information of the four separate overhead variances. When overhead costs are recorded in total and there is no differentiation between actual fixed and actual variable overhead incurred, three-way analysis of variance is common. Note that information is lost with each level of aggregation. In order to evaluate performance to take proper action, managers may need the more disaggregated information. Compression into a two-way analysis yields the term *controllable* for the aggregation of the two variable overhead variances and the fixed overhead spending variance. The application variance is, by implication, uncontrollable.

Managers may very well want to disaggregate overhead variances on a different basis. First, as discussed above, the application variance has little or no use for planning and control decisions. Thus, managers may want to delete this variance from their reports. In addition, rather than using the formal variance labels (e.g., variable overhead efficiency variance), managers may want to break overhead down into a line-by-line comparison of actual costs versus budget. This is probably the most meaningful way to disaggregate overhead items. Special attention can be paid to both big individual costs and large differences between actual and planned costs.

MARKETING VARIANCES

The discussion to this point has involved how profits are affected when production costs for a product differ from standard. Profits are also affected by changes in sales price and sales volume. As with production variances, marketing variances can be presented in a summary form (aggregated) or can be disaggregated. In addition, we can also move from the one-product company to a multi-product firm.

Single-Product Firm

If a company has but one product, then there can be two marketing variances: *sales price variance* and *sales volume variance*. These variances are similar to the two basic variable cost variances. Since marketing variances are designed to reflect changes in profits caused by changes in selling price and/or sales volume from budget, managers use contribution margin where costs are held at standard. This is especially important in the sales volume variance since, as is shown below, costs would cancel themselves out in the sales price variance. Thus, the two single-product marketing variances are:

Sales Price Variance = (actual price − budgeted price) × actual quantity
sold

Sales Volume Variance = (actual quantity sold − budgeted quantity sold)
× budgeted contribution margin

Multi-Product Companies

When a firm has more than one product, then the sales volume variance can be broken down into two pieces: *sales mix* and *sales volume*. For example, assume that the Sylvia Company produces two products with prices, costs, and volume as follows:

	Planned	Actual
Product A		
Sales price per unit	$30	$25
Production cost per unit	17	
Sales volume	100,000 units	114,000 units
Product B		
Sales price per unit	$10	$15
Production cost per unit	3	
Sales volume	100,000 units	76,000 units

Several observations can be made before a manager calculates various marketing variances. First, plans called for a total of 200,000 units to be sold with a 50/50 mix between the two products. Second, Product A sold at a price lower than expected while Product B sold at a price higher than budget. Third, only 190,000 units were sold and proportionately more Product A was sold than Product B (114,000/190,000 = 60 percent Product A). As a summary, then, we expect an unfavorable volume variance, a mix variance reflecting the change from plans, and sales price variances reflecting both favorable and unfavorable results. The actual variances are shown in Exhibit 9-5.

Exhibit 9-5
Two-Product Case Sales Variances

Actual Volume Actual Price Actual Mix Budgeted Cost	Actual Volume Budgeted Price Actual Mix Budgeted Cost	Actual Volume Budgeted Price Budgeted Mix Budgeted Cost	Budgeted Volume Budgeted Price Budgeted Mix Budgeted Cost
114,000 ($25 − $17) + 76,000 ($15 − $3) = $1,824,000	114,000 ($30 − $17) + 76,000 ($10 − $3) = $2,014,000	95,000 ($30 − $17) + 95,000 ($10 − $3) = $1,900,000	100,000 ($30 − $17) 100,000 ($10 − $3) = $2,000,000

Sales Price Variance
$V_p = \$190,000\ U$

Sales Mix Variance
$V_m = \$114,000\ F$

Sales Volume Variance
$V_v = \$100,000\ U$

In this disaggregated form, management has calculated three variances:

Sales price variance	$190,000 Unfavorable
Sales mix variance	114,000 Favorable
Sales volume variance	100,000 Unfavorable
Total	$176,000 Unfavorable

One more stage of disaggregation can be added here by dividing the sales price variance into its two components: $570,000 U for Product A and $380,000 F for Product B. Note how much information is hidden by the summarizing of these two parts into one sales price variance. Aggregation tends to lose information.

As explained above, management could aggregate the volume and mix variances into one part using weighted average contribution margins as follows:

budgeted weighted average contribution margin = (.5 × $13) + (.5 × $7) = $10

and

sales price variance	= $1,824,000 − (190,000 × $10) =	$76,000 U
sales volume variance =	(200,000 − 190,000) × $10 =	100,000 U
Total		$176,000 U

While the total of the variances is the same ($176,000 unfavorable), note the difference in the variances not only in numbers but also in usefulness to managers. The major shortcoming of the combined variances is the anomaly of using the weighted average contribution margin of $10 when the mix has changed from 50/50 to 60/40. This throws all the calculations out of synch.

There is a question as to whether a weighted average contribution margin really has much use in sales mix and sales volume variances. Note that the mix variance is favorable if the actual mix of products sold has a greater percentage of products with higher contribution margins. Thus, with an actual mix of 60/40 instead of 50/50, our illustration shows a favorable sales mix variance since Product A has a higher contribution margin than Product B. It has been suggested by Peles[8] and others that our notion of marketing variances relies on the independence of prices and quantities. We segment our analysis as if raising the price does not affect volume sold. In most situations, this is not realistic. Thus, it is to our advantage to keep as many details available in our variance analysis so that (1) variances are not obscured or washed out by one another and (2) enough detail exists so that interdependence can be tracked and analyzed.

---

[8] Yorem C. Peles, "A Note on Yield Variance and Mix Variance," *The Accounting Review* (April 1986), pp. 325–329.

Market Size and Market Share Variances

We can further divide the sales variances into two components reflecting changes in market size and in market share. This ties in with the discussion of controllable and uncontrollable variances above. First, if the market for a firm expands, then, assuming that the company's market share remains constant, we would expect a favorable sales volume variance. However, if the firm did not cause the market to rise, then this is an uncontrollable variance. Second, no matter what the overall market does, the firm should assess whether its marketing department gained in market share. Thus, these two variances can be defined as follows:

market size variance = (actual total market volume − budgeted total market volume) × budgeted market share × budgeted contribution margin

market share variance = (actual market share − budgeted market share) × actual total market volume × budgeted contribution margin

In a two-product case, there can be market share and market size variances for both products separately. Assume the following for Sylvia's Products A and B:

	Product A	Product B
Budgeted total market volume	1,000,000	1,000,000
Actual total market volume	950,000	800,000
Budgeted market share	10%	10%
Actual market share[a]	12%	9.5%
Budgeted contribution margin	$13	$7

[a]where 114,000/950,000 = 12 percent and 76,000/800,000 = 9.5 percent

The two variances for each product would be calculated as follows:

Product A
market size variance   = (950,000 − 1,000,000) (.10) ($13) = $65,000 *U*
market share variance = (.12 − .10) (950,000) ($13)   =   247,000

Product B
market size variance   = (800,000 − 1,000,000) (.10) ($7) = 140,000 *U*
market share variance = (.095 − .10) (800,000) ($7)   =   28,000 *U*
Total $14,000 *F*

Note that the sum of these four variances is the same as the sum of the sales mix and sales volume variances calculated above. This is just another way of evaluating the efforts of the marketing department.

In summary, management can calculate sales price, mix, and volume variances in multi-product settings. In addition, with budgeted and actual market information, they can divide the volume part of the variances (which include mix and volume) by other dimensions and get variances for market size and market share. All can be useful in evaluation of decisions and managers.

PRODUCTION MIX AND YIELD VARIANCES

Much in the same way as managers can calculate sales mix and volume variances, they can also use the same principles for calculating production mix and yield variances. However, for there to be meaning to these variances, some basic conditions must exist. Let us use the example of an automobile. Obviously the full production of a finished product involves many inputs of various type and cost for materials, labor, and overhead. In some sense, the final automobile is a mix of these inputs. However, most of these inputs are not interchangeable. One could not, say, add an additional rear seat instead of putting in a window. Thus, for materials at least, managers would calculate separate material price and use variances for all the inputs that are independent of one another. The same would hold true for independent labor and overhead functions.

In some cases, however, inputs are exchangeable for each other. For example, if a firm is producing an animal feed, differing combinations of raw materials can be used to achieve an end result that includes necessary fiber, protein, vitamins, minerals, and so on. If the price of, say, corn goes too high, another grain and/or supplement can be partially substituted for the corn. This changes the input mix.

A natural partner with an input mix variance is a *yield variance*. This variance maps the relationship between inputs and outputs. Some input-output relationships are one-to-one while others are not. If raw materials need to be processed so that there is some shrinkage due to the process or due to testing, for example, there would be more inputs used than outputs achieved on a regular basis. This would be taken care of in standard quantities required.

With these ideas and conditions in mind, we can look at the two variances. The logic follows the discussion about marketing mix and volume variances. If the actual mix of interchangeable inputs has a weighted standard cost that is greater than the standard mix, then there is an unfavorable mix variance. If the inputs used to achieve the output are greater than standard, then there is an unfavorable yield variance.

The Horse Feed Company uses linear programming to help it decide how to minimize its costs in producing feed. Constraints relate to marketability of the feed. The objective function, results, and sensitivity analysis for a current product are shown in Exhibit 9-6.

Exhibit 9-6
Horse Feed Company
Linear Programming Solution Feed Content and Cost

```
MIN      .3 CORN + .5 OATS + .45 BARLEY
SUBJECT TO
       2)    CORN <= .5
       3)    CORN + OATS + BARLEY = 1
       4)    .15 CORN + .2 OATS + .1 BARLEY >= .14
       5)    .1 CORN + .25 OATS + .35 BARLEY >= .25
END

LP OPTIMUM FOUND AT STEP 4
         OBJECTIVE FUNCTION VALUE

  1)        .417500000
```

VARIABLE	VALUE	REDUCED COST
CORN	.300000	.000000
OATS	.250000	.000000
BARLEY	.450000	.000000

ROW	SLACK OR SURPLUS	DUAL PRICES
2)	.200000	.000000
3)	.000000	-.006250
4)	.000000	-1.375000
5)	.000000	-.875000

```
NO. ITERATIONS = 4

RANGES IN WHICH THE BASIS IS UNCHANGED:
```

OBJ COEFFICIENT RANGES

VARIABLE	CURRENT COEF	ALLOWABLE INCREASE	ALLOWABLE DECREASE
CORN	.300000	.175000	INFINITY
OATS	.500000	INFINITY	.110000
BARLEY	.450000	.183333	.350000

RIGHTHAND SIDE RANGES

ROW	CURRENT RHS	ALLOWABLE INCREASE	ALLOWABLE DECREASE
2	.500000	INFINITY	.200000
3	1.000000	.088889	.133333
4	.140000	.060000	.020000
5	.250000	.060000	.040000

The optimal mix calls for a cost of $0.4175 with the following mix of materials:

Material	Percent	Price	Price per pound
Corn	0.30	$0.30	$0.0900
Oats	0.25	0.50	0.1250
Barley	0.45	0.45	0.2025
			$0.4175

Assume that the price for oats dropped from $0.50 to $0.38. Since this drop exceeds the limits shown in Exhibit 9-6, a new optimal solution is called for. Before taking into account the idea of forecasting and opportunity cost variances, let us look at mix and yield variances based on using the mix suggested in Exhibit 9-6. The full analysis of price, mix, and yield variances is shown in Exhibit 9-7, based on producing 100,000 pounds of feed.

Since the managers followed the original formulation called for in the linear programming solution, all that is shown is a price variance of $3,000 F. The mix and yield are as prespecified. Let us change the situation a bit and say that management wants to change the standards to reflect what they should have done given the change in grain prices. A new optimal solution given an oat price of $0.38 per pound calls for 100 percent oats and no corn or barley. An analysis of price, mix, and yield is shown in Exhibit 9-8.

Exhibit 9-7
Production Price, Mix, and Yield Variances
Horse Feed Company

	AQ/Input AP/Input Actual Input Mix	AQ/Input SP/Input Actual Input Mix	AQ—Total SP/Input Standard Input Mix	SQ—Total SP/Input Standard Input Mix
Corn	30,000 lb @ $0.30	30,000 lb @ $0.30	30,000 lb @ $0.30	30,000 lb @ $0.30
Oats	25,000 lb @ $0.38	25,000 lb @ $0.50	25,000 lb @ $0.50	25,000 lb @ $0.50
Barley	45,000 lb @ $0.45 $38,750	45,000 lb @ $0.45 $41,750	45,000 lb @ $0.45 $41,750	45,000 lb @ $0.45 $41,750

$3,000 F   0   0
price   mix   yield

Exhibit 9-8
Price, Mix, and Yield Variances—Revision of Standards
Horse Feed Company

	AQ/Input AP/Input Actual Input Mix	AQ/Input SP/Input Actual Input Mix	AQ—Total SP/Input Standard Input Mix	SQ—Total SP/Input Standard Input Mix
Corn	30,000 lb @ $0.30	30,000 lb @ $0.30	0 lb @ $0.30	0 lb @ $0.30
Oats	25,000 lb @ $0.38	25,000 lb @ $0.38	100,000 lb @ $0.38	100,000 lb @ $0.38
Barley	45,000 lb @ $0.45 $38,750	45,000 lb @ $0.45 $38,750	0 lb @ $0.45 $38,000	0 lb @ $0.45 $38,000
	0 price	$750 *U* mix	0 yield	

If standards reflect both the new mix and new price for oats, then there is only a mix variance of $750 reflecting the opportunity cost lost due to using the old mix given a new optimal solution. From our perspective of forecasting and opportunity cost variances, this $750 unfavorable variance could be classified as either depending on whether management had the opportunity to react to the change in prices or not.

So far we have illustrated a price variance with no mix or yield variance, and a mix variance with no price or yield variance. The following example takes all three factors into account. Assume that grain prices are within the bounds called for in the original linear programming solution but that purchases cannot be made based on the exact standard prices used. Also assume that a large order came in and that there was an insufficient amount of barley available to meet the order. Thus, the manager had to alter the optimal mix. Finally, due to some spoilage, they had to use more inputs than called for to yield the required outputs.

First, given the additional constraint on resources, a new linear programming solution was run as shown in Exhibit 9-9. Then, after production was completed, a variance analysis was calculated as shown in Exhibit 9-10. Note that actual prices for grains are reflected in that exhibit.

The prices for grains were within the bounds called for in the original optimal solution. The additional linear programming constraint in Exhibit 9-9 reflects that for the order, no more than 25 percent of the inputs could be

Exhibit 9-9
Horse Feed Company
Limit Barley—New Constraint

```
MIN        .3 CORN + .5 OATS + .45 BARLEY
SUBJECT TO
        2)    CORN <= .5
        3)    CORN + OATS + BARLEY = 1
        4)    .15 CORN + .2 OATS + .1 BARLEY >= .14
        5)    .1 CORN + .25 OATS + .35 BARLEY >= .25
        6)    BARLEY <= .25
END
LP OPTIMUM FOUND AT STEP 1
```

```
        OBJECTIVE FUNCTION VALUE

 1)           .454166700

VARIABLE          VALUE        REDUCED COST
    CORN          .166667          .000000
    OATS          .583333          .000000
  BARLEY          .250000          .000000

     ROW     SLACK OR SURPLUS     DUAL PRICES
     2)          .333333          .000000
     3)          .000000         -.166667
     4)          .026667          .000000
     5)          .000000        -1.333333
     6)          .000000          .183333

NO. ITERATIONS = 1

RANGES IN WHICH THE BASIS IS UNCHANGED:

                    OBJ COEFFICIENT RANGES
VARIABLE         CURRENT          ALLOWABLE         ALLOWABLE
                 COEF             INCREASE          DECREASE
    CORN         .300000          .200000           INFINITY
    OATS         .500000          INFINITY          .110000
  BARLEY         .450000          .183333           INFINITY

                    RIGHTHAND SIDE RANGES
     ROW         CURRENT          ALLOWABLE         ALLOWABLE
                 RHS              INCREASE          DECREASE
     2           .500000          INFINITY          .333333
     3          1.000000          .200000           .100000
     4           .140000          .026667           INFINITY
     5           .250000          .025000           .050000
     6           .250000          .200000           .250000
```

Exhibit 9-10
Price, Mix, and Yield Variances—Limited Supply
Horse Feed Company

	AQ/Input AP/Input Actual Input Mix	AQ/Input SP/Input Actual Input Mix	AQ—Total SP/Input Standard Input Mix	SQ—Total SP/Input Standard Input Mix
Corn	18,000 lb @ $0.33	18,000 lb @ $0.30	17,159 lb @ $0.30	
Oats	60,000 lb @ $0.45	60,000 lb @ $0.50	60,080 lb @ $0.50	96,000 lb @ $0.45417
Barley	25,000 lb @ $0.46	25,000 lb @ $0.45	25,750 lb @ $0.45	
	$44,440	$46,650	$46,775	$43,594

$210 *F* price $125 *F* mix $3,181 *U* yield

barley. The new cost of $0.4541667 per pound is greater than the old solution of $0.4175. However, management had the opportunity to react in this case and to alter the mix. It is unclear why the mix of inputs did not meet the percentages specified in Exhibit 9-9. Perhaps a spoilage problem was detected during the manufacturing process and additional grain was added to make up for it.

The savings in oats outweighed the higher prices in corn and barley for a favorable price variance. It is important to isolate each part of that variance so that the swings in prices of each commodity are shown. The mix variance is favorable since more lower price grains were used than called for in the optimal solution. Finally, with inputs totaling 103,000 pounds and output of only 96,000 pounds, there is an unfavorable yield variance of 7,000 pounds at the weighted average cost of $0.4541667 or $3,178 (the variance in Exhibit 9-10 reflects rounding).

TOTAL DISAGGREGATION OF VARIANCES

Up to this point, both aggregated and disaggregated variances have been illustrated. In fact, looking at the discussion regarding marketing variances, different disaggregations may be possible. The following material demonstrates a way that managers can organize variance analysis and choose the level of disaggregation they desire. This work is based on an article by Shank and Churchill.[9]

As an illustration, the information contained in Exhibit 9-11 will be used. The major difference between this illustration and those that preceded it is in the area of market size and share. Here we assume that the market size is for all products (like a finite market for automobiles, given a mix of

Exhibit 9-11
Brodie Paints
Budget and Actual Data

Budget/Standard

| | Flat Wallpaint | | Semigloss Enamel | | |
	Latex	Oil	Latex	Oil	Total
Sales (gallons)	10,000	500	5,000	1,500	17,000
Price/gallon	$17.00	$16.00	$20.00	$19.00	
Variable cost/gallon	5.00	5.00	6.00	6.00	
Contribution margin	12.00	11.00	14.00	13.00	
Total contribution margin	$120,000	$5,500	$70,000	$19,500	$215,000
Common costs					40,000
Income					$175,000

Actual

| | Flat Wallpaint | | Semigloss Enamel | | |
	Latex	Oil	Latex	Oil	Total
Sales (gallons)	9,000	600	6,000	1,800	17,400
Price/gallon	$17.50	$16.50	$20.50	$19.50	
Variable cost/gallon	5.10	5.00	6.20	6.00	
Contribution margin	12.40	11.50	14.30	13.50	
Total contribution margin	$111,600	$6,900	$85,800	$24,300	$228,600
Common costs					41,000
Income					$187,600

Basic Analysis

Actual income	$187,600
Budgeted income	175,000
Income variance	$12,600 F

[9] John Shank and Neil Churchill, "Variance Analysis: A Management-Oriented Approach," *The Accounting Review* (July 1972), pp. 549–555.

models offered by a manufacturer), and that market share involves the whole product line and not each individual product in the line separately.

As shown in Exhibit 9-11, Brodie Paints has four products for interior painting: latex flat wallpaint, oil flat wallpaint, latex semigloss enamel, and oil semigloss enamel. The idea of this example is to use this basic information and to see the various levels of variances that could usefully be calculated. As a beginning, a very basic analysis is the difference between budgeted profit of $175,000 and actual profit of $187,600. There is a favorable *income variance* of $12,600. This is the most aggregated variance we can calculate, and it provides a good starting point for analysis.

Exhibit 9-12 takes the $12,600 favorable difference in income and breaks it down into cost-volume-profit related categories. Overall variances are shown for revenues, variable costs, contribution margin, fixed costs, and the total variance of income.

The next level of disaggregation deals with just changes in income caused by marketing volume differences between plans and actual sales. In Exhibit 9-13, actual sales levels are combined with standard contribution margins to yield income of $182,000. This is compared to budgeted sales at standard contribution margins of $175,000 and there is a marketing volume variance of $7,000 favorable. "Other variances" comprise the difference between the known total variance of $12,600 favorable and the $7,000 marketing volume variance.

The next level shows the marketing price variance, a breakdown of the $7,000 favorable marketing volume variance into its mix and volume components, and a summary of variable cost and fixed cost variances. This level is reflected in Exhibit 9-14. Compare the results in this exhibit with those in Exhibit 9-12. Variances in revenues, variable costs, and contribution margins in Exhibit 9-12 tend to hide causality that begins to be revealed in Exhibit 9-14. Changes in mix and volume will change variable costs even if variable cost per unit remains at standard.

Exhibit 9-12
Brodie Paints
General Category Variances

LEVEL ONE

	Actual	Budgeted	Variance	
Revenues	$325,500	$306,500	$19,000	F
Variable costs	96,900	91,500	5,400	U
Contribution margin	228,600	215,000	13,600	F
Period costs	41,000	40,000	1,000	U
Income	187,600	175,000	12,600	F

Exhibit 9-13
Brodie Paints
Marketing Volume Variance

LEVEL TWO
Actual sales at standard contribution margin

	Flat Wallpaint		Semigloss Enamel		
	Latex	Oil	Latex	Oil	Total
Sales (gallons)	9,000	600	6,000	1,800	17,400
Price/gallon	$17.00	$16.00	$20.00	$19.00	
Variable cost/gallon	5.00	5.00	6.00	6.00	
Contribution margin	12.00	11.00	14.00	13.00	
Total contribution margin	$108,000	$6,600	$84,000	$23,400	$222,000
Common costs					40,000
Income					$182,000

Budgeted income at actual sales levels	$182,000	
Budgeted income	175,000	
Marketing volume variance	$7,000	F
Actual income	$187,600	
Budgeted income at actual sales levels	182,000	
Other variances	$5,600	F
Total variance	$12,600	F

An analysis of this level indicates that semigloss enamel rose in total as a percentage of sales (44.82 percent actual versus 38.23 percent budgeted). This accounts for the favorable mix variance. Total sales were 400 gallons over projection and prices exceeded expectations by $0.50 for all products. In this level, we force the variable cost variances by backing out the total marketing variances and the known fixed cost variance from the total $12,600 favorable income variance.

Exhibit 9-15 (page 374) illustrates the next level of disaggregation. First, the $5,059 favorable marketing volume variance is broken down into market size and market share variances. Next, the mix and price variances are disaggregated into portions for each product. Finally, the $2,100 variable cost variance total is shown on a product-by-product basis. With additional information, another level of disaggregation could show the various material, labor, and variable cost variances in total and by product.

Exhibit 9-14
Brodie Paints
Marketing Variances

LEVEL THREE

	AQ/Product Actual Price Budgeted Cost Actual Mix	AQ/Product Budgeted Price Budgeted Cost Actual Mix	AQ-Total Budgeted Price Budgeted Cost Standard Mix	Budgeted Volume Budgeted Price Budgeted Cost Standard Mix
Flat latex	112,500	108,000	122,824	120,000
Flat oil	6,900	6,600	5,629	5,500
Semigloss latex	87,000	84,000	71,647	70,000
Semigloss oil	24,300	23,400	19,959	19,500
	-------	-------	-------	-------
	230,700	222,000	220,059	215,000

	Price	Mix	Volume
	8,700 F	1,941 F	5,059 F
			Aggregated
			7,000 F

Where:

MIX				
	Budget	Percent	Actual	Percent
Flat latex	10,000	0.5882	9,000	0.5172
Flat oil	500	0.0294	600	0.0345
Semigloss latex	5,000	0.2941	6,000	0.3448
Semigloss oil	1,500	0.0882	1,800	0.1034
	17,000	1.0000	17,400	1.0000

Marketing price	$8,700	F
Marketing mix	1,941	F
Marketing volume	5,059	F
Total marketing	15,700	F
Total variance	12,600	F
Other variances	(3,100)	U
Fixed cost variance	(1,000)	U
Variable variance	(2,100)	U

Finally, Exhibit 9-16 (page 375) shows a summary of all the variances that have been calculated and ties them to the basic income variance of $12,600 favorable. This illustration is meant to spur thinking about ways to present variance information. Managers must decide on levels of detail (aggregation) for presentation of information to corporate officers, to marketing managers, to manufacturing managers, and the like. Do not use the suggested levels of disaggregation presented in the example as *the* way to present variances. This is merely *an* idea—one for you to build on and modify as appropriate to a situation.

Exhibit 9-15
Brodie Paints
Disaggregation of Variances

LEVEL FOUR

```
                Budgeted    Actual
Total market    142,000    130,000
Total sales      17,000     17,400
Market share     0.1197      0.1338
Avg. CM          $12.65
```

Market Size Variance = (130,000 - 142,000) (.1197) ($12.65) =   (18,169) U

Market Share Variance = (.1338-.1197) (130,000) ($12.65) =   23,228 F

                                        Marketing volume variance   5,059 F

Disaggregation of mix variance

	Budgeted Price Budgeted Cost Actual Mix	Budgeted Price Budgeted Cost Standard Mix	Details of Mix Variance
Flat latex	108,000	122,824	(14,824) U
Flat oil	6,600	5,629	971 F
Semigloss latex	84,000	71,647	12,353 F
Semigloss oil	23,400	19,959	3,441 F
	222,000	220,059	1,941 F

Disaggregation of price variance

	AQ/product Actual Price Budgeted Cost Actual Mix	AQ/product Budgeted Price Budgeted Cost Actual Mix	Details of Price Variance
Flat latex	112,500	108,000	4,500 F
Flat oil	6,900	6,600	300 F
Semigloss latex	87,000	84,000	3,000 F
Semigloss oil	24,300	23,400	900 F
	230,700	222,000	8,700 F

Disaggregation of variable cost variance

	AQ Sold	Std. VC	Actual VC	Variance
Flat latex	9,000	$5.00	$5.10	(900) U
Flat oil	600	$5.00	$5.00	0
Semigloss latex	6,000	$6.00	$6.20	(1,200) U
Semigloss oil	1,800	$6.00	$6.00	0
				(2,100) U

Exhibit 9-16
Brodie Paints
Summary of Variances

Summary of All Variances

Marketing price	Flat latex	$4,500	F
	Flat oil	300	F
	Semigloss latex	3,000	F
	Semigloss oil	900	F
	Total	8,700	F
Marketing mix	Flat latex	(14,824)	U
	Flat oil	971	F
	Semigloss latex	12,353	F
	Semigloss oil	3,441	F
	Total	1,941	F
Marketing volume			
	Market size	(18,169)	U
	Market share	23,228	F
	Total	5,059	F
Fixed cost variance		(1,000)	U
Variable cost variances	Flat latex	(900)	U
	Flat oil	0	
	Semigloss latex	(1,200)	U
	Semigloss oil	0	
	Total	(2,100)	U
Total of all variances		12,600	F

VARIANCES AND NEW TECHNOLOGY

The presentation so far has relied on the basic notion that most materials and labor (as well as related variable overhead) will behave as specified in our basic examples of cost-volume-profit and standard cost variance analysis. If portions of heretofore variable costs become fixed in nature due to new technology or for other reasons, the basic idea remains, but the details change. Note that the emphasis in the preceding section is on product analysis and on marketing variances. Changes in the fixed or variable portions of manufacturing costs would be reflected in the details of manufacturing variances. The core idea is the same—the details will differ.

However, there should be some dramatic changes in variances that go beyond the idea of what is fixed and what is variable. As long as there have been variances, managers have complained that they are not timely. Even in the best of circumstances, the manufacturing accounting system does not generate variances and, therefore, variance reports until after the end of a period. There is no opportunity to use information coming from the accounting system to avoid variances as they are happening. Variance reports become after-the-fact summaries of what happened and may form the basis for future corrective action.

One of the benefits of computer-integrated manufacturing (CIM) is the ability to monitor production as the manufacturing process is taking place. Thus, there are real-time variances. When defects are occurring or when machines are moving out of tolerance, there will be immediate feedback to the operating personnel. They, in turn, can take actions that will minimize variances since corrections are taking place while production continues and not after the end of an accounting period.

Certain variances might disappear. If the just-in-time material philosophy is adopted, suppliers will be held more accountable for component and raw material quality. By extending the reach of the corporation into its suppliers, the material use variance might be all but eliminated when combined with real-time variances. In this CIM environment there is a real question about the role of all the traditional standard cost variances. Should they be eliminated for management accounting purposes? Should they only exist to tie standard costing into financial reports? Are they still valuable as control devices after the end of a period? Can managers develop new variance measures that will yield useful and timely information?

VARIANCE REPORTING

Computers allow managers to calculate many different variances and to present them in various ways. Not only do manufacturing accounting packages allow for several options, but also spreadsheet analysis can produce the same or even expanded results. Exhibits 9-11 through 9-16, for example, were generated by a single interrelated spreadsheet. However, the calculation of variances is only the beginning. Two other aspects are as important as the variances themselves. One direction is an analysis of a variance. Why did it occur? Should management investigate a variance (will the cost outweigh the benefit)? These are the types of questions that are addressed in Chapter 10. The second issue is how to present variance information to management. While both of these issues are related, let us look at the presentation issue here.

The issue of variance reporting involves some of the same questions asked in Chapter 1. Some of these are form, order, and format questions. Should variances be presented in the order of marketing, then production? Should variances be listed in descending monetary order? in alphabetical order? favorable and then unfavorable? unfavorable and then favorable? If there is real-time reporting of actual performance, what variance-type information should be available to managers on microcomputers linked to the production process?

Should there be exception reporting with only variances that exceed some percentage level (such as 10 percent over or under standard) or some dollar level (such as $5,000) being reported? This option is available in basic computer manufacturing accounting packages.

What is the level of detail that should be presented? This issue is partially addressed in the discussion above. Should graphs or charts be used in a presentation? Should last period's variances be compared to this period's? How much is useful information and how much will be disregarded? Should a verbal analysis accompany the list of variance figures? If causes or remedies have been identified, should they be shown? How long should variance information wait for analysis to take place? This is a balance between timeliness and completeness.

Our discussion in Chapter 1 shows that the choices we make can affect how variances are perceived by a manager. This area is a good example of how we can generate much data and information and of the need to make conscious choices of how and when to present this information.

SUMMARY

Variances are the comparison of actual performance against some relevant benchmark. The basis for comparison might be standard costs or might incorporate actual or adjusted-actual costs from prior periods. Within the chapter we illustrated a basic standard cost variance structure as well as appropriate marketing variances in single- and multi-product settings. These variances are presented as an illustration of the issues involved in variance analysis rather than as a model for all companies to use. In order to aid in operational control, managers must establish what variances seem useful. They will also determine the best basis for comparison; what variances to report in monetary and in nonmonetary terms; levels of aggregation; and the form, order, and format of variance reports. As with any planning or control system, managers should review the structure for variance calculation and reporting on a regular basis to make sure that it is still fulfilling the objectives for which it was created. If there have been changes in the internal and/or external environment that warrant changes in the system, then managers should rethink and revise as appropriate. With this as background, the next chapter will go beyond a variance itself and ask why it occurred and whether it is wise to try to investigate it.

PROBLEMS AND CASES

9-1. Mix and Yield Variances (CMA)

Energy Products Company produces a gasoline additive, Gas Gain. This product increases engine efficiency and improves gasoline mileage by creating a more complete burn in the combustion process.

During the production process careful controls are required to ensure that the proper mix of input chemicals is achieved and that evaporation is controlled. If the controls are not effective, there can be loss of output and efficiency.

The standard cost of producing a 500-liter batch of Gas Gain is $135. The standard materials mix and related standard cost of each chemical used in a 500-liter batch are as follows.

Chemical	Standard Input Quantity in Liters	Standard Cost per Liter	Total Cost
Echol	200	$0.200	$ 40.00
Protex	100	0.425	42.50
Benz	250	0.150	37.50
CT-40	50	0.300	15.00
	600		$135.00

The quantities of chemicals purchased and used during the current production period are shown in the schedule below. A total of 140 batches of Gas Gain were manufactured during the current production period. Energy Products determines its cost and chemical usage variations at the end of each production period.

Chemical	Quantity Purchased	Total Purchase Price	Quantity Used
Echol	25,000 liters	$ 5,365	26,600 liters
Protex	13,000 liters	6,240	12,880 liters
Benz	40,000 liters	5,840	37,800 liters
CT-40	7,500 liters	2,220	7,140 liters
Total	85,500 liters	$19,665	84,420 liters

Required:
1. Calculate the purchase price variances by chemical for Energy Products Company.

2. Calculate the total material usage variance related to Gas Gain for Energy Products Company and then analyze this total usage variance into the following two components:
   a. total mix variance.
   b. total yield variance.

9-2. Variance and Responsibility (CMA)

Maidwell Company manufactures washers and dryers on a single assembly line in its main factory. The market has deteriorated over the last five years and competition has made cost control very important. Management has been concerned about the materials cost of both washers and dryers. There have been no model changes in the past two years and economic conditions have allowed the company to negotiate price reductions in many key parts.

Maidwell uses a standard cost system in accounting for materials. Purchases are charged to inventory at a standard price with purchase discounts considered an administrative cost reduction. Production is charged at the standard price of the materials used. Thus, the price variance is isolated at time of purchase as the difference between gross contract price and standard price multiplied by the quantity purchased. When a substitute part is used in production rather than the regular part, a price variance equal to the difference in the standard prices of the materials is recognized at the time of substitution in the production process. The quantity variance is the actual quantity used compared to the standard quantity allowed with the difference multiplied by the standard price.

The materials variances for several of the parts Maidwell uses are unfavorable. Part No. 4121 is one of the items that has an unfavorable variance. Maidwell knows that some of these parts will be defective and fail. The failure is discovered during production. The normal defective rate is 5 percent of normal input. The original contract price of this part was $0.285 per unit; thus, Maidwell set the standard unit price at $0.285. The unit contract purchase price of Part No. 4121 was increased $0.04 to $0.325 from the original $0.285 due to a parts specification change. Maidwell chose not to change the standard, but to treat the increase in price as a price variance. In addition, the contract terms were changed from n/30 to 4/10, n/30 as a consequence of negotiations resulting from changes in the economy.

Data regarding the usage of Part No. 4121 during December is as follows.

• Purchases of Part No. 4121	150,000 units
• Unit price paid for purchases of Part No. 4121	$0.325
• Requisitions of Part No. 4121 from stores for use in products	134,000 units
• Substitution of Part No. 5125 for Part No. 4121 to use obsolete stock (standard unit price of Part No. 5125 is $.35)	24,000 units
• Units of Part No. 4121 and its substitute (Part No. 5125) identified as being defective	9,665 units
• Standard allowed usage (including normal defective units) of Part No. 4121 and its substitute based upon output for the month	153,300 units

Maidwell's material variances related to Part No. 4121 for December were reported as follows.

Price variance	$7,560.00 U
Quantity variance	1,339.50 U
Total material variances	
for Part No. 4121	$8,899.50 U

Bob Speck, the Purchasing Director, claims the unfavorable price variance is misleading. Speck says that his department has worked hard to obtain price concessions and purchase discounts from suppliers. In addition, Speck has indicated that engineering changes have been made in several parts, increasing their price even though the part identification has not changed. These price increases are not his department's responsibility. Speck declares that price variances simply no longer measure the Purchasing Department's performance.

Jim Buddle, the Manufacturing Manager, thinks that responsibility for the quantity variance should be shared. Buddle states that manufacturing cannot control quality arising from less expensive parts, substitutions of material to use up otherwise obsolete stock, or engineering changes that increased the quantity of materials used.

The Accounting Manager, Mike Kohl, has suggested that the computation of variances be changed to identify variations from standard with the causes and functional areas responsible for the variances. The following system of materials variances and the method of computation for each was recommended by Kohl.

Variance	Method of Calculation
Econcomics variance	Quantity purchased times the changes made after setting standards that were the result of negotiations based on changes in the general economy.
Engineering change variance	Quantity purchased times change in price due to part specifications changes.
Purchase price variance	Quantity purchased times change in contract price due to changes other than parts specifications or the general economy.
Substitutions variance	Quantity substituted times the difference in standard price between parts substituted.
Excess usage variance	Standard price times the difference between the standard quantity allowed for production minus actual parts used (reduced for abnormal scrap).
Abnormal failure rate variance	Abnormal scrap times standard price.

Required:

1. Discuss the appropriateness of Maidwell Company's current method of variance analysis for materials and indicate whether the claims of Bob Speck and Jim Buddle are valid.
2. Compute the materials variances for Part No. 4121 for December using the system recommended by Mike Kohl.
3. Indicate who would be responsible for each of the variances in Mike Kohl's system of variance analysis for materials.

9-3. Flexible Budgets (CMA)

Wielson Company employs flexible budgeting techniques to evaluate the performance of several of its activities. The selling expense flexible budgets for three representative monthly activity levels are shown below.

Representative Monthly Flexible Budgets for Selling Expenses

Activity measures:			
Unit sales volume	400,000	425,000	450,000
Dollar sales volume	$10,000,000	$10,625,000	$11,250,000
Number of orders	4,000	4,250	4,500
Number of salespersons	75	75	75
Monthly expenses:			
Advertising and promotion	$ 1,200,000	$ 1,200,000	$ 1,200,000
Administrative salaries	57,000	57,000	57,000
Sales salaries	75,000	75,000	75,000
Sales commissions	200,000	212,500	225,000
Salesperson travel	170,000	175,000	180,000
Sales office expense	490,000	498,750	507,500
Shipping expense	675,000	712,500	750,000
Total selling expense	$ 2,867,000	$ 2,930,750	$ 2,994,500

The following assumptions were used to develop the selling expense flexible budgets.

- The average size of Wielson's salesforce during the year is planned to be 75 people.
- Salespersons are paid a monthly salary plus commission on gross dollar sales.
- The travel costs are best characterized as a step variable cost. The fixed portion is related to the number of salespersons, while the variable portion tends to fluctuate with gross dollar sales.
- Sales office expense is a mixed cost with the variable portion related to the number of orders processed.
- Shipping expense is a mixed cost with the variable portion related to the number of units sold.

A salesforce of 80 persons generated a total of 4,300 orders resulting in a sales volume of 420,000 units during November. The gross dollar sales amounted to $10.9 million. The selling expenses incurred for November were as follows.

Advertising and promotion	$1,350,000
Administrative salaries	57,000
Sales salaries	80,000
Sales commissions	218,000
Salesperson travel	185,000
Sales office expense	497,200
Shipping expense	730,000
Total	$3,117,200

Required:

1. Explain why flexible budgeting is a useful management tool.
2. Explain why the selling expense flexible budgets presented above would not be appropriate for evaluating Wielson Company's November selling expenses, and indicate how the flexible budget would have to be revised.
3. Prepare a selling expense report for November that Wielson Company can use to evaluate its control over selling expenses. The report should have a line for each selling expense item showing the appropriate budgeted amount, the actual selling expense, and the monthly dollar variation.

9-4. Aggregated Variances (CMA)

Handler Company distributes two home-use power tools to hardware stores—a heavy duty $\frac{1}{2}$" hand drill and a table saw. The tools are purchased from a manufacturer that attaches the Handler private label to the tools. The wholesale selling prices to the hardware stores are $60 each for the drill and $120 each for the table saw.

The 19X2 budget and actual results are presented below. The budget was adopted in late 19X1 and was based upon Handler's estimated share of the market for the two tools.

During the first quarter of 19X2, Handler's management estimated that the total market for these tools would actually be 10 percent below its original estimates. In an attempt to prevent Handler's unit sales from declining as much as industry projections, management developed and implemented a marketing program. Included in the program were dealer discounts and increased direct advertising. The table saw line was emphasized in this program.

Handler Company
Income Statement for the Year Ended December 31, 19X2
(000s omitted)

	Hand Drill		Table Saw		Total		
	Budget	Actual	Budget	Actual	Budget	Actual	Variance
Sales in units	120	86	80	74	200	160	40
Revenue	$7,200	$5,074	$9,600	$8,510	$16,800	$13,584	$(3,216)
Cost of goods sold	6,000	4,300	6,400	6,068	12,400	10,368	2,032
Gross margin	$1,200	$ 774	$3,200	$2,442	$ 4,400	$ 3,216	$(1,184)
Unallocated costs							
Selling					$ 1,000	$ 1,000	
Advertising					1,000	1,060	$ (60)
Administration					400	406	(6)
Income taxes (45%)					900	338	562
Total unallocated costs					$ 3,300	$ 2,804	$ 496
Net income					$ 1,100	$ 412	$ (688)

Required:
1. Analyze the unfavorable gross margin variance of $1,184,000 in terms of
   a. sales price variance.
   b. cost variance.
   c. volume variance.
2. Discuss the apparent effect of Handler Company's special marketing program (i.e., dealer discounts and additional advertising) on 19X2 operating results. Support your comments with numerical data where appropriate.

9-5. Comprehensive Review of Variances (CMA)

Allglow Company is a cosmetics manufacturer specializing in stage makeup. The company's best selling product is SkinKlear, a protective cream used under the stage makeup to protect the skin from frequent use of makeup. SkinKlear is packaged in three sizes—8 ounces, one pound, and three pounds—and regularly sells for $21.00 per pound. The standard cost per pound of SkinKlear, based on Allglow's normal monthly production of 8,000 pounds, is as follows.

Cost Item	Quantity	Standard Cost	Total Cost
Direct materials			
Cream base	9.0 oz.	$0.05/oz.	$0.45
Moisturizer	6.5 oz.	0.10/oz.	0.65
Fragrance	0.5 oz.	1.00/oz.	0.50
			$ 1.60
Direct labor[a]			
Mixing	0.5 hr.	$4.00/hr.	$2.00
Compounding	1.0 hr.	5.00/hr.	5.00
			7.00
Variable overhead[b]	1.5 hr.	$2.10/hr.	3.15
Total standard cost per pound			$11.75

[a]Direct labor dollars include employee benefits.
[b]Applied on the basis of direct labor hours.

Based on these standard costs, Allglow prepares monthly budgets. Presented below are the budgeted performance and the actual performance for May 19X6, when the company produced and sold 9,000 pounds of SkinKlear.

Contribution Report for SkinKlear for the Month of May 19X6

	Budget	Actual	Variance
Units	8,000	9,000	1,000 F
Revenue	$168,000	$180,000	$12,000 F
Direct material	12,800	16,200	3,400 U
Direct labor	56,000	62,500	6,500 U
Variable overhead	25,200	30,900	5,700 U
Total variable costs	$ 94,000	$109,600	$15,600 U
Contribution margin	$ 74,000	$ 70,400	$ 3,600 U

Barbara Simmons, Allglow's President, was not pleased with these results; despite a sizeable increase in the sales of SkinKlear, there was a decrease in the product's contribution to the overall profitability of the firm. Simmons has asked Allglow's Cost Accountant, Brian Jackson, to prepare a report that identifies the reasons why the contribution margin for SkinKlear has decreased. Jackson has gathered the information presented below to help in the preparation of the report.

May 19X6 Usage Report for SkinKlear

Cost Item	Quantity	Actual Cost
Direct materials		
Cream base	84,000 oz.	$ 4,200
Moisturizer	60,000 oz.	7,200
Fragrance	4,800 oz.	4,800
Direct labor		
Mixing	4,500 hr.	18,000
Compounding—manual	5,300 hr.	26,500
Compounding—mechanized	2,700 hr.	13,500
Compounding—idle	900 hr.	4,500
Variable overhead		30,900
Total variable cost		$109,600

While doing his research, Jackson discovered that the Manufacturing Department had mechanized one of the manual operations in the compounding process on an experimental basis. The mechanized operation replaced manual operations that represented 40 percent of the compounding process.

The workers' inexperience with the mechanized operation caused increased usage of both the cream base and the moisturizer; however, Jackson believed these inefficiencies would be negligible if mechanization became a permanent part of the process and the workers' skills were improved. The idle time in compounding was traceable to the fact that fewer workers were required for the mechanized process. During this experimental period, the idle time was charged to direct labor rather than overhead. The excess workers could either be reassigned or laid off in the future. Jackson also was able to determine that all of the variable manufacturing overhead costs over standard could be traced directly to the mechanization process.

Required:
1. Prepare an explanation of the $3,600 unfavorable variance between the budgeted and actual contribution margin for SkinKlear during May 19X6 by calculating the following variances.
   a. Sales price variance.
   b. Material price variance.
   c. Material quantity variance.
   d. Labor efficiency variance.
   e. Variable overhead efficiency variance.
   f. Variable overhead spending variance.
   g. Contribution margin volume variance.

2. Allglow Company must decide whether or not the compounding operation in the SkinKlear manufacturing process that was mechanized on an experimental basis should continue to be mechanized. Calculate the variable cost savings that can be expected to arise in the future from the mechanization. Explain your answer.

9-6. Change of Standards Variance

The manufacturing accounting system of the Furr and Purr Pet Food Company contains information on the actual inputs and original standards given units of production, and has the ability to incorporate information on changes in standard prices and quantities, as ingredients for the products are used in different mixes given changing price conditions.

On one basic product, Manx Mix, a feed supplement, the following ingredients were being used with the following standard prices:

	Per Pound of Food
Fish oil supplement	$^{2}/_{3}$ lb. at $0.20/lb.
Soy-based supplement	$^{1}/_{3}$ lb. at $0.25/lb.

This production mix was based on the results of a linear program as shown below, where A is fish oil supplement, B is vegetable-based supplement, and C is soy-based supplement.

```
MIN       $0.20A  +  $0.40B  +  $0.25C
SUBJECT   TO
          2)      A  +    B  +     C=     1   total  must  equal  1  pound
          3)    .2A  +  .4B  +  .35C>=   .25 niacin  content  (percent)
          4)    .5A  +  .2B  +  .28C>=   .4  calcium content  (percent)

          OBJECTIVE  FUNCTION  VALUE

     1)        .216666700


VARIABLE          VALUE        REDUCED  COST
        A         .666667         .000000
        B         .000000         .133333
        C         .333333         .000000


     ROW  SLACK  OR  SURPLUS   DUAL  PRICES
     2)              .000000      -.133333
     3)              .000000      -.333333
     4)              .026667       .000000
```

During the month of May, 10,000 pounds of Manx Mix were produced using the following materials:

Fish oil supplement	7,300 pounds ($1,460)
Vegetable-based supplement	1,300 pounds ($ 325)
Soy-based supplement	1,800 pounds ($ 450)

During the month, due to a change of prices in the vegetable-based supplement, 5,000 pounds were made using the original mix, and 5,000 were made using a new mix.

Required:
1. Using the actual prices of the three ingredients after the price change for the vegetable-based supplement, what is the new mix suggested by a linear programming solution?
2. The cost system uses the original standards for the month and any changes in standards (revised standards) are compared to the original. Calculate meaningful standard cost variances given the original, revised, and actual data.

9-7. Are Variances Useful?

At a recent conference on changes in accounting due to changes in manufacturing processes, some of the discussants stated that standard costs and standard cost variances lead to dysfunctional behavior and, at best, are too little, too aggregated, and too late to do managers any good.

One person said that variances give wrong signals to managers. Say a manager sees a favorable labor efficiency variance. The manager might think that anything favorable is good. This is dysfunctional since, if a company is going to be more productive (and competitive), fixed standards will slow them down. The argument is that actual costs are a much better way to assess effectiveness and efficiency.

Required:
Comment on the above discussion. Research and cite appropriate articles to support your arguments.

9-8. Market Size and Market Share Variances

Shankhill Corporation expected to sell 30,000 units of product but only sold 28,800. The market was down 10 percent from what was expected. Standard contribution margin per unit is $4. Shankhill's management had budgeted a 30 percent share of the market.

Required:
1. If the market size variance is $12,000 U, what is the size of the budgeted and the actual total market?
2. What is the market share variance?
3. Comment on the usefulness of breaking the sales volume variance into market size and market share variances.

9-9. Disaggregation of Variances[10]

At the end of 1923, Al Kapon, vice president of the Chicago Amusement Company, stared out of the window of his posh west-side office in dismay. His expectations for a highly profitable year were dashed. The disappointing results appear here:

[10] This problem is based on an original problem by Professor Jack Blann.

	Plan	**Actual**
Sales	$500,000	$456,000
Direct material	$ 50,000	$ 48,000
Direct labor	200,000	201,000
Variable overhead	100,000	92,000
Fixed overhead	100,000	98,000
Profits	$ 50,000	$ 17,000

Planned sales were 50,000 units out of a planned market of 100,000 units (each unit is a bottle of the firm's single product). Sales turned out to be only 48,000 units, while the market as a whole was 105,000 units. Taxes are not a consideration for this company.

Actual results included an average selling price of $9.50 per unit, material costs of $48,000 for 100,000 quarts bought and used, 40,000 direct labor hours at standard rates (no one dared ask for more), and a production run of 48,000 units.

Standards established by a committee of top guns in the company were:

Price	$10.00/unit
Materials (2 quarts @ $0.50)	1.00
Direct Labor (0.80 hrs. @ $5/hr)	4.00
Variable Overhead (@ $2.50/DLH)	2.00
Fixed Overhead	2.00

Required:
Analyze the preceding data using the format of the Brodie Paint example in Exhibits 9-11 through 9-16. This assignment should be done using an electronic spreadsheet program. All parts should be tied together by cell formulas. Go into as much detail as you can (as many levels as possible). Prepare a printout of the results as well as of the formulas.

9-10. Variance Reports

The Doonsberry Division of Zonker Enterprises produces footballs, basketballs, and soccer balls for home, school, and professional use. The following is a variance report issued on January 11, 19X1, for production during November 19X0:

Variance Report, Footballs—Model H25

Sales variances	$1,200 F
Production variances:	
Material use variance	$ 300 U
Labor rate variance	200 U
Labor efficiency variance	800 U
Variable overhead efficiency variance	600 U
Material price variance	400 F
Variable overhead rate variance	100 F
Fixed overhead spending variance	1,000 F
Fixed overhead application variance	400 F

Required:
Comment on this report and offer suggestions for improvement.

9-11. Variances—A Chance to Review Standards

The standards for overhead in the Kermit Glove Company were set using linear regression and correlation analysis. Based on this analysis, variable overhead was set at $1.10 per direct labor hour. After the first six months of operations, the plant manager has pointed to the following variable overhead variances and has asked that they be investigated:

**Variable Overhead Spending Variance,
January–June, 19X1**

	Production Level	Variance
January	3,000 units	$ 500 F
February	3,500	1,000 U
March	4,000	100 U
April	4,200	500 F
May	3,800	500 U
June	3,300	100 U

The production manager states that the last six months are typical of good production and he does not see why there has been this big swing in variances. Further investigation reveals that the data used for the standards are as follows:

Direct Labor Hours	Overhead Costs
7,200	$11,982
6,600	10,721
5,800	9,552
6,300	10,004
8,030	12,017
6,850	11,325
7,500	12,031
6,700	11,197
6,500	10,578
7,850	12,040
7,000	11,930
8,120	12,006
5,500	9,505

It takes two labor hours to produce one unit based on standard costs. The efficiency variances have been fairly minimal over the last six months.

Required:
1. The production manager says that the stated variances do not seem reasonable to him. Check the standards for variable overhead by calculating a regression equation by hand, calculator, or computer. What reply do you make to the production manager?
2. Plot the original data. Does this change your thinking? Explain.

9-12. Variance Reports—A Case

The World's Fair Printing Company, located in a large Midwest city with plants throughout Ohio and Indiana, is a large printer of books and catalogs. The company was founded in the 1920s with a plant in Dayton. Over the ensuing years several suburban and rural plants have been built. Currently the company does $200 million in sales annually. The corporate headquarters are in Dayton. The general organizational structure is mostly decentralized with respect to all functions except finance and sales. These functions are carried out and coordinated by the corporate headquarters.

The Troy, Ohio, plant primarily prints catalogs for various stores and mail-order companies. The plant itself consists of a preparatory department where the plates for the offset presses are made, a pressroom containing 15 offset presses, a bindery where the sections of each catalog are collected, bound, and made ready for shipment, and a shipping department where orders are staged and shipped by truck and rail.

Purchasing consists of paper, ink, and preparatory, binding, and shipping supplies. Paper contracts are negotiated companywide by a committee consisting of the various plant managers under the direction of the vice president of production at corporate headquarters. Paper contracts tend to be long-term insofar as supply commitments are concerned, but prices vary with the market. Several mills supply paper to the Troy plant. Ink contracts for both price and quantity are negotiated by each plant manager. In some plants there are various suppliers; in other plants an ink company has installed an in-house plant for producing ink right next to the particular production facility. This is the case at Troy. The purchasing department at each plant is responsible for the various supplies that are bought. Aluminum of a certain weight and thickness as well as various supplies and chemicals are needed for the preparatory department. Photographic materials also must be purchased, although they usually come from a major supplier such as Kodak. Wire, glue, and other supplies must be purchased for binding and shipping. The contracting for boxes and bags is handled separately from that for paper for printing. In the case of boxes and bags, the local purchasing department makes the necessary contacts.

The operations of the preparatory department are as follows: material is sent in from various customers in what is called camera-ready form. This means that all type has been set, sized, and pasted down onto thin sheets of cardboard, so that only one photo is needed per page of type. Photographs are provided loose, showing any cropping and sizing that is necessary. Thus, each photograph will require one photo. This camera-ready art work is taken to the camera room, where large horizontal cameras take pictures of both the type and the photographs needed for each page. Film is processed through an automatic film-processing machine and is given to a worker at a light table (a large table with a piece of glass on top and fluorescent lights underneath) to put together into eight-page groupings. The presses are set up so that each part of a catalog that is printed is basically a sixteen-page section. There are eight pages on each side of this section. Depending on the size of the press used, 16, 32, or 48 pages may be printed at one time. After the worker has assembled eight pages using special paper and tape, a contact print of the finished sheet (sometimes called an eight-page flat) is made on another large piece of film.

In another part of the preparatory department, thin sheets of aluminum are coated with a special chemical substance that is heat and light sensitive. The full eight-page negatives are placed on top of the aluminum plates. This sandwich is exposed to high-intensity light, which hardens all the material on the aluminum exposed through clear areas in the film. The printing plate is put through a chemical process by which the soft areas (those areas that were black on the negative) are washed away. A caustic substance is used to etch into the plate, and a copper solution is introduced into this area. When this process is completed, the remaining treated area of the plate is removed. As a final result, all areas that will print have been filled with a copper substance, and all areas that will not print remain aluminum. The plate is then treated with a preservative and sent to the press room. Given the number of presses at the Troy plant and the average length of production runs, an average of 50 to 60 plates is produced in each eight-hour shift. The plant generally runs three shifts a day.

The general cost accounting system for the Troy plant, like that for most of the other plants in the company, is basically job order costing. The costs are accumulated by each catalog for analysis by both the production department and the sales department.

Required:

Plant management has just instituted a standard cost system in the preparatory department. Expected costs have been developed for the various aspects of the production process in this department. You have been asked to prepare a recommendation for variance reports reflecting the performance of the preparatory department. The variance reports will be used as appropriate by various levels of management. Part of your recommendation should include the audience and format of your reports. State all assumptions you have made. If you have questions that need to be answered before final recommendations are made, make sure to list these questions.

9-13. Quality Considerations (CMA)

As part of its cost control program, Tracer Company uses a standard cost system for all manufactured items. The standard cost for each item is established at the beginning of the fiscal year, and the standards are not revised until the beginning of the next fiscal year. Changes in costs, caused during the year by changes in material or labor inputs or by changes in the manufacturing process, are recognized as they occur by the inclusion of planned variances in Tracer's monthly operating budgets.

Presented below is the labor standard that was established for one of Tracer's products, effective June 1, 19X0, the beginning of the fiscal year.

Assembler A labor (5 hours @$10/hour)	$ 50.00
Assembler B labor (3 hours @$11/hour)	33.00
Machinist labor (2 hours @$15/hour)	30.00
Standard cost per 100 units	$113.00

The standard was based on the labor being performed by a team consisting of five persons with Assembler A skills, three persons with Assembler B skills, and two persons with machinist skills; this team represents the most efficient use of the company's skilled employees. The standard also assumed that the quality of material that had been used in prior years would be available for the coming year.

For the first seven months of the fiscal year, actual manufacturing costs at Tracer have been within the standards established. However, the company has received a significant increase in orders, and there is an insufficient number of skilled workers available to meet the increased production. Therefore, beginning in January, the production teams will consist of eight persons with Assembler A skills, one person with Assembler B skills, and one person with Machinist skills. The reorganized teams will work more slowly than the normal teams; and, as a result, only 80 units will be produced in the same time period that 100 units would normally be produced. Faulty work has never been a cause for units to be rejected in the final inspection process, and it is not expected to be a cause for rejection with the reorganized teams.

Furthermore, Tracer has been notified by its material supplier that a lower quality material will be supplied beginning January 1. Normally, one unit of raw material is required for each good unit produced, and no units are lost due to defective material. Tracer estimates that 6 percent of the units manufactured after January 1 will be rejected in the final inspection process due to defective material.

Required:
1. Determine the number of units of lower quality material that Tracer Company must enter into production in order to produce 35,720 good finished units.
2. Without prejudice to your answer in Part 1 assume that Tracer Company must manufacture a total of 50,000 units in January to have sufficient good units to fill the orders received.
   a. Determine how many hours of each class of labor will be needed to manufacture a total of 50,000 units in January.
   b. Determine the amount that should be included in Tracer's January operating budget for the planned labor variance caused by the reorganization of the labor teams and the lower quality material, and indicate how much of the planned variance can be attributed to (a) the change in material and (b) the reorganization of the labor teams. Be sure to support your answer with appropriate calculations.

9-14. Introduction of Standard Cost System (CMA)

Windsor Healthcare Inc. (WHI), a manufacturer of custom-designed home healthcare equipment, has been in business for 15 years. Miriam Blanc, the founder and company president, originally began designing equipment for her chronically-ill son in an effort to keep him out of the hospital as much as possible. As word spread among healthcare professionals, she made the equipment available to others. Now, WHI has grown to the point where some of its products have become standards of the industry and are being manufactured in large quantities.

Last year, in an effort to monitor and control the costs of their products, Blanc and the controller, Susan Isacson, decided to implement a standard cost system. Isacson took great pride in her work, and she personally guided the recently hired cost accounting manager, David Natali, in the research, development, and implementation of the standards. Isacson and Natali used production figures for the past three years and spent considerable effort perfecting exact calculations to four decimal places. They did not include other company personnel in the standard-setting process since they considered this to be purely an accounting issue.

Isacson and Natali finished the project and distributed the standards with a cover memo six months ago. The memo explained the usefulness of the standards as a basis of comparison between the planned costs for each product and the incurred costs. Reports were to be issued monthly for tracking performance. When the difference between these costs created an unfavorable variance, i.e., the incurred costs were higher than the standard costs, then Natali would investigate the problem. In order to keep the standards up-to-date, reviews would be conducted annually.

John Reisner, WHI's production manager, has complained repeatedly about the standards to his superior, James Henry, vice president of operations. Reisner claims the standards are unrealistic, already out-of-date, and stifle motivation by only concentrating on unfavorable variances. As an example, he cited on-going quality concerns which have always dictated timely product improvements at WHI. Their newest innovation, the use of titanium in their Speedy Wheelchairs, increased material costs but decreased labor time. The net result was no change in total production cost. When Reisner explained that the unfavorable material variance is offset by the favorable labor variance, Natali agreed to make a "mental" adjustment. However, while the continuing favorable labor variance suggests that the workers are more productive than expected, there are indications that the workers have been slowing down on the wheelchair production line.

Isacson and Blanc cannot understand why product costs are not now under better control since all unfavorable variances are rigorously researched.

Required:
1. Describe several characteristics associated with the successful introduction and operation of a standard cost system.
2. A standard cost system can have a strong impact on both costs and employees.
   a. Describe at least three ways that a standard cost system strengthens management cost control.
   b. Describe at least two reasons why a standard cost system may negatively impact the motivation of production employees.
3. Discuss several reasons why Windsor Healthcare Inc.'s standard cost system has not been successful.

9-15. Variances in Service Industry (CMA)

Mountain View Hospital has adopted a standard cost accounting system for evaluation and control of nursing labor. Diagnosis Related Groups (DRGs), instituted by the U.S. government for health insurance reimbursement, are used as the output measure in the standard cost system. A DRG is a patient classification scheme that perceives hospitals to be multiproduct firms, where inpatient treatment procedures are related to the numbers and types of patient ailments treated. Mountain View Hospital has developed standard nursing times for the treatment of each DRG classification, and nursing labor hours are assumed to vary with the number of DRGs treated within a time period.

The nursing unit on the fourth floor treats patients with four DRG classifications. The unit is staffed with registered nurses (RNs), licensed practical nurses (LPNs), and aides. The standard nursing hours and salary rates are as follows.

**Fourth Floor Nursing Unit
Standard Hours**

DRG Classification	RN	LPN	Aide
1	6	4	5
2	26	16	10
3	10	5	4
4	12	7	10

Standard Hourly Rates

RN	$12.00
LPN	8.00
Aide	6.00

For the month of May 19X9, the results of operations for the fourth floor nursing unit are presented below.

Actual Number of Patients

DRG 1	250
DRG 2	90
DRG 3	240
DRG 4	140
	720

	RN	LPN	Aide
Actual hours	8,150	4,300	4,400
Actual salary	$100,245	$35,260	$25,300
Actual hourly rate	$12.30	$8.20	$5.75

The accountant for Mountain View Hospital calculated the following standard times for the fourth floor nursing unit for May 19X9.

DRG Classification	No. of Patients	Standard Hrs/DRG			Total Standard Hrs		
		RN	LPN	Aide	RN	LPN	Aide
1	250	6	4	5	1,500	1,000	1,250
2	90	26	16	10	2,340	1,440	900
3	240	10	5	4	2,400	1,200	960
4	140	12	7	10	1,680	980	1,400
					7,920	4,620	4,510

The hospital calculates labor variances, using a flexible budgeting approach, for each reporting period by labor classification (RN, LPN, Aide) since the hospital does not have data to calculate variances by DRG. Labor mix and labor yield variances are also calculated since one labor input can be substituted for another labor input. The variances are used by nursing supervisors and hospital administration to evaluate the performance of nursing labor.

Required:
1. Calculate the total flexible budget variance for the fourth floor nursing unit of Mountain View Hospital for May 19X9, indicating how much of this variance is attributed to
    a. labor efficiency, and to
    b. rate differences
2. a. Calculate the labor mix variance for the fourth floor nursing unit of Mountain View Hospital. (Use whole hours and whole cents in all calculations.)
    b. Explain the significance of the labor mix variance calculated in Part 2a.
3. a. Calculate the labor yield variance for the fourth floor nursing unit of Mountain View Hospital. (Use whole hours and whole cents in all calculations.)
    b. Interpret the meaning of the labor yield variance calculated in Part 3a.

9-16. Variance Reporting (CMA)

Terry Travers is the manufacturing supervisor of the Aurora Manufacturing Company which produces a variety of plastic products. Some of these products are standard items that are listed in the company's catalog, while others are made to customer specifications. Each month, Travers receives a performance report displaying the budget for the month, the actual activity for the period, and the variance between budget and actual. Part of Travers' annual performance evaluation is based on his department's performance against budget. Aurora's purchasing manager, Bob Christensen, also receives monthly performance reports, and is evaluated in part on the basis of these reports.

The most recent monthly reports had just been distributed, on the 21st of the following month, when Travers met Christensen in the hallway outside their offices. Scowling, Travers began the conversation, "I see we have another set of monthly performance reports hand-delivered by that not very nice junior employee in the budget office. He seemed pleased to tell me that I was in trouble with my performance again."

Christensen: "I got the same treatment. All I ever hear about are the things I haven't done right. Now, I'll have to spend a lot of time reviewing the report and preparing explanations. The worst part is that the information is almost a month old, and we spend all this time on history."

Travers: "My biggest gripe is that our production activity varies a lot from month to month, but we're given an annual budget that's written in stone. Last month, we were shut down for three days when a strike delayed delivery of the basic ingredient used in our plastic formulation, and we had already exhausted our inventory. You know that, of course, since we had asked you to call all over the country to find an alternate source of supply. When we got what we needed on a rush basis, we had to pay more than we normally do."

Christensen: "I expect problems like that to pop up from time to time—that's part of my job—but now we'll both have to take a careful look at the report to see where charges are reflected for that rush order. Every month, I spend more time making sure I should be charged for each item reported than I do making plans for my department's daily work. It's really frustrating to see charges for things I have no control over."

Travers: "The way we get information doesn't help, either. I don't get copies of the reports you get, yet a lot of what I do is affected by your department, and by most of the other departments we have. Why do the budget and accounting people assume that I should only be told about my operations even though the president regularly gives us pep talks about how we all need to work together, as a team?"

Christensen: "I seem to get more reports than I need, and I am never getting asked to comment until top management calls me on the carpet about my department's shortcomings. Do you ever hear comments when your department shines?"

Travers: "I guess they don't have time to review the good news. One of my problems is that all the reports are in dollars and cents. I work with people, machines, and materials. I need information to help me this month solve this month's problems—not another report of the dollars expended last month or the month before."

Required:
1. Based upon the conversation between Terry Travers and Bob Christensen, describe the likely motivation and behavior of these two employees resulting from Aurora Manufacturing Company's variance reporting system.
2. When properly implemented, both employees and companies should benefit from variance reporting systems.
   a. Describe the benefits that can be realized from using a variance reporting system.
   b. Based on the situation presented above, recommend ways for Aurora Manufacturing Company to improve its variance reporting system so as to increase employee motivation.

Chapter 10

Variance Investigation

"You stopped breathing once when you were five weeks old. Did I ever tell you that?"

No, she certainly hadn't.

"I was about to take a bath and then I thought I'd better check the crib, so I went in and you weren't moving at all. I thought you were dead. I snatched you up and tore out of the house to the Jensens and pounded on the door, and right then you let out a cry. Anyway, we took you to the doctor."

"What did he say?"

"He wasn't sure. He didn't think it was a seizure. I guess it was just one of those things that happens sometimes." Then she got up to make a salad for supper.[1]

---

[1] Garrison Keillor, *Lake Wobegon Days* (New York: Viking Penguin, Garrison Keillor, 1985), pp. 138–139.

Calculating variances allows managers to see if there is a difference between some predicted level of resource use and actual resources consumed. If variances are to be used as a source of corrective and adaptive action as well as a basis for helping to evaluate how a segment or segment manager is performing, managers are interested in seeing if a cause can be found and if something can be learned about the variance. This chapter covers variance investigation: why variances occur, when to investigate, cost-benefit trade-offs, what can be considered a normal variation around standards, and what to do after investigation.

Variances are simply indicators—much like the temperature gauge of a car going into "red." Reasons for this signal include: the gauge is faulty, the thermostat on the radiator is stuck, the radiator cap is faulty, the radiator itself has a leak, a hose has broken, fluid levels in the radiator are down, and so on. Other reasons could be linked to different parts of the automobile such as the engine or the air-conditioning or heating system. If you are going to investigate the rising temperature, you will probably stop the car and look for visible signals of the source of the problem (steam, water escaping). Given the signals as well as your own expertise with these matters, you will assess whether to proceed with the journey or whether to call a tow truck. The reasons for the signal vary from a faulty message to quite costly causes. There are interdependencies that can exist as well. Most manufacturing variances can follow this same model as can the variance investigation process. It's a matter of looking at signals, asking questions about the information behind the signal, and seeing if the cause can be found and corrected. Sometimes, as in the opening quote, it's just a seemingly random happening and no cause can be found.

CONCERNS OF INVESTIGATION

Managers are concerned about what corrective actions are warranted and possible and how to assign responsibility for variances. Variances have economic consequences and can be interrelated. Thus, managers are interested in why a variance occurred and how it might be related to other parts of the business or other managers' actions. In addition, some variances might show that the norms are no longer applicable. This opens up a discussion and analysis of what actions to take. The first question, then, is why variances occur.

WHY VARIANCES OCCUR

Managers are concerned with causality of variances so that they can decide how to avoid unfavorable variances (or possibly repeat favorable variances) in the future. In addition, there may be an interrelationship among variances.

For example, unfavorable variances in one area might have been caused by actions that yielded favorable variances in another area. As an illustration, substandard work in a previous department may have produced favorable material use and labor and variable overhead efficiency variances in that department. However, the succeeding department may have a difficult time (increased time, scrap, rework) with those subassemblies and have unfavorable variances as a result. Thus, it is not enough to know that a variance occurred. Managers also need to find out why and how it is interrelated with other variances. As another item of concern, determining cause also allows managers to see if standards should be revised due to a permanent change in prices, quality, or technology.

While it is difficult to find an all-inclusive set of categories to describe why variances occur, we can develop some basic classifications. First, variances can be the result of inaccurate data. A second reason for variances is a change in costs (price standard) or production conditions (quantity standard) that warrant a change in standard costs. Third, variances can be the result of random happenings—something that is unlikely to occur on an ongoing basis. Finally, variances can be the result of especially efficient or inefficient operations.

Inaccurate Data

Variances may be the result of incorrect data. Costs can be recorded incorrectly all the way from receiving material to the shipping of final products. A good control system will contain procedures to check the accuracy of the system itself. Were costs recorded in the proper accounts? Were data collected correctly and accurately reported? Were separable costs properly differentiated from joint costs? How was overhead applied? These can be difficult questions, depending on the complexity of the system.

Products and services can go through many departments. The more data that have to be recorded, the more exposure there is for possible errors. In a hospital, for example, records may travel with a patient from admitting through the emergency room, X-ray, the pharmacy, and ultimately to a floor where the patient is put into a room. Different people handle the records under differing states of pressure. There may have been a multiple-vehicle accident so that the emergency room and X-ray resources are taxed to their limit. This may result in some wrong information being posted regarding a particular patient's costs or the total number of patients treated in a given period of time. Good system management will tend to prevent errors by having good procedures. Careful control checks will allow many errors to be detected before they affect variances. However, errors can and do occur.

It is possible that data are intentionally inaccurate. Managers get to know when and how variances are reported to upper management. For example, if only variances that exceed $1,000 or are at least plus or minus 10 percent of standard will be reported, a manager may try to control his variance levels so that few if any exceptional variances happen. Thus, if a certain shift (day, week) is particularly efficient, the manager may not report how well it did but, rather, may "save" the additional efficiency for the next shift (day, week) when production may be down a bit. This presents an interesting problem; accountants must be as alert to variances that regularly show little or no deviation from normal limits as they are of variances that exceed these limits.

Out-of-Date Standards

In Chapter 9 we discussed variances that are caused by standards being out of date. The most common reason that standard costs are dated is a change in costs. Material costs change as competitive pressures and the economy change. Labor or contracted service costs change over time due to new contracts, cost-of-living adjustments, and the like.

Standards may have been set with the idea that new equipment would be in place by a certain time. During the transition period while the old equipment is still being used, standards will be out of date. Standards for jobs entailing crews may be based on a certain experience level of an average crew. A telephone company may have standards on installation based on a crew with a predicted level of experience. If, say, due to rapid expansion of service within an area, crews needed to be split up and many new hires were added to the installation teams, then existing standards of performance would be inaccurate and should be adjusted at least during the learning experience time of the new people.

There can be a difference between estimating standards and production standards. For example, a particular job may have been estimated based on a certain routing of the job through departments and personnel and machinery within those departments. However, when the job was ready to be produced, operating managers may reroute the job due to capacity and cost needs of the time. The estimating standards and variances from these standards will be a good way to see if the operating managers made correct decisions in such cases, but a new set of standards for the job, based on what costs should have been given the routing selected, must be used to evaluate operational performance. (Note how this is similar to the ideas of forecasting and opportunity cost variances discussed in Chapter 9.) Many computer-based manufacturing accounting systems allow for these two variances to be calculated on a regular basis. In addition, the change of standard variance outlined in the previous chapter allows managers to recognize that standards have changed but also to tie records back to original budgets and standards so there is a trail for the control system.

Random Happenings

Not all variances can be attributed to a particular set of causes. Some variances are not ongoing in nature and, even if a cause can be found, are not likely to recur in a subsequent period. When managers establish standards, they do so with the realization that both standard input cost and standard use are based on expected values. Historical data are often used as a basis for standard costs. Perhaps regression analysis has been used. If so, then management has a good idea of not only the expected costs but also a range of expected deviations from that cost (by use of the standard error of the regression coefficient, the standard error of the estimate, or standard error of the forecast). Thus, managers expect some random fluctuation to occur around the standards. Control charts and control limits discussed below allow a tracking of such variation.

Special Conditions

A particular operation may have experienced either a special efficiency or inefficiency. The most common example of this is what managers call an *out-of-control* condition. The word *control* in this context means within usual cost limits. If, say, managers believe that standard costs plus or minus two standard deviations is a proper range for operating values, these are the control limits. If a process moves outside these limits on what seems a permanent basis, it is classified as out of control. Trends become especially important in determining if and how a process is out of control. These trends, as illustrated in our discussion of control charts as well as the use of Bayesian revision, for example, allow managers to schedule preventative maintenance before costs (and variances) get too much out of line.

WHEN TO INVESTIGATE

Once data have been checked and standards have been updated as appropriate, managers must decide if the size and the cost of a variance warrant an investigation. The basic question is whether the expected benefits of investigation are greater than the expected costs of that investigation. While the expected-value model presented below is simplistic, it is a practical way that managers make this decision.

Variances Reported by Exception

A usual way to begin to identify at least which variances should be candidates for investigation is to set up screening criteria. For example, a usual screen would be variances that exceed some dollar amount (such as $1,000) or that are over (or under) standards by some set percentage (such as 10 percent). Any variance that meets one or both of these criteria might be large enough both to report and to investigate.

Cost versus Benefit

Once likely variances are identified, then managers can use an expected-value model to assess if investigation is called for. In the basic model, we identify that an investigation can have two outcomes: *success* or *failure*. If the investigation is successful, managers can determine causality and can correct the variance. Later we will expand the discussion to include situations where a cause can be found but the variance may not be correctable.

As with most models, we start off assuming certainty about some of the parameters. Assume that there is a cost (C) of investigation that is certain and there is a benefit (B) that is also known and certain. In most cases, we assume that the benefit is the cost of the variance, which will disappear the next period if a corrective action is taken by management. As stated, there are two outcomes if investigation is undertaken: success or failure. Managers will have to assess the probability of success (with the probability of failure being 1-*probability of success*). With this in mind, we have the following set of circumstances:

	Success	Failure
Investigate	+$	–$
Do not investigate	0	0
	P	1 – p	**Probability of success**

If the benefit of investigating is less than the cost of the investigation, then, obviously, no investigation is called for based on expected values, even if *p(success)* = 1.00. The table above shows that if we investigate and are successful, the benefit will exceed cost. If managers investigate in vain, the company is out the cost of investigation and reaps no benefits. If managers choose not to investigate, there are neither costs nor benefits.

As an example, assume that a company has incurred a variance where the cost of an investigation is $400 and the expected benefits are $750. Also assume that the probability of finding a correctable cause [*p(success)*] is 40 percent. In this case, the payoff table would look like the following:

	Investigation		
	Success	**Failure**	**Expected Value**
Investigate	$750 – $400	– $400	– $100
Do not investigate	0	0	0
p(success)	0.40	0.60	

The expected value (*EV*) of investigation is ($350)(0.40) − ($400)(0.60) = −$100. Therefore, it is better from an expected-value viewpoint not to investigate since the *EV* (do not investigate) = $0.

Another way of looking at this is that there is a 40 percent chance of receiving the $750 gross benefit if management investigates while there is a 100 percent chance of spending the $400 cost. Since the expected benefit is only $300 (0.40 x $750) while the cost is $400, there is a $100 disadvantage to investigating.

It is possible to generalize from the above discussion and payoff table. Managers would want to investigate if the expected benefits are greater than the expected costs. If we identify *p(success)* as *P*, then, using the example given above, managers would investigate if *PB* > *C*. We see that *PB* is $300 and *C* is $400. Here, *PB* < *C* and we do not investigate.

It is important to do some sensitivity analysis using this relationship. What would *P* have to be so that managers would be indifferent between investigating and not investigating? In such a case, the expected benefits would exactly equal the expected costs. This is the point where

$$PB = C \quad \text{or} \quad P = C/B$$

In the example above, C/B = $400/$750 = 0.533333. At this point (as you should verify) the expected costs and the expected benefits both equal $400.

Costs, benefits, and the probability of success may not be easy to estimate. Managers also run the risk of investigating when there really is no correctable variance (such as a random occurrence) and incurring a cost with no possibility of a benefit. Sometimes they chance not investigating (not believing the situation is out of control or thinking the size of the benefit is smaller than it turns out to be) when they really should have. It is important to know the parameters of this simple model and to do sensitivity analysis. If the *p(success)* is estimated to be, say, 0.50, a manager may choose to investigate even though this figure is below the breakeven suggested by the expected-value model. Thus, managers will want to look at costs and benefits as well as the probability of success to find out what combination of these three variables will push an answer toward the decision to investigate or not investigate.

CONTROL LIMITS AND CHARTS

This section and the next address ways that managers can gain a better perspective about the investigation decision, a view that extends beyond the expected-value model above. If a manager is deciding whether to commit resources for an investigation, it is useful to see cost or use trends that have occurred over time. While a variance may itself be within the usual bounds defined as "normal" by managers, costs may be drifting upward (downward) toward these limits. Control limits and control charts allow managers to highlight variances that seem out of bounds and to monitor ongoing trends as well.

Statistical Control Limits

Control limits and control charts are most useful when there is a way to measure the attributes of production output. For example, packages of frozen orange juice can be weighed, can be tested for the quality of the frozen concentrate, and so on. Manufactured parts can be measured to see if they meet engineering specifications. Waste as a percentage of material use can be measured.

In most firms, there is a testing procedure that relies on sampling production. Samples are a way to come to a conclusion about an entire population without the expense of looking at everything produced. However, not all production should be sampled, since some sampling will destroy the product. Samples would be collected hourly, each shift, daily, weekly, or monthly depending on the process, costs of sampling, and so on. Each sample will have a mean and a range (dispersion) of values around the mean. Each mean is $\bar{x}_i$ and each sample has a standard deviation of $\sigma_{\bar{x}}^2$. As more samples are accumulated, managers can calculate a grand mean of all samples, $\bar{\bar{X}}$, (called X double-bar) and that grand mean will be the manager's estimate of the true cost, measurement, or attribute of all production, μ.

Since the normal distribution assumption is robust, managers usually set up control limits and testing procedures that incorporate a normal distribution. If there are a small number of observations, then a manager may use a t distribution instead.[2] The variance of sample means, $\sigma_{\bar{x}}^2$, is calculated by dividing the true variance of costs by the sample size. This is noted as

$$\sigma_{\bar{x}}^2 = \frac{\sigma_{\bar{x}}^2}{n}$$

Note that this variance decreases as the number of samples, n, increases. Much in the same way managers use $\bar{\bar{X}}$ to estimate μ, the true variance of costs is estimated by s, the sample standard deviation. This is

$$s = \sqrt{\frac{\Sigma(x_i - \bar{x})^2}{n-1}}$$

---

[2] Actually, the use of a t distribution is warranted when the variance of a sample is unknown. However, as the number of observations increases, the values of the t distribution, as shown in a t-table, approach values for a normal distribution (a Z-table). Finally, even if the underlying variable has an unknown distribution, the distribution of sample means will be normal.

As a result of sampling, then, managers can establish a standard (which may be based on the grand mean) and a measure of variation (the sample standard deviation). Then, using either normal or *t*-tables, they can determine upper and lower bounds that are acceptable to them. It is usual that either two or three standard deviations form at least the upper bound. Bounds may be truncated due to marketing considerations or governmental regulations. Thus, bounds may not be symmetrical.

Illustration: Navigator Juices

Navigator Juices produces a frozen orange juice concentrate in 16-ounce cans. Let us say that U. S. government standards require that foods labeled as containing a certain weight (volume) of food must contain at least 98 percent of that weight or, in this case, 15.68 ounces (0.98 × 16). Managers would want an overall mean of about 16 ounces. While they are allowed a lower value (i.e., 15.68 ounces) customers and consumer advocate groups would complain if average contents were not at the stated weight level. Past experience has shown that an expected standard deviation should be about 0.2 ounces. This would mean that an approximate 95 percent confidence interval of weight would be from 15.6 ounces to 16.4 ounces. Assume that Navigator Juices has sampled 15 days of production as follows:

Concentrated Frozen Orange Juice

Sample	Weight					$\bar{x}$ Mean	R Range
1	16.49	15.66	15.48	16.53	15.49	15.93	1.04
2	15.64	15.81	16.53	15.02	16.96	15.99	1.94
3	15.75	16.08	15.89	16.40	15.35	15.90	1.05
4	16.69	15.97	15.82	16.22	16.30	16.20	0.86
5	17.00	16.29	16.89	15.28	16.39	16.37	1.71
6	15.05	16.94	16.77	15.88	16.07	16.14	1.90
7	16.88	15.17	15.89	16.95	16.66	16.31	1.78
8	16.71	16.31	16.69	15.35	15.04	16.02	1.67
9	15.26	15.72	15.05	16.12	15.69	15.57	1.07
10	16.03	15.82	16.09	16.58	16.08	16.12	0.76
11	15.06	16.40	15.44	15.84	16.02	15.75	1.33
12	16.92	15.37	16.11	15.02	16.00	15.88	1.90
13	16.36	15.17	16.41	15.72	16.92	16.12	1.75
14	15.90	16.65	15.23	16.72	15.62	16.02	1.49
15	15.89	16.20	15.21	15.70	16.38	15.88	1.17
				Grand mean ($\bar{\bar{X}}$)		16.01	

Note that the grand mean is 16.01, very nearly the 16 ounces as desired.

Control Charts

Management has set a range of 15.6 to 16.4 ounces and a mean of 16 ounces. This is a 95 percent control range of (about) 16 +/– (1.96)(0.20). To view ongoing trends, managers can chart both the means and ranges of samples to look at trends. The 16.4 ounces is called an *upper control limit* or UCL and the 15.6 ounces is a *lower control limit* or LCL. Figures 10-1 and 10-2 show control charts both for mean and for range. Both are necessary, since merely looking at the chart for means can obscure some big ranges that might show that the filling machines are out of adjustment (the *out-of-control* condition discussed earlier).

Figure 10-1 shows that the LCL has been violated once. Sample 9 has a mean of 15.57, below the 15.6 lower control limit. Note that sample 5 is close to the upper control limit. No apparent pattern exists in this chart. UCL and LCL can also be set for range as depicted in Figure 10-2. Obviously, 0.00 is the LCL for range. Most samples show a range of 1.0 ounces or above. In addition there seems to be a cyclical pattern of ranges going up and down. Compare Figures 10-1 and 10-2. While sample 2, for example, has a mean near the desired 16 ounces, the range within that sample is almost 2 ounces. This is a good illustration of why managers use both mean and range control charts. It seems from this investigation that there is a problem and that

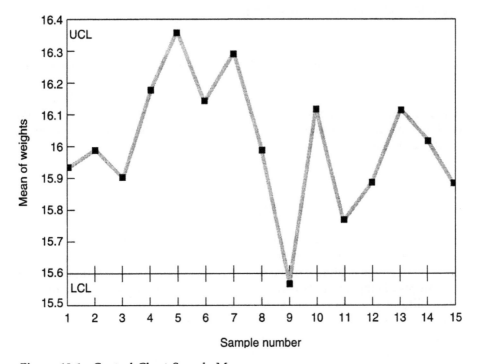

Figure 10-1 Control Chart Sample Means

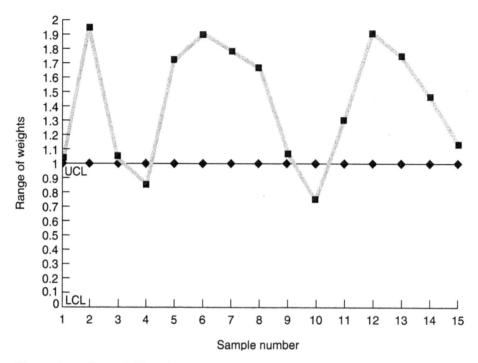

Figure 10-2   Control Chart Sample Ranges

managers may seek more samples and will go to the factory floor to see if they can solve this problem.

In this case managers would not wait for a full 15 samples to take action. Ongoing testing and charts mean that managers have daily or hourly records to view, and they can take investigative and corrective action as soon as trends seem clear.

BAYESIAN REVISION AND VARIANCE INVESTIGATION

Bayesian revision of probabilities is a method that managers can use to update their estimates of whether a process is in or out of control. Bayes' theorem, in essence, allows managers to combine their preexisting estimates of a process being in control with new information. This yields a revised probability of the process being in control.

As we discussed earlier, Bayesian revision is not widely used by operating managers. In some ways, it seems too complex to operationalize. However, the notion of revising prior information with updated information and coming to a conclusion is valid. Thus, this discussion is included in order to make you more familiar not only with the Bayesian model but also with the idea of formally revising and updating estimates in an orderly fashion.

We will assume that a company has an operating process that can be either in or out of control. Our illustration of Navigator Juices shows such a process. Control charts give some indication if the machine that fills orange juice containers is operating within normal bounds (*in control*) or is in need of adjustment due to widely fluctuating results (*out of control*).

In a simple case, we can assume that there is some distribution of values that managers would consider in control. For the weight of juice, Navigator's managers set a mean of 16 ounces with a standard deviation of 0.2 ounces. If this is a normal distribution (and we will assume it is), this *in-control* distribution can be depicted as shown in Figure 10-3.

Let us also assume that the juice machinery goes out of balance because major maintenance is needed. Past experience from company records shows that if the machine is out of control then the mean fill is 17 ounces while the standard deviation remains 0.2 ounces.[3] Figure 10-4 shows both the in- and the out-of-control distributions. Assume that a new set of samples was taken by the managers of Navigator Juices and that the mean result of all the samples (the grand mean) was 16.7 ounces. This mean value is also shown in Figure 10-4.

We need some additional information before we can use Bayes' theorem. First, we need the probability that managers had assessed that the process was in control *before* the new set of samples was taken. Given the last set of data shown in the illustration of control charts, let us say that managers estimate that *p(in control)* = 0.6. Secondly, we will need to be able to get exact probabilities to see what the likelihood is that the new grand mean

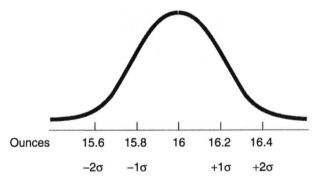

Figure 10-3   In-Control Distribution

---

[3] This is a limiting assumption since we would expect that, if a process is out of control, the variance of values around the mean would be greater than if it were in control. A later example will show how to handle such situations.

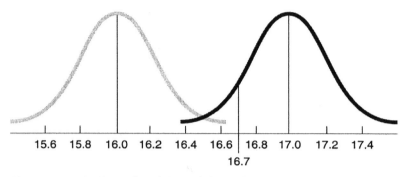

Figure 10-4   In-Control and Out-of-Control Distributions

comes from a distribution that is in control or from one that is out of control.[4] This information is shown in Table 10-1:

TABLE 10-1

$\dfrac{x - \mu}{\sigma}$	Ordinate
0.25	0.38667
0.50	0.35207
0.75	0.30114
1.00	0.24197
1.25	0.18265
1.50	0.12952
1.75	0.08628
2.00	0.05399
2.25	0.03174
2.50	0.01753
2.75	0.00909
3.00	0.00443
3.25	0.00203
3.50	0.00087
3.75	0.00035
4.00	0.00014

---

[4] Most Z-tables are used to estimate the probability of something within a range of values. These tables are based on the *cdf* (cumulative density function) of the distribution and, therefore, cumulative values are shown. Thus, using a Z-table, managers could answer the question *what is the probability that a mean of 16.7 or greater could occur given an in-control distribution?* However, we want to know the probability of a mean of *exactly* 16.7 given an in-control distribution. This is found by referring to a *pdf* (probability distribution function) table—Table 10-1.

We are interested in the following estimates:

p(in control)   *p(out of control)*
p(observation | in control)   *p(observation | out of control)*

Since the *p(out of control)* is equal to 1-*p(in control)*, it is 1 – 0.6 or 0.4. The two conditional probabilities (called *likelihoods*) can be ascertained from Table 10-1. As with a Z-table of cumulative normal probabilities, a manager must first standardize the distribution by taking the difference between the observation and the mean and dividing it by the standard deviation. This is done as follows:

In Control	**Out of Control**
$\dfrac{16.7-16}{0.2} = 3.5$	$\dfrac{16.7-17}{0.2} = 1.5$

Even at this point (before any formal math analysis has taken place) we can see that there is a higher likelihood that the observation of 16.7 ounces comes from an out-of-control distribution rather than one that is in control. This is true since the observation is much closer to the mean of the out-of-control distribution than it is to the mean of the in-control distribution (1.5 standard deviations versus 3.5).

Probability revision using Bayes' theorem is stated as follows: the probability that the process is in control *given* the observation [*p*(in control | observation)] equals

$$\frac{p(\text{observation} \mid ic) \cdot p(ic)}{p(\text{observation} \mid ic) \cdot p(ic) + p(\text{observation} \mid ooc) \cdot p(ooc)}$$

where   *ic* = in control
       ooc = out of control

In this case, this would yield the following:

$$\frac{(0.00087)(0.60)}{(0.00087)(0.60) + (0.12952)(0.40)} = 0.009975$$

Thus, while managers had a *prior probability* of 60 percent that the process was in control, the revised (*posterior*) probability is only about 1 percent given the mean of 16.7 ounces on a group of samples. This is additional information that managers can use to assess if they want to investigate the situation.

More usual cases involve a larger standard deviation for out-of-control conditions than exists for in-control. Thus, while the standard deviation for an in-control distribution may be 0.2 ounces, the standard deviation for the out-of-control distribution may be 0.3 ounces, for example. If this occurs, then the likelihoods (also called *ordinates*) must be scaled by dividing them by the appropriate standard deviation. (With 0.3 ounces as the new standard deviation, the ordinate is now 0.24197.) Thus, managers would divide as follows:

$$0.00087/0.2 = 0.004 \quad \text{and} \quad 0.24197/0.3 = 0.8066$$

These scaled likelihoods would then be used in the Bayesian revision model to yield the following:

$$\frac{(0.004)(0.60)}{(0.004)(0.60) + (0.8066)(0.40)} = 0.0074$$

With uneven variances, the two distributions would look quite different, as is shown in Figure 10-5. The out-of-control distribution is more dispersed, given its higher standard deviation. The results of using scaled ordinates, given a higher standard deviation for one of the distributions, yields a lower posterior probability of the process being in control. In this case the change is not really dramatic (0.009975 versus 0.0074), but it can be when the current observation falls not so far away from the mean of either distribution.

Bayesian revision is presented here as a general idea. It may not be possible to use this model fully. Evidence shows that managers do not act as strict Bayesians.[5] Thus, managers may not be willing to accept the results that a Bayesian revision yields. They may make subjective changes to these results or may act more conservatively than the revision suggested by the model. However, this is a valuable model to present and to discuss even if

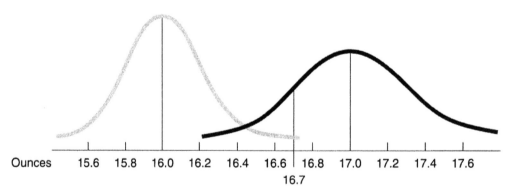

| Ounces | 15.6 | 15.8 | 16.0 | 16.2 | 16.4 | 16.6 | 16.8 | 17.0 | 17.2 | 17.4 | 17.6 |

16.7

Figure 10-5   Observation of 16.7 Ounces

[5] See Robert H. Ashton, *Studies in Accounting Research #17: Human Information Processing in Accounting*, Sarasota, Fla.: American Accounting Association (1982), Chapter 5, and P. Slovic and S. Lichenstein, "Comparison of Bayesian and Regression Approaches to the Study of Information Processing in Judgment," *Organizational Behavior and Human Performance* (November 1971), pp. 649–744.

it is not used in its full quantitative form. The basic premise that existing information should be updated given new information is a good one. Thus, even if managers do not actually use Bayesian revision, they can use the basic idea it contains quite successfully.

INVESTIGATION WITH TOC, JIT, TQC, AND ZERO DEFECTS

In an advanced manufacturing and competitive environment, we would expect a heightened effort to find out why a variance occurred. In addition, variances outside of norms should be a real exception. Thus, with virtual zero defects (five parts per million, for example), any defect is looked upon as an important matter and it is thoroughly investigated. Some Japanese firms believe that a variance is to be treasured because of what can be learned about the process and will allow managers to avoid further problems.

Investigation in a firm that follows TQC, TOC, activity-based costing, or any of the other newer models concentrates on looking at global issues rather than individual variances. Performance measures are based on overall success and, therefore, variance analysis and investigation are also based on that criterion. Proponents of TOC want to maximize throughput while minimizing inventory and operating expenses. Companies with activity-based costing look closely at transactions and the long- and short-term causes of resource consumption. JIT companies want to minimize any buffer stocks. All of these models employ some method of variance analysis. It is really the idea of what the relevant variances are given the model and what signals to follow and investigate. It gets back to the earlier example of the automobile and a signal that the water temperature is rising toward the danger zone; variance investigation is a matter of logic and based on the particular circumstances of a business.

AFTER INVESTIGATION—THEN WHAT?

Standard cost variances and variance investigation serve at least two purposes. First, as part of the control phase of management information, variances allow responsibility and causality to be determined. Secondly, however, standard cost variances and variance investigation are part of the planning phase of the next period. Managers are not looking for ways to lay blame for variances. They are looking for ways to improve profits (reduce cost) by taking action given the results achieved from production (or from services rendered).

Determining New Standards

Change-of-standards variances have been discussed. These can occur if, say, prices have changed in the marketplace and existing standards are out of date. Standards may be changed if new technology changes the nature of production or services. In addition, management may not always be able to resolve an out-of-control situation. Costs may preclude a permanent adjustment or overhaul of a machine. Thus, at least for the near term, standards should be adjusted to reflect a new cost reality.

Maximization Models

Companies use many maximization models, the most popular of which is linear programming. These models are based on specific costs and constraints. If variance investigation reveals that elements of the model have changed beyond the limits shown in the sensitivity analysis for these models, then new objective functions and/or constraints are needed and the model should be rerun. This concept is illustrated in Chapter 6. Even simple models may have to be adjusted. CVP analysis and sensitivity analysis for that model may have to be redone, given new parameters of costs or volume capabilities.

Investigating Favorable Variances

Too often discussion centers on unfavorable variances. Control charts and Bayesian revision, for example, focus on what happens if a process is going out of control. There are good reasons for looking just as carefully at favorable variances; most manual or computer-based management-by-exception reports of variances show both favorable and unfavorable variances.

Variances may be interconnected and dependent. Thus, a favorable variance in one department or aspect of cost may be the cause of an unfavorable variance in another area. Poor quality of raw materials or semifinished goods can affect costs in a following area. Excellent quality workmanship can result in equally excellent results in a subsequent department. The first may yield an unfavorable variance, but the second may be favorable and outweigh the additional cost in the first department.

If something is going on that is good, then managers want to take note of it. Perhaps favorable variances can be investigated in order to see how a particular manager's techniques and style give rise to lower costs (or higher sales). Managers need to be recognized for helping the company. It would be a shame to just concentrate on unfavorable variances and to ignore successes that managers have achieved.

Managers also have to be wary about what they stress in variance analysis. If one area is stressed too much, it may be addressed but other areas might be neglected. If, say, defective parts are highlighted as a key area for concern, it is possible that workers will raise costs to an extent that it would be less costly to have some defective parts.[6]

Analysis: The Key

Managers (and students) become enamored with numbers and sometimes forget that numbers are not answers but, at best, are information that is useful in *analysis*. Therefore, finding the numerical answer of whether the cost of investigation is lower than the expected benefit, creating control charts, using Bayesian revision, or reporting a list of standard cost variances is just the beginning. Managers must *use* these pieces of information to analyze the problems at hand and to come up with solutions or with questions that need additional information to answer. In many ways, the numerical "answers" are easy to obtain and do not take as much time as the more difficult analysis and decision making that must follow these numbers.

BEYOND THE TECHNIQUES

Some variances cannot be easily investigated using the models discussed so far. If we look at the marketing variances in Chapter 8, for example, it is hard to see how we can apply a cost-benefit expected-value model to, say, a market share variance. However, since variances are used to evaluate an agent's behavior, a trend in variances (gaining an understanding through a history) allows a manager to decide when to investigate a variance, even if in an informal way. Given the principal-agent relationship discussed in Chapter 8, managers will look beyond and into the variances when it's appropriate to do so.

SUMMARY

Managers are interested in going beyond just calculating variances. They want to know why a variance occurred, if a cause can be found, whether corrective action can be taken, who or what is responsible for a variance, etc. Variance investigation should be based on the nature of the variances calculated, a cost-benefit trade-off of the investigation process, and how to integrate variances and variance investigation with other management philosophies or evaluation techniques.

---

[6] Managers following the Japanese methods of manufacturing may argue that this conclusion cannot happen. They want absolutely zero defects.

PROBLEMS AND CASES

10-1. Questions About Variances

Required:
Respond to each question or comment independently.
1. A friend has just read some material on variances and says to you, "I would think you would want to really look at all variances and find out why they happened no matter what their size. Oh, I might overlook a $10 variance, but anything that is bigger should be investigated."
2. "It would seem to me," another student says, "that if the production variances are bad, then the person in charge of that production facility should be held responsible for the poor performance."
3. A friend has done a problem to find a critical value for the probability of success in investigating a variance. Your friend tells you, "So I solved the problem and found the answer to be 58 percent. How am I ever going to know in a practical setting whether the probability of success is 58 percent?"

10-2. Control Chart

The Stark Company maintains a standard costing system and keeps a set of control charts like the one below, which relates to direct labor cost per unit of a particular model carpet. The firm investigates a variance when the actual unit cost goes outside the limits drawn on the chart.

Required:
1. Using the firm's criterion for investigating a variance, when would it first investigate direct labor cost for carpet model 397?
2. Do you have any suggestion for the firm?

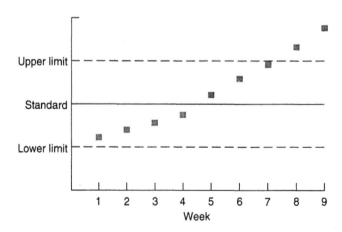

Control Chart—Direct Labor, Model 397

10-3. Variance Investigation

The Suarez Company's controller has determined that it costs $200 to investigate a variance and that in one out of five cases investigated corrective action is possible. A variance of $500 unfavorable has just been reported. Because of a major overhaul of equipment scheduled for a month from now, any savings would last only a month if corrective action could be taken.

Required:
Should the variance be investigated?

10-4. Variance Investigation: Expected Values

Phoenix, Inc., has experienced a $2,500 unfavorable variance. The production manager believes there is a 30 percent chance that the variance is a unique occurrence and will not continue. The manager believes that if an investigation is made, the chance of correcting the variance is 40 percent (therefore, the chance of not correcting it is 60 percent). It costs $700 to investigate a variance. It is expected that the most that will be lost if the variance continues is $3,000.

Required:
1. Calculate the expected costs of investigating and of not investigating the variance.
2. Should an investigation be made?

10-5. Variance Investigation: Expected Values

Current variance reports from the Cunningham Company shows an unfavorable $1,500 variance this month. The production supervisor has analyzed past data and estimates that about 30 percent of the time a variance of this size is experienced there is nothing wrong with the process and the variance stops. When there is a problem with the process, about 60 percent of the time the variance continues for two additional months (at $1,500 per month) and 40 percent of the time it continues at $1,500 per month for three months.

Just investigating the variance would cost Cunningham $600. A correctable problem usually occurs about 40 percent of the time (for either 2-month or 3-month variances). If a correctable cause is found, it is estimated that another $400 would be spent to solve the problem.

Required:
Determine the expected costs of investigating and of not investigating.

10-6. High Productivity Through Statistical Analysis

An article in *People* magazine (September 8, 1980) discussed Dr. W. Edwards Deming and his work in Japan and the United States regarding statistical analysis. The article reminds us that "Made in Japan" used to be a joke and a synonym for shoddiness. Today Japanese products are highly regarded for their quality. Dr. Deming was instrumental in working with industry in Japan and is currently working with industry in the United States to increase quality and productivity.

Asked why American industry has not adopted his methods, Dr. Deming criticized it for not being willing to commit to a long training program for all workers.

He added: "And, to my horror, I have discovered that most American companies think they already have statistical control of quality. What they have is lots of printouts full of irrelevant and out-of-date information."

Dr. Deming asserted that management has much more responsibility in declining productivity than do the workers. As an example, he discussed the purchase of inferior material that caused unfavorable efficiency variances in the production line. Management had not directed its attention to the correlation between material quality and production efficiency. Asked what could be done about ineffective management, he said:

> For one thing, our business schools have to change. Their graduates get good economics, law, finance—overall a good education. But they don't teach statistical methods in research and production. For instance, they don't teach the connection between what people need, the cost of materials and what can be produced economically.

He went on to recommend using statistical methods to improve quality. He criticized final inspection of products or inspection at major assembly points as being inefficient and ineffective. Instead, he said, we must rely more on the statistical methods available to us for quality control.

Required:
Comment on the philosophy espoused by Dr. Deming in light of the material presented in this chapter.

10-7. Explaining Variances (CMA)

The financial results for the Continuing Education Department of BusEd Corporation for November 19X8 are presented below. Mary Ross, president of BusEd, is pleased with the final results but has observed that the revenue and most of the costs and expenses of this department exceeded the budgeted amounts. Barry Stein, vice president of the Continuing Education Department, has been requested to provide an explanation of any amount that exceeded the budget by 5 percent or more.

Stein has accumulated the following facts to assist in his analysis of the November results.

1. The budget for calendar year 19X8 was finalized in December 19X7, and at that time, a full program of continuing education courses was scheduled to be held in Chicago during the first week of November 19X8. The courses were scheduled so that eight courses would be run on each of the five days during the week. The budget assumed that there would be 425 participants in the program and 1,000 participant days for the week.

2. BusEd charges a flat fee of $150 per day of course instruction, i.e., the fee for a three-day course would be $450. BusEd grants a 10 percent discount to persons who subscribe to its publications. The 10 percent discount is also granted to second and subsequent registrants for the same course from the same organization. However, only one discount per registration is allowed. Historically, 70 percent of the participant day registrations are at the full fee of $150 per day and 30 percent of the participant day registrations receive the discounted fee of

$135 per day. These percentages were used in developing the November 19X8 budgeted revenue.

Food charges per participant day (lunch/coffee breaks)	$ 27
Course materials per participant	8
Instructor fee per day	1,000

3. The following estimates were used to develop the budgeted figures for course related expenses.
4. A total of 530 individuals participated in the Chicago courses in November, 19X8, accounting for 1,280 participant days. This included 20 persons who took a new, two-day course on pension accounting that was not on the original schedule; thus, on two of the days, nine courses were offered, and an additional

Full fee registrations	704
Discounted fees	
Current periodical subscribers	128
New periodical subscribers	128
Second registrations from the same organization	320
Total participant day registrations	1,280

instructor was hired to cover the new course. The breakdown of the course registration was as follows.

5. A combined promotional mailing was used to advertise the Chicago program and a program in Cincinnati that was scheduled for December, 19X8. The incremental costs of the combined promotional piece was $5,000, but none of the promotional expenses ($20,000) budgeted for the Cincinnati program in December will have to be incurred. This earlier than normal promotion for the

Full fee registrations	140
Discounted registrations	60
Total participant day registrations	200

Cincinnati program has resulted in early registration fees collected in November as follows (in terms of participant days).

6. BusEd continually updates and adds new courses, and includes $2,000 in each monthly budget for this purpose. The additional amount spent on course development during November was for an unscheduled course that will be offered in February for the first time.

Barry Stein has prepared the quantitative analysis of the November 19X8 variances shown on page 418.

BusEd Corporation
Statement of Operations—Continuing Education Department
November 19X8

	Budget	Actual	Favorable/ (Unfavorable) Dollars	Favorable/ (Unfavorable) Percent
Revenue				
Course fees	$145,500	$212,460	$ 66,960	46.0
Expenses				
Food charges	$ 27,000	$ 32,000	$ (5,000)	(18.5)
Course materials	3,400	4,770	(1,370)	(40.3)
Instructor fees	40,000	42,000	(2,000)	(5.0)
Instructor travel	9,600	9,885	(285)	(3.0)
Staff salaries and benefits	12,000	12,250	(250)	(2.1)
Staff travel	2,500	2,400	100	4.0
Promotion	20,000	25,000	(5,000)	(25.0)
Course development	2,000	5,000	(3,000)	(150.0)
Total expenses	$116,500	$133,305	$(16,805)	(14.4)
Revenues over expenses	$29,000	$ 79,155	$ 50,155	172.9

BusEd Corporation
Analysis of November, 19X8 Variances

Budgeted revenue			$145,500	
Variances:				
Quantity variance				
[(1,280 − 1,000) × $145.50]	$40,740	F		
Mix variance [($143.25 − $145.50) × 1,280]	2,880	U		
Timing difference ($145.50 × 200)	29,100	F	66,960	F
Actual revenue			$212,460	
Budgeted expenses			$116,500	
Quantity variances				
Food charges [(1,000 − 1,280) × $27]	$ 7,560	U		
Course materials [(425 − 530) × $8]	840	U		
Instructor fees (2 × $1,000)	2,000	U	$ 10,400	U
Price variances				
Food charges [($27.00 − $25.00) × 1,280]	$ 2,560	F		
Course materials [($8.00 − $9.00) × 530]	530	U	2,030	F
Timing differences				
Promotion	$ 5,000	U		
Course development	3,000	U	8,000	U
Variances not analyzed (5 percent or less)				
Instructor travel	$ 285	U		
Staff salaries and benefits	250	U		
Staff travel	100	F	435	U
Actual expenses			$133,305	

Required:
After reviewing Barry Stein's quantitative analysis of the November variances, prepare a memorandum addressed to Mary Ross explaining the following.
1. The cause of the revenue mix variance.
2. The implication of the revenue mix variance.
3. The cause of the revenue timing difference.
4. The significance of the revenue timing difference.
5. The primary cause of the unfavorable total expense variance.
6. How the favorable food price variance was determined.
7. The impact of the promotion timing difference on future revenues and expenses.
8. Whether or not the course development variance has an unfavorable impact on the company.

10-8. Decision to Investigate

Standard costs for the Crawford Frozen Foods Company include the following for one of its largest-selling products:

Standard Material Costs
Chinese Beef and Asparagus Dinner per 8-oz Package

Choice grade sirloin strips, 8 oz uncooked weight at $3/lb	$1.50
California select thin asparagus, 3 oz uncooked weight at $1.50/lb	0.28
Secret blend of herbs and spices, ½ oz.	0.20

The production process starts in the food preparation department, where all raw foodstuffs are cut. From there, the raw foods go to the cooking department, where workers combine the ingredients according to Crawford's recipes. Portion control is very important from the standpoint of cost as well as that of quality and consistency. Foods shrink when cooked; it is expected that the net weight of a package after shrinkage is 8 ounces. Management has set up control limits as follows, using a 3-sigma range for the finished product:

$\overline{X}$: 7.92 to 8.16 oz
R: 0 to 0.12 oz

Crawford is limited by federal government rules to providing packages that weigh no less than 99 percent of the stated weight. Thus, while the upper control limit is 3 sigmas, the lower limit is truncated for $\overline{X}$.

During February the following samples were taken at random over a one-week period:

Sample	Work Shift	Sample Packages 1	2	3	4
1	1	7.95	8.09	8.06	8.03
2	2	8.16	8.13	8.18	8.11
3	2	8.14	8.19	8.12	8.15
4	1	8.05	7.93	8.07	8.05
5	1	8.05	8.03	8.02	8.15
6	2	8.12	8.20	8.15	8.17

Required:
1. Plot the data on $\bar{X}$ and R charts.
2. On the basis of these data, what recommendations would you make to the managers of Crawford?

10-9. Developing Control Charts

Rather than calculating control limits for $\bar{X}$ (and $\bar{R}$) by using $\bar{X}$ and $\sigma_{x'}$ tables are available to use just $\bar{X}$ and $\bar{R}$ in the calculations. Under this method, control limits for $\bar{\bar{X}}$ are

$$\bar{\bar{X}} \pm F\bar{R}$$

where F is a factor (Exhibit 1) for 3 standard deviations (a confidence interval of 99.73 percent using the normal distribution). Limits for $\bar{R}$ are

upper limit: $U\bar{R}$
lower limit: $L\bar{R}$

where U and L (Exhibit 2) also are 3 standard deviations from the mean, $\bar{R}$. In both cases, n refers to the number of items in each sample.

Assume the Tercela Company produces a chemical called Plake that is delivered to customers in 5-pound buckets. As part of cost control it is important to check that the net weight of each bucket of Plake is within reasonable limits of 5 pounds. On January 28 management sampled production runs over an eight-hour shift. The weights found in Exhibit 3 were recorded for samples taken at random during each hour.

Required:
1. Using the techniques described above, establish upper and lower control limits for $\bar{X}$ and $\bar{R}$.
2. Use the techniques in the chapter to confirm a 3-standard-deviation UCL and LCL calculated for $\bar{X}$ and $\bar{R}$ in Part 1.

Exhibit 1 **Control-Limit Factor for $\bar{X}$ Charts, F**			**Exhibit 2** **Control-Limit Factors for R Charts,** **U and L**		
n	F		n	U	L
2	1.880		2	3.268	0.000
3	1.023		3	2.574	0.000
4	0.729		4	2.282	0.000
5	0.577		5	2.114	0.000
6	0.483		6	2.004	0.000
7	0.419		7	1.924	0.076
8	0.373		8	1.864	0.136
9	0.337		9	1.816	0.184
12	0.266		12	1.716	0.284
14	0.235		14	1.671	0.329
16	0.212		16	1.636	0.364

Exhibit 3
Tercela Company Production Runs

Hour	Samples (in Pounds)					
	1	2	3	4	5	6
1	5.22	5.06	4.97	5.11	5.02	5.03
2	4.95	5.18	5.08	5.00	5.06	5.12
3	5.11	5.09	5.06	5.13	5.10	5.01
4	4.98	5.00	5.06	4.96	5.07	5.10
5	5.05	5.18	5.01	5.15	5.01	5.09
6	5.11	5.04	5.06	5.10	5.18	5.20
7	5.07	5.11	5.08	4.99	5.00	5.02
8	5.13	5.02	5.09	5.08	5.15	5.10

10-10. When to Investigate

Frank Strout, manager of Midcourse, Inc., has been accumulating data over several years concerning the costs, benefits, and probability of success when seemingly excessive variances have been investigated. These data show that about 90 percent of the time that material use is higher than 2 ½ standard deviations from standard, the process can be considered out of control. Past records also show that use under 2 ½ standard deviations from standard means that there is an 85 percent chance the process is in control.

Required:
1. What is the probability that the process is in control given each of the following situations?

a.

Standard Cost per Unit	σ
Material — 3 lb at $4	$1
Actual use — 1,000 units produced using $15,000 of materials at standard prices	

b.

Standard Cost per Unit	σ
Material — 4 gal at $5	0.2 gal
Actual use — 1,000 units produced using 4,400 gal	

2. If we assume that the cost to investigate variances is $1,500 and the expected savings are $2,000 in Part 1a, what is the breakeven point for investigation? Would you investigate in this case? What about Part 1b?

10-11. Linear Programming and Variance Investigation

Many companies use linear programming to help them in resource allocation. The constraint on labor time, for example, may include standard times for each different unit produced. If actual times vary either favorably or unfavorably beyond some point, the company would be better off to produce a different mix than the mix of products called for using a linear programming solution.

Assume that cost data for the Egrad Company are as follows:

	Product 1	Product 2
Sales price	$20.00	$21.00
Materials at $1/lb	3.00	5.00
Labor at $2/hr	5.00	4.00
Overhead	6.00	4.80
Margin	$ 6.00	$ 7.20

Constraints are as follows:

Materials	200 lb
Labor	100 hr

Required:
1. Use a computer solution or a graphical analysis and solve the product mix called for by a linear program.
2. What level of labor would be required to change the solution reached in item 1? [*Hint*: Use sensitivity analysis as developed in Chapter 6.]
3. During the current month, variances on product 1 for 1,000 equivalent units were as follows:

Material use variance	$ 600 U
Labor efficiency variance	$1,200 U

If these variances are investigated and found to be rather permanent in nature, should the production be changed or kept the same? If it is changed, what is the new solution?

10-12. Bayesian Revision

Harris Stowe, the production manager of Redeye Manufacturers, has been developing data on one of the main pieces of manufacturing equipment. As a cost accountant, you have been using these data in looking beyond simple variance calculations. The main forming machine usually produces parts that are within standard tolerances. For example, the standards for a #80-H shaft include a diameter of 2.5 cm and an acceptable variance of 0.01 cm. However, internal parts of the machine are subject to wear. Past experience indicates that when average diameter is 2.9 cm and the variance is 0.09 cm, the process is out of control and repairs are called for costing $38,000 at current prices. During December, production data combined with standard costs showed $8,000 in unfavorable variances associated with the production of #80-H shafts. You have been asked to give Mr. Stowe information to help him decide whether to order the $38,000 overhaul. December production reports show an average diameter for #80-H shafts of 2.75 cm.

Required:
If management is currently 90 percent confident that a variance of 10 percent or less means that the production process is within normal ranges of tolerance, calculate

an updated probability estimate for Mr. Stowe, given the current production information. (See Table 10-1 on page 408.)

10-13. Investigation Decision

In Assignment 10-12 you were asked to calculate the posterior probability that the forming process was in control. Assume Redeye management thinks that if $38,000 is spent on an overhaul, there is only an 80 percent chance they can solve an out-of-control situation. Also assume that if the process is out of control, abnormal variances will be $90,000 per year.

Required:
Using a one-year time frame, should management order an overhaul? (Use the information you calculated in the previous assignment.)

10-14. Expected Values and EVPI (CMA)

The Wentworth Company manufactures modular furniture for the home and uses a monthly variance system to control costs of the manufacturing departments. Edward Collins is the supervisor of the Assembly Department and is reviewing the monthly variance analysis for November that is shown below.

Standard cost of production materials	$275,000
Materials price variance	-0-
Materials quality variance—unfavorable	19,000
Actual cost of production materials	$294,000

Collins has gathered the following information to assist him in deciding whether or not to investigate the unfavorable materials quantity variance.

Estimated cost to investigate the variance	$4,000
Estimated probability that the Assembly Department is operating properly	90%
If the Assembly Department is operating improperly:	
Estimated cost to make the necessary changes	$8,000
Estimated present value of future unfavorable variances that would be saved by making the necessary changes	$40,000

Required:
1. Recommend whether or not Wentworth Company should investigate the unfavorable materials quantity variance. Support your recommendation by
   a. preparing a payoff table for use in making the decision.
   b. computing the expected value of the cost of each possible action.
2. Edward Collins is uncertain about the probability estimate of 90 percent for proper operation of the Assembly Department. Determine the probability estimate of the Assembly Department operating properly that would cause Collins to be indifferent between the two possible actions.
3. Assume a consultant is hired to advise Wentworth Company and is able to predict accurately the state of the operations in the assembly department. Compute the expected value of the consultant's perfect information.

10-15. Investigating Standard Cost Variances in the Mesa Corporation[7]

The Mesa Corporation, a medium-sized manufacturing firm, uses injection molding machines to produce a variety of custom-ordered products for the airline and automotive industries. Recent recessionary pressures in the economy have negatively affected both the airline and the automotive industries. The major airline and auto firms are "squeezing" their suppliers, including Mesa. Consequently, there is a lot of pressure to control costs.

Adrian Bates is the production superintendent for Mesa (see the partial organization chart for Mesa in Figure 1). Adrian's job requires both an engineering degree and an MBA degree. In addition, she must have considerable practical experience gained from working in various line and support functions for Mesa. This duality

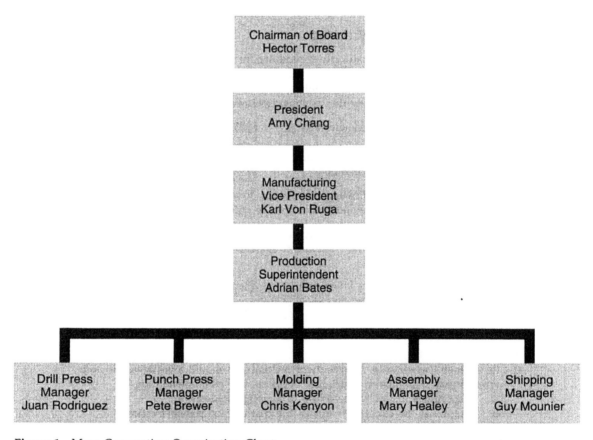

Figure 1   Mesa Corporation Organization Chart

[7] Robert Capettini, Chee W. Chow, and James E. Williamson, "Instructional Cases: The Proper Use of Feedback Information," *Issues in Accounting Education*, (Sarasota, Fla.: American Accounting Association) Vol. 7, No. 1 (Spring 1992), pp. 37–56.

of education and experience is necessary because she needs to aid managers in solving production problems, in using management accounting information, and in using techniques to control production costs.

One of Ms. Bates' subordinates, Chris Kenyon, manages the Molding Department of Mesa Corporation. Mr. Kenyon has asked Ms. Bates' opinion about some perceived problems in his department and a potential solution which he is considering. Based on his rudimentary knowledge of cost control and some feedback data from recent production reports, Mr. Kenyon thinks that one of the standards in his department may be outdated. As a proposed solution, he is considering revising the standard of expected average usage of plastic which is used as a benchmark to signal an out-of-control machine.

While the job description for a production department manager does not require a college degree, Chris' job does require an elementary knowledge of cost-control techniques, as well as a good functional knowledge of production procedures and some basic interpersonal management skills necessary for working with people. Chris fulfilled the educational requirements by attending a community college for two years, where he took some basic math, engineering, and statistics courses; a production course; and an introduction to managerial accounting course.

The Molding Department has 12 identical molding machines (Machines A through L) which produce subassemblies for various products. When a machine is properly adjusted, it uses an average of 100 pounds of plastic (with a standard deviation of 3 pounds) to produce a subassembly. When a machine is not properly adjusted, it uses an average of 110 pounds of plastic (with a standard deviation of 5 pounds) to produce a subassembly. Since it is quite costly to adjust the machines, adjustments are made only when variances indicate that a machine might be out-of-control.

Mr. Kenyon's responsibilities include determining which variances should be investigated and whether the existing standard is correct or should be revised. The primary criterion underlying his decisions is to minimize the department's production costs per subassembly. Figure 2 illustrates the situation in Mr. Kenyon's department. The bell-shaped curve on the left represents the distribution of the material usage per unit of output when a machine is in-control. The mean of this distribution, $C_i = 100$, is used as the performance standard. The bell-shaped curve on the right is the distribution of material usage when a machine is out-of-control. The mean of this distribution, C_o, is 110. Since performance is typically subject to a multitude of random factors, actual material usage may be lower (a favorable variance) or higher (an unfavorable variance) than C_i when a machine is in-control. Likewise, random factors may cause material usage to be higher or lower than C_o even when a machine is out-of-control. These situations are reflected in the overlap of the two distributions.

Table 1 illustrates the two basic types of decision errors which increase the cost of producing the subassemblies. The rows of the table indicate the two alternative actions which Chris may take, while the columns indicate the two alternative states of nature which can occur. A Type I error results in the cost of an unnecessary investigation when a machine is actually in-control and does not need adjustment. A Type II error results in the cost of continuing to use too much plastic by not adjusting a machine which is actually out-of-control. Type I errors are caused by large random unfavorable variances from the in-control distribution. Type II errors are caused by large random favorable variances from the out-of-control distribution.

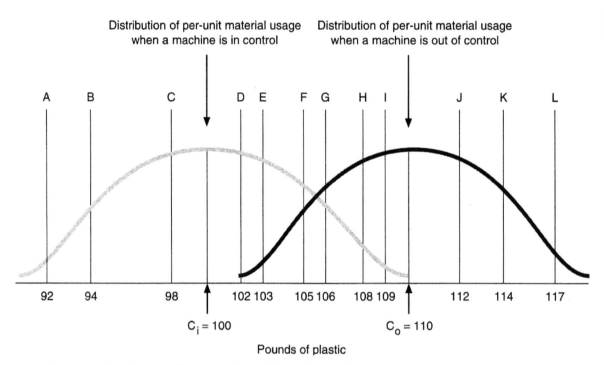

Figure 2 Distribution of In-Control and Out-of-Control Costs with the Twelve Machines

TABLE 1
Decision Table for Variance
Investigation Decision

	Machine is In-Control	**Machine is Out-of-Control**
Investigate	Type I Error	Correct Decision
Do not Investigate	Correct Decision	Type II Error

Recently, Mr. Kenyon received the variance report (shown in Table 2) for the 12 machines in his department. The observations from these 12 machines also are shown in Figure 2. The report shows usage variances, from the standard quantity of 100 pounds, ranging from a favorable 8 pounds to an unfavorable 17 pounds. Because Mr. Kenyon did not want to incur excessive and unnecessary investigation costs, he decided to have the firm's mechanic inspect and adjust only those machines with unfavorable variances two or more standard deviations from the standard (machines G, H, I, J, K, and L). From his investigations the mechanic found machines G and H to be in-control while machines I, J, K, and L were out-of-control (see Table 3).

TABLE 2
Direct Materials Standard Variance Reports for Twelve Illustrative Machines

Observation from Machine	Pounds of Plastic Used	Standard Pounds of Plastic	Variance	
A	92	100	FAV	8
B	94	100	FAV	6
C	98	100	FAV	2
D	102	100	UNFAV	2
E	103	100	UNFAV	3
F	105	100	UNFAV	5
G	106	100	UNFAV	6
H	108	100	UNFAV	8
I	109	100	UNFAV	9
J	112	100	UNFAV	12
K	114	100	UNFAV	14
L	117	100	UNFAV	17

TABLE 3
Mechanic's Report of the Physical Inspection of Six Machines

In-Control Machines		Out-of-Control Machines	
	Lbs. Used		Lbs. Used
G	106	I	109
H	108	J	112
		K	114
		L	117
Total Usage	214	Total Usage	452
Average Usage	107	Average Usage	113

Mr. Kenyon feels that knowing the means of both the in-control distribution and the out-of-control distribution is necessary to making sound investigation decisions. Based upon the mechanic's findings, Mr. Kenyon was considering revising the standard quantity allowed for production of the subassemblies from 100 to 108 pounds of plastic per unit; this is the standard which would have prevented the Type I errors resulting in the unnecessary investigation costs associated with machines G and H. He also was considering revising the expected mean usage of an out-of-control machine from 110 to 113 pounds of plastic per unit.

As Chris Kenyon's boss, Adrian Bates is concerned that Chris might be wasting resources by doing unnecessary investigations. However, Ms. Bates also is concerned that if Chris does not do enough investigations, the resultant lower quality may cause the product to be rejected by the airline and automotive firms. This may lead to expensive rework or loss of profitable contracts with these industries.

Required:

Suppose that you are Adrian Bates who has been asked to evaluate Chris Kenyon.

1. Has Chris Kenyon performed his job well?

2. Which of the 12 machines would you have investigated (i.e., which cost variances do you think were caused by a machine NOT being in proper adjustment)? Why?

3. Why were the means of the two distributions (when a machine is properly adjusted and when a machine is not properly adjusted), based on the variances selected for investigation, higher than what Chris Kenyon thought they were?

4. Re-estimate the means of the two distributions. Is the mean plastic usage of 100 pounds when a machine is in proper adjustment still an appropriate standard or is 108 or some other number a better standard? Is the existing mean plastic usage of 110 pounds when a machine is not in proper adjustment still an appropriate estimate of the mean of that distribution or is 113 or some other number a better estimate?

5. What methods can you suggest to improve Chris Kenyon's ability to update, in the future, the means of the two distributions?

Chapter 11

Allocation Issues

The butcher he killed a calf, a nice, young adolescent bull. Being a modern butcher, he then called upon his engineer, his secretary, and his figurers three to appear and perform a cost allocation on the carcass.

What price veal?" quoth he, "and what price hide? How much did the meat on this animal cost me? How much did the hide cost in its present undressed state? My rate of profit must be the same, too, on the bones and hoofs, so tell me the cost per pound of each."

Thereupon and for many days thereafter the figures flew freely. The bull was spread upon the dissecting table and treated from every angle and by every method. And finally the city health authorities came and carted them all away.

There has been a lot of good bull used up in allocations, but the original bull remains unallocated.[1]

---

[1] Charles S. Reed, "Veal, Hide and By-Products," *Electrical World* (August 27, 1927).

At least since World War II, competition has forced firms to differentiate their output and to undertake multiproduct operations. During the same 50-year span, white collar workers displaced blue collar workers, production became more capital intensive, more automated, and more computerized. The costs of labor increasingly were determined by long-term contracts and passed from variable to semi-fixed or fixed. As a consequence of these and other major trends, the need to allocate costs, both as relevant data for operations and as guides to pricing policy, grew proportionately.

Yet, during the same period, the term 'cost allocation' was anathema. Economists and accountants never wearied of pointing out that practically all cost allocations were arbitrary, dysfunctional, sterile, unnecessary and/or useless. . . . What obviously was needed was that methods of cost allocations be proposed that could be justified theoretically, whether on behavioral, organizational or economic grounds.[2]

Managers are increasingly aware that they should trace costs to units, batches, products, processes, and plants. This is the focus of activity-based costing (ABC) and activity-based management (ABM). However, once these costs are traced to their appropriate level, managers are still left with the question of whether to assign such costs to the cost object even though there is no clear way to trace them. At the same time, financial accounting rules require that all product costs be assigned to units of product so that inventory and cost of goods sold can be valued according to GAAP for external reports to, among others, stockholders, debt holders, and regulatory agencies.

There has been an ongoing debate among academics and practicing accountants for decades, as alluded to in the introductory quotations. On one side are those that say that allocations are arbitrary and can cause dysfunctional decisions. On the other hand are proponents who say that allocations are useful and aid in decision making. Clearly managers allocate; thus, any discussion of the topic must take this reality into account. These are not easy

[2] Rene P. Manes and C. S. Agnes Cheng, *The Marginal Approach to Joint Cost Allocation: Theory and Application*, Studies in Accounting Research #29 (Sarasota, Fla.: American Accounting Association, 1988), p. 212.

arguments to reconcile nor is there an easy answer. In this chapter, we look at these contrary points of view and see what is happening in practice.

ALLOCATION: A DEFINITION

In Chapter 2, we introduced the idea of tracing costs to a cost object. All costs can be traced to some level (e.g., unit, batch, product, process, plant) with, in this example, unit being the lowest and plant the highest. Costs that are traceable to units are usually variable (materials, variable labor, etc.). Costs traced to a batch, product, process, or plant are by definition not traceable to units. If we assign such costs to a lower level than that to which they are traceable (e.g., assign plant costs to units), we are *allocating*.

Cost assignment can be looked at as a spectrum. On one end are costs that can be traced directly with cost objects. For example, assume we run a simple regression (and it meets all appropriate objective and subjective tests of usefulness) where machine hours (MH) was the independent variable and electricity cost the dependent variable. If we find that there is a relationship of \$4/MH, then an additional 100 machine hours should cause power costs to rise by about \$400. This is a *one-to-one* relationship.[3] If we amend this example to one where the dependent variable is related to several independent variables and we get a significant regression, the result is a *many-to-one* relationship. Neither one-to-one nor many-to-one relationships will be called allocations in the context of this discussion, since they both result in tracing costs.

On the other hand, if we have a cost that is traceable to, say, the plant level and it is divided up among several cost objectives even though there is no causal or statistical relationship to make this division, the division of such a cost is an *allocation*. Examples of cost allocations include depreciation, where the original purchase price of an asset is allocated to various periods; joint product costs that are divided up among resulting products to value inventory and to price those products; and service department costs, whose costs are ultimately divided among operating departments. In general, this chapter will deal with such *one-to-many* divisions of costs. Thomas calls these allocations notional, figure shuffling. They do not represent economic reality but rather just accounting numbers.[4] This is in contrast to other authors, such as Manes and Cheng, who are quoted at the beginning of the chapter. Such authors believe there are strong reasons to allocate—and that there are economic grounds to do so.

---

[3] The terms and idea for this section come from Arthur L. Thomas, *A Behavioural Analysis of Joint-Cost Allocation and Transfer Pricing*, Arthur Andersen & Co. (1977) and Stipes Publishing Company (1980). This book contains an excellent bibliography in this area.

[4] Arthur L. Thomas, "Cash-Flow Reporting as Allocation-Free Disclosure: A Polemic," Working Paper No. 136, University of Kansas (1980).

THE PERVASIVENESS OF ALLOCATIONS

There has always been a contrast between basic managerial accounting analysis for internal decision making and what has traditionally been thought of as cost accounting: product costs for financial accounting. Such techniques and philosophies as ABC, ABM, and TOC are just newer versions of this basic analytical framework in management accounting. For internal decisions regarding pricing, adding or dropping products, acquiring new capital assets, and segment performance evaluation, for example, managers are concerned with incremental costs. In basic cost-volume-profit analysis, we classify costs as either variable or fixed and look at contribution margin. At the simplest level, variable costs are traceable to the product level and fixed costs are common to the process or plant. We explore how allocating fixed costs to the product level can lead to poor decisions since the notion of *fixed cost per unit* is, by definition, a contradiction. Fixed costs per unit change as the denominator (units) changes. However, even with this basic knowledge, we freely allocate fixed production costs to units of product to value inventory and cost of goods sold for financial accounting.

Product costs for financial accounting (which reflect manufacturing) include direct materials, direct labor, variable factory overhead, and fixed factory overhead as productive inputs. Included in these costs can be many allocations. For example, assume there is a joint process that involves all four cost inputs. Say that three products are generated out of this joint process. The joint costs must be divided among these three products for inventory valuation of finished goods (and possibly work in process) and for cost of goods sold. Costs may be used as a basis for pricing or market prices may be used as a basis for dividing costs.

Depreciation is allocated to periods of time (years, for example), using criteria derived from financial accounting (or tax accounting) requirements. Then, the yearly portion of that asset's cost is assigned to units of product by some overhead allocation scheme using actual, normal, or standard costing. The same asset in different companies producing the same end products may be handled in several different but acceptable ways across time (choice of depreciation method) and within a time period (choice of how to apply overhead). All methods are considered "correct." This is an example of allocations being arbitrary. If managers can allocate in several different ways that each lead to "correct" results, how are we to choose among these methods to find one that is uniquely the best? You can begin to see some of the problems that critics address.

Depreciation is included in factory overhead calculations. Besides allocations like depreciation, there are allocations of plant management costs, of service department costs (computer, maintenance, and employee cafeteria, for example), and of other costs that are common to several departments and/or products. Managers can choose among many different bases to allocate (apply) overhead. Again, within fairly broad bounds, any resulting inventory values are "correct." Thus, one-to-many allocations and the issues they raise are everywhere in product costing.

Going beyond the need for full-cost accounting for inventory valuation, allocations can be seen in divisional performance reports. Divisions may be assigned portions of central office expense. For example, the Night and Day Company operates several convenience stores in a major metropolitan area. The company has a central office that includes the president, central purchasing, accounting, personnel administration, maintenance people, overall supervision of the stores, and so on. Each month the company's accounting system generates an income statement for each of the 30 stores the company owns. As a part of that income statement, each store is charged a management fee and a maintenance fee. Thus, income per store includes allocations of the central office expenses. Resulting income is used to evaluate how stores and their managers are performing. These issues will be explored later.

This chapter will address two main areas of allocations that affect product costing: service department allocations and joint-cost allocations. In addition, the chapter will contrast what is presently used by business against other ideas that have been proposed for allocation.

THEORY VERSUS PRACTICE

One of the leaders in criticizing all one-to-many allocations has been Arthur Thomas. His 1969 and 1974 *Studies in Accounting Research* monographs[5] set the stage for much of the current debate in this area. In a later work, he said the following to illustrate what he calls the total ambiguity of allocations:

> . . . consider the manuscript before you. It is the product of at least four essential inputs: paper, ink . . . , a program (stored in my grey matter as I type this) and a printer. Let us suppose that someone wishes to allocate the output (manuscript) among these four inputs, in order to specify how much of it each input contributed.
>
> One could argue that the entire output should be allocated to the paper (and, thereby, none to other inputs) on the grounds that, lacking paper, there would be *no* manuscript, only a smudge. But one could equally argue that the output should instead be allocated entirely to the ink, the program or the printer. For instance, with a different program you might be reading *Moby Dick*. The point, of course, is that the exercise is foolish. This manuscript is a joint consequence of *all* of its inputs, and attempts to determine each input's individual contributions to it have the same logical form as joint-cost allocations.[6]

---

[5] Arthur L. Thomas, *The Allocation Problem in Financial Accounting Theory*, Studies in Accounting Research No. 3 (1969) and *The Allocation Problem: Part II*, Studies in Accounting Research No. 9 (1974). Sarasota, Fla.: American Accounting Association.
[6] Thomas, "Cash Flow Reporting as Allocation-Free Disclosure" (1980), pp. 1–2.

Thomas's paper is directed at allocation-free financial accounting in this case, but that cannot be achieved unless allocations are eliminated in management accounting as well.

As a contrast to this point of view, Fremgen and Liao[7] studied companies' actual practices of allocating indirect costs to divisions. About 90 percent of the companies said that they allocated corporate costs to remind managers that these costs exist and must be covered by operations. Around 46 percent stated that allocating costs would stimulate managers to whom the allocations were made to pressure the providing managers to control their costs. Finally, 23 percent said that they allocated corporate costs to encourage the use of services.[8]

More recently, authors have been trying to see how theory is applied in practice. Manes and Cheng[9] wrote a monograph describing an approach to joint-cost allocation. In addition, as part of their study, they applied their ideas at several companies. Manes and Cheng also challenge Thomas and propose that allocations are useful and can lead to good decisions, as we explore below.

Thus, there is a division between those who say that allocations are arbitrary and can lead to dysfunctional and/or suboptimal decisions and those who think there is a need for allocations in order to promote certain behavior and to make better decisions. The key is behavior, and many writers have taken the position that since allocations seem to be here to stay, the best course of action is to provide methods that will promote the behavior that management wants: *behavior* or *goal congruence* with central office management's desires.[10] The following sections outline not only the most common ways that companies allocate but also alternative methods that have been proposed for such allocations.

SERVICE DEPARTMENT ALLOCATIONS

Service, or support, departments are non-value-added departments since they are not involved in actually producing goods. Examples include engineering, maintenance, building services, data processing, food services, and so on. Some of these departments (such as personnel) provide services to both operating and other service departments while others might only use resources to work with one or the other types of areas.

One of the key aspects of service departments is whether to source such support internally and, if so, how to price the service to others within the

[7] James M. Fremgen and Shu S. Liao, *The Allocation of Corporate Indirect Costs* (New York: National Association of Accountants, 1981).

[8] Fremgen and Liao, Table 5–2, p. 61.

[9] Manes and Cheng, *The Marginal Approach to Joint Cost Allocation.*

[10] Thomas (1977) calls this behavior congruence with central-office-optimal decisions.

organization. It is the objective of such pricing to promote rational use choices by those receiving the service. Managers who purchase services from support departments should believe the prices they pay are fair.

Actual fairness (as opposed to a perception of equity) means that separable incremental costs are charged to the departments that cause them. If, say, a manufacturing department needs a very large mainframe computer to assist in the manufacturing process but the needs of the other operating and service departments call for a much smaller computer, the incremental cost of the larger computer (both investment and operating costs) would be charged to the causing department. Equity also comes into play in the original definition offered for allocation: the division of a one-to-many cost. When there is a one-to-one or a many-to-one *relationship* of cost and activity, a doctrine of fairness (and accuracy) would be to use that relationship to assign costs. This will be explored in detail under variable service department costs below.

If a service department is perceived as charging too much for its services, an operating manager may either choose to do without such services or to seek them in other ways that might be more costly to the company as a whole. Say that a computer department charges what a using manager thinks is too high a price. Even though the computer center has no incremental costs for serving the department in the short run, it has established a pricing structure for its services. If there were no price (or too low a price), managers would be tempted to overuse the computer as a free good. In that case the company would be faced with the problem of adding staff, hardware, and software, which comprise real costs. However, the manager who refuses services because of prices seen as too high may be making a dysfunctional decision if such services could generate useful information for that manager. Buying separate computers for a department or contracting with an outside computer service bureau could also be suboptimal from the company's perspective.

VARIABLE SERVICE DEPARTMENT COSTS

When service department costs are mainly variable or when managers can distinguish between variable and fixed costs, the variable costs should be assigned using the reciprocal method. This system bases costs on actual use of services. This is a one-to-one mapping of costs and is not allocation. This is an introduction to the use of the reciprocal method, which is explored in more detail later in the chapter.

Assume that a steel company mines its own coal and generates its own electricity. The steel plant itself requires 250,000 tons of coal and needs 10,000,000 KwH of electricity. In addition, each 100 KwH of electricity requires 1 ton of coal, and mining 1 ton of coal uses about 10 KwH. The variable cost to produce a kilowatt hour, apart from the cost of coal, is $0.10, and the variable cost to mine a ton of coal, apart from the cost of electricity, is about $8. By the use of the reciprocal method of assigning costs, management can determine the adjusted variable cost of each of these services. In addition, linear programming can be used to yield answers in this type of problem.

While the electricity and coal needs of the steel plant are specified, the total needs are not. To find out total needs, the following equations are set up and solved:

$$T = 250{,}000 + 0.01K$$
$$K = 10{,}000{,}000 + 10T$$

where K = KwH of electricity needed and T = tons of coal needed. This relationship is based on the facts that each KwH needs 1/100th of a ton of coal and each ton of coal requires 10 KwH. Solving for these two unknowns yields 388,889 tons of coal and 13,888,889 KwH of electricity.

In order to find the adjusted variable costs for each service department, the following equations must be solved:

$$k = \$0.10 + 0.01t$$
$$t = \$8.00 + 10k$$

This results, as you should verify, in k (the variable cost of a KwH of electricity) equaling $0.20 and t (the variable cost of a ton of coal) $10.00. These equations recognize that the cost per KwH is $0.10 plus the cost of the 1/100th ton of coal needed to generate each KwH. The same logic holds true for the coal costs.

An alternate formulation would be based on percents of use. Exhibit 11-1 shows the set-up and solution of this example. While unadjusted costs for coal and electricity are $8 and $0.10, respectively, full variable costs are $10 and $0.20. These can be used as shadow prices to determine the savings that would be generated if one or the other department were closed down. For example, if the coal mine were closed down, how much would the company be willing to pay for each ton of coal? With no coal mine, there would be no need for electricity to be generated for the mine. Thus electric needs would be the 10,000,000 KwH for the plant. Coal needs would be the 250,000 tons for the plant plus another 100,000 tons for the electric generation department.

10,000,000 KwH × $0.10 out-of-pocket costs for electricity = $1,000,000
350,000 tons × outside cost per ton for coal = $3,500,000

We know that the total out-of-pocket costs for coal and electricity are $4,500,000 when produced in house (388,889 × $8 plus 13,888,889 × $0.10 = $4,500,000). Thus, we can spend up to $3,500,000 for coal or $10 per ton. This matches the full cost calculated above. Verify by the same logic that

Exhibit 11-1
Variable Service Department Costs
Reciprocal Allocation

	Service Performed for			
Service Done by	**Coal Mining**	**Electricity**	**Plant**	**Total**
Coal Mining	0	138,889	250,000	388,889
Electricity	3,888,889	0	10,000,000	13,888,889
		Percents		
Coal Mining	0	0.35714	0.64286	
Electricity	0.28	0	0.72	

K' = total variable cost of electricity
T' = total variable cost of coal
$K' = \$1,388,889 + 0.35714\,T'$
$T' = \$3,111,112 + 0.28 \quad K'$

Total costs are unadjusted variable costs times total needs
   (e.g., $388,889 \times \$8 = \$3,111,112$)

$K' = \$2,777,769$
$T' = \$3,888,887$

These yield variable costs per service unit of
$\$2,777,769/13,888,889 = \$0.20$ for electricity
$\$3,888,887/3,888,889 \quad = \$10$ for coal

the marginal cost for electricity would be $0.20 if it were bought from a local utility while coal production was maintained.

Linear Programming

A minimization problem can be set up with the original information that will show the total amount of tons and KwH needed as well as the adjusted costs of the two services. The objective function and constraints are as follows:

$$\text{Min } \$0.10K + \$8T$$
s.t.
$$K - 10T \geq 10,000,000$$
$$-0.01K + T \geq \quad 250,000$$

The results show a cost of $4,500,000 and solution values for K and T of 13,888,889 KwH and 388,889 tons. The dual prices are the adjusted variable costs of $0.20 for electricity and $10 for coal. Finally, the sensitivity analysis yields the needs for coal if it were bought on the outside and the needs for electricity if it were bought on the outside. The allowable decrease is shown as 12,500,000 KwH and 350,000 tons respectively. You should verify these conclusions by running the above linear programming formulation.

SERVICE DEPARTMENT ALLOCATIONS

Many service department costs cannot be traced. However, at least for financial accounting purposes, managers must choose some way to fairly allocate such costs to operating departments and then to units of product. This section deals with allocating service department costs to operating departments.

Basic Methods to Allocate Service Department Costs

The major problem is in allocating fixed service department costs. Such costs are common to the service department and, unless certain fixed costs are directly associated with providing a specific service to one other department, they comprise the usual one-to-many allocation problem we have been discussing. There are three ways that are used by many companies to allocate service department costs. They are the direct method, the step (or step-down) method, and the reciprocal method.

Service to Other Service Departments   Some service departments deal only with operating departments while others also serve other supporting departments. For example, while the maintenance department might only be concerned with operating machinery, the janitorial service cleans both service and operating areas. The differentiation of the three allocation methods is not only in the technique but also in how this inter-service department activity is handled. In the direct method, inter-service-department service is ignored; in the step method it is partially recognized; in the reciprocal method it is fully recognized.

Self-Service   The cafeteria serves food to cafeteria employees. The maintenance department maintains its own machinery. These are examples of self-service. All three methods ignore self-service. In the reciprocal method the ultimate allocations to operating departments will be the same whether self-service is included or excluded.

The Ultimate Objective   In applying techniques, it is easy to lose sight of the ultimate objective of the process. Service department costs must be assigned in some way so that they appear as an expense on the income statement or are included as part of inventory values on the balance sheet.

This is very similar to how direct labor and factory overhead are handled. Thus, all the allocation methods yield an allocation of service department costs to operating departments of the company so that these costs can be assigned to units of product. That is the objective of any of these techniques.

Bases for Allocation   As with overhead application, companies must choose a basis to allocate service department costs.[11] When there are substantial variable costs to assign, companies should try to find a causal variable much in the same way that overhead is applied using direct labor hours or machine hours. In allocating service department costs, some common measures are *square feet* for some building services, *employees* for things like personnel and a cafeteria, a measure of *use* (like CPU time) for computer service, and so on. With a predominance of fixed service department costs to allocate, the choice of method is arbitrary because there is no causal variable (one-to-many allocation).

Dual Bases   Some companies choose to allocate fixed costs using a different basis than that chosen for variable costs. As we have discussed, the assignment of variable costs should be on as much of a one-to-one foundation as is possible through engineering studies and/or through the use of statistical techniques such as linear regression. Fixed costs might be based on a measure of capacity. For example, if a company buys a piece of maintenance machinery to handle a peak need for service in the busiest months of a seasonal production schedule, such a purchase was made for capacity reasons. Departments should share in that cost based on their needs at peak as well as their ongoing needs over the year.[12]

Direct Method

Exhibit 11-2 contains the basic information for the examples that will follow. The Sale Company has three service departments (personnel, computer services, and building services) and two operating departments (forming and assembling). Direct costs for each service department are shown in the

---

[11] A useful source is old Cost Accounting Standards Board pronouncements such as CAS 403, "Allocation of Home Office Expense to Segments" and CAS 418, "Allocation of Direct and Indirect Costs." Also see Patricia James Bost, "Do Cost Accounting Standards Fill a Gap in Cost Allocation?" *Management Accounting* (November 1986), pp. 34–36.

[12] This discussion can be applied to regulatory problems in the electric utility industry. Arguments involve hundreds of millions of dollars of allocation of fixed utility costs. For example, how much should each customer class be responsible for needs of power at peak and how much for ongoing needs? If a utility only needed to provide power for peak needs, it could buy light-duty generating machinery. With heavy ongoing demand, much heavier generating equipment is bought. This equipment is more expensive to install, but will last given the heavy use required of it and will have lower operating costs given heavy demand. This is a good analogy for some fixed service department costs and equipment.

Exhibit 11-2
The Sale Company
Basic Data

| Service Performed by | Services Performed for | | | | | | Total Without Self-service |
	Personnel	Computer Services	Building Services	Forming	Assembling	Total	
Personnel	10	20	10	30	40	110	100 employees
Computer Services	2,360	5,000	4,960	19,955	19,955	52,230	47,230 processing time
Building Services	3,500	2,500	1,000	9,000	5,000	21,000	20,000 square feet
Costs before allocation	$40,000	$70,000	$10,000				
Percents							
Personnel		20.00%	10.00%	30.00%	40.00%	100.00%	
Computer Services	5.00%		10.50%	42.25%	42.25%	100.00%	
Building Services	17.50%	12.50%		45.00%	25.00%	100.00%	

exhibit. Assume that these are all (or mostly) fixed in nature at this point. The upper part of Exhibit 11-2 shows that there are different allocation bases for each of the three service departments: employees for personnel, processing time for computer use, and square feet for building services. As discussed above, self-service is ignored in these methods. Thus, the percents of use shown in the lower part of the exhibit are without self-service.

In the *direct method*, service department costs are allocated only to producing departments. Thus, no use of the computer for, say, the personnel department is recognized. Exhibit 11-3 shows the allocation of these costs using the direct method. The new percents that are shown are based only on use by operating departments. Thus, for example, there are 70 employees in the two operating departments. Forming has $30/70 = 42.86$ percent (rounded) and Assembling has $40/70 = 57.14$ percent of the employees. You should verify the percents for computer and building services.

Remembering the ultimate objective of service department allocation, it is good practice to check to make sure that all of the costs were allocated. This is much like a cost of production report verifies costs and units in dealing with process costing. All $120,000 in service department costs have been allocated.

Exhibit 11-3
The Sale Company
Direct Method

Service Performed by	Services Performed for					
	Personnel	Computer Services	Building Services	Forming	Assembling	Total
Personnel				42.8571%	57.1429%	100.00%
Computer Services				50.0000%	50.0000%	100.00%
Building Services				64.2857%	35.7143%	100.00%
Costs before allocation	$40,000	$70,000	$10,000			$120,000
Allocation of Personnel	($40,000)			$17,143	$22,857	
Allocation of Computer Services		(70,000)		35,000	35,000	
Allocation of Building Services			(10,000)	6,429	3,571	
				$58,572	$61,428	$120,000

Step Method

The *step (or step-down) method* is illustrated in Exhibit 11-4. In this allocation technique, managers must choose an order to allocate service department costs. Perhaps the order is based on the amount of unallocated costs. With this criterion, the order of allocation will be computer services, personnel, and building services. Some managers choose to allocate first the department that provides the most service to other service departments. This would yield personnel, building services, and computer services with 30 percent, 30 percent, and 15.5 percent respectively (with the order of the first two determined by size of unallocated costs). With the step method, inter-department costs are partially recognized. Once an order has been established, costs of the first service department are allocated to the rest of the service departments and the operating departments based on the percents of use shown in Exhibit 11-2. Once that has been done, the next service department is allocated with two changes. First, costs have been added to the direct costs and this total is now allocated. Second, a service department whose costs have already been allocated is ignored and no new costs are allocated to it. This process is repeated until all service department costs are allocated.

Exhibit 11-4 shows the result of two orders of allocation: size of direct costs and service provided to other service departments. This is another

Exhibit 11-4
The Sale Company
Step Method

A. Allocate by size of unallocated costs

Service Performed by	Services Performed for					
	Personnel	Computer Services	Building Services	Forming	Assembling	Total
Computer Services	5.00%		10.50%	42.25%	42.25%	100.00%
Personnel			12.50%	37.50%	50.00%	100.00%
Building Services				64.29%	35.71%	100.00%
Costs before allocation	$40,000	$70,000	$10,000			$120,000
Allocation of Computer Services	$ 3,498	($70,000)	$ 7,351	$29,575	$29,575	
Allocation of Personnel	(43,498)		5,437	16,312	21,749	
Allocation of Building Services			(22,788)	14,650	8,139	
				$60,537	$59,463	$120,000

B. Allocate by percent of services performed for service departments

Service Performed by	Services Performed for					
	Personnel	Computer Services	Building Services	Forming	Assembling	Total
Personnel		20.00%	10.00%	30.00%	40.00%	100.00%
Building Services		15.15%		54.55%	30.30%	100.00%
Computer Services				50.00%	50.00%	100.00%
Costs before allocation	$40,000	$70,000	$10,000			$120,000
Allocation of Personnel	($40,000)	$ 8,000	$ 4,000	$12,000	$16,000	
Allocation of Building Services		2,121	(14,000)	7,636	4,242	
Allocation of Computer Services		(80,121)		40,061	40,061	
				$59,697	$60,303	$120,000

layer of choice (some say arbitrary) that can result in a different final assignment of costs. Thus, using the direct method and two different ways to apply the step method, the following allocations result:

	Forming	Assembling
Direct	$58,571	$61,429
Step (A)	60,537	59,463
Step (B)	59,697	60,303

This is a range of almost $2,000 or about 2 percent of total costs.

Reciprocal Method

In the *reciprocal method* of allocating service department costs, all the service that each department gives to all other departments, be they service or operating, is recognized. Managers can arrange a set of equations that reflect that the full cost of a service department not only includes the separable unallocated cost but also includes that department's share of the costs of services provided to it. For The Sale Company, the following set of equations would reflect these relationships.

$$P = \$40,000 \qquad\quad + 0.05C \ + 0.175B$$
$$C = \$70,000 + 0.20P \qquad\quad + 0.125B$$
$$B = \$10,000 + 0.10P + 0.105C$$

where: *P*, *C*, and *B* represent the full costs of the three service departments, Personnel, Computer Services, and Building Services respectively.

One of the most confusing parts about the reciprocal allocation method is setting up the basic equations. The percents all come from Exhibit 11-2 on page 440. Looking at the equation for personnel costs, for example, the full costs of the personnel department (*P*) are the $40,000 in direct costs from that department plus 5 percent of computer costs (since the computer department does 5 percent of its work *for* the personnel department) plus 17.5 percent of the costs of building services (and building services does 17.5 percent of its work *for* personnel).

These are three equations with three unknowns. This system of equations can be solved by dealing with simultaneous equations for simple problems, but use matrix manipulation (and/or linear programming) for solving larger problems.[13] As you should verify, the solution to the above would yield the following values:

$$P = \$48,241$$
$$C = \$82,585$$
$$B = \$23,496$$

---

[13] If a company had, say, 25 service departments, the resulting equations would be too cumbersome to solve by hand.

Do not be alarmed that these total more than the $120,000 to allocate. Exhibit 11-5 shows the results of using these figures to allocate costs to all service and all operating departments. Note that the sum of the allocations to the operating departments still adds up to $120,000 (some rounding error).

Matrix Solution

Larger problems require the use of matrices for solution. Not only is such a solution necessary for larger problems, but a matrix solution also provides additional information, demonstrated below.

We can rearrange the basic relationship equations on the previous page as follows so that the unallocated costs are all to the right of the equal sign:

$$P - 0.05C - 0.175B = \$40,000$$
$$-0.20P + C - 0.125B = \$70,000$$
$$-0.10P - 0.105C + B = \$10,000$$

Thus, all the figures pertaining to each service department's provisions of service to other service departments are in one column while the rows are still the relationship needed to find the full cost for each service department, given work provided by other service departments. In matrix form the values

Exhibit 11-5
The Sale Company
Reciprocal Method

Service Performed by	Services Performed for					
	Personnel	Computer Services	Building Services	Forming	Assembling	
Personnel		20.00%	10.00%	30.00%	40.00%	100.00%
Computer Services	5.00%		10.50%	42.25%	42.25%	100.00%
Building Services	17.50%	12.50%		45.00%	25.00%	100.00%
Costs before allocation	$40,000	$70,000	$10,000			
Costs to allocate	$48,241	$82,585	$23,496			
Allocation of Personnel	($48,241)	$ 9,648	$ 4,824	$14,472	$19,296	
Allocation of Computer Services	4,127	(82,585)	8,673	34,893	34,893	
Allocation of Building Services	4,112	2,937	(23,496)	10,573	5,874	
				$59,938	$60,063	$120,001

we are trying to find (P, C, and B) form a column vector, x. The coefficients of the service departments form a matrix, A. Finally, the unallocated (direct) costs of each department form a column vector, b. In matrix notation this is

$$
\begin{matrix} & A & \\ \begin{bmatrix} 1 & -0.05 & -0.175 \\ -0.20 & 1 & -0.125 \\ -0.10 & -0.105 & 1 \end{bmatrix} \end{matrix}
\begin{matrix} x \\ \begin{bmatrix} P \\ C \\ B \end{bmatrix} \end{matrix}
=
\begin{matrix} b \\ \begin{bmatrix} \$40,000 \\ \$70,000 \\ \$10,000 \end{bmatrix} \end{matrix}
$$

which is $Ax = b$. To solve, multiply both sides of the equation by A^{-1}, the inverse of matrix A. The inverse of A, if it exists,[14] when multiplied by the matrix A, will yield an identity matrix I. (An identity matrix has ones in the major diagonal and zeros in all other cells.) Thus,

$$A^{-1}A = I$$

If both sides of the basic relationship of $Ax = b$ are multiplied by the inverse, then

$$A^{-1}Ax = A^{-1}b$$

Finally, using the identity relationship established above,

$$Ix = A^{-1}b$$

Since any matrix multiplied by an identity matrix is unchanged, the above is the same as

$$x = A^{-1}b$$

The matrix inverse and the solution using matrix algebra are shown below.

$$
\begin{bmatrix} 1.033295 & 0.071591 & 0.189775 \\ 0.222495 & 1.028715 & 0.167526 \\ 0.126691 & 0.115174 & 1.036567 \end{bmatrix}
\begin{bmatrix} 40,000 \\ 70,000 \\ 10,000 \end{bmatrix}
=
\begin{bmatrix} 48,241 \\ 82,585 \\ 23,496 \end{bmatrix}
$$

Allocations to the operating department are made as they were in Exhibit 11-5: multiply the percents of service provided to each operating department times the adjusted value of costs for the service department.[15] The results will be the same as Exhibit 11-5.

---

[14] If the determinant of the inverse equals zero, for example, then an inverse does not exist.
[15] Many computer programs that solve for reciprocal service department allocations use matrix algebra to do the final allocations. The matrix formed by the percentages under Forming and Assembling in Exhibit 11-5 would be multiplied by the x matrix to get the final allocations.

The elements in the main diagonal of the inverse matrix above are useful. If the company were deciding whether to buy computer services on the outside, for example, how much computer time would it have to purchase? Remembering that there is a reciprocal relationship between services, an elimination of computer services in house affects all service departments because they supply services to the computer department. By dividing the total needs of 47,230 (see Exhibit 11-2 on page 440) by the corresponding element in the main diagonal above of 1.028715, the internal needs of computer time bought from another source would be 47,230/1.028715 = 45,912.

JOINT-COST ALLOCATIONS

Some products are the result of a joint manufacturing process. While goods such as automobiles are made one at a time along assembly lines, other processes yield several joint products. An example would be an oil refinery where crude oil is refined into, say, gasoline, diesel, and motor oil among other products. The cost of the crude oil as well as the conversion costs to the point of production of identifiable separate products (called the *split-off point*) are allocated to the joint products. This is a one-to-many allocation as previously defined.

Managers deal with major joint products differently from minor by-products of a joint process. Thus, methods to allocate joint costs are usually divided between main products (sometimes called joint products) and by-products.

Joint-Product Allocation Methods

Exhibit 11-6 contains basic data that will be used in the following examples. The Election Company has three joint products that are manufactured in a common process: Bondite, Woodite, and Senite. In the illustrations that follow, all three products will be considered main products. Three common bases of allocating joint-product costs are *net realizable value, constant gross margin,* and *relative sales value.* The basic data in Exhibit 11-6 show that there are $150,000 in common costs to allocate to the joint products. In each of the three allocation methods the *sales value of production* will play a part in the actual division of costs. It is important to remember that the objective is to allocate joint production costs to production achieved. Thus, actual sales are irrelevant (unless dealing with a perishable product) and managers focus on the sales value of production. In addition, Exhibit 11-6 shows that there can be a sales value at split off as well as a sales value when a product reaches a final finished stage. Certain products are salable in an unfinished form. For example, raw gasoline could be sold, or raw stock could be further processed and have other chemicals added to it to yield a high-octane

Exhibit 11-6
Joint-Product Allocation: Basic Data
Election Company

	Bondite	Woodite	Senite	Total
Units produced from joint process	4,000	5,000	1,000	
Selling price of final product	$ 31	$ 51	$ 5	
Total revenue	$124,000	$255,000	$5,000	$384,000
Separable costs after split off	30,000	50,000		80,000
Revenue less separable costs	$ 94,000	$205,000	$5,000	$304,000
Selling price at split off	$ 10			
Total revenue—sale at split off	$ 40,000			
Joint costs of process				$150,000

final product. Finally, some products require additional costs beyond split off in order to finish them for final sale. Since the products have been identified, such costs may be separable. It is possible, however, that once the main common process is finished, certain of the products go through other joint processes and the allocation scheme needs to be layered to accommodate this reality.

Net Realizable Value   The *net realizable value* of a product is defined as the price of that product less any separable costs to get it to the point of sale. Net realizable value (NRV) can be interpreted in at least two ways. In one way (labeled *A* in Exhibit 11-7) the relevant sales figures to use are the NRV's at the first possible point of sale. Thus, since Bondite can be sold at split off, its NRV will be $40,000 (there are no separable costs to get Bondite ready for sale at split off). The net realizable value method for allocating the common costs uses the relative NRV's of all the products, as is illustrated in Exhibit 11-7. The other definition of NRV (shown as *B* in Exhibit 11-7) uses the NRV of the best sales options open to the company. Bondite can be sold at split off for $40,000. However, with additional processing costs of $30,000, it can be sold for a total of $124,000. Thus, this is the better opportunity for Election Company's managers. Therefore, the relative NRV's used to allocate joint costs are based on selling all products in their final form. (There are several instances where the cost of further processing is more than the incremental revenue that would be achieved. In those cases, the intermediate product (product at split off) would be the best sales option and that NRV would be used in the allocation.) The definition of NRV can

Exhibit 11-7
Net Realizable Value
Election Company

	Bondite	Woodite	Senite	Total
Net Realizable Value—A	$40,000	$205,000	$5,000	$250,000
Percent	16.00%	82.00%	2.00%	100.00%
Allocation of joint costs	$24,000	$123,000	$3,000	$150,000
Net Realizable Value—B	$94,000	$205,000	$5,000	$304,000
Percent	30.92%	67.43%	1.64%	100.00%
Allocation of joint costs	$46,382	$101,151	$2,467	$150,000

substantially affect allocation of joint costs, as this illustration shows. The objective is to allocate costs that occur prior to split off. If split-off values exist for all products, one can argue that they should be used as the basis to divide costs. However, if split-off values do not exist (there is no intermediate market), then NRV based on the first available point of sales may be a reasonable substitute for these values. The NRV method is based on the notion of an ability to bear: the more valuable a product, the more common costs should be assigned to it since it has the ability to bear such costs.

Constant Gross Margin   A second way of allocating joint costs is the *constant gross margin* method. This technique forces the gross margin for all products to be the same as the gross margin of the joint process as a whole. This is illustrated in Exhibit 11-8. The joint process taken as a whole has a gross margin of 40.10 percent (rounded). Common costs are allocated (as you should verify) so that Bondite, Woodite, and Senite all have gross margins of 40.10 percent. The rationale is that since there is no way to differentiate these costs among the products, all should earn the same percent of profits.

Relative Sales Value   In the *relative sales value* method, joint costs are allocated by using the relative sales values of the products.[16] This is illustrated in Exhibit 11-9. This technique is based on the same rationale as the net realizable value method: the ability to bear costs. However, it ignores separable costs and, therefore, may allocate so much of the joint cost as to show a loss for a product. Say separable costs for Senite were $4,000 instead of zero. The following allocations would take place under the net realizable value and the relative sales value schemes.

---

[16] Relative sales value can be at final sale of the product, or at the first point of sale (i.e., split-off value if it exists).

Net Realizable Value

	Bondite	Woodite	Senite	Total
Net Realizable Value—A	$40,000	$205,000	$1,000	$246,000
Percent	16.26%	83.33%	0.41%	100.00%
Allocation of joint costs	$24,390	$125,000	$ 610	$150,000
Net Realizable Value—B	$94,000	$205,000	$1,000	$300,000
Percent	31.33%	68.33%	0.33%	100.00%
Allocation of joint costs	$47,000	$102,500	$ 500	$150,000

Exhibit 11-8
Constant Gross Margin
Election Company

	Bondite	Woodite	Senite	Total
Total revenues				$384,000
Total separable costs				80,000
Total joint costs				150,000
Gross margin				$154,000
Gross margin as percent of sales				40.10%
Revenue	$124,000	$255,000	$5,000	$384,000
Separable costs	30,000	50,000	0	80,000
Revenue less separable costs	94,000	205,000	5,000	304,000
Required gross margin at 40.10%	49,729	102,266	2,005	154,000
Allocation of joint costs	$ 44,271	$102,734	$2,995	$150,000

Exhibit 11-9
Relative Sales Value
Election Company

	Bondite	Woodite	Senite	Total
Revenue	$124,000	$255,000	$5,000	$384,000
Relative revenue	32.29%	66.41%	1.30%	100.00%
Allocation of joint costs	$ 48,438	$ 99,609	$1,953	$150,000

There is a slight profit that can be achieved from Senite ($5,000 less separable and joint costs of $4,500). Contrast this to the relative sales value method below.

Relative Sales Value

	Bondite	Woodite	Senite	Total
Revenue	$124,000	$255,000	$5,000	$384,000
Relative revenue	32.29%	66.41%	1.30%	100.00%
Allocation of joint costs	$ 48,438	$ 99,609	$1,953	$150,000

Here Senite will have a loss of $953 ($5,000 less $1,953 in common costs and $4,000 in separable costs). Parenthetically, all methods can produce nonmeaningful numbers.[17] For example, the constant gross margin method would allocate cost as follows:

Constant Gross Margin

	Bondite	Woodite	Senite	Total
Total revenues				$384,000
Total separable costs				84,000
Total joint costs				$150,000
Gross margin				$150,000
Gross margin as percent of sales				39.06%
Revenue	$124,000	$255,000	$5,000	$384,000
Separable costs	30,000	50,000	4,000	84,000
Revenue less separable costs	94,000	205,000	1,000	300,000
Required gross margin	48,438	99,609	1,953	150,000
Allocation of joint costs	45,563	105,391	(953)	150,000

It makes little sense to have a negative allocation of costs. Costs are being removed from Senite so that it can achieve the overall 39 percent gross margin since its separable margin has been reduced to 20 percent.

While these three methods comprise the main ways to allocate joint costs of main products, other ways exist to allocate. For example, one could allocate based on units of product or relative product weights. These methods have little merit unless the products have equal values or weights. Otherwise, there might be some seemingly unfair divisions of costs.

---

[17] Thomas may argue that all methods produce useless results for decision making.

Marginal Approach

Cheng and Manes[18] illustrate a marginal approach to joint-cost allocation. They show a basic one-period model that allows managers to make production decisions about the use of joint processes. They propose an example where there is a single joint process using a joint material (X). Each pound of X yields ½ of unit A, 1 unit of B, and 2 units of C. In addition, managers have estimated the expected demand for products A, B, and C as 20, 25, and 10 units respectively for the next period.

Exhibit 11-10 reflects the basic facts and relationships in this illustration. The contribution margins (CM) (column 4) are selling price less any separable costs for each product beyond the split-off point. While product A has the highest CM per unit, from a marginal cost perspective, product B has the highest CM per resource ($8 per pound of X). Thus, managers would want to have capacity of the joint process set at 25 pounds. This would yield 12.5 units of A (25 × ½), 25 units of B (25 × 1), and 50 units of C (25 × 2). With these production levels, there would be unfilled demand of 7.5 A (20 – 12.5) and oversupply of 40 C (10 – 50). This oversupply would either have to be held, sold, or disposed of.

This one-period model can be examined using linear programming. Exhibit 11-11 shows the linear programming objective function and constraints as well as the solution and sensitivity analysis.[19] The values for production and sales are as derived above as is the value of the joint process, X. Unfilled demand and oversupply are also shown. New information

Exhibit 11-10
Cheng and Manes Illustration
Basic Information

(1) Joint Product	(2) Budget Estimate of Demand	(3) Budget Estimate of Sales Quantities in terms of X	(4) Contribution Margin/Unit of product	(5) Contribution Margin/Pound in terms of X
A	20 units	40 pounds	$12.00	$6.00
B	25 units	25 pounds	8.00	8.00
C	10 units	5 pounds	0.50	1.00

The cost of raw material X, including separable costs of the joint process, is $11 per pound.

[18] C. S. Agnes Cheng and Rene P. Manes, "The Marginal Approach to Joint Cost Allocation: A Model for Practical Application," *Journal of Management Accounting Research*, Vol. 4, (Sarasota, Fla.: American Accounting Association, Fall 1992), pp. 44–63. This article is a condensation of Manes and Cheng, *The Marginal Approach to Joint Cost Allocation*.

[19] This is the same as the appendix in Cheng and Manes, "The Marginal Approach to Joint Cost Allocation." A full discussion of the linear programming formulation is found in Manes and Cheng, *SAR #29*.

Exhibit 11-11
Cheng and Manes
Linear Programming Solution

Problem Formulation

```
MAX       12 AS + 8 BS + 0.5 CS - 11 X     objective function using
                                            CM/unit
SUBJECT TO
       2) - X + 2 AP =    0                 resource use relationships
       3) - X + BP =   0
       4) - X + 0.5 CP =    0
       5)   AS - AP <=   0                  sales must be no more than
                                            production
       6)   BS - BP <=   0
       7)   CS - CP <=   0
       8)   AS <=   20                      demand
       9)   BS <=   25
      10)   CS <=   10
END

Where:    AS = Product A sold     AP = Product A produced
          BS = Product B sold     BP = Product B produced
          CS = Product C sold     CP = Product C produced
```

Solution and Sensitivity Analysis

```
          OBJECTIVE FUNCTION VALUE
1)        80.0000000

VARIABLE          VALUE          REDUCED COST
      AS       12.500000            .000000
      BS       25.000000            .000000
      CS       10.000000            .000000
       X       25.000000            .000000
      AP       12.500000            .000000
      BP       25.000000            .000000
      CP       50.000000            .000000

   ROW    SLACK OR SURPLUS     DUAL PRICES
    2)             .000000        6.000000
    3)             .000000        5.000000
    4)             .000000         .000000
    5)             .000000       12.000000
    6)             .000000        5.000000
    7)           40.000000         .000000
    8)            7.500000         .000000
    9)             .000000        3.000000
   10)             .000000         .500000
```

Exhibit 11-11 (continued)

RANGES IN WHICH THE BASIS IS UNCHANGED:

OBJ COEFFICIENT RANGES

VARIABLE	CURRENT COEF	ALLOWABLE INCREASE	DECREASE
AS	12.000000	10.000000	6.000000
BS	8.000000	INFINITY	3.000000
CS	.500000	INFINITY	.500000
X	-11.000000	5.000000	3.000000
AP	.000000	10.000000	6.000000
BP	.000000	5.000000	3.000000
CP	.000000	2.500000	1.500000

RIGHTHAND SIDE RANGES

ROW	CURRENT RHS	ALLOWABLE INCREASE	ALLOWABLE DECREASE
2	.000000	15.000000	25.000000
3	.000000	20.000000	15.000000
4	.000000	INFINITY	20.000000
5	.000000	7.500000	12.500000
6	.000000	20.000000	15.000000
7	.000000	INFINITY	40.000000
8	20.000000	INFINITY	7.500000
9	25.000000	15.000000	20.000000
10	10.000000	40.000000	10.000000

includes the shadow prices for rows 2, 3, and 4, which are the allocations of the joint cost of X ($11): $6 is allocated to A, $5 to B, and $0 to C. A second set of shadow prices (rows 5, 6, and 7) show the allocation of joint costs to one unit each of the three products that remain unsold at the end of the period. Up to 7.5 additional units of A, the marginal value is the CM of $12 per unit given the unfilled demand. For B, demand is being filled exactly (25 units). The marginal value of $5 reflects the allocation of the joint cost of X referred to above. Finally, sensitivity analysis shows the ranges in which the basic solution holds.

Cheng and Manes propose that if demand and price/costs remain relatively stable over several periods, this model can be used in make-or-buy and special order decisions. Thus, for example, if this company can purchase product B at a cost lower than $5 per unit (say, $4 per unit), managers should choose to buy rather than to make *if* they can meet demand of product C. In this case, with B being purchased from the outside, the minimum production of the joint process will have to yield 10 units of C in order to meet demand; this means that X will be 5 pounds to produce 10 units of C.

With 5 pounds in the joint process, only 20 units of B would be purchased on the outside and 5 made internally.[20] The proof of the above is as follows:

1. If the company makes all products internally, the resulting contribution margin is $80, as shown in Exhibit 11-11.
2. If they purchase 20 units of B externally and set the joint process at 5 units of X, they will make 2.5 A (5 × ½ × $12 = $30), 5 B (5 × 1 × $8 = $40), and 10 C (5 × 2 × $0.50 = $5) for a total contribution margin of $75 *less* the joint cost of $55 (5 × $11) *plus* 20 units of B purchased outside at $4 per unit, which yields another $80 in CM (20 × ($8 − $4)). This totals $100 ($75 − $55 + $80) or $20 better than the basic solution (the $1 savings in cost from the outside compared to the shadow price times the 20 units purchased on the outside).

As you should prove to yourself, the above solution that produces a CM of $100 is better than any other combination of production/purchase decisions. For every increment in the joint process above 5, the company would make less money. The basic idea is that for every pound of X that is *not* processed, the company saves $11. This is compared to lost CM on A of $6 per pound of X, or a net of $5.

Cheng and Manes go on to show how this model works for special orders. Going back to the basic solution and using product B again, if a firm offers to buy B at *more* than $5 per unit, the company will be better off up to a maximum of 15 units (after which there would be excess A produced). At 10 additional units of B to be sold for $7 each, for example, the company would incur additional costs of $11 × 10 = $110 for the joint process while CM would go up by $130 (5 A @ $12 ($60) plus 10 B @ $7 ($70))[21] for a net increase of $20 in profits. This amounts to the $2 per unit difference between the shadow price for B of $5 and its special order selling price of $7.

Let us return to the arguments regarding the usefulness of joint-cost allocations at this point. This example, although simplified, illustrates that the allocation of the joint cost of X yields meaningful information to managers for decisions that require knowledge of marginal costs (e.g., make-or-buy or special order). If allocations provide useful information that leads to good decisions, then such allocations seem appropriate. However, this is a limited model. Cheng and Manes state that "at the infant stage of applying the marginal approach, we should only recommend application of the basic, one-period model or possibly a multi-period model based on one seasonal cycle."[22] Even so, this model does allow us to raise doubts about unequivocally denouncing allocations as causing dysfunctional behavior.

---

[20] Remember that the proportion of output resulting from the joint process is fixed.
[21] Product C is ignored since any additional production would just yield more excess inventory. The example does not explicitly include the cost of holding or disposing of such inventory, but this could be built in.
[22] Cheng and Manes, "The Marginal Approach to Joint Cost Allocation," p. 59.

By-Product Allocations

Companies may have welcome (or unwelcome) by-products of a joint manufacturing process. In general, by-products have much lower value than main products and probably would not have been produced unless the main product was made. For example, rice hulls are sold for animal bedding and other uses. It would not be economically justified to grow rice just for the hulls; they are a by-product of growing rice for grain.

Sometimes companies get a by-product that they do not want, one that has a negative impact. For example, there is much controversy about whether emissions from coal-fired electric generation facilities cause acid rain. Such emissions may be an undesirable by-product of power production. We also have problems in disposing of freon, used tires, and waste oil. We will not discuss negative by-products.

The two main ways of allocating common costs to by-products are called *net realizable value* and *other income*. Assume the Election Company chooses to classify Senite as a by-product while keeping Bondite and Woodite as main products. Exhibit 11-12 shows the two methods under this assumption.

Under the *net realizable value* allocation, joint costs are assigned to the by-product exactly equal to the net realizable value of the by-product. Thus, Senite will have a $5,000 inventory value (all joint costs in this case) but

Exhibit 11-12
Election Company
Senite as By-Product

	Senite	
Net Realizable Value Method		
Revenue of by-product	$5,000	
Separable cost	0	
Net realizable value	$5,000	
Joint cost allocated to by-product	$5,000	
Joint costs to be allocated to main products		$145,000
Value of inventory of by-product	$5,000	
Income from by-product at sale	0	
Other Income Method		
Revenue of by-product	$5,000	
Separable cost	0	
Net realizable value	$5,000	
Joint cost allocated to by-product	0	
Joint costs to be allocated to main products		$150,000
Value of inventory of by-product	0	
Income from by-product at sale	$5,000	

will yield zero income when the inventory is sold since revenues are also $5,000. After the net realizable value of $5,000 has been assigned to the by-product, the remaining joint costs ($145,000) can be allocated to the main products by any method management chooses.

Under *other income method*, no common costs are assigned to the by-product; rather sales of it are treated as other income. Thus, unless the by-product has some separable costs, there will be a zero inventory value. Common costs to be allocated to the main products remain at $150,000.

Both these methods can be criticized. In the net realizable value allocation, no income is generated by the by-product. Income is assigned only to main products. This may not seem reasonable. Under the other income method, by-products usually have no inventory value. The sale of the by-product has future value to the firm. Thus, it would seem justified that an inventory value be established to reflect that fact.

Decision Making and Joint-Cost Allocations

The focus of joint-cost allocation seems to be on inventory valuation. While there is a major emphasis on product costing, cost allocations have an effect in other areas. Pricing may be set based on costs. For example, many government contracts are priced on a cost plus fee basis. Thus, the costs assigned to a product affect the selling price; the higher the costs, the higher the profit. In addition, managers may be responsible for product lines. Allocated costs affect perceived profitability of joint products. If market prices are fairly low for a product in comparison to its separable and allocated joint costs, it is possible that incorrect decisions may result in such areas as advertising resources, marketing efforts, and so on. Note that it is almost impossible to get a true picture of costs for different products when there are joint manufacturing costs that are allocated.

JOINT VERSUS SEPARATE COSTS OR SERVICES

Companies may have the option of buying products externally or producing them as a part of a joint process. In the case of services (the next topic of discussion) managers may have the option of providing a service themselves (or purchasing it through an outside vendor) or of availing their departments of common services provided by the company (or through a common outside vendor). Any allocation scheme should promote decisions that will be the most efficient and most effective for the company as a whole. Ayres discusses how allocations affect how coalitions are formed.[23] A

---

[23] Frances L. Ayres, "Models of Coalition Formation, Reward Allocation and Accounting Cost Allocations: A Review and Synthesis," *Journal of Accounting Literature* (Spring 1985), pp. 1–31. This article contains an excellent bibliography.

coalition, in this case, consists of two or more departments that band together to use a common service. Ayres outlines four properties of normative allocation models. They are:

1. *Core Membership.* If an allocation method is in the core, it is not possible for any subcoalition of departments to achieve lower costs if they break off from the overall coalition. As an example, assume that four departments are sharing computer services and are being allocated these common costs. Also assume that these costs in total are less than any other combination of ways to get the same computer service. If a department were to buy its own computer, the allocation method would be in the core if the costs of that separate computer were greater than the allocated common costs from the coalition of the four departments.
2. *Full Cost Allocation.* All joint costs must be allocated. (While this was not explicitly stated in the discussion about joint-product cost allocation, it was an implicit part of all of those models.)
3. *Neutrality with respect to decision making.* An allocation method should not affect decision making. Thus, if no allocations were made, a decision should be the same as when allocations are used. This is based on the assumption that allocations do cause dysfunctional decisions. As will be discussed under return on investment in Chapter 15, this assertion is open to question.
4. *Fairness.* This includes sharing in the benefits or changes in costs in a way that is deemed fair by managers. For example, if two departments use the same amount of a service, it would seem fair to charge them the same cost.[24]

Several authors have dealt with the notion of coalitions being formed to buy services that were heretofore bought separately by the coalition members. For example, Moriarity[25] proposes that if there is a savings from forming a coalition, these savings should be apportioned based on the relative share of costs each member of the coalition had before the savings were made. In one of his examples, he assumes that a janitorial service has been charging $200 a month to clean the executive offices and $1,000 a month to clean the plant. If a full-time employee were to do both jobs, the total cost would be $1,080 or a savings of $120 per month. Under Moriarity's plan, the office would receive 200/1,200 of the savings or $20 and the plant would receive 1,000/1,200 of the savings or $100. Other authors have pointed out that this method may result in the cost of the service allocated to a department

---

[24] Ayres, p. 18.
[25] Shane Moriarity, "Another Approach to Allocating Joint Costs," *The Accounting Review* (October 1975), pp. 791–795.

being greater than the cost of obtaining it separately, and the total cost can be less than the cost to provide it internally.[26]

Thomas compares some of the common ways to allocate joint product costs as well as other methods (such as Moriarity's). The following example is drawn from Thomas.[27] Assume the following facts regarding four joint products:

| Joint costs of process: | $9 | | | |
	A	B	C	D
Sales price	$21	$10	$18	$13
Separable costs to finish	7	12	15	5
Net realizable value	14	(2)	3	8

Assume that the joint costs will be incurred if any of the four products is produced but could be avoided if all production ceased. This example also assumes that processing beyond split off is the preferred option from a profit perspective. Also assume that the company could buy batches of these four products on the outside market with costs of $18, $13, $11, and $22 respectively. The sum of outside costs, $64 ($18 + $13 + $11 + $22), is greater than the total cost of producing them internally, $48 ($9 + $7 + $12 + $15 + $5). Finally, the company does have the option of engaging in the joint process but only producing some of the output. Thus, if only Product A were made, and the other three products were not made, A would have a total cost of $16 (common cost of $9 plus separable cost of $7). While this is cheaper than buying Product A on the outside ($16 versus $18), this same condition does not hold for all products. Product B's external price is $13, while its cost would be $21 if it were the only product produced; Product C's price is $11 compared to $24 internally. However, Product D would also be produced less expensively alone ($14) as compared to the external market price ($22). Thus, we have the following:

	A	B	C	D
Price to purchase externally	$18	$13	$11	$22
Cost to make by itself	16	21	24	14
Best cost option to company	16	13	11	14

The Moriarity approach is explained above in general. Under this method, the savings of $16 ($64 − $48) would be divided among the joint products according to their share of the best cost option to the company. The

[26] See Joseph G. Louderback, "Another Approach to Allocating Joint Costs: A Comment," *The Accounting Review* (July 1976), pp. 683–685; and Shane Moriarity, "Another Approach to Allocating Joint Costs: A Reply," *The Accounting Review* (July 1976), pp. 686–687.
[27] Thomas, *A Behavioral Analysis* . . . This example is from Chapter 2, pp. 32–35.

savings would not be generated unless all four products were produced internally. Thus, the allocation of costs would be

$$A = \$16 \times (\$48/\$54) = \$14.22$$
$$B = \$13 \times (\$48/\$54) = 11.56$$
$$C = \$11 \times (\$48/\$54) = 9.78$$
$$D = \$14 \times (\$48/\$54) = 12.44$$

The total of this allocation procedure is $48, the total cost to make all these products internally. Note that the denominator in the above is the sum of the best option to the company ($54 = $16 + $13 + $11 + $14). Both separable and joint costs are allocated under this method. The allocation of the $9 of joint costs can be found by subtracting the separable costs from the total allocated costs for each product.

Another approach was suggested by Louderback[28] as an improvement on Moriarity, where joint costs are allocated using a ratio of (external costs to acquire a product less internal costs to finish the product)/(total external costs to acquire all products less total internal costs to process after split off). However, if the costs to process further are greater than the external market price (as in Product C), that product is ignored in the calculations (and no joint costs are assigned to it). If it were included, a negative joint cost would be assigned. As explored above, this does not make intuitive sense. Thus, the following allocations of joint costs would occur:

$$\text{Product A} \quad \$9 \times (18 - 7)/(53 - 24) = \$3.41$$
$$\text{Product B} \quad \$9 \times (13 - 12)/(53 - 24) = 0.31$$
$$\text{Product D} \quad \$9 \times (22 - 5)/(53 - 24) = 5.28$$

The table below shows a comparison of four methods of allocating joint costs: net realizable value (NRV), relative sales value (RSV), the Moriarity method (M), and the Louderback (L) method.[29]

	NRV	RSV	M	L
Joint cost allocation				
Product A	$5.48	$9.26	$7.22	$3.41
Product B	(0.78)	(4.26)	(0.44)	0.31
Product C	1.17	(1.06)	(5.22)	0.00
Product D	3.13	5.06	7.44	5.28
Sum	$9.00	$9.00	$9.00	$9.00

---

[28] Louderback, "Another Approach to Allocating Joint Costs."
[29] Thomas uses two more methods that are adaptations of the Moriarity and Louderback methods in his presentation, but leaving them out here does not harm the discussion.

	NRV	RSV	M	L
Total Cost				
Product A	$ 12.48	$16.26	$14.22	$10.41
Product B	11.22	7.74	11.56	12.31
Product C	16.17	13.94	9.78	15.00
Product D	8.13	10.06	12.44	10.28
Sum	$ 48.00	$48.00	$48.00	$48.00
Book profit				
Product A	$ 8.52	$ 4.74	$ 6.78	$10.59
Product B	(1.22)	2.26	(1.56)	(2.31)
Product C	1.83	4.06	8.22	3.00
Product D	4.87	2.94	0.56	2.72
Sum	$14.00	$14.00	$14.00	$14.00

Several things can be seen from the table. There is a large range of allocation of joint costs and, therefore, profits for each product. Since any of these methods are deemed acceptable in financial accounting,[30] the inventory values and resulting incomes would be considered "correct." Three of the four methods allocate a *negative* joint cost to some products. Only the Louderback method does not. The relative sales value method shows that Product B has a profit of $2.26 when there is an incremental loss of $2 ($10 selling price less $12 in separable costs) for the product. This does not make sense from either a planning or a product costing–income perspective. This comparison makes it clear that while the total profits of the joint process are $14 in each case, the ways of allocating these profits to products differ quite a bit.

There are many other methods to deal with joint-cost allocation. Some are quite complex, such as Shapley's[31] and others. However, the main points have been developed in this discussion. Allocation methods can yield results that seem unappealing from a product costing perspective. A basic problem in allocations is one of behavior: central office management wants its lower-level managers to make decisions that are in the best interests of the company as a whole and different allocation methods may cause different coalitions to form or may inhibit the formation of any coalitions. This discussion will now be extended into service department pricing.

---

[30] Negative income would violate the lower-of-cost-or-market rule.

[31] L. S. Shapley, "A Value for n-Person Games," in H. W. Kuhn and A. W. Tucker, eds., *Contributions to the Theory of Games* (Princeton, N.J.: 1953), pp. 307–317; Shapley and Shubik, "On Market Games," *Journal of Economic Theory* (June 1969), pp. 9–25; and Shapley and Shubik, "On the Core of an Economic System with Externalities," *American Economic Review* (September 1969), pp. 678–684. Also see such articles as John S. Hughs and James H. Scheiner, "Efficiency Properties of Mutually Satisfactory Cost Allocations," *The Accounting Review* (January 1980), pp. 85–95; Susan S. Hamlen et al., "The Use of the Generalized Shapley Allocation in Joint Cost Allocation," *The Accounting Review* (April 1980), pp. 269–287.

PRICING SERVICES

The previous discussion shows that in decentralized companies, for segment managers to agree to buy services, a coalition must be formed and prices must be deemed fair or reasonable. When a support department sells its services to other departments within the company, the prices they charge are called *transfer prices*, the topic of Chapter 15. There are at least two aspects to consider when deciding if a transfer of services is going to take place: What is appropriate from the firm's point of view and what from the perspective of a manager of a buying department?

A company bases sourcing decisions on many factors, including price, quality, availability, and personnel considerations. Any choice is based on current and expected needs for services. Obviously, the firm's managers are interested in controlling costs, whether for purchased or in-house services. When buying from an outside source, use brings incremental costs to the company. If a company pays a janitorial service $20 per hour for its workers, then any additional use will actually cost $20 per hour.

However, let us compare that to an internal service where incremental use might not cause incremental costs. For example, based on a survey and many meetings among managers, a company decides to purchase a set of computer hardware and software, linking them all with a fiber optic network. The data processing department is in charge of these resources and will set a price for their use. If the price is too low, managers might be tempted to use the services quite freely and strain the system's ability to keep up. Terminals would be added and use would go beyond that originally contemplated. This results in, for example, response time on the system becoming longer and a long queue for color plotter time. As a result of this overload, data processing managers might make a case to upper management that they have too few resources and seek to expand those they have. However, the problem might be in the pricing. Using managers were getting a signal from the system that the cost of a service was low. With little or no cost, managers would use the system well beyond what they had contracted for and, perhaps, in an inefficient way.

This problem can be illustrated by looking at capacity problems within public utilities. An electric utility in an area where summer usage is high due to hot weather is faced with having enough capacity to handle the situation. If prices are set so that consumers pay the same amount for electricity summer and winter and there is no difference for time of day use, the signal to the market place is that they can use electricity at any time and there is no consequence of this action. However, in late August when it's 90 degrees or more in the late afternoon, the utility is faced with a serious capacity problem. Even worse than the computer illustration above, the utility must have capacity in place to meet demand. However, the pricing of the service affects such demand. By using marginal cost pricing, the utility would be giving correct information to potential users: it costs more to provide electricity on summer afternoons than late summer evenings and it costs more in summer versus winter. Such pricing will allow more efficient capacity decisions.

Thus, companies are faced with charging prices that will promote appropriate use of resources. Prices might include a dual basis as discussed earlier: a capacity charge plus a charge for incremental costs. Further, as we explore in Chapters 14 and 15, it's important that prices charged to one manager are not affected by use of other managers.

SUMMARY

This chapter deals with the problems of allocating common costs to many cost objectives. One-to-many allocations are deemed arbitrary in the sense that there are many acceptable ways of allocating joint costs and there is no way theoretically to distinguish which is best. The notion of coalition forming, fairness, and equity which lead, hopefully, to behavior congruent decisions seem to be most important.

While there are many ways that allocations are included in accounting numbers, this chapter discusses service department allocations and joint-product cost allocations.

Service department allocations include methods such as direct, step, and reciprocal allocation. When variable costs are to be assigned, the reciprocal allocation method yields the best mapping of a relationship between use and incremental cost. Both matrix and linear programming solutions are useful in large allocation problems using the reciprocal method. Changes in the manufacturing environment may mean the blurring of the lines between service and manufacturing departments and/or the elimination of a two-stage allocation process so that service department costs are directly assigned to products. In joint-product cost allocations, common methods such as net realizable value, constant gross margin, and relative sales value are illustrated. These are compared to other notions of allocation such as Manes and Cheng, Moriarity, and Louderback methods to demonstrate the variety of results that come when companies try to allocate the joint costs (and, therefore, the joint profits) of a process.

The argument about allocation remains. While allocations are firmly entrenched in our financial and managerial accounting, we can continue to question their use in areas of planning and control as well as the financial accounting numbers that result from their use in income statements and balance sheets.

PROBLEMS AND CASES

11-1. Joint Cost Allocation (CMA)

Talor Chemical Company is a highly diversified chemical processing company. The company manufactures swimming pool chemicals, chemicals for metal processing companies, specialized chemical compounds for other companies, and a full line of pesticides and insecticides.

Currently, the Noorwood plant is producing two derivatives, RNA-1 and RNA-2, from the chemical compound VDB developed by Talor's research labs. Each week 1,200,000 pounds of VDB are processed at a cost of $246,000 into 800,000 pounds of RNA-1 and 400,000 pounds of RNA-2. The proportion of these two outputs is fixed and cannot be altered because this is a joint process. RNA-1 has no market value until it is converted into a product with the trade name Fastkil. The cost to process RNA-1 into Fastkil is $240,000. Fastkil wholesales at $50 per 100 pounds.

RNA-2 is sold as is for $80 per hundred pounds. However, Talor has discovered that RNA-2 can be converted into two new products through further processing. The further processing would require the addition of 400,000 pounds of compound LST to the 400,000 pounds of RNA-2. The joint process would yield 400,000 pounds each of DMZ-3 and Pestrol—the two new products. The additional raw material and related processing costs of this joint process would be $120,000. DMZ-3 and Pestrol would each be sold for $57.50 per 100 pounds. Talor management has decided not to process RNA-2 further based on the analysis presented in the schedule below. Talor uses the physical method to allocate the common costs arising from joint processing.

| | RNA-2 | Process Further | | Total |
		DMZ-3	Pestrol	
Production in pounds	400,000	400,000	400,000	
Revenue	$320,000	$230,000	$230,000	$460,000
Costs				
VDB costs	$ 82,000	$ 61,500	$ 61,500	$123,000
Additional raw materials				
(LST) and processing				
of RNA-2		60,000	60,000	120,000
Total costs	$ 82,000	$121,500	$121,500	$243,000
Weekly gross profit	$238,000	$108,500	$108,500	$217,000

A new staff account who was to review the analysis above commented that it should be revised and stated, "Product costing of products such as these should be done on a net relative sales value basis not a physical volume basis."

Required:
1. Discuss whether the use of the net relative sales value method would provide data more relevant for the decision to market DMZ-3 and Pestrol.
2. Critique the Talor Company's analysis and make any revisions that are necessary. Your critique and analysis should indicate:
   a. whether Talor Chemical Company made the correct decision.
   b. the gross savings (loss) per week of Talor's decision not to process RNA-2 further, if different from the company-prepared analysis.

11-2. Joint Products and By-Products (CMA)

Doe Corporation grows, processes, cans, and sells three main pineapple products—sliced pineapple, crushed pineapple, and pineapple juice. The outside skin is cut off in the Cutting Department and processed as animal feed. The skin is treated as a by-product. Doe's production process is as follows:

- Pineapples first are processed in the Cutting Department. The pineapples are washed and the outside skin is cut away. Then the pineapples are cored and trimmed for slicing. The three main products (sliced, crushed, juice) and the by-product (animal feed) are recognizable after processing in the Cutting Department. Each product is then transferred to a separate department for final processing.
- The trimmed pineapples are forwarded to the Slicing Department where the pineapples are sliced and canned. Any juice generated during the slicing operation is packed in the cans with the slices.
- The pieces of pineapple trimmed from the fruit are diced and canned in the Crushing Department. Again, the juice generated during this operation is packed in the can with the crushed pineapple.
- The core and surplus pineapple generated from the Cutting Department are pulverized into a liquid in the Juicing Department. There is an evaporation loss equal to 8 percent of the weight of the good output produced in this department, which occurs as the juices are heated.
- The outside skin is chopped into animal feed in the Feed Department.

The Doe Corporation uses the net realizable value method (relative sales value method) to assign costs of the joint process to its main products. The by-product is inventoried at its market value.

A total of 270,000 pounds were entered into the Cutting Department during May. The schedule presented below shows the costs incurred in each department, the proportion by weight transferred to the four final processing departments, and the selling price of each end product.

Processing Data and Costs
May 19X1

Department	Costs Incurred	Proportion of Product by Weight Transferred to Departments	Selling Price per Pound of Final Product
Cutting	$60,000		none
Slicing	4,700	35%	$0.60
Crushing	10,580	28	0.55
Juicing	3,250	27	0.30
Animal feed	700	10	0.10
Total	$79,230	100%	

Required:

1. The Doe Corporation uses the net realizable value method to determine inventory values for its main products and by-products. Calculate:
    a. the pounds of pineapple that result as output for pineapple slices, crushed pineapple, pineapple juice, and animal feed.
    b. the net realizable value at the split-off point of the three main products.

    c.   the amount of the cost of the Cutting Department assigned to each of the three main products and to the by-product in accordance with corporate policy.

    d.   the gross margins for each of the three main products.

2.   Comment on the significance to management of the gross margin information by main product.

3.   In the production of joint products either a by-product or scrap could be generated.

    a.   Distinguish between a by-product and scrap.

    b.   Would the proper accounting treatment for scrap differ from that for by-products? Explain your answer.

11-3. Fairness of Cost Allocations

Joe Farinella, a local landscaper, worked for Keith Tenney. For $30.00 per week Farinella mowed the grass, trimmed the hedges, and weeded the planted areas around the house. Ralph Myer, Tenney's next-door neighbor, asked the landscaper for a quote to perform the same services for him. Farinella replied that the charge would be $27 if he came on a day other than Monday, the day he did the Tenney work, but would charge a total price to Tenney and Myer of $40 if he could do both the same day.

Tenney and Myer agreed to having the service done on the same day and to pay Farinella a total of $40. They are unsure of how to divide the cost and have come to you for advice.

Required:

List a few fair ways that Tenney and Myer could split the $40 cost. Give a rationale for each method. Choose one method as "best" and justify your choice.

11-4. Allocation Issues in Public Facilities

The town of Lake Wobetide is in a resort area. About 2,500 of the 10,000 houses in the town are owned by people who occupy them only during the summer season, which runs for about four months in that area.

While there are a few water wells, most water comes from the town water supply. The current charge for water is $2.50 per thousand gallons. An association of year-round residents has petitioned the city management for a change in the rate. They think that the summer users pay too little for water use as compared to the full-time residents. They especially point to the fact that there is no minimum charge for water so that summer residents only pay when they use water in the summer.

The city manager wants to be fair and only wants to recover the costs for the system. Currently, $2,000,000 are the annual fixed costs and, at annual consumption of 900,000,000 gallons, variable costs are $0.20 per thousand gallons.

Required:

1.   You have been asked by the city manager to recommend a series of plans to charge water costs. Develop a set of pricing methods along with a list of each method's strengths, weaknesses, whether it favors one consumer group or the other, and what signals it gives to consumers. Finally, choose one method as your recommendation and justify your choice.

2.   Would your choice have been affected by the climate of the area (e.g., is Lake Wobetide in upper Wisconsin, southern Illinois, or southern Alabama)?

3.   Explain how this is a question of accounting theory.

11-5. Joint Products and By-Products

Toklas Manufacturing produces several chemicals used in pasture and pond maintenance. Most come from a single joint process. While some of the products are ready to sell at split off, others either need further processing before sale or could be changed into different products with further processing.

In the first part of the process, the Distilling Department, Algebase and Weedbase are produced. In addition, a rodent prevention chemical (Rodent Rid) is produced as a by-product.

Algebase goes through a second processing department, Pond Chemicals, where it is refined into Algekill and Poolcide. Poolcide can be sold as is, but Algekill is further processed to yield Algepond and Algekill Plus.

Weedbase can be sold to local farming organizations as it comes from the Distilling Department or can be further processed to yield CornWeed and SoyWeed in the Farm Chemicals Department.

Sales prices for the various products are as follows:

Poolcide	$20/gallon
Algepond	17
Algekill Plus	22
Weedbase	30
CornWeed	35
SoyWeed	40
Rodent Rid	3

Standard costs during the month were $83,000 in the first department yielding 8,000 gallons of Algebase and 4,000 gallons of Weedbase. In the Pond Chemicals Department, common costs were $10,000 during the month; the 8,000 gallons of Algebase were turned into 4,000 gallons of Poolcide and 4,000 gallons of Algekill. These 4,000 gallons were, in turn, refined into 2,000 gallons of Algepond and 2,000 gallons of Algekill Plus at a cost of $1,500. Separable costs in the Pond Chemicals Department were $12,000 for Poolcide and $7,000 for Algekill Plus.

Common costs in the Farm Chemicals Department were $34,200; the 4,000 gallons of Weedbase were turned into 3,000 gallons of CornWeed and 1,000 gallons of SoyWeed. Separable costs were $50,000 for CornWeed and $7,000 for SoyWeed. In addition, costs to ready the by-product for market were $1,000.

Required:

1. Using an electronic spreadsheet, enter the facts for this case on a template in a data section.
2. Using your template and the basic data, allocate joint costs for the main products by physical volume and for the by-product by the other income method. Show all allocations, assignment of separable costs, and profit for each product (assuming all were sold).
3. Repeat part 2 except use the net realizable value method to allocate joint costs for main products and the by-product.
4. What choices do you have to make in order to proceed with part 3?
5. Repeat parts 3 and 4 except use the constant gross margin method for the main products and the net realizable value method for the by-product.

11-6. Allocation of Joint Product Costs (CMA)

Alderon Industries is a manufacturer of chemicals for various purposes. One of the processes used by Alderon produces SPL-3, a chemical used in swimming pools; PST-4, a chemical used in pesticides; and RJ-5, a by-product that is sold to fertilizer manufacturers. Alderon uses the net realizable value of its main products to allocate joint production costs, and the first-in, first-out (FIFO) inventory method to value the main products. The by-product is inventoried at its net realizable value, and this value is used to reduce the joint production costs before the joint costs are allocated to the main products. The ratio of output quantities to input quantities of direct material used in the joint process remains consistent from month to month.

Data regarding Alderon's operations for the month of November, 19X9 are presented below. During this month, Alderon incurred joint production costs of $1,702,000 in the manufacture of SPL-3, PST-4, and RJ-5.

November 19X9 Operations

	SPL-3	PST-4	RJ-5
Finished goods inventory in gallons (11/1/X9)	18,000	52,000	3,000
November sales in gallons	650,000	325,000	150,000
November production in gallons	700,000	350,000	170,000
Sales value per gallon at split off	none	$ 3.80	$0.70*
Additional processing costs	$874,000	$816,000	none
Final sales value per gallon	$ 4.00	$ 6.00	none

* Disposal costs of $0.10 per gallon will be incurred in order to sell the by-product.

Required:
1. Determine Alderon Industries' allocation of joint production costs for the month of November, 19X9. Be sure to present appropriate supporting calculations.
2. Determine the dollar values of the finished goods inventories for SPL-3, PST-4, and RJ-5 as of November 30, 19X9.
3. Alderon Industries has an opportunity to sell PST-4 at the split-off point for $3.80 per gallon. Prepare an analysis showing whether Alderon should sell PST-4 at the split-off point or continue to process this product further.

11-7. Negative Allocations of Joint Costs

The discussion in the chapter shows various methods that can yield a negative allocation of a joint cost to a product or department. In other words, instead of costs being increased by the allocation process, they are decreased.

Required:
Comment on negative allocations. Justify when such allocations are useful. Also discuss when a negative allocation yields what seems a meaningless result.

11-8. Variable Service Department Costs

The Electronics Division of Will Industries had the following relationship between service and operating departments in the month of June:

Service Performed by	Data Processing	Engineering	Fabrication	Assembly
Data Processing	0%	20%	30%	50%
Engineering	25%	0%	60%	15%

The total variable costs before reciprocal allocations and activities for the service departments in June are:

Data Processing	$45,000	30,000	CPU units
Engineering	75,000	6,000	hours

where: CPU units are a measure of time used on the central processing unit of the mainframe computer.

Required:
1. Comment on the use of the CPU units and hours as a basis for allocating activity for these two departments. When would each be appropriate and when inappropriate?
2. Using the matrix procedure illustrated in the chapter, what are the total variable costs for each of the service departments? What is the adjusted variable cost per unit of service for each department?
3. Determine the amounts of variable service department costs that would be assigned to each production department.
4. What are the external needs of data processing if an outside firm were hired and the internal department shut down? Independently, what are the external engineering needs if that service were contracted outside the company?
5. Demonstrate that if the firm buys data processing services from an outside supplier at the adjusted variable cost per CPU unit calculated in part 2, it will show the same total variable costs in total that it now does ($120,000).

11-9. Equitable Cost Assignment Basis (CMA adapted)

Marfrank Corporation is a manufacturing company with six functional departments—Finance, Marketing, Personnel, Production, Research and Development (R&D), and Information Systems—each administered by a vice president. The Information Systems Department (ISD) was established in 19X8 when Marfrank decided to acquire a new mainframe computer and develop a new information system.

While systems development and implementation is an ongoing process at Marfrank, many of the basic systems needed by each of the functional departments were operational at the end of 19X9. Thus, calendar year 19Y0 is considered the first year when the ISD costs can be estimated with a high degree of accuracy. Marfrank's president wants the other five functional departments to be aware of the magnitude of the ISD costs by reflecting the allocation of ISD costs in the reports and statements prepared at the end of the first quarter of 19Y0. The allocation of ISD costs to each of the departments was based on their actual use of ISD services.

Jon Werner, vice president of ISD, suggested that the actual costs of ISD be assigned on the basis of the pages of actual computer output. This basis was suggested because reports are what all of the departments use in evaluating their operations and making decisions. The use of this basis resulted in the following:

Department	Percentage	Allocated Cost
Finance	50	$112,500
Marketing	30	67,500
Personnel	9	20,250
Production	6	13,500
R&D	5	11,250
Total	100	$225,000

After the quarterly reports were distributed, the Finance and Marketing Departments objected to this method. Both departments recognized that they were responsible for most of the output in terms of reports, but they believed that these output costs might be the smallest of ISD costs and requested that a more equitable basis be developed.

After meeting with Werner, Elaine Jergens, Marfrank's controller, concluded that ISD provided three distinct services—systems development, computer processing represented by central processing unit (CPU) time, and report generation. She recommended that a predetermined rate be developed for each of these services from budgeted annual activity and costs. The ISD costs would then be assigned to the other functional departments using the predetermined rate times the actual activity used. Any difference between actual costs incurred and costs assigned to the other departments would be absorbed by ISD.

Jergens and Werner concluded that systems development could be charged on the basis of hours devoted to systems development and programming, computer processing based on CPU time used for operations (exclusive of database development and maintenance), and report generation based on pages of output. The only cost that should not be included in any of the predetermined rates would be purchased software; these packages were usually acquired for a specific department's use. Thus, Jergens concluded that purchased software would be charged at cost to the department for which it was purchased. In order to revise the first quarter assignment, Jergens gathered the information on ISD costs and services shown in Tables 1 and 2, respectively.

Required:
1. a. Develop predetermined rates for each of the service categories of ISD—systems development, computer processing, and report generation.
   b. Using the predetermined rates developed in part 1a, determine the amount each of the other five functional departments would be charged for services provided by ISD during the first quarter of 19Y0.
2. With the method proposed by Elaine Jergens for charging the ISD costs to the other five functional departments, there may be a difference between ISD's actual costs incurred and the costs assigned to the five user departments.
   a. Explain the nature of this difference.

TABLE 1
Information Systems Department Costs

	Estimated Annual Costs	Actual First Quarter Costs	Percentage Devoted To		
			Systems Develop.	Computer Processing	Report Generation
Wages and benefits					
Administration	$100,000	$25,000	60%	20%	20%
Computer operators	55,000	13,000		20	80
Analysts/programmers	165,000	43,500	100		
Maintenance					
Hardware	24,000	6,000		75	25
Software	20,000	5,000		100	
Output supplies	50,000	11,500			100
Purchased software	45,000	16,000*	—	—	—
Utilities	28,000	6,250		100	
Depreciation					
Mainframe computer	325,000	81,250		100	
Printing equipment	60,000	15,000			100
Building improvements	10,000	2,500		100	
Total department costs	$882,000	$225,000			

*Note: All software purchased during the First Quarter of 19Y0 was for the benefit of the Production Department.

TABLE 2
Information Systems Department Services

	Systems Development	Computer Operations (CPU)	Report Generation
Annual capacity	4,500 hours	360 CPU hours	5,000,000 pages
Actual usage during First Quarter—19Y0			
Finance	100 hours	8 CPU hours	600,000 pages
Marketing	250	12	360,000
Personnel	200	12	108,000
Production	400	32	72,000
R&D	50	16	60,000
Total usage	1,000 hours	80 CPU hours	1,200,000 pages

    b.   Discuss whether this proposal by Jergens will improve cost control in ISD.

    c.   Explain whether Jergens' proposed method of charging user departments for ISD costs will improve planning and control in the user departments.

3. What part of this process is more accurate costs and what part more equitable allocation?

11-10. Allocation of Fixed and Variable Service Department Costs

Alphareta Industries has three service departments and four production departments. Alphareta uses standard costs and, therefore, first allocates fixed and variable service department costs at budget to the operating departments. Then these costs are combined with the budgeted overhead costs in each department in order to establish a standard rate per labor hour or per machine hour as deemed appropriate. Costs are finally allocated to units of production through the application of standard overhead.

The following information is for May 19X7, for service departments A, B, and C, and operating departments D, E, F, and G:

	Service			Operating					
	A	B	C	D	E	F	G	Total	Units
A	10%	10%	15%	15%	10%	20%	20%	100%	30,000
B	5	15	20	20	5	25	10	100	15,000
C	15	15	5	5	20	20	20	100	10,000

Total variable costs (at standard) before reciprocal assignment were:

Department A	$51,000
Department B	15,100
Department C	27,500

Separable departmental budgeted fixed costs for the month were:

Department A	$30,000
Department B	10,000
Department C	5,000

Management states that, on average, inter-service-department use was about normal in May. However, the distribution of the percentage of service to the operating departments was a bit off. Capacity requirements had been based on the following:

	Service			Operating				
	A	B	C	D	E	F	G	Total
A	10%	10%	15%	15%	10%	20%	20%	100%
B	5	15	20	15	15	15	15	100
C	15	15	5	10	15	20	20	100

Required:
In the following requirements, you will need to use the matrix method (as illustrated in the chapter) and either an electronic spreadsheet template or a computer program to do the required matrix inversion.

1. Assign variable service department costs to all departments using the reciprocal method.
2. Allocate fixed service department costs to all departments on the basis of planned capacity.

3. Using the information from the main diagonal elements of the inverted matrix, what are the external needs for each service department? Explain what these external needs represent.
4. What are the adjusted variable costs per unit of service for each service department? Explain what these adjusted variable costs mean.
5. How can information from this process be used in standard cost variance analysis? Explain fully and, if possible, create an illustration to help in your explanation.

11-11. Linear Programming and Allocation of Fixed Costs

In an article by Robert S. Kaplan and Gerald L. Thompson,[32] the authors propose that the traditional method for allocating fixed overhead can be misleading for pricing and other management decisions. It is possible that using traditional methods will show that a product is unprofitable when, in fact, it is profitable but being penalized under the allocation method.

The authors suggest some rules that help in allocating fixed costs so that the resulting margins are useful for managerial decisions. The proof is that the same product-mix decision would be made both before and after fixed-cost allocation. A basic premise of the proposed technique is that overall profits are positive (total contribution margin exceeds total fixed costs). In addition, the authors assume perfectly competitive markets so that prices for all products are given.

Fixed overhead costs can either be traceable to a particular scarce resource or common to all resources. Note that fixed overhead relates to resources and not to products.

After a linear programming solution (using contribution margins per unit in the objective function) has been obtained indicating production mix, the rules for allocating fixed overhead are as follows:

Common Fixed Overhead   Allocate common fixed overhead over all products in proportion to the total imputed value of the scarce resources employed in their production. This means that the contribution margin for each product should be multiplied by a constant k, where k = common fixed costs divided by the $1 \times n$ vector of the shadow prices of the resources multiplied by the $n \times 1$ vector of the total resources available (right-hand sides of the constraints).

Traceable Fixed Overhead   There are two rules here:
1. When the shadow price for a resource is greater than or equal to the average traceable fixed overhead per unit of capacity of that resource (traceable fixed overhead divided by total resource availability), then for each product multiply the average traceable fixed overhead per unit of capacity by the number of resource units required (hours, for example) to produce each product.
2. However, if the shadow price of a resource is less than the average traceable fixed overhead per unit of capacity of that resource do the following:
    a. Multiply the shadow price by the number of resource units required for one unit of a particular product.

---

[32] "Overhead Allocation via Mathematical Programming Models," *The Accounting Review* (April 1971), pp. 352–364.

    b. Assign that number to the product in question.

    c. Any excess of average traceable fixed overhead per unit of capacity over the shadow price should be treated as if it were common fixed overhead as in the first rule. Consider the following example:

```
MAX        X₁ + .5 X₂
SUBJECT TO
           2)  3 X₁ +  2 X₂ <=  12   machine 1
           3)  5 X₁        <=  10   machine 2
```

$$MAX \quad X_1 + .5\, X_2$$
$$\text{SUBJECT TO}$$
$$2) \quad 3 X_1 + 2 X_2 \le 12 \quad \text{machine 1}$$
$$3) \quad 5 X_1 \le 10 \quad \text{machine 2}$$

```
           OBJECTIVE FUNCTION VALUE

1)              3.50
```

VARIABLE	VALUE	REDUCED COST
X_1	2.000000	.000000
X_2	3.000000	.000000

ROW	SLACK OR SURPLUS	DUAL PRICES
2)	.000000	.250000
3)	.000000	.050000

RANGES IN WHICH THE BASIS IS UNCHANGED:

OBJ COEFFICIENT RANGES

VARIABLE	CURRENT COEF	ALLOWABLE INCREASE	ALLOWABLE DECREASE
X_1	1.000000	INFINITY	.250000
X_2	.500000	.166667	.500000

RIGHTHAND SIDE RANGES

ROW	CURRENT RHS	ALLOWABLE INCREASE	ALLOWABLE DECREASE
2	12.000000	INFINITY	6.000000
3	10.000000	10.000000	10.000000

THE TABLEAU

ROW	(BASIS)	X_1	X_2	SLK 2	SLK 3	
1	ART	.000	.000	.250	.050	3.500
2	X_2	.000	1.000	.500	-.300	3.000
3	X_1	1.000	.000	.000	.200	2.000

Required:

(*Hint*: treat the fixed overhead as per unit information so that you can adjust your objective function to reflect full costs rather than just variable costs. Reference to the original article may be useful.)

1. Assume that the company incurs a common fixed overhead of $2.50. There is no traceable fixed overhead. Allocate the $2.50 between X_1 and X_2 using the rules proposed above so that the resulting linear programming model yields an optimal product mix the same as the above solution.

2. Now assume that the company incurs common fixed overhead of $0.90 and traceable fixed overhead of $1.20 for machine 1 and $0.40 for machine 2. Allocate the total fixed overhead of $2.50 between X_1 and X_2 so that the resulting linear programming model yields the original product mix.

3. Finally, assume that the company incurs a common fixed overhead of $0.70 and traceable fixed overhead of $1.20 for machine 1 and $0.60 for machine 2. Again allocate the total fixed overhead of $2.50 between the two products so that the resulting linear programming solution yields the original product mix.

4. Comment on this method of allocating fixed overhead. What are its strengths and its weaknesses?

11-12. Allocations and Equity

Four people own residential property that is accessed by a rock road leading from a state highway. The road is 5/10 of a mile in length with the first person's (Tenney's) property along both sides of the road for the first 3/10 of a mile. The second person's (Berger's) property is only along the north side of the road. His driveway is at the 3/10-of-a-mile mark. The third property (Sharpe) is along the south side of the road with her driveway 4/10ths of a mile down the road. The final property (Desloge) is situated totally at the end of the road (5/10ths of a mile from the state highway); none of this property touches the road except the driveway. In addition, the Tenney property has a house on one side of the road and a barn on the other side, the Berger property has a house, the Sharpe property has a house, and the Desloge property has no buildings on it nor are there plans to build in the foreseeable future.

Mr. Berger wants to pave the roadway along its entire length. He argues that this will improve the property values in what is now a growing residential area. The bid to pave the road 10 feet wide is $50,000. The Tenneys want to maintain the road as is but agree that if an equitable apportionment of the costs can be achieved, they will participate. Sharpe is willing to go along either way, but Ms. Sharpe has made it clear that she lives on a fixed income. Therefore, she can only participate if her share of costs is limited. In addition, she is very worried about ongoing maintenance costs if the road were to be paved. Finally, Desloge does not want to participate at all in the paving project.

Required:
1. What criteria should be used to develop a plan for paving the road?
2. Develop at least three ways to divide the paving cost. State how the criteria you developed above were met for each plan.
3. Choose one of the plans you developed and clearly present the rationale for your choice.
4. What other issues are important in this situation? How do you recommend dealing with these issues?

11-13. Computer Service Corporation[33]

The Setting:

Meeting Notice
Subject: Allocation of parts overhead to products
Purpose: To decide on an equitable method
Location: Executive Conference Room
Time: 1:00 p.m. Thursday

Attendees
John Stevens, President, Computer Service Corporation
Don Vawter, President, Complex Systems Division
Linda Westbrook, President, Common Systems Division
Larry Walters, Corporate Director of Accounting

Transcript:

The meeting to decide on an equitable method of allocating parts overhead was held on schedule. The following is a transcript of the discussion.

John Stevens: Good afternoon. For some time now, you have been studying various methods of allocating parts overhead to the products we service. As I understand it, no agreement has been reached on a single method that is acceptable to all. I'm pleased with the effort you have been making, but also feel it is important we come to an agreement and I feel that we can reach agreement before we adjourn today.

To reach agreement, each of you will have to put aside, to some extent, your division's particular interest and focus on a financial approach that is in the best interest of the total corporation. I am convinced that our final agreement will turn on a way of allocating this important element of service cost to products based on an association that best recognizes cause and effect.

To price our services properly, we must eliminate the product inequities inherent in our current method which, as you know, allocates parts overhead to each product serviced based on the proportionate share of the cost of direct parts used. There are, of course, difficulties in associating indirect costs to product in a practical and cost efficient manner. These points, I am sure, will come out as each of you has an opportunity to state your position on the current and proposed methods.

Larry, would you start us off by reviewing our current method in detail and reminding us why it was put in place when it doesn't seem to work well for anyone today.

Larry Walters: Thanks a whole lot for the terrific lead in, John. Or should I say set up!

Fact is, there was no disagreement with the current method when it was adopted ten years ago. Of course, we had fewer than 25 products then, and they were all large, complex systems. It wasn't until our product line began to grow and the products became substantially different in complexity that the inequities developed. Before I go any further in reviewing today's method, however, let me run through the definitions and elements of direct parts cost and parts overhead, just to make sure we're all starting from the same point.

---

[33] This problem is used with the permission of the Institute of Management Accountants.

Cost Definitions:
Direct Parts Cost: The cost of parts which can be associated with a single product.

Parts Overhead Cost: The cost of parts which cannot be directly associated with a single product and the cost of storing and distributing parts.

Cost Elements:
Direct Parts Cost: The cost of parts used in servicing a product. The single product being serviced is identified on the service report. This cost is referred to as "product usage."

Parts Overhead Cost:
1. Nonproduct Usage—The cost of parts used which cannot be associated with a single product because
    a. the part is "low value" and need not be reported (to keep administrative and processing costs to a minimum low value parts costing less than $10 are not reported);
    b. the association cannot be made because of reporting error.
2. Inventory Variance—The cost of parts lost, as identified by a physical inventory.
3. Parts Scrap—The cost of parts scrapped either because of defects, being surplus, or being obsolete.
4. Distribution–The cost of operating the distribution centers which store and distribute all parts for service.

Any questions? Well then, enough for definitions. Let's go on to our current method. Today's method is simply to calculate each product's percent of direct parts cost and apply it to parts overhead. For example (L. Walters presented the following chart).

	Direct Parts Cost	Percentage	Parts Overhead Cost	Total Cost
Product A	$32,000	33.33	$20,000	$ 52,000
Product B	16,000	16.67	10,000	26,000
Product C	48,000	50.00	30,000	78,000
Total	$96,000	100.00	$60,000	$156,000

The problem with this method is that the Common Systems Division is being overcharged for the products it services for the following reasons:

• Their distribution costs are proportionately lower because they use a significantly higher percentage of common parts. They, in fact, have and need fewer parts in stock to meet their service requirements.
• Because of parts commonality related to the products they service, they have significantly less scrap.

While it's a fact that Common Systems is being overcharged, we haven't changed the accounting methods because Don has not accepted any of the new methods proposed. But Linda has a proposal which might be acceptable. Linda, would you take over at this point?

Linda Westbrook: Thanks, Larry. John, I agree with Larry's presentation of my division's problem. We considered various ways to improve the allocation of costs and settled on this approach as the most practical.

- Allocate non-product usage to products based on product usage or direct parts cost.
- Allocate the other elements of parts overhead cost to product based on the parts inventory by product.

A parts inventory by product would be established by associating each part number with a product. For unique parts, this is simple. All of the inventory for these parts would be associated with the unique product. For common parts, an allocation would be made to each product based on usage.

This approach could be implemented in a few months. The only thing we are lacking is agreement to implement. Don, are you willing to go along with what I've described? Or do you have objections to my proposal?

Don Vawter: John, if you were to decide based on these two presentations, Complex System's financial measurements would be adversely affected.

I don't disagree with anything that Larry or Linda said. My problem is that they have left out a couple of important facts.

First, they failed to mention that those low value parts, which do not require reporting, are mostly used by Common Systems. To allocate them based on usage would unfairly charge my division.

Second, they propose to allocate the other elements of parts overhead based on inventory "value." Inventory value will allocate too much cost to Complex Systems because we have the most expensive parts but, at the same time, we occupy a much smaller share of inventory space and have a significantly lower number of units in inventory.

To sum up, I agree that our present method leaves a lot to be desired, but I request that we don't change unless we can satisfy all of our concerns.

Required:
1. What are the objectives of allocating costs to product?
2. Given the above scenario, what other basis might be used to allocate cost to product?
3. Identify which elements of cost would be included within each product allocation method.

11-14. Home Builders Association versus St. Louis County Water Company[34]

This case examines cost allocation issues in a regulatory environment. The St. Louis County Water Company (SLCWC) is an investor-owned, for-profit utility regulated by the Public Service Commission of Missouri (PSC). At the time of this case, SLCWC had filed a request for a rate increase with the PSC. The Home Builders Association of St. Louis (HBA) intervened in the rate process to request a change in the way SLCWC allocated indirect payroll costs to its Construction operations.

---

[34] Michael L. Costigan and Maurice L. Hirsch, Jr., *Journal of Accounting Education*, Vol. II (New York: Pergamon Press, 1993), pp. 151–175.

At least three constituencies have a stake in this allocation problem: the HBA, the PSC, and the SLCWC shareholders and managers. In addition, the Public Counsel's office of the State of Missouri has the role of seeing that the residential consumers are represented in rate proceedings. However, in this case the Public Counsel's role is passive.

Part A of the case first provides a background on the PSC and the process of rate regulation at the PSC. Next, background information is presented on the SLCWC and the allocation method currently in use. Finally, a description of the HBA and its concern over the allocation method is presented. The case asks you to consider this allocation process from the point of view of (1) accounting theory and (2) each of the three major stakeholders.

Part B of the case reviews three alternative allocation schemes: one proposed by SLCWC and two proposed by a consultant to the HBA. This part of the case asks you to consider these proposals and discuss whether they offer improvements over the PSC method.

Part C describes the resolution of the case and summarizes the experience of SLCWC in the first year following the case. It also can stand by itself since it illustrates generic cost allocation issues that came to light after the rate case. Your instructor will distribute Part C after discussion of Parts A and B.

Part A

Background on Rate Regulation and the PSC and PSC Staff   The PSC consists of both commissioners and staff. The commissioners are appointed by the Governor of Missouri and these commissioners hire the staff. Commissioners serve for a three-year term and can be reappointed. While both the commissioners and the staff work for the PSC, it is not uncommon for the agenda of these two groups to be different. Thus, even though the staff works under guidelines and policies established by the commissioners, they might take a different approach to a problem than the commission itself. In addition, in some cases, staff might hire outside consultants to deal with a specific aspect of a problem or to better represent a particular class of consumers (e.g., the residential class).

As with most utilities, the SLCWC is a monopoly, one that supplies water throughout St. Louis County, Missouri. It is the PSC's responsibility to regulate such monopolies for the good of the citizens of the state. Specifically, the PSC is interested in the rate of return that utilities earn. Thus, they look at the rates a utility charges (its revenues), the costs it wants to expense against such revenues, and the assets it says are employed to generate the regulated service (its asset base). The PSC allows utilities to set water rates so that they earn enough revenue to (1) cover certain expenses (operation and maintenance costs, depreciation, and various taxes) and (2) earn an authorized rate of return. The PSC determines the "authorized rate of return" for a regulated utility by considering the comparable earnings for a company of comparable risk. (At the time of this case, the authorized rate of return for SLCWC was 10.53%.)

A water utility requests permission from the PSC to change its water rates when it earns (or wants to earn) a return different from its authorized rate of return or when it is earning less than the authorized rate of return. Given increases in operating costs, SLCWC was requesting rates to allow it to achieve its authorized rate of return. The utility decides on the amount of rate increase that it requests by comparing its operating profit for a recent 12-month period (revenues from the current rate structure less operation and maintenance costs, depreciation, and various taxes) to the operating profit that would allow it to earn its authorized rate of return (the authorized rate of return times the asset base, which is the value of the water utility's assets used and useful in serving its customers). Exhibit 1 shows a streamlined example of this calculation.[35]

SLCWC has followed a policy of requesting rate increases every other June. Under state law, the PSC has 11 months to consider a rate request, thus SLCWC adjusts their rates every other May. During this 11-month approval period, PSC staff (auditors, attorneys, engineers, etc.) study the company's rate request and make recommendations to the PSC. In addition, other stakeholders (e.g., public interest groups and, in this case, the HBA) have the right to intervene in the process to suggest changes in the rate request. This can include looking at the approved rate of return and the expenses and/or assets ascribed to regulated business. In addition, many cases deal with how overall revenue (and return) will be divided among various customer classes (e.g., residential, mercantile, industrial, public, etc.) or between regulated and non-regulated parts of a business (e.g., supplying water versus construction of water mains). In this case, the HBA filed as an intervenor and entered testimony suggesting a change in how payroll costs are allocated to Construction, a non-regulated part of the business.

Background on the SLCWC   The water company's operations can be classified into two broad areas: Operations and Maintenance (O&M) and Construction. At SLCWC, O&M includes the normal operations of the water company such as providing water and sewer service, billing, collecting, and servicing accounts. Construction includes two activities. First, the SLCWC spends a significant amount of time and money maintaining the water system, updating its water lines, and moving water

Exhibit 1
Calculation of Requested Rate Increase

Revenue from current rate structure		$ 63,000,000
Expenses:		
Operations and Maintenance	$ 33,000,000	
Depreciation	3,000,000	
Taxes (40%)	10,800,000	
Total		$ 46,800,000
Earnings from current rate structure		$ 16,200,000
Total asset base		$180,000,000
Authorized rate of return from the PSC		10%
Earnings allowed		18,000,000
Earnings from current rate structure		16,200,000
Revenue deficit (after tax)		$ 1,800,000
divide by (1 − t)		.60
Rate increase (before tax)		$ 3,000,000

---

[35] All exhibits are based on approximate numbers available from SLCWC and PSC documents.

lines because of roadwork projects. Second, SLCWC performs construction activities for contractors such as connecting new developments to the water system.

SLCWC's activities are carried out through five departments: Distribution, Engineering, Production, Administration, and Executive. Non-management personnel in Distribution, Engineering, and Production maintain timecards which allow their salaries to be directly traced to O&M or Construction. The rest of the salaries incurred at SLCWC are indirect costs which are either allocated to O&M or capitalized as Construction.

Costs allocated to O&M become expenses and, therefore, lower income. This means that SLCWC can request a rate increase from the PSC to achieve its approved rate of return. On the other hand, indirect payroll costs allocated to Construction are capitalized. If such costs relate to construction needed for repairs, upgrading, or highway relocation work, they become part of the asset base paid for by the stockholders and increase the revenue that SLCWC can request over the depreciable life

Exhibit 2
Outline of the Allocation Problem at SLCWC

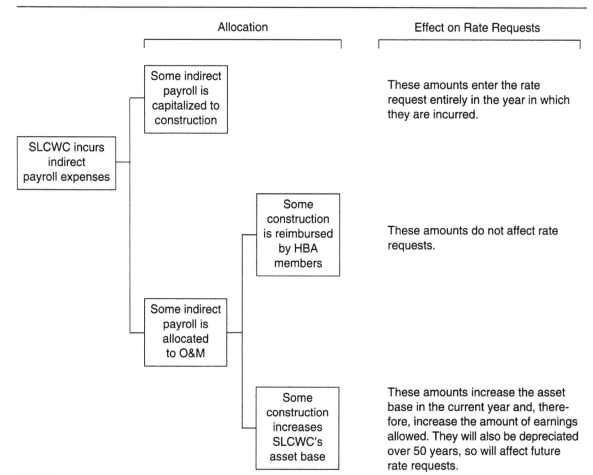

of the assets (50 years, on average).[36] If they are assignable to work performed under contract for developers, they are billed to such developers. In turn, when the work is completed to, say, extend a water main into a new housing development, the developer who has paid the water company for the work is then required to donate the asset to SLCWC. Exhibit 2 summarizes this allocation process and the effect that it has on rate increase requests from SLCWC. From the SLCWC's point of view, they would rather have as many costs as possible classified as O&M since they can be expensed in the year incurred instead of capitalized and expensed over 50 years. From a developer's perspective, the less costs that are allocated to Construction, the lower the construction bill for building water mains. Thus, from both sides, the more costs allocated to O&M the better.

Summary of the Current Allocation Method   The current allocation method, described as a *rolled-up allocation*, was devised by the staff of the PSC and went into effect two years prior to the current case. The notion of a rolled-up allocation assumes that the appropriate basis for allocating a manager's salary is the composite capitalization rate (percent) for all employees supervised by that manager. Exhibit 3 outlines this method as it is used at SLCWC and Exhibit 4 provides a numerical example of the allocation.

Note that the initial basis for the allocation is the amount of non-manager salary traceable to construction from timecards maintained by employees in Distribution, Engineering, and Production. The percent of salaries traced to Construction from these timecards is used to allocate a portion of manager salaries to Construction in each department. A composite capitalization rate (Ratio A) is computed from these departments.

Based on the assumption that employees in Administration supervise all of the employees in Distribution, Engineering, and Production, the composite capitalization rate computed for Distribution, Engineering, and Production (Ratio A) is used to capitalize a portion of salaries from Administration. A new composite capitalization rate (Ratio B) is then computed.

Finally, based on the assumption that employees in the Executive Office supervise all of the employees in Distribution, Engineering, Production, and Administration, the composite capitalization rate (Ratio B) is used to capitalize a portion of salaries from the Executive Office to Construction.

Construction and the HBA   The HBA represents homebuilder developers in the St. Louis area. When a developer wants to build a subdivision or set of apartments, it is that builder's responsibility to bring water service on site. The owners of SLCWC are not interested in expanding service themselves since that would require additional equity capital or increased borrowing. Therefore, they require that developers contract to build main extensions and donate the completed work to SLCWC. Developers, such as members of the HBA, can either get SLCWC or an independent contractor to build such facilities at the developer's expense. At the time of this case, it was the norm for SLCWC to do almost 100 percent of main extension

---

[36] Assets donated from developers, such as HBA members, are not included in the asset base that is used as the denominator in determining if the company's actual return matches its approved rate of return.

work due to (1) the engineering roadblocks erected by SLCWC (as alleged by the HBA) and/or (2) competitive bidding favors SLCWC. However, during the two years that the current allocation procedure was in place, members of the HBA became concerned about the amount charged by SLCWC for construction activities.

SLCWC charges homebuilders for construction activities based on a pricing scheme established at the beginning of each year. SLCWC begins the pricing process by

Exhibit 3
Outline of SLCWC's "Rolled-Up"
Allocation of Indirect Costs to Construction

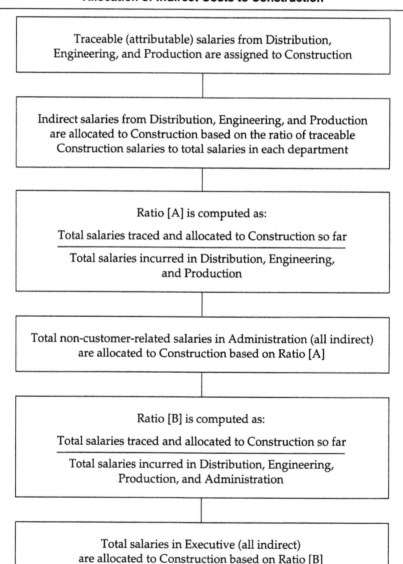

EXHIBIT 4
PSC Staff Allocation Method for construction Related Costs

Panel A: Allocation

Step 1

Responsibility Center	Distribution	Engineering	Production	Total
Center number	5000	6000	8000	Total
Total labor	$ 5,300,000	9,500,000	$1,100,000	$15,900,000
Manager Salaries	($ 1,000,000)	($3,000,000)	($ 300,000)	
Nonmanager Labor	$ 4,300,000	$6,500,000	$ 800,000	
Amount traceable to				
construction from timecards	$ 255,000	$3,100,000	$ 475,000	
% allocated to construction	5.93%	47.69%	59.38%	
Manager Salaries	$ 1,000,000	$3,000,000	$ 300,000	
Amount of manager salary				
allocated to construction	$ 59,302	$1,430,769	$ 178,125	
Total to construction	$ 314,302	$4,530,769	$ 653,125	$ 5,498,196

Ratio [A] $5,498,196/$15,900,000   34.58%

Step 2

Responsibility Center	Administration	
Center number	7000	
Total labor	$2,665,000	
Customer service	($ 300,000)	
Noncustomer labor	$2,365,000	
times Ratio [A]	34.58%	
Amount of Administration salary		
allocated to construction		$ 817,814

Total to Construction from Departments
5000, 6000, 8000 & 7000 $ 6,316,000

Ratio [B] $6,316,010/$18,565,000   34.02%

Step 3

Reponsibility Center	Executive	
Center number	9000	
Total labor	$ 325,000	
times Ratio [B]	34.02%	
		$ 110,568

Total cost to Construction $ 6,426,578

Panel B: Summary

Responsibility Center	Total	Capitalized to Construction	Expensed to Operations
Distribution	$ 5,300,000	$ 314,302	$ 4,985,698
Engineering	9,500,000	4,530,769	4,969,231
Administration	2,665,000	817,814	1,847,186
Production	1,100,000	653,125	446,875
Executive	325,000	110,568	214,432
Total	$18,890,000	$6,426,578	$12,463,422
%	100.00%	34.02%	65.98%

estimating the amount of costs expected to be traced and allocated to construction in the upcoming year. These allocated costs are based on SLCWC's fully allocated cost of construction in the previous year. Next the level of construction activity experienced in the previous year is used to compute a basic price for construction. Different prices are charged based on the diameter of the line installed and the number of feet required. For example, in 1991, SLCWC charged $32.08 per foot for a 6-inch diameter line running 400 feet or less. For each foot over 400 feet and up to 1,000 feet, the additional charge was $21.43 per foot. For each foot over 1,000 feet and up to 4,000, the additional charge was $18.38 foot. There were equivalent costs for 8-inch pipe.[37]

The homebuilders are billed in advance for any construction based on this price structure. (In addition, since the enactment of the 1986 Tax Act, developers also must contribute an additional 34 percent to cover federal income taxes on the contributed assets.) If the actual cost of construction proves to be less than the bid from SLCWC, the excess is rebated to the homebuilders. If the actual cost of construction exceeds the amount charged to the homebuilders, SLCWC bears this extra cost.

Homebuilders also receive rebates from SLCWC as homeowners connect to the system and as fireplugs are installed on the system. The logic for these rebates is that the water company benefits from the connection of new customers and from the addition of fireplugs. The size of these rebates is based on the present value of SLCWC's estimated revenue from water use over an infinite time period. All parties are agreed that the method for such rebates is fair.

At the time that SLCWC filed for its latest increase in rates, HBA members felt that construction charges from SLCWC were excessive. While they had no quarrel with traceable costs incurred by SLCWC, they were concerned about the amount and composition of the indirect salaries allocated to Construction. The problem is more complicated than the normal supplier/customer relationship because any change in the amount of payroll cost allocated to Construction, a non-regulated part of the business, must be approved by the PSC since the allocation affects rates charged to water company customers, the regulated portion of operations.

Required:

1. Using theoretical arguments, evaluate the allocation method currently in use at SLCWC.
2. Consider the three classes of stakeholders (the PSC, the HBA, and SLCWC).
   a. As a representative of the HBA, how would you like to see this allocation process change?
   b. As a stockholder (or an employee) of SLCWC, what is your position concerning this allocation process?
   c. As a member of the PSC, why is this allocation important to you?

Part B

This section of the case reviews three alternative allocation schemes. The first was actually used by SLCWC in a previous period before the PSC mandated a change

---

[37] At times SLCWC opts to put in pipe larger than 6- or 8-inch pipes in order to meet potential future demand in an area. However, in such cases, SLCWC only bills a developer either 6- or 8-inch rates based on the needs of the development itself.

to the system described in Part A. The other two alternatives were proposed by the HBA as a replacement for the system described in Part A.

SLCWC Study Method   In response to criticisms raised by PSC Staff in a 1987 rate case, SLCWC undertook a study to determine the appropriate percent of costs to be allocated to Construction. The SLCWC distributed a questionnaire to its vice presidents, managers, and supervisors who did not keep their time based on a daily time sheet or other similar recording device. Each of these people was asked to evaluate his/her efforts for each quarter of the year in nine categories in terms of percent of time spent. Construction-related functions in the questionnaire were Construction, Capital Budget Preparation, and Capital Budget Review. For managers who did keep time sheets, these records were used to assign costs to O&M or to be capitalized.

Study working papers show that the study method first assigned to operations both direct payroll costs and those payroll costs to be assigned as the result of the survey and then proceeded with a rolled-up allocation similar to that proposed by PSC Staff. Based on the percent of O&M payroll over total payroll assigned so far from a center, managers' salaries were allocated to O&M. As managers' salaries were allocated, new percents [O&M payroll (including managers) over total payroll to that point] were calculated. These percents were used for higher-level allocation (e.g., the vice president for the area). For upper-level managers, including those in center 9000, this type of rolling up of allocation percentages was used to allocate costs to O&M. The balance of costs (total payroll less costs assigned to O&M and billed to others) was assigned to be capitalized.

Because the method is designed to assign all payroll costs either to operations or to construction, it is unclear how costs beyond those associated with effort based on the surveys (or other measures of activity) should be allocated. The study allocates these costs using a rolled-up allocation method similar to the PSC method described above. The results of this study are shown in Exhibit 5.

HBA Consultant's Method   In the testimony prepared by the HBA and submitted to PSC as part of the proceedings, a consultant proposed two allocation methods. One is a modification of the SLCWC method described above while the other is based entirely on avoidable cost.

Exhibit 5
Allocation Method from SLCWC Study

Responsibility Center	Total	Capitalized to Construction	Expensed to Operations
Distribution	$ 5,300,000	$ 265,000	$ 5,035,000
Engineering	9,500,000	3,250,000	6,250,000
Administration	2,665,000	200,000	2,465,000
Production	1,100,000	600,000	500,000
Executive	325,000	70,000	255,000
Totals	$18,890,000	$ 4,385,000	$14,505,000
%	100.00%	23.21%	76.79%

The first proposal from the consultant is based on the contention that the costs that were allocated to construction over and above those assigned based on the surveys and other measures of activity should not be allocated to construction at all. As shown in Exhibit 6, the original SLCWC figures were adjusted to remove the annualized wages of managers and officers. These costs ($236,000) were allocated to operations and to construction based on rolling up percentages in the SLCWC study. The consultant argued that while it is commendable to identify costs with effort, there is no rationale to just assign whatever is left over under the notion that you *have* to assign all costs. It is interesting that no surveys were filled out by officers in the Executive group. In discussions with the SLCWC, the consultant concluded that there was no real way for these people to identify what portions of their time were spent on different functions. It is also interesting that the SLCWC and/or the officers and managers in this group did not even make a rough estimate of operations versus construction activity. The consultant contends that Exhibit 6 shows as complete an assignment of costs as is reasonable.

The consultant's second proposal was based entirely on avoidable costs. Avoidable costs are the costs that would be saved in the long run if the SLCWC decided to get out of the construction business entirely. Avoidable costs were identified by the

Exhibit 6
Consultant's Revision of Allocation Method from SLCWC Study

Panel A: Adjustments to SLCWC amounts (to remove all officer payroll)

Distribution	Managers	$ 7,400
	Vice President	5,200
Engineering	Managers	38,500
	Vice President	31,200
Administration	Managers	1,800
	Controller	5,400
	Vice Presidents	6,900
Production	Managers	25,800
	Vice Presidents	43,800
Executive	All	70,000
	Total	$236,000

Panel B: Revised Allocation

Responsibility Center	Total	Capitalized to Construction	Expensed to Operations
Distribution	$ 5,300,000	$ 252,400	$ 5,047,600
Engineering	9,500,000	3,180,300	6,319,700
Administration	2,665,000	185,900	2,479,100
Production	1,100,000	530,400	569,600
Executive	325,000	—	325,000
Totals	$18,890,000	$4,149,000	$14,741,000
%	100.00%	21.96%	78.04%

consultant and SLCWC staff. They reviewed each job within the company and classified each based on whether or not the position would be eliminated if SLCWC were to cease doing construction. The results of that discussion are shown in Panel A of Exhibit 7. It is important to note that the only A&G costs capitalized to construction in Exhibit 7 are $48,000 from Administration. No costs are capitalized to construction from Distribution and only $72,000 is capitalized from Production. The balance of the costs capitalized to construction are costs that are direct to construction and incurred in Engineering.

Panel B of Exhibit 7 summarizes cost assignment with only the avoidable costs (identified in Panel A of Exhibit 7) allocated to Construction.

Exhibit 7
Avoidable Cost Allocation Method from HBA Consultant Study

Panel A: Avoidable Costs

	Current	Eliminate	Per Person Current Payroll	Total Current	Payroll Saved
Engineering—Construction					
Non-Union					
Asst. Construction Supervisor	1	1	$33,000	$33,000	$33,000
Suprv. Const-Crew Chiefs	1	1	51,000	51,000	51,000
Distribution Crew Chief	13	13	38,000	494,000	494,000
Relief Distribution Cre Chief	1	1	38,000	38,000	38,000
Secretary II	2	1	24,000	48,000	24,000
Union					
Worker, Construction	52	52	28,500	1,482,000	1,482,000
Operator, Const. Equip.	22	13	30,500	671,000	396,500
Chauffeur, Trucking	11	9	28,500	427,500	256,500
Mechanic, Garage	6	2	29,500	177,000	59,000
Temporary					
Construction Worker	3	3	21,500	64,500	64,500
Construction Equipment Operator	1	1	30,500	30,500	30,500
Engineer Tech I—Cnst	6	6	23,500	141,000	141,000
Construction Crew Chief	1	1	35,000	35,000	35,000
Trucking Chauffeur	3	2	28,500	85,500	57,000
Total Engineering					$3,162,000
Administration—General Accounting					
Union					
Clerk, Accounting	1		26,000	26,000	
Clerk, Accounts Payable	2		24,000	48,000	
Clerk, Asst Acc/Payr Acct	1		24,000	24,000	
Clerk, Cash Recs Control	1		26,000	26,000	
Clerk, Inventory	1		26,000	26,000	
Typist, Clerk II—Acct	1		18,000	18,000	
Clerk, Payroll	2		24,000	48,000	
Saved positions		2			48,000
Total Administration					48,000

Exhibit 7 (continued)

Production—System Engineering
  Non-Union

Suprv, System Engineer	1	40,500	40,500
Mgr, System Engineering	1	60,000	60,000
Engineer I, System	4	30,500	122,00
Engineer II, System	2	33,500	67,000
CADD/Drafing Tech I	1	22,500	22,500
Engineer Tech I	2	22,000	44,000
Engineer Tech III	1	28,000	28,000
Mgr, Eng & Spec Projects	1	48,500	48,500
Engineer II, Project	1	38,500	38,500
Saved positions		2	72,000

Total Production   72,000

                                                    $4,465,000 $3,282,000

Panel B: Summary

Responsibility Center	Total	Capitalized to Construction	Expensed to Operations
Distribution	$ 5,300,000		$ 5,300,000
Engineering	9,500,000	3,162,000	6,338,000
Administration	2,665,000	48,000	2,617,000
Production	1,100,000	72,000	1,028,000
Executive	325,000	—	325,000
Totals	$18,890,000	$3,282,000	$15,608,000
%	100.00%	17.38%	82.62%

One can ask the question if it's possible for the SLCWC to cease doing construction work. With highway relocation work and replacement work, even if economic activity stopped, there would be plenty of construction. However, depending on how much the SLCWC charges as compared to others in the marketplace, it is possible that (1) contractors would choose to purchase construction elsewhere, and (2) rather than keeping a smaller crew to handle only its own work, SLCWC would choose to employ an outside contractor and shut down its construction operations.

Required:
1. Are any of these methods better than the one currently in place? Why or why not?
2. Which of all the methods is best for the SLCWC? for the HBA? for the water customers? What criteria have you chosen to define "best"?

Part 4

Information
for Planning
and Evaluation

Chapter 12

Strategic Management

If accountants are to enhance their role in the strategic management of the organization, they must "fish where the fish are"; to wit, they must utilize the advances in managerial accounting theory and information technology to develop sophisticated and responsive accounting systems needed to both support and lead organizational strategy. Changes are needed in traditional managerial accounting systems if one is to address management concerns with shrinking product life cycles and increases in new product variety, new product introductions, quality, automation, process improvements, complexity, and need for specific support increase. . . .

An enhanced understanding of the strategy and strategic management processes will place the accountant in a better position to avoid major pitfalls in attempts to harmonize the strategic aspects of the accounting system with the organizational strategy. The managerial accountant may then, through creative adaptation of the accounting mechanism, support organizational strategic management and enhance the organization's ability to survive and prosper.[1]

The swirl of new events and altered circumstances make it incumbent on managers to continually reassess their company's position and prospects, always checking for *when* it's time to steer a new course and adjust the mission. The key question here is "What new directions should we be moving in *now* to get ready for the changes we see coming in our business?"[2]

This chapter begins a section on planning and control. As with the chapters that precede it, it also ties back to the basic ideas proposed in Chapters 1–3: planning and control in light of the information needs of managers in a dynamic environment. *Strategic management* includes planning, implementation, and control. The planning phase (sometimes called *strategic planning* or *strategy formulation*) involves designing a mission, setting goals and objectives, and establishing strategies to achieve them. This planning process includes assessing the internal and external environment of a business and looking at the strengths and weaknesses of the company. Managers measure how a company is doing to accomplish its strategic goals in the control phase. The objective of this chapter is to discuss strategic management and management accounting's role in strategic planning, implementing, and controlling. Specifics about segment and manager performance evaluation, which are part of the control process, are covered in Chapter 14.

A company's strategic plan is an organizing framework. Everything that a company does should be oriented to and coordinated with its strategic

---

[1] Richard J. Palmer, "Strategic Goals and Objectives and the Design of Strategic Management Accounting Systems," *Advances in Management Accounting*, Vol. 1 (Greenwich, Conn.: JAI Press, 1992), pp. 200–201.

[2] Arthur A. Thompson and A. J. Strickland III, *Strategic Management: Concepts and Cases*, 6th ed. (Homewood, Ill.: Richard D. Irwin, 1992), pp. 24–25.

plan. For example, in the discussion about capital asset acquisition in Chapter 13, each time managers look at an investment opportunity, they should ask themselves how a project or a new piece of equipment fits into the strategic plan of the company. How will it help the company accomplish its mission? The same holds true for control: all measures should relate back to the mission, goals, and objectives in the plan. Even short-term measures such as cash flow, return on investment, and market share should relate to the plan. However, measures should go beyond looking at whether the existing plan is being achieved. In addition, as alluded to in the introductory quote by Thompson and Strickland, managers should be measuring what is happening both inside and outside the organization so that they will be prepared to change mission, goals, objectives, and strategies as situations warrant. Therefore, *strategic management* means

1. Assessing the external environment of a business
2. Judging a company's strengths and weaknesses
3. Establishing a mission along with goals and objectives
4. Implementing strategies to accomplish goals and objectives
5. Measuring how effectively and efficiently the mission is being accomplished through the strategies, objectives, and goals
6. Measuring changes in the firm's external and internal environment
7. Altering the mission, goals, objectives, and strategies as appropriate

You can see how this ties into earlier discussion. For example, the Theory of Constraints (TOC), just-in-time (JIT), activity-based costing (ABC) and management (ABM), and value chains are ways that managers can plan, implement, and control in light of the company's mission, goals, and objectives. These management tools should be integral to strategic management.

DEVELOPING A STRATEGIC PLAN

In establishing a strategic plan, managers want to look into the future and establish a plan and course of action to guide the company over a multi-year time horizon. On one hand, the plan must be specific enough to provide a basis for ongoing action and evaluation. On the other hand, it cannot be so fixed that managers have a hard time adapting to important changes in the environment. Thus, when planning for, say, a three- to five-year time horizon, managers want to answer the following questions, not only from the perspective of here and now but also what the answers are projected to be after five years.

1. What is the environment that the company is facing?
2. What is the firm's current strategy and how is it working?
3. What is the long-range direction of the business?
4. What are the company's major areas of business? What are the market segments that are being addressed? What needs does it fill? What are the resources that the company has?

5. What are the capabilities (human, financial, physical) available? What are the firm's strengths and weaknesses?
6. What competitors are there to contend with and how does the company compare to them?
7. Given available opportunities as well as existing threats to a company, what are reasonable objectives and goals?
8. Given objectives and goals, what are the strategies to achieve them? What resources and time frame are required to achieve these goals?
9. What kind of monitoring program can be established to track progress toward desired ends?

The first few questions help managers define what kind of business the company is in, a key to developing its mission. For example, an accounting firm can define that it is in the tax preparation and auditing business. If this is an acceptable definition, objectives can be set and resources expended to achieve these objectives *given* the definition of major areas of business, competitors, and market segments. However, if an accounting firm defines its major area of business as consulting on all information needs, this entails a different set of market assessments, resource capabilities, products, and so on. Too often companies ignore these basic questions. This leaves the door open for different managers to have different ideas about the basic definition of the company. What can result is a chaotic attempt to meet unrelated (and uncommunicated) goals. Since these questions are related to a company's mission, let us now look at mission, goals, and objectives.

MISSION, GOALS, AND OBJECTIVES

Many companies establish a *mission statement*. Usually, this is simple and straightforward. The mission statement is the cornerstone for all other planning. It should clearly outline what business the company is in and its basic values or service characteristics in a way that will motivate managers, attract customers, and inform (and excite) investors and creditors. Exhibit 12-1 shows some current mission statements from various companies. These examples are presented to show a variety of companies and formats. In reading each statement, think about the following questions:

1. Does the statement clearly define the business the company is in? How narrow or broad is this definition?
2. What is it saying about values relating to customers, suppliers, employees, or other stakeholders?
3. What is included about resources, technology, and methods to achieve ends?
4. Is the statement forward-looking? Is it static? Does it incorporate the ability to change?
5. To whom do you think the statement is addressed (e.g., managers, customers, financial analysts, etc.)? .

Exhibit 12-1
Mission Statements

The following are all from annual reports:

The Mead Corporation (1990)
MISSION: TO BE NUMBER ONE IN CUSTOMER SATISFACTION

It may be the shortest mission statement of all the *Fortune 500* companies.

"We asked ourselves a simple question some time ago," explains Mead's president, Steve Mason—"How would we like Mead to be described 10 years from now? A good many thoughtful, intelligent answers were proposed, but this one had universal appeal:

'Mead is number one in customer satisfaction in all of its businesses.'

"That answer points the way to competitive success, financial success and the person success of our people. Pursuing that vision highlights the concept of customer satisfaction and makes it the key strategy in every business," Mason emphasizes.

"It also requires that we look closely at our customers to identify those whose needs we can satisfy better than anyone else. But above all, this is a mission which challenges each employee. Every one of us has customers. If we're in the woodyard, the pulp mill is our customer; If we're in the pulp mill, then the paper mill is our customer; It may be the local printer or one of the world's greatest publishers. It may a law firm, a toymaker or a fourth-grader who buys a Mead notebook."

IBM (1991)
IBM is in the business of helping people solve problems through the use of advanced information technologies. IBM creates value by offering products and services that help customers succeed. These offerings include: services, software, systems, products, and technologies.

Throughout its worldwide marketing and services companies, business partners, and strategic alliances, IBM offers unique solutions and skills to address each customer's individual needs. IBM manufacturing and development businesses and key alliances provide timely and competitive offerings to meet the demands of the markets IBM serves.

The Washington Post Company—Newspaper Division (1990)
"As alternative media proliferate in the 1990s, enabling Americans to experience news as it happens, the newspaper will continue to evolve into a one-stop supermarket of information that helps readers understand and cope with a complex world presented in fragments elsewhere.

"We will dig more deeply, inform more fully, explain more expertly and remain more authoritative. We will continue to find and publish important information that would never reach citizens without us. We will protect the unique relationship of trust we have with our readers.

"We will emphasize vivid writing, appealing design, dramatic photography, informative graphics and helpful packaging. We will focus more on such special interests as health, recreation, money management, technology, lifestyles, the arts, popular culture, science and education.

"With a far larger audience every day than any single competitor in our market, we are invigorated rather than daunted by the challenge of remaining a necessity for our readers this decade and beyond."

Leonard Downie, Jr.
Managing Editor
The Washington Post

Exhibit 12-1 (continued)

Campbell Soup Company (1991)
STRATEGIC PRECEPTS

The precepts which guide our strategies are very simple yet very final. They provide a framework for evaluating the validity of long-term proposals. The precepts are:

1. PRIME PURPOSE—BUILD SHAREOWNER WEALTH

The prime purpose of the Company is to reward risk bearers by building long-term shareowner wealth. Dividend growth is fundamental while long-term stock appreciation is prime. Stock appreciation is driven by business performance and especially by delivering superior results in approximate consonance with expert projections.

2. DRIVING FORCE—BRAND POWER

The Company's success and longevity have been founded on value-added, competitively superior branded products. Consumer repeat purchase, the foundation of every strong brand franchise, derives from products providing superior satisfaction.

While high quality is basic, a product-driven company must keep on the cutting edge of change with innovation, while striving to achieve and maintain a low-cost product status. A strong research and development and consumer market research focus is essential.

3. CONTROLLING FORCE—BRAIN POWER, PEOPLE POWER

People control the destiny of a company. In a highly competitive and money-driven business world, quality people must be attracted and developed.

While building shareowner wealth is the prime company purpose, it should be achieved in the context of scrupulous morality, honorable partnerships and a pursuit of excellence with integrity. Product quality is a sacred trust and can only be entrusted to talented and caring individuals. The climate for personal growth should encourage individual risk bearing and teamwork with rewards linked to results. "Adding Value" is an ongoing expectation. The final measurement of superior people performance is the mix of reputation and business results versus competition.

4. COMPANY ENDURANCE—PRESERVATION OF INDEPENDENCE

A company can live forever. The ultimate challenge for each succeeding management is to protect the Company's heritage while adjusting to and actually creating change over the long term. The final determinant in resisting an outside thrust for control is superior performance in building shareowner wealth.

Besides mission statements for the company as a whole, each business unit should also have its own mission. Govindarajan and Shank propose that such statements should be organized around *build, hold,* or *harvest.*[3] **Build** means an emphasis on increasing the unit's market share. This can have a

---

[3] Vijay Govindarajan and John K. Shank, "Strategic Cost Management: Tailoring Controls to Strategies," *Journal of Cost Management* (New York: Warren, Gorham, & Lamont, Fall 1992), pp. 14–24.

negative impact on short-term earnings and cash flow. **Hold** means retaining the position the unit has in the market. The authors cite IBM's high market share position in the mainframe computer market as an example of a company in a hold position. They also propose that cash outflows about equal cash inflows for such a mission. Firms that **harvest** means that they are "maximizing short-term earnings and cash flow, even at the expense of market share."[4] In this case, you would expect the unit to provide cash to other parts of the company. Thus, in using measures to assess performance, a subject covered in Chapter 14, managers should be aware of the unit's mission and how that would affect income and cash flow.

A mission statement is not something that is created in a vacuum: managers must assess the environment and the company's capabilities before a statement is written. Imagine, for example, stating that a company's mission is to provide leading-edge service to its customers when the company is faced with limited cash resources in a changing technological environment. Thus, in setting its mission, managers need a good deal of information. The management accountant can be a source of such information.

Management Accounting and the Mission Statement

Palmer[5] talks about how a strategic management accounting system (SMAS) can affect the mission statement. In defining what products or services a company will offer (and the markets it will serve), a well-developed SMAS allows managers to know the separable costs associated with these products or services. This is where ABC comes into play; its real value is more in strategic management than in just knowing short-term margins. After conversion to ABC, it may become apparent that certain products or services cannot be produced profitably. If the current mission statement includes meeting every customer's demands, no matter how small the order, and managers now find that the cost of this is too great, the mission statement should be altered.

Production technology is also an important component of a mission statement. This means knowing what kind of human and physical resources are needed and available given the financial resources at hand. If managers are using TOC, bottlenecks in the production process are addressed and the mission statement can be tailored around these resources. This goes beyond just technology and includes quality and throughput time. As we explore in Chapter 13, looking at technology is more than an analysis of discrete projects. It involves harder questions of interaction among and between human, financial, and physical resources to accomplish the company's mission.

---

[4] Govindarajan and Shank, p. 15.
[5] Palmer, "Strategic Goals and Objectives and the Design of Strategic Management Accounting Systems."

Goals and Objectives

Once a company has established its mission, the next step is to set goals and objectives to meet the mission. As companies move from a mission statement to goals and objectives, they become more specific. *Goals and objectives* must allow managers to (1) establish specific strategies and (2) assess if the goals and objectives are being met. Thus, if a company is entering the international market, a goal must say more than "make our presence known in the international market." Perhaps the goal should be to achieve a certain market share for specific products in specific countries with yearly objectives for the next five years. Thus, managers must establish both short-term and longer-term goals and objectives to achieve the mission.

Thompson and Strickland[6] propose that objectives should relate to *financial performance* and to *strategic performance*; both must be accomplished for the company to survive and to grow. *Financial objectives* relate to growth in revenue, cash balances, profit (or contribution) margins, the ability to pay dividends, meeting certain ratios to fulfill current loan agreements or to attract expanded financing, etc. *Strategic objectives* involve market share, quality, technological gains, competitive costs as compared to others in industry, customer service, time between order placement and delivery, and so on. It is possible that financial and strategic objectives will conflict with one another. While a company might want to attain a certain market share, it might not have the borrowing capability or cash flow to achieve this goal. In such cases, managers must make trade-offs and see how these compromises affect the mission itself.

Much of the literature about budgeting includes setting tough but attainable goals. This same concept is important in looking at goals to achieve strategic ends. We will develop this discussion more in Chapter 14. However, as you know from your own experience (perhaps in this course), challenging goals are meant to motivate; goals that are too easy to achieve are not highly regarded; and goals that are really out of reach can be demotivating.

Finally, and parallel to annual budgeting, goals and objectives must be defined at each level of management. If the goal is to achieve a 10 percent market share for a product line in France, this can be divided into several areas. For example, the sales force would have certain objectives regarding particular customers, and production would have goals relating to costs and quality. Within both sales and production, these goals can be further defined for lower-level managers.

Strategies

Strategies are the action plans to accomplish goals and objectives. If the goal is to cut costs of production by 10 percent, strategies could include negotiating

---

[6] Thompson and Strickland, *Strategic Management*, Chapter 2.

with suppliers, having regular meetings with line workers, moving equipment to allow for a more efficient work flow (e.g., a manufacturing cell), cutting raw material and in-process inventories as part of a JIT system, etc. Each goal or objective will have its own set of strategies for each appropriate level of the company. Therefore, in an ongoing monitoring process, there is a clear trail of what actions are supposed to do and whether these strategies are accomplishing the goals and objectives. This allows managers to change or amend strategies (and goals and objectives) as actual performance is measured against plans and expectations.

Before looking at control, let us first go back and look at the kinds of analyses that a company must perform in order to come up with its mission, goals, and objectives. Strategy formulation requires analysis of both the firm's capabilities and external environment. One of the primary goals in strategic management is to align the company with its environment: What are the threats and opportunities that could affect the company over the next three to five years? How can the company position itself to maximize its opportunities while defending against possible threats?

EXTERNAL ANALYSIS

From establishing a mission through setting specific strategies, a company must look at the external and internal environment that it faces. Environmental analysis takes place at two levels: the firm's immediate industry environment and the broader macro environment, which includes looking at governmental regulations, political and societal concerns, economic factors, technology, and the marketplace.

Governmental Regulation and Political Concerns

Regulation involves not only the specific rules that different governmental agencies have affecting a business but also the regulatory climate. Regulation and concern about governmental intervention goes from the local to the federal level. Recently, a midwestern division of a national company was bought from the parent by a combination of its employees and outside investors. In assessing the environment, managers and potential investors looked at concerns with the EPA (was there any pollution to clean up?), the state insurance board (would they allow self-funding for workers compensation insurance?), and local taxing authorities (was real estate tax abatement possible?). Not only is the investment itself affected by answers to these questions, but such concerns can also affect the goals and objectives. For example, without self-funding for workers compensation, cash flows would be adversely affected so that growth plans would have to be significantly revised.

Major oil spills and both state and federal regulations regarding pollution influence the major oil companies. Disasters such as the Alaska oil spill feed the flames of those who want more regulation. The knowledge of the finite amount of oil available coupled with environmental concerns regarding air quality affect the automobile industry. Not only are fuel consumption and exhaust emissions regulated, but also passive restraints are legislated given a public concern about highway deaths. The recent collapse of the savings and loan industry and the weakness in the banking industry have brought about a whole new set of regulations and enforcement standards. Companies often respond to these pressures by including specific value statements in their mission. See, for example, Campbell Soup's statement in Exhibit 12-1. In addition, there is no doubt that such regulations or threat of regulations affects goals, objectives, and strategies.

Certain industries have become deregulated. For example, the airline industry was deregulated with effects on the size and number of surviving companies, routes flown, age of aircraft kept, and ownership. Deregulation in financial institutions might have contributed to goals and strategies that brought about the collapse of a whole segment of the industry. The breakup of AT&T coupled with the rise of personal computers, cellular telephones, information networks, and cable television, for example, have had a serious impact not only on the "baby Bell" companies but also on competing companies and on firms that were in different parts of the value chain.

Regulated utilities face another set of challenges. For example, state public service commissions issue orders affecting how costs are allocated. The St. Louis County Water Company allocates construction costs to operations (expensed in year incurred) and to capital assets (amortized over 40 years) according to a formula negotiated with the Public Service Commission of Missouri. The Water Company not only does construction for its own needs (replacing worn out water lines and relocating mains due to highway construction), but also has been the major contractor for laying new mains paid for by private developers of subdivisions and shopping centers. The allocation methodology ordered by the Public Service Commission coupled with changes in the environment (curtailed building in the early 1990s) has altered the ability of the company to be a competitive supplier of construction service. This affects its mission, goals, and strategies.

Litigation is a growing concern for many companies. The Big Six accounting firms recently issued a statement of position regarding what they see as a liability crisis and its impact on the accounting profession.[7] The conclusion of this report is that the increasing amount of litigation and its cost can threaten the long-term survival of the Big Six firms, will substantially increase the cost of auditing, will hurt companies trying to raise capital due

---

[7] Arthur Anderson & Co., Coopers & Lybrand, Deloitte & Touche, Ernst & Young, KPMG Peat Marwick, and Price Waterhouse, *The Liability Crisis in the United States: Impact on the Accounting Profession*, August 6, 1992.

to increased costs from underwriters, attorneys, and accountants who must defend themselves, will engender risk-reduction actions from professionals such as not performing services that are seen as open to litigation, and will hurt the recruiting of excellent people to the profession due to apprehension about potential liability. Litigation and perceived liability can also lead to governmental queries and action. Certainly this has an impact on defining the scope of business of a company. Other regulations that can affect businesses include tax laws (including payroll taxes for programs such as Social Security and health care), labor laws, and export regulations.

International Politics and Environment

This past decade has seen some wrenching changes in the international scene. It's tough to know what will happen next or what the ripple effect will be from what has occurred so far. Changes in the international environment present both opportunities (new markets) and threats (new competition) that can affect firm profitability. Pacific Rim countries like Japan and Korea became dominant players not only in the production arena but also in international finance markets. The changes in Europe with the potential of dropping of tariffs among the Common Market and a more unified governmental and/or financial structure will affect how companies compete. The disintegration of the Soviet Union and the ensuing ethnic wars are a factor to deal with. The reunification of Germany was coupled with a recession that affected governmental policies. North American free trade agreements, like those in Europe, affect where parts are made given different costs. Thus, when developing a strategic management plan, managers must assess what is happening in the world that will affect their company, whether it is selling goods or services only in the United States or abroad or both. The changes we are witnessing are a good example of an area of the environment that has been fairly static for a long period but now is dynamic: nothing can be taken for granted when projecting into the future.

Economic Conditions

The early 1990s have seen a recession. Profitability in the areas of construction, airline travel, and consumer goods, for example, is strongly tied to economic conditions. In addition, there has been a change in the power structure of unions; far fewer companies are unionized and even in organized plants, workers often have had to take wage reductions to keep their jobs. The media have been full of reports of wage concessions in the airline and automobile industries among others. The general weakness of the economy (along with a reduction of defense spending) has left many highly qualified people out of work. Recently a small bank holding company in a rural area advertised for a controller and received over 80 applications from qualified personnel within a week. A manufacturer in Ohio looking for an engineer/accountant to implement an ABC program had only to go to a single defense contractor who had laid off a significant part of their work force to find several qualified people. Thus, among other things, the economic conditions affect the availability and cost of human resources.

The economy also affects the cost of money. Interest rates were low in the early 1990s. This allows companies with lower-cost funds to expand or to bring their technology into a competitive position. However, it also affected exchange rates adversely. While a slow economy poses a threat in some areas, it presents an opportunity in others.

Technology

Some industries have very rapid changes in technology while others do not. Technology can affect productive resources and the products themselves. When a company faces a fairly stable technology, their mission, goals, and objectives will be to capitalize on existing techniques and to exploit them as much as possible. In contrast, if a company is involved in an industry with rapidly changing technology and it does not respond as quickly as its competitors, it runs the risk of going out of business. In Chapter 13 we illustrate what can happen with a business if it chooses *not* to invest in an asset that would make it technologically competitive.

Managers have to decide whether to be leaders or followers in technology. Available resources often interplay with management's desires in this area since you can only do what you are able to do. Knowing the technological environment as well as the company's ability to keep at the cutting edge allows managers to develop goals and objectives and strategies to achieve them.

The Market and Competition

Many companies develop an *industry profile* looking at products, resources, raw materials, and competitors. Thompson and Strickland pose seven questions regarding an industry and competitive analysis:[8]

1. What are the chief economic characteristics of the industry?
2. What factors are driving change in the industry and what impact will they have?
3. What competitive forces are at work in the industry and how strong are they?
4. Which companies are in the strongest/weakest competitive position?
5. Who will likely make what competitive moves next?
6. What key factors will determine competitive success or failure?
7. How attractive is the industry in terms of its prospects to above-average profitability?

---

[8] Thompson and Strickland, *Strategic Management*, pp. 57–58.

The answers to these questions affect everything from the mission to strategies.

Chief Economic Characteristics   An industry's chief economic characteristics include its overall size; where competition takes place (locally, regionally, domestic, international); the size and number of competitors; the size and number of potential customers; how differentiated both producers and buyers are (segmentation); the cost of entry and of maintaining a competitive position; and possible economies of scale and/or ability to experience a learning curve.

Factors Driving Change   In some industries, governmental action causes change. We have already explored changes caused by regulation or deregulation. Mergers play an important part in some industries. Consider what is happening in the banking and airline industries today as there are fewer and fewer competitors. Changes in technology can affect both equipment and products, as we have discussed. Economic and political forces can affect raw materials, components, production, the financial market, and customers.

Certainly one of the most discussed factors driving change in many industries has been lower-cost products from companies in other countries. There has been a cry for American companies to become "world class" in costs and quality. The introduction and acceptance of ABC, ABM, JIT, TOC, TQM, and other operating philosophies and techniques were spurred in part by the realization that the market had changed in a dramatic way, one that could not be ignored by just doing business as usual.

Change can also be caused by public concern. Recent years have seen the effects on the tobacco industry, for example. We have moved from warnings on cigarette packages to banning of smoking on domestic airline flights to smoke-free buildings and areas. Other concerns about health affect the cost to bring certain products to market.

Competitive Forces   Some companies are in a friendly competitive environment while others deal with tough competition. Firms need to defend against competitive forces because competition puts downward pressure on firm profits. As firms face greater competition they are often forced into costly strategic moves like lowering prices, increasing advertising, building a better product, offering better service, and so on. Managers need a good understanding of their industry's competitive structure in order to develop a strategy that best positions them to minimize the potential cost of competition.

Summary

In order to develop their mission, goals, objectives, and strategies for a reasonable timeframe, companies must assess the threats and opportunities that exist in the external environment. In different ways, companies are affected by governmental regulation, political and social issues, the economy, changes in technology, and the competitive environment. In addition, a company must look within itself to see strengths and weaknesses.

INTERNAL ANALYSIS

An internal analysis helps managers develop plans in light of the history, current status and capabilities, and strengths and weaknesses of the company. Current reality is the basis for future planning: you start from where you are now and move from there. An internal analysis also involves a close look at how the company matches with actual or potential competitors (products, quality, cost, etc.).

Assessing Strengths and Weaknesses

Looking at a company's strengths and weaknesses allows a reality check: Where are we before we decide what to do next? A starting point is to clearly identify current strategy and assess how it is doing. Investigation can take on the structure of the company with questions dealing with administration, research and development, sales, production, and so on. Exhibit 12-2 is a sample of a set of questions that can be asked in an internal analysis. There are many other questions that can be addressed, but this exhibit provides an idea about internal assessment. The objective of any set of questions is not only to establish a history but also to spur thinking about improvements. Analysis should fairly evaluate areas of strength where the company should maintain that strength as well as areas of weakness that need to be improved. Gathering this information helps build a strategy that capitalizes on a company's distinctive strengths (things the company does better than its rivals) while minimizing its weaknesses.

Another stage of this assessment is to ask questions about each product. Questions include specific sales performance, analysis of costs (such as ABC), and where products are in their life cycles, as well as questions about quality, design, and performance. The result is a set of pluses and minuses about each product. In addition, the company can ask the same questions about business functions and products, albeit in a more abbreviated form, regarding their competition. This is part of the industry analysis discussed above.

Value Chain

In Chapter 3, we discussed the idea of value chain and its importance in strategic management. Certainly an internal analysis must include where a company sees itself on the value chain. This goes back to the definition of

Exhibit 12-2
Internal Analysis Questions

1. Central Administration
   a. What is the organizational structure and is it cohesive?
   b. What is the practice regarding decentralization versus centralization?
   c. Who are the prime movers and decision makers? Who is dominant?
   d. How are decisions made?
   e. Is the organization structured in the most efficient way to meet both short- and long-term needs?
2. Human Resources
   a. Do well-qualified people occupy all critical positions?
   b. Is there a need for training or recruiting for short- or long-term needs?
   c. How can excess needs of one area serve restricted availability in others?
   d. Is there a turnover problem with key personnel?
   e. How are critical positions filled? Can internal supply and quality meet needs?
   f. How are issues of equal opportunity being addressed?
   g. What are the rewards and will they keep key personnel motivated?
3. Marketing
   a. How are products distributed?
   b. What is being done to improve sales activity?
   c. How are customer needs monitored?
   d. How are the company's products differentiated in the market?
   e. What is the history of products over the last five to ten years?
   f. How does pricing affect sales? Are we a price leader or price follower?
   g. What is the history of pricing in the near term?
   h. How sensitive are profits to changes in prices?
   i. How do terms of sale (e.g., discounts or warranties) affect sales?
   j. How is advertising used and is it effective?
   k. How are products delivered and is this a key factor of success?
   l. How are new markets defined and/or new client groups identified and pursued?
4. Engineering and Research
   a. What is the level of technology in the industry and how does the company compare to it?
   b. How are changing customer needs addressed?
   c. How are new products developed?
   d. How are manufacturing and operations planning conducted?
   e. What are existing or anticipated bottlenecks in manufacturing?
   f. What are the costs for research and for operations engineering?
5. Manufacturing
   a. What is the basic structure of operations?
      1.) How are products made? What is the sequence of operations?
      2.) What is the cost of each operation?
      3.) How is plant space utilized by each operation?
      4.) How labor or machine intensive is each operation? Can any operation be more automated? How can robotics be used?
   b. How are operations standardized?
   c. What lead time is required for items like component acquisition and scheduling?
   d. How much time does each operation take?

Exhibit 12-2 (continued)

   e. How is productivity measured?

   f. Does the technology define the product or do the products define the technology?

   g. What is the location, age, size, and capacity of each facility?

   h. What is the investment in each facility in plant and equipment and what investment is anticipated?

   i. How are costs defined as variable and fixed?

   j. How do costs relate to sales?

   k. How is overhead defined and applied?

   l. How are costs allocated?

   m. What controls exist to monitor costs?

6. Finance

   a. How is financial performance measured?

   b. What is specific financial performance by segment including:

     1. cash flow

     2. controllable income

     3. return on investment and/or residual income

7. Systems

   a. What are the means for communicating accounting information? marketing information? manufacturing information?

   b. What is done by hand and what is computerized?

   c. Is there an integrated system of information?

   d. How are decisions made on the form, order, and format of information?

what business the company is in, one of the prime aspects of a mission statement. Going back to the example of an accounting firm, the value chain of providing information to internal, external, and regulatory users is broad. A firm must define what part of the chain seems appropriate given its external and internal analysis.

STRATEGIC MANAGEMENT AND ACCOUNTING

Palmer[9] poses that management accountants can help in establishing the mission, goals, and objectives; assessing the opportunities and threats in the external and internal environment; and implementing the strategic plan itself. Earlier we discussed financial objectives as compared to strategic objectives. Management accountants can see if there are sufficient financial resources available to achieve strategic objectives.

Accountants are supposed to question assumptions. Therefore, they can be helpful in looking at the mission, goals, objectives, and strategies to make

---

[9] Palmer, "Strategic Goals and Objectives and the Design of Strategic Management Accounting Systems."

sure that they seem consistent and appropriate. Our review of Exhibit 12-1 included several questions about clarity, and the discussion about establishing goals and objectives involved writing them in such a way that managers could set up measures of success. Management accountants can be part of this process making sure that the parts of strategic management are clearly communicated and measurable.

More and more management accountants are being required to move outside the realm of financial and quantitative measures. We will see more of this in Chapter 14. Being involved in an external and internal analysis allows management accountants to increase their skills in nonfinancial and qualitative areas.

In implementation, management accountants must provide useful information and analysis to other managers. They must establish *key success factors* that allow managers to see how strategies are or are not leading to achieving goals and objectives. In addition, as conditions change, management accountants must make sure that the accounting system changes, too. It's good to point out again in this chapter on strategic management that management accounting is future oriented and any SMAS must also be flexible enough to let managers know when changes are necessary.

Govindarajan and Shank state that a strategic cost management system must respond to the mission, goals, and objectives of the company. For example, budgeting is affected by whether a unit has a build, hold, or harvest mission. With a build mission, the budget is more of a short-term planning tool, standard costs are not important in assessing performance, flexible budgeting for manufacturing cost control is not very important, and behavior is controlled more than output. With a harvest mission, the budget is a control tool ("document of restraint"), standard costs are important in assessing performance, flexible budgeting for manufacturing cost control is important, and output is controlled more than behavior.[10] In addition, Govindarajan and Shank propose that budget revisions will be more frequent and managers will have more impact on formulations of budgets in units with a build mission.

Perhaps the greatest part of strategic management is stressing that all activities within the firm should be consistent with the firm's strategies. For management accountants, this means that we will only adopt JIT or TOC operating philosophies, for example, as part of the strategic management process rather than looking at them as isolated ideas. The whole concept of ABC and ABM makes even more sense when coupled with the mission, goals, and objectives of the company. Without such a link, implementing ABC would be sterile.

---

[10] Govindarajan and Shank, "Strategic Cost Management," Exhibit 2, p. 18.

SUMMARY

Strategic management involves long-term planning, implementing, and controlling. Strategic plans should include a mission statement, goals and objectives to achieve the mission, and strategies to achieve the goals and objectives. In establishing its mission, goals, and objectives, companies analyze the external and internal environment looking at strengths and weaknesses, opportunities and threats. Management accountants are part of the strategic management process by analyzing basic assumptions, taking part in defining the mission, goals, and objectives, establishing ways to measure success, and participating in external and internal analyses. Strategic management provides a framework for all the actions managers take and how they are assessed.

PROBLEMS AND CASES

12-1. Mission Statements

Exhibit 12-1 on pages 494–495 shows the mission statement from large corporations. Based on these statements and a review of the major lines of business each pursues, draw up a list of possible goals and objectives for these corporations for ther next two years.

12-2. Strategic Planning and Management Accounting (CMA)

Strategic and long-range planning generally are considered to consist of four activities—defining the objectives of an organization, establishing the program to achieve the objectives, determining the resources required to support the objectives, and identifying "benchmarks" of progress toward achieving the objective. The management accounting function is involved with many aspects of these processes.

Required:
For the four activities of strategic and long-range planning identified above:

1. Describe what is involved in each activity, and
2. Discuss the role of the management accounting function in each activity.

12-3. Product Strategies (CMA)

Marval Products manufactures and wholesales several different lines of luggage in two basic types—soft-side and molded. Each luggage line consists of several different pieces, all of which are in different sizes. At least one line is a complete set of luggage designed to be used by both men and women, but some lines and styles are designed specifically for men or women. Some lines also have matching attaché cases. Luggage lines are discontinued and introduced as tastes change or as product improvements are developed.

Marval Products also manufactures luggage for large retail companies according to each company's specifications. This luggage is marketed under the retail companies' own private label rather than the Marval label.

Marval has been manufacturing several lines of luggage under its own label and private lines for one or more retail companies for the last ten years.

Required:
1. Identify and discuss the factors Marval Products needs to consider in its periodic review of long-term product strategy including any decisions with respect to new and/or existing products.
2. Identify and discuss the factors Marval Products needs to consider when developing its sales component of the annual budget.

12-4. Mission Statement—Not-for-Profit Organization

The Paso Fino Horse Association, Inc., a not-for-profit corporation, is an association of the owners of Paso Fino Horses. The Association, which was founded over 20 years ago, represents a naturally gaited horse from Colombia, Puerto Rico, and other Caribbean and Central and South American countries. The current horse population for the breed is 10,000, quite small when compared to that of breeds such as the Quarter Horse or Arabian.

The 3,000 plus members mostly engage in pleasure riding and in horse shows. There is some competitive trail riding, but it is limited at present. Members vary from professional trainers and large breeders to people who own just one horse. The national organization is run from a central office and has an annual operating budget of about $700,000 gained mostly from dues, registration fees, and show fees. The organization is governed by a board elected from about 20 regional groups.

In 19X5 the Long Range Planning Committee for the Association developed a mission statement for the group: To promote the Paso Fino breed to the American public.

Required:
1. What business is this organization in? Give your rationale. (*Hint:* Consider the competition.)
2. How can this mission statement be put into operation with specific strategies?

12-5. Planning at a Regional Theater

The Midwest Regional Theater, located in the suburbs of a large city, has just celebrated its twentieth birthday. The theater was founded by a group of community citizens that wanted to bring quality professional theater to the area with the type of drama that could not be found in touring national companies. Theaters of this type are usually founded by a theater professional who brings his or her artistic image to the area and persuades the community to give financial support to it.

After the first artistic director, who was there for ten years, there has been a succession of acting artistic directors and artistic directors over the past few years. Finally, a person who had been with the organization for several years was chosen artistic director, and a new sense of stability began to emerge.

The theater was currently in debt because its most recent artistic director had gone way over budget and had presented a mediocre season. The debt was manageable in the short run, but the Board of Directors was uneasy about it. All the endowment of the theater was pledged as collateral for a loan; thus, there was no financial flexibility left in the organization.

About 60 percent of the theater's revenues came from subscriptions and from single ticket sales. A recent trend of dropping subscriptions had been reversed. Last year a total of 12,000 seats had been sold, but 14,000 looked possible in the upcoming year. At its highest, subscriptions had been 20,000; the theater could easily handle 24,000 subscribers over the run of a show. There were five shows in the mainstage area and four in a smaller studio space, and a children's theater (funded by corporations and corporate gifts) toured the area.

The balance of the funding came from a community arts foundation, local entertainment taxes, some federal and state arts money, and the bulk from private contributions from individuals and from corporations.

While the theater occupied its own space, there was a serious chance that the owner of the building would move to oust the theater if a new regional shopping mall and condominiums could be developed in this area. The lease was for 10 years, but the owner could cancel with 24 months' notice.

The Board and the staff think that the theater is at a crossroads and that strategic planning is called for. You have been retained to help the Board and staff begin this process.

Required:
Based on the city assigned by your instructor, use the strategic planning model and real-world information to begin to formulate how this theater should proceed. Be as specific as you can. You should prepare a presentation as if you were going to hold a weekend seminar with some members of the Board and staff to get the plan started.

12-6. Expansion into Another City

Phil and Scrubby's Car Wash is a chain of filling stations/car washes located in Denver. After 15 years in the Denver area, management believes that the local market is saturated and is looking for new market areas. Robyn Kitchen, president, has identified several cities for expansion, with Salt Lake City, Tulsa, and Kansas City leading the list.

A basic car wash unit takes about an acre of ground. In addition to ground cost, the building and equipment cost about $400,000. The petroleum supplier usually invests in the facility as well putting in about $100,000 in pumps, tanks, lights, and a canopy.

Kitchen is concerned, since the company has never ventured out of its basic area before. Current operations are run from a central office where supervision, accounting and finance, warehousing of chemicals and parts, and maintenance are housed. It would take several units in another city to warrant a regional operations center. Until that time, functions that could not be run out of the central office would be handled at the individual car wash units.

Required:
1. What are the environmental concerns for this company?
2. How would you begin to address the internal strengths and weaknesses?
3. What management issues should be addressed with units in a new city?
4. What specific strategies do you think might be employed in this expansion?

12-7. Pro Form Statements and Strategic Plans (CMA)

TabCo has been in business for eight years. The company experienced slow growth in its early years, but was very profitable.

Don Feinberg was hired by TabCo's Board of Directors two years ago to serve as the Chief Executive Officer. Feinberg changed the company's operations significantly. The results of his efforts have been striking. Sales have increased dramatically and at a faster rate than profits. Dollar profits are considered satisfactory. The increase in sales appears to be the consequence of four specific factors:

- Carrying larger inventory balances and a wider range of products in stock to reduce back orders and canceled orders.
- Liberalizing sales credit terms and collection policies to allow customers longer payment periods.
- Extending credit to a riskier class of customers.
- Advertising the products more aggressively.

Feinberg intends to maintain the following financial relationships:

- Year-end investments in inventory should be approximately 20 percent of the cost of goods sold of the next fiscal year.
- The net accounts receivable balance should be approximately one sixth of the current year's sales.
- Advertising expenditures should be at least 10 percent of the sales dollars.
- Inventories should be financed by trade creditors by having accounts payable at about one third of the current assets exclusive of cash.

The Board of Directors has been pleased with the results to date. The following objectives, as adopted by the Board, are being met and are to be continued unchanged.

- Regular sales growth.
- Regular profit growth.
- A 20 percent annual increase in dividends.
- Debt consisting only of regular trade credit and the outstanding mortgage on a warehouse.

Feinberg believes that sales should continue to increase at 40 percent annually for the next several years if his policies are continued and the financial relationships he looks for are met. However, the increased sales will require more warehouse capacity. In expectation of future growth, Feinberg intends to enter into a long-term operating lease for a warehouse. This warehouse will cost $200,000 per year, but should provide adequate capacity for the next 8 to 15 years. The lease on the warehouse currently rented will not be renewed.

The financial statements for the fiscal year just ended are presented on page 510.

TabCo
Statement of Income and Retained Earnings
For the Year Ended May 31, 19X3
($000s omitted)

Sales	$3,000
Less costs and expenses	
Cost of goods sold	$2,000
Variable labor costs	200
Fixed labor costs	35
Warehouse facilities	
Depreciation	165
Rent	50
Advertising costs	250
Interest	120
Total costs and expenses	$2,820
Income before taxes	$ 180
Income tax (40%)	72
Net income	$ 108
Add retained earnings June 1, 19X2	842
Deduct cash dividends	(50)
Retained earnings May 31, 19X3	$ 900

TabCo
Statement of Financial Position
May 31, 19X3
($000s omitted)

Assets

Cash	$ 370
Accounts receivable (net)	400
Inventories	500
Total current assets	$1,270
Warehouse (net of accumulated depreciation)	2,000
Total assets	$3,270

Equities

Accounts payable	$ 300
Accrued interest[a]	120
Mortgage payable current[a]	200
Total current liabilities	$ 620
Mortgage payable	1,000
Total liabilities	$1,620
Capital stock	750
Retained earnings	900
Total equities	$3,270

[a]Annual principal payment of $200,000 and accrued interest at 10%.

Required:
1. Assume Don Feinberg's plans and financial relationships can be accomplished and the expected sales growth is achieved. Prepare for TabCo:
   a. Pro-forma Statement of Income and Retained Earnings for the fiscal year ending May 31, 19X4.
   b. Proforma Statement of Financial Position as of May 31, 19X4.
   All costs and expenses not specifically addressed will be incurred at the same rates/amounts as experienced in the fiscal year ended May 31, 19X3.
2. Would the objectives of TabCo's Board of Directors be met for the 19X3–19X4 fiscal year? Explain your answer.

12-8. Strategies for Growth (CMA)

Unlike many companies in its industry, OreWood Products has the financial resources to endure slow periods in its base market. OreWood owns its own timberlands and has low debt levels that contribute to its strength. Both sales and earnings over the last decade have fluctuated sharply above and below an 8 percent compound annual growth trend-line. The fluctuations are characteristic of the industry, but the growth rate is above average for the industry, as is OreWood's return-on-assets.

OreWood's common stock is widely held and traded in the over-the-counter-market. The stock currently is selling for six times earnings. OreWood is the fifth largest wood products company in the United States and is about one third the size of its biggest competitor. The company is organized into three divisions.

One division is responsible for managing the timberlands that are large enough to meet OreWood's wood fiber needs and for providing surplus logs for sale outside the company. Most of these timberlands were acquired in the early part of this century at a cost which is minuscule compared to current fair market value.

A second division operates three large mills that produce lumber and plywood for the residential and light commercial building markets. Historically sensitive to business cycles, there are now two structural changes that will affect business. New wood technologies enable the production of lumber and plywood from previously unusable tree species grown in the southeastern United States. Sharply higher shipping costs are the second change, putting products from the Pacific northwest at a cost disadvantage in the eastern and midwestern markets.

OreWood's third division operates two paper mills that produce kraft paper for use in making cardboard boxes. This market also is sensitive to business cycles and shipping costs. There are frequent periods of unused production capacity partly due to the huge size of new paper mills. Both paper mills—and the three lumber and plywood mills—were built in the Pacific northwest prior to 1950 and have been expanded regularly since then.

The Board of Directors has been reviewing the long-run direction of OreWood. Several members of the Board have suggested that OreWood consider the acquisition and merger route to growth. The Board concluded that OreWood should formulate a strategy for growth.

Important factors that should be considered in this growth strategy are the company profile (i.e., where it is) and company objectives (i.e., where it wants to be).

Required:
1. Identify and discuss the key categories that should be included in the company profile prepared by the management of OreWood Products.
2. Describe specific, important considerations that would lead OreWood Products to consider using acquisition and merger activities as part of its growth strategy.
3. To select an acquisition and merger candidate, OreWood Products probably would employ a screening procedure to evaluate potential candidates and then select a candidate from those that satisfy the screening criteria.
    a. Identify significant screening criteria OreWood could use in evaluating merger and acquisition candidates.
    b. Discuss criteria OreWood should use to select one candidate from the group of final candidates.

12-9. Evaluation of Objectives and Strategies (CMA)

The Brockman Co. became a subsidiary of Planto Industries in early 19X9 when Sid Brockman, founder and President, sold it to Planto. At Planto's request, Brockman, along with his Controller, Sales Manager, and Plant Manager continued to manage the subsidiary. The three members of this team report to the appropriate corporate officer for their function as well as to Brockman. This management team has been together for many years and had made Brockman Co. very successful. Planto looks for solid management in its acquisitions, establishes minimum controls, and give subsidiary managements extensive freedom.

The Brockman management has gotten along well with Planto management. The only area of friction between the Brockman team and Planto is Planto's insistence that the subsidiary develop stable as well as growing earnings. Historically, Brockman Co. had experienced short-term earnings swings, but over its life there had been significant growth in sales and earnings.

Brockman has called a meeting of his team for the purpose of developing a strategy that could be used to moderate the variations in earnings. The strategy should not cause major changes in the nature of the business and should not have a detrimental economic impact (i.e., not affect net cash flows over a two-year period). In addition, any actions considered should not strain the subsidiary's relationship with Planto management. The following recommendations were made during the meeting:

1. Vary the useful lives on new asset acquisitions within appropriate limits depending upon need for earnings.
2. Adjust percentage estimates for accounts receivable bad debts to the extent possible.
3. Review inventory stocks and idle machinery in periods of high earnings to establish obsolescence write-offs.
4. Change to weighted average inventory methods to reduce the effect of production variations on cost.
5. Sell or inventory scrap materials as needed to change revenues.
6. Arrange short-term leases for assets, with the option to purchase, in years of high earnings.

7. Delay or accelerate manufacture and delivery of product to those customers who are flexible regarding delivery dates.

8. Vary the customer credit policy as needed to increase or decrease revenues.

Required:

1. Is the requirement for stable as well as growing earnings an appropriate objective for Planto Industries to ask of the Brockman management? Explain your answer.

2. For each of the eight recommended actions, explain whether the act described will have a detrimental economic impact (i.e., affect net cash flows in a two-year period) on Brockman Co. (Disregard income tax considerations.)

3. For each of the eight recommended actions, explain whether the act described would be considered an acceptable subsidiary response by Planto's management to its desire to achieve stable but growing earnings.

12-10. Strategies, Policies, and Behavior (CMA)

Western Corporation is a holding company with three subsidiaries—an electric utility, a natural resource development company, and an electronics manufacturer. Western is regarded as a utility because the utility subsidiary accounts for over 65 percent of revenues and net income. Virtually all of Western's officers and top executives have risen through the utility. The presence of the other subsidiaries is unusual for a utility. The diversification plus perceptive management have served Western well. The recent hard times for utilities had some impact on Western, but the company emerged in sound condition.

Western's diversification is a coincidental result arising from its policy of acquiring other electric utilities. One utility acquisition included a coal deposit, and from that beginning, other deposits and development activities were added to form the natural resource subsidiary. Similarly, another acquisition included a telephone company that provided the basis for the electronics manufacturing subsidiary.

The acquisition of other electric utilities no longer presents the growth opportunities it did in the past. Western has already acquired virtually all of the smaller utilities in its region that make a reasonable fit with Western. A proposed merger with another large utility would face strong opposition from state and federal regulators. Future economic expansion within Western's territory is now the main growth opportunity of the electric utility. However, the region's economy has been depressed, and the five-year forecast is not optimistic.

Western's strategy for expanding the other two subsidiaries has been to respond to offers initiated by sellers rather than to seek acquisitions actively. This strategy has resulted in the expansion and profitability of the electronics subsidiary. However, the natural resource subsidiary is another matter. Heavily dependent on coal, it has closely tracked the coal market's recent boom and bust. The coal market's future is uncertain. As the result of top management's dismay over the depressed coal market, Western has completed its initial strategic planning exercise. The following statements of strategy for each subsidiary were developed to formulate the basis for the master plan.

- *Electric Utility.* The key variables for this subsidiary are efficient operations and effective relations with regulators. Maximum generation of cash for use in further diversification by the corporation's other subsidiaries is the principal objective for the electric utility.

* *Natural Resources.* An orderly divestiture of low potential assets is the initial objective. Once the divestitures are accomplished, formulating an acceptable profit and growth strategy for the remaining units is the main objective of the natural resource subsidiary.
* *Electronics.* The corporation's discretionary resources are to be employed to support the growth and diversification of this subsidiary. The future officers of Western are to be developed here.

These strategy statements were part of the strategic plan presented to Western's Board of Directors. The Directors' only debate was whether Western should sell the entire natural resource subsidiary rather than parts of it. In the end, the statements, as presented, received the Board's approval. Following the Board's action, all three statements were circulated to managers throughout the three units and described as the corporation's "new marching orders."

Required:
1. Identify corporate practices or policies that must be present within Western Corporation for the strategic plan to be effective.
2. Several important characteristics differentiate Western Corporation's three subsidiaries.
   a. Identify these distinguishing characteristics.
   b. Describe how these characteristics influenced the formation of a different strategy for each subsidiary.
3. Discuss the likely effects of the three strategy statements on the behavior of both the top management and the middle management of the electric utility subsidiary of Western Corporation.

12-11. Regulation (CMA)

Within the last two decades, U.S. businesses moved from an era of minimal regulation limited to antitrust and employment legislation to the current environment that includes compliance with numerous social regulations. Businesses no longer have the freedom to design and produce products without regard to social considerations, nor do they have complete control over marketing practices and pricing policies. Social regulations have had an enormous impact on businesses, causing economic and continuity concerns. Despite the fact that there has been criticism against overregulation by the government, polls indicate that the majority of Americans continue to support most forms of social regulation.

Listed below are five agencies that have been created for the implementation and administration of social regulations.

* Food and Drug Administration (FDA).
* Consumer Product Safety Commission (CPSC).
* Environmental Protection Agency (EPA).
* Occupational Safety and Health Administration (OSHA).
* Equal Employment Opportunity Commission (EEOC).

Required:

1. Discuss the general reasons for the dramatic increase in the social regulation of business during the last two decades.
2. For each of the five areas of social regulation administered by the agencies listed above,
    a. describe the social concerns that gave rise to each area of social regulation.
    b. discuss how each area of social regulation has impacted the business community.

12-12. Strategies (CMA)

Sovera Enterprises, an expanding conglomerate, was founded 35 years ago by Emil Sovera. The company's policy has been to acquire businesses that show significant profit potential; if a business fails to attain projected profits, it is usually sold. Presently, the company consists of eight businesses acquired throughout the years; three of these businesses are described below.

LaBue Videodiscs produces a line of videodisc players. The sale of videodisc players has not met expectations, but the management of LaBue believes that the company will succeed in being the first to develop a moderately priced videodisc recorder/player. Market research predicts that the first company to develop this product will be a star.

Ulysses Travel Agencies also showed potential, and the travel industry is growing. However, Ulysses' market share has declined for the last two years even though Sovera has contributed a lot of money to Ulysses' operations. The travel agencies located in the midwest and eastern sections of the country have been the biggest drain on resources.

Reddy Self-Storage was one of the first self-storage companies to open. For the last three years, Reddy has maintained a large market share while growth in the self-storage market has slowed considerably.

Ron Ebert, chairman of Sovera, prepared the agenda for the company's annual planning meeting where the present businesses were evaluated and strategies for future acquisitions were formulated. The following statements of strategy for each of the subsidiary companies discussed were formulated as the basis for the master plan.

*   *LaBue Videodiscs.* Sovera's discretionary resources are to be employed to support the growth of this business. The future officers of Sovera are to be developed here.
*   *Ulysses Travel Agencies.* An orderly disposal of the least profitable locations is the initial objective. Once the disposals are complete, an acceptable profit and growth strategy for the remaining locations will be formulated.
*   *Reddy Self-Storage.* The strategy for this company is to maintain efficient operations and maximize the generation of cash for use in the further development of Sovera's other companies.

These strategy statements were part of the strategic plan presented to Sovera's Board of Directors. The Directors' only debate was whether Sovera should sell the entire Ulysses organization rather than parts of it. However, the Board approved all three statements as presented and circulated them to managers throughout the three units as the corporation's "new marching orders."

Required:
1. Identify corporate policies and practices needed for strategic planning to be effective.
2. Identify at least four general characteristics that differentiate the three businesses identified above, and describe how these characteristics influenced the formation of a different strategy for each business.
3. Discuss the likely effects of the three strategy statements on the behavior of the top management and middle management of each of the three businesses.

12-13. Accounting Information and Strategies[11]

Background

The AC&B Reliable Transportation Company (AC&B) is a major provider of rail transportation with routes extending over 19 states, the District of Columbia, and Canada. It hauls various commodities, ranging from bulk materials, such as coal, paper and chemicals, to consumer goods. Last year, over 6 million shipments were carried over AC&B's 24,000 miles of track.

AC&B and the other major railroads have been experiencing a dramatic revitalization in recent years, due in large part to the passage of the Staggers Act in 1980. This legislation was intended to relieve railroads of the more onerous aspects of governmental regulation.

Prior to 1980, railroads were unable to react to changing market conditions in a timely fashion. Rates were set via tariffs—government approved schedules of mandatory point-to-point rates. Changing these tariffs could be accomplished only by a joint conference with shippers and other railroads or, failing this, by the Interstate Commerce Commission.

Across-the-board rate changes (adjustments for inflation and so on) were gained by petitioning the ICC—a process that normally took up to several months. Other normal marketing tools such as volume discounts and long-term contracts were prohibited before 1980. In addition, exit from markets, principally by abandoning underutilized trackage, was via costly, time-consuming legal proceedings.

After deregulation, however, railroads were given the freedom to price traffic without government sanction, enter long-term contracts, and to abandon unprofitable markets. This loosening of regulation, in turn, caused radical changes in management's approach to marketing its traffic. On the one hand, railroads could now meet head-on the challenge of competing with truckers—to whom the railroads were steadily losing market share. Railroad sales agents could now quote spot prices, change train schedules (including adding new trains), and enter incentive contracts as truckers always had.

On the other hand, these new freedoms not only required a shift in orientation to market-driven decisions, but created new demands for cost information that heretofore had not been readily available.

---

[11] This problem is used by permission of the Institute of Management Accountants.

Cost Data Availability

Railroad accounting systems were the principal source of cost information before railroad deregulation. AC&B's systems are designed to provide a level of detail to satisfy: (1) management budgetary controls and (2) regulatory reporting to the Interstate Commerce Commission.

Management accounting data for AC&B is responsibility-based; i.e., all expenses (other than certain corporate charges such as depreciation expense) are assigned to groups within the corporate organization structure. Further breakdowns define the type of expense, location (if appropriate) and special purpose. For example, freight car inspection labor can be identified to the second-shift work crew at a particular terminal.

The management accounting details "roll up" with each layer of the company's organization, providing budgetary controls that correspond with supervisory responsibilities. In addition, statistical data are available which are utilized to derive unit costs and for other analyses. Examples of these statistics include labor hours, certain material units, and volume data (ton-miles).

Interstate Commerce Commission reporting data is somewhat different in that it is oriented to system-wide operations, as opposed to responsibility-based expenses. Statistics are similarly derived on a system-wide basis. All regulatory proceedings involving this data, such as pricing and line abandonment studies, work off system averages that have been "smoothed" for period-to-period fluctuations.

Demands for Additional Cost Data

While AC&B's accounting systems provide a very high level of detail, there are numerous "gaps" which have appeared as a result of the changing needs of AC&B's marketing managers. Most of these gaps involve costs associated with train operations—since these expenses can be only indirectly associated with specific trains or specific freight cars.

The following are typical requests from the marketers:

1. Costs for a particular train or shipment, rather than costs that are responsibility specific.
2. The cost of adding an additional freight car to a particular train.
3. The effects on costs of utilizing otherwise surplus freight cars.
4. The effect on costs of "backhauls" to origin points (the return trip for freight cars).
5. The profitability of a particular branchline, including a breakeven analysis based on changing traffic volumes.

AC&B's Finance Department, although acknowledging the need for this additional cost data, questions whether it is practical to upgrade the accounting systems to respond to the marketing manager's requests. Exhibits 1 through 3 present some preliminary analyses performed by the Finance Department.

Required:

1. What types of changes does AC&B need to make to its accounting systems in order to upgrade the cost information? In what circumstances would accounting data be inappropriate for pricing decisions?
2. How can incremental cost information be derived from the types of accounting data that are currently available?

Exhibit 1
AC&B Reliable Transportation Company
Operating Income Statement 19X5 (Millions of Dollars)

Rail revenues	$4,772.6
Rail expenses	
Engineering Department	464.0
Mechanical Department	
Overhauls	110.0
Maintenance	526.2
Total mechanical	636.2
Car hire—net	275.6
Transportation Department	
Road crews	398.5
Yard crews	227.2
Fuel	361.8
Other transportation expenses	717.9
Total	1,705.4
Administrative departments	
Damaged lading	20.3
General claims	110.0
Uncollectible accounts	8.6
Salaries, etc.	391.5
Total	530.4
Fixed expenses (unassigned)	
Depreciation	251.5
Long-term leases	153.1
Other	135.2
Total fixed expenses	539.8
Total rail expenses	4,151.4
Operating income	$ 621.2

Notes:

1. The Engineering Department is responsible for maintenance of track and other line-of-road properties.

2. The Mechanical Department maintains all rolling stock; heavy overhauls are performed on a cycle basis; all other maintenance is as needed.

3. Car hire represents the daily rent expense associated with use of "foreign" freight cars on AC&B's track, net of rent income from AC&B's cars similarly used on other railroads' track.

4. The Transportation Department's activities principally involve movement and handling of freight cars (loaded with shippers' lading or empty). Road crews man trains operating between terminals and to shipper facilities, while yard crews perform switching and other terminal functions related to assembling trains.

5. Administrative departments manage, among other things, handling of claims for shippers' goods damaged in transit, general claims from employees and other accidents, and collection of accounts receivable.

6. Long-term leasing of freight cars, locomotives and certain real properties is a common financing practice for AC&B.

Exhibit 2
Cost Element Treatment

Element	Management Accounting	ICC Reporting
Engineering	Actual expenses by track gang or other organization unit; can be specific to geographic location	Actual by functional category; e.g., repairs to crossties, cleanup of derailments, etc.
Mechanical		
Programs	Actual by shop crew or other organization unit; also specific to car types and locomotive number	Actual by work function; e.g., locomotive repairs, dismantling retired freight cars, etc.
Maintenance	Same as mechanical programs	Grouped with mechanical programs
Car hire	Actual rental income/expense by car type	Actual rental income/expense in total
Transportation		
Train crews	Actual wages + fringes by train number; train type available	Actual in total
Yard crews	Actual wages + fringes by yard assignment	Actual in total
Fuel	Actual purchasing and ending inventory by issuing location	Actual, prorated to road vs. yard operation
Administration		
Damaged lading	Estimated by major commodity using trend analysis	Estimated, prorated to road vs. yard operation
General claims	Estimated by organization unit based on number of incidents and standard rates	Estimated to engineering, mechanical, transportation, etc., on type of accident
Uncollectible receivables	Estimated in total, using trend analysis	Same
Fixed		
Depreciation	Estimated by asset category (freight car type, rail, ties, etc.)	Same
Long-term leases	Actual by asset type (freight car, track, etc.)	Same

Exhibit 3
Cost Variability

Element	Fixed	Variable	Comments
Engineering	X		
Mechanical			
Programs		X	Variable with car-miles/locomotive-miles; discretionary as to timing
Maintenance		X	Variable with usage or programs
Car hire			
Expense		X	Variable as to "foreign" car usage
Income		X	Variable as to owned cars used by "foreign" railroads
Transportation			
Road train crews		X	Variable with number of trains and length of haul
Yard crews		X	Variable with cars handled at terminals
Fuel		X	Variable with tonnage and distance
Agencies	X		
Administration			
Lading damage		X	Variable with traffic tonnage and length of haul
General claims		X	Variable with car-miles/locomotive-miles
Uncollectible accounts		X	Variable with revenues, although affected by economic conditions
Salaries, etc.	X		
Fixed			
Depreciation	X		
Long-term leases	X		

Chapter 13

Capital Budgeting: Some Complex Concerns

The commonly used present value model evaluates cash flows against present industry and firm conditions and assumes that those conditions will remain constant throughout the projected life of the asset or project. Clearly this is not the case. If new equipment is not purchased, present equipment will not continue to produce at a constant level while requiring equivalent maintenance and repair costs. If innovative projects are not initiated by the firm, competitors will initiate similar projects that will change the competitive nature of the industry.[1]

A review of the literature reveals two principal criticisms of existing capital budgeting procedures: failure to deal systematically with qualitative (subjective) project selection criteria and failure to link capital budgeting decisions formally to business strategy.[2]

---

[1] David H. Sinason, "A Dynamic Model for Present Value Capital Expenditure Analysis," *Journal of Cost Management* (New York: Warren, Gorham, & Lamont, Spring 1991), p. 41.
[2] Thomas F. Monahan, Matthew J. Liberatore, and David E. Stout, "Decision Support for Capital Budgeting: A Model for Classroom Presentation," *Journal of Accounting Education*, Vol. 8 (London: Pergamon Press, 1990), p. 225.

The basics of discounted cash flow analysis have been a part of management practice for decades. A recent survey shows that large firms use discounting for replacement decisions (60 percent), expansion of existing operations (86 percent), expansion into new operations (87 percent), foreign operations (79 percent), abandonment decisions (62 percent), and high technology decisions (75 percent).[3] However, as the opening quotations show, there are some areas where we can expand our understanding and application of the capital budgeting model. Specifically, managers should address how they can best incorporate how changes in the internal or external environment affect their analyses of capital projects. This means dealing with the changing base line concept (things are *not* going to stay the same if you do not invest), looking at the interrelationships of financial, human, and physical resources in achieving long-term strategic goals, how subjective matters can be realistically included in analysis, and how to deal with shorter life cycles and changing patterns of risk. These along with other topics of interest in this area form the content of this chapter. This material assumes the reader has a general knowledge about the basic discounted-cash-flow models (net present value and internal rate of return). If not, Appendix 13A is a review of these methods. In addition, Appendix 13B reviews the applicable parts of the current tax law, the Tax Reform Act of 1986.[4]

The first part of the chapter covers the various stages of capital budgeting analysis and the abandonment decision. This is followed by the concept of relevant discount rate, a comparison of the present-value models, and preference rules for choosing capital projects with and without constraints. This sets the stage for the next section dealing with risk (sensitivity analysis) and then one on investing in the new manufacturing and competitive environment. This is followed by discussion of expected monetary value and expected utility analysis. Finally, we deal with capital rationing and investing versus financing issues.

Throughout this discussion, keep in mind the issues raised in Chapters 2 and 3 such as activity-based costing and management (tracing costs and looking at what activities cause a resource to be in place or used), Theory of Constraints (maximizing throughput while minimizing inventory and operating cost), and just-in-time and manufacturing cells (changing the nature of work assignments and the amount of space/capital/resources needed for inventory management, handling, and storage). In addition, any discussion of capital budgeting has strong ties to Chapter 12 on strategic planning.

---

[3] Thomas Klammer, Bruce Koch, and Neil Wilner, "Capital Budgeting Practices—A Survey of Corporate Use," *Journal of Management Accounting Research*, Vol. 3 (Sarasota, Fla.: American Accounting Association, Fall 1991), Table 1, p. 118.

[4] Tax laws have had a way of changing during the last ten years. The objective of including some details of the 1986 act is more to have you look at and apply *an* act rather than to bind you to any particular set of rules. If you understand the basics, then using any set of regulations is relatively easy.

THE STAGES OF CAPITAL BUDGETING

There are five stages for capital budgeting: the *identification stage*, where opportunities tied to strategic management are identified; the *development stage*, where managers work on developing projects and estimating cash flows in concert with adopted strategies, goals, and objectives; the *selection stage*, which is the subject of much of this chapter; the *implementation stage*, where a chosen project is undertaken; and the *control stage*, where managers evaluate how projects are performing in light of original estimates. The control stage involves the life cycle of each project and, ultimately, should give information to managers as they evaluate whether to continue a project or to abandon it.

As managers coped with changes in the internal and external environment about ten years ago, Pinches criticized how academicians seemed to cover capital budgeting. Specifically he said that too much attention was paid to technique and not enough to the identification, development, and control (post audit) stages.[5] As we discussed, managers are just now coming to grips with how to measure the effects of improved quality, customer satisfaction, and delivery time, for example. In this section, we will look at how managers might identify projects, develop them so that they can be evaluated, and then, once adopted, how they can look back on the decision-making process (perform a post audit). Finally, we will look at the abandonment decision.

Identification Stage

Chapter 12 on strategic planning includes a discussion about how objectives, goals, and strategies follow the adoption of a mission statement. Everything else should follow the mission statement and be congruent with it. Managers can focus their efforts in identifying new investment opportunities based on how they fit into the mission of the company as well as the particular objectives, goals, and strategies that are part of the strategic plan. Deciding *where* to invest is an important part of strategic planning. Timing may play an important role as specific goals need to be met. The external and internal analyses that are part of the strategic planning process allow managers to better identify appropriate projects and to deal with the risk associated with each proposed investment.

Development Stage

Once opportunities have been identified, managers need to develop information so that specific strategies can be evaluated by DCF analysis. Besides

---

[5] George E. Pinches, "Myopia, Capital Budgeting and Decision Making," *Financial Management* (Autumn 1982), p. 6.

the common and more easily quantifiable costs and benefits from a particular option, managers should address the more difficult areas referred to above. For example, new projects may include a new flow of materials and a more machine/robot pacing of manufacturing. This may have an effect on in-process inventory as well as raw materials and finished goods. Training costs and recruitment activity may be changed to include new needs. There may be a positive (or a negative) effect on employee morale, on product quality, on delivery, and on other items that should be quantified as part of the DCF analysis. Our discussion of capital budgeting seems too often to imply that we are looking at quite discrete projects. In reality, managerial choices in one area may have effects in many other areas of the company.

Evaluating Decisions: The Post Audit

The idea of a post audit of the decision, or control phase, is increasing in popularity. Klammer et al. report that 86 percent of the companies surveyed did a post audit of major projects. This is up 10 percent over eight years in their survey.[6] The ultimate evaluation is whether the strategy adopted achieves the goals and objectives that it was meant to address. These goals and objectives may relate to market penetration, product quality and innovation, cash return for corporate equity and debt holders, and so on. The control phase, then, should include analyses showing how these goals and objectives are being met. The evaluation scheme should be analogous to standard cost variance analysis: What is the "standard" for comparison and what are the variances (controllable and uncontrollable) from that benchmark?

The control phase should also include an updating of the original set of estimates and assumptions. Is the original estimated economic life still valid? Have cash inflow or outflow expectations changed? What has happened to the reinvestment rate, the tax laws, the estimated salvage value, and so on?

Have there been changes in the basic assessments that underlie the strategic plan? Has the economy changed? What has been the competitors' reaction to a project? What has happened technologically? Has the mission of the company changed and how does this change affect the strategies the company is pursuing? These are a sample of the questions that can be asked in the control stage. With enough changes, managers can also ask if it is time to abandon a segment or project. The focus is on the project, *not* the manager. It is important to extract blame from this process so the company can secure a more accurate assessment.

The Abandonment Decision

When companies are faced with a constraint on available capital, any funds that could be freed from existing projects for productive investments should

---

[6] Klammer, et al., "Capital Budgeting Practices," Table 8, p 128.

be investigated. Since companies have alternate uses for their funds, the continuance of a segment or investment project should yield cash returns that exceed the opportunity costs of the alternate uses. If not, the company may want to abandon the project. One question that can be asked is whether the present value of the remaining cash flows from a project exceed the cash that could be realized if the assets were sold now. This, in turn, can be divided into two questions:

1. What is a project's updated NPV? If it is negative, then other options can be explored.
2. If a project has a positive ongoing NPV, are there more advantageous ways that the company could invest funds that could be realized by selling the project now?

A decision to abandon a project can be caused by many reasons. The basic mission of a company may change so that the continuance of the project does not fit into the new corporate image. As an example, a Midwest chain of department stores had a car-wash division with car-wash facilities in the malls where their retail department stores were located. Corporate management redefined the mission of the company and decided to sell (abandon) this division even though it was a profitable use of funds.

The economic environment may change. Consider a plant nursery that was built in the suburbs of a city before housing and commercial development moved that far. At a certain point, the value of the land may exceed the present value of the nursery business and the nursery may choose to go out of business or to relocate farther away; in any case, the current site would be abandoned. Abandonment can also be caused by the shortening of the life cycle of a product or process.

The analysis for an abandonment decision takes about the same format as the original investment analysis. For example, expected values of future flows can be estimated along with the probabilities of different states of nature and either by a decision-tree analysis or through simulation, the option of closing, selling, abandoning can be compared to that of continuing operations. At times, due to government regulations, changes in the corporate mission, or other reasons, the decision to abandon may be fairly perfunctory since it may be the only viable option a company has.

A COMPARISON OF THE BASIC PRESENT-VALUE MODELS

With the stages of capital budgeting as a background, the next subject is a comparison of the basic discounted-cash-flow (DCF) models, *net present value* (NPV) and *internal rate of return* (IRR).[7] The use of these basic models begins

---

[7] There is a third model, *present-value index* or *benefit-cost ratio*, which is not explored here since it is not widely used in practice.

with an assumption of virtual certainty about all parameters and variables and also assumes risk neutrality of the decision maker.[8] The decision rule for a single project for these two models is to accept a project if

$$NPV > 0 \text{ at the relevant discount rate } (k)$$
$$IRR > k$$

Inherent in these decision rules is the relevant discount rate, k.

Relevant Discount Rate

The **relevant discount rate** is the rate that managers use to discount cash flows in the NPV model or as a minimum rate against which to judge the IRR of those cash flows. In the main, the relevant discount rate relates to the weighted-average cost of capital that a firm faces. However, there are alternate ways of looking at the relevant discount rate (also called just the *discount rate* or the *hurdle rate*) that incorporate adjustments for performance goals and various aspects of risk. Unfortunately, many examples illustrating capital budgeting analysis include an assumed discount rate. In practice, deciding on what rate to use can be quite difficult. It is important to know the foundation for the relevant discount rate as a basis for deciding if and when to change it in the analytical process. At its most basic, k is related to the cost to the firm of debt and equity funds.

Weighted-Average Cost of Capital   Corporations raise funds from several sources including debt and equity financing. The concept of weighted-average cost of capital (WACC) is to find the average cost of such funds. Projects must earn at least the WACC in order for companies to pay their debt and provide a return to equity investors.

Investors look for a cash return on their investment.[9] Holders of common stock, in the main, are willing to invest a sum equaling the present value of an infinite stream of dividends.[10] While it is theoretically possible to describe the cost of common stock (the required return investors demand), this is complicated by the various forms of equity investment available as well as the many risk/reward structures of investors.

---

[8] In addition, as discussed under the section on relevant discount rate, there is an implicit assumption that all projects under consideration have about the same risk characteristics.

[9] Companies also look for a cash return on their investment. Accounting measures of profitability in the main do not reflect such a return per se.

[10] In publicly traded companies, the collective behavior of equity investors (their collective risk characteristics) determines the price they are willing to pay for a stock given such a stream of projected dividends. In smaller companies, the different risk preferences of investors complicates the scene and makes it harder to use a single rate to reflect overall desired returns.

Bond holders look at the present value of the stream of interest payments from the bond as well as the present value of the face value of the bond received at maturity. Again, there are a variety of bond instruments available with some differences in risk characteristics and/or conversion features. Thus, finding the average cost of debt can be complicated.

Current tax laws provide that payment of dividends is not deductible to a corporation but payment of interest is. Tax deductibility affects the net cost of funds to a company. A company has, say, 50 percent common stock and 50 percent bonds. The stock was sold for $20 per share and has a projected dividend of $2 per share. Bonds (sold at par) mature in ten years and have an 8 percent coupon rate. With a 40 percent average tax rate for the company, the WACC will be 7.4 percent [(10% return on equity × 0.50) + (8% return on debt × (1 − 0.40) × 0.50) = 7.4%].[11]

The many forms of debt and equity as well as the changing markets for securities cause the practical establishment of the WACC to be hard to accomplish. However, there is some general agreement that the WACC is a measure of the overall riskiness of the firm and there are substitute ways to assess the relevant discount rate.[12]

Riskiness of the Firm   One way to approximate the WACC is to look at the relative riskiness of the firm in relation to the marketplace. In the United States, the best measure of a riskless rate of return would be various U.S. Treasury issues. Corporate offerings are considered more risky by investors than U.S. government notes. Thus, the WACC can be the riskless rate in the economy plus a risk premium reflecting the riskiness of the firm. Companies can gain some measure of the riskiness of the firm through how banks evaluate them (i.e., the more points above the prime rate that a bank wants from a loan, the more risk the bank perceives). This does not imply that bond or stock rates are tied to the corporate prime lending rate (or that this rate is riskless); however, loans tied to that rate are a good indicator of how at least one segment of the financial community assesses the risk of the company.

Portfolio Rate of Return   A practical way to assess a rate of return is to look at the actual return being generated by the existing set of financial, human, and physical assets being employed at a company. If we look at the cash being generated over the long term by this portfolio, we can see the current relevant rate of return. This can be used not only for evaluating other projects, but also as a basis to see if the return is sufficient. Looking at

---

[11] This assumes the common stockholder is looking at in infinite stream of dividends and that bonds, purchased at face value, are held to maturity and are redeemed at face value. These are not unreasonable assumptions.

[12] Proponents of the capital asset pricing model (CAPM) might argue this conclusion. However, it is still a reasonable statement.

the firm as a portfolio of assets also focuses managers' attention on the integration of all the parts of the company; this might keep managers from thinking about a particular capital project as if it were completely independent of the rest of the company.

While it is possible to look at overall returns, it is more problematic to look at returns from individual projects. In some ways, this parallels the discussion in Chapter 3 about the Theory of Constraints: managers should not look at returns of individual products separately since everything interconnects. Unless a company has quite separate facilities and products, it is difficult to assess the return from any single project or even from a group of assets separate from the return for the entire company. If a company is looking to acquire an entirely new facility in a new line of business, there is a fair amount of separability from the rest of the company. However, if managers are looking at adding a new printing press in a plant with eight other presses, it is more difficult to separate the costs and benefits of that single piece of equipment from the rest of the facility. We get into some severe tracing problems in addition to the problem of assuming that projects/products affect the company discretely.

Goal-Oriented Discount Rate   Using the base of WACC, projects must at least earn the cost of funds to a company. Some companies establish **goal-oriented discount rates** or **hurdle rates** that are in excess of the firm's WACC. Chapter 12 on strategic planning includes establishing specific goals, objectives, and strategies given the mission of the organization. These might include a rate of return higher than the WACC. While WACC might be 10 percent, managers might decide to adopt new projects that return 12 percent or higher if the firm wants to accent financial growth. In addition, as we will see in the discussion about capital rationing later in this chapter, raising the discount rate is a reasonable way to screen projects when cash availability is constrained.

Risk-Adjusted Discount Rate   Although the idea of uncertainty and risk is assumed away in basic DCF models, different projects frequently have different risk characteristics. Managers might decide to alter the usual discount rate to incorporate the risk level of a particular project.[13] This is especially true as managers look at new technology and ways of managing and organizing how goods are produced. In some cases, managers are faced with analyzing a completely new way of doing things. There are no external references that they can use as part of the analysis. On one hand, the risk of such a new project is increased since the installation and operating characteristics are unknown (other than straight engineering estimates). This would call for increasing the discount rate. On the other hand, others

---

[13] Klammer, et al., "Capital Budgeting Practices," p. 123, report that 40 percent of the firms responding raise the required rate of return as a way to deal with risk.

argue that there are benefits to, say, reorganizing work flows into manufacturing cells, going to JIT, increasing quality, etc. that cannot be fully quantified (the *subjective factor*). Since it is difficult to put such benefits in annual monetary terms, one approach is to *lower* the discount rate.[14] This artificially increases the present value of the better quantified cash flows. Once managers choose a relevant discount rate and find the NPV and/or IRR of various proposals, the next step is to rank projects for possible implementation.

Ranking Projects Without Constraints

When several projects are mutually independent (managers can only choose one) and there are no constraints on resources (e.g., available investment capital),[15] managers would probably look at the NPV and/or IRR of the projects and pick the one with the highest value. However, there can be a conflict between the different DCF techniques when ranking projects. Consider the following mutually independent projects:

	Project	
	A	**B**
Original investment	$1,500	$1,500
Cash flow		
Year 1	1,150	0
Year 2	1,150	2,500
NPV @ 10%	$ 496	$ 566
IRR	34%	29%

While Project A has the higher IRR, Project B has the higher NPV. Since A returns cash flows faster than B, the IRR is higher. When the relevant discount rate, k, is lower than the IRR (as it is in this case), there is a heavy weight on funds returned early since the IRR model implicitly assumes that all intermediate cash flows will be reinvested at the internal rate of return. Thus, the IRR model implies that $1,150 received at the end of Year 1 could be reinvested at 34 percent.

Exhibit 13-1 shows in numbers and Figure 13-1 graphically shows the net present values of Projects A and B at different discount rates. Project B has a higher NPV than A at any discount rate less than about 18 percent, which is the indifference point or crossover rate. Above that rate, A has the higher NPV so there is no conflict in ranking the two projects. When the relevant discount rate is below 18 percent (such as 10 percent in the illustration), managers are faced with conflicting answers by the two DCF models. They

---

[14] However, this might open the door to some game playing by managers.
[15] Acquiring capital assets is a strategic decision. The list of relevant projects could be generated as a response to a bottleneck constraint (in TOC terms). However, the constraints alluded to here would not be constraints as defined by TOC.

Exhibit 13-1
Net Present Value Crossover

	Project A	Project B	
Investment	($1,500)	($1,500)	
Cash flow			
Year 1	1,150	0	
Year 2	1,150	2,500	

Discount Rate	Net Present Value	Net Present Value	Difference
5%	$638	$768	($129)
6%	608	725	(117)
7%	579	684	(104)
8%	551	643	(93)
9%	523	604	(81)
10%	496	566	(70)
11%	469	529	(60)
12%	444	493	(49)
13%	418	458	(40)
14%	394	424	(30)
15%	370	390	(21)
16%	346	358	(12)
17%	323	326	(3)
18%	300	295	5
19%	278	265	13
20%	257	236	21
21%	236	208	28
22%	215	180	36

must choose between A and B, depending on the DCF model they believe more relevant. From a cash flow perspective, it is more likely that the better choice is Project B when $k < 18$ percent because of the inability to be assured that the firm can maintain such a high rate of return (e.g., 29 or 34 percent).[16]

Inherent Problems in DCF Models

The problems above deal with choosing between mutually exclusive alternatives where different DCF models may rank these projects differently. There are other ranking problems with IRR. The IRR model also can yield confusing results given a certain pattern of cash flows. In addition, all DCF techniques suffer from a basic problem: how to reinvest intermediate funds.

---

[16] In this discussion, we are assuming that all other things about the two projects are equal. That includes risk, subjective factors, and the like.

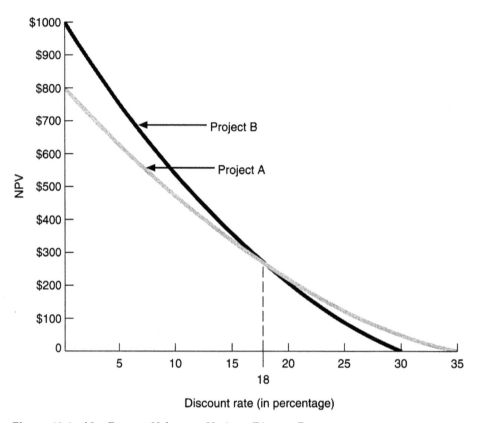

Figure 13-1   Net Present Values at Various Discout Rates

Loss of Scale   As a relative measure, the IRR removes the scale of the project. Consider the choice between two mutually exclusive alternatives with one yielding a 50 percent IRR and the other an 8 percent IRR; the first looks much better than the second. However, if the first is an investment.of $10 and the second one of $10,000, the second looks better than the first *assuming* that the $9,990 difference could only be invested at rates less than 8 percent.

Multiple Rates of Return   Usual cash flows may include one or more periods of net negative flows (outflows) followed by years of net positive cash flows (inflows). However, if cash flows change from negative to positive and back to negative again, use of the IRR model may result in more than one internal rate of return.[17] These uncommon flows can be caused, for example, by major maintenance during the project that over-powers inflows for a year. Also, using IRR to compare incremental flows such as the difference between two projects may result in multiple IRR's.

---

[17] The contrast is between one sign change (−, + or even +, −) and multiple sign changes (e.g., −, −, +, +, +, −, +, +, −, +).

In this case, while one project has a lower cost in Year 0 and a higher net cash inflow in Year 1, it may have a lower cash inflow in Year 2. Thus, there would be a sign change when looking at the difference between the two projects of −, +, − and possible multiple internal rates of return.

Assume the following set of cash flows:[18]

Year 0	−$234,050
Year 1	552,250
Year 2	− 324,300

Solving for the IRR yields about 10 percent and 26 percent, as is illustrated by Exhibit 13-2, an electronic spreadsheet analysis of the problem. The net present value at different interest rates is graphed in Figure 13-2. Note that the net present value equals zero at both 10.07 and 25.89 percent, thus satisfying the IRR criterion.

Exhibit 13-2
Multiple Internal Rates of Return

A	B	C	D	E	F
4	Time Period		Cash Flows		
5	0		($234,050)		
6	1		552,250		
7	2		(324,300)		
8					
9					
10	NPV at	6%	($1,590)	where formula for NPV is	
11		8%	($687)	@NPV(C10,D5..D7)	
12		10%	($19)		
13		12%	$447		
14		14%	$738		
15		16%	$879		
16		18%	$891		
17		20%	$792		
18		22%	$598		
19		24%	$322		
20		26%	($21)		
21		28%	($423)		
22					
23					
24	Actual IRR's		0.1006858	where formula for IRR is	
25			0.2588526	@IRR(.10,D5..D7)	
				@IRR(.26,D5..D7)	

---

[18] See Joseph G. Louderback and Charles W. McNichols, "A Note on Net Present Value and Internal Rate of Return Functions in Electronic Spreadsheets," *Journal of Accounting Education*, (London: Pergamon Press, Fall 1986), pp. 113–116, for additional discussion of this idea.

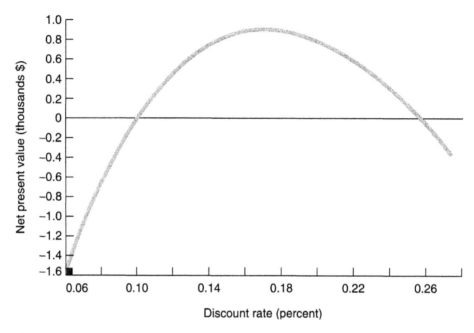

Figure 13-2   Plot of Net Present Values

The general rule of thumb is that there can be as many rates of return as there are changes in the signs of the cash flows year to year. The result is a basically useless measure.[19] Several authors have devised a scheme for using IRR even in this situation, but most managers would find any interpretation counterintuitive.[20]

The Reinvestment Assumption   All DCF models have an inherent assumption about the reinvestment of funds received during the life of the project. Perhaps the most problem-free reinvestment assumption is that if a company uses its WACC as the relevant discount rate and if it receives enough funds from various projects, it may be fair to assume that these intermediate funds (positive net inflows received during the life of the project) can be reinvested on average at the WACC rate. However, much in the same way that a particular loan or other source of funds used for a specific project may be different than the WACC of the firm, there may not be reinvestment opportunities available at the WACC for funds coming from a project. Perhaps funds can be invested at a rate greater than (or less than) the WACC. Thus, the NPV model is flawed if it is not possible to invest intermediate funds on average at about the discount rate used in the DCF analysis.

---

[19] Some authors would say that the IRR is useful if the second and any additional IRR's are well outside the range of normal discount rates.

[20] Some examples are found in various texts on capital budgeting. See Appendix B—Selected References.

When risk-adjusted or goal-oriented rates are used in NPV analyses, there is a problem since these rates are usually above the WACC.

The internal rate of return model inherently assumes the reinvestment of funds at the IRR. Take an investment opportunity with a 25 percent IRR. The company may not have any sources to reinvest funds received from that investment anywhere near 25 percent. If the firm cannot reinvest funds at or near the IRR, then there is some question about the validity of the IRR as a true rate of return.

In practice, most managers adopt the NPV model as the least flawed and are willing to use k to discount cash flows. However, one way to deal with the reinvestment assumption is to use terminal values instead of present values to build in specific estimates about the reinvestment of each year's cash flows.[21] This adds another layer of estimates to a model already burdened with estimates; moreover, managers are not used to looking at the terminal value of a project in, say, 2001 versus the present value of a project now.

SENSITIVITY ANALYSIS: DEALING WITH UNCERTAINTY

Sensitivity analysis is a widely adopted way that managers can deal with risk.[22] Basic DCF analysis includes specific values for such variables as the original investment cost, economic life of the asset/project, incremental changes in working capital, yearly operating flows (or savings), startup costs and timing, ongoing and major maintenance, marginal tax rate over time, tax life and depreciation base, net salvage value, relevant discount rate, and a reinvestment rate over time. In reality, there is risk associated with many of these original values. While management might be able to lock in the original investment cost and how assets will be depreciated for tax purposes, other aspects of the analysis are less certain and difficult to estimate. Sensitivity analysis is a naïve way that managers can look at what would happen if certain estimates were wrong. **Sensitivity analysis** involves either changing one variable at a time (while holding all other variables constant) or changing several variables to see the impact on NPV and/or IRR.

Economic Life

Managers are faced with ever-shortening life cycles for equipment and products. Technology in some areas moves at an exponential pace where

---

[21] See Appendix B—Selected References—for various texts on capital budgeting and finance, most of which deal with terminal values.

[22] Klammer et al., "Capital Budgeting Practices," p. 124, report that 67 percent of the companies surveyed use sensitivity analysis to deal with risk.

something might be outdated almost when it is installed. If you have been in the market for a personal computer, you know the feeling. Just when you think you want to jump in and replace what you have (or purchase your first computer), advances are made and you are unsure what to do. **Economic life** (or useful life) is the time period of the life cycle of the asset/product. There is a real difference between *economic life* and *physical life*. An asset might be capable of producing for many years to come, but if there is no need for the things it can make, its economic life is over. New machines can also become available that produce at a higher quality and/ or lower cost. However, the existence of newer technology does not, by itself, end an asset's economic life. To go back to the personal computer example, if you have a perfectly good computer that performs the types of functions you need at a reasonable speed and cost, then even if there are newer generations of computers, the useful life of your existing equipment is still going on. With larger and larger amounts being spent on capital assets (especially when there is computer-integrated manufacturing involved), managers want to see the consequences of economic lives that are shorter than the one they used in their original DCF analysis.

Changes in Other Variables

Except for a very few figures that can be established fairly well at the outset of the project, others will have different uncertainty associated with them. If a company is embarking on a completely new technology (e.g., wave soldering in the 1980s), they have little experience about operating and maintenance costs. Salvage values are affected by changes in technology, too. Recent history shows how the WACC can change downward due to a recession. This is contrasted to an upward pressure in times of high inflation (a subject we cover later in the chapter).

Basic Sensitivity Analysis

Managers are evaluating a single project illustrated in Exhibit 13-3. The NPV is over $60,000 given all the estimates about various variables. In Exhibits 13-4, 13-5, and 13-6, managers have varied their estimates first of the relevant discount rate, next of changes in yearly operating flows, and, finally, both of these together. When changes are taken together, the NPV falls to a negative value.

Discounted Payback

A way to deal with sensitivity analysis and economic life is to use *discounted payback* or *breakeven net present value*. **Discounted payback** is the number of years it will take to yield NPV = 0. Obviously, one can just look at the useful life variable or can also look at other variables at the same time. In Exhibits 13-3 through 13-6, there is a line showing the cumulative present value. For example, in Exhibit 13-3, ignoring the salvage value (which is not

Exhibit 13-3
Basic Information and Analysis

DATA SECTION

Discount rate	10%
Tax life of asset	7
Depreciation method	ACRS
Cost of asset	$250,000
Salvage value	1,000
Working capital changes	
Year 0	50,000
Year 1	0
Year 2	0
Recovery in last year	50,000
Economic life of project	8
Tax rate	40%

Operating flows	
Year 1	$60,000
Year 2	75,000
Year 3	90,000
Year 4	90,000
Year 5	90,000
Year 6	90,000
Year 7	90,000
Year 8	90,000

ANSWER SECTION

YEARS	0	1	2	3	4	5	6	7	8
Investment	(250,000)								
TED		14,280	24,490	17,490	12,490	8,930	8,930	8,930	4,460
Working capital	(50,000)								50,000
Net salvage value									600
Operating flows		36,000	45,000	54,000	54,000	54,000	54,000	54,000	54,000
Total	(300,000)	50,280	69,490	71,490	66,490	62,930	62,930	62,930	109,060
PVIF	1.0000	0.9091	0.8264	0.7513	0.6830	0.6209	0.5645	0.5132	0.4665
Present value	(300,000)	45,709	57,430	53,711	45,414	39,075	35,522	32,293	50,877
Cum PV	(300,000)	(254,291)	(196,861)	(143,150)	(97,736)	(58,662)	(23,139)	9,154	60,031

Net present value	$60,031
Internal rate of return	14.91%

Exhibit 13-4

Sensitivity Analysis—Change in Discount Rate

DATA SECTION

Discount rate	12%
Tax life of asset	7
Depreciation method	ACRS
Cost of asset	$250,000
Salvage value	1,000
Working capital changes	
Year 0	50,000
Year 1	0
Year 2	0
Recovery in last year	50,000
Economic life of project	8
Tax rate	40%

Operating flows

Year 1	$60,000
Year 2	75,000
Year 3	90,000
Year 4	90,000
Year 5	90,000
Year 6	90,000
Year 7	90,000
Year 8	90,000

ANSWER SECTION

YEARS	0	1	2	3	4	5	6	7	8
Investment	(250,000)								
TED		14,280	24,490	17,490	12,490	8,930	8,930	8,930	4,460
Working capial	(50,000)	0	0	0	0	0	0	0	
Net salvage value									600
Operating flows		36,000	45,000	54,000	54,000	54,000	54,000	54,000	54,000
Total	(300,000)	50,280	69,490	71,490	66,490	62,930	62,930	62,930	109,060
PVIF	1.0000	0.8929	0.7972	0.7118	0.6355	0.5674	0.5066	0.4523	0.4039
Present value	(300,000)	44,893	55,397	50,885	42,256	35,708	31,882	28,466	44,048
Cum PV	(300,000)	(255,107)	(199,710)	(148,825)	(106,569)	(70,861)	(38,979)	(10,513)	33,535

Net present value	$33,535
Internal rate of return	14.91%

Exhibit 13-5

Sensitivity Analysis—Change in Operating Flows

DATA SECTION

			Operating flows	
Discount rate	10%		Year 1	$50,000
Tax life of asset	7		Year 2	60,000
Depreciation method	ACRS		Year 3	70,000
Cost of asset	$250,000		Year 4	70,000
Salvage value	1,000		Year 5	70,000
Working capital changes			Year 6	70,000
Year 0	50,000		Year 7	70,000
Year 1	0		Year 8	70,000
Year 2	0			
Recovery in last year	50,000			
Economic life of project	8			
Tax rate	40%			

ANSWER SECTION

YEARS	0	1	2	3	4	5	6	7	8
Investment	(250,000)								
TED		14,280	24,490	17,490	12,490	8,930	8,930	8,930	4,460
Working capital	(50,000)	0	0	0	0	0	0		50,000
Net salvage value									600
Operating flows		30,000	36,000	42,000	42,000	42,000	42,000	42,000	42,000
Total	(300,000)	44,280	60,490	59,490	54,490	50,930	50,930	50,930	97,060
PVIF	1.0000	0.9091	0.8264	0.7513	0.6830	0.6209	0.5645	0.5132	0.4665
Present value	(300,000)	40,255	49,992	44,696	37,217	31,624	28,749	26,135	45,279
Cum PV	(300,000)	(259,745)	(209,754)	(165,058)	(127,841)	(96,217)	(67,468)	(41,333)	3,946

Net present value	$3,946
Internal rate of return	10.34%

Exhibit 13-6
Sensitivity Analysis—Change in Operating Flows and Discount Rate

DATA SECTION

Discount rate	12%
Tax life of asset	7
Depreciation method	ACRS
Cost of asset	$250,000
Salvage value	1,000
Working capital changes	
Year 0	50,000
Year 1	0
Year 2	0
Recovery in last year	50,000
Economic life of project	8
Tax rate	40%

Operating flows

Year 1	$50,000
Year 2	60,000
Year 3	70,000
Year 4	70,000
Year 5	70,000
Year 6	70,000
Year 7	70,000
Year 8	70,000

ANSWER SECTION

YEARS	0	1	2	3	4	5	6	7	8
Investment	(250,000)								
TED		14,280	24,490	17,490	12,490	8,930	8,930	8,930	4,460
Working capital	(50,000)	0	0	0	0	0	0	0	
Net salvage value									600
Operating flows		30,000	36,000	42,000	42,000	42,000	42,000	42,000	42,000
Total	(300,000)	44,280	60,490	59,490	54,490	50,930	50,930	50,930	97,060
PVIF	1.0000	0.8929	0.7972	0.7118	0.6355	0.5674	0.5066	0.4523	0.4039
Present value	(300,000)	39,536	48,222	42,344	34,629	28,899	25,803	23,038	39,201
Cum PV	(300,000)	(260,464)	(212,242)	(169,898)	(135,269)	(106,370)	(80,567)	(57,529)	(18,328)

Net present value	($18,328)
Internal rate of return	10.34%

material in this illustration), the project will have to go seven years in order to achieve a positive NPV. This jumps to eight years in Exhibits 13-4 and 13-5. (In Exhibit 13-6 there is never a positive NPV within the original time frame. The project would have to last longer than eight years to get to present-value breakeven.)

Inflation

Inflation is not a universal problem. However, certain industries and certain parts of the world experience significant inflation. It's an important topic especially in light of companies competing in a world marketplace. DCF models can incorporate inflation if both the cash flows and the discount rate are adjusted for specific estimates of inflation.

When managers forecast that cash flows from operations are going to be $100,000 a year for five years and use that constant amount in a DCF analysis, they are implicitly saying that there is going to be no inflation over that period of time. Since the WACC would probably include some factor for inflation by its very nature, using the even flows with k = WACC would be a mismatched set.

Inflation affects some nominal costs, such as operating flows, directly. If materials or labor will rise over time or if prices will rise given inflationary pressure, this should be included in the analysis by making estimates of future prices and costs. Other flows, such as the tax shield of depreciation, are affected by the inflation in the discount rate rather than directly adjusted for inflation themselves. The real result is a loss of purchasing power for such flows, much in the same way that people on fixed incomes lose purchasing power with inflation.

In the most basic analysis, operating flows can be adjusted by the expected rate of inflation, and the discount rate can be similarly adjusted. Say there is a project with a discount rate of 10 percent (ignoring inflation) and cash flows are expected to be a nominal $100,000 per year. As you should be able to confirm, cash flows including 5 percent inflation over five years would be

Year 1	$105,000
Year 2	110,250
Year 3	115,763
Year 4	121,551
Year 5	127,628

Discount rates also rise with inflation as investors and lenders must meet their own inflation-adjusted needs. The discount rate is adjusted in the same way that cash flows are: multiply the discount rate times the inflation factor. Thus, the present-value interest factor for one year at 10 percent with a 5 percent inflation factor is

$$1/(1 + 0.10)^1 (1 + 0.05)^1 = 0.8658$$

This specific calculation can be generalized by raising both factors in the denominator to the power of t, years in the future.

If all flows were adjusted upward by 5 percent and then discounted downward by 5 percent again, the result would be the same as if inflation were ignored. However, since some flows are affected by inflation and others are not, the analysis should include specific estimates. This can get complicated in the sense that different flows may be affected by different inflation factors. While the economy may be rising at a 5 percent inflation factor, materials or labor or other costs may be affected more or less than that overall average. While it may be possible to establish specific estimates of each cost's relevant inflation rate, the manager is then faced with a choice of how to adjust the relevant discount rate for inflation. Should the manager use the inflation rate in the general economy? for the industry? some weighted rate based on estimates in the analysis? All may be appropriate given the estimates and the data. Spreadsheet sensitivity analysis is useful in such cases to see how sensitive the DCF results are to changes in various inflation factors. An example of how to deal with inflation when there is a known inflation index (factor) is illustrated in Exhibit 13-7. This exhibit uses the same data as Exhibit 13-3 on page 537.

The only change between Exhibit 13-3 and 13-7 involves the inflating of the cash flows by an annual rate of 4 percent and the matched change in the relevant discount rate to 14.4 percent (1.10 × 1.04 = 1.144 or 14.4 percent). Below is a comparison of the DCF values from the two exhibits.

	Original Example	Inflation Example
Net present value	$60,031	$35,081
IRR	14.91%	17.49%
Relevant discount rate	10.00%	14.40%

Why is the NPV lower but the IRR higher? Inflation has taken its toll on the tax effect of depreciation and the recovery of working capital and the salvage value. These numbers remained the same but were subject to a higher discount rate due to inflationary pressure. However, the IRR is calculated on nominal cash flows—which are up when compared to the original example. This anomaly is yet another reason to suspect the value of the IRR.

INVESTING IN THE NEW MANUFACTURING AND COMPETITIVE ENVIRONMENT

There has been much written in recent years about the need to make U.S. firms more competitive in the world marketplace. In some cases, this means abandoning older ways of doing things and adopting a new perspective on how to manage the firm as well as what equipment to have in place. To meet the challenges of the market, companies have to produce goods that

Exhibit 13-7
Inflation Adjusted Data and Discount Rate

DATA SECTION		Inflation	4%
Discount rate	14.40%		
Tax life of asset	7	Operating flows	
Depreciation method	ACRS	Year 1	$60,000
Cost of asset	$250,000	Year 2	78,000
Salvage value (gross)	1,000	Year 3	97,344
Book value	0	Year 4	101,238
Tax on gain/loss	(400)	Year 5	105,287
Salvage value (net)	600	Year 6	109,499
Working capital changes		Year 7	113,879
Year 0	50,000	Year 8	118,434
Year 1	0		
Year 2	0		
Recovery in last year	50,000		
Economic life of project	8		
Tax rate	40%		

ANSWER SECTION									
YEARS	0	1	2	3	4	5	6	7	8
Investment	(250,000)								
TED		14,280	24,490	17,490	12,490	8,930	8,930	8,930	4,460
Working capital	(50,000)	0	0	0	0	0	0	0	50,000
Net salvage value									600
Operating flows		36,000	46,800	58,406	60,743	63,172	65,699	68,327	71,060
Total	(300,000)	50,280	71,290	75,896	73,233	72,102	74,629	77,257	126,120
PVIF	1.0000	0.8741	0.7641	0.6679	0.5838	0.5104	0.4461	0.3900	0.3409
Present value	(300,000)	43,951	54,472	50,692	42,756	36,798	33,293	30,127	42,991
Cum PV	(300,000)	(256,049)	(201,577)	(150,884)	(108,128)	(71,330)	(38,037)	(7,910)	35,081

Net present value	$35,081
Internal rate of return	17.49%

are cost and quality competitive and that can be delivered in a timely fashion. As stated at the outset of this chapter, notions of ABC/ABM, TOC, JIT, and strategic management are all involved in changing American businesses. In addition, as we discuss in Chapter 14, managers are looking at ways to evaluate the performance of segments (and their managers) based on both financial and nonfinancial outcomes. In this section, we look at the problems and challenges facing managers when evaluating capital asset acquisitions in this new environment.

The Moving Baseline Concept

In traditional DCF analysis, a project is evaluated as if it were discrete to the costs or revenues of the balance of the firm. With a new emphasis on quality and throughput, managers are now asking the question, "What happens to our firm in the long run if we do *not* invest in this new equipment or technology?" This is the idea of a **moving baseline**: instead of looking at the rest of the company as remaining status quo if no investment is made, specifically incorporate estimates about the *decrease* in business with no investment.[23] Thus, for example, if new equipment is going to be used to manufacture a significant component for the company's products, instead of just looking at the cost characteristics of the new equipment (acquisition cost, operating costs, maintenance, etc.), managers should also look at how sales would be affected if the new equipment were not purchased.

Assume that a company is currently generating cash flow of $150,000 annually. In some cases, managers assume that this cash flow will continue regardless of whether new equipment is purchased. However, in this situation, not investing in advanced manufacturing equipment would put it at a competitive disadvantage in quality, delivery, or cost. Exhibit 13-8 contains the basic information for this illustration. The first column shows the cash flows by year for an investment in new technology assuming no interrelationship with the rest of the company. The second column is continuing cash flows of the company at $150,000 per year again assuming independence between the new project and the other cash flows. The third column recognizes what will happen to other cash flows if the investment is not made (this is the moving baseline). Determining these estimates is another part of going beyond the project itself and seeing the effect of actions on long-term goals. Columns 2 and 3 are graphed in Figure 13-3.

Column 4 of Exhibit 13-8 shows the cash flows of the project adjusted for what would be lost if there were no investment. For Year 2, for example, while the status quo shows a cash flow of $150,000, the adjusted cash flow for the rest of the company if no investment is made is $0; therefore, there

---

[23] Some of this discussion and the illustration that follows come from Robert A. Howell and Stephen R. Soucy, "Capital Investment in the New Manufacturing Environment," *Management Accounting* (New York: National Association of Accountants, November, 1987), pp. 26–32.

Exhibit 13-8
Moving Baseline Illustration
(Figures in thousands of dollars)

Year	(1) Unadjusted Project Cash Flows	(2) Status Quo Other Cash Flows	(3) No Investment Other Cash Flows	(4) (1) + [(2) − (3)] Adjusted Project Cash Flows	(5) Project Cumulative Present Value	(6) Adjusted Project Cumulative Present Value
0	−450	150	150	−450	−450	−450
1	−420	150	75	−345	−822	−755
2	−240	150	0	−90	−1,010	−826
3	0	150	−75	225	−1,010	−670
4	240	150	−150	540	−862	−339
5	420	150	−225	795	−634	93
6	450	150	−300	900	−418	525
7	450	150	−375	975	−227	940
						$k = 13\%$

Source: Howell and Soucy, "Capital Investment in the New Manufactured Environment," pp. 30*ff.*

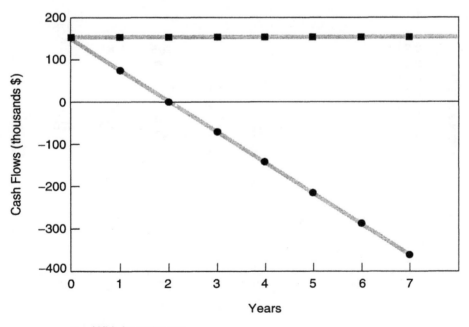

■ = With investment
● = Without investment

Figure 13-3   Other Cash Flows

is a savings of avoiding losing business if the investment of $150,000 is made, which adds to the unadjusted cash flow of the project of –$240,000 and yields –$90,000. The cash flows with and without the moving baseline are graphed in Figure 13-4.

If management were to look at the project by itself (with a relevant discount rate of 13 percent), the net present value would be –$227 thousand, as reflected in column 5 of Exhibit 13-8. Managers might be inclined to reject such a project. However, as column 6 shows, by including the moving baseline, the NPV is $940 thousand. These cumulative present values are graphed in Figure 13-5. From this illustration, you can see the value of incorporating what might happen in the rest of the company if an investment is not made.

Difficulties in Appraising Investments

Various authors reflect the problems that managers are having in coming to some conclusion about purchasing major new equipment. There are many ways that companies can incorporate new technology (sometimes called *advanced manufacturing technology* or *AMT*). Some companies are trying more extensive use of robotics. Others are looking toward computer-integrated manufacturing (CIM) where all machinery is linked and run by computers

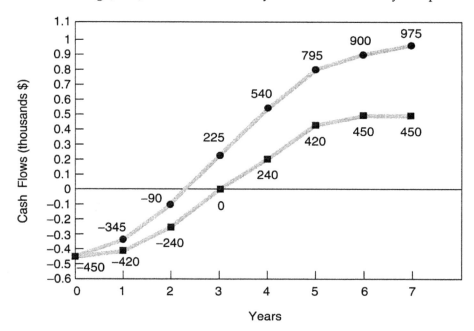

Figure 13-4   Project Cash Flows

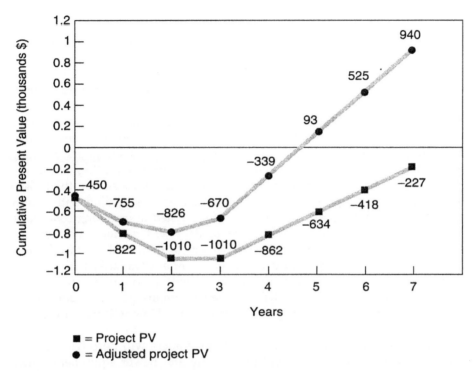

■ = Project PV
● = Adjusted project PV

Figure 13-5   Cumulative Present Values

and human attendants are more service than line personnel. Manufacturing cells are a way that existing and new equipment can be realigned on the factory floor to have minifactories making complete components or products. We also have flexible manufacturing systems (FMS), computer-aided design (CAD), computer-aided manufacturing (CAM), and so on. Managers must now decide how to adapt their analyses to incorporate all the issues that arise with various parts of AMT.

A Longer Period of Negative Cash Flows   Investments in highly sophisticated equipment may not pay off as soon as we have assumed in more traditional analysis. It might take several years before these projects start showing the overall savings projected. This is coupled with the possibility that the economic or useful life of the project might be relatively short. Thus, managers are uneasy about the large initial capital outlay coupled with a longer period before benefits are clearly shown.

Difficulty in Estimating Annual Flows   Traditional analysis puts a great deal of emphasis on establishing the annual operating flows from a project. Managers estimate product volume, prices, incremental costs of production, and other costs associated with operation (e.g., ongoing and periodic maintenance, computer programming requirements). With some new technologies, however, managers are having a harder time coming up with adequate estimates. They might have no real frame of reference in a new area: no one has done this before. All they can do is to rely on engineering estimates, which can cause problems. For example, during the 1980s, a midwestern manufacturer bid on and received a contract from the Department of Defense to produce a new type of fairly expensive radio. Part of the production technology to be used was wave soldering, a way to have almost perfect solders of key components. Managers used estimates of what they thought it would cost to buy the equipment, get it set up and running properly, and operate on an ongoing basis. Unfortunately, they found out that some of their basic estimates were way off the mark so that the project ended up with a significant loss. This company was dealing with a new product and a process that had not been fully tested in operating conditions.

Managers are also faced with how to deal with softer estimates: the effect of better quality, increased customer satisfaction, or shorter lead times, for example. With a new product, managers are always faced with estimating demand and the price that the market is willing to pay. Let us say that a company decides to move to JIT management philosophy and adopts some new manufacturing technology at the same time. How will this affect sales of existing products that had been manufactured using other equipment? Managers will also want to look at how customers will perceive the company given its new management philosophy and newer equipment. There might be a positive effect on other product lines even though they continue to be made on existing equipment. This also goes back to the moving baseline concept: the whole thing should be looked at in reverse (lost business) if such new equipment is not installed.

Much is said about quality and the comparison of U.S. goods versus those made in other countries. U.S. automobile makers have long been faced with the perception by American consumers that vehicles made in other countries (and even those made in U.S. factories of foreign manufacturers) are higher in quality than U.S. brands. These automakers have invested hundreds of millions of dollars revamping manufacturing. In looking at an analysis of these investments, managers are faced with estimating how long it will take public perception to catch up with what they see as a quite improved reality regarding quality.

Changes in Working Capital   One of the biggest savings from both newer management philosophies such as JIT or TOC, from reorganizing production into manufacturing cells, and from advanced technology is to permanently reduce capital invested in raw materials, work in process, and finished goods. In the traditional analysis of cash flows for a new project, it was usually anticipated that working capital would rise at the outset of the project's life and then would fall to its preproject level at the end of the project's economic life. Now we are saying that working capital will *fall* at the beginning. Since this change often results from how a plant is organized and managed, such a reduction should not be reversed at the end of a project's useful life. Thus, managers are not only faced with estimating the impact on working capital given proposed changes, but also they will show this only as a savings at the beginning of the project and will assume that they will not increase it again at its end.

New Evaluation Methods

The basic DCF analysis provides managers with a starting point. In a previous section we discussed a way to deal with risk associated with managers' original estimates: sensitivity analysis. However, as discussed above, there is more to analyzing a proposal than just looking at the numbers, even if we can try to put some numbers on some of the intangibles (e.g., effect on customer satisfaction). In addition, as illustrated in the moving baseline concept and in Chapter 12, managers want to see how any new project is going to move the company toward its goals. Engwall proposes a multiple-attribute decision model or MADM whereby management can incorporate critical factors in how they rank projects.[24] He proposes that all projects be looked at and ranked on

1. Financial quantitative factors, including NPV, operating profit margin, level of investment, and level of savings
2. Nonfinancial quantitative factors, including throughput time, process yield, schedule attainment, and lead time
3. Qualitative factors, such as whether the new process is required for a new product, whether the investment would improve an existing process, whether it would yield ongoing cost reductions, how it contributed to basic research and development, and how it would affect technology or product obsolescence

He proposes that managers measure what they can and then place values on each of these factors for each project. However, rather than keeping measures in dollars, Engwall suggests all values would have to be converted into some scale (such as 0 to 5). Thus, for example, any project with an NPV of greater than $5 million might get a value of 5, those with from $2.5 to $5 million a value of 4, and so on. All the critical factors for each project would be so valued. These individual values would be multiplied by weights for the relative importance of each factor; all the weights would be in percents and would have to add to 100 percent. Then, to incorporate some element of risk assessment, each weighted value would be multiplied by a confidence level factor, a number between 0 and 1. Thus, if a manager feels fairly certain about the NPV results, she might give that a confidence factor of

---

[24] See the article by Richard L. Engwall, "Investment Evaluation Technologies," *Journal of Cost Management* (New York: Warren, Gorham, & Lamont, Spring 1988), pp. 40–44, for a complete discussion of this model.

0.9. However, if her confidence about how this would affect throughput time is lower, she might assign a confidence factor of 0.6 or less. Finally, the adjusted weighted values would be summed for each project. This then allows for an overall ranking of projects using the MADM. Engwall offers the examples of a low-risk standalone project as compared to a high-risk flexible manufacturing system. These are illustrated in Exhibit 13-9.

However, as with all models, managers should be careful to apply a rule of common sense here: Are the final rankings logical? If not, then managers should reexamine the critical factors, the values assigned for each factor, the weights, and the confidence level they have for each factor. Such a model needs subjective adjustment and testing in order for it to work. It also cannot remain static as needs and priorities change over time.

EXPECTED MONETARY VALUE AND EXPECTED UTILITY

This section explores some of the fundamentals of capital budgeting under conditions of uncertainty. Up to this point in the discussion, we have assumed either certainty or have used sensitivity analysis to deal with riskiness in estimates. However, managers can incorporate notions of expected monetary value and/or expected utility in their analyses.

Expected Value Analysis

Assume that mangers are evaluating a single project and think that there are several events that can affect cash flow. The estimated cash flows by each event as well as the probabilities for each event are shown in Exhibit 13-10. The expected net present value [E(NPV)] is $145 as shown in the exhibit.

As with any use of expected value and discrete probabilities, managers should recognize that (1) even though they are modeling the problem as though there is a zero probability of any other NPV than the five shown, in reality there may be other NPV's that are possible; (2) while the E(NPV) = $145, actual results would be –$100, 0, $150, $210, or $300 for a single project if the discrete points are taken literally; and (3) the use of expected value in decision making is valid when managers use this criterion on a regular basis so that the probabilities have a chance to work over many trials.

While a measure of central tendency is useful, managers also like to know some measure of dispersion such as the standard deviation. The formula to calculate the variance of a discrete distribution is reflected in Exhibit 13-10; it is the sum of the squared deviations from the mean weighted by the probability of each event occurring. The standard deviation is $130. Thus, with a mean of $145 and a standard deviation of $130, managers can assess the probability of achieving a positive net present value. If we assume a normal distribution and transform our estimates from a discrete distribution to a continuous one, the z value is –1.12 [(0 – 145)/130] yielding a

Exhibit 13-9
Example of MADM Evaluation[25]

A. Low-Risk Standalone Project

Critical Factor	Weight A	Value B	Confidence Level C	Total (AxBxC)
Financial Quantitative				
Net present value	20	3	1.0	60
Operating profit margin	25	2	1.0	50
Level of investment	5	4	1.0	20
Level of savings	5	2	1.0	10
Nonfinancial Quantitative				
Throughput time	7	2	1.0	14
Process yield	15	2	1.0	30
Schedule attainment	3	2	1.0	6
Lead time	5	2	1.0	10
Qualitative				
Process	5	1	1.0	5
Basic R&D	2	0		0
Technology obsolescence	5	2	1.0	10
Product obsolescence	3	0		0
Total	100			215

B. High-Risk Flexible Manufacturing System

Critical Factor	Weight A	Value B	Confidence Level C	Total (AxBxC)
Financial Quantitative				
Net present value	20	0		0
Operating profit margin	25	5	0.7	88
Level of investment	5	2	0.7	7
Level of savings	5	4	0.7	14
Nonfinancial Quantitative				
Throughput time	7	4	0.9	25
Process yield	15	4	0.9	54
Schedule attainment	3	4	1.0	12
Lead time	5	3	1.0	15
Qualitative				
Process	5	3	1.0	15
Basic R&D	2	0		0
Technology obsolescence	5	4	1.0	20
Product obsolescence	3	0		0
Total	100			250

---

[25] Engwall, Exhibits 2 and 3, p. 43.

Exhibit 13-10ᵃ
Net Present Value and Expected Monetary Value

Events	1	2	3	4	5
Cash flows					
Year 0	($500)	($500)	($400)	($300)	($500)
Year 1	103	132	149	140	219
Year 2	103	132	149	140	219
Year 3	103	132	149	140	219
Year 4	103	132	149	140	219
Year 5	103	132	149	140	219
NPV @ 10%	($100)	$0	$150	$210	$300
p(event)	10%	20%	25%	20%	25%
E(NPV) 145 =	-10 +	0 +	37 +	42 +	75
VARIANCE					
NPV	-100	0	150	210	300
PNV-E (NPV)	-244	-144	5	65	156
Deviation					
squared	59,609	20,797	28	4,248	24,213
p(event)	10%	20%	25%	20%	25%
Weighted value	5,961	4,159	7	850	6,053
Variance		17,030			
Standard deviation		$130			

ᵃThere is rounding shown. The spreadsheet actually uses unrounded figures.

$p(\text{NPV} > 0)$ of about 87 percent. Managers could also use the discrete data to get an assessment of $p(\text{NPV} > 0)$, which would be 70 percent ($0.25 + 0.20 + 0.25 = 0.70$).

Managers can also compare this project to another that, say, has an E(NPV) of $180 and a standard deviation of $150. The expected monetary value (EMV) decision criterion when comparing two projects would be as follows:

1. If both projects have the same standard deviation, choose the one with the higher EMV.
2. If both projects have the same EMV, choose the one with the lower standard deviation.
3. If one project has both a higher EMV and a higher standard deviation compared to the other, then the managers' risk attitude comes into play.[26]

---

[26] Remember that the manager is acting as an agent for the owners of the business. Thus, a manager's risk attitude should reflect the manager's role as agent.

Expected Utility

Managers do not always strive to maximize the expected monetary value.[27] If a manager simply uses expected monetary values as the single criterion for choosing, the choice is risk neutral since it did not include any measure of dispersion (variance). However, managers and the firms they work for are not always risk neutral. For example, say that a company is looking at an opportunity that could yield a NPV from –$500,000 to $1,000,000. Even if the E(NPV) were to equal $400,000, managers may not invest if the loss of $400,000 or $500,000 would bankrupt or severely injure the company or severely damage their careers.

The same notions of expected utility discussed in Chapter 8 apply here. Assume that the utility function of the manager assessing this project for the firm is $100/\ln$ (NPV), a risk-averse function. Exhibit 13-11 shows that the expected utility [E(U)] is negative. Therefore, the risk-averse manager would not accept this project even though the EMV is positive. You should verify the utility figures shown in the exhibit.

Expected Value and a Portfolio of Projects

In some cases, managers evaluate opportunities that are not mutually exclusive. Consider a new firm that is evaluating several lines of business

Exhibit 13-11
Net Present Value and Expected Utility

Events	1	2	3	4	5
Cash flows					
Year 0	($500)	($500)	($400)	($300)	($500)
Year 1	103	132	149	140	219
Year 2	103	132	149	140	219
Year 3	103	132	149	140	219
Year 4	103	132	149	140	219
Year 5	103	132	149	140	219
NPV @ 10%	($100)	$0	$150	$210	$300
U(NPV)	0.00	-94.98	19.96	18.71	17.53
p(event)	10%	20%	25%	20%	25%
E(U) -5.88 =	0.00	-19.00 +	4.99 +	3.74 +	4.38

[27] This discussion does not include the notion of *satisficing* rather than *maximizing* but brings into play risk aversion.

and has prepared net present value analyses for each area. They could adopt one or more product lines and, therefore, would have a portfolio of projects. If only one product is made (one project accepted), managers could assess risk using sensitivity analysis or expected value as discussed above. However, once more than one investment is undertaken, management has a portfolio of projects and they need to know how the projects interact with one another: Are they independent or dependent?

The notion of independence can take on several meanings. First, it is possible that some products are *technologically dependent* in that they use the same machinery or are the result of a common joint process. Other projects may be dependent in the *marketplace*; tires for new cars are dependent on new car production. The notion of dependence or independence used here is a *statistical* one: Are the cash flows from one project dependent on the cash flows from another project? If so, then there is dependence between the projects.

Assume that an investment opportunity is as follows:

Year 0	−$40,000
Year 1	25,000
Year 2	17,500
Year 3	10,000

If the relevant discount rate is 6 percent, this project has a positive net present value of $7,128. However, if these cash flows represent one of two possible states of nature, then this project may not be as attractive as it now seems. Exhibit 13-12 shows the expected cash flows for this opportunity (Project A) given two events (states of nature) that can occur. The expected net present value is -$508. In this case, managers would probably choose to reject Project A based on expected monetary value.

However, assume that there is another project that is being considered at the same time, Project B. Cash flows given the same two events (such as a strong or weak economy, for example) are shown in Exhibit 13-13 along with NPV's and E(NPV) for Project B. The variances for both projects are shown in Exhibit 13-13 as well. Note that Project B does well given Event 2 and does poorly given Event 1. This is the exact opposite of Project A.

The variance of two projects (A and B in this example) is

$$\text{Variance (A + B)} = \text{Variance(A)} + \text{Variance(B)} + 2\,\text{Cov(A,B)}$$

where Cov(A,B) is the covariance of the two projects. The covariance measures the relationship between projects and is defined as

$$\text{Cov(A,B)} = E[NPV(A) * NPV(B)] - E[NPV(A)] * E[NPV(B)]$$

The covariance can also be expressed as

Exhibit 13-12
Expected Value-Project A

Relevant discount rate   6%

Year	0	1	2	3	NPV
Project A					
Event 1	($40,000)	$25,000	$17,500	$10,000	$7,128
Event 2	(40,000)	20,000	10,000	7,500	($5,599)
EMV	p(event 1)			0.4	$2,851
	p(event 2)			0.6	(3,359)

				E(NPV)	($508)

Variance

		NPV(A)	NPV(A)^2
	Event 1	$7,128	$50,813,175
	Event 2	(5,599)	31,349,080
	EV	($508)	$39,134,718

			Standard Deviation
	E(NPV^2) − E(NPV)^2 = Variance		
Variance A	39,134,718 − 258,146 = $38,876,572		$6,235

$$Cov(A,B) = \sigma_A * \sigma_B * \rho_{AB}$$

where ρ_{AB} is a measure of association much like r in linear regression and takes on values from −1 to 1. The size and the sign of the covariance (−$33,674,641) show that there is a strong negative correlation between the two projects. Thus, when adopting both projects, not only will the combined expected value be positive ($2,530) but also the standard deviation of the two projects together is less than one project by itself ($834 versus $6,235).

To see the effect of changes in ρ_{AB}, look at the bottom of Exhibit 13-13. The lowest variance (and standard deviation) is achieved when there is perfect negative correlation—the case that seems to exist given the calculated value of the covariance. If the projects were positively correlated, then when one was successful, the other would also be successful; when one failed, the other would fail as well. With ρ_{AB} of zero, either the two projects are statistically independent, or the figures just yield a covariance of 0. With independence, one project does not relate to the other, and the variance of the two projects would just be the sum of the independent variances [$68,045,333 = $38,876,572 + $29,168,761].

When managers choose a portfolio that has a strong positive ρ_{AB}, there is a better chance of making a larger net present value if there is success and

Exhibit 13-13
Variance and Covariance Analysis

Relevant discount rate   6%

	Year	0	1	2	3	NPV
Project A						
Event 1		($40,000)	$25,000	$17,500	$10,000	$7,128
Event 2		(40,000)	20,000	10,000	7,500	($5,599)
EMV						
p(event 1)				0.4		$2,851
p(event 2)				0.6		(3,359)

				E(NPV)		($508)
Project B						
Event 1		($50,000)	$10,000	$30,000	$12,000	($3,576)
Event 2		(50,000)	15,000	35,000	15,000	$7,448
EMV						
p(event 1)				0.4		($1,430)
p(event 2)				0.6		4,469

				E(NPV)		$3,038

Variances

	NPV(A)	NPV(A)²	NPV(B)	NPV(B)²	NPV(A)*NPV(B)
Event 1	$7,128	$50,813,175	($3,576)	$12,788,809	($25,491,959)
Event 2	(5,599)	31,349,080	7,448	55,475,909	(41,702,742)
EV	($508)	$39,134,718	$3,038	$38,401,069	($35,218,429)

	E(NPV²)	E[NPV(A)]*E[NPV(B)]		E(NPV)²	=	Variance	Standard Deviation
Variance A	39,134,718	–		258,146	=	$38,876,572	$6,235
Variance B	38,401,069	–		9,232,308	=	$29,168,761	$5,401

E[NPV(A)*NPV(B)] – E[NPV(A)]*E[NPV(B)] = Covariance

Covariance   (35,218,429) – (1,543,788) = (33,674,641)

Sensitivity analysis on Rho:

Rho	Cov(A,B)	Var(A + B)	Standard Deviation (A+B)	EV(A+B)
1	33,674,641	135,394,615	11,636	2,530
0.5	16,837,321	101,719,974	10,086	2,530
0	0	68,045,333	8,249	2,530
-0.5	(16,837,321)	34,370,692	5,863	2,530
-1	(33,674,641)	696,051	834	2,530

a greater probability of losing more (given failure) as well. In addition, the variance can be quite a bit larger with a strong positive relationship. On the other hand, with a negative ρ_{AB}, gains are dampened, but there is a lower chance of losing a great deal. The variance of the two projects is at its lowest point when there is perfect negative correlation between the projects. Using these basic principles of portfolio analysis, managers can reduce overall risk. Thus, a risk-averse manager is able consciously to lower the risk of one project by adopting another project that is negatively correlated to the first.

This same analysis is possible with more than two projects. The formula for the total variance would be expanded to incorporate all the relationships. Thus, for a two-project example, there is one covariance since there is only one pair of projects that can be related. In a three-project illustration, there are three covariances since there are three different pairs that can be considered. The number of covariances goes up as the number of opportunities rises.

Some Problems with Capital Budgeting and Uncertainty

Before leaving the area of capital budgeting under conditions of uncertainty, we should note that there are problems associated with the method illustrated in this section. An earlier warning bears repeating: expected value can be reasonable only when enough projects are evaluated so that the law of large numbers allows the notion of average and standard deviation a chance. In addition, as with the discussion about cost-volume-profit under conditions of uncertainty, there can be distribution assumption problems that would negate the use of a normal distribution (e.g., if expected sales are normally distributed and expected contribution margin is also normally distributed, the multiplication of the two together yields a distribution that is *not* a normal distribution). For these reasons, managers tend to investigate conditions under uncertainty by using spreadsheet sensitivity analysis, by employing statistical analyses like expected net present value on a basic level, or by using simulation techniques. People underestimate the probability that extreme values can occur through chance. Thus, even if there are a large number of trials (e.g., 1,000 iterations in a simulation), there still can be bad outcomes.

INVESTING DECISION VERSUS FINANCING DECISION

While many managers try to combine the decision of whether to invest with the decision about the form of financing that will be the most beneficial to the firm, this may lead to incorrect decisions. The *investing decision* should be made quite separately from the *financing decision*. The issue is not whether to invest and buy or invest and lease. The questions are whether to invest and *then* whether to buy (through borrowing, use of excess cash, and so on), or to lease.

The Investing Decision

The investing decision is based on whether the present value of the cash flows from an opportunity discounted at the relevant hurdle rate exceeds the cost of the project. Present-value analysis incorporates the weighted-average cost of capital in the discount rate. This rate is an implicit opportunity cost of funds to the company. Specific financing in the analysis of cash flows can lead to erroneous conclusions or incorrect figures. For example, if managers used a WACC of 10 percent as the discount rate and then included principal and interest payments based on the same economic life and 10 percent, the analysis would be flawed since financing would have been included twice: once in the discounting of cash flows, and once in the specific loan payments. The investing decision is whether to invest. The financing decision follows the investing decision and is dependent on it: *Given* the decision to invest, what is the best way to finance a project?

Consider a company that has estimated the cash flows for a project as follows:

cost of project:	$200,000
annual cash flows—10 years	33,000/year
net present value at 10 percent	2,770

Thus, from a quantitative view, this is an acceptable project; it has a positive NPV at the relevant cost of capital or hurdle rate. However, suppose that instead of looking at the original investment as $200,000, the managers had looked at an offer the manufacturer had made to delay payment to the end of the first year of the project and then to pay $240,000. Thus, instead of using a cost of $200,000 in Year 0, managers used a cost of $240,000 in Year 1. This would yield a present value at 10 percent of –$866 as you should verify. In this case, managers may turn down the project. What has happened is that the manufacturer has, in essence, loaned the company $200,000 for a year and has charged $40,000 or 20 percent interest for that year. Even if the interest is deductible and would cost a net of, say, $24,000 at a marginal tax rate of 40 percent, including the specific financing flows has clouded the analysis and can lead to dysfunctional decisions.

Other examples could be constructed showing that a project is not acceptable when judged against the relevant after-tax hurdle rate but looks acceptable when financing is included in the analysis. Some would argue that it would be wise to accept a project in this case since it is earning more than the cost to finance it. This is the major fallacy with looking at the investing and financing decisions at the same time. *Remember that managers have decided that all projects should return at least the weighted-average cost of capital or the goal-oriented discount rate.* This has been set as the basic decision hurdle. Accepting projects that are below the relevant discount rate violates this basic decision and the notion of opportunity cost. Rejecting projects that would be financed above the average unfairly raises the discount rate above the opportunity cost.

Managers do successfully combine an analysis of discounted cash flows and one of how to finance a project. However, such a combination is fraught with problems and, more often than not, contains errors of logic and can lead to poor decisions. For this reason, it is wise to completely separate the investing decision from the financing decision.

Leasing versus Buying

Leasing is one form of financing. Since it is treated differently from other forms of financing, it has been common to compare leasing versus buying. Two things should be noted at the outset. First, the tax treatment of leases is not tied to how leases are handled on the books for financial accounting purposes. Thus, it is not important whether a lease is classified an operating lease or a capitalized lease.[28] Second, the term *buying*, as used in "leasing versus buying," has many meanings. Companies can buy assets using excess available cash, using cash borrowed from a bank or other lending institution, or using cash from equity or debt offerings, to name some general sources of cash. Thus, to simplify the analysis, managers can compare the costs of leasing to the cost of buying, given the best form of financing. If managers have compared all sources of financing they would employ if the company owned an asset and decided to borrow money from an insurance company at 12 percent, this would be the relevant "buy" alternative to be compared with the costs of leasing. Finally, the only costs that are compared in the decision to invest or to buy (and borrow in this case) would be the incremental cash flows of each alternative. Given management's decision to invest in an asset, the question becomes, what is the best form of financing?

If a firm owns an asset, it can depreciate the asset and reap the tax shield from the depreciation. On the other hand, the company is liable for any and all after-tax costs of the asset, including such expenses as maintenance, personal property taxes, and so on. Any interest that is incurred to purchase the asset is deductible. Principal payments are not deductible for taxes.

When an asset is leased, the leasing company takes the depreciation. However, the lessee can deduct the entire lease payment from income and thereby reduce taxes. In addition, some leases include maintenance or personal property taxes, for example. It is important to know what is included in the lease so a comparison can be made on an equal basis to the cost of owning.

There have been many algorithms suggested for the comparison of leasing versus buying. The purpose of these methods is to derive the implicit interest rate included in the lease. We can accomplish the same end by setting up two tables showing cash flows for owning and cash flows for

---

[28] An exception to this would be difference between taxable income and book income that could invoke provisions of the alternate minimum tax.

leasing. The cash flows from both options can be discounted at the opportunity cost for owning (e.g., the specific bank interest rate or opportunity cost of investing excess cash rather than using it to purchase an asset). If the present value of the cost of owning is less than the present value of the cost of leasing, then the effective interest rate in the lease is higher than the opportunity cost of funds for owning. Managers can also find the interest rate that forces the cost of owning to exactly equal the cost of leasing. This is the effective interest rate of the lease.

Exhibit 13-14 shows the cost of owning an asset and borrowing funds at 10 percent (6 percent after taxes) compared to leasing the asset. All differential cash flows are shown in the exhibit. The present value of the cost of the lease is more than the present value of the cost of owning and borrowing. Thus, the effective or implicit interest rate of the lease is more than 10 percent. As shown in Exhibit 13-15, the effective rate of the lease is 7.86 percent after taxes or 13.1 percent before taxes, the rate that forces the cash flows from leasing to equal the cash flows from owning.

Both Exhibit 13-14 and Exhibit 13-15 were created using an electronic spreadsheet program. Once the values have been entered in the data section of the worksheet, managers can find the effective interest rate by varying the percent until the present value of the two sets of flows is about equal. In addition, a generic form of this lease-versus-own spreadsheet can be adapted for all such decisions by managers.

CAPITAL RATIONING

Choosing among projects when there is no limit on available funds is based on a single criterion for each DCF model: which projects have a positive NPV or an IRR over the relevant discount rate. However, firms are often faced with constrained funds either through internal rationing or through external rationing.

Managers may decide to use only a certain amount of funds for capital projects over the next year or so. Perhaps they do not want to stretch outside funding opportunities or want to retain some cash for emergencies. They may have an acceptable balance of debt and equity and do not want to change this particular mix. This is an internal limit on funds. On the other hand, managers may find that funds are not readily available on the market at rates they are willing to pay. While finance theory states that there is a strong capital market and that funds are available at some rate,[29] this rate may be just too high. This leads to an external limit on funds.

Thus, due to an internal funds constraint, a company may not be able to invest in all projects that have, say, a positive net present value at the relevant discount rate based on WACC. Three methods are proposed to

---

[29] See Ezra Solomon, "The Arithmetic of Capital Budgeting," *Journal of Finance* (April 1956).

Exhibit 13-14
Financing Through a Loan or Through a Lease

```
DATA SECTION
Cost of asset           $100,000
Tax life                   5 years
Type of depreciation    ACRS
Cost of loan              10% After-tax cost  6%
Marginal tax rate         40%

Lease payments-each year $ 26,000
Life of lease              5 years
```

COST OF OWNING

Year	0	1	2	3	4	5	6
Investment	($100,000)						
Tax shield of depreciation		$ 8,000	$12,800	$7,680	$4,608	$4,608	$2,304
PVIF	1.0000	0.9434	0.8900	0.8396	0.7921	0.7473	0.7050
Present value	($100,000)	$ 7,547	$11,392	$6,448	$3,650	$3,443	$1,624
Present value of the cost of owning	($ 65,895)						

COST OF LEASING

	0	1	2	3	4	5	6
Lease payments (net)	($ 15,600)	($15,600)	($15,600)	($15,600)	($15,600)		
Present value	($ 15,600)	($14,717)	($13,884)	($13,098)	($12,357)		
Present value of the cost of leasing	($ 69,656)						

Exhibit 13-15
Effective Interest Rate of Lease

DATA SECTION
Cost of asset $100,000
Tax life   5 years
Type of depreciation   ACRS
Cost of loan   13.10% After-tax cost 7.86%
Marginal tax rate   40%

Lease payments—each year $ 26,000
Life of lease   5 years

COST OF OWNING

Year	0	1	2	3	4	5	6
Investment	($100,000)						
Tax shield of depreciation		$ 8,000	$12,800	$ 7,680	$4,608	$4,608	$2,304
PVIF	1.0000	0.9271	0.8596	0.7969	0.7389	0.6850	0.6351
Present value	($100,000)	$ 7,417	$11,002	$ 6,120	$3,405	$3,157	$1,463

Present value of
the cost of owning   ($ 67,436)

COST OF LEASING

	0	1	2	3	4	5	6
Lease payments (net)	($ 15,600)	($15,600)	($15,600)	($15,600)	($15,600)		
Present value	($ 15,600)	($14,463)	($13,409)	($12,432)	($11,526)		

Present value of the
cost of leasing   ($ 67,431)

solve the capital rationing dilemma: solution by inspection, solution by raising the discount rate, and solution through mathematical programming.

Solution by Inspection

One way to find the group of projects that will yield the highest total NPV given funds availability is to look at the list of projects and come to a solution by inspection. Assume that a company is considering four projects and the relevant discount rate is 10 percent. The cash flows and net present values of the projects are shown in Exhibit 13-16. While all have positive NPV's, project D has the highest NPV even though it has the most cash needs overall. If we assume that cash is limited to $40,000 in Year 0, the combinations of projects management could accept are as follows (assuming that management would invest up to $40,000 in total and that the projects are not mutually exclusive):

Combination	Cash Use	Total NPV
B	$30,000	$ 6,000
A and C	40,000	10,801
A and D	40,000	16,002
C and D	40,000	18,801

If none of these projects are mutually exclusive, the best combination is C and D.

While it is relatively simple to enumerate the possible combinations in a choice involving these four investment opportunities, inspection can become unwieldy with several projects. Even with four projects, there can be several combinations that fit given constraints. Imagine a problem with twenty or thirty projects, and it readily becomes apparent that other methods need to be investigated given capital rationing.[30]

Exhibit 13-16
Capital Rationing
Illustrative Data

	Project			
	A	**B**	**C**	**D**
Year 0	($20,000)	($30,000)	($20,000)	($20,000)
Year 1	10,000	10,000	(30,000)	(50,000)
Year 2	5,313	9,546	19,000	27,295
Year 3	5,313	9,546	19,000	27,295
Year 4	5,313	9,546	19,000	27,295
Year 5	5,313	9,546	19,000	27,295
NPV @ 10%	4,001	6,000	6,800	12,001

[30] With, say, 20 projects, there would be 2^n combinations or 2^{20}, which is over 1,000,000 ways to combine the 20 projects . . . and this is before any constraints are considered.

Solution by Raising the Discount Rate

Another way to solve the capital rationing problem is to raise the discount rate and see what projects still have positive NPV's. Managers could establish a rate higher than the WACC, for example, and choose only those projects that exceeded that rate. Exhibit 13-17 extends Exhibit 13-16 by adding on figures showing the net present value of the four projects at discount rates ranging from the assumed WACC of 10 percent up to 20 percent. Project C drops out at 16 percent, D at 18 percent, B at 19 percent, and A at 20 percent. (In many ways, ranking by raising the discount rate is much like ranking by using the IRR's of each project. The difference is that it is applied using sensitivity analysis rather than solving for the IRR.) Thus, one reason for using a goal-oriented discount rate may be to choose among projects in a capital rationing setting. If managers had chosen, say, a hurdle rate of 18 percent, then Projects A and B would be selected. However, with a cash constraint of $40,000 in year 0, only B can be implemented with a total NPV of $6,000, lower than the solution of C and D with a combined NPV of $18,001.

Exhibit 13-17
Capital Rationing
Solution by Raising Discount Rate

	Project			
	A	**B**	**C**	**D**
Year 0	($20,000)	($30,000)	($20,000)	($20,000)
Year 1	10,000	10,000	(30,000)	(50,000)
Year 2	5,313	9,546	19,000	27,295
Year 3	5,313	9,546	19,000	27,295
Year 4	5,313	9,546	19,000	27,295
Year 5	5,313	9,546	19,000	27,295
NPV @ 10%	4,001	6,000	6,800	12,001
11%	3,476	5,126	5,476	10,130
12%	2,979	4,300	4,233	8,374
13%	2,509	3,520	3,066	6,726
14%	2,063	2,781	1,970	5,178
15%	1,640	2,082	941	3,725
16%	1,239	1,421	(26)	2,361
17%	858	794	(934)	1,079
18%	497	201	(1,787)	(126)
19%	155	(362)	(2,589)	(1,257)
20%	(171)	(894)	(3,343)	(2,320)

Mathematical Programming Solutions

Capital rationing problems can become quite complex. Management may have cash constraints in several years. Adopting projects means a series of cash inflows and/or cash outflows in each year depending on the particular group of projects chosen. With a large list of projects that last over several years and some cash projections about availability over those same years, solution by inspection becomes difficult and raising the discount rate does not deal with limited funds over several years.

Assume that besides the $40,000 limit on funds in Year 0 for the four projects shown in Exhibit 13-16, there is a $60,000 limit on funds in Year 1. While this problem could be made more complex by adding cash constraints over several years, the first two years are binding since there are no planned cash outflows from any of these projects after Year 1. An integer program[31] could be set up as follows with positive numbers in the constraints denoting cash needs.

$$\text{Max } \$4,001 \text{ A} + \$6,000 \text{ B} + \$6,800 \text{ C} + \$12,001 \text{ D}$$
$$\text{S. t.}$$
$$20,000 \text{ A} + 30,000 \text{ B} + 20,000 \text{ C} + 20,000 \text{ D} <= \$40,000$$
$$-10,000 \text{ A} - 10,000 \text{ B} + 30,000 \text{ C} + 50,000 \text{ D} <= 60,000$$
$$\text{A, B, C, D} = 0 \text{ or } 1$$

This is solved using an integer program since managers have to adopt or reject a whole project. The cash flows in Exhibit 13-16 are shown for Years 0 and 1 in the constraints. The objective function is to pick that set of projects that will yield the highest total NPV given the constraints. The solution to this problem is to invest in Projects A and D with a total NPV of $16,001. All $40,000 is used in Year 0, while there is $20,000 left unused in Year 1 (−$10,000 + $50,000 = $40,000 and $60,000 is available). In this relatively simple case, you can verify this solution without the use of a computer-based integer programming model. However, with, say, twenty or thirty opportunities and cash constraints covering several years, mathematical programming becomes a welcome option. Several microcomputer programs are available to make these computations easy to accomplish.[32]

The solution above is based on the assumptions that funds cannot be transferred between periods, that managers know the cash flows with relative certainty, and that the projects are independent. While these assumptions may weaken the model in some sense, managers can perform sensitivity analysis to see how changes affect the combination chosen using mathematical programming. Simulation can be used in the face of uncertainty to estimate variable values for use in an integer programming solution.

---

[31] This discussion assumes some basic knowledge of linear programming and integer programming. (See Chapter 6.)

[32] One easy-to-use package is *LINDO* by Linus Schrage (The Scientific Press, 1991).

SUMMARY

While managers have embraced basic discounted cash flow techniques for many years, they are being challenged today to change how they use these techniques and to make DCF analysis part of a bigger and more integrative view of how capital asset acquisition decisions affect the entire company. Chapters 2, 3, and 12 especially emphasize how managers are looking more closely at *management* instead of just *cost* and how decisions affect corporate strategy. The opening quotations of this chapter set the stage for the issues in capital budgeting: managers should look not only at the financial numbers associated with projects but also at the nonfinancial quantitative factors and the qualitative factors. In addition, projects should not be viewed discretely but should be examined as part of overall strategy. This includes investigating what would happen if a project is not adopted, the moving baseline concept.

More attention should also be given to the project identification and development stages. This ties in well with the notion of wanting projects to relate to the overall corporate goals. A post audit of a decision allows managers to look at whether these goals have been achieved.

Managers are concerned with risk since many projects involving advanced manufacturing techniques call for large investments in unproven processes. Methods to deal with risk include sensitivity analysis, looking at some way to weight other parts of an analysis by a confidence factor, simulation, and the like. More formal risk analysis can include looking at portfolios and measures of variation. In addition, managers' utility functions can be included in analyses.

Finally, we looked at financing versus investing decisions, which includes the lease-versus-own option, and we looked at problems brought about by capital rationing. This whole chapter's set of concerns is built on a basis of the basic strengths and weaknesses of DCF models, particularly NPV and IRR.

This chapter is a brief summary of some of the complexities found in capital budgeting. It really is an introduction to these areas, one that can be expanded by reviewing relevant material from not only the area of cost management but also finance.

❖ *APPENDIX 13A*

DISCOUNTED-CASH-FLOW MODELS: A REVIEW

TIME VALUE OF MONEY

Money has a time value. If one were to be offered $100 today or $100 a year from now, most people would want the $100 today. If invested, the funds would be worth more than $100 in a year. If in need of a $100 loan, receiving the $100 today means that borrowing could be delayed for a year with resulting savings in interest cost.

The sum of $100 received today and invested at 10 percent would yield $110 in a year. Thus, $110 is the *future value* in one year of $100 received today and invested at 10 percent. You can verify that $121 would be the future value in two years of $100 received today at 10 percent. In reverse, $100 is the *present value* at 10 percent of receiving $110 a year from now, and it is the present value at 10 percent of receiving $121 two years from now.

In formula form the future value of a single sum is

where $FV = PV\,(1 + i)^t$

FV = future value

PV = present value

i = rate of interest

t = time indicator (usually expressed in year terms)

this can be rewritten as

$$PV = FV(1 + i)^{-t}$$

or

$$PV = FV\frac{1}{(1 + i)^t}$$

Most capital projects involve cash flows that occur over several periods of time. Merely summing the cash flows received over, say, ten years would ignore the time value of money. Thus, managers need to convert all cash flows into a single period of time through discounted-cash-flow (DCF) or present-value models.

DCF MODELS

There are two basic present-value or DCF models: net present value (NPV), internal rate of return (IRR). Assume the cash flows for a capital project shown below.

January 1, 19X0 – invest	$1,100
December 31, 19X0 – receive	500
December 31, 19X1 – receive	600
December 31, 19X2 – receive	700

Note the early simplifying assumptions of this model: the original investment takes place on the first day of the project (usually termed *Time Period* or *Year 0*) and the other cash flows (either negative or positive) are received (spent) on the last day of each year. Each of the DCF models translates the nominal flows from all three years of this project and puts them in present-value terms as of Year 0. In both models, there is one unknown. While some of the other variables may be estimated, each model solves for just one unknown.

Net Present Value   The net present value (NPV) model is a sum of the present values of the cash flows (inflows and outflows) over the life of a project *given* a required discount rate.[33] Thus, the only unknown is the sum of the present values. All other variables—including cash flows, the life of the project, relevant tax considerations, and the relevant discount rate—are given (estimated). Using values from Table A-3 at the end of the book, the NPV's of the illustration at 8, 12, and 30 percent are as follows:

Time Period	Cash Flow	PV @ 8%	PV @ 12%	PV @ 30%
Year 0	−$1,100	−$1,100	−$1,100	−$1,100
Year 1	500	463	446	385
Year 2	600	514	478	355
Year 3	700	556	498	319
NPV		$ 433	$ 323	−$ 42

The NPV of a project goes down as the relevant discount rate goes up, holding all else constant. At some point, around 30 percent in this example, the NPV is negative.

Internal Rate of Return   When the net present value of a project is exactly zero, the present value of the future flows exactly equals the Year 0 net flows. The internal rate of return (IRR) solves for the rate of interest (discount rate) that will force the NPV to be zero. Thus, the unknown in the IRR model is the discount rate. NPV is given as zero.

In the illustration above, the IRR must be somewhere below 30 percent since the NPV is negative at 30 percent. You should be able to verify by hand (using a calculator) or by an electronic spreadsheet and using the formula for present value (present-value interest factor = $(1 + i)^{-t}$ where $t = 1$, 2, and 3) that the IRR is about 27.5 percent. Remember that the formula refers to a single sum received in the future. Since, in this illustration, there are single sums in each of three years, the formula should be applied separately to each cash flow and the sum of all four years (including the nondiscounted flows from Year 0) yields the NPV.

---

[33] The discussion in the body of the chapter refers to the relevant discount rate as k rather than i, a more general term.

❖ *APPENDIX 13B*

TAX REFORM ACT OF 1986

Under the 1981 and 1982 Tax Acts, most capital assets dealt with in capital budgeting decisions could be depreciated over a five-year life using the Accelerated Cost Recovery System (ACRS) regardless of the economic or physical life of the assets. In addition, an investment tax credit (ITC) of up to 10 percent was allowed, giving what amounted to a government discount on capital acquisitions. The Tax Reform Act of 1986 eliminated the ITC and seems to combine the philosophy of the 1981 and 1982 Acts (accelerated depreciation) along with prior legislation (depreciation is over an asset's economic life rather than, say, over five years regardless of projected life). What resulted is a very complex tax system.

A couple of warnings before we proceed. First, this is not meant to be a tax course. Therefore, the details of the Act are not stressed, only the basic framework of the Act. Second, this discussion involves only personal property (as contrasted to real property).

CLASSES OF ASSETS

Under the 1981 and 1982 Acts, capital assets were generally classified as having a five-year life. Some shorter-lived assets could be written off over three years. There were other classes of assets under these Acts, but they did not generally pertain to assets we are concerned with (e.g., amusement parks or sewer systems).

Under the 1986 Act, assets can fall into a three-year, five-year, seven-year, ten-year, fifteen-year, or twenty-year class. Classes are based on the ADR (Asset Depreciation Range) or midpoint life of the asset. This concept is linked to physical life. It looks as if the general class-lives that will concern us will be the five- and seven-year classes. The seven-year class includes any property with an ADR midpoint of 10 years or more and less than 16 years and property with no ADR midpoint that is not specifically assigned to another class. If one can establish that an asset has an ADR midpoint of more than 4 years but less than 10 years, a five-year class can be used. Note that the same asset in different types of industries can be in different classes.

The term "ADR midpoint" is used. If a company places several assets in service (say new desks or microcomputers) at the same time, they will wear out over a range of time. The ADR midpoint is the middle of that range. The IRS has established the ADR for several types of assets.

It may be difficult at times to determine the life of an asset for depreciation purposes. If no instructions are given, use the class that seems to fit the particular asset being acquired in the problem you are doing. Thus, if a project lasts about five years, use a five-year life. If it lasts about seven or eight years, use a seven-year life. You might consider using an electronic spreadsheet to aid in your numerical analysis. With such a spreadsheet, you can try a couple of reasonable depreciation lives and see the effect on net present value and/or internal rate of return.

CHOICES OF DEPRECIATION METHODS

Under the 1981 and 1982 Acts, a five-year asset could be depreciated over five years using ACRS or over six years using a modified straight-line (SL) method. With the 1986 Act, all assets are depreciated over a time period that is one year longer than their asset-class lives. Thus, for example, seven-year assets are depreciated over eight years. With the exception noted below, assets get one-half year depreciation in the first year of service and one-half year in the final year of service.

Three ways of depreciating an asset are possible: ACRS, SL, and an alternative depreciation system. There are complications under the 1986 Act when the book value of an asset does not equal the tax basis of the asset. It is possible that a corporation would be liable for an alternative minimum tax under certain circumstances. Thus, the choice of a depreciation method (and life) may be influenced not only by the present value of the tax shield from each depreciation method, but also the tax consequences that may be caused by value differences between the financial and tax books.

However, from a present-value perspective, the ACRS method yields the highest present value of the tax shield from depreciation. We will assume that companies will use ACRS unless a particular problem calls for SL depreciation. We will assume that the alternate method will not be used. SL depreciation is handled much as it was under the 1981 and 1982 Acts: one-half year depreciation in the first and final years and full SL depreciation for other years. The ACRS methods are 200 percent and 150 percent declining balance methods that cross over to SL when it is advantageous to do so (see Exhibit 13B-1).

DISPOSITION AND SALVAGE VALUE

As with the 1981 and 1982 Acts, the 1986 Act states that the expected salvage value should not be deducted from the original price of the asset. However, under prior legislation there could be no depreciation in the year

Exhibit 13B-1
Annual Recovery (Percent of Original Depreciable Basis)

Recovery Year	3 Year 200% db	5 Year 200% db	7 Year 200% db	10 Year 200% db	15 Year 150% db	20 Year 150% db
1	33.00	20.00	14.28	10.00	5.00	3.75
2	45.00	32.00	24.49	18.00	9.50	7.22
3	15.00	19.20	17.49	14.40	8.55	6.68
4	7.00	11.52	12.49	11.52	7.69	6.18
5		11.52	8.93	9.22	6.93	5.71
6		5.76	8.93	7.37	6.23	5.28
7			8.93	6.55	5.90	4.89
8			4.46	6.55	5.90	4.52
9				6.55	5.90	4.46
10				6.55	5.90	4.46
11				3.29	5.90	4.46
12					5.90	4.46
13					5.90	4.46
14					5.90	4.46
15					5.90	4.46
16					3.00	4.46
17						4.46
18						4.46
19						4.46
20						4.46
21						2.25
Sum	100.00	100.00	100.00	100.00	100.00	100.00

of disposition. Under the 1986 Act, companies get one-half year of depreciation in the year an asset is sold (assuming it is sold before it is fully depreciated).

SPECIAL RULE FOR PURCHASES IN THE FINAL QUARTER OF THE YEAR

If the aggregate tax basis of assets placed in service in the final quarter of the year exceeds 40 percent of the aggregate basis of all assets placed in service during the entire year, then *all* assets follow a mid-quarter rule. Under this rule, the depreciation for the first year is based on the number of quarters that each asset was in service. Assets placed in service any time during a quarter are treated as if they were placed in service at mid-quarter. Thus, an asset bought in June would get first-year depreciation of 7½ months; an asset bought in July would get first-year depreciation of 4½ months. With most of the projects that you evaluate, it will be difficult to determine if a purchase is in the fourth quarter of a year and if that purchase comprises more than 40 percent of all assets put into service during the year. Thus, we will assume that this special provision does not apply to projects under evaluation.

PRESENT VALUE OF THE TAX SHIELD OF MODIFIED ACRS DEPRECIATION (MACRS)

Exhibit 13B-1 shows the annual recovery depreciation percentages based on the guidelines in the 1986 Act. Note that this table assumes (1) the asset

Exhibit 13B-2
Present Value of Tax Shield from Depreciation
Tax Reform Act of 1986

To use the following table, choose an asset class and the relevant after-tax discount rate. Multiply the asset's original cost by the table value and also by the marginal tax rate for the company to get the present value of the tax effect of depreciation. For example, the present value of the tax shield from depreciation for an asset costing $100,000 in the five-year life with a relevant discount rate of 10 percent and a 40 percent marginal tax rate is

$$\$100,000 \times 0.7733 \times 0.40 = \$30,932$$

Discount Rate	3 Year	5 Year	7 Year	10 Year	15 Year	20 Year
6%	0.8932	0.8526	0.8155	0.7649	0.6548	0.5867
7%	0.8773	0.8315	0.7902	0.7344	0.6154	0.5440
8%	0.8619	0.8113	0.7661	0.7059	0.5796	0.5062
9%	0.8469	0.7919	0.7432	0.6792	0.5470	0.4725
10%	0.8324	0.7733	0.7214	0.6541	0.5173	0.4424
11%	0.8183	0.7553	0.7007	0.6306	0.4901	0.4154
12%	0.8046	0.7381	0.6809	0.6084	0.4652	0.3911
13%	0.7913	0.7215	0.6621	0.5875	0.4423	0.3691
14%	0.7784	0.7055	0.6441	0.5678	0.4212	0.3492
15%	0.7659	0.6902	0.6269	0.5492	0.4018	0.3311
16%	0.7537	0.6753	0.6105	0.5317	0.3839	0.3146
17%	0.7418	0.6611	0.5948	0.5150	0.3672	0.2995
18%	0.7302	0.6473	0.5798	0.4993	0.3518	0.2856
19%	0.7190	0.6340	0.5654	0.4843	0.3375	0.2729
20%	0.7081	0.6211	0.5516	0.4702	0.3242	0.2612
21%	0.6974	0.6087	0.5384	0.4567	0.3118	0.2503
22%	0.6870	0.5968	0.5257	0.4439	0.3001	0.2403
23%	0.6769	0.5852	0.5135	0.4317	0.2893	0.2310
24%	0.6671	0.5740	0.5018	0.4201	0.2791	0.2223
25%	0.6575	0.5631	0.4906	0.4090	0.2695	0.2142

will be depreciated using MACRS, and (2) the mid-quarter convention does not apply.

Exhibit 13B-2 gives the present-value factor to use to get the tax effect from depreciation for an asset, given an asset class and a relevant discount rate. Thus, if an asset cost $100,000 and were in the seven-year class, with a relevant discount rate of 10 percent and a marginal tax rate of 38 percent, the present value of the tax shield from depreciation would be

$$\$100,000 * 0.7214 * 0.38 = \$27,413.20$$

PROBLEMS AND CASES

13-1. Reinvestment of Funds

The managers of Saxton Company are evaluating a new project. The initial cost is $200,000 and is expected to have an eight-year economic life. Depreciation is based on current tax laws and a five-year tax life. There is no expected salvage value. Operating flows before taxes of 40 percent and not including the tax effect of depreciation are expected to be $10,000 in the first year, $20,000 in year two, $60,000 in years three through six, $30,000 in year seven, and $20,000 in year eight. There are no working capital needs for this project.

In an assessment of the cost of capital, the Vice President of Finance, Harry Rich, believes that a pre-tax rate of 12 percent is appropriate. However, Mr. Rich also thinks that interest rates are falling and that, starting in year three, any reinvestment of funds will be at a 9 percent pre-tax rate.

Required:
1. Using an electronic spreadsheet analysis, find the net present value and the internal rate of return of this project, ignoring specific assumptions about reinvestment of funds.
2. Using the template developed in part 1, incorporate specific reinvestment assumptions in your analysis and find the net present value and internal rate of return for the project.
3. How is the terminal-value method different from your analysis in part 2? Develop a terminal-value analysis for the project and compare the results with part 2.
4. Make a recommendation to management that includes appropriate spreadsheet printouts as exhibits. Explain your recommendation and justify the inclusion of specific reinvestment assumptions.

13-2. Capital Rationing

Stan South, the president of Apex Arms, is evaluating six projects. Each is expected to last six years and the original investment and net after-tax cash flows are as follows. The hurdle rate is 10 percent.

Year	A	B	C	D	E	F
Invest	0	($10,000)	($20,000)	($25,000)	($25,000)	($15,000)	($40,000)
Cash flow	1	1,000	4,000	12,000	4,000	4,000	5,000
	2	2,000	5,000	10,000	5,000	4,000	8,000
	3	2,000	6,000	7,000	6,000	4,000	12,000
	4	4,000	8,000	1,000	7,000	4,000	17,000
	5	5,000	5,000	2,000	8,000	4,000	12,000
	6	5,000	3,000	2,000	9,000	4,000	5,000

Required:

1. Using an electronic spreadsheet analysis, find the net present values and the internal rates of returns of each of these six projects.
2. If these projects were mutually exclusive, what would be your ranking of the projects? Justify your choice. If there is a difference in ranking among projects using different criteria, explain what causes those differences. Use your electronic spreadsheet template and modify the data to illustrate your points.
3. If these projects are not mutually exclusive and cash availability was $75,000 in the year of investment, what projects would you choose (solution by inspection)?
4. If these projects are not mutually exclusive and the company needs $20,000 a year for years one and two to be generated by these projects to meet other needs, what projects would you select? Use integer programming to solve this part.
5. If cash needs in year one were changed to $24,000, what would be the integer programming solution to part 4?

13-3. Sensitivity Analysis and Bidding (CMA Adapted)

Wardl Industries is a manufacturer of standard and custom-designed bottling equipment. Early in December, 19X3 Lyan Company asked Wardl to quote a price for a custom-designed bottling machine to be delivered on April 1, 19X4. Lyan intends to make a decision on the purchase of such a machine by January 1 so Wardl would have the entire first quarter of 19X4 to build the equipment.

Wardl's standard pricing policy for custom-designed equipment is 50 percent markup on full cost. Lyan's specifications for the equipment have been reviewed by Wardl's Engineering and Cost Accounting Departments, and they made the following estimates for raw materials and direct labor.

Raw materials		$256,000
Direct labor	11,000 DLH @ $15	165,000

Manufacturing overhead is applied on the basis of direct labor hours. Wardl normally plans to run its plant 15,000 direct labor hours per month and assigns overhead on the basis of 180,000 direct labor hours per year. The overhead application rate of 19X4 of $9.00/DLH is based upon the following budgeted manufacturing overhead costs for 19X4.

Variable manufacturing overhead	$972,000
Fixed manufacturing overhead	648,000
Total manufacturing overhead	$1,620,000

The Wardl production schedule calls for 12,000 direct labor hours per month during the first quarter. If Wardl is awarded the contract for the Lyan equipment, production of one of its standard products would have to be reduced. This is necessary because production levels can only be increased to 15,000 direct labor hours each month on short notice. Furthermore, Wardl's employees are unwilling to work overtime.

Sales of the standard product equal to the reduced production would be lost, but there would be no permanent loss of future sales or customers. The standard product whose production schedule would be reduced has a unit sales price of $12,000 and the following cost structure.

Raw materials		$2,500
Direct labor	250 DLH @ $15	3,750
Overhead	250 DLH @ $ 9	2,250
Total cost		$8,500

Lyan needs the custom-designed equipment to increase its bottle-making capacity so that it will not have to buy bottles from an outside supplier. Lyan Company requires 5,000,000 bottles annually. Its present equipment has a maximum capacity of 4,500,000 bottles with a directly traceable cash outlay cost of $0.15 per bottle. Thus, Lyan has had to purchase 500,000 from a supplier at $0.40 each. The new equipment would allow Lyan to manufacture its entire annual demand for bottles and experience a raw material cost savings of $0.01 for each bottle manufactured.

Wardl estimates that Lyan's annual bottle demand will continue to be 5,000,000 bottles over the next five years, the estimated economic life of the special purpose equipment. Wardl further estimates that Lyan has an after-tax cost of capital of 15 percent and is subject to a 40 percent marginal income tax rate, the same rates as Wardl.

Required:

1. Wardl Industries plans to submit a bid to Lyan Company for the manufacture of the special purpose bottling equipment.
   a. Calculate the bid Wardl would submit if it follows its standard pricing policy for special purpose equipment.
   b. Calculate the minimum bid Wardl would be willing to submit on the Lyan equipment that would result in the same profits as planned for the first quarter of 19X4.

2. Wardl Industries wants to estimate the maximum price Lyan Company would be willing to pay for the special purpose bottling equipment.
   a. Calculate the present value of the after-tax savings in directly traceable cash outlays that Lyan could expect to realize from the new special purpose bottling equipment.
   b. Identify the other factors Wardl would have to incorporate in its estimate of the maximum price Lyan would be willing to pay for the equipment.
   c. Show how the cost savings (part 2a) and the other factors (part 2b) would be combined to calculate the estimate of the maximum price Lyan would be willing to pay for the equipment. List any assumptions.

13-4. Data for Decisions (CMA Adapted)

In mid-19X2 U.S. Metal Corporation introduced a major product line to a new marketing area in southwestern Ohio. Public acceptance of the product line has exceeded original expectations. U.S. Metal's management believes this level of demand will continue through December 19X8.

The company had planned to serve the area directly from its Chicago plant where the customers would obtain the product f.o.b. Chicago. However, the high demand cannot be handled effectively in this manner. The management has identified two alternatives which could be initiated in January 19X3.

1. Continue to manufacture the product in Chicago but establish a warehouse 300 miles away in Dayton, Ohio, to distribute the product.
2. Provide a manufacturing, warehousing, and distribution facility in the Dayton area. This facility would not be operational until January 19X5. Consequently, a temporary warehouse would still have to be used during the first two years of the project.

Customers would obtain the product f.o.b. Dayton under both alternatives.

Bill Minnick, Controller, has agreed to prepare an analysis to compare the two alternatives. He gathered the following facts for analysis.

- The Chicago plant has sufficient capacity to manufacture the additional product volume expected to be demanded in the new marketing area. Only maintenance and insurance costs are expected to increase at the Chicago plant as a result of the additional manufacturing volume. These costs are expected to be $20,000 higher than normal in 19X3 and can be expected to increase by $3,000 annually as long as the product line is manufactured in Chicago.
- U.S. Metal can lease sufficient warehouse space in Dayton for $24,000 annually. A lease agreement can be arranged for this amount for any period from two to six years. The annual lease payment would be due on December 31 for the following year.
- Warehousing personnel would be hired to manage and operate the warehouse. The annual initial warehousing cost, excluding the lease payment, is estimated at $50,000. This amount is expected to increase by 10 percent annually.
- Five truckloads of product per day, 250 days per year, would be shipped from Chicago to the Dayton warehouse by common carrier as long as the product is manufactured in Chicago. Each truckload would average 30,000 pounds. One common carrier has quoted U.S. Metal a freight rate of $1.00 per hundredweight for a 30,000 pound truckload ($300) plus a 20 percent fuel surcharge applied on the total freight charge for the one-way trip between Chicago and Dayton. The fuel surcharge is expected to continue at the same percentage through 19X8 but the freight rate per hundredweight for a 30,000 pound truckload is expected to increase each year as presented below.

19X4	$1.10
19X5	1.25
19X6	1.40
19X7	1.50
19X8	1.60

- A building suitable for manufacturing, warehousing, and distributing the product line can be obtained in Dayton for $50,000 annually on a twenty-year lease. The lease would be signed December 31, 19X2, so that the equipment installation could be started on January 1, 19X3. The lease payments would be remitted on December 31 for the following year.

- The Dayton warehousing operations and personnel would be transferred from the original leased warehouse to the combined facility in January 19X5. Because all functions would be in the same facility, annual warehousing personnel costs would be 10 percent lower than the cost of maintaining a separate warehouse as described in the first alternative.
- The estimated total cost of the manufacturing equipment for the Dayton plant is $1.2 million. The equipment would be acquired and paid for as follows:

December 19X2	$ 510,000
December 19X3	450,000
December 19X4	240,000
	$1,200,000

The equipment would be fully operational in January 19X5.

- The new equipment at the Dayton plant would be capable of manufacturing the product line at the same rate and costs, exclusive of maintenance and insurance, experienced at the Chicago plant. Annual maintenance and insurance costs for the Dayton equipment are expected to be $70,000 the first year the equipment is operational and increase $5,000 annually thereafter during the life of the project.
- The new equipment would have a twenty-year estimated economic life with no estimated salvage value at the end of twenty years. The company would use the Accelerated Cost Recovery System (ACRS) to write off the cost of the new manufacturing equipment for tax purposes, using a five-year life.
- If the market for the product line lasts only through 19X8 as forecasted, the company could use the plant and equipment for other products. Minnick estimates U.S. Metal could sell the Dayton equipment in December 19X8 for $900,000 if the equipment is no longer needed. The building could be subleased for $50,000 per year for the remaining term of the lease when it is no longer needed.
- U.S. Metal is subject to a 40 percent tax rate on operating income. Assume that taxes are paid in the year in which the transactions occur.

Required:
Calculate the after-tax cash flows for the period 19X2 through 19X8 by year for each of the two alternatives being considered by U.S. Metal Corporation, assuming that U.S. Metal will use discounted cash flow techniques in its decision process.

13-5. Data for Decisions (CMA Adapted)

Everhope Company has acquired a large tract of land bordering the ocean and has subdivided it into lots. There are three types of lots designed to sell at three different prices as shown below.

Because of the relatively complex sewage requirements for oceanfront lots, the variable costs for developing this type of property total approximately $12,000 each. Oceanview lots are the least costly to develop with variable costs amounting to $6,000

Lot Type	Selling Price
Oceanfront	$50,000
Oceanview	30,000
Ocean access	15,000

each. Ocean access lots require more road construction cost than the others, bringing the total variable development cost for this type of lot to $8,000.

Everhope sells lots for a 10 percent down payment and then conveys the buyer's promissory note for the balance, with recourse, to a financial institution in exchange for the remaining 90 percent of the cash. If the buyer defaults, Everhope must pay the 90 percent back to the financial institution, but Everhope keeps the 10 percent down payment and takes the lot back into its inventory.

The variable costs do not have to be incurred again to resell a defaulted lot. However, a buyer who defaults typically does some alterations that require restoration. In addition, there are legal costs involved in a repossession. The average amounts of both these costs are shown below.

Default Cost	Amount
Restoration	40% of selling price
Legal costs	$2,000 per repossession

Everhope uses several methods for attracting potential customers. They have gained sufficient experience to permit estimation of the cost and default risk associated with each method of attracting customers.

Method of Attracting Customers	Annual Cost	Probability of Default
Direct mail	$20,000	.30
National magazine ads	50,000	.10
National newspaper ads	30,000	.10
Agents	[a]	.10
Local promotion	10,000	.05

[a]Sales made through agents require payment of a 6% commission at the time of the sale. This commission is not recovered in the event of a default.

Everhope is also in a position to estimate the number of each type of lot which would be sold to customers attracted by each method during the next year. These estimates are shown below.

Method of Attracting Customers	Number of Lots Sold			
	Oceanfront	Oceanview	Ocean Access	Total
Direct mail	0	10	40	50
National magazine ads	5	20	20	45
National newspaper ads	5	10	20	35
Agents	5	10	20	35
Local promotion	5	10	5	20
Total	20	60	105	185

Even though the present supply of lots will carry the firm far into the future, the president is reluctant to use direct mail because of the high probability of default and the low average value of a sale to one of these customers.

Required:
1. Based on the information presented, perform an analysis to determine the before-tax profit or loss to Everhope Company of selling lots by direct mail.
2. If Everhope Company could legally limit direct mail customers to purchasing only ocean access lots, would this be a desirable action for the company to take? Support your answer with an appropriate analysis.
3. Everhope Company has used its experience to estimate the cost and default risk associated with the various methods of attracting customers.
   a. Discuss the problems Everhope could have by basing its estimates entirely on past experience.
   b. Identify information that Everhope could obtain from external sources that would be of value in making estimates of cost and default risk.

13-6. Sensitivity Analysis

The Cosette Company is analyzing a project costing $200,000 with an expected economic life of six years and, according to the accountants for the firm, a tax life of five years, using current tax laws. The marginal tax rate is 40 percent and the after-tax hurdle rate is 10 percent.

Required:
1. If straight-line depreciation under the current tax laws is used, what must the minimum before-tax cash flows be to yield a net present value of $10,000?
2. If ACRS depreciation is used, what must pretax cash flows be to yield a net present value of $10,000?
3. If the cash-flow needs are different between parts 1 and 2, explain the difference.
4. If pretax cash flows from operations (not including the tax effect of depreciation) are expected to be $50,000 annually, what must the purchase price of the asset be to yield a net present value of $10,000, using ACRS depreciation?
5. Redo part 4 but assume the tax life of the asset is only three years instead of five. Explain why the asset value changes in the direction it does.

6. Assuming a five-year tax life, if annual after-tax cash flows (excluding the tax effect of depreciation) are $33,500 and the cost of the asset $214,500, what must the after-tax discount rate be, using ACRS depreciation, to yield a net present value of $10,000?

13-7. Discounted Payback

The managers of Namfar Products have developed a basic net-present-value analysis of a new project that involves free-choice vitamins and minerals for poultry feeding. These are entirely natural, and the managers think that this product may well fit in with recent concerns about using steroids in chickens and other fowl.

New manufacturing equipment costing $500,000 would be purchased. While they believe the economic life of the project will be up to ten years, current tax laws allow a five-year tax life using ACRS depreciation. There would be little if any salvage value for the equipment at the end of its life since it is special purpose in nature. Initial plans call for a $100,000 advertising campaign in the first year and $40,000 a year thereafter. Changes in working capital would be $200,000 immediately and another $100,000 in a year.

The company has a 40 percent marginal tax rate, including federal, state, and local taxes. The firm believes this project to be risky and is using an 18 percent risk-adjusted hurdle rate. Annual fixed costs of production are expected to be $500,000, not including depreciation.

Required:
1. Using a ten-year economic life and assuming all cash flows occur at the end of each period, what is the total annual pretax contribution margin that is needed to break even on a net-present-value basis?
2. If operating flows before taxes and not including the tax effect of depreciation are $400,000 annually, how many full years would it take to break even on a net-present-value basis? If you have to make any assumptions in this analysis, make sure to list and justify them.

13-8. Inflation

At a meeting of the Finance Committee of the Tracy Company, a project was discussed. The initial investment would be $240,000; working capital requirements are $20,000 immediately and another $10,000 in a year. The current tax laws apply, and ACRS depreciation over a five-year tax life will be allowed. The marginal tax rate is 40 percent, and the after-tax hurdle rate that the committee used is 9 percent. Cash flows before taxes or the effect of depreciation are expected to be as follows:

Year 1	-$10,000
Year 2	60,000
Year 3	80,000
Year 4	100,000
Year 5	100,000
Year 6	70,000
Year 7	50,000

Required:
1. Using an electronic spreadsheet, lay out the cash flows and find the net present value and the internal rate of return of this project.

2. During the meeting the subject of inflation was raised. Current inflation has been running about 3 percent a year, but there is fear that inflation will rise. What would happen if, say, inflation were to be running at a 5 percent rate? Redo your analysis from part 1 and incorporate the effect of inflation.

13-9. Expected Values and Portfolio Considerations

Meryl Halpern, chief financial officer of Cardinal Manufacturing, has obtained the following information about the costs on a proposed capital project as well as the probabilities of these flows occurring. She considers the source of the estimates to be reliable.

	Event 1	Event 2	Event 3	Event 4	Event 5
Invest	−$100,000	−$100,000	−$100,000	−$100,000	−$100,000
Year 1	25,000	20,000	20,000	20,000	20,000
Year 2	30,000	25,000	25,000	30,000	20,000
Year 3	50,000	45,000	30,000	30,000	25,000
Year 4	30,000	25,000	35,000	30,000	30,000
Year 5	20,000	20,000	40,000	20,000	35,000
p(Event)	20%	20%	20%	25%	15%

Required:
1. What is the expected net present value of this project at a 10 percent discount rate? What is the variance for the project?
2. Mrs. Halpern also is considering the following project. The probabilities of the five events occurring is the same for both projects.

Invest	−$120,000	−$120,000	−$120,000	−$120,000	−$120,000
Year 1	40,000	30,000	30,000	20,000	20,000
Year 2	40,000	40,000	30,000	30,000	30,000
Year 3	45,000	40,000	40,000	45,000	35,000
Year 4	30,000	30,000	40,000	30,000	35,000
Year 5	25,000	20,000	20,000	25,000	20,000

Independent from the analysis in part 1, what is the expected net present value of this second project? the variance?
3. These two projects are being considered together and Mrs. Halpern is worried about how independent they are from one another. What is the variance of the two projects with a ρ_{AB} of 1, 0.5, 0, −0.5, and −1? Explain the change in the variance as the dependence between the two projects changes. How does this type of analysis help Mrs. Halpern in her decision-making process?
4. How would a company go about finding the value of the covariance between or among proposals?

13-10. Leasing versus Purchasing

An analysis of a new piece of equipment that would improve productivity at Bunte Company shows a positive net present value when discounted at 10 percent, the after-tax hurdle rate established by management. Bunte's marginal tax rate is 40 percent. The question now facing management is how to finance the project. Prior to working up the cost estimates associated with the new equipment, Robin Henry, Vice President of Finance, had contacted the company's local banking connection and had also discussed the purchase with a leasing company that Bunte had done business with over the years.

The bank offered a fixed-rate loan for four years at $16\frac{2}{3}$ percent interest on the unpaid balance. The loan would be for the original purchase price of $80,000. The asset can be depreciated using three-year ACRS under the most current tax laws.

The leasing company stated that a lease would be $29,000 per year paid at the beginning of each year over a four-year period. Included in the lease, however, is $1,000 a year for expected maintenance that Bunte would have to pay if they owned rather than leased the equipment.

Required:
1. From a financial perspective, which form of financing yields a lower cost to Bunte Company? What is the effective after-tax interest rate on leasing?
2. What are the advantages and disadvantages to Bunte Company of owning? of leasing? If you were advising Robin Henry, which form of financing would you choose? Justify your choice.

13-11. Leasing versus Purchasing (CMA Adapted)

LeToy Company produces a wide variety of children's toys, most of which are manufactured from stamped parts. The Production Department recommended that a new stamping machine be acquired. The Production Department further recommended that the company only consider using the new stamping machine for five years. Top management has concurred with the recommendation and has assigned Ann Mitchum of the Budget and Planning Department to supervise the acquisition and to analyze the alternative financing available.

After careful analysis and review Mitchum has narrowed the financing of the project to two alternatives. The first alternative is a lease agreement with the manufacturer of the stamping machine. The manufacturer is willing to lease the equipment to LeToy for five years even though it has an economic useful life of ten years. The lease agreement calls for LeToy to make annual payments of $62,000 at the beginning of each year. The manufacturer (lessor) retains the title to the machine and there is no purchase option at the end of five years. This agreement would be considered a lease by the Internal Revenue Service.

The second alternative would be for LeToy to purchase equipment outright from the manufacturer for $240,000. Preliminary discussions with LeToy's bank indicate that the firm would be able to finance the asset acquisition with a 15 percent term loan.

LeToy would depreciate the equipment, using ACRS and a five-year tax life.

All maintenance, taxes, and insurance are the same under both alternatives and are paid by LeToy. LeToy requires an after-tax cut-off return of 18 percent for investment decisions and is subject to a 40 percent corporate income tax rate on both operating income and capital gains and losses.

Required:

1. Calculate the relevant present value cost of the leasing alternative for LeToy Company.
2. Calculate the relevant present value cost of the purchase alternative for LeToy Company.

13-12. Capital Budgeting and New Manufacturing Technologies

Computer integrated manufacturing implies an even more capital-intensive manufacturing environment for some companies. Even today, some firms have second and third shift operations with no operating employees on the shop floor. The lights in the plant are out and are turned on only if a problem occurs and a service person has to respond.

Required:
(In responding to the following, you should use not only the text but also outside reading sources to develop your thoughts.) How does the new manufacturing environment and stress on world-class competition affect the identification, development, selection, and control stages of capital budgeting? This should be an in-depth discussion, and, if possible, real illustrations should be used.

13-13. Junior Executive[34]

Junior Executive has been assigned the task of determining whether his company should trade in its old airplane and purchase a new one. The company manufactures and sells highly specialized, complex machinery which often requires extensive technical selling, installation, and subsequent service. The machinery is sold primarily to electric motor manufacturers and utilities throughout the midwest. The machine installations allow wire in armatures, dynamos, and motor cores to be wound automatically, saving large amounts of cost—if the machines work correctly.

The company airplane is used in the business for two purposes: (1) to transport company executives to plants of potential new customers or to bring the executives of potential customers to the company's home office (or other installations) for sales demonstrations, and (2) to provide quick trouble shooting and repair service to customers. The latter is very important for the machinery installations are very sensitive and when they break down, the whole process stops with copper wire all over the place.

The problem involves whether to replace a single-engine Bonanza F33A airplane with a twin-engine Baron 58 model. Only the Baron is under consideration as the replacement plane because of the president's preference (she is also a pilot). The company is considering the larger plane for two reasons. First, its greater seating capacity will allow more people to be transported for sales demonstrations. Second, its ability to fly in adverse weather conditions will result in even faster repair service, thus enhancing the firm's reputation for reliable service.

---

[34] This problem is adapted from an original problem by Earl A. Spiller, Jr., "Capital Expenditure Analysis: An Incident Process Case," *The Accounting Review*, 56:1 (January 1981), pp. 158–165. Used by permission.

The president of the company, when asked, replied that it was impossible to quantify the increased value of the larger airplane because of the two factors mentioned above. She thinks it is significant. Instead, she has asked Junior to estimate by how much the new airplane would have to increase yearly sales to justify its purchase.

Currently, the company is using a four-seat Bonanza purchased a year ago on January 5, 19X9, at a cost of $170,000. The airplane has flown over 1,000 hours during the first year. It is common practice to have an engine exchange every 1,600–1,700 flying hours with this type of aircraft. Because the Bonanza will be scheduled within the year for this overhaul, the president thinks that now is the ideal time to consider buying a larger airplane.

The larger aircraft being considered is a six-seat Baron. The dealer has offered the Baron at a cash price of $570,000. The Bonanza would be sold for $136,000 as a used airplane.

The company has been in business only four years. The first two years were ones of organization and rapid growth and are not considered typical. The company is privately held with most of the stock owned by the president, the president's family, and key employees.

Junior has come to you early in 19Y0 and has asked you to help him. He has access to all company data but has trouble deciding which data are relevant or how to formulate the decision framework. He must report to the president within a couple of weeks.

Required:
You will be a member of a team that will consult with Junior Executive. You will be meeting with Junior Executive and submit questions to him. The results of your analysis will be a complete written report to Junior recommending actions and supporting these recommendations with appropriate financial and other data. Specifically, Junior is interested in a careful analysis taking into consideration all relevant quantitative factors, tax considerations, and the time value of money to help him decide what increase in sales volume would be necessary to justify economically the outright purchase of the Baron. He is also interested in other factors that might affect this decision.

Some Specific Directions
Not unlike some recent college graduates, Junior Executive is an overflowing fountain of relevant and irrelevant information. He knows a lot of answers; however, he sometimes has trouble asking the right questions or understanding questions asked by others.

You may ask questions of Junior, and he will try to provide an answer. The more specific your questions, the more likely Junior will be able to answer them. He tends to become very verbose in dealing with broad general types of questions.

Junior would like to be able to meet with you personally at any time to answer questions, but his busy schedule will not allow time. (He caddies for the president frequently.) However, you may ask questions in two ways.

1. You may submit questions or requests for additional information in written form by placing your questions in Junior's mailbox, which he shares with your instructor. The questions should be neatly presented and in duplicate (Junior wants to retain one copy of your questions so he can learn to ask proper questions).

2. Junior will meet with your team one or two times for up to 15 minutes a meeting. It is strongly suggested that you carefully schedule these meetings and have them well planned. Use them to clarify what you have learned from written questions and to follow up on any ambiguities.

Each team is to conduct its investigation and analysis *completely independently* of any other team. Junior Executive is known for sometimes supplying different answers to the same question asked by different teams.

You probably will find it very helpful to set up your analytical model using a computer spreadsheet. In this way, variables can be changed and you will not have to reevaluate your answer manually. In addition, you might want to do some sensitivity analysis.

13-14. Post Audits of Capital Budgeting Projects at the Bernardo Company[35]

The Bernardo Company is experiencing an extended period of corporate growth. Its compounded growth rate over the past five years has been in excess of 25 percent per year in sales and 20 percent per year in profits. Bernardo Company has invested heavily in a variety of capital projects to support this growth. The management of Bernardo Company, like many other contemporary firms, selects these capital projects based on their internal rates of return (IRRs), choosing only projects which are expected to yield IRRs of at least 15 percent.

Rosalind Stone has worked in the forecasting area for the Bernardo Company for the past five years and is currently a senior project supervisor. She is responsible for forecasting all future project cash flows and determining the IRRs for the projects assigned to her. The management of Bernardo Company requires a master's degree for the individual holding her position because of the level of sophisticated analytical techniques required to perform these forecasts. While not specifically required for her job, Rosalind also is a Certified Management Accountant (CMA). She currently has a team of four junior forecasters working for her; however, she is ultimately responsible for the accuracy of each project's forecasted profitability. Her team evaluates capital machinery requests for several different operations.

Leslie Kaplan is Rosalind's boss; he is the manager responsible for forecasting throughout the Bernardo Company. Mr. Kaplan is responsible for evaluating Rosalind's performance. Over the past five years, Rosalind has consistently received very high ratings from Leslie Kaplan. Recently, the Bernardo Company has initiated a program for post audits of their capital budgeting decisions. Mr. Kaplan has gathered information on eight projects which Ms. Stone and her team had evaluated three years ago. The results are somewhat disturbing to Mr. Kaplan. He feels that the corporate politics are such that Rosalind should not feel any pressures to make particular projects "look good," and he did not think that the team's estimates were biased. Nevertheless, he is puzzled by what seem to be discrepancies between Rosalind's projections and the results of those projects (labeled A through H as shown in Table 1).[36]

---

[35] Robert Capettini, Chee W. Chow, and James E. Williamson, "Instructional Cases: The Proper Use of Feedback Information," *Issues in Accounting Education*, Vol. 7, No. 1 (Sarasota, Fla.: American Accounting Association, Spring 1992), pp. 37–56.

[36] All of the projects subjected to post audits were approximately of the same scale and the same expected economic life.

TABLE 1
True and Estimated Internal Rates of Return for Eight Competing Projects

	Project	True IRR	Estimated IRR
	A	?	9%
	B	?	14%
	C	13%	17%
	D	14%	16%
	E	?	14%
	F	17%	16%
	G	?	14%
	H	25%	28%
Average estimated IRRs for all 8 projects			16%
Average IRR for Projects C, D, F, and H		17.25%	19.25%

When the Bernardo Company's hurdle rate of 15 percent was compared to Ms. Stone's estimates, projects C, D, F, and H were selected. Ms. Stone had estimated an average IRR of 19.25 percent for these four projects. However, the post audits show that an average IRR of only 17.25 percent had been realized and that two of the projects, C and D, had realized IRRs below 15 percent. Because of these results, Mr. Kaplan is considering raising the hurdle rate from 15 percent to 17 percent on future projects where Rosalind's team will perform the evaluation.

Required:
Suppose that you are Leslie Kaplan and you have to evaluate Rosalind Stone.

1. Has Rosalind Stone performed her job well?
2. Which projects would you have chosen? Why?
3. If Ms. Stone's estimates, on average, were unbiased, why were the selected projects' actual IRRs, on average, lower than estimated IRRs (i.e., how did this error or bias arise)?
4. What methods can you suggest to improve Rosalind Stone's performance in the future?

Chapter 14

Segment and Managerial Performance Evaluation

Traditional performance measurement systems concentrate on sales, net income, return on investment, and earnings per share for corporate officers and gross profit, labor and machine productivity, overhead absorption, and actual versus budget performance for plant and product line managers. However, while these tools have been effective barometers of an organization's financial and operating performance, the changing manufacturing environment requires adaptation of old measures and creation of new performance measurements that direct managers toward the objectives of long-run profitability, high quality, low inventories, fixed asset utilization, contribution margins, throughput, and employee satisfaction.[1]

---

[1] Robert A. Howell, James D. Brown, Stephen R. Soucy, and Allen H. Seed III, *Manufacturing Accounting in the New Manufacturing Environment* (Montvale, N.J.: Institute of Management Accountants, 1987), p. 49.

Performance measures must be highly correlated with shareholder wealth creation—the ultimate mission of U.S. corporations. . . . The principal role of executive compensation programs is to motivate executives, through appropriate rewards, to make decisions, and take actions that contribute to the creation of shareholder wealth.

. . . Internal business performance measures that lead to shareholder wealth creation can be used. These measures include *financial measures*, which predict future stock price movements and dividend payouts, and *nonfinancial measures*, which measure the company's success in gaining and maintaining a competitive advantage in the marketplace.

Performance measures must be consistent with the company's organizational and management environment, taking into consideration strategic financial management, executive ability to control results, and the company's culture and management style. . .

Performance measures must be consistent with the company's compensation philosophy and objectives, which determine the role of compensation in influencing behavior.[2]

Operational control encompasses management's need to see if business segments and their managers are performing up to expectations. The notion of control can go from the smallest business unit within a company (say, a particular production department) or a particular order all the way to looking at major divisions and the company as a whole. This chapter mainly deals with divisions and their managers, but many of the major points are equally applicable to smaller business segments.

---

[2] Seymour Burchman, "Choosing Appropriate Performance Measures," in *Executive Compensation: A Strategic Guide for the 1990s,* Fred F. Foulkes, editor (Boston: Harvard Business School Press, 1991), pp. 190–192.

Segment and managerial performance evaluation have evolved over the past years; these changes are, quite naturally, in concert with the changes in the external and internal environment that companies face. Thus, as managers implement ABC/ABM, TQC, JIT, TOC, and updated strategic management practices (as outlined in Chapter 12), they also are rethinking how to evaluate business units and segment managers. In this chapter, we explore the basis for decentralization, traditional financial measures of performance, more recent concerns dealing with nonfinancial quantitative and qualitative measures of success, issues relating to performance measures in different countries and given different cultures, and, finally, an introduction to issues involving managerial compensation and bonuses.

DECENTRALIZATION

Centralization or decentralization refers to the organization of a company and, specifically, to how low in the organizational structure decisions are made. The more independent the manager, the more decentralized the structure. For example, assume that a company has two plants. If central management decides what products each of these plants makes; what prices are charged; what inter-plant transfers should take place and at what price; inventory levels of raw, semifinished, and finished goods; and so on, then the organization is centralized. However, if local managers make these decisions, then a form of decentralized management is in place. Again, the depth of decentralization can best be measured by how low in the organization important decisions are made. Decentralization-centralization is a continuum, and companies and divisions within companies can fall all along this scale. Two elements are important in deciding the extent of decentralization: how to decentralize (what segments and bases for these segments) and why to decentralize.

Types of Business Segments

Traditionally, business segments have been defined by how they will be evaluated using *financial* measures. Thus, we have cost, revenue, income, and investment centers. While there have been many improvements in evaluation techniques, financial measures (in traditional or in modified form) still are at the heart of seeing how well segments and their managers are doing.

If the central office assesses a segment based on its control of costs, then, appropriately, the division is called a *cost center*. Examples of cost centers are service departments. These segments are designed to provide services to other departments and do not produce a final good or service that is sold externally. Service departments include maintenance, computer services, employee cafeterias, and other examples as illustrated in Chapter 11 in the discussion on allocating service department costs. Departments like research and development can also fall into the cost center category.

In the next chapter we discuss transfer pricing, the prices charged for goods transferred from one decentralized division to another. If a division produces a product that has no outside market and must be sold to another division of the company, the selling division can be a cost center since it is not directly responsible for revenue and is captive to the buying division. Thus, cost centers do not refer just to service departments.

If a segment is responsible for revenues alone, it can be a *revenue center*. Examples of such segments are rare and would include a sales division. However, even in such a division, there would be some costs, and these costs would be included in the evaluation of how well or poorly the segment was doing. Thus, such a department would probably be an *income center* where local managers would be assessed on both revenues and costs. Other income centers include divisions where few capital assets are employed. Income centers would be especially useful in service organizations that are people intensive.

Finally, if a segment not only creates revenue and incurs costs but also uses assets, it can be termed an *investment center*. Most manufacturing divisions would be investment centers since they employ substantial capital assets. Service businesses can also have investment centers since many services require substantial assets (e.g., hospitals, computer service bureaus). The question management asks in evaluating this kind of center is whether the assets employed are yielding an adequate return: a subject that is full of problems, as is explored below.

These definitions are, by implication, based on traditional financial accounting measures of success: income, return on investment, return on sales, return on equity, etc. There are other financial measures that can also be employed. Goldratt proposes measuring throughput, inventory, and operating expenses (as discussed and defined in Chapters 2 and 3 and reviewed below). While these measures are different in focus, their intent is the same: from a financial perspective, how well are we doing? One of the major differences, however, would be that Goldratt and others who support the Theory of Constraints (TOC) would probably not bother with titles such as cost, revenue, income, or investment centers; instead, segments would be evaluated appropriately on throughput, inventory, and operating expenses without the need for titles.

The main point remains, even with changes in the measures used: decentralization involves dividing a company into segments, divisions, strategic business units (SBU's), or any other name where the focus is on divisional autonomy and, therefore, evaluating the segment as a separate entity. The level of decentralization might not be equal across all units within a company. Thus, given the notion of evaluating managers on what they can control, seeing how well we think managers and segments are doing must be specific to the level of authority vested in a segment.

Bases for Decentralization

The general type of segments is but one decision that management must make. It includes the concept of controllability of revenues and costs in one paradigm or throughput, inventory, and operating expenses in another. A second decision involves how to decentralize: What is the optimum organizational structure for the firm? The optimum organizational structure should be responsive to internal and external environmental complexity. How complex is the marketplace? Is there a special need for expertise in raw material buying? What type of manufacturing process is employed? Are some products made in high-technology, robotics plants? These are some of the questions that can be asked about internal and external environmental complexity. As a result of such questions and other planning, control, and organizational concerns, companies can be segmented on several different bases.

Geographical Area   Multinational firms may often decentralize along geographical areas. Different countries mean different regulations and cultures. In addition, product groups may be quite specific to an area. For example, certain countries yield raw materials while others are sources of low-cost labor. Even within this country, companies may be divided geographically. Products and/or sales might be best managed from more localized management.

Products   One of the most obvious ways to divide a company is along product lines. Thus, a vehicle manufacturer may have a division for passenger automobiles, one for light-duty trucks, and one for heavy-duty trucks. A computer manufacturer may divide along the lines of personal computers and business computers. This type of decentralization is not limited to product-oriented companies. In public accounting, for example, the basic divisions are service lines: auditing, tax, and management advisory services.

Types of Customers   There can be a basic division between private and governmental customers. Other divisions can be wholesale and retail, large and small, and industrial and consumer, for example.

Technology   Segments can be defined based on particular plants or manufacturing processes that are technologically similar. Plants that generate several joint products are good examples of segmentation along technology lines.

Reasons for Decentralization

Before a company can decide how to classify a segment and the basis for decentralization, central management must have decided that decentralization was the best response to the environment. There are several benefits that are proposed for choosing a decentralized form of management.

Response to Environmental Complexity   If management is faced with a mature product in an industry with static technology, there is less need for decentralization than in a company facing uncertainties in all areas. Thus, decentralization is a response to technological and environmental complexity. The more complex the reality that faces management, the more there is a need for experts within smaller areas of concern to deal with business decisions. Complexity almost forces decisions to be made at lower levels of management since there is neither the time nor the expertise available for upper management to make important decisions. The idea of decentralization as a response to the environment facing the company leads to other reasons for and benefits from decentralization.

Cost of Information   The accumulation and transmission of information is costly. (Chapter 8 discusses information economics as a way to determine the expected net benefits of information.) Imagine having to forward enough information to top management so that the central office could make all decisions. This would be quite costly. The more complex the environment, the more costly it is to educate upper management and to generate the type, quality, and quantity of information needed for centralized decisions. Thus, the cost of information (which includes opportunity costs for productive time wasted in the accumulation, education, and transmission process) is an important reason to decentralize.

Timeliness   The more uncertain the environment, the more timely decisions need to be made. If decisions can be made on a corporate level once a month for, say, production volume in a fairly certain marketplace, then there are few reasons to decentralize based on timeliness. However, consider the trader on the floor of a commodity exchange where seconds can make the difference between profit and loss on raw material purchases or price hedging. In this case, the trader cannot take the time to consult with higher management. While certain policies may be set at a higher level, the trader can deal autonomously within these guidelines. Uncertainty on several levels can lead to the need for more timely decisions and, therefore, more decisions on important items by lower-level managers.

Motivation and Training   One of the early reasons that was proposed for decentralization is motivation. Much in the same way that participation in the budgeting process is based on the notion that managers feel more a part of the process and, therefore, are more invested in achieving the budget, decentralized managers may feel that they are more in business for themselves and be more motivated.

If a manager has real control over operations and decisions, she may perform better than if she perceives herself as just taking orders and being part of a large bureaucracy. In addition, managing a segment can be good training for larger responsibilities. Thus, upper management can hold a lower-level manager responsible for revenue generation, cost control, human resource development, and long-term asset acquisition, for example, as a way to train that manager for higher positions within the company with expanded responsibilities in some or all of these areas.

Ability to Evaluate Segments   Decentralization usually includes performance reports by each segment. With a centralized management, there is a reduced ability to evaluate how parts of the business are doing since departmental reports may not reflect responsibility. With proper segmentation, however, managers can create ways to see how each division is faring and can develop standards to evaluate managerial performance as well.

Therefore, within the basic idea that decentralization is a response to organizational needs (especially technological and environmental complexity), managers can define business segments.

Decentralization and Strategic Management in the 1990s

There are good reasons for managers to decentralize a company as outlined above. In addition, however, given today's competitive environment, there are reasons to limit the amount of decentralization managers experience. Strategic management and the ability to adapt rapidly to a changing environment seem to be the hallmarks of modern management. As such, it is possible that parent company management will specify certain policies regarding segment decision making that will, in effect, virtually centralize some decisions. For example, managers at a midwest division of a national company were evaluating an investment in some expensive, high-technology equipment in the mid 1980s. The parent company is owned by a large Japanese firm. While the parent company encouraged the segment to define the local markets that the new equipment would serve, and therefore come up with the specifications for the equipment, they gave segment managers a list of Japanese equipment manufacturers that were to comprise the sole vendor list. Part of this had to do with value chain decisions that the parent company had made as part of their long-term strategic planning process.

Large corporations are faced with hard economic times in the early 1990s. As a result, their managers might choose to look to core businesses and to dispose of those segments not associated with that core. In addition, corporate policies might be set to limit the kinds of businesses, processes, equipment, and products that are acceptable for their various segments. However, decentralization has never meant that *all* decisions are made at the segment level. Decisions regarding capital structure, debt limits, and extending credit, for example, are usually made by the parent organization. What we are seeing, then, is really a fine tuning of the decentralization structure rather than moving away from it. However, it's important to see that an organization's structure is directly linked to its strategic plan and the most effective way to achieve that plan. With this basic outline of decentralization as a foundation, we can proceed to a discussion of financial and nonfinancial measures of performance.

FINANCIAL MEASURES OF PERFORMANCE

Traditional financial accounting measures of performance include book income, return on investment (ROI), and residual income (RI). Other measures are return on equity, return on capital employed, return on sales, cash flows, contribution margin, and sales and sales growth.[3]

Evaluation and Reward

One of the results of divisional performance evaluation is a set of extrinsic rewards to divisional managers. Thus, if a segment does well, its managers may expect rewards in the form of promotions, salary increases, bonuses, and additional perquisites. If the division does poorly, expectations of these rewards are diminished. Managers are quick to perceive what actions will lead to rewards.

Evaluating a decentralized unit's performance means establishing a set of criteria for success. If central office management uses, say, accounting book income, there will be a definition of how that income is determined and some annual or multiyear goals to be achieved. Upper management hopes that an evaluation scheme not only gives them a true picture of how a division is doing, but also that the reward system coupled with that evaluation will motivate managers to achieve desired ends.

The key phrases that are used are *goal congruence* or *behavior congruence*. Both refer to lower-level managers making decisions on behalf of their divisions that will not only benefit themselves, but will also maximize the opportunities available to the overall company. If managers operate in a way that benefits themselves at the expense of the company, this is called *dysfunctional* or *suboptimal behavior*.

Thus, in order for decentralization to work, segments must be evaluated in a way that not only gives an accurate picture of current performance and,

---

[3] See Kenneth Merchant, *Rewarding Results: Motivating Profit Center Managers* (Boston: President and Fellows of Harvard College, 1989), Chapter 1, and Howell et al., *Manufacturing Accounting in the New Manufacturing Environment*, Chapter 4.

hopefully, future potential, but also the reward system that flows from the evaluation should promote congruent behavior. The subject of reward systems is covered in more detail later in the chapter. However, the discussion of specific evaluation measures that follows is based on the premise that the choice of a method and how it is used have behavioral consequences.

Accounting Measures of Segment Performance

The most commonly used measures to evaluate segment performance are historical-accounting based. Divisional income, ROI, and/or RI are all based on book income and book investment, where applicable.

Return on Investment   ROI is defined as income divided by investment. In its most common form, historical-cost divisional income is divided by historical-cost net divisional assets (as of the beginning of the period and after subtracting accumulated depreciation to that point). Different ways to define income and investment are discussed in a following section. ROI is a ratio and, like internal rate of return, it obscures the size of a project or a division. Consider the following divisions of a company. The Retail Products Division has a much higher investment base and higher income than the Wholesale Products Division, but the ROI of the latter is greater than the former. If one were to evaluate divisions solely on the basis of ROI, managers might conclude that the Wholesale division is better.

	Retail Products Division	Wholesale Products Division
Divisional income	$ 3,000,000	$ 500,000
Divisional investment	15,000,000	2,000,000
Return on investment	20%	25%

One of the most common criticisms of ROI is that it can lead to dysfunctional behavior on the part of managers. A manager who is being rewarded based on the divisional ROI may not be willing to accept projects that will lower that manager's overall ROI average even if such projects are in the best interests of the company as a whole. In addition, there are cases where a project that is not acceptable from the company's criteria may look advantageous from the manager's perspective.

For example, assume a manger is evaluating the investment opportunities shown in Exhibit 14-1 using discounted-cash-flow (DCF) techniques as illustrated in Chapter 13 and that the relevant hurdle rate is 15 percent. From the company's perspective, the best project seems to be #8703 since it has the highest net present value (NPV) and internal rate of return (IRR). Project #8701 is acceptable, but not as good as #8703. Project #8702 is unacceptable based on the 15 percent hurdle rate.

Exhibit 14-1
ROI and Discounted Cash Flows

| | Project 8701 | | | Project 8702 | | | Project 8703 | | |
	After-Tax Cash Flow	Net Income	Annual ROI	After-Tax Cash Flow	Net Income	Annual ROI	After-Tax Cash Flow	Net Income	Annual ROI
Year 0	($11,000)			($11,000)			($11,000)		
Year 1	3,500	1,300	11.82%	5,000	2,800	25.45%	(2,000)	(4,200)	-38.18%
Year 2	3,500	1,300	14.77%	6,000	3,800	43.18%	(1,000)	(3,200)	-36.36%
Year 3	3,500	1,300	19.70%	1,000	(1,200)	-18.18%	6,000	3,800	57.58%
Year 4	3,500	1,300	29.55%	1,000	(1,200)	-27.27%	8,000	5,800	131.82%
Year 5	3,500	1,300	59.09%	1,000	(1,200)	-54.55%	25,000	22,800	1,036.36%
Net present value	$637			($338)			$6,481		
IRR	17.78%			12.85%			27.87%		

Where: annual depreciation on all projects is straight-line over the life of the project.

If we consider these investments from a manager's point of view, we can see the possibility of dysfunctional decision. If the manager's division is currently yielding a 20 percent ROI, that manager may not be willing to accept projects #8701 or #8703. With both projects, average ROI will drop in the near term. The large negative ROI figures for project 8703 may not be acceptable to the manager. However, project 8702, the one that is unacceptable from the company's perspective, adds to divisional ROI in the short run. This is an illustration of the conflict between DCF methods and evaluation criteria. If the manager is looking for short-term rewards or anticipates a promotion within a couple of years, that manager may adopt projects that are suboptimal in the long run and reject others that would benefit the company over their lives.

Residual Income   One way to focus on the dollars rather than on the ratios is to use *residual income* to evaluate divisional performance. *Residual income* (RI) in its most common form is historical-cost divisional income less net beginning-of-the-period investment times a required rate of return. The required rate of return may be based on the cost of capital or some hurdle or goal-oriented rate much in the same way that the relevant discount rate is determined in DCF analysis. In the sense that there is a net (residual) income after a charge for the use of assets, RI is analogous to NPV.

If evaluation of the original illustration on page 595 is recast in terms of residual income and a required return of 15 percent, the Retail and Wholesale divisions would be assessed as follows:

	Retail Products Division	Wholesale Products Division
Divisional income	$ 3,000,000	$ 500,000
Divisional investment	15,000,000	2,000,000
Return on investment	20%	25%
Residual income (at 15%)	$ 750,000	$ 200,000

Much in the same way NPV adds scale to DCF analysis, using RI adds dollar scale to divisional performance evaluation. If a project has a positive residual income, it will add to an existing residual income of a division and would, therefore, be acceptable even if there is the potential to reject it using ROI. Thus, for example, if there were a project that had ROI's lower than the divisional average in its early years but had positive residual income in that same time period, it might be accepted under the RI evaluation criterion.

However, there is room for potential conflict with DCF analysis even using RI. Residual income is still income based. If managers adopt the basic philosophy explored in Chapter 13 that they want a cash return for cash investment, income or residual income may not be a good measure of that return. In addition, RI is just as susceptible to giving false short-term signals. For example, the same problems that appeared in evaluating the projects in Exhibit 14-1 using ROI are just as evident when using RI. Exhibit 14-2 shows the residual income for the three projects.

Using RI seems to be no help in this case. Project 8702 still adds to residual income in the short term even though it is not acceptable based on the 15 percent relevant discount rate. Projects 8701 and 8703 show negative residual incomes in the first years and may be rejected on that basis much in the same way that they were rejected using ROI.

The discussion to this point shows the possible weaknesses associated with return on investment and, to some extent, with residual income. However, ROI especially continues to be one of the most used measures of performance. One way that any of the income-based measures can be used more effectively is to set target levels for a segment. Thus, if a new project would decrease a segment's ROI in the short run, upper management can negotiate a lower short-run ROI. This process is akin to the annual budgeting process and would be handled using the same type of participation and procedure.

Cash Measures of Performance

If cash return on cash investment is the major criterion in making long-term asset acquisition decisions, it is also a way to evaluate the project during its life.

Defining cash flow can be complex. It can be as simple as historical-cost income plus depreciation, the rough measure that is often used in DCF analysis for annual cash flow from operations. However, one could also include changes in working capital caused by a project. Collection and payment patterns that are a result of a project or division provide more or less cash in any period due to timing differences.

Problems exist with using cash flow. Much in the same way that it is often hard to determine separable, controllable divisional or project income for ROI or RI measures, it is also difficult to determine separable, controllable cash flows from a division or project. In addition, there may be a behavioral problem since managers are more used to looking at income-based measures that include items like depreciation and may be uncomfortable with cash-based evaluation. However, the use of cash flow does tie to the original criteria for accepting and continuing any investment: cash return on that investment. Cash flow also gives management a measure of resource availability for future investments, dividends, and other uses of cash.[4]

Cash flow should be a measure of current performance since it can be a reflection of the change in cash over a specific period of time. Therefore, it should not be hampered with the historical-cost nature of most accounting measures. However, even some cash-based measures are meant to evaluate

---

[4] There are many managers who think that dividends, for example, can be paid from retained earnings. However, if there is not enough cash to pay those dividends, money must be secured at a cost to pay them.

Exhibit 14-2
Residual Income and Discounted Cash Flows

	Project 8701			Project 8702			Project 8703		
	After-Tax Cash Flow	Net Income	Annual RI	After-Tax Cash Flow	Net Income	Annual RI	After-Tax Cash Flow	Net Income	Annual RI
Year 0	($11,000)			($11,000)			($11,000)		
Year 1	3,500	1,300	(350)	5,000	2,800	$1,150	(2,000)	($4,200)	(5,850)
Year 2	3,500	1,300	(20)	6,000	3,800	2,480	(1,000)	(3,200)	(4,520)
Year 3	3,500	1,300	310	1,000	(1,200)	(2,190)	6,000	2,800	2,810
Year 4	3,500	1,300	640	1,000	(1,200)	(1,860)	8,000	5,800	5,140
Year 5	3,500	1,300	970	1,000	(1,200)	(1,530)	25,000	22,800	22,470
Net present value									
	$637			($338)			$6,481		
IRR	17.78%			12.85%			27.87%		

Where: annual depreciation on all projects is straight-line over the life of the project.

historical performance. Ijiri has proposed a corporate recovery rate (CRR) that is a ratio with the numerator cash flow (including changes in working capital and proceeds from sales of fixed assets) and the denominator total assets (with fixed assets valued at gross book value).[5] With historical-cost gross assets in the denominator, this measure may have some of the same problems as ROI and RI.

Other Views of Traditional Financial Measures

A current criticism of income, ROI, and RI is reflected as follows:

> Bottom-line financial and strategic measures of profitability, return on investment (ROI) . . . are valid performance measures, but they are reported too late and are not specific enough to allow mid-course corrections and remedial action to be taken.[6]

Cross and Lynch go on to state that traditional measurements are financially driven (past focus) and are limited in flexibility since a financial accounting system is being used to provide managerial information. They say that historical financial measures are not necessarily linked to operations strategy.[7] The major problems, then, are whether traditional financial measurements can be made to be future oriented and linked with strategic management.

Goldratt has another perspective and, interestingly enough, does not criticize return on investment or income, per se. In fact, he proposes that what we are really trying to do is to increase income and make a better return for investors—that the goal is "to make more money now and in the future."[8] While looking at net income and ROI as "bottom line" measures capable of seeing if the goal is being reached, Goldratt says these measures are not capable of allowing managers to see what impact local actions have on the overall goal. He goes on from there to define measures that will: throughput, inventory, and operating expenses. *Throughput* is "the rate at which the system generates money through sales." It is sales less the cost of materials and purchased components used in goods sold.[9] *Inventory* is "all the money the system invests in purchasing things the system intends to sell."[10] This is a more inclusive term than we are used to in financial accounting. It includes raw materials and components purchased but not in goods

---

[5] Yuri Ijiri, "Recovery Rate and Cash Flow Accounting," *The Financial Executive* (March 1980), pp. 54–60.

[6] Kelvin Cross, and Richard Lynch, "Accounting for Competitive Performance," in *Emerging Practices in Cost Management*, Barry J. Brinker, ed. (New York: Warren, Gorham, & Lamont, 1990), p. 412.

[7] Cross and Lynch, Exhibit 1, p. 412.

[8] Eliyahu M. Goldratt, *The Haystack Syndrome: Sifting Information Out of the Data Ocean* (Croton-on-Hudson, N.Y.: Eliyahu M. Goldratt, 1990), p. 14.

[9] Goldratt, pp. 19–20.

[10] Goldratt, p. 23.

sold, the raw material and component portion of work in process and finished goods, and the machines and buildings used in production. Finally, *operating expenses* are "all the money the system spends in turning INVENTORY into THROUGHPUT."[11] The objective is to increase throughput while controlling what is invested in inventory and spent in operating expenses. Goldratt argues that these are the important measures of performance rather than the traditional financial measures. If these measures are attended to and controlled, then the "bottom line" measures of income and return on investment will be taken care of—a result of the process. He redefines these measures in his terms. Thus, **income** becomes throughput less operating expenses and **return on investment** uses his definitions of income over inventory. In addition, income cannot be subdivided into any product-related measures (gross profit, for example), as we discussed in Chapter 11; any such division has to include allocations. As the next section shows, there are other definitions of how to measure income and investment than those proposed by Goldratt.

MEASURING INCOME AND INVESTMENT

Traditional financial measures involve the use of accounting book income and either net or gross assets when calculating ROI or RI. In addition, ROI is often divided into the following parts:

$$ROI = \frac{sales}{investment} \times \frac{income}{sales}$$

The first measure is called *turnover* while the second is *return on sales*. Sales are current while parts of income and investment are based on historical costs that may not be relevant today. Imagine, for instance, a capital-intensive company whose major assets were purchased 15 years ago. Depreciation and the investment base may be quite outdated compared to today's costs and expected technological life. Thus, companies need to investigate alternate definitions of income and of investment to achieve a useful measure of segment performance.

What to Include in Income and Investment

While much of the following discussion focuses on how to value income and/or investment, a basic question precedes these decisions: What will be included in income and what in investment? Income measures can be divisional contribution margin, divisional controllable income (with no allocations from

---

[11] Goldratt, p. 29.

outside the division), or accounting net income, including all separable as well as allocated common costs. The definition of income has an effect on how that measure is perceived by upper and by lower management. In addition, the choice of, say, divisional separable income instead of fully allocated accounting income will mean a different target return.

Investment can include just physical assets, or it can include working capital (cash, receivables, inventories, payables, and so on). With central management of cash, managers will have to decide whether to include only separable cash balances or that portion of the corporate cash balance that is attributable to the division. Obviously, the more that is included in investment, the higher the denominator in ROI or the required return in RI.

Gross or Net Assets

To this point in the discussion we have assumed that the investment base in ROI or RI is net assets valued at the beginning of a period. With the use of net book value, measures like ROI and RI tend to rise over time. Consider a division with stable income over several years. As income remains the same, the net asset value drops as a function of depreciation over time. Thus, the denominator falls in ROI and the required return on investment decreases in RI, and these measures increase as a function of time. The manager is not doing any better, but the measures of success are increasing. In fact, even if income decreases a bit, it is possible that ROI will rise if the net book value falls faster than income. One advantage of gross book value, then, is that it holds the investment base for ROI and RI constant over time—based on the original value of the asset. The disadvantage, however, is that continually low ROI's may cause dysfunctional decisions, as discussed earlier.

There is another argument for the use of gross values. Companies can choose among several different depreciation methods. Current financial accounting choices are now influenced heavily by tax regulations that may impose an alternate minimum tax when financial book value differs from the tax basis of an asset. Thus, divisions that acquire assets over time may employ different depreciation methods within the division and different methods from those adopted by other divisions of the same company. The use of net book value with difffering depreciation methods yields measures that are not comparable division to division.

Gross values penalize divisions with older assets. The life-cycle issues raised later show that cash flows will start to decrease in the aging phase, as will accounting income. The assets in an aging division are probably fully depreciated from an accounting point of view and should be reflected as such from a technological assessment of the division. Since the definition of an asset is something that has future worth to a company, it is unfair to value aged assets at their original investment value since that does not reflect a reasonable measure of opportunity cost to the division. Thus, there are reasons in favor of and in opposition to the use of both a net and a gross value for investment.

Other Bases for Defining Income and Investment

Financial accounting provides several different measures of income other than historical cost. These include constant dollar accounting, current value accounting, and exit value accounting.

Constant Dollar Accounting   Constant dollar (or price-level-adjusted) accounting emphasizes the purchasing power of money. If a company paid, say, $300,000 for a piece of equipment ten years ago and there has been a general inflation of 5 percent over that time, the asset valued in today's dollars would be worth (gross value):

$$\$300,000 \times (1.05)^{10} = \$488,700$$

Thus, if that asset were purchased today it would cost $488,700.[12] The idea of constant dollar accounting is to adjust all historical costs so that they reflect current purchasing power. Generally this is done by looking at indices such as the Gross National Product Implicit Price Deflator or the Wholesale Price Index. There are specific indices for various industries that can be used.

There is a problem with general price-level adjustments, however. It may be true that the dollar has lost value over time with the cumulative effect of inflation, but a general index may not reflect the purchasing power within a particular industry or even for a particular company. Different divisions may experience different inflationary pressures. Any across-the-board effort to adjust prices may lead to figures that are not comparable division to division.

Current Value Accounting   Current value (or replacement cost) accounting refers to the cost of replacing current productive capacity and existing inventory. Note that this does not imply that a company would buy the same equipment it has; managers would replace manufacturing capacity with whatever is now available in the market. Thus, replacement equipment might contain robotics features while existing equipment is labor-intensive. Replacement cost or current value, however, would only reflect the remaining life of existing productive assets. Replacement costs would, therefore, have to be reduced by an assumed accumulated depreciation.

Managers are responsible for the assets under their control. The historical cost of these assets may not be a good measure of the responsibility entrusted to managers. Current values reflect a better way to assess investment. Managers would all be on the same basis since all assets would be

---

[12] This assumes that technology has not changed over time so that the same asset could be purchased today.

valued at current replacement value. However, current values may not represent the opportunity cost of assets or inventory.

Exit Value Accounting   Exit values are the amounts management could get if they sold existing equipment and inventories. Using sales value is justified on an opportunity cost basis; if the company continues to employ assets that could be sold, it gives up the opportunity of using the cash gained from sale in another productive way. When asset acquisition decisions are made, the notion of net present value is based on finding out if a project can earn more than the opportunity cost of funds. This same measure could be brought into play with segment performance evaluation through exit values. Using market resale prices may be especially appropriate with divisions in the mature and aging stages where abandonment is an ongoing option.

Present-Value Accounting

The idea of using present values can take on at least two different forms. In the more theoretically based alternative, assets would be valued at the present value of anticipated future cash flows. However, finding a value that managers would agree to may be quite complex. In addition, while we model discounted cash flow analysis based on the specific return of one, or a related group of, asset(s), it may be more difficult in practice to assign specific cash flows to each piece of equipment; some sort of aggregation may be necessary.

If it is possible to estimate specific cash flows for each asset, management can use present-value (or compound-interest) depreciation. The idea of present-value depreciation is to tie the expected return from a project (its internal rate of return) to the measure of income to be used in ROI or RI calculations. The procedure for using compound-interest depreciation is as follows:

1. Given the cash flows expected from a project, find the internal rate of return (IRR).
2. Determine annual income for the first year by multiplying the beginning-of-the-year asset value by the IRR.
3. Assuming that cash flow equals income plus depreciation, subtract calculated income from projected cash flow. The result is depreciation for the period.
4. Deduct the depreciation from the beginning-of-the-year asset value and repeat steps 2, 3, and 4 until there are no more cash flows.

An example is shown in Exhibit 14-3. This example has been constructed with even cash flows in order to show that the depreciation rises over time with this method.

The project lasts four years. The internal rate of return is 15 percent given the investment value of $1,000,000 and the annual cash flows of $350,265. You should verify that the beginning-of-the-year investment value for each year is the present value of the remaining cash flows from the project.

Exhibit 14-3
Compound-Interest Depreciation

Year	(a) [Prior Value − (d)] Investment at Beginning of Year	(b) Cash Flow	(c) [(a) × 0.15] Income at 15%	(d) [(b) − (c)] Depreciation Expense
1	$1,000,000	$ 350,265	$150,000	$ 200,265
2	799,735	350,265	119,960	230,305
3	569,430	350,265	85,414	264,851
4	304,579	350,265	45,686	304,579
Total		$1,401,060	$401,060	$1,000,000

One of the appealing aspects of compound-interest depreciation is that the ROI is held constant at the IRR. Each year's income is, by definition, based on the IRR times the asset value. Thus, there is a constant ROI. This eliminates two objections to ROI using historical-cost depreciation: there are no low early year ROI's, and ROI does not rise inappropriately in later years. Residual income under this method would be positive as long as the required rate of return is less than the IRR of the project, or 15 percent in this illustration.

Present-value depreciation is not popular in actual use. Managers seem to be wary of increasing depreciation. In addition, changes in estimates of cash flows over time will change the IRR and will cause a recasting of at least future planned depreciation expense and income. Finally, there are acquisitions that are not made on a present-value basis, including assets to address governmental regulation issues (pollution, for example) or to address social issues faced by the company. For example, in order to keep operating, the EPA required a midwestern company to invest $2 million in equipment to combat air pollution. In these cases, this type of depreciation (and income determination) would seem inappropriate.

Implicit Capital Investment: An Adjustment to ROI

Sinclair and Schwartz offer an alternative to present value depreciation: implicit capital investment.[13] Their objective is to find a measure that will give the same message to a manager as discounted cash flow analysis—a link of the investment and the evaluation criteria. Exhibit 14-4 shows their basic example. The project involves putting $78,850 in a *nondepreciable* investment. The first part of Exhibit 14-4 shows the cash flows from this investment and the net present value (NPV) at 10 percent as well as the internal rate

---

[13] Kenneth P. Sinclair, and Eli Schwartz, "Reconciling Cash Flow Decision Making and Accounting Performance Evaluation," *Journal of Cost Management* (New York: Warren, Gorham, & Lamont, Fall 1987), pp. 25–31.

Exhibit 14-4
Implicit Capital Investment

I. Basic Illustration: Discounted Cash Flow Analysis of Project[1]

Discount Rate 10%

Year	0	1	2	3	4	5	6	7	8	9	10
Invest	($78,850)										
											$78,850
Cash flows		$1,000	$2,000	$4,000	$8,000	$16,000	$32,000	$28,000	$24,000	$20,000	16,000
Total		1,000	2,000	4,000	8,000	16,000	32,000	28,000	24,000	20,000	94,850

NPV	$30,795
IRR	15.01%

II. Implicit Capital Investment (ICI)[2]

	1	2	3	4	5	6	7	8	9	10
Asset base $78,850	$85,735	$92,309	$97,539	$99,293	$95,886	$92,479	$89,072	$85,664	$82,257	$78,850
Cash flows	1,000	2,000	4,000	8,000	16,000	32,000	28,000	24,000	20,000	16,000
ICI adjustment	6,885	6,574	5,231	1,754	(3,407)	(3,407)	(3,407)	(3,407)	(3,407)	(3,407)
Adjusted income	7,885	8,574	9,231	9,754	12,593	28,593	24,593	20,593	16,593	12,593
ROI	10.00%	10.00%	10.00%	10.00%	12.68%	29.82%	26.59%	23.12%	19.37%	15.31%

Where: ICI adjustment is (cost of capital) × (net book value of asset at beginning of period) − (projected net income after taxes in that period).

Example: Year 1 ICI = (0.10) × ($78,850) − ($1,000) = $6,885. This amount is added to the beginning-of-the-period asset value to get $85,735 as the ending value for Year 1 (beginning value for Year 2).

Notes: 1. Modified from Sinclair and Schwartz, "Reconciling Cash Flow Decision Making," Exhibit 2, p. 27.
2. Modified from Sinclair and Schwartz, "Reconciling Cash Flow Decision Making," Exhibits 4 and 5, pp. 29–30.

of return (IRR). The authors propose that ROI is an inappropriate measure since, as you should verify, it will rise over time from 1 percent in the first year to 41 percent in Year 6 and, finally, will fall to 20 percent in Year 10. As with other criticisms of ROI, Sinclair and Schwartz argue that since the ROI of the project does not exceed the cost of capital until after the fourth year, managers might not be willing to invest in this project.

With this in mind, they propose a modified ROI model with an implicit capital investment (ICI) to fill the gap between traditional ROI and the required rate of return (10 percent in their example). The second part of Exhibit 14-4 shows the calculation of the ICI, an adjustment to investment in the early years when traditional ROI is less than the cost of capital. Thus, an adjustment would be needed for the first four years of this project. After traditional ROI exceeds the relevant cost of capital, then the ICI adjustment would be amortized on a straight-line basis over the remaining life of the project. The result is an ROI that is always at or above the relevant cost of capital, thus encouraging managers to invest in projects that they otherwise might not if evaluated by traditional ROI.

Note, however, that ROI still rises over time. This same project could be recast in the context of present-value depreciation. In Exhibit 14-5, two forms of present-value depreciation are illustrated. In the first part, present-value depreciation is set to achieve ROI equal to the IRR of about 15 percent. In the second part, excess present value is added to the original investment and depreciation is set to achieve the hurdle rate of 10 percent. In both examples, ROI remains constant over the life of the investment, an aspect not reflected in the Sinclair and Schwartz model.

OTHER MEASURES OF PERFORMANCE

Besides the traditional and amended *quantitative financial* measures of performance, there are also both *nonfinancial quantitative* and *qualitative* measures. In their 1985 survey, Howell et al. list the following as important measures among their respondents (listed in order of preference):

Product quality
Labor productivity
Delivery performance/customer service
Market share
Market growth
Throughput rate
Material yield
Product development performance
Equipment productivity
Manufacturing flexibility
Technological capability[14]

---

[14] Howell, et al., *Manufacturing Accounting in the New Manufacturing Environment*, Figure 29, p. 52.

Exhibit 14-5
Comparison of ICI with Present Value Depreciation

I. Present-Value Depreciation: ROI at IRR

Year	0	1	2	3	4	5	6	7	8	9	10
Net asset	$78,850	$89,682	$101,139	$112,316	$121,169	$123,351	$109,861	$98,346	$89,104	$82,474	$78,850
Income		11,832	13,457	15,177	16,854	18,182	18,510	16,485	14,757	13,371	12,376
Cash flows		1,000	2,000	4,000	8,000	16,000	32,000	28,000	24,000	20,000	16,000
Depreciation		(10,832)	(11,457)	(11,177)	(8,854)	(2,182)	13,490	11,515	9,243	6,629	3,624
ROI		15.01%	15.01%	15.01%	15.01%	15.01%	15.01%	15.01%	15.01%	15.01%	15.01%

II. Modified Present-Value Depreciation: (Asset + Positive NPV) and 10 Percent ROI

Year	0	1	2	3	4	5	6	7	8	9	10
Net asset	$109,645	$119,609	$129,570	$138,527	$144,380	$142,818	$125,099	$109,609	$96,570	$86,227	$78,850
Income		10,964	11,961	12,957	13,853	14,438	14,282	12,510	10,961	9,657	8,623
Cash flows		1,000	2,000	4,000	8,000	16,000	32,000	28,000	24,000	20,000	16,000
Depreciation		(9,964)	(9,961)	(8,957)	(5,853)	1,562	17,718	15,490	13,039	10,343	7,377
ROI		10.00%	10.00%	10.00%	10.00%	10.00%	10.00%	10.00%	10.00%	10.00%	10.00%

McNair et al. expand this list to include

Design for manufacturability
Zero defects
Minimize raw material and component inventory
Zero lead time
Minimize process time
Optimize production
Matching demand directly to production
Zero set-up time
Zero finished goods inventory
Control of non-value-added costs in the management cost structure
Minimize total life cycle cost[15]

Green et al. consider performance measures in a JIT environment as McNair, et al. do and offer an illustration of a list of measures to consider from the AT&T New River Valley Works:

Number defective (parts per million)
First pass quality percent yield
On-time percent shipped
Manufacturing interval (hours)
Work-in-process inventory and turnover
Finished goods inventory and turnover
Cost of scrap
Scrap percent of output
Line disruptions
Percent of personnel cross trained[16]

McDonald's has long incorporated quality, service, and cleanliness (QSC) in evaluating individual stores. Others argue that companies will not succeed without continuous improvement. For example, Goldratt's recent revision of *The Goal*[17] seems to be partially spurred by making sure readers know that instituting TOC and looking at throughput, inventory, and operating expenses is not enough by itself; management must always look for new bottlenecks—a process of continual improvement. All these authors also stress that it's important that these measures be seen in an integrated way: how managers are achieving the goals and objectives of the company rather than how they might be optimizing some local measures irrespective of global company outcomes.

---

[15] C. J. McNair, William Mosconi, and Thomas Norris, *Meeting the Technology Challenge: Cost Accounting in a JIT Environment* (Montvale, N.J.: Institute of Management Accountants, 1988), pp. 197–211.
[16] F. B. Green, Felix Amenkhienan, and George Johnson, "Performance Measures and JIT: U.S. Companies Are Revamping Traditional Cost Systems," *Management Accounting* (February 1991), p. 53.
[17] Eliyahu Goldratt, *The Goal*, 2nd ed. (Croton-on-Hudson, N.Y.: Dr. Eliyahu M. Goldratt, 1992).

Multiple Performance Criteria

Chan and Lynn propose that managers and segments should be evaluated by multiple performance criteria and provide a model for such analysis.[18] In providing a rationale for the need for multiple performance criteria, they state:

> Financial measures are deficient not only because they can be abused but also because they purport that financial health is the only goal of the organization, a focus which results in management's myopic pursuit of short-run profit maximization.[19]

They then look at the reasons why single measures are used by many firms and the costs and benefits of using multiple measures. They want to relate performance measures to strategic management: achieving the goals of the company. However, they expand the discussion of such behavior by stating:

> Organizational theory suggests that goals arise from the organization itself, namely from transactions and contracting among power coalitions within the organization. Whether or not the information system captures the goals of the dominant coalition and tries to define appropriate evaluation criteria relating to those goals, such politically-based goal structures exist. . . . Expanding the criteria in the performance evaluation scheme from the single financial indicator to multiple measures can allow different perspectives to be incorporated into the goal set through participation of those to be evaluated.[20]

They then go on to point out that even though people understand the need for multiple measures, actual evaluation most often still uses a single measure. To combat this, they propose an *analytic hierarchic process*, a computational algorithm that synthesizes multiple inputs from those involved in the evaluation process (managers being evaluated and those doing the evaluation). These participants look at different criteria in pairs to develop an ordinal ranking of the criteria. For example, these authors use leadership, human relations skills, and financial management ability as criteria. Each of the three pairs of these criteria would be compared by participants who would choose one criterion from each pair as more important. These choices are then weighted by a ratio scale of 1 to 9 for relative importance of one criterion over another (e.g., leadership is four times more important than human relations skills). Using an algorithm involving matrices and eigenvalues, managers can be assessed on these multiple criteria.[21] The authors propose that their model's biggest contribution is

---

[18] Yee-Ching Lilian Chan and Bernadett Eleanor Lynn, "Performance Evaluation and the Analytic Hierarchy Process," *Journal of Management Accounting Research*, Vol. 3 (Fall 1991), pp. 58–87.

[19] Chan and Lyon, p. 60.

[20] Chan and Lyon, p. 62–63.

[21] For an example of such calculations, see Exhibit 1 of this article. It's less important here to give such calculations than it is to explore the basis for such a model.

that it provides a systematic approach to weighting performance criteria to provide a comprehensive performance measure. Such a measure can be used to assess the overall performance of the organization (or segment), to rank organizations or segments of organizations, to serve as input into incentive compensation schemes, and as an input into decisions about the organization or segment. Rather than an arbitrary weighting to determine the comprehensive measure, the input to the analytic hierarchy process can be used to methodically poll opinions of the constituents about factor priorities so that the resultant comprehensive measure is, in fact, a product of constituents' preferences and rankings.[22]

Other authors have less complex methods to include multiple criteria in segment and managerial performance evaluation. For example, Maisel proposes what he calls a *balanced scorecard approach*. He says that measures of success should relate to customers, business process, human resources, and finance and that these measures should all be tied to the basic strategies and values of the company.[23] The idea is to not only avoid letting financial measures be the sole determinant of success but also to expand the measures used in each area and relate all areas to one another and to the strategic plan of the company.

Life Cycle and Segment Evaluation

The concept of life cycle enters a company's choice of evaluation methods for its divisions. Consider divisions in each of the four stages of life cycle. Division A is just starting out. Its products are new and at the technological forefront of the field. While a few products have just been introduced, there is a considerable amount of research and development still being pursued to refine existing products and to bring out enhanced, or new generation, products. Division B is several years ahead of Division A, but along the same path. It is growing steadily as it establishes its market and the reliability of its products. Division C is more mature. Its products are not new in the marketplace but still command a significant share. Technology in its area is fairly stable and may change only when the nature of the product changes. Finally, Division D is in an aging industry. The latest technological changes of any substance took place ten years ago. It would cost too much to retool this division to compete against newer firms in third-world countries.

---

[22] Chan and Lyon, "Performance Evaluation," p. 67.
[23] Lawrence S. Maisel, "Performance Measurement: The Balanced Scorecard Approach," *Journal of Cost Management* (New York: Warren, Gorham, & Lamont, Summer 1992), p. 49.

Seed[24] identifies these four types of divisions as being in the embryonic, growth, mature, and aging stages of the life cycle. He proposes that there are three major financial factors to explore: revenues, income, and net cash flow. Revenues should build through the first two stages and peak as a division moves from the growth to the mature stage. Net income starts off as a loss in the embryonic stage and grows with its maximum during the middle of the mature stage. Net cash flows are negative during the embryonic stage and some of the growth stage and reach their highest positive point as a division moves from the mature to the aging stage. This means that measures like ROI have little significance in some of the stages of the cycle.

Seed suggests that the embryonic stage should be measured by specific technological milestones achieved, market share, project cost, and budgeted cash outflows. In the growth stage, measurements would include market share, profit margins (and contribution margins), ROI, cash flow (which is expected to change from negative to positive during this stage), and improvements in productivity. During the mature stage, measures that continue are profit margins, ROI, cash flow (expected to be positive), and improvements in productivity. However, market share should be established, and a new emphasis should emerge to control operating costs in this fairly steady-state environment. Finally, in the aging stage, a company is looking to harvest its investment. This is a maintenance phase where companies continually evaluate when to abandon an area. Measures of success include cash inflows, profit margins, and operating costs.

Managers are faced with a difficult task when designing measures to evaluate short-range and long-range performance of divisions and of managers. While accounting-based measures are popular, these measures can affect managerial performance since they are tied to compensation plans. In addition, competing in today's marketplace seems to dictate an expanded set of evaluation measures to incorporate other measures of success, such as increases in quality or productivity or use of human assets. Finally, any measure must be in relation to life-cycle stages. However, with the basic use of measures like accounting income, ROI, and RI, there are improvements that can be made to make these measures more useful, as we discussed earlier.

INTERNATIONAL INFLUENCES

In recent times, there has been much written about Japanese management. In addition, researchers are reporting the results of field studies in several countries. This section reviews some of these findings and compares and contrasts them to earlier parts of the chapter.

---

[24] Allen H. Seed, III, "Using Cash Flows to Measure Business Unit Performance," *Corporate Accounting* (New York: Warren, Gorham, & Lamont, Summer 1983), pp. 14–19.

Japanese Evaluation Methods

Sakurai studied accounting practices in Japan through interviews and mail surveys.[25] He reports that although ROI has been widely criticized in the United States (see discussion above regarding possible dysfunctional behavior promoted by ROI), important researchers in Japan have advocated its use. However, many practitioners have continued to use financial accounting book income since (1) stockholders are not pressuring management to increase dividends or ROI and (2) the rapid business expansion in Japan between 1950 and the early 1970s promoted active investment in land, buildings, and equipment. Investments grew in value, loans were available at low interest rates, and managers focused on short-term profits.[26] If the conditions of this period had remained, the emphasis on short-term profits would have resulted in long-term growth and profits.

Sakurai goes on to point out that his surveys in 1984 and 1988 showed the use of absolute profit decreasing. In his 1976 survey, over 70 percent of the 1,000 companies responding said that ordinary profit, earnings before taxes, or net income after taxes were part of their corporate goals.[27] In his 1988 mail survey, absolute profit was used by 45 percent of the companies while return on sales (ROS) was used by 37 percent of those responding. He noted a special affinity for ROS with "assembly-oriented companies producing a variety of products."[28] He proposes that ROS is appropriate in this environment since (1) it's virtually impossible to get ROI on individual products; (2) it fits in well with target costing, a technique favored by Japanese managers; (3) ROI is ineffective in high-tech companies since the size of the capital investment needed might make managers reject projects improperly; and (4) there is no pressure from stockholders to achieve a particular ROI.[29]

However, Sakurai believes that Japanese managers implicitly use ROI in other ways. Specifically, they use *both* ROS and turnover rather than just ROI as a summary measure. In addition, he argues that target costing and JIT would naturally lead to the use of ROS and turnover. With JIT, managers want to reduce inventory to almost zero. This, in turn, increases turnover. By setting ROS goals, managers can then use JIT and target costing to maximize profits.

---

[25] Michiharu Sakurai, "The Influence of Factory Automation on Management Accounting Practices: A Study of Japanese Firms," in *Measures for Manufacturing Excellence*, Robert S. Kaplan, editor (Boston: Harvard Business School Press, 1990), pp. 39–62. This article also contains a good bibliography of Sakurai and others in this field.

[26] Sakurai, pp. 53–55.

[27] Sakurai, Table 2-6, p. 55.

[28] Sakurai, p. 55.

[29] Sakurai, p. 56.

Martin et al. also report on Japanese management accounting.[30] They point out that accounting and control systems in the United States tend to focus on reporting about past performance while Japanese accounting systems are tied into strategic planning and are meant to influence managers' behavior. Rather than dealing with meeting some budget, Japanese managers are more interested in using planning and feedback as a way to remain flexible in the light of a changing environment. This has an effect not only on measures such as ROI but also on how Japanese managers view standard costs and standard cost variances, a subject treated earlier in the book. As a result of these two studies, it seems that Japanese firms use both ROS and turnover but still concentrate on accounting-based financial performance measures. However, their measures are also related to continuous improvement and remaining flexible in the marketplace.

Studies in Other Countries

Merchant and Riccaboni report on a field study conducted at the Fiat Group in Italy.[31] Their study includes an analysis of the management-by-objective (MBO) program the Fiat Group implemented to reward managers. For profit centers, awards under this program are based on net profit before taxes and net financial position (a sum of mid- to long-term debt, both from institutions and from the parent company). Nonfinancial measures include

> increasing sales in specific market segments; completing an acquisition, divestment, or reorganization; improving quality, asset management, or customer service; and introducing new products or processes.[32]

The authors point out that Fiat Group has been successful during the period that the MBO system has been in place and that the managers credit the system with some of that success. However, they point out that some managers are worried that the system does not well balance short- and long-term concerns. As a result, these managers recommended an increased weight for nonfinancial measures. In addition, managers will be asked to relate current actions to the achievement of long-term objectives.

Merchant and Riccaboni conclude that there do not seem to be differences in how the Fiat Group, an Italian company, deals with incentives and how they are dealt with in the United States. Citing surveys they and others have conducted in the United States, they show that the Fiat program and those

---

[30] James, R. Martin, Wendi K. Schelb, Richard D. Snyder, and Jeffrey S. Sparling, "Comparing U.S. and Japanese Companies: Implications for Management Accounting," *Journal of Cost Management*, Vol. 6, No. 1 (New York: Warren, Gorham, & Lamont, Spring 1992), pp. 6–14.

[31] Kenneth A. Merchant and Angelo Riccaboni, "Evolution of Performance-Based Management Incentives at the Fiat Group," in *Performance Measurement, Evaluation, and Incentives*, William J. Bruns, Jr., ed. (Boston: Harvard Business School Press, 1992), p. 96.

[32] Merchant and Riccaboni, p. 73.

in other companies they studied are similar in that they heavily weight financial measures of performance while also considering some nonfinancial measures and use preset budget targets as a standard for achievement.[33]

Summary

There are significant differences between management accounting as it is being practiced in the United States as compared to other countries, notably Japan. As earlier discussion has highlighted, in order for U.S. companies to become more competitive in the world marketplace, their managers must tie their actions to overall strategic management. The similarities and differences we can see between performance evaluation techniques here and in other countries are also tied to strategic management: financial quantitative, nonfinancial quantitative, and qualitative measures should all be tied to the long-run strategic goals of the organization. As such, there is no difference that seems caused by one culture or another. Rather it is in a general management philosophy that can flourish in most cultures.

PERFORMANCE EVALUATION REPORTS

No matter what country an organization is in, one of the foundation principles of responsibility accounting and performance measurement is to focus on controllable factors. Thus, regardless of the technique chosen or the measures used, controllability is important. Performance reports should therefore stress controllable items; any noncontrollable factors should be clearly separated and labeled as such.

The basic concept of decentralization and divisional autonomy includes holding a manager responsible for the revenues and costs under her or his control. However, this idea sometimes is lost in setting up evaluation reports. Some upper managers think that allocations of common costs are just as important to show in divisional reports as are separable costs. While it would be theoretically better to show just separable revenues and costs in each product and divisional area, there is pressure to show all costs in reports. As a response to both the need to separate controllable from uncontrollable costs and revenues as well as a way to show all costs, some companies use a *tiered contribution analysis* report.[34] The format of a tiered contribution

---

[33] Merchant and Riccaboni, p. 90. There are other similarities between Italian and U.S. firms reported, but they are not germane to this discussion.

[34] This concept is used by Arthur Andersen & Co., and the discussion is enhanced by *Cost Management, Functional Practice Guidelines, Principles and Concepts* (Chicago: Arthur Andersen & Co., 1983), Chapter 5.

analysis starts off with separable revenues and variable costs of manufacturing. A manufacturing contribution margin (called *variable manufacturing contribution* in the illustration) is followed by separable manufacturing fixed costs and a *total manufacturing contribution* (similar to gross profit). Selling and administrative costs are deducted to yield a *marketing contribution*. Finally, common corporate costs are allocated to get to profit (loss).

Exhibits 14-6 and 14-7 show a tiered contribution analysis for the Computer Division of Snow, Inc. Exhibit 14-6 shows the two product groups within the division (personal computers and printers), corporate/unallocated costs, and a column for the division as a whole. Costs that are not separable by product group or are costs allocated to the division by corporate headquarters are placed in the corporate/unallocated column. For example, divisional management allowed $250 in discounts and allowances, there are $8,000 in divisional fixed selling and distribution costs, and there are $39,500 of divisional and corporate general and administrative costs to allocate. In this illustration, management has decided to allocate corporate/unallocated costs based on relative variable manufacturing margin.

While the personal computer group shows a net profit, the printer group shows a loss after the allocation of common costs. Looking at separable margins (marketing contribution), the personal computer group shows $62,670 (49.9 percent), while the printer group shows only $13,985 (15.5 percent). An analysis even at this level shows why these margins are so different. Variable and fixed manufacturing costs as well as variable selling and distribution costs are much higher for the printer group.

Exhibit 14-7 shows a breakdown of the information for the printer group. There are two printers: a standard model and a deluxe model. While the standard model shows marketing contribution of $21,175 (38.5 percent), the deluxe model shows a loss of $7,190 (–20.4 percent). Further analysis shows that the deluxe model has a negative total manufacturing contribution.

Some of the issues of allocation discussed in Chapter 11 arise in this presentation. Management has chosen to allocate based on the variable manufacturing contribution. This choice affects indicated income and can distort upper management's perception about profitability. Other choices of allocation include total manufacturing contribution, marketing contribution, and defined contribution. The table below shows the different income numbers generated by each of the allocation bases. You should verify these results.

	Income Before Taxes		
Allocation Bases	**Personal Computers**	**Printers**	**Total**
Variable manufacturing contribution	$32,572	($3,667)	$28,905
Total manufacturing contribution	29,231	(326)	28,905
Marketing contribution	23,630	5,275	28,905
Defined contribution	23,630	5,275	28,905

Exhibit 14-6
Tiered Contribution Analysis
Computer Division—Snow, Inc.

	Division Total		Personal Computers		Printers		Corporate/ Unallocated
	$	%	$	%	$	%	$
Gross revenue	215,700	100.0%	125,500	100.0%	90,200	100.0%	0
Discounts and allowances	2,140	1.0%	1,890	1.5%	0	0.0%	250
Net revenue	213,560	99.0%	123,610	98.5%	90,200	100.0%	(250)
Manufacturing costs							
Direct/Variable at standard	67,610	31.3%	34,500	27.5%	33,110	36.7%	0
Variances	7,310	3.4%	2,510	2.0%	4,800	5.3%	0
Direct manufacturing contribution	138,640	64.3%	86,600	69.0%	52,290	58.0%	(250)
Manufacturing costs— indirect/variable	19,220	8.9%	11,170	8.9%	8,050	8.9%	0
Variable manufacturing contribution	119,670	55.4%	75,430	60.1%	44,240	49.0%	(250)
Manufacturing costs—fixed	24,160	11.2%	8,750	7.0%	15,410	17.1%	0
Total manufacturing contribution	95,260	44.2%	66,680	53.1%	28,830	32.0%	(250)
Selling and distribution							
Direct/Variable	11,445	5.3%	2,880	2.3%	8,565	9.5%	0
Indirect/Variable	7,410	3.4%	1,130	0.9%	6,280	7.0%	0
Fixed	8,000	3.7%	0	0.0%	0	0.0%	8,000
Marketing contribution	68,405	31.7%	62,670	49.9%	13,985	15.5%	(8,250)
General and administrative expenses							
Indirect/Variable	14,500	6.7%	0	0.0%	0	0.0%	14,500
Fixed	25,000	11.6%	0	0.0%	0	0.0%	25,000
Defined contribution	28,905	13.4%	62,670	49.9%	13,985	15.5%	(47,750)
Allocations	0	0.0%	30,098	24.0%	17,652	19.6%	47,750
Profit (before taxes)	28,905	13.4%	32,572	26.0%	(3,667)	-4.1%	0

Exhibit 14-7
Tiered Contribution Analysis
Printer Group

	Printers Total		Standard Model		Deluxe Model	
	$	%	$	%	$	%
Gross revenue	$90,200	100.0%	$55,000	100.0%	$35,200	100.0%
Discounts and allowances	0	0.0%	0	0.0%	0	0.0%
Net revenue	90,200	100.0%	55,000	100.0%	35,200	100.0%
Manufacturing costs						
Direct/Variable at standard	33,110	36.7%	13,750	25.0%	19,360	55.0%
Variances	4,800	5.3%	500	0.9%	4,300	12.2%
Direct manufacturing contribution	52,290	58.0%	40,750	74.1%	11,540	32.8%
Manufacturing costs—						
indirect/variable	8,050	8.9%	4,950	9.0%	3,100	8.8%
Variable manufacturing contribution	44,240	49.0%	35,800	65.1%	8,440	24.0%
Manufacturing costs—fixed	15,410	17.1%	5,550	10.1%	9,860	28.0%
Total manufacturing contribution	28,830	32.0%	30,250	55.0%	(1,420)	–4.0%
Selling and distribution						
Direct/Variable	8,565	9.5%	5,225	9.5%	3,340	9.5%
Indirect/Variable	6,280	7.0%	3,850	7.0%	2,430	6.9%
Marketing contribution	13,985	15.5%	21,175	38.5%	(7,190)	–20.4%
Allocations	17,652	19.6%	14,285	26.0%	3,368	9.6%
Profit (before taxes)	(3,667)	–4.1%	6,890	12.5%	(10,558)	–30.0%

Since there are no separable general and administrative expenses, the results from marketing contribution and defined contribution are the same. Note how indicated income rises (loss is reduced) for the printer group as the allocation base changes. These same allocation choices lead to different product profits. For example, since both total manufacturing contribution and marketing contribution are negative for deluxe printers, a *negative* amount of common costs would be allocated using either of these bases. This does not seem a fair way to allocate.

MANAGERIAL EVALUATION AND REWARDS

Corporate management must be careful to evaluate a business segment separately from its managers. A manager in a high technology division may look better than that person really is if the division is growing mostly because of exogenous factors. A manager of an aging division may be reaping extraordinary returns given the situation, even though measures like ROI or RI would show poor segment performance compared to divisions earlier in their life cycles. Thus, evaluating managers should be separate from evaluating their divisions.

Given the situation at hand, the stage of a division in its life cycle, the target levels of appropriate measures of success, how did the manager do? What are the key factors of success of the segment? How did the manager address these factors? These are the types of questions that should be asked when evaluating a manager. The next question is how to use rewards to motivate managers to achieve desired results.

Expectancy theory[35] is a model of motivation. Under this theory, motivation is determined by a combination of intrinsic (self-based) rewards/feelings for having engaged in an effort, intrinsic rewards/feelings for having succeeded in the effort, and extrinsic (external) rewards for having succeeded. These intrinsic and extrinsic rewards are weighted by probabilities of achieving success and of getting a reward given success, as appropriate. This and other models of motivation propose that rewards affect performance. The major question, then, is what types of rewards promote what types of action. In the discussion below, we will explore some of the options open to management.

Income-Based Rewards

Many salary increases and/or bonuses paid to managers are based on financial accounting numbers such as income, target ROI, and target RI. There are several choices that affect these numbers. In the example of the Computer Division of Snow, Inc., group managers for personal computers and for printers would have, say, different bonuses depending on the allocation base for common costs. Other choices such as inventory valuation (LIFO, FIFO, various combinations, etc.) affect income. The same issues raised above in income and investment definition (historical cost versus some other base) come into play here as well. In addition, the issue of controllability is important: Does the income number used for bonus calculation include only controllable items?

The issue at hand is behavior congruence: Will the manager act in the best interests of the corporation? This is the key element of compensation and bonus plans. If a manager thinks that the measures used to evaluate his performance (or that of his division) are unfair, he may try to manipulate results to the detriment of the company as a whole. Given the wide array of options open in determining historical-cost income, managers have the opportunity to affect their own bonuses in a dysfunctional way.

---

[35] See, for example, J. Ronen and J. L. Livingstone, "An Expectancy Theory Approach to the Motivational Impacts of Budgets," *The Accounting Review* 50:4 (October 1975), pp. 671–685.

Noncash Compensation

Part of the satisfaction that a manager may achieve is based on the general working conditions that the manager faces. Office location and size, private secretary or administrative assistant, access to personal computers, and so on are important. In fact, for certain managers, the trappings of power may be more motivating than a bonus. While a corner office or attending a conference in Florida are external rewards (given by upper management), they lead to internal satisfaction (intrinsic rewards) for engaging in everyday business.

Stock and Near-Stock Bonuses

In publicly listed companies, managers may receive stock in the corporation, stock options to buy stock at fixed prices, or a cash compensation based on stock price movement.

Stock   Managers may get a specific numbers of shares of stock based on income targets, for example. Stock awards are based on performance and continued employment with the company. Companies may set performance goals based on, say, the strategic plan for several years. Receiving stock would be based on achieving these longer-term goals.

Stock (or any other bonus, for that matter) that relies on an annual measure may promote short-term actions that are dysfunctional from a longer-term perspective. The advantage of awards based on longer-term goals may be more goal-congruent behavior. Note, however, that stock bonuses can have the same limitations as cash bonuses if they are based on accounting measures such as income or earnings per share.

Stock Options   Stock options are the right to buy stock in the future based on a fixed price set at the time the options are issued. At the time of issuing, it is common that the options are priced somewhere near the current market value of the stock. Thus, if the company is successful, the stock price should rise and the manager can acquire stock at a price that is then less than market. Many options have expiration dates and/or include an escalation of the price for the stock as a function of time. Current tax laws dictate how stock options are treated from both the corporate and the manager's tax perspective.

A basic problem with stock options (or any plan that is tied to stock prices) is that the stock price may not behave solely on factors under the control of the company. Shifts in general interest rates, trade embargoes, the behavior of the United States dollar against other currencies, to name a few reasons, may affect stock prices upward or downward in contrast to company performance. Thus, stock-price-based rewards, like stock options, may have problems.

Near-Stock Bonuses   Rather than issuing stock or awarding stock options, some companies base a cash reward system on movements in stock price. Thus, managers may be awarded units in a bonus plan that are linked to stock prices. As the stock price moves, so does the value of the unit. Many of these plans are ways to defer cash bonuses and to link the bonus program with long-term goals and results.

Golden Handcuffs and Golden Parachutes

New terms entered the bonus and compensation picture in the 1980s: *golden handcuffs* and *golden parachutes*. The first term, golden handcuffs, refers to deferred bonuses that are not awarded unless the executive is still employed with the company. It is the object of these plans to make the future awards so appealing that the opportunity cost of moving to another company would be more than the salary and bonus that could be achieved by such a move.

The wave of mergers (both friendly and unfriendly) of the 1980s spurred many management groups to have *golden parachutes* written into their employment contracts. In essence, if the company were to be dissolved, merged, or otherwise combined with another company, there would be provisions to pay existing management large sums of money as compensation for their losing their jobs. While the motivation of these plans included making takeovers more costly and compensating for real loss, the results may have been quite expensive and not always in the best interests of the stockholders.

In a mid-1980s case, managers of a large corporation were faced with the prospects of unfriendly takeover bids from several sources. In this case, management had large stock holdings as well. As a result of these bids, the board of directors and senior management first decided to sell off assets that were not achieving target results (making less than the opportunity cost of funds). In the face of continued threats, management decided to dissolve the company and to sell all its operating groups and assets. In doing so, management was due money under the golden parachute clauses in its contracts. What was the best option available for all the stockholders? Was the best option the dissolution of the company and the distribution of cash to stockholders (the action taken), or was it better to reorganize the company and to continue on as an entity? It is possible that, because managers would not receive additional compensation anywhere near the amounts received by dissolution, managers acted in a way counter to stockholder interests.

This is just an introduction to compensation plans. The objective is to demonstrate the ways that such plans can motivate (positively or negatively) and how managerial performance and rewards are tied in accounting numbers to segment performance evaluation. The biggest problem with both segment and managerial performance evaluation has been the emphasis on short-term results. Even though managers adopt strategic plans with long-term goals, most corporations still use annual results for evaluation and compensation. Relying on annual results may well lead to a diminished ability to compete in the world marketplace in the future.

Merchant provides us with one of the best studies of executive compensation.[36] In this field study, he proposes that the three basic flaws in executive compensation contracts are

1. Emphasis in short-term income manipulation at the expense of long-term investments. Such contracts place great weight on short-term earnings.
2. When results are not linked to rewards or when too much of a segment manager's reward is based on corporate performance, motivation is hurt.
3. Some contracts include rewards that have no motivational impact; thus, they are unnecessary.[37]

He states that

> The ideal motivational contract for employees in reasonably simple, self-contained, stable work situations has six primary characteristics: (1) performance measures that are congruent with the overall corporate goal of maximizing shareholder value; (2) controllable results measures; (3) accurate results measures; (4) preset and challenging performance standards; (5) rewards that are meaningful, but at minimum cost; and (6) simplicity.[38]

In addition to the measures discussed above, he says that his studies show that a particularly important part of any contract, even if it's unwritten, is the ability for segment managers to be promoted if they perform well over time.[39] This list can also include the criteria listed in the quote by Burchman at the beginning of this chapter.

In addition to looking at criteria, there are other aspects of executive compensation to consider. Lawler says:

> Executive compensation perhaps has its biggest impact on the culture and structure of an organization. It can signal what is valued and serve as a role model in such areas as performance appraisal, employee involvement, open communication, and putting the long-term success of the organization above self-interest. It can be a major driver of the degree to which the organization is differentiated by horizontal levels. In short, executive compensation systems have an organizational impact that goes far beyond their impact on the executives who are directly affected by them.[40]

---

[36] Merchant, *Rewarding Results: Motivating Profit Center Managers.*

[37] Merchant, p. 7.

[38] Merchant, p. 23.

[39] Merchant, p. 41.

[40] Edward E. Lawler, III, "The Organizational Impact of Executive Compensation," in *Executive Compensation: A Strategic Guide for the 1990s,* Fred K. Foulkes, editor (Boston: President and Fellows of Harvard College, 1991), p. 148.

SUMMARY

Performance evaluation is changing in concert with changes in other aspects of management. Companies are placing a greater emphasis on long-term performance and the ability to adapt as the external or internal environment changes. While decentralization still remains a viable way to organize a company, the range of how segments and their managers are evaluated is evolving. Financial measures such as book income, return on investment, and return on sales, for example, are being either reexamined and modified in their traditional form or redefined such as under the Theory of Constraints. In addition, more than lip service is being paid to quantitative nonfinancial measures and qualitative measures of performance. Finally, measures and how executives are compensated for reaching their goals must be carefully related to the long-term strategy of the company.

PROBLEMS AND CASES

14-1. Information for Decision Making[41]

Once upon a time many, many years ago there lived a feudal landlord in a small province of Western Europe. The landlord, Baron Coburg, lived in a castle high on a hill. He was responsible for the well-being of many peasants who occupied the lands surrounding his castle. Each spring as the snow began to melt, the Baron would decide how to provide for all his peasants during the coming year.

One spring, the Baron was thinking about the wheat crop of the coming growing season. "I believe that 30 acres of my land, being worth five bushels of wheat per acre, will produce enough wheat for next winter," he mused, "but who should do the farming? I believe I'll give Ivan and Frederick the responsibility of growing the wheat." Whereupon Ivan and Frederick were summoned for an audience with Baron Coburg.

"Ivan, you will farm on the 20-acre plot of ground and Frederick will farm the 10-acre plot," the Baron began. "I will give Ivan 20 bushels of wheat for seed and 20 pounds of fertilizer. (Twenty pounds of fertilizer are worth two bushels of wheat.) Frederick will get 10 bushels of wheat for seed and 10 pounds of fertilizer. I will give each of you an ox to pull a plow, but you each will have to make arrangements with Feyador the Plowmaker for a plow. The oxen, incidentally, are only three years old and have never been used for farming, so they should have a good 10 years of farming ahead of them. Take good care of them, because an ox is worth 40 bushels of wheat. Come back next fall and return the oxen and the plows along with your

---

[41] Adapted from W. T. Andrews, "Another Improbable Occurrence," *The Accounting Review* (Sarasota, Fla.: American Accounting Association, April 1974), pp. 369–370.

harvest." Ivan and Frederick thanked the Baron and withdrew from the Great Hall, taking with them the things provided by the Baron.

The summer came and went, and after the harvest Ivan and Frederick returned to the Great Hall to account to their master for the things given them in the spring. Ivan said, "My Lord, I present you with a slightly used ox, a plow, broken beyond repair, and 223 bushels of wheat. Unfortunately, I owe Feyador the Plowmaker three bushels of wheat for the plow I got from him last spring. And, as you might expect, I used all the fertilizer and seed you gave me last spring. You will also remember, my Lord, that you took 20 bushels of my harvest for your own personal use."

Frederick spoke next. "Here, my Lord, is a partially used ox, the plow, for which I gave Feyador the Plowmaker three bushels of wheat from my harvest, and 105 bushels of wheat. I, too, used all my seed and fertilizer last spring. Also, my Lord, you took 30 bushels of wheat several days ago for your own table. I believe the plow is good for two more seasons."

"You did well," said the Baron. Blessed with this benediction the two peasants departed.

After they had taken their leave, the Baron began to contemplate what had happened. "Yes," he thought, "they did well, but I wonder which one did better?"

Required:
1. In evaluating the performance of Ivan and Frederick, what measures should Baron Coburg use to answer his question? Justify your choices.
2. Use the measures you propose in part 1 and evaluate the performance of Ivan and Frederick for the most recent growing season. Which did better and why have you come to that conclusion?

14-2. Criteria for Decentralization (CMA)

Pittsburgh-Walsh Company (PWC) is a manufacturing company whose product line consists of lighting fixtures and electronic timing devices. The Lighting Fixtures Division assembles units for the upscale and mid-range markets. The Electronic Timing Devices Division manufactures instrument panels that allow electronic systems to be activated and deactivated at scheduled times for both efficiency and safety purposes. Both divisions operate out of the same manufacturing facilities and share production equipment.

PWC's budget for the year ending December 31, 19X0, is shown at the bottom of the next page and was prepared on a business segment basis under the following guidelines.

- Variable expenses are directly assigned to the incurring division.
- Fixed overhead expenses are directly assigned to the incurring division.
- Common fixed expenses are allocated to the divisions on the basis of units produced which bear a close relationship to direct labor. Included in common fixed expenses are costs of the corporate staff, legal expenses, taxes, staff marketing, and advertising.
- The production plan is for 8,000 upscale fixtures, 22,000 mid-range fixtures, and 20,000 electronic timing devices.

PWC established a bonus plan for division management that requires meeting the budget's planned net income by product line, with a bonus increment if the division exceeds the planned product line net income by ten percent or more.

Shortly before the year began, the CEO, Jack Parkow, suffered a heart attack and retired. After reviewing the 19X0 budget, the new CEO, Joe Kelly, decided to close the lighting fixtures mid-range product line by the end of the first quarter and use the available production capacity to grow the remaining two product lines. The marketing staff advised that electronic timing devices could grow by 40 percent with increased direct sales support. Increases above that level and increasing sales of upscale lighting fixtures would require expanded advertising expenditures to increase consumer awareness of PWC as an electronics and upscale lighting fixture company. Kelly approved the increased sales support and advertising expenditures to achieve the revised plan. Kelly advised the divisions that for bonus purposes the original product line net income objectives must be met, but he did allow the Lighting Fixtures Division to combine the net income objectives for both product lines for bonus purposes.

Prior to the close of the fiscal year, the division controllers were furnished with preliminary actual data for review and adjustment, as appropriate. These preliminary year-end data reflect the revised units of production amounting to 12,000 upscale fixtures, 4,000 mid-range fixtures, and 30,000 electronic timing devices and are presented at the top of the next page.

The controller of the Lighting Fixtures Division, anticipating a similar bonus plan for 19X1, is contemplating deferring some revenues into the next year on the pretext

Pittsburgh-Walsh Company
Budget for the Year Ending December 31, 19X0
(in thousands of dollars)

| | Lighting Fixtures | | Electronic | Totals |
	Upscale	Mid-range	Timing Devices	
Sales	$1,440	$770	$800	$3,010
Variable expenses				
Cost of goods sold	720	439	320	1,479
Selling and administrative	170	60	60	290
Contribution margin	550	271	420	1,241
Fixed overhead expenses	140	80	80	300
Segment margin	410	191	340	941
Common fixed expenses				
Overheads	48	132	120	300
Selling and administrative	11	31	28	70
Net income (loss)	$ 351	$ 28	$192	$ 571

Pittsburgh-Walsh Company
Preliminary Actuals for the Year Ending December 31, 19X0
(in thousands of dollars)

| | Lighting Fixtures | | Electronic | |
	Upscale	Mid-range	Timing Devices	Totals
Sales	$2,160	$140	$1,200	$3,500
Variable expenses				
Cost of goods sold	1,080	80	480	1,640
Selling and administrative	260	11	96	367
Contribution margin	820	49	624	1,493
Fixed overhead expenses	140	14	80	234
Segment margin	680	35	544	1,259
Common fixed expenses				
Overheads	78	27	195	300
Selling and administrative	60	20	150	230
Net income (loss)	$ 542	$ (12)	$ 199	$ 729

that the sales are not yet final, and accruing in the current year expenditures that will be applicable to the first quarter of 19X1. The corporation would meet its annual plan and the division would exceed the 10 percent incremental bonus plateau in the year 19X0 despite the deferred revenues and accrued expenses contemplated.

Required:
1. a. Outline the benefits that an organization realizes from segment reporting.
   b. Evaluate segment reporting on a variable cost basis versus an absorption cost basis.
2. a. Segment reporting can be developed based on different criteria. What criteria must be present for division management to accept being evaluated on a segment basis?
   b. Why would the management of the Electronics Timing Devices Division be unhappy with the current reporting and how should the reporting be revised to gain their acceptance?
3. Explain why the adjustments contemplated by the controller of the Lighting Fixtures Division are unethical by citing the specific standards of competence, confidentiality, integrity, and/or objectivity from **Statements on Management Accounting Number 1C**, "Standards of Ethical Conduct for Management Accountants."

14-3. Segment Performance (CMA)

John Arnston recently has been appointed Chief Operating Officer of Parton Co. Arnston has a manufacturing background and most recently managed the heavy machinery segment of the company. The business segments of Parton range from heavy machinery to consumer foods.

In a recent conversation with the company's chief financial officer, Arnston suggested that segment managers be evaluated on the basis of the segment data appearing in Parton's annual financial report. This report presents revenues, earnings, identifiable assets, and depreciation for each segment for a five-year period. He raised this issue because he thought that evaluating segment managers by using the same type of information often used to evaluate the company's top management would be appropriate.

Parton's chief financial officer has expressed his reservations to Arnston about using segment information from the annual financial report for this purpose. He has suggested that Arnston consider other ways to evaluate segment management performance.

Required:
1. Identify the characteristics of segment information in the annual financial report that would lead Parton's chief financial officer to have reservations about its use for the evaluation of segment management performance.
2. Are the best interests of the company likely to be served if segment managers are evaluated on the basis of segment information in the annual financial report? Explain your answer.
3. Identify and explain the financial information you would recommend Arnston obtain when evaluating segment management performance.

14-4. Responsibility Accounting (CMA)

Kelly Petroleum Company has a large oil and natural gas project in Oklahoma. The project has been organized into two production centers (Petroleum Production and Natural Gas Production) and one service center (Maintenance).

Maintenance Center Activities and Scheduling

Don Pepper, Maintenance Center Manager, has organized his maintenance workers into work crews that serve the two production centers. The maintenance crews perform preventive maintenance and repair equipment both in the field and in the central maintenance shop.

Pepper is responsible for scheduling all maintenance work in the field and at the central shop. Preventive maintenance is performed according to a set schedule established by Pepper and approved by the production crew managers. Breakdowns are given immediate priority in scheduling so that downtime is minimized. Thus, preventive maintenance occasionally must be postponed, but every attempt is made to reschedule it within three weeks. Preventive maintenance work is the responsibility of Pepper. However, if a significant problem is discovered during preventive maintenance, the appropriate production center supervisor authorizes and supervises the repair after checking with Pepper.

When a breakdown in the field occurs, the production centers contact Pepper to initiate the repairs. The repair work is supervised by the production center supervisor. Machinery and equipment sometimes need to be replaced while the original equipment is repaired in the central shop. This procedure is followed only when the time to make the repair in the field would result in an extended interruption of operations. Replacement of equipment is recommended by the maintenance work crew supervisor and approved by a production center supervisor.

Routine preventive maintenance and breakdowns of automotive and mobile equipment used in the field are completed in the central shop. All repairs and maintenance activities taking place in the central shop are under the direction of Pepper.

Maintenance Center Accounting Activities

Pepper has records identifying the work crews assigned to each job in the field, the number of hours spent on the job, and parts and supplies used on the job. In addition, records for the central shop (jobs, labor hours, parts and supplies) have been maintained. However, this detailed maintenance information is not incorporated into Kelly's accounting system.

Pepper develops the annual budget for the Maintenance Center by planning the preventive maintenance that will be needed during the year, estimating the number and seriousness of breakdowns, and estimating the shop activities. He then bases the labor, part, and supply costs on his plans and estimates and develops the budget amounts by line item. Because the timing of the breakdowns is impossible to plan, Pepper divides the annual budget by 12 to derive the monthly budget.

All costs incurred by the work crews in the field and in the central shop are accumulated monthly and then allocated to the two production cost centers based upon the field hours worked in each production center. This method of cost allocation has been used on Pepper's recommendation because he believed that it was easy to implement and understand. Furthermore, he believed that a better allocation system was impossible to incorporate into the monthly report due to the wide range of salaries paid to maintenance workers and the fast turnover of materials and parts.

The November cost report for the Maintenance Center that is provided by the Accounting Department follows.

Production Center Manager's Concerns

Both production center managers have been upset with the method of cost allocation. Furthermore, they believe the report is virtually useless as a cost-control device. Actual costs always seem to deviate from the monthly budget and the proportion charged to each production center varies significantly from month to month. Maintenance costs have increased substantially since 19X0, and the production managers believe that they have no way to judge whether such an increase is reasonable.

The two production managers, Pepper, and representatives of corporate accounting have met to discuss these concerns. They concluded that a responsibility accounting system could be developed to replace the current system. In their opinion, a responsibility accounting system would alleviate the production managers' concerns and accurately reflect the activity of the Maintenance Center.

Required:

1. Explain the purposes of a responsibility accounting system, and discuss how such a system could resolve the concerns of the production center managers of Kelly Petroleum Company.
2. Describe the behavioral advantages generally attributed to responsibility accounting systems that the management of Kelly Petroleum Company should expect if the system were effectively introduced for the Maintenance Center.

3. Describe a report format for the Maintenance Center that would be based upon an effective responsibility accounting system, and explain which, if any, of the Maintenance Center's costs should be charged to the two production centers.

Oklahoma Project
Maintenance Center Cost Report
For the Month of November 19X2
(in thousands of dollars)

	Budget	Actual	Petroleum Production	Natural Gas Production
Shop hours	2,000	1,800		
Field hours	8,000	10,000	6,000	4,000
Labor-electrical	$ 25.0	$ 24.0	$ 14.4	$ 9.6
Labor-mechanical	30.0	35.0	21.0	14.0
Labor-instrumentation	18.0	22.5	13.5	9.0
Labor-automotive	3.5	2.8	1.7	1.1
Labor-heavy equipment	9.6	12.3	7.4	4.9
Labor-equipment operation	28.8	35.4	21.2	14.2
Labor-general	15.4	15.9	9.6	6.3
Parts	60.0	86.2	51.7	34.5
Supplies	15.3	12.2	7.3	4.9
Lubricants and fuels	3.4	3.0	1.8	1.2
Tools	2.5	3.2	1.9	1.3
Accounting and data processing	1.5	1.5	0.9	0.6
Total	$213.0	$254.0	$152.4	$101.6

14-5. Different Evaluation Criteria

The Angel Company has several divisions. Of these, three divisions (Globe, Universe, and Enterprise) all are in mature industries. Data for these divisions appear below (in millions of dollars).

	Division		
	Globe	Universe	Enterprise
Sales	$320	$450	$1,200
Income	32	40	90
Investment	160	240	600
Depreciation (included in income)	20	30	80

Current assets and liabilities remain fairly constant from year to year. Angel Company requires a minimum ROI of 10 percent.

Required:

1. Rank the divisions in order of their contribution to the firm, using at least three different criteria.

2. Choose the one ranking criterion that you believe to be the best and justify your choice.

3. If these divisions had been in the growth stage, would your response to part 2 have changed? How and why?

14-6. Decentralization (CMA)

RNB is a bank holding company for a state-wide group of retail consumer-oriented banks. The bank holding company was formed in the early 1960s by a group of young investors who believed in a high level of consumer services. The number of banks owned by the holding company expanded rapidly. These banks gained visibility through their experimentation with innovations such as free-standing 24 hour automated banking machines, automated funds transfer systems, and other advances in banking services.

RNB's earnings performance has been better than most other banks in the state. The founders organized and continue to operate RNB on a highly decentralized basis. As the number of banks owned grew, RNB's executive management delegated more responsibility and authority to individual bank presidents. The bank presidents are viewed by RNB as a "linking pin" to its executive management. Although certain aspects of each bank's operations are standardized (such as procedures for account and loan applications and salary rates), bank presidents have significant autonomy in determining how each individual bank will operate.

The decentralization has led each of the banks to develop individual marketing campaigns. Several of them have introduced unique "packaged" accounts that include a combination of banking services. However, they sometimes fail to notify the other banks in the group as well as the executive office of their plans and programs. One result has been inter-bank competition for customers where the market areas overlap. Also, the corporate marketing officer had recently begun a state-wide advertising campaign that conflicted with some of the individual banks' advertising. Consequently, there have been occasions when customers and tellers have experienced both confusion and frustration, particularly when the customers attempt to receive services at a bank other than their "home" bank.

RNB's executive management is concerned that there will be a slight decline in earnings for the first time in its history. The decline appears to be attributable to reduced customer satisfaction and higher operating costs. The competition among the state's banks is keen. Bank location and consistent high quality customer service are important. RNB's 18 banks are well located and the three new bank acquisitions planned for next year are considered to be in prime locations. The increase in operating costs appears to be directly related to the individual banks' aggressive marketing efforts and new programs. Specifically, expenditures increased for the advertising, and for the special materials and added personnel for the "packaged" accounts.

For the past three months RNB's executive management has been meeting with the individual bank presidents. The purpose of the meetings is to review RNB's recent performance and seek ways to improve it. One recommendation that appeals to the RNB's executive management is to change the organization to a more centralized structure. The specific proposal calls for a reduction in individual bank autonomy and creation of a centralized Individual Bank Management Committee. The committee would consist of all bank presidents and be chaired by a newly created position, Vice-President of Individual Bank Operations. The individual banks' policies, expected to conform to overall RNB plans, would be set by consensus of the committee. RNB's executive management feels that this participative management approach will be a "fair trade" for the loss of autonomy by the individual bank presidents.

Required:
1. Discuss the advantages attributed to a decentralized organizational structure.
2. Identify disadvantages of a decentralized structure, supporting each disadvantage with an example from RNB's situation.
3. The proposed "more centralized" structure is said by RNB's executive management to include the "participative management approach."
   a. Define the concept "participative management."
   b. Does RNB's recommended approach include participative management? Use information from the situation to support your answer.

14-7. Evaluation Criteria (CMA)

The Jackson Corporation is a large, divisionalized manufacturing company. Each division is viewed as an investment center and has virtually complete autonomy for product development, marketing, and production.

Performance of division managers is evaluated periodically by senior corporate management. Divisional return on investment is the sole criterion used in performance evaluation under current corporate policy. Corporate management believes return on investment is an adequate measure because it incorporates quantitative information from the divisional income statement and balance sheet in the analysis.

Some division managers complained that a single criterion for performance evaluation is insufficient and ineffective. These managers have compiled a list of criteria which they believe should be used in evaluating division managers' performance. The criteria include profitability, market position, productivity, product leadership, personnel development, employee attitudes, public responsibility, and balance between short-range and long-range goals.

Required:
1. Jackson management believes that return on investment is an adequate criterion to evaluate division management performance. Discuss the shortcomings or possible inconsistencies of using return on investment as the sole criterion to evaluate divisional management performance.
2. Discuss the advantages of using multiple criteria versus a single criterion to evaluate divisional management performance.
3. Describe the problems or disadvantages which can be associated with the implementation of the multiple performance criteria measurement system suggested to Jackson Corporation by its division managers.

14-8. Performance Measures (CMA)

Divisional mangers of SIU Incorporated have been expressing growing dissatisfaction with the current methods used to measure divisional performance. Divisional operations are evaluated every quarter by comparison with the static budget prepared during the prior year. Divisional managers claim that many factors are completely out of their control but are included in this comparison. This results in an unfair and misleading performance evaluation.

The managers have been particularly critical of the process used to establish standards and budgets. The annual budget, stated by quarters, is prepared six months prior to the beginning of the operating year. Pressure by top management to reflect increased earnings has often caused divisional managers to overstate revenues and/or understate expenses. In addition, once the budget had been established, divisions were required to "live with the budget." Frequently, external factors such as the state of the economy, changes in consumer preferences, and actions of competitors have not been adequately recognized in the budget parameters that top management supplied to the divisions. The credibility of the performance review is curtailed when the budget cannot be adjusted to incorporate these changes.

Top management, recognizing the current problems, has agreed to establish a committee to review the situation and to make recommendations for a new performance evaluation system. The committee consists of each division manager, the Corporate Controller, and the Executive Vice-President who serves as the chairman. At the first meeting, one division manager outlined an Achievement of Objectives System (AOS). In this performance evaluation system, divisional managers would be evaluated according to three criteria:

- Doing better than last year—Various measures would be compared to the same measures of the prior year.
- Planning realistically—Actual performance for the current year would be compared to realistic plans and/or goals.
- Managing current assets—Various measures would be used to evaluate the divisional management's achievements and reactions to changing business and economic conditions.

A division manager believed this system would overcome many of the inconsistencies of the current system because divisions could be evaluated from three different viewpoints. In addition, managers would have the opportunity to show how they would react and account for changes in uncontrollable external factors.

A second division manager was also in favor of the proposed AOS. However, he cautioned that the success of a new performance evaluation system would be limited unless it had the complete support of top management. Further, this support should be visible within all divisions. He believed that the committee should recommend some procedures which would enhance the motivational and competitive spirit of the divisions.

Required:
1. Explain whether or not the proposed AOS would be an improvement over the measure of divisional performance now used by SIU Incorporated.
2. Develop specific performance measures for each of the three criteria in the proposed AOS which could be used to evaluate divisional managers.
3. Discuss the motivational and behavioral aspects of the proposed performance system. Also, recommend specific programs which could be instituted to promote morale and give incentives to divisional management.

14-9. Measuring Productivity (CMA)

Productivity, defined as output divided by input, has been the center of attention recently because of the general below average performance of United States industries. Productivity improvement is vital to maintaining an increased standard of living for the consumer and industry. Additionally, improved productivity is necessary if companies wish to remain competitive and improve their profitability.

Productivity is often directly associated with profitability because both are measures of performance. In addition, improved productivity is assumed to result in improved profits. While there are many similarities, distinct differences do exist. Profits represent the significant financial measure in a business enterprise while productivity measures represent a significant physical measure.

Because productivity influences the accounting performance measures, and because productivity measures represent one type of performance measure, the management accountant should participate in the development and implementation of productivity measures.

Many companies have already developed measures of productivity. For example, one manufacturing firm employs the rather simplistic measure:

$$\frac{\text{Total revenue}}{\text{Total labor costs}}$$

A company in a regulated industry developed the following productivity evaluation from its work measurement system:

$$\frac{\text{Total applicable standard hours}}{\text{Total actual reported hours}}$$

where:

total applicable standard hours equals job activity times standard hours allowed per activity.

An equipment manufacturer uses the following productivity measure with values expressed in terms of a base year.

$$\frac{\text{Sales billed}}{\text{Direct costs incurred to produce and sell product or service}}$$

Each of these three measures is an attempt to evaluate the effect of various input factors on physical output.

Required:
1. Comment on the validity of this statement: "Productivity is just another ratio and, when considered by itself, suffers from the same shortcomings as any other ratio analysis."
2. What criteria should the management accountant consider in the initial implementation of a productivity measurement and analysis program?
3. Discuss the attributes and deficiencies of any two of the three productivity measures presented in the problem.

14-10. Evaluation and Pricing (CMA)

The Fiore Company manufactures office equipment for sale to retail stores. Tim Lucas, Vice-President of Marketing, has proposed that Fiore introduce two new products to its line—an electric stapler and an electric pencil sharpener.

Lucas has requested that Fiore's Profit Planning Department develop preliminary selling prices for the two new products for his review. Profit Planning is to follow the company's standard policy for developing potential selling prices using as much data as available for each product. Data accumulated by Profit Planning regarding these two new products follow.

	Electric Stapler	Electric Pencil Sharpener
Estimated annual demand in units	12,000	10,000
Estimated unit manufacturing costs	$10.00	$12.00
Estimated unit selling and administrative expenses	$ 4.00	Not available
Assets employed in manufacturing	$180,000	Not available

Fiore plans to employ an average of $2,400,000 of assets to support its operations in the current year. The condensed pro forma operating income statement presented below represents Fiore's planned goals with respect to cost relationships and return-on-assets employed for the entire company for all of its products.

Fiore Company
Pro Forma Operating Income Statement
For the Year Ending May 31, 19X5
($000 omitted)

Revenue	$4,800
Cost of goods sold (manufacturing costs)	2,880
Gross profit	$1,920
Selling and administrative expenses	1,440
Operating profit	$ 480

Required:
1. Calculate a potential selling price for the:
   a. electric stapler using return-on-assets pricing.
   b. electric pencil sharpener using gross margin pricing.
2. Could a selling price for the electric pencil sharpener be calculated using return-on-assets pricing? Explain your answer.
3. Which of the two pricing methods—return-on-assets pricing or gross margin pricing—is more appropriate for decision analysis? Explain your answer.
4. Discuss the additional steps Tim Lucas is likely to take after he receives the potential selling prices for the two new products (as calculated in part 1) to set an actual selling price for each of the two products.

14-11. Compensation Plans (CMA)

Pre-Fab Corporation, a relatively large company in the manufactured housing industry, is known for its aggressive sales promotion campaigns. Pre-Fab's innovative advertising and sales strategies have resulted in generally satisfactory performance in the last few years.

One of Pre-Fab's objectives is to increase sales revenue by at least 10 percent annually. This objective has been attained. Return on investment is considered good and had increased annually until last year, when net income decreased for the first time in nine years. The latest economic recession could be the cause of the change, but other factors such as sales growth discount this reason.

A significant portion of Pre-Fab's administrative expenses are fixed, but the majority of the manufacturing expenses are variable in nature. The increases in selling prices have been consistent with the 12 percent increase in manufacturing expenses. Pre-Fab has consistently been able to maintain a companywide manufacturing contribution margin of approximately 40 percent. However, the manufacturing contribution margin on individual product lines varies from 25 to 55 percent.

Sales commission expenses increased 30 percent over the past year. The prefabricated housing industry has always been sales oriented and Pre-Fab's management has believed in generously rewarding the efforts of its sales personnel. The sales force compensation plan consists of three segments.

- A guaranteed annual salary which is increased annually at about a 6 percent rate. The salary is below industry average.
- A sales commission of 9 percent of total sales dollars. This is higher than the industry average.
- A year-end bonus of 5 percent of total sales dollars to each sales person when their total sales dollars exceed the prior year by at least 12 percent.

The current compensation plan has resulted in an average annual income of $42,500 per sales employee compared with an industry annual average of $30,000. However, the compensation plan has been effective in generating increased sales. Further, the sales department employees are satisfied with the plan. Management, however, is concerned about the financial implications of the current plan. They believe the plan has caused higher selling expenses and a lower net income relative to the sales revenue increase.

At the last staff meeting the Controller suggested that the sales compensation plan be modified so that sales employees could earn an annual average income of $37,500. The Controller believed that such a plan still would be attractive to its sales personnel and, at the same time, allow the company to earn a more satisfactory profit.

The Vice-President of Sales voiced strong objection to altering the current compensation plan because employee morale and incentive would drop significantly if there were any change. Nevertheless, most of the staff believed that the area of sales compensation merited a review. The President stated that all phases of a company operation can benefit from a periodic review, no matter how successful they have been in the past.

Several compensation plans known to be used by other companies in the manufactured housing industry are:

- straight commission as a percentage of sales.
- straight salary.
- salary plus compensation based upon sales to new customers.
- salary plus compensation based upon contribution margin.
- salary plus compensation based upon sales unit volume.

Required:

1. Discuss the advantages and disadvantages of Pre-Fab Corporation's current sales compensation plan with respect to:
    a. the financial aspects of the company.
    b. the behavioral aspects of the sales personnel.
2. For each of the alternative compensation plans known to be used by other companies in the manufactured housing industry, discuss whether the plan would be an improvement over the current plan in terms of:
    a. the financial performance of the company and
    b. the behavioral implications for the sales personnel.

14-12. Incentive Plans (CMA)

Galaxy Inc. is a multi-division organization offering a diversified line of products and services. A brief synopsis of Galaxy's four divisions is presented below.

*   Star Manufacturing is a maker of athletic equipment that currently is enjoying steady growth. Its market is very competitive and dependent on the economy.
*   Sun Appliances is the holder of exclusive patents on medical equipment. The market has monopolistic characteristics and is limited. The division is highly profitable but has little potential for growth. Considerable investments have been made in research and development.
*   Venus Services is a newly acquired division that offers financial services and is geared to capture the market for the expanding financial needs of professional women. It has strong growth and profit potential.
*   Comet Engineering is a civil engineering firm. A majority of its contracts are with state and local governments. Profit margins are restricted by cost plus fixed fee contracts.

James Wright, Galaxy's President, would like to introduce an incentive plan that would reward the performance of key personnel. He knows, however, that these plans can fail if they are not carefully formulated and properly implemented. Wright's previous employer had an incentive plan based on corporate profit improvement that resulted in "managed" earnings and a seesaw record of "good" and "bad" years.

In order to study the feasibility of an incentive plan for Galaxy, Wright has asked Alice Fischer, Manager of Budgets and Standards, to draft a proposal. Fischer's incentive plan proposal for Galaxy contains the following conditions and guidelines.

*   The performance of the manager and key personnel of each division would be measured against the division's annual operating plan. The division operating plan would have been prepared by the division manager and approved by corporate management during the annual budgeting process.
*   The minimum acceptable level of performance would be 90 percent of the division's budgeted operating income prior to corporate and capital allocations; no bonuses would be paid for performance below this level. For every percentage point achieved above the minimum acceptable level of performance, one percent of the division's operating income would be put into the division's bonus fund. The maximum bonus fund contribution any division can receive without the review of the Compensation Committee of the Board of Directors is 20 percent of divisional budgeted operating income (for achieving 110 percent of the budgeted operating income).

- The performance of each division would be reviewed by the Compensation Committee of the Board of Directors prior to distribution of the bonus funds. The committee would have the authority to adjust the bonus funds on its judgment of the following factors.
  a. Nonquantitative achievements such as planning, executive development, and community relations.
  b. Decisions to incur major expenses in the current year that will benefit only future profits, or conversely, the avoidance of expenses that should have been incurred.
  c. Uncontrollable external influences such as regulatory actions, strikes, material shortages, and accounting and tax changes.

The adjustment of any bonus fund upward or downward may not exceed 15 percent of the fund.

Required:
1. Discuss the advantages and disadvantages generally associated with the use of incentive plans.
2. For the incentive plan proposal prepared by Alice Fischer for Galaxy:
   a. evaluate the provisions included in the proposal.
   b. discuss how the plan provisions could be expected to influence the behavior of the key management personnel in each of Galaxy's four divisions.

14-13. Live Case Study

Required:
Based on data from publicly available sources or, preferably, based on interviews with an organization (manufacturing, service, not-for-profit) in your area, address some of the major concerns regarding organizational structure including, but not limited to, the following:

1. How decentralized or centralized is the organization?
2. Are segments cost, revenue, income, or investment centers?
3. What bases were used to decentralize?
4. How complex is the environment? the technology?
5. How are segments evaluated? What monetary and nonmonetary measures are used?
6. Analyze the strengths and weaknesses of the organizational structure and procedures. Are they appropriate? Include in your analysis how structure and procedures tie in with strategic planning and how life-cycle issues are being addressed.

14-14. Forms of Decentralization

In the chapter, various reasons were developed why and how firms chose to decentralize. A firm's organizational structure might change over time as the environment changes.

Required:
Choose a Fortune 500 firm. Using Moody's as well as other sources such as *Fortune*, *Forbes*, *The Wall Street Journal*, *Harvard Business Review*, and the like as resource

materials, describe the organizational form and the level and type of decentralization of the company at least 20 years ago and today. Try to find out as much as you can about how the firm is decentralized and why it chose that form. State clearly why you think the firm either stayed with the same form and type of decentralization over time or why it changed. For example, if a firm originally formed divisions based on functional (product) areas and now is decentralized based on geographic regions, develop both facts and your own opinions about why such a change was made and whether it seemed warranted.

14-15. The Information Services Division[42]

Background

As with many companies, the DRM Hotel chain has recently experienced an unprecedented boom in the processing of data, resulting in the creation of a relatively large data processing division (information services division or ISD). This division has become a high profile department servicing virtually every facet of the company. In the beginning, this department reported directly to the chief executive officer, rather than one of the operating groups or users; this was done to avoid any intergroup conflicts of interest that might arise should such a reporting structure be in place. A brief history of ISD is given in Exhibit 1.

For the past several years the cost and staffing of ISD increased at a far greater rate than the cost increases experienced in other divisions within the company. Some recent actual and budgeted cost figures are given in Exhibit 2. During this same time DRM was experiencing severe financial problems. The rationalization for the ISD cost increase was that the greater the degree of computerization, the greater would be the ability of the company to operate with leaner staffs and thus achieve net cost reductions. To obtain the staff reductions, however, it was going to be necessary to

---

Exhibit 1
History of ISD

ISD was created in 19X1 out of DRM's Micor subsidiary, which developed and maintained its own hardware and software, as well as provided data processing services. ISD's primary purpose at that time was to (a) rationalize the existing data processing operations and (b) develop a new reservation system.

ISD is DRM's in-house data processing group and is responsible for all nongaming data processing functions, namely

- Rooms Reservation Systems
- Financial and Accounting Systems
- Operational Data Bases

Its principal customers are

- RINA—An independent, arms-length organization which handles the promotion of DRM's hotel system (company-owned and franchised) through the operation of a centralized reservation system as well as through marketing programs.

---

[42] This problem is used by permission of the Institute of Management Accountants.

Exhibit 1 (continued)

- Hotel Group
- Corporate Group

The principal departments within ISD are:

Data Processing
- Responsible for the running of the hardware itself, together with the development and maintenance of operating systems.

Corporate Systems Development
- Responsible for the development and maintenance of financial applications software together with the operational data bases.

Reservation Systems
- Responsible for the development and maintenance of the operating and applications software for the reservation system.

Telecommunications
- Responsible for the communications software between hardware devices (whether within the executive office complex or between hotels, the reservations centers, and the host computers at headquarters) as well as telecommunications hardware systems (telexes, telephones, data and voice lines, and teleconferencing).

Out of this mandate came the broad strategy for the 19X2–19X6 period:
- Replacing the then existing mainframes and peripherals with more powerful equipment.
- Converting and, where necessary, upgrading all application systems to run on the new machines.
- Developing, in-house, a customized reservation system at least equal to that of Holiday Inns and American Airlines.

In addition, ISD was to ensure that DRM was poised to take advantage of technological advances as they took place. In this five-year time period, the PC revolutionized business needs of data processing, and users had a major impact on what was going to occur within the business environment. During this period, ISD undertook (in appropriate chronological order) the following activities:
- Ordered an upgraded mainframe on which to develop the reservation system, plus a second mainframe to serve initially as a backup to the original system, but that also had the capabilities of running the financial and operating systems. In addition, new disk and tape drives plus other necessary peripheral hardware and software required to support this system were acquired.
- Developed and implemented the reservation system based upon the functional specifications given by users.
- Converted approximately 35 financial and operating application programs to the new mainframe.
- Acquired and implemented new software packages for general ledger, fixed assets, payroll, capital spending, and order entry.
- Converted word processing to an all PC-based system. Efforts to centralize to a host mainframe and develop LAN's (Local Area Networks) has been, for now, put on the back burner.
- Replaced the backup mainframe with a newer, more powerful mainframe.

Exhibit 2
DRM, Inc.
Information Services Division
Costs—19X3 to 19X6

	19X3 Actual	19X4 Actual	19X5 Budget	19X5 Actual	19X6 Budget
Payroll related	$2,928	$3,862	$ 5,559	$3,289	$3,149
Line costs	579	847	673	841	764
Rental	1,265	1,251	1,951	1,475	1,540
Maintenance	684	529	1,013	629	761
Professional	125	172	212	12	141
Supplies	153	172	323	182	277
T&E	95	166	387	76	148
Loss on disposal	95	359	398		
Depreciation	300	354	1,260	346	580
Other	353	408	223	357	111
Total	$6,577	$8,120	$11,999	$7,207	$7,471
Annual increase	—	23.5%	47.8%	(11.2)%	3.7%
Headcout					
Budget	99	100	134		
Actual	98	123		76	76

Information Services Division
19X3 Actual RINA, Hotel and Corporate Costs

	Total	RINA	Hotels	Corporate
Direct costs				
Data processing	$3,073	$1,536		$1,537
Corporate systems	624			624
Reservations systems	592	592		
Total direct costs	4,289	2,128		2,161
Indirect costs				
Corporate communications				
—telephone	579		$ 579	
—other	641	318	323	
Divisional administration	673	334	339	
Depreciation	300	149	151	
Loss on disposal	95			95
Total indirect costs	2,288	801	1,392	95
Total costs	$6,577	$2,929	$1,392	$2,256

Exhibit 2 (continued)

Information Services Division
19X4 Actual RINA, Hotel and Corporate Costs

	Total	RINA	Hotels	Corporate
Direct costs				
Data processing	$3,338	$1,669		$1,669
Corporate systems	720			720
Reservations systems	799	799		
Total Direct Costs	4,857	2,468		2,389
Indirect costs				
Corporate communications				
—telephone	800		800	
—other	860	437	423	
Divisional administration	871	443	428	
Depreciation	400	203	197	
Loss on disposal	332			332
Total indirect costs	3,263	1,083	1,848	332
Total costs	$8,120	$3,551	$1,848	$2,721
Allocated in 19X3	$6,577	$2,929	$1,392	$2,256
Percent increase	23.5%	21.2%	32.8%	20.6%

develop on-line systems that would allow employees to directly access up-to-date information and thus eliminate the need for the layers of analysts, and operators, who were required to extract information from the available data.

While in the beginning it was recognized that the ISD users should be allocated the costs of ISD, the big questions became (a) what level of costs should the users accept, (b) what cost control the users should have over the tremendous increase in DP costs (which were not being matched by net reductions in the overhead costs of the user groups), and (c) what was the "bottom line" that ISD and users should be measured by—before or after allocated costs?

Cost Responsibilities

Upon the formation of ISD, the allocation of costs to users was done using a very simple formula (see Exhibit 3). Although the face of ISD changed along with the increase in costs, the method of allocating costs remained the same, but with the following limitation.

The charge to DRM's third party marketing organization, RINA, rose so fast that it was not able to afford the extra charges. Hence it was necessary for DRM to put a "cap" on what was being charged each year to RINA. This "cap," however, did not inhibit RINA's requests for changes and upgrades in the systems it used, principally the reservations system (both hardware and software), thereby contributing to ISD's cost spiral.

Exhibit 3
Allocation of Costs

Data Processing
- Allocate 50 percent to RINA, and 50 percent to corporate.
- Systems so intermingled—cannot identify costs with users.

Corporate Systems
- Used on financial systems reporting to Executive Vice President-Finance, and thus 100 percent to corporate.

Reservations
- Relates to reservation system, and thus 100 percent to RINA.

All Other Departments
- As overhead costs, pro-rata with the above costs, but with the corporate portion charged to hotels. The only exception is that 100 percent of telephone costs goes to hotels.

The corporate group's allocated costs were driven largely by the cost of hardware acquired, together with the systems development staff, and the operating software required to run the nonreservations hardware. As the corporate group was not in a position to control the capital spending of ISD, or the additional support required, the costs going into the corporate budgets (and reported to outside shareholders) grew rapidly each year.

The hotel group picked up the balance of the costs including the RINA costs not absorbed, but as the hotel group had as much control over ISD's spending habits as did corporate, their bottom line costs also rose.

The net result was that users were quite upset with ISD. This was clearly evident at the presentation of the ISD budget to users. The meetings reflected a combination of skepticism and histrionics. The only consensus was that all parties concerned had significantly different views on what was required by way of data processing services.

Management's Response
Definitive responses from management came in two distinct phases:

Spectrum   The first step in the solution was to introduce a project management system know as Spectrum. This system addressed two groups of users: RINA and DRM. Spectrum provided for two committees for each user—one for large projects and another for all others. The size of the projects to be reviewed by each committee was arbitrarily set at:

Large—greater than 1,000 man hours
Small—40 hours to 1,000 man hours
Controlled by ISD—less than 40 hours (maintenance only)

The intent was to have each committee staffed by users who were to prioritize the various systems upon their merits. The involvement of ISD in these committees was one of technical support only; they had no votes in the final prioritization. A large committee, which consisted of the heads of each of the Company's business groups, only met once or twice in total but the small project committees met monthly.

These committees, although somewhat bureaucratic, did serve a very important purpose—they managed to identify and document who was asking for what projects, and they were able to identify quite clearly those which were of doubtful usefulness or would yield minimal returns on investment. Accordingly, such projects were effectively canceled by virtue of the fact that they received low priorities and were passed over in order to address the higher priority tasks.

There were also instances where ISD became the sponsor—or user—(such as with word processing), and at times certain conflicts of interest occurred. These committees addressed the needs of not only the applications software, but also the capital expenditures. It also put effective controls on the hiring of application systems programmers.

Reporting Structure   The second step was a change in the reporting structure. In the middle of 19X5, the Company was reorganized, addressing certain cost problems and correcting the system. In this change, ISD now reported to the president of the hotel group. The rationale for this action was that reservations and hotel accounting were a significant part of the ISD job description, and the hotel group was the most prolific user. It also allowed this user, who had become the sink-hole for unallocated costs, to exercise a certain amount of cost control.

Required:
1. To whom do you feel ISD should report?
2. Should costs of ISD be assigned to user departments, and if so, how should such costs be assigned?
3. Assuming users are responsible for their "bottom line," is it fair to have them measured on costs they cannot control; how might they control such costs?

14-16. Industrial Chemicals Company[43]

Background
In 19X5, events which were thought about and planned for the past several years in the Industrial Chemicals Company culminated in the most significant change in the company's 80-plus year history. A major corporate restructuring was announced including the purchase of a large U.S. based pharmaceutical company, for $2.8 billion.

In February of 19X6, the Chairman of the Board and Chief Executive Officer told a reporter for a major financial magazine: "We felt that if we were to build a strong technology base of biology and biotechnology that would simultaneously serve agriculture, animal nutrition, and health care, we could build a unique powerhouse backing it up in a way that companies in these individual businesses couldn't do, and we've built it." The changes initiated were thus not merely pruning and trimming, but changing the very direction of the company by getting out of commodity chemicals and into more innovative areas.

The magazine article made a key observation in its February 10 issue:

> A major problem looms: Can the remaining product lines support the level of research needed to make a major impact on biotechnology? Earnings for the first three quarters of 19X5 dropped and the company expects to show a loss for the fourth quarter, even before write-offs on closed chemical plants.

---

[43] This problem is used by permission of the Institute of Management Accountants.

The company suffered further losses in the silicon wafer business, in which it invested close to $500 million since 19X1. And it was hurt by the sharp downturn in the farm economy. For 19X6, however, analysts estimate earnings of $4.50 per share vs. $3 last year before special charges.

The chairman of the board was well aware of the major concern as to the remaining product lines' capability to support the level of research needed to make a major impact in biotechnology. In fact, as 19X5 drew to a close, he commissioned a special subgroup of the Executive Management Committee (the EMC is the senior management group dealing with major strategic and operational issues) to review the company's overall R&D spending, its affordability and priorities, and bring back recommendations to the EMC in time for inclusion in the 19X6 budgeting process.

In addition to wrestling with the affordability and priority of research programs controlled within the operating units of the company, the EMC subcommittee also focused on the corporately managed R&D effort as to both affordability and organizational placement in terms of operations and control. Views among the subcommittee on this latter issue were varied. The most significant differences in viewpoint are characterized as follows:

> One perspective was to disassemble the corporate R&D effort and place it directly with the businesses being supported wherever possible with, of course, all costs moving directly to those units. The operating unit manager would then be held accountable for the "bottom line" results and would have direct control over all R&D. R&D would thus be moored to managers with a future obligation to commercialize successfully.
>
> Another perspective reasoned that if biotechnology was in fact to be the cornerstone of the transformation of the company, there must be a minimum threshold below which discovery efforts must not go. This viewpoint further reasoned that such effort must be managed corporately and not turned over to operations. Retention of control at the corporate level would insure a long-term focus and avoid susceptibility to cutbacks during times of short-term profit pressure.

A major part of the 19X5 restructuring was a thrust to study and decentralize all corporate staff units to the fullest extent possible into the operating units that are held accountable for overall financial results. The corporate R&D group was to undergo perhaps one of the most substantial reviews of all corporate staff groups.

Research and Development
From a total corporate perspective, the R&D effort falls into three classifications:

> Class I—Maintain existing businesses: This effort is associated with managing existing business assets, maintaining competitiveness of products in existing businesses, and supplying technical service.
> Class II—Expand existing businesses: R&D associated with expanding existing business assets, expanding markets of existing products, or substantially lowering costs of existing processes.
> Class III—Create new businesses: R&D associated with creating new business assets.

Exhibit 1 is a summary of total R&D costs from 19X0–19X4 within these three categories. Exhibit 2 provides comparative data on overall R&D spending for the company and its new acquisition against competitors.

Organizationally, each of the operating units administers its own R&D efforts which cut across all three categories above. In very simple terms, the operating unit is relatively self-sufficient across all three categories where technology *already exists*. They "purchase" some support services from the corporate R&D group as described later. In terms of performance assessment for incentive compensation, the operating unit R&D groups are tied to the "bottom line" results achieved by their respective units.

Corporate R&D

The corporate R&D group, in addition to providing support services to the operating unit's R&D efforts, is primarily responsible for required *new technology* in creating new businesses. At the point in time in the product invention time line when new-technology-based products reach a level of commercial viability, these programs are "handed off" to an operating unit R&D group for eventual movement to commercialization. In the past several years, this corporate R&D group has been successful in "inventing" and "handing off" commercial leads despite some operating unit reluctance to fund the research costs. In these instances, funding sometimes remained with corporate R&D after the "hand-off." The performance assessment for incentive compensation applied to corporate R&D is the total corporation's achievement of "bottom-line" results weighted by the level of success in "handing off" product leads to operating units and keeping the new product discovery pipeline filled with potential products with high probability of commercial success.

A more detailed description of the corporate R&D group follows.

The corporate research and development group is headed by a senior vice president reporting to the chairman of the Board and CEO. The organization, before the 19X5 restructuring, is depicted in Figure 1 (page 647).

The central research laboratory group consists of an information center (20 percent of its costs are charged to operating units on a fee-for-service basis), an MIS facility, bioprocess development and cell culture groups (which are essentially involved in devising production processes for biotechnology-based products), a

Exhibit 1
R&D Costs by Major Category

	19X4		19X3		19X2		19X1		19X0	
	Amount	Percent	Amount	Percent	Amount	Percent	Amount	Percent	Amount	Percent
Class I—Maintain existing businesses	$107	29%	$ 92	32%	$ 84	32%	$ 80	34%	$ 76	37%
Class II—Expand existing businesses	81	22	68	23	65	24	62	27	65	31
Class III—Create new businesses	150	40	102	35	78	30	55	24	44	21
Other—Unclassified	32	9	28	10	37	14	36	15	23	11
Total	$370	100%	$290	100%	$264	100%	$233	100%	$208	100%

Exhibit 2
19X4 R&D Expenditures for the Chemical Industry

	Sales ($M)	R&D as % of Sales	Net Income
Industrial Chemicals (preacquisition)	$6,691	5.5%	$439
Competitors			
1	1,340	4.7	(21)
2	9,508	2.8	380
3	3,857	6.1	216
4	3,328	2.8	161
5	11,418	4.4	549
6	35,915	11.0	1,431
7	10,734	4.0	623

19X5 R&D for the Drug Industry

	Sales ($M)	R&D as % of Sales
Pharmaceutical (preacquisition)	$1,246	9.6%
Competitors		
1	4,700	4.2
2	4,450	5.1
3	40	12.6
4	60	5.7
5	160	6.3
6	3,295	11.0
7	296	14.4
8	3,600	11.0
9	4,000	6.5
10	1,224	3.1
11	700	6.9
12	560	5.4
13	1,910	8.7
14	3,190	9.5
15	2,300	8.0
16	1,835	4.8
17	949	13.5
18	2,000	10.5
19	3,280	6.2

physical sciences center (a central analytical chemistry group providing very specialized and highly skilled support to many users across the company—65 percent of this group's costs are charged out directly on a fee-for-service basis), a group called controlled delivery which develops vehicles for the transfer of pharmaceutical and animal science products into the living systems within which they must act, and a chemistry group providing very specialized skills for both conventional and

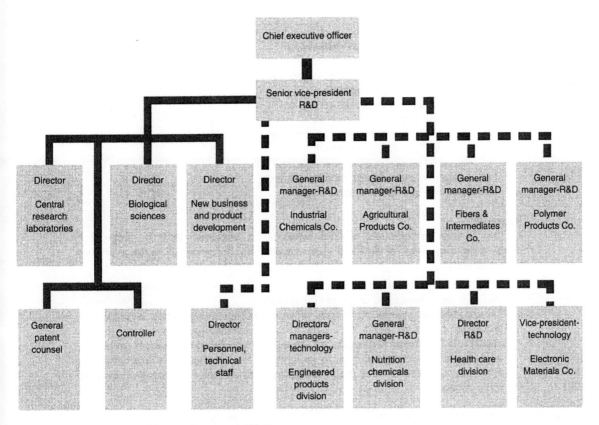

Figure 1   Organization Chart—Corporate R&D

biotechnology process chemistry (about 25 percent of this group's costs are charged directly on a fee-for-service basis). In addition to the direct fee-for-service chargeouts described above, a portion of the costs of this central research laboratory group (primarily the bioprocess development and cell culture groups) is assigned to the biological sciences segment. The remaining costs, along with overall corporate R&D administrative costs, are allocated as a part of corporate charges.

The biological sciences group has been the major focal point for new technology in the pharmaceutical and animal sciences area. It supports plant sciences for the agricultural unit as well. The costs for the biological sciences group are reported as being for new direction basic research. Also controlled within corporate R&D and reported in this segment are the costs of key university relationships supporting basic and applied biomedical, crop chemicals, and animal sciences research efforts.

The patent group has always been decentralized with a patent counsel and staff assigned to each operating unit reporting on a "dotted line" basis to the operating unit and administratively to the general patent counsel. Thus about 80 percent of patent cost is already directly borne by operating units with the remainder allocated as a part of corporate charges.

The "bottom line" of the above operating unit/corporate R&D cost picture was as follows when 19X5 ended:

		Percentage
Directly controlled and administered by operating units		80%
Controlled and administered by corporate research and development		
Charged to operating units on fee-for-service basis.	4%	
Allocated to operating units as "corporate charge" based upon net investment.	3	
Reported as part of biological sciences segment (new direction basic research).	13	20
Total research and development cost		100%

Required:

As the Controller reflected on the information obtained and the important issues being addressed by the EMC subcommittee, the following thoughts and questions surfaced:

1. Would operating unit control of our key R&D growth programs enhance or mitigate our chances of meeting our goals?
2. I know there'll be pressure to level off our R&D spending across the company, including corporate R&D. We've got to make sure we get more "bang for our R&D buck" in terms of prioritizing those efforts to go after the most promising commercial opportunities if we're going to achieve our goals in biotechnology! How can we be sure we're prioritizing these efforts toward increased commercial success?

14-17. Polymer Products Company[44]

Background

In 19X6, the Polymer Products Company was a multinational company engaged in the manufacture of a diverse line of products including chemical and agricultural products, synthetic fibers, electronic materials, pharmaceuticals, process controls, and fabricated products. Sales in 19X6 were $6.8 billion with the following breakdown for operating units and major markets:

Operating Unit	Percent	Major Markets	Percent
Agricultural Products	17	Agriculture	18
Baker Controls	9	Capital Equipment	13
Chemicals		Construction and	
Polymer Products	16	Home Furnishings	13
Industrial Chemicals	20	Food	13
Synthetic Fibers	13	Personal Products	14
Electronic Materials and		Pharmaceuticals	11
Fabricated Products	5	Motor Vehicles	10
Health Care	10	Other	8
Sweeteners	10		
	100		100

---

[44] This problem is used by the permission of the Institute for Management Accountants.

For the past seven years, the firm has been gradually restructuring its core businesses (polymer products, industrial chemicals, and synthetic fibers) by withdrawing from those product lines that do not support the firm's long-term strategy, or which are not expected to produce adequate long-term results.

Polymer's management carefully examined each business unit and decided to fully support only those that had the current or future potential to compete successfully in selected markets. Businesses which appeared unlikely to produce returns that exceeded the company's cost of capital have been, or will be, divested or shut down.

As 19X5 ended, the company changed the financial reporting of its operating unit segments to more closely align it with the restructuring and to better reflect the company's operations. The 19X5 operating unit segments were as follows:

Agricultural Products
   Crop Chemicals
   Animal Sciences
Chemicals
Electronic Materials
Baker Controls
Pharmaceuticals
Sweeteners
Oil & Gas (This business was sold during the 4th Quarter of 19X5).

Synthetic fibers, industrial chemicals, polymer products, and the majority of the fabricated products business unit were combined to form the new "chemicals" segment. Two new segments, sweeteners and pharmaceuticals, resulted from the 19X5 acquisition of a major health care company. The electronics business was made a separate segment, and the separations business—previously a part of fabricated products—was transferred to Baker Controls since it served similar process control equipment markets. The former biological sciences segment, which was composed of animal nutrition products, the health care division, and corporate research & development expense not charged to operating units, was eliminated. The animal nutrition segment became a component of agricultural products called "animal sciences," while the health care division was merged with the pharmaceuticals segment of the newly acquired company. Corporate research and development expenses included in the biological sciences segment were being studied. For external and internal reporting these overheads were retained at the corporate level and not assigned to the operating units.

Company Performance Measurement Philosophy

Until the start of the decade, Polymer focused on a "performance income" measure of an operating unit's results. The "performance income" internal reporting system assigned only directly controllable elements of sales, cost of goods sold, marketing, administrative, and technical expenses, as well as working capital, to the operating units. Indirect or non-controllable elements, such as the cost of corporate staff support groups, interest expense and income, foreign currency gains and losses, and taxes were pooled corporately. Various "formulae" were applied to assign the aggregate of these "net corporate charges" to the operating units for determining a pro forma net income, return on capital employed, and net cash flow. As a result, these overall "bottom line" indicators of business unit performance were only directionally representative.

As the current decade began, some of the company's core businesses matured and began to decline. Declining margins and profitability quickly brought an awareness to management of the need to shift business strategies and/or businesses. Faced with difficult divestment/investment/acquisition decisions, top management soon recognized the need for a more accurate measurement and understanding of worldwide operating unit results. The myriad of "special studies" which preceded the restructuring program often revealed dramatically different business results than the formula-derived indicators. Some examples of the problems encountered are provided below:

1. Under the "formula" approach, currency gains and losses were treated as a component of net corporate charges. If a product were sold to a French customer on 180-day terms, the selling business unit reflected the full sales value at the then current exchange rate, leaving the company exposed to devaluation of the French franc. If the devaluation occurred, performance of the operating unit involved was not affected but the company results were.

2. Under the "formula" approach, all operating units applied an average worldwide tax rate to compute a pro forma net income, return on capital employed, and net cash flow. When a business unit had a choice to source the same product from Belgium or the U.K., a dilemma was created. Although costs were nominally higher in the U.K., lowering a unit's performance income, the company was in a non-tax position there which dramatically improved net income. However, by reporting business results using an average worldwide tax rate, all product sourcing from the U.K. appeared disadvantageous. The company, because of its internal reporting practices, ran the risk of not taking full advantage of its tax loss carry-forward situations in various pricing and sourcing decisions.

3. Under the "formula" approach, all operating units applied an average interest expense and interest income rate per dollar of capital employed as a result of including "net corporate charge" in their net income computation. Two anomalies resulted from this practice. First, businesses operating in hyperinflationary countries generated significant amounts of interest expense due to the fact that net finance expense rates were high and the local subsidiaries were generally highly leveraged. Because average worldwide interest expense rates were used in the corporate formula, all businesses shared in this unusual cost—even if they had no presence in these countries. And second, emerging businesses with rapidly expanding capital needs drained corporate cash, while mature businesses with contracting capital bases generated most of the internal funds. Because average worldwide interest income rates were used in the corporate formula, businesses consuming cash received an ever increasing share of interest income, while those generating cash received a declining share—exactly the reverse of what might be considered "equitable."

Because of the inadequacies of the current internal reporting system, top management wanted a new performance measurement technique which brought operating management's attention to "all" the financial impacts of a business decision. To accomplish this, it was decided in 19X2 that as many of the income statement and balance sheet items as were practicable would be identified with, and charged to, each operating unit. It was further intended that each operating unit would then be measured by their achievement against goals established for net income, return on capital employed, and net cash flow. The definitions to be used for return on capital employed and net cash flow are provided below:

$$\text{return on capital employed} = \frac{\text{net income} + \text{after-tax interest expense}}{\text{average capital employed}}$$

net cash flow = net income + depreciation and obsolescence − capital expenditures − change in (receivables + inventory + other current assets + net capitalized interest + investments and miscellaneous assets + net corporate assets) + change in (deferred taxes + minority interest + other liabilities)

Note: average capital employed = operating unit net worth

Because of the significant changes created by the new internal reporting system, and the fact that many factors which were only partially or indirectly controlled were to be incorporated into the measurement of business results, upper management anticipated adverse line manager reaction. To begin reporting "all" the financial impacts of a business decision, without creating internal upheaval, the asset management program was "sold" on the premise that it was intended to "measure the business, not necessarily the manager." When incorporating business results in the performance evaluation process, managers were initially encouraged to avoid blindly accepting the "bottom line" results without at least judgmentally incorporating controllability aspects. Although upper level management performance evaluations required little mitigation, lower level manager's results clearly needed some interpretation.

The incentive compensation system for upper management was also changed for 19X3 to reward directors and officers based upon their relative success in achieving annual budgets established for the above measures. The total corporate annual incentive award is determined in part based upon where "bottom line" earnings fall relative to a narrow target range determined at the beginning of each year. The award was initially designed to cascade down the organization. As a result, a similar quantitative assessment of "bottom line" earnings was made annually at the operating and business unit levels to determine if lower level managers also qualified for an award based on their business's contribution to total corporate results. The incentive award methodology gradually evolved in the 19X4-X6 timeframe. In 19X6, although the total amount of the incentive award was corporately determined, the CEO assigned specific amounts to each operating unit. It was then up to the head of each unit to determine how the award was to be assigned within his organization. For 19X7, each operating unit designed its own incentive award system, tailored to blend the "bottom line" with other performance measures. The corporate system awards are presented two-thirds in cash and one-third in restricted stock, which is accessible only after three years and only if stock prices meet certain appreciation tests. This latter feature was recently added to bring long-term dimension to the program in addition to the near-term annual income/cash flow results focus.

Before this new reporting and management scheme (called "Asset Management"), the amount of corporately "pooled" costs allocated as a corporate charge was nearly 4 percent of worldwide sales. After the asset management program was instituted, along with selected decentralization of certain corporate staff groups, these corporately pooled costs were less than 1.5 percent of worldwide sales.

Required:
Discuss the relative merits of the performance income measure and the asset management program as bases for the evaluation of managers' performance.

14-18. BP America[45]

John Bishop, Corporate Controller of BP America, gazed out his office window on the 37th floor of the BP America Building, admiring the activities of the ice breakers that were clearing the shipping lanes on Lake Erie. He was contemplating this year's upcoming negotiations between the "businesses" and the "staff departments" to determine the costs of, and responsibility for, centrally provided services. (See Exhibits 1 and 2 for lists of businesses and staff departments.) His thoughts faded to last year, which saw the beginning of the end of the old cost allocation system and the dawning of a new, more imaginative and innovative process for managing corporate charges. He was trying to imagine how this year's procedure would differ from last year's, what guidelines to use to judge its success, and what new problems possibly could arise.

Exhibit 1
BP America Businesses

BP Exploration	BP Nutrition
BP Oil	Carborundum Division
BP Chemicals	BP America Ventures
BP Advanced Minerals	Research and
BP Titanium Minerals	Development
BP Minerals	Chase Brass
BP Coal	Kaldair

Exhibit 2
BP America Staff Departments

Audit
Control
Finance
Planning
Tax
Law
Executives
Administrative Services
Information Management
Other Administrative and Information Services
Human Resources
External Affairs—Cleveland
Federal Government Affairs
State Government Affairs
Public Affairs
Patent and License
Health, Safety, and Environmental Quality

---

[45] This problem is used by the permission of the Institute of Management Accountants.

Background

BP America was formed from the combination of Standard Oil and BP North America. The original link between BP and Standard Oil was forged in 1970 when, in exchange for an increased shareholding in Standard Oil, BP transferred to the company its crude oil leases at Prudhoe Bay on the North Slope of Alaska, along with some other upstream and downstream assets. That arrangement brought together BP's large oil reserves in Alaska and the marketing expertise of the long-established American company. In 1987, a total merger of the two companies occurred when BP purchased the minority shareholding in Standard Oil, and BP America was formed. Along with the physical exchange of assets, Standard Oil, in becoming BP America, also had to wrestle with the cultural and philosophical attitudes of a new global parent.

The 1970s and 1980s saw significant changes in the oil industry. By the 1980s, a higher degree of concentration and more intensive competition was evident, which forced BP America to reconsider both its internal and external business methodologies. One of the outcomes was greater responsibility passing out from the center of the organization to the individual businesses, creating a more decentralized company. Sir Peter Walters, Chairman of BP, described this as "central control over strategy and delegation of business operating decisions." The result was more day-to-day decision-making at lower levels in the organization. The change also affected accountability for costs at both the corporate and business levels.

Historically, central costs were divided by the corporate staff into (1) costs directly applicable to the businesses and (2) corporate costs. The business-related costs were allocated from internal cost centers to the businesses using several allocation bases, including headcount, billable hours, and space occupied. Corporate costs were defined as all costs controlled by the CEO which benefitted the corporation as a whole, not individual businesses per se. These included items solely related to the CEO's activities, such as Planning, Control, and Executives.

New Procedures

Although the old allocation process was not considered "broken," top management believed that a change was necessary to adhere to the new philosophy of increased profit responsibility of the businesses. A new procedure was initiated to encourage a buyer/seller relationship between the central staff departments and their primary "customers," the businesses. The BP America CEO also was considered to be one of the customers of the staff departments because of his stewardship role over corporate costs, which were re-named "stewardship costs." The staff departments and their customers were required to negotiate both the level of services to be provided and the amounts to be charged for services. Under this scheme, each staff department was required to:

1. demonstrate value for dollars spent to convince its customers to use its services;
2. be competitive with respect to alternatives—for example, services from third parties; and
3. insure the satisfaction of its customers.

Conversely, the businesses had the option to:

1. continue to use the BP America corporate staff at negotiated charges;
2. purchase services from external sources;

3. perform services themselves; or
4. do without services, if expected costs were greater than expected benefits.

From a corporate viewpoint, this procedure:

1. decreased corporate overhead by dispersing more costs to users;
2. made the businesses aware of the value of corporate services; and
3. helped eliminate inefficient or unnecessary services.

John Bishop mentally reviewed the mechanics of the process. About a year ago, Robert "Bob" Horton, then CEO of BP America, had created the Business Forum. This group, comprised of the BP America business heads and senior corporate staff, introduced the new buyer/seller procedure. Bishop considered this a masterstroke, because it focused the business heads on the need to more accurately distribute central costs between stewardship and the businesses. Effectively, the process took business-related activities out of stewardship and placed them in the businesses. It also ensured the businesses' total involvement from the start.

At a meeting of the Business Forum, each staff department presented its operating plan for the year. Items presented were as follows:

1. role and mission of the staff department;
2. input expected from businesses for the staff department to be able to fulfill its responsibilities;
3. expected headcount and budgeted costs of the staff department; and
4. a review of services provided to businesses, billing procedures for these services, and expected annual charges.

The Business Forum then provided a recommendation to the CEO of BP America on the appropriate distribution of costs between stewardship and the businesses. The chairman of the Forum, Bill Johnson, insisted on agreement; silence was considered to be consent. The Business Forum also made recommendations to eliminate activities that the group no longer considered to be needed. However, at no point did the Business Forum attempt to carry out the role of negotiator or mediator between individual buyers and sellers. James Ross (who replaced Robert Horton as CEO in April 1988) immediately endorsed this entire process.

The Discussion

Bishop's thoughts were interrupted by David Sourwine, Controller, Headquarters and Treasury, who was arriving for a meeting on this very subject. After exchanging pleasantries, they got down to business:

JB: "Let's look at where we've been and where we're going this year with the annual review of corporate charges."

DS: "As I recall, the overall process worked pretty well last year, although there is no doubt that it was a dramatic change for some people. Of the $141 million of budgeted costs, only $11 million was in disagreement after the first cut, and we managed to whittle that down to $1.1 million. One of the problems was that some of the staff departments were uncomfortable with being challenged, both on what they do and their associated costs. They felt they were being put in an adversarial position, which wasn't necessary."

JB: "Yes, and some of the business heads believed that staff departments didn't attack their costs vigorously enough. I have a feeling it may be very different this time around. And it's our responsibility to get the job done with as little residual ill will as possible. I know that James Ross wants us to develop an atmosphere in which constructive challenge is healthy and expected."

DS: "When is the Business Forum meeting this year?"

JB: "In April, when it will review the process and remind everyone that they should prepare in advance for the staff/business discussions. And this time we'll make sure that everyone understands the costs which have to be borne by the businesses and can't be hidden in stewardship any longer."

DS: "A couple of the businesses seemed to be "playing games" last year—deliberately negotiating low charges and then not reducing the amounts of services they used."

JB: "There are no free lunches. We'll have to make sure that everyone knows this. We'll also have to stress that the businesses must think longer-term. They must realize that if they decide not to use corporate services this year or if they underestimate their expected usage, these services may not be available when they want them. BP America cannot reduce its corporate headcount and costs one year and then go back into the market to re-hire the next. And of course, Mr. Ross and the CEO Committee have the power to oversee the process for the overall good of BP America. Ross has to be satisfied that any changes made are in the corporation's best interests."

DS: "I've heard rumors that some of the people in corporate staff are worried the businesses will try to unreasonably reduce billing rates."

JB: "One purpose of this process is to satisfy the businesses that they're getting value for the dollars they spend on services. If they really don't want what the corporate departments are providing, that will certainly come out in the wash."

DS: "Do you believe Mr. Ross is expecting the stewardship costs to be reduced again this year?"

JB: "If you are referring to the $16 million shifted last year from stewardship to the businesses, I don't think he will expect the same to happen again. However, I believe the potential exists for some further transfers of business-related costs from stewardship. Also, recall that James Ross said this year he will not pick up any discrepancies, like the $1.1 million of unbilled service he absorbed into stewardship last year."

Required:
1.   Should BP America's corporate staff departments be designated as profit centers? If so, should they be allowed to solicit businesses outside the corporation?
2.   What measure(s) should be used to evaluate the performance of staff departments?
3.   BP America recently sold BP Minerals, a business which accounted for over 10 percent of the corporation's assets. What effect would you expect this sale to have on corporate staffing requirements under the new chargeout procedures?
4.   What effect would you expect the new procedures to have on total corporate costs?

14-19. Centerior Energy Corporation (A)[46]

> The challenge of operating efficiently is spelled out in the rate agreement. Our interim goal is to reduce annual operation and maintenance expense (other than fuel and purchased power) by $40 million to $100 million by 1991. No Company activity is off limits where cost-cutting is concerned, except where cost-cutting would reduce the quality of our service to customers or endanger our employees or the public.
>
> Centerior Energy Corporation
> 1988 Annual Report

Background

Centerior Energy Corporation was created in 1985 as a holding company for the Cleveland Electric Illumination Company (CEI) and Toledo Edison (TEd). CEI and TEd are electric utilities serving market areas in northeastern and northwestern Ohio, respectively. As a result of the formation of Centerior Energy, Centerior Service Company was formed to provide administrative and engineering services to CEI and TEd. Centerior Energy Corporation and Centerior Service Company operate under the rules and regulations of the SEC for public utility holding companies; Centerior Service Company, CEI, and TEd are regulated by the Federal Energy Regulatory Commission (FERC) and the Public Utilities Commission of the State of Ohio (PUCO).

The rate agreement referred to in the above excerpt became effective on February 1, 1989. Additional rate increases were to follow in 1990 and 1991. The PUCO attached to this rate agreement a requirement that Centerior Energy not only establish fair and reasonable productivity standards for generating units but also reduce the costs of operating and maintaining the units' generating capacity. After the February 1, 1989 rate increase, CEI's and TEd's prices to residential customers for 500 kilowatt-hours of service were $10.10 and $11.30 per kilowatt-hour, respectively. (See Exhibit 1 for a chart of typical electric billings as of January 1, 1989 in selected northern cities.)

Although revenues had increased since 1986, operating income at Centerior had decreased, due principally to growth in operation and maintenance expense as well as in depreciation and amortization. Centerior was especially concerned about managing the operation and maintenance expense because of its dramatic recent growth and its immediate demands for cash for current operating purposes. (See Exhibit 2, page 658, for three years' comparative results of operations for Centerior Energy.)

Accounting Systems

In the early 1950s, TEd had developed concepts for activity accounting which accumulated costs at a relatively low level of aggregation to activities such as maintaining poles, operating boilers, and replacing transformers. In addition, TEd had developed allocation systems that assigned indirect costs on the basis of standards which reflected flexible activity levels. TEd's accounting system had been in place for about 35 years without major changes. Upper, middle, and lower management had become accustomed to managing their activities using reports that captured costs at the activity level.

CEI's accounting system, on the other hand, captured costs at a much higher level of aggregation. It was used to control labor and material costs at the operating

---

[46] This problem is used by permission of the Institute of Management Accountants.

Exhibit 1
Typical Electric Billings
Residental Prices Per KWH
(January 1, 1989)

New York	$.1272
Philadelphia	.1235
Akron	.1137
Gary	.1076
Pittsburgh	.1051
Newark, NJ	.1050
Chicago	.1014
Toledo*	.1001
Hartford	.0993
Cleveland*	.0927
Boston	.0884
Detroit	.0877
Buffalo	.0846
Dayton	.0828
Erie	.0812
Baltimore	.0751
Milwaukee	.0741
Columbus	.0718
Cincinnati	.0711
Washington, D.C.	.0507

*Centerior Energy service areas.
Note: Assumes 500 KWH per month usage.

department level on a monthly basis. These costs were assigned directly to departments rather than to activities. Indirect costs were accumulated at headquarters and allocated monthly to the operating departments. First-line managers were unaccustomed to receiving cost reports from the accounting system. For the most part, the accounting and work management systems were not compatible with each other. Accounting cost information was provided only to executive and middle management.

The manner in which the two operating companies budgeted for costs differed dramatically, reflecting differences in the cost systems. TEd's budget was prepared by estimating activity levels throughout the entire organization for the budget period. Costs were subsequently traced to activities across departmental lines. CEI budgeted at the department level, without the same emphasis on tracing the impact of one department's operating decisions on other units of the company.

Management Accounting Response

"There were really two parts of our charge to create a new accounting system for Centerior Energy," explained Jack Flick, the corporation's Manager of Accounting Systems. "First, as our part of the company-wide commitment to reduce operating costs, we were expected to implement a system or systems that would streamline the accounting functions within Centerior. Prior to the rate agreement there were 45 accountants at Centerior Service, 180 at CEI, and 65 at TEd, for a total of 290.

Exhibit 2
Centerior Energy Corporation
Results of Operations

	For the years ended December 31,		
	1988	1987	1986
Operating Revenues:			
Electric	$2,037,560	$1,911,985	$1,882,838
Steam heating	—	13,371	12,953
	$2,037,560	$1,925,356	$1,895,791
Operating Expenses:			
Fuel and purchased power	391,401	470,466	522,281
Other operation and maintenance	865,632	642,594	550,874
Depreciation and amortization	264,824	214,421	141,009
Taxes, other than federal income taxes	268,550	207,521	194,925
Perry Unit 1 and Beaver Valley Unit 2 deferred operating expenses	(188,209)	(87,623)	—
Federal income taxes	123,697	105,912	138,181
	1,725,895	1,553,291	1,547,270
Operating Income	$ 311,665	$ 372,065	$ 348,521

Top management challenged us to create and implement a corporation-wide accounting system that would reduce that number.

"Second, the PUCO placed a challenge before us to manage our costs more effectively. To do that we had to think in terms of an overall cost management system that would satisfy the regulatory requirements. Our biggest hurdle was in the immense difference in cost management traditions in the two operating companies, CEI and Toledo Edison. Even though Toledo Edison's system was based on concepts which we believed to be sound, its age—about 35 years—and its dedicated computer system—which was pretty inflexible—presented very real problems. It was not possible to make adjustments to the old system in order to fix it adequately for the 1990s.

"CEI was entirely different. Its accounting system was even older and conceptually never had reached the level of costing activities. Especially difficult for us were the problems created by the system of cost allocation. For example, repair departments were allocated actual costs of the warehouse on a monthly basis according to the number of actual requisitions. That meant that everybody tried to requisition warehouse items in the busy summer months and avoid requisitions in the winter when little work was done. Repair units would inflate their requisitions in the summer and stockpile parts. This is only one of a multitude of ways in which the costing system created management problems."

Required:

1. Based on the brief description of CEI's and TEd's accounting systems, identify their cost objects. How does any difference in cost objects relate to management control and cost management problems that may arise from the affiliation of the two companies?

2. Should accounting systems remain decentralized to the operating companies or be centralized at Centerior Service Company?
3. What are the benefits and costs of an activity-based approach to cost attribution, budgeting, and management performance evaluation throughout Centerior Energy?

Chapter 15

Transfer Pricing

Many Ph.D. dissertations in accounting explore the theoretical never-never land of transfer pricing, thereby assuring the writer a life of almost complete obscurity. We have read a number of these dissertations and suggest that you wait for the movie.[1]

The transfer pricing problem is a difficult and frustrating one. Although there has been substantial interest in this problem among academics, many managers regard it as unsolved or unsolvable.[2]

When companies are decentralized and segments looked upon as profit or investment centers, the divisions often sell goods or services to one another. *Transfer prices* are the prices that they charge. Companies establish policies regarding transfers (e.g., Is a division forced to buy internally or can it buy

---

[1] Daniel P. Keegan, and Patrick D. Howard, "Transfer Pricing for Fun and Profit," *Review*, No. 3, Price Waterhouse (1986), p. 38.

[2] Robert C. Eccles, *The Transfer Pricing Problem: A Theory for Practice* (Lexington, Mass.: D. C. Heath, 1985), p. 1.

elsewhere?) and the prices charged (e.g., Can a division charge less than it does to outside customers?) and also administer the policies (e.g., If a dispute arises between a selling and buying division, what should be done next?). This chapter deals primarily with transfers made between decentralized divisions of companies that are viewed as investment centers. The main points are also applicable to service department transfers as discussed in Chapter 11.

Consider a general case where one division of a company manufactures a component that is used by another division of the same company to produce a final product that is sold externally to the company. Also assume that the two divisions are treated as independent investment centers and that measures of income are used when evaluating these divisions. Thus, the price that the manufacturing division charges the buying division for the component will affect accounting income for each division. From a corporate perspective, however, the profit on any final product is the price of that product when sold externally less the costs to manufacture it. While the profit for each division is changed if one division pays another more or less money for a part of a final product, the profit to the overall company remains unchanged since out-of-pocket *costs* are unchanged. Thus, transfer pricing involves the allocation of the overall corporate profit on a product to each of the divisions involved in its production. Since that allocation affects profits, measures of divisional performance such as return on investment (ROI) or residual income (RI) are changed as transfer prices change. It is by nature, therefore, a behavioral issue: given the transfer pricing policies, their administration, and the transfer prices that have been set, will managers act in a way that maximizes the profits of the company? Will managers perceive the entire transfer pricing system to be fair? Because the basic problem is behavioral, there are no uniformly applicable solutions. Each company must come to a solution that works for the managers in that company. However, there are guidelines that help in resolving this difficult area.

SOME BASIC ISSUES

In a decentralized company, managers of cost, profit, and investment centers have varying degrees of autonomy to make critical decisions that affect their divisions. With complete decentralization, managers can decide whether to make a part within the segment, buy that part from another division of the company, or buy it from an outside vendor. To achieve the most profit for the company, that decision should include choosing a source of supply with the lowest cost.[3] Incremental costs to make a component within the division

---

[3] There are issues of delivery and quality that also affect decisions. These are also costs but are ignored at this point in the discussion.

include both differential variable and fixed costs. With external sources incremental costs to the buying division consist of the transfer price from another division (the selling division) or the price from an outside supplier.

From the buying division's perspective, it is a make-or-buy decision where there is one source of making (the division itself) and there are two sources of buying (another division or an outside company). From the company's perspective, this make-or-buy decision has two sources of making (two different divisions within the company) and one source of buying (the outside vendor). Because there is this difference in perspective, managers of decentralized divisions may make decisions that seem optimal for their divisions (income, ROI, and/or RI go up) but are not optimal for the overall company. It is possible that transfer pricing policies, administration, and transfer prices will encourage managers to choose, say, an outside vendor when, from a corporate-cost standpoint, the optimal decision is to buy from another division.

BASES FOR TRANSFER PRICES

From either an accounting or an economic point of view, there are some basic ways that transfer prices can be set. Market price (or an estimate of market price) seems to be a ceiling for a transfer price, while some notion of incremental or marginal cost is the floor.

Market Prices

Market prices refer to the price that a selling division can get for its product in the external market or the price at which a buying division can purchase the product in the marketplace. With some *intermediate goods* (the term used to define a part or subassembly that could be transferred from one division to another) there is an external market while with others there is not.

A buying division would rarely be willing to pay another division of the same company a price that exceeds the market place. In fact, since there would be little or no selling expenses nor the possibility of an uncollected account receivable with an internal sale, buying divisions will want a price that is less than the market price.

From the company's view, the market price (reduced by any costs saved by selling internally) is the opportunity cost when a selling division is at full capacity. Sales at less than market result in lost business that would have been at market prices. In this case, the division and the company are best served if transfers occur at market.

The basic advantage of using market prices is that they allow each division to be evaluated on a standalone basis. Measures of income have more validity when market prices are used. Managers are encouraged to treat their divisions as independent companies and to buy from whatever source seems the best under current market conditions.

However, there are some limitations to the use of market prices. First, a market may not exist for an intermediate product. Take the case of the transmission division of an automobile company. There may be no external market to buy the transmissions that the assembly division needs. In this case, divisions may approximate market by either basing prices on like products manufactured in the market or by marking up costs of production in the same manner that they would for an outside sale.

Second, if a division is a captive of another division (there is no source of supply except that division or there is no source of sales except the other division), then there is a real question about using income-based measures to evaluate the division. A captive selling division that provides 100 percent of its output to another division may well be evaluated as a cost center. A captive buying division that needs all its products from other divisions of the company may be evaluated as a revenue center. In these cases there is dependence between the divisions, and it would be best if they were evaluated together as a single unit. Finally, there are some market-based transfer prices that can lead to suboptimal decisions as a later discussion about transfer pricing theory shows.

Cost-Based Prices

If a segment is not at capacity, then incremental cost is the opportunity cost of selling to another division. From the economist's perspective, incremental cost is marginal cost: the cost to provide the next unit of production. However, most accountants and managers treat incremental variable costs (and any differential fixed costs) as a good approximation of marginal cost.

The base for a transfer price, then, is variable cost. The selling division would look the best if actual variable cost were used since any cost overruns would be passed on to the buying division. However, the buying division would like to use standard variable costs since they would not think it fair to pay for possible inefficiencies of the selling division. Say that a part had a standard cost of $50 but actual costs were $55. The managers of the selling division would have no incentive to control costs if they could sell these parts at $55 each. If the standards are accurate, the $50 standard cost reflects what the part should have cost, and any costs above that amount hurt the division and the company. The other side of the coin is that if the selling division is more efficient than standard (say costs are held to $47), it gets to keep the favorable $3 per unit variance and improve its income. In both cases, however, the buying division can plan its own costs since it will purchase the part at $50, the standard variable cost.

While standard variable cost and any incremental fixed costs associated with a transfer are the opportunity costs to the company when excess capacity exists, some managers want to recover full costs of production. Absorption costing assigns fixed cost to product on a unit basis. While fixed cost per unit actually changes as the number of units changes, it is most common to establish the full cost of a product at the beginning of a year and to use that cost for the entire year regardless of changes in production levels. Full costs include nondifferential costs such as common departmental, factory, and/or divisional costs that would not change if sales to another division were dropped. The defense of full costs is found when they are used as a basis for estimating market prices. When no market exists for an intermediate good, standard full costs plus a usual markup may be as good a way as possible for a selling division to approximate the market.

An alternative to standard full costs is variable costs plus a sum that reflects capacity use of the buying division. For example, if the selling division is buying new equipment, they may face a choice of what size, quality, or capacity of equipment to purchase. With sporadic purchases from other divisions, managers may choose equipment that has limited capacity and/or uses different technology. However, if ongoing business from another division of the company affects that decision, then these capacity costs should be passed on to the buying division. While the full capacity costs are common to all the products in the selling division, the buying division is responsible for their share of that capacity.

Opportunity Costs

Thus, from the company's point of view, the market price (when it exists) is the opportunity cost when the selling division is at capacity. In the same way, variable cost plus incremental fixed cost and/or some share of capacity is the opportunity cost when there is excess capacity or when capacity has been established exclusively for internal transfers of goods. However, a conflict exists since managers of decentralized segments may not share these assessments and may make decisions in the best interest of the division that turn out to be suboptimal for the overall company.

ADMINISTERING TRANSFER PRICING

It would be unfair to try to isolate a transfer price from the entire process that surrounds a final sourcing decision and the transfer price itself. If transfer pricing is to be useful and perceived as fair, then it must result from clearly articulated policies. Once policies have been set, then they must be administered. Questions that arise at this stage involve how formal a transfer price-setting mechanism a company wants, how often transfer prices are revised, and how conflicts between divisions are resolved.

Policies

Administration should flow naturally from basic policy decisions. In the discussion of strategic planning in Chapter 12, policies are the result of the

goals and objectives that are generated as a response to the mission statement of the company. Consider a company where managers have decided
that the best strategy to achieve overall corporate goals, objectives, and
mission is to divide the company into decentralized units on a geographical
basis. Thus, each production plant is a decentralized segment. Assume a strategic decision is to evaluate each division as a cost center. Finally, assume that
management has decided that the only time components will be ordered from
outside sources is when a division just is not qualified to make them. These
are a consistent set of strategies. With captive sellers and buyers of intermediate products, it makes it difficult to assess divisions as profit or investment
centers if significant transfers take place. Any transfer pricing policy should
be in concert with these basic decisions. Perhaps management has decided that
transfers should be based on a division of the final market price of the completed product. Thus, the selling division would receive revenue made up of
standard incremental costs plus a share of income. This same amount would
be used as a cost for the buying division. Madison[4] criticizes using cost-based
transfer prices between cost centers since motivation is affected adversely. Thus,
a market-based price may be preferable, as in this example.

Administration

Policies as natural consequences of the strategic planning process need to
be matched with administration. For example, if policies are based on the
notion that divisions are to be viewed as free-standing businesses and profit
centers, then direction from upper management and conflict resolution take
on a different meaning than if the divisions are captive to one another and
transfers are mandated. In the former case, central management should take
much more of a hands-off approach to resolving disputes between divisions.
Divisional managers should make their own decisions and arrive at agreed-
upon transfer prices *if* a transfer is to take place. Central office managers
would only come into play when divisional managers brought them in or
when the issue at hand was deemed so important to the mission of the
company that the central office decided to intervene in order to centralize
the decision.

The Price Waterhouse study revealed several ways companies deal with
conflict resolution. There can be appeal processes, a transfer pricing committee overseeing all transfers, a general set of accounting and financial
policies that must be followed, and the like.[5]

Administration also involves the day-to-day collection of information
needed for transfer prices to be established. Part of the information-collection

[4] Roland L. Madison, "Responsibility Accounting and Transfer Pricing: Approach with
Caution," *Management Accounting* (January 1979), pp. 25–29.
[5] See Price Waterhouse, *Transfer Pricing Practices of American Industry* (Price Waterhouse, 1984),
p. 10.

process are policies governing the sharing of information. Will the buying division know what costs are incurred by the selling division? How will the buying division validate the market prices used as bases for transfer prices? The Price Waterhouse study revealed that about three fourths of the buying divisions did not know the true costs of the component they were buying from another division. What is surprising is that only one third of the companies had a policy to keep such information confidential.[6]

Companies also have to decide when to change transfer prices. If market-based prices are used, should transfer prices be changed as often as the market changes, or will, say, a quarterly adjustment be adequate? Perhaps some set of bounds can be established so that prices are adjusted quarterly or whenever the bounds are violated. Thus, if bounds of plus or minus 10 percent are adopted, a transfer price would remain in place unless the market changed by more than 10 percent in either direction.

TRANSFER PRICING THEORY

As the two quotes at the beginning of the chapter show, there seems to be a gap between the theory of transfer pricing and its practice. Keegan and Howard,[7] after surveying the practices of 74 of the largest industrial companies in the United States, concluded that the only viable transfer price is market-based. They believe that cost-based prices are fine for classroom discussion and an accounting exercise, but market-based prices are called for when a company adopts a decentralized strategy.[8] On the other hand, Eccles[9] interviewed 144 managers at 13 companies and concludes that transfer prices should be based on full costs when a selling profit center is not viewed as a distinct business for both internal and external sales, but that market-based transfer prices are called for when it is viewed as a distinct business. In addition, Eccles discusses other forms of transfer pricing policy he found in his interviews. In order to understand this conflict, we will first review the basic academic theories, their strengths, and their weaknesses.

Economic Theory

Early attempts to set transfer pricing policy were based on marginal prices and marginal costs. Basic economic analysis involves the point where mar-

---

[6] Price Waterhouse, 1984), pp. 14–15. The authors of the study (Keegan and Howard—see footnote 1) concede that some of the responses in this area are inconsistent and further study is needed to draw conclusions.

[7] Keegan and Howard, "Transfer Pricing for Fun and Profit."

[8] The implication here is that the company is actually decentralized and not just nominally so.

[9] Eccles, *The Transfer Pricing Problem*, Chapter 1.

ginal cost equals marginal revenue. The conclusion of this theory is that market prices are ideal transfer prices when (1) there is perfect competition for the intermediate product, or (2) the selling division is operating at capacity (which was discussed earlier). Only under these two conditions will buying and selling divisions make goal-congruent decisions using market-based transfer prices.

Perfect Competition   From an economist's point of view, perfect competition means that the selling division can sell all it wants to of a product at the same price. Once a price is set, it will not change no matter how many units of the product are sold. Thus, marginal revenue for the selling division equals the external market price. The selling division will maximize its profits when its marginal cost equals the outside market price. This output level may or may not be at capacity, depending on the marginal cost structure of the division.

From the company's perspective, the opportunity cost of any unit of intermediate product, given the output level chosen by the selling division, would be the market price of that product. This is true since the selling division could sell all its output on the external market at that price. Even the buying division is optimizing output since it will choose an output level for a final product where its marginal revenue equals its marginal cost. If the buying division uses fewer intermediate products than the selling division makes, the excess can be sold on the external market. If the buying division needs more units than the selling division is willing to produce, with perfect competition the buying division can buy its excess needs on the open market at the same price. However, examples of perfect competition are hard to find. Therefore, while it is nice to see that optimal decisions would be made under conditions of perfect competition, this does not give much guidance to the normal operating manager.

Imperfect Competition   With imperfect competition, a selling division cannot sell all it wants to at a fixed price. As quantity goes up, price goes down. Optimal output for the selling division is again found at the point where marginal cost equals marginal revenue. Since marginal cost for the buying division increases as the transfer price rises, the higher the price that the selling division charges, the lower the amount that will be made of the final product. Looking at profits for the overall company, however, the output choice of the buying division may not be optimal.

Assume that a buying division makes a product with a variable cost (excluding the transfer price of a component) of $60, that the division could sell 26,000 units of final product on the open market at $180 each or 34,000 units at $160 each, and that the variable cost of the component purchased from the selling division is $20. Finally, assume that besides internal sales the selling division could sell 14,000 units of the component on the open market at $50 or 20,000 at $40.[10]

Looking at the *selling division*, they can achieve the following contribution margins on external sales:

Sell 14,000: 14,000 ($50 − $20) = $420,000
Sell 20,000: 20,000 ($40 − $20) = $400,000

Thus, the higher-price option is better for the selling division. It seems natural that if the selling division can get $50 from outside buyers, it will also want $50 each for this product from another division.

From the company's point of view, the *buying division* has the following options for its sales of the final product:

Sell 26,000: 26,000 ($180 − $60 − $20) = $2,600,000
Sell 34,000: 34,000 ($160 − $60 − $20) = $2,720,000

Costs include the variable costs of both divisions. The best output choice is 34,000 final units. If the transfer price is set at $50, however, the manager of the buying division will be looking at the following income estimates:

Sell 26,000: 26,000 ($180 − $60 − $50) = $1,820,000
Sell 34,000: 34,000 ($160 − $60 − $50) = $1,700,000

The manager would be better off setting an output level of 26,000 units in this case. This would be suboptimal for the company as a whole.

At what price would the buying division manager be willing to sell 34,000 units? If the manager can show a profit of $1,820,000 and sell 34,000 units, there would be an economic indifference point. A total contribution margin of $1,820,000 for 34,000 units would be $53.53 (rounded) per unit. This could be achieved if the transfer price were $46.47 ($160 − $60 − $x = $53.53). Thus, if the buying division's manager can get the selling division to lower the transfer price from $50 to $46.47 (or lower), the buying division would be as well (or better) off if it produced 34,000 units.

The selling division could sell 26,000 components to the buying division at $50 and earn a contribution margin of $780,000 ($30 × 26,000). Thus, managers of that division would want $780,000 in total sales of 34,000 components to the buying division. This is a contribution margin of $22.94 ($780,000/34,000) or a price of $42.94 when variable costs are added. Therefore, with the selling division needing a minimum of $42.94 and the buying division wanting a maximum transfer price of $46.47, there is negotiating room to find a solution suitable to both divisions.

---

[10] It does no harm to this analysis to simplify the choices that are open to the managers of both divisions. If there is a problem with even these simple assumptions, adding complexity just adds to the problem.

Assumptions of Economic Analysis   As with most models there are assumptions that are part of this analysis. It is assumed that the divisions are independent both in demand and in technology. This means that the price that one division charges does not affect the demand of the other division. In addition, the output of one division cannot affect the output of another division. If divisions compete for the same scarce resources this would not be true. Finally, there is the assumption that an intermediate market exists. If it does not, then there is no independence between divisions and this type of economic analysis does not hold up. In fact, dependence gives rise to the basic question whether the divisions should be treated as separate profit centers for evaluation purposes.

Economic analysis is based on marginal costs and marginal revenues as defined by economists. It is doubtful if managers have the ability under existing accounting and information systems to find marginal costs. In addition, marginal costs can ignore fixed costs as sunk. Many managers will find this unreasonable since they have been schooled in the idea of full costs. Finally, this procedure assumes that managers will share information so that proper transfer prices can be set. This may encourage gaming and misinformation among managers so that divisional profits can be increased.

Accounting Theory

Accounting theory is based on the notion of opportunity cost to the firm and the interrelationship between transfer pricing and divisional performance evaluation. From the opportunity cost perspective, the basic premise is that standard variable cost is the lowest transfer price and is the base when excess capacity exists. Market price is the opportunity cost at full capacity, as has been discussed.

If no external market exists for the intermediate product, the opportunity cost when at full capacity is the standard variable cost of the component plus the contribution margin that would be made on goods that must be limited if the transfer takes place. Linear programming can help with this estimate since shadow prices show lost contribution margins for constrained resources.

Mathematical Programming   Mathematical programming has been suggested as a way to solve the transfer-pricing problem. The objective is to maximize corporate profits. Divisions inform central management about costs, resource use, and resource availability as well as revenue from outside sales. A linear (or integer) program is run that yields the optimum transfers of components between division and external sales of components and final goods. In addition, transfer prices are set by the model.

However, academics and practitioners criticize the use of mathematical programming. First, since the process relies on accurate information, managers have the opportunity to supply data that is in their favor. Again, gaming and misinformation may be promoted. Secondly, with such a centralized notion of quantities and transfer prices, decentralization becomes limited. As discussed in Chapter 14, decentralization means that decisions are made lower down in the organization. Programming centralizes decisions on output and prices, the key to a division that is being evaluated as a standalone business.

Dual Prices   Accountants recognize that the success of a transfer pricing system rests on whether managers are making goal-congruent decisions. In an earlier illustration, managers of the buying and selling divisions may be able to come to an agreed-upon price since a negotiating range existed in that example. What happens, say, if there is no negotiating range in prices? Managers may make decisions that seem best for their divisions but are not optimal for the company as a whole.

The problem lies in divisional performance evaluation using accounting-based income numbers. Assume a case where a transfer is in the best interests of the company but using either market-based or standard-variable-cost-based transfer prices would encourage one manager or the other to deal with outside sources or markets. If the selling division were allowed to show revenue based on market prices while the buying division were to show cost based on standard variable cost plus incremental fixed costs, both divisions' incomes would be maximized and the transfer could take place. This process is called *dual pricing*. Since profits for the overall company are not affected given any transfer price that is charged, it is a simple matter to use dual prices and to eliminate their effects during consolidation of accounting records for corporate reporting. However, managers may not like a system that reflects different values for the two divisions.

Negotiated Transfer Prices   Inherent in the discussion to this point has been the option for managers to negotiate transfer prices. If there is a negotiating range, then managers can decide between themselves if the transfer is to take place and at what price. In a fully decentralized company, corporate management would intervene only if an impasse developed in the negotiation process.

Critics of negotiation state that the transfer price will depend on the negotiating skills of each party and, therefore, the resulting price may not yield a reasonable divisional income figure. The counterargument is that negotiation skills are part of being a good manager. Managers must negotiate with buyers and suppliers as well as with contract labor, for example. If these results are included in segment performance evaluation, why should negotiated transfer prices be any different?

Another criticism of negotiation has to do with the relative power of the managers. If a buying division has other sources but a selling division has no other way to sell its output, the selling division is really a captive of the buying division and negotiation is not reasonable due to the power imbalance.

The same would be true in reverse if the buying division had no source of supply other than from the selling division, but the selling division had other customers it could serve on the outside market.[11]

Finally, if transfer pricing involves the allocation of the profit of a final good among the divisions that produced it, managers may see this as a zero-sum game: there are winners and losers since there is only a finite amount to be divided in the transfer pricing process. While a transfer price may be set, it is possible that it will result in a spirit of noncooperation and gaming on sharing information. However, studies of transfer-pricing practices show that negotiation is a part of real-world transfer pricing.

TRANSFER PRICING IN PRACTICE

Neither economic nor accounting theory seems to provide an integrated and practical framework for transfer pricing. At this point, let us look at what companies are actually doing.

Surveys of Actual Practice

Some of the most recent studies on actual transfer-pricing practice are by Vancil and by Price Waterhouse.[12] Exhibit 15-1 shows the breakdown of actual practice from Vancil's 1978 study.

About half of the companies Vancil surveyed use cost-based systems while half use market-based systems. Of the market-based prices, half of these are a result of negotiation.[13] It is interesting to note in this survey that the use of variable cost (either actual or standard) is found in only about 5 percent of the companies while some form of full cost or full cost plus a markup is found in over 40 percent of the cases. This is counter to the notion of economic and accounting theorists. It is possible that users of full-cost-based methods do so as an approximation of market. However, it is also possible that full costs are perceived by managers as being the real opportunity costs to their divisions. Having been conditioned by financial accounting's concept of product costs, managers may feel more at ease with full costs than any other concept. In addition, even though a transfer at anything above variable cost would be profitable for a division that is not at capacity, divisional income would not go up for transfers at variable cost. Why would a

---

[11] See Arthur L. Thomas, *A Behavioural Analysis of Joint-Cost Allocation and Transfer Pricing* (Stipes, 1980), for a good discussion of relative power in the negotiating process.

[12] Price Waterhouse, *Transfer Pricing Practices of American Industry.*

[13] Eccles, *The Transfer Pricing Problem*, argues that negotiated prices should not be listed as part of market-based transfer prices since they are administratively different in nature from either cost- or market-based prices (page 43).

Exhibit 15-1
Transfer Pricing Policies

Cost-Based Policies			
Variable cost			
Actual	1.7%		
Standard	2.9		
Total		4.6%	
Full cost			
Actual	13.0		
Standard	12.5		
Total		25.5	
Cost plus		16.7	
Total cost based policies			46.8%
Market-Based Policies			
Market price			
Competitor's price	11.7		
Market price	19.3		
Total		31.0	
Negotiation		22.2	
Total market based policies			53.2
		100.0%	100.0%

Source: Richard F. Vancil, *Decentralization: Managerial Ambiguity by Design* (Dow Jones-Irwin: Financial Executives Research Foundation, 1979), Exhibit B-10, p. 180.

manager commit capital resources to provide goods for another division and receive no incremental income for the effort?

Keegan and Howard[14] refer to the Price Waterhouse 1984 study and state that 31 percent of the responding companies use cost-based transfer prices while 69 percent use market-based prices. This more recent study is more heavily skewed toward market-based prices. Keegan and Howard include negotiated prices and dual prices as subsets of market-based prices in their discussion.

What the Studies Suggest

Keegan and Howard reject cost-based transfer pricing systems and call them an accounting exercise. In contrast, market-based prices are consistent with decentralization and evaluating decentralized segments. If the selling division is to be evaluated as an independent business, then divisional managers should base transfer prices on market. Sales to other divisions are viewed no differently from sales to external buyers. Much in the same way that prices are negotiated with outside buyers, 72 percent of the companies in the survey reported that negotiation was part of internal transfer prices.[15]

[14] Keegan and Howard, "Transfer Pricing for Fun and Profit."
[15] Keegan and Howard, p. 41.

These authors conclude that some form of market-based transfer prices is the only reasonable method. They include notions of negotiation and conflict resolution as well as the possibility of dual prices in how market prices can be used.

Eccles sees transfer pricing as a natural extension of basic strategies of a company.[16] In his study he differentiated between those companies that had a strategy of vertical integration and those that did not. Vertical integration means that there are ongoing and important transfers of intermediate goods within the company. This strategy implies that managers of the divisions are directed to buy/sell within the company when that option is open.

Recent trends within the automobile industry in the United States provide good examples of strategies involving vertical integration. During the 1980s, there has been a trend by many of the major manufacturers to open the sources for parts to outside vendors. Old notions of vertical integration being less costly seem to be tempered by current union contracts. The automobile manufacturer is bound by a general union wage and conditions contract for all its divisions. These costs may be much higher than an outside contractor pays. In 1987, General Motors announced that its long-standing policy of being virtually fully vertically integrated would be abandoned for a more open policy that sought outside sources for many of its needed parts.

Since vertical integration means mandated transfers of goods, the next question is how the buying and selling divisions are viewed. If they are evaluated as autonomous segments for all their internal and external sales, then market prices seem the most appropriate transfer prices. If they are not seen as independent divisions, then cost-based transfer prices should be used.

When there is not a strategy of vertical integration, Eccles suggests that companies use what he calls exchange autonomy. In essence, the divisions are treated as wholly independent divisions, standalone business entities. As such, managers are encouraged to make whatever decisions are in the best interest of the division. For a transfer to take place, both parties must arrive at a transfer price that is mutually agreeable.

Finally, Eccles suggests that dual pricing is always an alternative to all transfer-pricing situations. Thus, companies may revert to dual pricing as a means of conflict resolution. In addition, negotiation seems a general part of the fabric of transfer pricing.

TRANSFER PRICING AND LIFE CYCLE

The life cycle of a product has an effect on transfer pricing much as it has an effect on divisional performance evaluation as discussed in Chapter 14.

---

[16] See Eccles, *The Transfer Pricing Problem*, pp. 7ff.

Divisions that have products in the embryonic, growth, mature, and/or aging stages have different needs in transfer pricing. While a selling division may have a component in the mature stage, the buying division's final product may be in its embryonic stage. This situation sets up a new dimension to be considered.

Take the different stages of a life cycle from the perspective of the selling division. In the embryonic stage, there may be no market price for a product. On the other hand, prices may be quite elastic since there is new technology that could benefit a buying division. Costs are not stable in this phase, research and development are continuing, and the division is acquiring and testing new production facilities. Thus, it may be difficult to set transfer prices from either the market or cost perspective.

As a product enters the growth stage, management of the selling division are interested in developing an ongoing market for their product. Hopefully design, cost, and quality issues have been resolved and the emphasis is on market share, profit margins, cash flow, and improvements in productivity as suggested by Seed.[17] Eccles suggests that the growth stage means a market-based transfer price as the selling division wants to gain market share and, therefore, would want to earn profits equally from internal and external sales.[18]

During the mature stage, the market is settled and the selling division is attempting to maintain its share. Cash flow and cost control are paramount. It is possible that there will be pressure on market prices as competition leads to additional capacity. While market prices are a reasonable transfer price, a buying division is now in a more powerful position in the negotiation process.

Relative power may shift even more dramatically to the side of the buying division as a product reaches the aging stage. Major decisions at this stage include when to abandon the product. Internal use may well be the only thing that is keeping a certain production line open. Thus, while the balance of power may lie with the selling division with the introduction of a product in the embryonic stage, this balance shifts to the buying division as the product moves through its life cycle.

TRANSFER PRICING AND MULTINATIONAL COMPANIES

The possibility of a more unified European trading community, the various new countries that are emerging within eastern Europe and Asia, and North American trading agreements have an effect on transfer prices. Various countries individually as well as in cooperation with other trading partners

---

[17] Allen H. Seed, III, "Using Cash Flows to Measure Business Unit Performance," *Corporate Accounting* (New York: Warren, Gorham, & Lamont, Summer 1983), pp. 14–19.

[18] See Eccles, *The Transfer Pricing Problem*, Chapter 9, for his discussion of life cycles and transfer pricing.

have regulations, tariffs, and income and other taxes that affect transfers. Political considerations are everywhere, including whether the U.S. president designates certain countries as *most favored nations* for trading. In addition, with different currencies, foreign exchange plays a part in how and when transfers are made. This is another part of the external environment that businesses face. Managers include these factors when deciding to establish (or abandon) foreign subsidiaries to make components or finished products.

MOTIVATION AND TRANSFER PRICING

As discussed in Chapter 14, segment performance evaluation (and, therefore, managerial evaluation) still heavily relies on financial accounting numbers. However, as the discussions in both Chapters 12 and 14 among others point out, managers are increasingly looking at measures to reflect how they are accomplishing the long-term strategic goals of the organization. As a result, the overreliance on accounting-based measures might change over time. Transfer pricing strategies, policies, and administration should all promote actions that not only advance segment financial quantitative measures but also lead to achieving the overall strategic direction of the company: optimal decisions will be made based on long-term considerations that will benefit not only the segment but the total organization. Therefore, the transfer pricing system should lead to congruent decisions by managers at all levels and performance rewards should be based on achieving strategic ends.

Since transfer pricing involves an allocation of profits of a final product among the divisions producing it, it is subject to the basics of allocation in Chapter 11: managers must perceive transfer prices and how they are administered as fair and reasonable. If not, then managers will try to manipulate the system for their own ends. Gaming can take place in sharing information about costs, capacity, and the like. Since negotiation seems integral to much transfer pricing, the whole negotiation process and the ability to appeal to higher authorities must seem fair as well. Managers should be motivated to cooperate as much as possible and to resolve problems in a way that will lead to future transfers between divisions as appropriate.

SUMMARY

While transfer pricing has been the subject of much theoretical argument over the years, both general economic and accounting theory seem too limited by assumptions or too narrow in scope to guide operating managers. What can be gleaned from theory is that companies should incorporate opportunity costs in transfer prices. At full capacity, the opportunity cost is based on market prices. When excess capacity exists, opportunity costs are related to incremental variable and fixed costs and/or some measure of capacity. In practice, it seems that more companies use market-based transfer prices than cost-based ones. Within the companies using cost-based prices, full costs seem to prevail counter to what theory predicts. Negotiation and dual prices are options that many companies employ.

Transfer prices cannot be viewed in a vacuum. Life-cycle issues are important, as are policies and administration regarding transfer prices. In addition, since transfer prices are part of the concept of decentralization and segment/managerial evaluation, all aspects of transfer pricing have behavioral consequences. It is not easy to prescribe the best transfer pricing system for a company. As with segment performance evaluation, many factors need to be considered, including how actions affect overall corporate strategies.

PROBLEMS AND CASES

15-1. Market-Based and Cost-Based Transfer Prices

The chapter develops arguments for the sole validity of market-based transfer prices as well as some legitimacy of cost-based prices.

Required

Using appropriate references, defend the use of both cost-based and market-based transfer prices. Develop examples as part of your discussion. Show both when it is useful and when it is inappropriate to use each basis.

15-2. Transfer Pricing and Service Departments

The Aldone Company operates several divisions in various industries. The major performance criterion for this decentralized company is return on investment. In fact, a large part of the bonus program for managers is tied to ROI. At this point, divisional ROI consists of direct profit by the division over divisional investment. Allocated corporate costs are not included in ROI calculations.

There is a central data processing department and the treasurer of the firm wants to develop a transfer pricing policy for this service. Recent trends to computerize the manufacturing facilities have required much programming time.

Since the data processing department is, in essence, producing a product, the treasurer wants to evaluate it as a profit center and wants to bill the divisions for services both directly used by the division and also for services performed for the corporate central administration. Since the major cost is programmer time, the treasurer has developed a standard hourly rate to be billed. However, the treasurer is still questioning whether to bill just for time or to build in a profit in the hourly rates.

There is no doubt that the movement to computer-integrated manufacturing and digital controlled machines was a major cause in the increase in programmer costs and general costs in the data processing department. The department now has an annual budget of over $300,000, and the treasurer thought it was high time that these costs be assigned to operating divisions based on an equitable transfer price.

Required:
1. As a divisional manager, prepare arguments against the proposed system.
2. As the treasurer, rebut the arguments you developed.

3. Make any recommendations that you think would help to make the system more acceptable to the divisional managers.

15-3. Alternate Transfer Prices (CMA)

DePaolo Industries manufactures carpets, furniture, and foam in three separate divisions. DePaolo's operating statement for 19X3 is shown in Exhibit 1.

Exhibit 1
DePaolo Industries
Operating Statement
For the Year Ended December 31, 19X3

	Carpet Division	Furniture Division	Foam Division	Total
Sales revenue	$3,000,000	$3,000,000	$4,000,000	$10,000,000
Cost of goods sold	2,000,000	1,300,000	3,000,000	6,300,000
Gross profit	$1,000,000	$1,700,000	$1,000,000	$ 3,700,000
Operating expenses				
Administrative	$ 300,000	$ 500,000	$ 400,000	$ 1,200,000
Selling	600,000	600,000	500,000	1,700,000
Total operating expenses	$ 900,000	$1,100,000	$ 900,000	$ 2,900,000
Income from operations before taxes	$ 100,000	$ 600,000	$ 100,000	$ 800,000

Additional information regarding DePaolo's operations are as follows:

- Included in Foam's sales revenue is $500,000 in revenue that represents sales made to the Furniture Division that were transferred at manufacturing cost.
- The cost of goods sold consists of the following costs:

	Carpet	Furniture	Foam
Direct material	$ 500,000	$1,000,000	$1,000,000
Direct labor	500,000	200,000	1,000,000
Variable overhead	750,000	50,000	1,000,000
Fixed overhead	250,000	50,000	
Total cost of goods sold	$2,000,000	$1,300,000	$3,000,000

- Administrative expenses include the following costs:

	Carpet	Furniture	Foam
Segment expenses			
Variable	$ 85,000	$140,000	$ 40,000
Fixed	85,000	210,000	120,000
Home office expenses (all fixed)			
Directly traceable	100,000	120,000	200,000
General (allocated on sales dollars)	30,000	30,000	40,000
Total	$300,000	$500,000	$400,000

• Selling expense is all incurred at the segment level and is 80 percent variable for all segments.

John Sprint, Manager of the Foam Division, is not pleased with DePaolo's presentation of operating performance. Sprint claimed, "The Foam Division makes a greater contribution to the company's profits than what is shown. I sell foam to the Furniture Division at cost and it gets our share of the profit. I can sell that foam on the outside at my regular markup, but I sell to Furniture for the well-being of the company. I think my division should get credit for those internal sales at market. I think we should also revise our operating statements for internal purposes. Why don't we consider preparing these internal statements on a contribution approach reporting format showing internal transfers at market?"

Required:

1. John Sprint believes that the intra-company transfers from the Foam Division to the Furniture Division should be at market rather than manufacturing cost for divisional performance measurement.
   a. Explain why Sprint is correct.
   b. Identify and describe two approaches used for setting transfer prices other than manufacturing cost used by DePaolo Industries and market price as recommended by Sprint.
2. Using the contribution approach and market-based transfer prices, prepare a revised operating statement by division for DePaolo Industries for 19X3 that will promote the evaluation of divisional performance.
3. Discuss the advantages of the contribution reporting approach for internal reporting purposes.

15-4. Cost-Based Transfer Pricing (CMA)

PortCo Products is a divisionalized furniture manufacturer. The divisions are autonomous segments with each division being responsible for its own sales, costs of operations, working capital management, and equipment acquisition. Each division serves a different market in the furniture industry. Because the markets and products of the divisions are so different, there have never been any transfers between divisions.

The Commercial Division manufactures equipment and furniture that is purchased by the restaurant industry. The division plans to introduce a new line of counter and chair units which feature a cushioned seat for the counter chairs. John Kline, the Division Manager, has discussed the manufacturing of the cushioned seat with Russ Fiegel of the Office Division. They both believe a cushioned seat currently made by the Office Division for use on its deluxe office stool could be modified for use on the new counter chair. Consequently, Kline has asked Russ Fiegel for a price for 100 unit lots of the cushioned seat. The following conversation took place about the price to be charged for the cushioned seats.

Fiegel: "John, we can make the necessary modifications to the cushioned seat easily. The raw materials used in your seat are slightly different and should cost about 10 percent more than those used in our deluxe office stool. However, the labor time should be the same because the seat fabrication operation basically is the same. I would price the seat at our regular rate—full cost plus 30 percent markup."

Kline: "That's higher than I expected, Russ. I was thinking that a good price would be your variable manufacturing costs. After all, your capacity costs will be incurred regardless of this job."

Fiegel: "John, I'm at capacity. By making the cushion seats for you, I'll have to cut my production of deluxe office stools. Of course, I can increase my production of economy office stools. The labor time freed by not having to fabricate the frame or assemble the deluxe stool can be shifted to the frame fabrication and assembly of the economy office stool. Fortunately, I can switch my labor force between these two

Office Division:
Standard Costs and Prices

	Deluxe Office Stool		Economy Office Stool
Raw materials			
Framing	$ 8.15		$ 9.76
Cushioned seat			
Padding	2.40		
Vinyl	4.00		
Molded seat (purchased)			6.00
Direct labor			
Frame fabrication (0.5 × $7.50/DLH)	3.75	(0.5 × $7.50/DLH)	3.75
Cushion fabrication (0.5 × $7.50/DLH)	3.75		
Assembly[a] (0.5 × $7.50/DLH)	3.75	(0.3 × $7.50/DLH)	2.25
Manufacturing			
Overhead (1.5DLH × $12.80/DLH)	19.20	(0.8DLH × $12.80/DLH)	10.24
Total standard cost	$45.00		$32.00
Selling price (30% markup)	$58.50		$41.60

[a]Attaching seats to frames and attaching rubber feet.

Office Division:
Manufacturing Overhead Budget

Overhead Item	Nature	Amount
Supplies	Variable—at current market prices	$ 420,000
Indirect labor	Variable	375,000
Supervision	Nonvariable	250,000
Power	Use varies with activity; rates are fixed	180,000
Heat and light	Nonvariable—light is fixed regardless of production while heat/air conditioning varies with fuel charges	140,000
Property taxes and insurance taxes	Nonvariable—any change in amounts/rates is independent of production	200,000
Depreciation	Fixed dollar total	1,700,000
Employee benefits	20% of supervision, direct and indirect labor	575,000
	Total overhead	$3,840,000
	Capacity in DLH	300,000
	Overhead rate/DLH	$12.80

models of stools without any loss of efficiency. As you know, overtime is not a feasible alternative in our community. I'd like to sell it to you at variable cost, but I have excess demand for both products. I don't mind changing my product mix to the economy model if I get a good return on the seats I make for you. Here are my standard costs for the two stools and a schedule of my manufacturing overhead."
[See the tables on the previous page for standard costs and overhead schedule.]
Kline: "I guess I see your point, Russ, but I don't want to price myself out of the market. Maybe we should talk to corporate to see if they can give us any guidance."

Required:
1. John Kline and Russ Fiegel did ask PortCo corporate management for guidance on an appropriate transfer price. Corporate management suggested they consider using a transfer price based upon variable manufacturing cost plus opportunity cost. Calculate a transfer price for the cushioned seat based upon variable manufacturing cost plus opportunity cost.
2. Which alternative transfer price system—full cost, variable manufacturing cost, or variable manufacturing cost plus opportunity cost—would be better as the underlying concept for an intra-company transfer price policy? Explain your answer.

15-5. Perfect Competition

The Prima Division of Gypsy Corporation makes a product that it can sell on the outside or can sell to another division of the same company, the Onza Division. Onza can use the product as a component in a product it makes. There is perfect competition in the market for the intermediate product.

Assume that the net marginal revenue for Onza is $200 - \$0.50Q$ (where net marginal revenue is the marginal revenue of the final product that Onza sells less any marginal cost of the final product but ignoring the transfer price of the component from Prima). This is derived from a net revenue function of $\$200Q - \$0.25Q^2 - \$400$. Also assume that the total cost for Prima producing the component is estimated to be $\$500 + \$8.00Q + \$0.25Q^2$. Q represents the quantity of units sold.

Required:
1. Graph net marginal revenue for Onza and marginal cost for Prima divisions. What quantity is indicated where production by Prima will equal purchases by Onza? Verify your results by solving mathematically for the point where marginal cost equals net marginal revenue.
2. What market price would be called for at this equilibrium point?
3. What would happen if the market price increased by $10 per unit? decreased by $10 per unit?
4. What would be the effect of no intermediate market for the component on the above analysis?

15-6. Policy Development and Administration

The Wings Company (Wings), a decentralized firm specializing in fast-food franchises and food production, was in the process of developing policies for transfer pricing as well as policies on how to administer the pricing method adopted.

Wings is in a growth industry in most of its divisions. Franchises deal with Mexican food, seafood, and health food. Producing divisions include many of the products that are sold in the restaurants. These divisions also sell to other restaurant chains and have products sold through local supermarkets.

The owners of the business are the chief operating officers of Wings. Divisional management consists of people hired from the outside or managers that came with divisions that were acquired by the company over the last couple of years. Growth has been swift with little time for real planning between and among the divisions.

You have been hired to help the managers of Wings in developing a transfer pricing policy and a way to administer that policy.

Required:
Develop a list of questions that you would like answered in order to help Wings' managers. What are the major issues to be addressed in this case?

15-7. Pricing Strategy[19]

Background

The New Brunswick Company is a mid-size subsidiary of the Sun Corporation that manufactures various textile and similar material composites. Sales are made to affiliate companies within the Sun Corporation, as well as to external companies. Approximately one-half of New Brunswick's sales are to affiliated companies.

New Brunswick's formal mission statement reads as follows:

> New Brunswick's mission is to develop and supply unique, cost effective fabrics and related nonconventional structures to proactively support the Sun Corporation's worldwide and professional markets.
>
> An extension of New Brunswick's mission is to capitalize on the resultant unique product and fabric capabilities, by developing profitable franchises in selective growth oriented consumer and industrial markets.
>
> This will be accomplished while satisfying the expectations of the company and fostering commitment, challenge and reward for our employees.

This statement has received wide approval from the corporate level and from the affiliate management boards. It serves as the driving force for New Brunswick's management and sets clear objectives.

The Product

Fifteen years ago, New Brunswick research began evaluating a fabric formation technology (originally developed by the Smith Company, a competitor), called "Super Weave." In this technology, fibers are entangled mechanically using water sprayed under high pressure. The resulting fabric is very cloth-like in appearance, feel and comfort. The Smith Company realized early on that this fabric would make an ideal barrier in the operating room. The new fabric would provide an effective disposable replacement for operating room drapes and gowns, providing a greater degree of sterility than had been attainable in the past.

Within the Sun Corporation's family of companies, Sanitech is responsible for asepsis within the operating room. To this end, Sanitech markets operating room apparel, gloves and disinfectants.

---

[19] This problem is used by permission of the Institute of Management Accountants.

Ten years ago, Sanitech began marketing operating room packs and gowns using the Smith fabric. While the franchise was successful, the relationship between supplier and customer did have drawbacks which the Sun Corporation, Sanitech and New Brunswick fully understood:

1. Product improvements made by Smith might not be exclusive to Sanitech in the future, as Smith could sell to Sanitech's competitors.
2. Smith's capacity versus Sanitech's demand.
3. Lack of a second source.
4. Fear of monopolistic pricing practices. (Figure 1 displays graphically the corporation's pricing concern. Smith's raw material cost changes are plotted against Smith's selling price.)

New Brunswick's Entry into the Market

Six years ago, New Brunswick developed a material equivalent to the "Super Weave" fabric for sale to Sanitech. Entering this business required New Brunswick to make a significant capital investment in plant and equipment. The total investment would approach 30 million dollars, the largest single investment in the company's long history. Given the Sun Corporation's policy of decentralized operating companies and New Brunswick's mission, New Brunswick's resources alone were used to fund the project. Additionally, Sanitech as the marketing company was at liberty to select the fabric which, from its perspective, would best meet its customers' requirements at the lowest cost to Sanitech.

New Brunswick's proposal was presented to the Executive Committee of the Sun Corporation who gave final approval for New Brunswick to proceed.

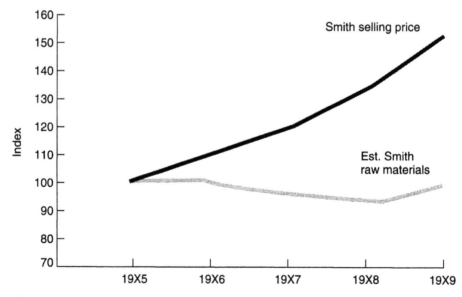

Figure 1 Raw Material Cost vs. Smith Pricing: 19X5–19X9

Smith's Response

Three years ago, New Brunswick began making fabric at comparable quality to Smith. However, New Brunswick found itself in a significantly changed market environment:

1. Concurrent with New Brunswick's entry, Smith's prices to Sanitech immediately dropped (Figure 2 plots the selling price).
2. Smith introduced pricing strategies which rewarded Sanitech for high volume and provided multi-year incentives.
3. With the exception of price escalation, Sanitech and Smith had developed an effective partnership since 19X5.
4. After several years of manufacturing, Smith had been able to maximize manufacturing efficiencies and achieve lower cost. New Brunswick realized it was at a cost disadvantage and could not price based on intercompany transfer formulas. (Normally, full cost plus a percent return on invested capital and working capital.)

New Brunswick understood very quickly and clearly that, in order to be successful, it must beat Smith's pricing and in the long run minimize manufacturing costs or New Brunswick would have to be content as a secondary source of supply.

New Brunswick's Problem

The Vice-President of Affiliate Marketing at New Brunswick requested the assistance of the chief financial officer in developing a plan that would enable New Brunswick to sell its product to Sanitech while achieving the following objectives:

1. Establish a price that is competitive while recovering the capital investment in a reasonable number of years.

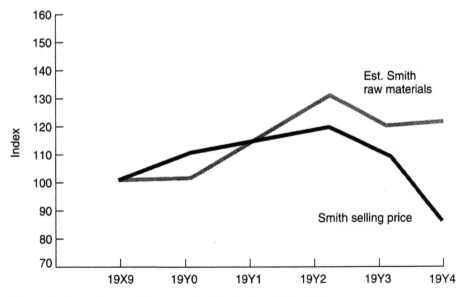

Figure 2   Raw Material Cost vs. Smith Pricing: 19X9–19Y4

2. Establish the longer term profitability for New Brunswick.
3. Provide the corporation with the lowest cost product over the long run.

Required:
1. How should New Brunswick develop its pricing strategy?
2. How should the benefit to the Sun Corporation be measured?
3. What might Smith's reaction be to your strategy?
4. Should vertically integrated corporations be forced to procure raw materials from other divisions?
5. Should intercompany pricing policy be inflexible?

15-8. Policy Issues[20]

Background

The Universal Medical Corporation is engaged in the manufacture and sale of a broad range of products in the health care field in most countries of the world. The company is organized on the principles of decentralized management and conducts its business through operating subsidiaries which are themselves, for the most part, integral, autonomous operations. Direct responsibility for each company lies with its operating management (headed by a president, general manager, or managing director) who reports directly or through a company group chairman to a member of the Executive Committee. In line with this policy of decentralization, each international subsidiary is, with some exceptions, managed by citizens of the country where it is located.

The company's international business is conducted by 130 subsidiaries manufacturing in 50 countries outside the United States and marketing in most countries of the world. In recent years, international businesses have accounted for 41 and 43 percent of the company's total sales and earnings, respectively. Last year's worldwide sales were $6.4 billion with pretax profits of $900 million. The company employs 75,000 people.

Management's Problem

Recently, the Vice President of Finance called a meeting of his fellow executives to discuss a growing problem. The participants in the meeting were:

Walt Jackson, Vice-President, Finance, CFO
Steve Edwards, Vice-President, International
Sara Roberts, Vice-President, Taxes
Mark Andrews, Corporate Treasurer
John Clark, Vice-President, General Controller

After welcoming the others, Jackson opened the meeting,

> The issue is cash . . . it's building up in our foreign companies and we need to bring it home. What I want today is your thoughts on what course of action we should recommend to the Executive Committee. Mark, would you recap our situation?

---

[20] This problem is used by permission of the Institute of Management Accountants.

At this point, Mark Andrews, Treasurer, described how the cash position of the foreign companies had grown; he believed that action was necessary to repatriate more earnings. In summarizing, he stated:

> Cash is building up in our foreign companies and we need to bring it home. It's our policy to minimize our exposure to exchange gains or losses. Right now, the dollar is starting to weaken, but that's beside the point. We're not in the currency trading business and our policy is to minimize exposure. I think that the obvious solution is to increase the flow of dividends from the international companies.

Sara Roberts, Vice President, Taxes, broke into the presentation,

> I have to disagree. That action will hurt our tax situation . . . we're already bringing home all the dividends that we can without attracting higher taxes. If we increase repatriated dividends, we'd have to pay more taxes to the U.S. Government on those foreign earnings.

John Clark nodded his head in agreement,

> That's right . . . we're already paying an effective rate of almost 50 percent on international earnings; it could go to 60 percent if we brought home all the earnings. If so, we'd have to reconsider the economic viability of some of those businesses. It could mean shutting down businesses in some countries.

Roberts continued,

> And, this is only half of the story. Right now a proposed tax bill has taken a turn for the worse in Washington. What they want us to do is allocate our U.S. research and administrative expenses proportionately against international. In other words, disallow deduction in the U.S., even though we would get no deduction overseas for those expenses. With 40 percent of our business foreign-sourced, this could be a monster of a problem.

After doing some rough calculations, John Clark stated,

> We could be talking about a 70 percent effective tax rate on international. That's ridiculous! And the way we manage those companies, we can't clearly identify the amount of U.S. expense allocable to international.

Trying to bring the conversation back to possible solutions, Jackson said,

> Wait a minute. The topic today is cash flow. Why don't we raise inter-company prices on exports from the U.S.?

Steve Edwards, who had been listening quietly to this point, broke into the conversation,

> That would really hurt . . . it's the new small companies that depend on sourcing from the U.S. They would suffer by higher prices. The larger companies are already self-manufacturing. Of course, perhaps we could look selectively at price increases on high margin products for adjustment.

Jackson then walked over to the chart board and put up Exhibit 1, which details the current ratios of research and administration expenses incurred by domestic and international operations.

John Clark interceded,

> Steve, I've been looking at that exhibit on the wall. The technical service fees are, in effect, a royalty we charge our international companies to recover R&D and corporate costs. Have you given any thought to increasing technical service fees?

Edwards responded,

> No way can I buy that. They're already paying 2 percent of sales. If we increase it, each and every company will have to go to their government to get acceptance of these increased charges for tax deductibility in their country.

Roberts then responded,

> But we could help them with justification and negotiations if needed. Maybe even adjust the fees country-by-country to get the most we can.

Clark was quiet for a moment. He then responded,

> But how can we motivate managing directors to do this when it reduces their earnings and margins? They will think that their bonuses will be affected.

Edwards said,

> Seriously, on their financial reports to corporate headquarters, they could add-back these additional fees . . . report what profits would have been . . . so that their Executive Committee member doesn't come down on them for lower margins.

Andrews looked concerned,

> Isn't that two sets of books? I've heard that other companies do it, but we have always avoided it for what I thought were ethical reasons.

Clark said,

> You may be right. Wouldn't that be sending the wrong signal to the companies? Does the Credo (Exhibit 2) give us any guidance on this matter?

Exhibit 1
Current Corporate Expenses as a Percent of Sales

	Domestic	International
Research and development expense	10.0%	4.0%
Technical service fees	(2.0)	2.0
General corporation and legal expense	4.0	
Total	12.0%	6.0%

Exhibit 2
The Company's Credo

We believe our first responsibility is to the doctors, nurses and patients,
to mothers and all others who use our products and services.
In meeting their needs everything we do must be of high quality.
We must constantly strive to reduce our costs
in order to maintain reasonable prices.
Customers' orders must be serviced promptly and accurately.
Our suppliers and distributors must have an opportunity to make a fair profit.

We are responsible to our employees,
the men and women who work with us throughout the world.
Everyone must be considered as an individual.
We must respect their dignity and recognize their merit.
They must have a sense of security in their jobs.
Compensation must be fair and adequate,
and working conditions clean, orderly and safe.
Employees must feel free to make suggestions and complaints.
There must be equal opportunity for employment, development
and advancement of those qualified.
We must provide competent management,
and their actions must be just and ethical.

We are responsible to the communities in which we live and work
and to the world community as well.
We must be good citizens—support good works and charities
and bear our fair share of taxes.
We must encourage civic improvements and better health and education.
We must maintain in good order
the property we are privileged to use,
protecting the environment and natural resources.

Our final responsibility is to our stockholders.
Business must make a sound profit.
We must experiment with new ideas.
Research must be carried on, innovative programs developed
and mistakes paid for.
New equipment must be purchased, new facilities provided
and new products launched.
Reserves must be created to provide for adverse times.
When we operate according to these principles,
the stockholders should realize a fair return.

Roberts said,

> I won't get into that argument, but these are the ways to go . . . bringing
> back cash that will be "sheltered" by allocated U.S. expenses. Meanwhile, I'll
> get busy with our friends in Washington . . . I don't think they understand

the potential adverse consequences on multinationals of their allocation proposals . . . certainly under the circumstances of our tremendous national trade deficit.

Jackson moved to wrap up the meeting:

So, how shall we position our recommendation to the Executive Committee? Intercompany price increases across the board or only on those products which yield a comfortable margin to the international companies? Increase technical service fees to whatever can be negotiated with the foreign governments, country by country? How can we get acceptance by the international managing directors? Is this a Credo issue? What's our response if they say that we're asking them to reduce the taxes they pay to their country's government because we have to pay more to the U.S. Government? Or, should we just tell them to *do it!*

Required:
1. What should be the Finance Division's recommendations to the Executive Committee? What factors should be considered in their recommendations?
2. Would your suggestion apply only to the Universal Medical Corporation or to all U.S. companies? What, if any, circumstances may influence your recommendation?
3. What are the responsibilities of a U.S. management to the employees, managers, communities, and governments of wholly owned subsidiaries operating in foreign countries?

15-9. Starglow Shampoo—Sourcing Surfactants[21]

Approximately two hundred shampoos currently on the market in the United States were rated in the February 1989 issue of *Consumer Reports*. One of the key performance measures that influenced the final ratings was, simply, did the shampoo clean hair effectively? Have you ever wondered just what chemical or ingredient in shampoo, or any other personal cleaning product, actually does the "cleaning"? Perhaps you have wondered why some cleaners seem to be more effective on blood, and less effective on grease, while others are exactly the other way around.

Surfactants

The key cleaning performance in personal care and household cleaning products is the type and concentration of *surfactant* used in the formulation. Surfactant is a generic term for a very wide range of synthetic detergent agents. These detergent agents are created via a chemical process that reacts alcohol with sulphur trioxide gas; the output of this process is a surfactant, a substance that has both an organic aspect (from the alcohol) and an inorganic aspect (from the SO_3). The organic aspect of the surfactant gives it the ability to mix with, dissolve, and clean oil, grease, and other organic type material from ourselves, our clothing, and our dishes. The inorganic aspect, from the SO_3, causes the surfactant to have an affinity for water. The

---

[21] James A. Anderson, "Sourcing Surfactants," *Journal of Accounting Education*, Vol. 10, No. 2 (New York: Pergamon Press, Fall 1992), pp. 357–374.

combination of these aspects creates a substance that likes grease, oil, and water, all at the same time—allowing the product to both clean effectively and to rinse out thoroughly with water. Since there are many different kinds of dirt, grease, etc., surfactants are formulated very specifically for the intended cleaning job. The alcohol inputs are varied, although most are petroleum based, and the manufacturing process is modified as needed.

Use of Surfactants in Starglow Shampoo

The formulation of any shampoo calls for the use of a surfactant that is effective on typical human hair and body oils. In Fall, 1989, the Black Hill, Virginia plant of the Andrews and Nutter Company (A&N) was using two surfactants in the production of its Starglow brand of shampoo: ALS and AE3S. Both are ammonium lauryl sulfate compounds, and both are currently purchased from the Wilmington, Delaware soap and detergent plant of A&N. These two plants are parts of different divisions within A&N; Black Hill is part of the personal-care division, while Wilmington is part of the laundry division. Consequently, the purchase of surfactants is done in accordance with the company's transfer pricing policy, which calls for transfers to be made at a price equal to the seller's full cost plus 5 percent markup.

The Wilmington plant specializes in the production of light duty detergents, such as used in dishwashing liquids, car wash formulations, and so on. It does not normally produce shampoo type surfactants; in fact, the Black Hill plant is the only customer for which Wilmington produces surfactants.

The quality of the surfactants delivered by Wilmington has been spotty. That fact has created some grumbling among the production people on the Starglow line; they are charged with minimizing costs of the product, and the inconsistent quality of surfactant does not make their job any easier.

Recently, the Finance staff at the Black Hill plant has begun to wonder about the possibility of finding another source of surfactants. They managed to assemble some preliminary information.

ALS and AE3S will be used in roughly equal quantities during 1989/90 for the planned production of 3,267,000 cases of Starglow Shampoo. (There are 90 ounces of Starglow per case.) In 1988/89, 8,875,222 pounds of ALS and 10,185,685 pounds of AE3S were used to make about 3.2 million cases of Starglow. In 1988/89, Wilmington charged Black Hill $0.226 per pound for ALS and $0.239 per pound for AE3S, including direct freight expense. The possible costs of inconsistent quality are not included in those figures.

The Dreary Lane Plant

In the middle 1980s, Andrews and Nutter had acquired another company's operations: those of the Carr and Armstrong Company (C&A). Among C&A's many assets was a plant very near A&N's Black Hill facility—the Dreary Lane plant. Dreary Lane was similar to Black Hill in that it concentrates on the production of personal care items, including the Prestiga line of shampoos. Like Starglow, the Prestiga brand requires the use of surfactants; unlike Black Hill, the Dreary Lane facility purchases surfactants from an outside source, the Boynton Company. The Dreary Lane plant currently uses about one half as much surfactant as does Black Hill. In 1988/89, it used 4,683,000 pounds each of ALS and AE3S. During that year, the Dreary Lane plant paid Boynton $0.32 per pound for ALS and $0.34 per pound for AE3S, excluding inbound freight.

Kansas City Plant

Black Hill's "sister" plant, the Kansas City, Kansas facility, produces more shampoo than the Black Hill and Dreary Lane plants combined. To support the production of its brands (different than Starglow), the Kansas City plant began producing its own surfactants in 1982. During 1988/89, Kansas City produced and used 70,500,000 pounds of ALS and AE3S of a type that is identical per A&N raw material specifications to the ALS and AE3S that Black Hill purchases from Wilmington.

Required:

You have been recently hired by the Black Hill plant as a management accountant. The Finance staff at Black Hill knew that, as with most production and sourcing decisions, several options probably existed, but they have been too busy lately so that they have been able to do little more than gather raw data from various company sources. They are willing to make available to you any data that they have, but time is short. (Your instructor will give you specific information regarding how you can obtain needed information from the Finance staff.)

The division controller is coming tomorrow, and wants to see a concrete proposal at that time. This will be your first independent task for the company. It is up to you to prepare the needed analysis.

Appendix A

TABLE A-1[1]

Area under the Normal Curve Between the Mean and Successive Values of z

Example: If $z = 1.87$, the area between the mean and 1.87 standard deviations is .46926 and the area to the right of z is .03074 (.50000 − .46926).

z	.00	.01	.02	.03	.04	.05	.06	.07	.08	.09
.0	.00000	.00399	.00798	.01197	.01595	.01994	.02392	.02790	.03188	.03586
.1	.03983	.04380	.04776	.05172	.05567	.05962	.06356	.06749	.07142	.07535
.2	.07926	.08317	.08706	.09095	.09483	.09871	.10257	.10642	.11026	.11409
.3	.11791	.12172	.12552	.12930	.13307	.13683	.14058	.14431	.14803	.15173
.4	.15542	.15910	.16276	.16640	.17003	.17364	.17724	.18082	.18439	.18793
.5	.19146	.19497	.19847	.20194	.20540	.20884	.21226	.21566	.21904	.22240
.6	.22575	.22907	.23237	.23565	.23891	.24215	.24537	.24857	.25175	.25490
.7	.25804	.26115	.26424	.26730	.27035	.27337	.27637	.27935	.28230	.28524
.8	.28814	.29103	.29389	.29673	.29955	.30234	.30511	.30785	.31057	.31327
.9	.31594	.31859	.32121	.32381	.32639	.32894	.33147	.33398	.33646	.33891
1.0	.34134	.34375	.34614	.34849	.35083	.35314	.35543	.35769	.35993	.36214
1.1	.36433	.36650	.36864	.37076	.37286	.37493	.37698	.37900	.38100	.38298
1.2	.38493	.38686	.38877	.39065	.39251	.39435	.39617	.39796	.39973	.40147
1.3	.40320	.40490	.40658	.40824	.40988	.41149	.41309	.41466	.41621	.41774
1.4	.41924	.42073	.42220	.42364	.42507	.42647	.42785	.42922	.43056	.43189
1.5	.43319	.43448	.43574	.43699	.43822	.43943	.44062	.44179	.44295	.44408
1.6	.44520	.44630	.44738	.44845	.44950	.45053	.45154	.45254	.45352	.45449
1.7	.45543	.45637	.45728	.45818	.45907	.45994	.46080	.46164	.46246	.46327
1.8	.46407	.46485	.46562	.46638	.46712	.46784	.46856	.46926	.46995	.47062
1.9	.47128	.47193	.47257	.47320	.47381	.47441	.47500	.47558	.47615	.47670
2.0	.47725	.47778	.47831	.47882	.47932	.47982	.48030	.48077	.48124	.48169
2.1	.48214	.48257	.48300	.48341	.48382	.48422	.48461	.48500	.48537	.48574
2.2	.48610	.48645	.48679	.48713	.48745	.48778	.48809	.48840	.48870	.48899
2.3	.48928	.48956	.48983	.49010	.49036	.49061	.49086	.49111	.49134	.49158
2.4	.49180	.49202	.49224	.49245	.49266	.49286	.49305	.49324	.49343	.49361
2.5	.49379	.49396	.49413	.49430	.49446	.49461	.49477	.49492	.49506	.49520
2.6	.49534	.49547	.49560	.49573	.49585	.49598	.49609	.49621	.49632	.49643
2.7	.49653	.49664	.49674	.49683	.49693	.49702	.49711	.49720	.49728	.49736
2.8	.49744	.49752	.49760	.49767	.49774	.49781	.49788	.49795	.49801	.49807
2.9	.49813	.49819	.49825	.49831	.49836	.49841	.49846	.49851	.49856	.49861
3.0	.49865									
4.0	.49997									

[1]Courtesy of Professor Lyn Pankoff, Washington University.

TABLE A-2[2]
Critical Values of Student's _t_ Statistic

Degrees of Freedom	Levels of Significance for One-Tailed Test				Degrees of Freedom	Levels of Significance for One-Tailed Test			
	.10	.05	.025	.005		.10	.05	.025	.005
1	3.078	6.314	12.706	63.657	16	1.337	1.746	2.120	2.921
2	1.886	2.920	4.303	9.925	17	1.333	1.740	2.110	2.898
3	1.638	2.353	3.182	5.841	18	1.330	1.734	2.101	2.878
4	1.533	2.132	2.776	4.604	19	1.328	1.729	2.093	2.861
5	1.476	2.015	2.571	4.032	20	1.325	1.725	2.086	2.845
6	1.440	1.943	2.447	3.707	21	1.323	1.721	2.080	2.831
7	1.415	1.895	2.365	4.499	22	1.321	1.717	2.074	2.819
8	1.397	1.860	2.306	3.355	23	1.319	1.714	2.069	2.807
9	1.383	1.833	2.262	3.250	24	1.318	1.711	2.064	2.797
10	1.372	1.812	2.228	3.169	25	1.316	1.708	2.060	2.787
11	1.363	1.796	2.201	3.106	26	1.315	1.706	2.056	2.779
12	1.356	1.782	2.179	3.055	27	1.314	1.703	2.052	2.771
13	1.350	1.771	2.160	3.012	28	1.313	1.701	2.048	2.763
14	1.345	1.761	2.145	2.977	29	1.311	1.699	2.045	2.756
15	1.341	1.753	2.131	2.947	30	1.310	1.697	2.042	2.750
					∞	1.282	1.645	1.960	2.576

To find the critical value for a two-tailed test, simply multiply the levels of significance by 2. That is, the values for the one-tailed test with significance of .10 are also those for a two-tailed test with .20 significance, and so on.

[2] Table courtesy of Jeannine A. Myer.

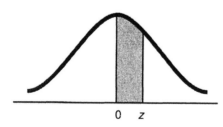

Graph for Table A-1

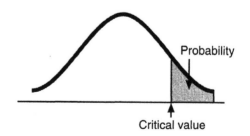

Graph for Table A-2

TABLE A-3
Present Value of $1

$$\frac{1}{(1+r)^t}$$

t/r	4%	5%	6%	7%	8%	9%	10%	11%	12%	13%	14%	15%	16%	17%	18%	19%
1	.9615	.9524	.9434	.9346	.9259	.9174	.9091	.9009	.8929	.8850	.8772	.8696	.8621	.8547	.8475	.8403
2	.9246	.9070	.8900	.8734	.8673	.8417	.8264	.8116	.7972	.7831	.7695	.7561	.7432	.7305	.7182	.7062
3	.8890	.8638	.8396	.8163	.7938	.7722	.7513	.7312	.7118	.6931	.6750	.6575	.6407	.6244	.6086	.5934
4	.8548	.8227	.7921	.7629	.7350	.7084	.6830	.6587	.6355	.6133	.5921	.5718	.5523	.5337	.5158	.4987
5	.8219	.7835	.7473	.7130	.6806	.6499	.6209	.5935	.5674	.5428	.5194	.4972	.4761	.4561	.4371	.4190
6	.7903	.7462	.7050	.6663	.6302	.5963	.5645	.5346	.5066	.4803	.4556	.4324	.4104	.3898	.3704	.3521
7	.7599	.7107	.6651	.6227	.5835	.5470	.5132	.4817	.4523	.4251	.3996	.3759	.3538	.3332	.3139	.2959
8	.7307	.6768	.6274	.5820	.5403	.5019	.4665	.4339	.4039	.3762	.3506	.3269	.3050	.2848	.2660	.2487
9	.7026	.6446	.5919	.5439	.5002	.4604	.4241	.3909	.3606	.3329	.3075	.2843	.2630	.2434	.2255	.2090
10	.6756	.6139	.5584	.5083	.4632	.4224	.3855	.3522	.3220	.2946	.2697	.2472	.2267	.2080	.1911	.1756
11	.6496	.5847	.5268	.4751	.4289	.3875	.3505	.3173	.2875	.2607	.2366	.2149	.1954	.1778	.1619	.1476
12	.6246	.5568	.4970	.4440	.3971	.3555	.3186	.2858	.2567	.2307	.2076	.1869	.1685	.1520	.1372	.1240
13	.6006	.5303	.4688	.4150	.3677	.3262	.2897	.2575	.2292	.2042	.1821	.1625	.1452	.1299	.1163	.1042
14	.5775	.5051	.4423	.3873	.3405	.2992	.2633	.2320	.2046	.1807	.1597	.1413	.1252	.1110	.0985	.0876
15	.5553	.4810	.4173	.3624	.3152	.2745	.2394	.2090	.1827	.1599	.1401	.1229	.1079	.0949	.0835	.0736
16	.5339	.4581	.3936	.3387	.2919	.2519	.2176	.1883	.1631	.1415	.1229	.1069	.0930	.0811	.0708	.0618
17	.5134	.4363	.3714	.3166	.2703	.2311	.1978	.1696	.1456	.1252	.1078	.0929	.0802	.0693	.0600	.0520
18	.4936	.4155	.3503	.2959	.2502	.2120	.1799	.1528	.1300	.1108	.0946	.0808	.0691	.0592	.0508	.0437
19	.4746	.3957	.3305	.2765	.2317	.1945	.1635	.1377	.1161	.0981	.0829	.0703	.0596	.0506	.0431	.0367
20	.4564	.3769	.3118	.2584	.2145	.1784	.1486	.1240	.1037	.0868	.0728	.0611	.0514	.0433	.0365	.0308
21	.4388	.3589	.2942	.2415	.1987	.1637	.1351	.1117	.0926	.0768	.0638	.0531	.0443	.0370	.0309	.0259
22	.4220	.3418	.2775	.2257	.1839	.1502	.1228	.1007	.0826	.0680	.0560	.0462	.0382	.0316	.0262	.0218
23	.4057	.3256	.2618	.2109	.1703	.1378	.1117	.0907	.0738	.0601	.0491	.0402	.0329	.0270	.0222	.0183
24	.3901	.3101	.2470	.1971	.1577	.1264	.1015	.0817	.0659	.0532	.0431	.0349	.0284	.0231	.0188	.0154
25	.3751	.2953	.2330	.1842	.1460	.1160	.0923	.0736	.0588	.0471	.0378	.0304	.0245	.0197	.0160	.0129
30	.3083	.2314	.1741	.1314	.0994	.0754	.0573	.0437	.0334	.0256	.0196	.0151	.0116	.0090	.0070	.0054
35	.2534	.1813	.1301	.0937	.0676	.0490	.0356	.0259	.0189	.0139	.0102	.0075	.0055	.0041	.0030	.0023
40	.2083	.1420	.0972	.0668	.0460	.0318	.0221	.0154	.0107	.0075	.0053	.0037	.0026	.0019	.0013	.0010
45	.1712	.1113	.0727	.0476	.0313	.0207	.0137	.0091	.0061	.0041	.0027	.0019	.0013	.0009	.0006	.0004
50	.1407	.0872	.0543	.0339	.0213	.0134	.0085	.0054	.0035	.0022	.0014	.0009	.0006	.0004	.0003	.0002

(continued)

TABLE A-3
(continued)

t/r	20%	21%	22%	23%	24%	25%	26%	28%	30%	32%	34%	36%	38%	40%	45%	50%
1	.8333	.8264	.8197	.8130	.8065	.8000	.7937	.7813	.7692	.7576	.7463	.7353	.7246	.7143	.6897	.6667
2	.6944	.6830	.6719	.6610	.6504	.6400	.6299	.6104	.5917	.5739	.5569	.5409	.5251	.5102	.4756	.4444
3	.5787	.5645	.5507	.5374	.5245	.5120	.4999	.4768	.4552	.4348	.4156	.3975	.3805	.3644	.3280	.2963
4	.4823	.4665	.4514	.4369	.4230	.4069	.3968	.3725	.3501	.3294	.3102	.2923	.2757	.2603	.2262	.1975
5	.4019	.3855	.3700	.3552	.3411	.3277	.3149	.2910	.2693	.2495	.2315	.2149	.1998	.1859	.1560	.1317
6	.3349	.3186	.3033	.2888	.2751	.2621	.2499	.2274	.2072	.1890	.1727	.1580	.1448	.1328	.1076	.0878
7	.2791	.2633	.2486	.2348	.2218	.2097	.1983	.1776	.1594	.1432	.1289	.1162	.1049	.0949	.0742	.0585
8	.2326	.2176	.2038	.1909	.1789	.1678	.1574	.1388	.1226	.1085	.0962	.0854	.0760	.0678	.0512	.0390
9	.1938	.1799	.1670	.1552	.1443	.1342	.1249	.1084	.0943	.0822	.0718	.0628	.0551	.0484	.0353	.0260
10	.1615	.1486	.1369	.1262	.1164	.1074	.0992	.0847	.0725	.0623	.0536	.0462	.0399	.0346	.0243	.0173
11	.1346	.1228	.1122	.1026	.0938	.0859	.0787	.0662	.0558	.0472	.0400	.0340	.0289	.0247	.0168	.0116
12	.1122	.1015	.0920	.0834	.0757	.0687	.0625	.0517	.0429	.0357	.0298	.0250	.0210	.0176	.0116	.0077
13	.0935	.0839	.0754	.0678	.0610	.0550	.0496	.0404	.0330	.0271	.0223	.0184	.0152	.0126	.0080	.0051
14	.0779	.0693	.0618	.0551	.0492	.0440	.0393	.0316	.0254	.0205	.0166	.0135	.0110	.0090	.0055	.0034
15	.0649	.0573	.0507	.0448	.0397	.0352	.0312	.0247	.0195	.0155	.0124	.0099	.0080	.0064	.0038	.0023
16	.0541	.0474	.0415	.0364	.0320	.0281	.0248	.0193	.0150	.0118	.0093	.0073	.0058	.0046	.0026	.0015
17	.0451	.0391	.0340	.0296	.0258	.0225	.0197	.0150	.0116	.0089	.0069	.0054	.0042	.0033	.0018	.0010
18	.0376	.0323	.0279	.0241	.0208	.0180	.0156	.0118	.0089	.0068	.0052	.0039	.0030	.0023	.0012	.0007
19	.0313	.0267	.0229	.0196	.0168	.0144	.0124	.0092	.0068	.0051	.0038	.0029	.0022	.0017	.0009	.0005
20	.0261	.0221	.0187	.0159	.0135	.0115	.0098	.0072	.0053	.0039	.0029	.0021	.0016	.0012	.0006	.0003
21	.0217	.0183	.0154	.0129	.0109	.0092	.0078	.0056	.0040	.0029	.0021	.0016	.0012	.0009	.0004	.0002
22	.0181	.0151	.0126	.0105	.0088	.0074	.0062	.0044	.0031	.0022	.0016	.0012	.0008	.0006	.0003	.0001
23	.0151	.0125	.0103	.0086	.0071	.0059	.0049	.0034	.0024	.0017	.0012	.0008	.0006	.0004	.0002	.0001
24	.0126	.0103	.0085	.0070	.0057	.0047	.0039	.0027	.0018	.0013	.0009	.0006	.0004	.0003	.0001	.0001
25	.0105	.0085	.0069	.0057	.0046	.0038	.0031	.0021	.0014	.0010	.0007	.0005	.0003	.0002	.0001	.0000
30	.0042	.0033	.0026	.0020	.0016	.0012	.0010	.0006	.0004	.0002	.0002	.0001	.0001	.0000	.0000	
35	.0017	.0013	.0009	.0007	.0005	.0004	.0003	.0002	.0001	.0001	.0000	.0000	.0000	.0000	.0000	
40	.0007	.0005	.0004	.0003	.0002	.0001	.0001	.0001	.0000	.0000						
45	.0003	.0002	.0001	.0001	.0001	.0000	.0000	.0000								
50	.0001	.0001	.0000	.0000	.0000											

TABLE A-4
Present Value of an Annuity of $1

$$1 - \frac{1}{\dfrac{(1+r)^t}{r}}$$

t/r	4%	5%	6%	7%	8%	9%	10%	11%	12%	13%	14%	15%	16%	17%	18%	19%
1	.9615	.9524	.9434	.9346	.9259	.9174	.9091	.9009	.8929	.8850	.8772	.8696	.8621	.8547	.8475	.8403
2	1.8861	1.8594	1.8334	1.8080	1.7833	1.7591	1.7355	1.7125	1.6901	1.6681	1.6467	1.6257	1.6052	1.5852	1.5656	1.5465
3	2.7751	2.7232	2.6730	2.6243	2.5771	2.5313	2.4869	2.4437	2.4018	2.3612	2.3216	2.2832	2.2459	2.2096	2.1743	2.1399
4	3.6299	3.5460	3.4651	3.3872	3.3121	3.2397	3.1699	3.1024	3.0373	2.9745	2.9137	2.8550	2.7982	2.7432	2.6901	2.6386
5	4.4518	4.3295	4.2124	4.1002	3.9927	3.8897	3.7908	3.6959	3.6048	3.5172	3.4331	3.3522	3.2743	3.1993	3.1272	3.0576
6	5.2421	5.0757	4.9173	4.7665	4.6229	4.4859	4.3553	4.2305	4.1114	3.9975	3.8887	3.7845	3.6847	3.5892	3.4976	3.4098
7	6.0021	5.7864	5.5824	5.3893	5.2064	5.0330	4.8684	4.7122	4.5638	4.4226	4.2883	4.1604	4.0386	3.9224	3.8115	3.7057
8	6.7327	6.4632	6.2098	5.9713	5.7465	5.5348	5.3349	5.1461	4.9676	4.7988	4.6389	4.4873	4.3436	4.2072	4.0776	3.9544
9	7.4353	7.1078	6.8017	6.5152	6.2469	5.9952	5.7590	5.5370	5.3282	5.1317	4.9464	4.7716	4.6065	4.4506	4.3030	4.1633
10	8.1109	7.7217	7.3601	7.0236	6.7101	6.4177	6.1446	5.8892	5.6502	5.4262	5.2161	5.0188	4.8332	4.6586	4.4941	4.3389
11	8.7605	8.3064	7.8869	7.4987	7.1390	6.8052	6.4951	6.2065	5.9377	5.6869	5.4527	5.2337	5.0286	4.8364	4.6560	4.4865
12	9.3851	8.8633	8.3838	7.9427	7.5361	7.1607	6.8137	6.4924	6.1944	5.9176	5.6603	5.4206	5.1971	4.9884	4.7932	4.6105
13	9.9856	9.3936	8.8527	8.3577	7.9038	7.4869	7.1034	6.7499	6.4235	6.1218	5.8424	5.5831	5.3423	5.1183	4.9095	4.7147
14	10.5631	9.8986	9.2950	8.7455	8.2442	7.7862	7.3667	6.9819	6.6282	6.3025	6.0021	5.7245	5.4675	5.2293	5.0081	4.8023
15	11.1184	10.3797	9.7122	9.1079	8.5595	8.0607	7.6061	7.1909	6.8109	6.4624	6.1422	5.8474	5.5755	5.3242	5.0916	4.8759
16	11.6523	10.8378	10.1059	9.4466	8.8514	8.3126	7.8237	7.3792	6.9740	6.6039	6.2651	5.9542	5.6685	5.4053	5.1624	4.9377
17	12.1657	11.2741	10.4773	9.7632	9.1216	8.5436	8.0216	7.5488	7.1196	6.7291	6.3729	6.0472	5.7487	5.4746	5.2223	4.9897
18	12.6593	11.6896	10.8276	10.0591	9.3719	8.7556	8.2014	7.7016	7.2497	6.8399	6.4674	6.1280	5.8178	5.5339	5.2732	5.0333
19	13.1339	12.0853	11.1581	10.3356	9.6036	8.9501	8.3649	7.8393	7.3658	6.9380	6.5504	6.1982	5.8775	5.5845	5.3162	5.0700
20	13.5903	12.4622	11.4699	10.5940	9.8181	9.1285	8.5136	7.9633	7.4694	7.0248	6.6231	6.2593	5.9288	5.6278	5.3527	5.1009
21	14.0292	12.8212	11.7641	10.8355	10.0168	9.2922	8.6487	8.0751	7.5620	7.1016	6.6870	6.3125	5.9731	5.6648	5.3837	5.1268
22	14.4511	13.1630	12.0416	11.0612	10.2007	9.4424	8.7715	8.1757	7.6446	7.1695	6.7429	6.3587	6.0113	5.6964	5.4099	5.1486
23	14.8568	13.4886	12.3034	11.2722	10.3711	9.5802	8.8832	8.2664	7.7184	7.2297	6.7921	6.3988	6.0442	5.7234	5.4321	5.1668
24	15.2470	13.7986	12.5504	11.4693	10.5288	9.7066	8.9847	8.3481	7.7843	7.2829	6.8351	6.4338	6.0726	5.7465	5.4509	5.1822
25	15.6221	14.0939	12.7834	11.6536	10.6748	9.8226	9.0770	8.4217	7.8431	7.3300	6.8729	6.4641	6.0971	5.7662	5.4669	5.1951
30	17.2920	15.3725	13.7648	12.4090	11.2578	10.2737	9.4269	8.6938	8.0552	7.4957	7.0027	6.5660	6.1772	5.8294	5.5168	5.2347
35	18.6646	16.3742	14.4982	12.9477	11.6546	10.5668	9.6442	8.8552	8.1755	7.5856	7.0700	6.6166	6.2153	5.8582	5.5306	5.2512
40	19.7928	17.1591	15.0463	13.3317	11.9246	10.7574	9.7791	8.9511	8.2438	7.6344	7.1050	6.6418	6.2335	5.8713	5.5482	5.2582
45	20.7200	17.7741	15.4558	13.6055	12.1084	10.8812	9.8628	9.0079	8.2825	7.6609	7.1232	6.6543	6.2421	5.8773	5.5523	5.2611
50	21.4822	18.2559	15.7619	13.8007	12.2335	10.9617	9.9148	9.0417	8.3045	7.6752	7.1327	6.6605	6.2463	5.8801	5.5541	5.2623

(continued)

TABLE A-4
(continued)

t/r	20%	21%	22%	23%	24%	25%	26%	28%	30%	32%	34%	36%	38%	40%	45%	50%
1	.8333	.8264	.8197	.8130	.8065	.8000	.7937	.7812	.7692	.7576	.7463	.7353	.7246	.7143	.6897	.6667
2	1.5278	1.5095	1.4915	1.4740	1.4568	1.4400	1.4235	1.3916	1.3609	1.3315	1.3032	1.2760	1.2497	1.2245	1.1653	1.1111
3	2.1065	2.0739	2.0422	2.0114	1.9813	1.9520	1.9234	1.8684	1.8161	1.7663	1.7188	1.6735	1.6302	1.5889	1.4933	1.4074
4	2.5887	2.5404	2.4936	2.4483	2.4043	2.3616	2.3203	2.2410	2.1662	2.0957	2.0290	1.9658	1.9060	1.8492	1.7195	1.6049
5	2.9906	2.9260	2.8636	2.8035	2.7454	2.6893	2.6351	2.5320	2.4356	2.3452	2.2604	2.1807	2.1058	2.0352	1.8755	1.7366
6	3.3255	3.2446	3.1669	3.0923	3.0205	2.9514	2.8850	2.7594	2.6427	2.5342	2.4331	2.3388	2.2506	2.1680	1.9831	1.8244
7	3.6046	3.5079	3.4155	3.3270	3.2423	3.1611	3.0833	2.9370	2.8021	2.6775	2.5620	2.4550	2.3555	2.2628	2.0573	1.8829
8	3.8372	3.7256	3.6193	3.5179	3.4212	3.3289	3.2407	3.0758	2.9247	2.7860	2.6582	2.5404	2.4315	2.3306	2.1085	1.9220
9	4.0310	3.9054	3.7863	3.6731	3.5655	3.4631	3.3657	3.1842	3.0190	2.8681	2.7300	2.6033	2.4866	2.3790	2.1438	1.9480
10	4.1925	4.0541	3.9232	3.7993	3.6819	3.5705	3.4648	3.2689	3.0915	2.9304	2.7836	2.6495	2.5265	2.4136	2.1681	1.9653
11	4.3271	4.1769	4.0354	3.9018	3.7757	3.6564	3.5435	3.3351	3.1473	2.9776	2.8236	2.6834	2.5555	2.4383	2.1849	1.9769
12	4.4392	4.2784	4.1274	3.9852	3.8514	3.7251	3.6059	3.3868	3.1903	3.0133	2.8534	2.7084	2.5764	2.4559	2.1965	1.9846
13	4.5327	4.3624	4.2028	4.0530	3.9124	3.7801	3.6555	3.4272	3.2233	3.0404	2.8757	2.7268	2.5916	2.4684	2.2045	1.9897
14	4.6106	4.4317	4.2646	4.1082	3.9616	3.8241	3.6949	3.4587	3.2487	3.0609	2.8923	2.7403	2.6026	2.4775	2.2100	1.9931
15	4.6755	4.4890	4.3152	4.1530	4.0013	3.8593	3.7261	3.4834	3.2682	3.0764	2.9047	2.7502	2.6106	2.4839	2.2138	1.9954
16	4.7296	4.5364	4.3567	4.1894	4.0333	3.8874	3.7509	3.5026	3.2832	3.0882	2.9140	2.7575	2.6164	2.4885	2.2164	1.9970
17	4.7746	4.5755	4.3908	4.2190	4.0591	3.9099	3.7705	3.5177	3.2948	3.0971	2.9209	2.7629	2.6206	2.4918	2.2182	1.9980
18	4.8122	4.6079	4.4187	4.2431	4.0799	3.9279	3.7861	3.5294	3.3037	3.1039	2.9260	2.7668	2.6236	2.4941	2.2195	1.9986
19	4.8435	4.6346	4.4415	4.2627	4.0967	3.9424	3.7985	3.5386	3.3105	3.1090	2.9299	2.7697	2.6258	2.4958	2.2203	1.9991
20	4.8696	4.6567	4.4603	4.2786	4.1103	3.9539	3.8083	3.5458	3.3158	3.1129	2.9327	2.7718	2.6274	2.4970	2.2209	1.9994
21	4.8913	4.6750	4.4756	4.2916	4.1212	3.9631	3.8161	3.5514	3.3198	3.1158	2.9349	2.7734	2.6285	2.4979	2.2213	1.9996
22	4.9094	4.6900	4.4882	4.3021	4.1300	3.9705	3.8223	3.5558	3.3230	3.1180	2.9365	2.7746	2.6294	2.4985	2.2216	1.9997
23	4.9245	4.7025	4.4985	4.3106	4.1371	3.9764	3.8273	3.5592	3.3254	3.1197	2.9377	2.7754	2.6300	2.4989	2.2218	1.9998
24	4.9371	4.7128	4.5070	4.3176	4.1428	3.9811	3.8312	3.5619	3.3272	3.1210	2.9386	2.7760	2.6304	2.4992	2.2219	1.9999
25	4.9476	4.7213	4.5139	4.3232	4.1474	3.9849	3.8342	3.5640	3.3286	3.1220	2.9392	2.7765	2.6307	2.4994	2.2220	1.9999
30	4.9789	4.7463	4.5338	4.3391	4.1601	3.9950	3.8424	3.5693	3.3321	3.1242	2.9407	2.7775	2.6314	2.4999	2.2222	2.0000
35	4.9915	4.7559	4.5411	4.3447	4.1644	3.9984	3.8450	3.5708	3.3330	3.1248	2.9411	2.7777	2.6315	2.5000	2.2222	2.0000
40	4.9966	4.7596	4.5439	4.3467	4.1659	3.9995	3.8458	3.5712	3.3332	3.1250	2.9412	2.7778	2.6316	2.5000	2.2222	2.0000
45	4.9986	4.7610	4.5449	4.3474	4.1664	3.9998	3.8460	3.5714	3.3333	3.1250	2.9412	2.7778	2.6316	2.5000	2.2222	2.0000
50	4.9995	4.7616	4.5452	4.3477	4.1666	3.9999	3.8461	3.5714	3.3333	3.1250	2.9412	2.7778	2.6316	2.5000	2.2222	2.0000

TABLE A-5
Present Value of ACRS Tax Shield

Discount Rate	Five-Year Assets	Seven-Year Assets
.08	.8113	.7662
.10	.7732	.7215
.12	.7381	.6810
.13	.7215	.6622
.14	.7055	.6442
.15	.6901	.6270
.16	.6753	.6106
.18	.6472	.5799
.20	.6211	.5517
.22	.5967	.5258
.25	.5631	.4907

Using Table A-5. Find the factor for the appropriate ACRS life and discount rate. Multiply that factor by the cost of the asset multiplied by the income tax rate. For example, for a $500,000 asset that qualifies for five-year treatment, 35 percent tax rate, and 12 percent discount rate, $500,000 × .35 × .7381 gives $129,168. Table A-5 gives the sums of the ACRS percentages multiplied by the present-value factors for each year during which depreciation is taken. Thus, the five-year factor at 10 percent is (rounded): (.20 × .9091) + (.32 × .8264) + (.192 × .7513) + (.115 × .6830) + (.115 × .6209) + (.058 × .5645).

Appendix B

Selected References

Allocation

Thomas, Arthur L., "Cash-Flow Reporting as Allocation-Free Disclosure: A Polemic," Working Paper No. 136 (Lawrence, Kans.: Univesity of Kansas, 1980).

Thomas, Arthur L., *A Behavioural Analysis of Joint-Cost Allocations and Transfer Pricing* (Stipes, 1980).

Thomas, Arthur L., *The Allocation Problem: Part Two*, Studies in Accounting Research #9 (Sarasota, Fla.: American Accounting Association, 1974).

Thomas, Arthur L., "Useful Arbitrary Allocations (with a Comment on the Neutrality of Financial Accounting Reports)," *The Accounting Review* (July 1971), pp. 472–479.

Thomas, Arthur L., *The Allocation Problem*, Studies in Accounting Research #3 (Sarasota, Fla.: American Accounting Association, 1969).

Behavioral Dimensions/Information

Ashton, Robert H., *Human Information Processing in Accounting*, Studies in Accounting Research #17 (Sarasota, Fla.: American Accounting Association, 1982).

Behling, Orlando, and Jesse F. Dillard, "Accounting: The Intuitive Challenge," *Accounting Horizons* (June 1987), pp. 35–42.

Bruns, W. J., Jr., and D. DeCoster, *Accounting and Its Behavioral Implications* (New York: McGraw-Hill, 1969).

Caplan, Edwin H., *Management Accounting and Behavioral Science* (Reading, Mass.: Addison-Wesley, 1971).

Demski, Joel S., *Information Analysis* (Reading, Mass.: Addison-Wesley, 1972).

Douglas, Patricia, "Reporting Accounting Information to Top Management," *Corporate Accounting* (Summer 1987), pp. 38–45.

Feltham, Gerald A., *Information Evaluation*, Studies in Accounting Research #5 (Sarasota, Fla.: American Accounting Association, 1972).

Ferris, Kenneth R., and J. Leslie Livingstone, *Management Planning and Control: The Behavioral Foundations*, rev. ed. (Columbus, Ohio: Publishing Horizons, 1987).

Flamholtz, Eric, *Human Resource Accounting* (Encino, Calif.: Dickenson, 1974).

Hopwood, Anthony, *Accounting and Human Behavior* (Englewood Cliffs, N.J.: Prentice-Hall, 1974).

Itami, Hiroyuki, *Adaptive Behavior: Management Control and Information Analysis*, Studies in Accounting Research #15 (Sarasota, Fla.: American Accounting Association, 1977).

Lammert, Thomas B., and Robert Ehrsam, "The Human Element: The Real Challenge in Modernizing Cost Systems," *Management Accounting* (July 1987), pp. 32–37.

Lev, Baruch, *Accounting & Information Theory*, Studies in Accounting Research #2 (Sarasota, Fla.: American Accounting Association, 1969).

Libby, Robert, *Accounting and Human Information Processing: Theory and Applications* (Englewood Cliffs, N.J.: Prentice-Hall, 1981).

Likert, Rensis, *The Human Organization* (New York: McGraw-Hill, 1967).

Madden, Donald L., and James R. Holmes, *Management Accountants: Responding to Change, An Exploratory Study* (Montvale, N.J.: National Association of Accountants, 1990).

McKinnon, Sharon M., and William J. Bruns, Jr., *The Information Mosaic: How Managers Get the Information They Really Need* (Boston: Harvard Business School Press, 1992).

Mock, Theodore J., *Measurement and Accounting Information Criteria*, Studies in Accounting Research #13 (Sarasota, Fla.: American Accounting Association, 1976).

Morris, William T., *Decision Analysis* (Columbus, Ohio: Grid, 1977).

Parker, Lee D., Kenneth R. Ferris, and David T. Otley, *Accounting for the Human Factor* (Sydney: Prentice-Hall of Australia Pty Ltd., 1989).

Pfeffer, Jeffrey, *Managing with Power: Politics and Influences in Organizations* (Boston: Harvard Business School Press, 1992).

Schiff, Michael, and Arie Y. Lewin, *Behavioral Aspects of Accounting* (Englewood Cliffs, N.J.: Prentice-Hall, 1974).

Schroder, H. M., M. J. Driver, and S. Struefert, *Human Information Processing: Individuals & Groups Functioning in Complex Social Situations* (New York: Holt, Rinehart, & Winston, 1967).

Shields, Michael D., and S. Mark Young, "A Behavioral Model for Implementing Cost Management Systems," *Journal of Cost Management* (Winter 1989), pp. 17–27.

Stokes, Carolyn R. and Kay W. Lawrimore, "Selling a New Cost Accounting System," *Journal of Cost Management* (Fall 1989), pp. 29–34.

Capital Budgeting

Bierman, Harold, Jr., and Seymour Smidt, *The Capital Budgeting Decision—Economic Analysis of Investment Projects*, 7th ed. (New York: Macmillan, 1988).

Clark, John, Thomas Hindelang, and Robert Prichard, *Capital Budgeting*, 3rd ed., (Englewood Cliffs, N.J.: Prentice-Hall, Inc., 1989).

Coulthurst, Nigel, "Justifying the New Factory," *Management Accounting* (U.K.) (April 1989), pp. 26–28.

Coulthurst, Nigel, "The New Factory," *Management Accounting* (U.K.) (March 1989), pp. 30–34.

Engwall, Richard L., "Investment Evaluation Methodologies," *Journal of Cost Management* (Spring 1988), pp. 40–44.

Herbst, Anthony F., *Capital Budgeting—Theory, Quantitative Methods, and Applications* (New York: Harper & Row, 1982).

Hertenstein, Julie H., *Introductory Note on Capital Budgeting Practices* (Boston: Harvard Business School 9-188-159, 1988).

Levy, Haim, and Marshall Sarnat, *Capital Investment and Financial Decisions*, 4th ed. (London: Prentice-Hall International (UK) Ltd., 1990).

Mecimore, Charles D., "Investment Justification: State of the Art," *Journal of Cost Management* (Summer 1987), pp. 65–67.

Mecimore, Charles D., and William G. Sullivan, *Cost Management Systems: A Digest of the Relevant Literature* (Montvale, N.J.: National Association of Accountants, and Arlington, Tex.: Computer Aided Manufacturing-International, 1987).

Osteryoung, Jerome S., *Capital Budgeting—Long-Term Asset Selection*, 2nd ed. (Columbus, Ohio: Grid, 1979).

Cost Management

Beaujon, George J., and Vinod R. Singhal, "Understanding the Activity Costs in an Activity-Based Cost System," *Journal of Cost Management* (Spring 1990), pp. 51–72.

Berliner, Callie, and James A. Brimson, editors, *Cost Management for Today's Advanced Manufacturing: The CAM-I Conceptual Design* (Boston: Harvard Business Schoool Press, 1988).

Beynon, Roger, "Change Management as a Platform for Activity-Based Management," *Journal of Cost Management* (Summer 1992), pp. 24–30.

Boer, Germain, *Use of Expert Systems in Management Accounting* (Montvale, N.J.: National Association of Accountants, 1989).

Brinker, Barry, editor, *Emerging Practices in Cost Management* (New York: Warren, Gorham, & Lamont, 1990).

Cooper, Robin, "Implementing an Activity-Based Cost System," *Journal of Cost Management* (Spring 1990), pp. 33–42.

Cooper, Robin, "The Two-Stage Procedure in Cost Accounting: Part Two," *Journal of Cost Management* (Fall 1987), pp. 39–45.

Cooper, Robin, "The Two-Stage Procedure in Cost Accounting: Part One," *Journal of Cost Management* (Summer 1987), pp. 43–51.

Cooper, Robin, "Does Your Company Need a New Cost System?" *Journal of Cost Management* (Spring 1987), pp. 66–69.

Cooper, Robin, and Robert S. Kaplan, "Activity-Based Systems: Measuring the Cost of Resource Usage," *Accounting Horizons*, Vol. 6, No. 3, (Sarasota, Fla.: American Accounting Association, September 1992), pp. 1–13.

Cooper, Robin, and Robert S. Kaplan, "How Cost Accounting Distorts Product Costs," *Management Accounting* (April 1988), pp. 20–27.

Frecka, Thomas J., and Robert McIlhatan, "Does Your Direct Labor-Based Cost System Make Sense?" *Journal of Cost Management* (Fall 1987), pp. 32–38.

Greene, Alice H., and Peter Flentov, "Managing Performance: Maximizing the Benefit of Activity-Based Costing," *Journal of Cost Management* (Summer 1990), pp. 51–59.

Hicks, Douglas T., "A Modest Proposal for Pricing Decisions: Ignore Depreciation Expense," *Management Accounting* (November 1992), pp. 50–53.

Hunt, Rick, Linda Garrett, and C. Mike Merz, "Direct Labor Cost Not Always Relevant at H-P," *Management Accounting* (February 1985), pp. 58–62.

Kaplan, Robert S., "In Defense of Activity-Based Cost Management," *Management Accounting* (November 1992), pp. 58–63.

Kaplan, Robert S., "The Four-Stage Model of Cost Systems Design," *Management Accounting* (February 1990), pp. 22–26.

Mecimore, Charles D., "The Difference Between a Cost Accounting System and a Cost Management System," *Journal of Cost Management* (Spring 1988), pp. 66–68.

Ostrenga, Michael R., "Activities: The Focal Point of Total Cost Management," *Management Accounting* (February 1990), pp. 42–49.

Rotch, William, "Activity-Based Costing in Service Industries," *Journal of Cost Management* (Summer 1990), pp. 4–14.

Seed, Allen H., III, "Improving Cost Management," *Management Accounting* (February 1990), pp. 27–30.

Steedle, Lamont F., editor, *World-Class Accounting for World-Class Manufacturing* (Montvale, N.J.: National Association of Accountants, 1990).

Woods, Michael D., "Completing the Picture: Economic Choices with ABC," *Management Accounting* (December 1992), pp. 53–57.

Finance and Economics

Baumol, William J., *Economic Theory and Operations Analysis*, 4th ed. (Englewood Cliffs, N.J.: Prentice-Hall, 1977).

Foster, George, *Financial Statement Analysis*, 2nd ed. (Englewood Cliffs, N.J.: Prentice Hall, 1986).

New Manufacturing Environment

Bennett, Robert E., James A. Hendricks, David E. Keys, and Edward J. Rudnicki, *Cost Accounting for Factory Automation* (Montvale, N.J.: National Association of Accountants, 1987).

Capettini, Robert, and Donald K. Clancy, editors, *Cost Accounting, Robotics, and the New Manufacturing Environment* (Sarasota, Fla.: American Accounting Association Management Accounting Section, 1987).

Cost Accounting for the 90s: The Challenge of Technological Change Proceedings (Montvale, N.J.: National Association of Accountants, 1986).

Dilts, David M., and Severin V. Grabski, "Advanced Manufacturing Technologies: What They Can Offer Management Accountants," *Management Accounting* (February 1990), pp. 50–53.

Fox, Robert E., "The Constraint Theory," in *Cases from Management Accounting Practice*, Vol. 8, James T. Mackey, editor (Montvale, N.J.: Institute of Management Accountants, 1992), pp. 1–16.

Goldratt, Eliyahu M., *The Haystack Syndrome: Sifting Information Out of the Data Ocean* (Croton-on-Hudson, N.Y.: North River Press, 1990).

Goldratt, Eliyahu M., and Jeff Cox, *The Goal: A Process of Ongoing Improvement*, 2nd ed. (Croton-on-Hudson, N.Y.: North River Press, 1992).

Hendricks, James A., "Applying Cost Accounting to Factory Automation," *Management Accounting* (December 1988), pp. 24–30.

Howell, Robert A., James D. Brown, Stephen R. Soucy, and Allen H. Seed III, *Management Accounting in the New Manufacturing Environment* (Montvale, N.J.: National Association of Accountants, 1987).

Howell, Robert A., and Michiharu Sakurai, "Management Accounting (and Other) Lessons from the Japanese," *Management Accounting* (December 1992), pp. 28–34.

Howell, Robert A., and Stephen R. Soucy, "Management Reporting in the New Manufacturing Environment, *Management Accounting* (February 1988), pp. 22–23.

Howell, Robert A., and Stephen R. Soucy, "Operating Controls in the New Manufacturing Environment," *Management Accounting* (October 1987), pp. 25–31.

Jeans, Mike, and Michael Morrow, "Management Accounting in AMT Environments: Product Costing," *Management Accounting* (U.K.) (April 1989), pp. 29–30.

Johnson, H. Thomas, and Robert S. Kaplan, *Relevance Regained: From Top-Down Control to Bottom-Up Empowerment* (New York: Free Press Division, Macmillan, 1992).

Johnson, H. Thomas, and Robert S. Kaplan, *Relevance Lost: The Rise and Fall of Management Accounting* (Boston: Harvard Business School Press, 1987).

Jonez, John W. and Michael A. Wright, "Material Burdening," *Management Accounting* (August 1987), pp. 27–31.

Juran, J. M., "Japanese and Western Quality: A Contrast in Methods and Results," *Management Review* (November 1978), pp. 27–45.

Kaplan/INC., "Accounting Critic Robert Kaplan," *INC.* (April 1988), pp. 55–67.

Lee, John Y., *Managerial Accounting Changes for the 1990s* (Reading, Mass.: Addison-Wesley, 1987).

McNair, C. J., William Mosconi, and Thomas Norris, *Meeting the Technology Challenge: Cost Accounting in a JIT Environment* (Montvale, N.J.: National Association of Accountants, 1988).

National Association of Accountants, *Statements on Management Accounting: Objectives of Management Accounting*, Statement No. 1B, June 17, 1982.

Troxler, Joel W., "Estimating the Cost Impact of Flexible Manufacturing," *Journal of Cost Management* (Summer 1990), pp. 26–32.

Performance Measures, Evaluation, and Control

Anthony, Robert N., *The Management Control Function* (Boston: Harvard Business School Press, 1988).

Anthony, Robert N., John Dearden, and Vijay Govindarajan, *Management Control Systems*, 7th ed. (Homewood, Ill.: Richard D. Irwin, 1992).

Armitrage, Howard M., and Anthony A. Atkinson, *The Choice of Productivity Measures in Organizations: A Field Study of Practice in Seven Canadian Firms* (Hamilton, Ontario: The Society of Management Accountants in Canada, 1990).

Bruns, W. J., Jr., editor, *Performance Measurement, Evaluation and Incentives* (Boston: Harvard Business School Press, 1992).

Foulkes, Fred F., editor, *Executive Compensation: A Strategic Guide for the 1990s* (Boston: Harvard Business School Press, 1991).

Kaplan, Robert S., editor, *Measures for Manufacturing Excellence* (Boston: Harvard Business School, 1990).

Keegan, Daniel P., Robert G. Eiler, and Charles R. Jones, "Are Your Performance Measures Obsolete?" *Management Accounting* (June 1989), pp. 45–50.

Lippa, Victor, "Measuring Performance with Synchronous Management," *Management Accounting* (February 1990), pp. 54–59.

McNair, C. J., Richard L. Lynch, and Kelvin F. Cross, "Do Financial and Non Financial Performance Measures Have to Agree?" *Management Accounting* (November 1990), pp. 28–31, 34–36.

Merchant, Kenneth, *Rewarding Results: Motivating Profit Center Managers* (Boston: Harvard Business School Press, 1989).

Michaels, Lawrence T., "A Control Framework for Factory Automation," *Management Accounting* (May 1988), pp. 37–42.

Ross, Gerald H. B., "Revolution in Management Control," *Management Accounting* (November 1990), pp. 23–27.

Ross, Gerald H. B., Howard Armitage, and Alexander Mersereau, "Management Accounting in Advanced Control Environments: Defining the Territory," *Journal of Cost Management* (Fall 1987), pp. 12–18.

Sinclair, Kenneth P., and Eli Schwartz, "Reconciling Cash Flow Decision Making and Accounting Performance Evaluation," *Journal of Cost Management* (Fall 1987), pp. 25–31.

Solomons, David, *Divisional Performance Measurement and Control* (Homewood, Ill.: Richard D. Irwin, 1965).

Spiller, Earl A., Jr., "Return on Investment: A Need for Special Purpose Information," *Accounting Horizons* (June 1988), pp. 1–9.

Stec, Stan, editor, "Information Please. What Are the Steps in a Cost Control System?" *Management Accounting* (February 1988), p. 65.

Turney, Peter B. B., editor, *Performance Excellence in Manufacturing and Service Organizations* (Sarasota, Fla.: American Accounting Association, 1990).

Quantitative Models
Bails, Dale G., and Larry C. Peppers, *Business Fluctuations: Forecasting Techniques and Applications*, 2nd ed. (Englewood Cliffs, N.J.: Prentice-Hall, 1993).

Bos, Theodore, and Paul Newbold, *Introductory Business Forecasting* (Cincinnati, Ohio: South-Western Publishing Co., 1990).

Bowen, Earl K., Gordon D. Prichett, and John C. Saber, *Mathematics with Applications in Management and Economics*, 7th ed. (Homewood, Ill.: Richard D. Irwin, 1993).

Keating, Barry, and J. Holton Wilson, *Business Forecasting* (Homewood, Ill.: Richard D. Irwin, 1990).

Kirkpatrick, Charles A., and Richard I. Levin, *Quantitative Approaches to Management*, 8th ed. (New York: McGraw-Hill, 1992).

Schweitzer, Marcell, Ernst Trossmann, and Gerald H. Lawson, *Break-Even Analysis: Basic Model, Variants, Extensions* (New York: Wiley, 1992).

Wu, Nesa, and Richard Coppins, *Linear Programming and Extensions* (New York: McGraw-Hill, 1981).

Research
Buckley, John W., Marlene H. Buckley, and Hong-Fu Chaing, *Research Methodology & Business Decisions* (Montvale, N.J.: National Association of Accountants and The Society of Management Accountants of Canada, 1976).

Corey, E. Raymond, *MBA Field Studies: A Guide for Students and Faculty* (Boston: Harvard Business School Publishing Division, 1990).

Hertenstein, Julie H., *FMC Corporation's Use of Current Cost Accounting* (Montvale, N.J.: National Association of Accountants, 1988).

Kaplan, Robert S., "The Evolution of Management Accounting," *The Accounting Review*, 59:3 (July 1984), pp. 390–418.

Kaplan, Robert S., "Measuring Manufacturing Performance: A New Challenge for Management Accounting Research," *The Accounting Review*, 58:4 (October 1983), pp. 686–705.

Wallace, Wanda A., *Accounting Research Methods: Do the Facts Speak for Themselves?* (Homestead, Ill.: Richard D. Irwin, 1991).

Yin, Robert K., *Case Study Research*, rev. ed. (Newbury Park, Calif.: Sage, 1989).

Zikmund, William A., *Business Research Methods*, 3rd ed. (Chicago: Dryden Press, 1991).

Strategic Management
Ansoff, H. Igor, *Implanting Strategic Management*, 2nd ed. (London: Prentice-Hall International, 1991).

Ansoff, H. Igor, *Corporate Strategy: An Analytical Approach to Business Policy for Growth and Expansion* (New York: McGraw-Hill, 1965).

Chandler, Alfred D., Jr., *Strategy and Structure: Chapters in the History of Industrial Enterprise* (Cambridge, Mass.: MIT Press, 1962).

Porter, Michael E., *Competitive Advantage: Creating and Sustaining Superior Performance* (New York: Free Press, 1985).

Porter, Michael E., *Competitive Strategy: Techniques for Analyzing Industries and Competitors* (New York: Free Press, 1980).

Reid, Peter C., *Well Made In America: Lessons from Harley-Davidson on Being the Best* (New York: McGraw-Hill, 1990).

Robinson, Michael A., editor, "Contribution Margin Analysis: No Longer Relevant/ Strategic Cost Management: The New Paradigm," *Journal of Management Accounting Research*, Vol. 2 (Fall 1990), pp. 1–32.

Shank, John K., and Vijay Govindarajan, *Strategic Cost Management: The New Tool for Competitive Advantage* (New York: Free Press Division, Macmillan, 1993).

Shank, John K., and Vijay Govindarajan, "Strategic Cost Management: The Value Chain Perspective," *Journal of Management Accounting Research* Vol. 4 (Fall 1992), pp. 179–197.

Shank, John K., and Vijay Govindarajan, *Strategic Cost Analysis: The Evolution from Managerial to Strategic Accounting* (Homewood, Ill.: Richard D. Irwin, 1989).

Thompson, Arthur A., and A. J. Strickland III, *Strategic Management: Concepts and Cases*, 6th ed. (Homewood, Ill.: Richard D. Irwin, 1992).

Transfer Pricing

Aranoff, Gerald, "Transfer Pricing for Short-Run Profit Maximization in Manufacturing," *Journal of Cost Management* (Fall 1990), pp. 37–43.

Borkowski, Susan C., "Environmental and Organizational Factors Affecting Transfer Pricing: A Survey," *Journal of Management Accounting Research*, Vol. 2 (Fall 1990), pp. 78–99.

Eccles, Robert G., *The Transfer Pricing Problem: A Theory for Practice* (Lexington, Mass.: D. C. Heath, 1985).

Eccles, Robert G., "Analyzing Your Company's Transfer Pricing Practices," *Journal of Cost Management* (Summer 1987), pp. 21–33.

Hirshleifer, Jack, "On the Economics of Transfer Pricing," *Journal of Business*, 29:3 (July 1956), pp. 172–184.

Keegan, Daniel P., and Patrick D. Howard, "Transfer Pricing for Fun and Profit," *Review*, No. 3, (Price Waterhouse, 1986), pp. 37–45.

Manes, Rene P., and C. S. Agnes Cheng, *The Marginal Approach to Joint Cost Allocation: Theory and Application*, Studies in Accounting Research #29 (Sarasota, Fla.: American Accounting Association, 1988).

Yost, Jeffrey A., *Intra-Firm Resource Allocation and Transfer Pricing Under Asymmetric Information: A Principal-Agent Analysis of Decentralized Decision-Making in a Multi-Division Firm*, dissertation presented to the Faculty of The Ohio State University, 1988.

Other

Landekich, Stephen, *Corporate Codes of Conduct* (Montvale, N.J.: National Association of Accountants, 1989).

Peavey, Dennis E., "Battle at the GAAP? It's Time for a Change," *Management Accounting* (February 1990), pp. 31–35.

Sundem, Gary L., Doyle Z. Williams, and John F. Chironna, "The Revolution in Accounting Education," *Management Accounting* (December 1990), pp. 49–53.

Vangermeersch, Richard, editor, *Relevance Rediscovered: An Anthology of 25 Significant Articles from the NACA Bulletins and Yearbooks 1919–1929*, Vol. I (Montvale, N.J.: National Association of Accountants, 1990).

Index